Educational and Psychological Research

A Cross Section of Journal Articles for Analysis and Evaluation

Third Edition

Mildred L. Patten

Editor

 Pyrczak Publishing

P.O. Box 39731 • Los Angeles, CA 90039

Although the author and publisher have made every effort to ensure the accuracy and completeness of information contained in this book, we assume no responsibility for errors, inaccuracies, omissions, or any inconsistency herein. Any slights of people, places, or organizations are unintentional.

Project Director: Monica Lopez.

Editorial assistance provided by Sharon Young, Brenda Koplin, Cheryl Alcorn, and Randall R. Bruce.

Cover design by Robert Kibler and Larry Nichols.

Printed in the United States of America.

ISBN 1-884585-45-0

CONTENTS

Continued →

True Experimental Research

Quasi-Experimental Research

Pre-Experimental Research

Causal-Comparative Research

Notes:

Introduction to the Third Edition

In this edition, you will find an entirely new set of research articles that illustrate a wide variety of approaches to research. By analyzing and evaluating them, you will become a skilled consumer of research. In addition, by studying them, you will learn how to conduct basic research and write research reports.

Like the previous editions, the Third Edition emphasizes research articles that employ straightforward research designs, emphasize basic statistics, and are on topics of interest to students in the social and behavioral sciences, with an emphasis on education and psychology.

I believe that all the articles in this collection provide valuable information. Note that some are reports on pilot studies in which researchers were trying out new methods, exploring new ideas on a small-scale basis, etc. Such pilot studies are valuable because they suggest promising hypotheses that may be explored later in more definitive studies.

From article to article, you will probably spot different weaknesses in research methodology. This should not surprise you because each investigator conducts research under a different set of limitations—such as limited financial support, access to subjects, availability of appropriate measuring tools, and so on. When applying evaluation criteria to the articles, keep in mind that your goal is to evaluate the methodology—not the researchers.

Answering the Questions in This Book

At the end of each article, there are two sets of questions. The *Factual Questions* help draw your attention to important methodological details. Field tests indicate that there is only one correct answer for each of these questions. The *Questions for Discussion*, on the other hand, are designed to stimulate classroom discussions. Each of these questions may have more than one defensible answer.

The lines in each article are sequentially numbered. Keeping track of the numbers on which you base your answers will prove helpful in your discussions with your instructor and other students.

About the Appendices

Appendix A contains a brief introduction to reading research articles. For those of you who have not read journal articles extensively, this appendix is a good place to start in this book.

Appendix B is a reprint of a classic article by Harry F. Harlow. His tongue-in-cheek discussion of the preparation of research articles from the perspective of a journal editor is both enjoyable and informative.

Appendices C and D provide research criteria that you can apply when evaluating the articles. In addition, your main textbook may contain a list of criteria. Your instructor will inform you which, if any, of these sets of criteria you are to apply.

Mildred L. Patten,
Editor

Article 1

Perceived Messages from Schools Regarding Adolescent Tobacco Use

Melanie Booth-Butterfield
West Virginia University

Robert Anderson
West Virginia University

Kimberly Williams
West Virginia University

ABSTRACT. This study conducted focus group interviews with 8th and 12th grade adolescent tobacco users to examine perceived messages from their school systems regarding tobacco use. This was part of a larger study sponsored by the CDC on adolescents' reasons for tobacco use. Two clear patterns of perceptions emerged. 1) Students perceive school systems to be hypocritical and to be sending contradictory messages regarding the use of tobacco. 2) The reward/punishment structure of public school systems may not be effective in deterring tobacco use among adolescents.

From *Communication Education, 49*, 196–205. Copyright © 2000 by National Communication Association. Reprinted with permission.

The problem of an individual's choice of unhealthy lifestyles has proven to be incredibly difficult to alter. Clearly, just having information about a risky health behavior such as unprotected sex or tobacco use is not
5 sufficient to cause elimination of the problems (Conner & Norman, 1998). Although it is estimated that 70% of cancer is attributable to lifestyle choices and environment, people persist in health behaviors that are proven harmful to them. For example, widespread community
10 and workplace campaigns to increase healthy diets often produce minuscule improvements overall, and no improvements in smoking cessation (e.g., Brownson et al., 1996; Lerman et al., 1997). Most smokers do not quit (or remain smoke-free), even though they make
15 three to five attempts to do so (Breslau & Peterson, 1996), and health problems may be even more serious for adolescent females who smoke than for adolescent males who smoke (Gold et al., 1996). Yet adolescents, especially females, persist in taking up smoking despite
20 acknowledgment of the well-publicized health risks.

Adolescent Tobacco Use

As educators, as well as taxpayers, we are interested in why adolescents continue to use tobacco, apparently heedless of the risk entailed. On a national level, Nelson and colleagues (1995) found that 1985
25 marked the end of several years' decline in smoking among white adolescents. No significant decrease was observed in that group during the years 1985–1991. In contrast, smoking declined among African American

youth between 1974–1991. Those researchers sug-
30 gested that the tobacco industry's targeting of that age group through advertising and promotion may partially account for the lack of decline in smoking among white teens even in the face of daunting physical risk (e.g., Barker, 1994; Pierce & Gilpin, 1995). They also sug-
35 gested that there has been an emergence of a group of high-risk adolescents who are more likely to experiment with smoking and who may have resisted school, parental, and media efforts to discourage smoking. The authors further speculated that since the ubiquitous
40 "just say no" campaigns emphasized illicit drugs as the target of what youth should "say no" to, adolescents may have perceived that cigarette smoking was a relatively acceptable activity.

A clear marker was observed in May 1996, when
45 the Centers for Disease Control and Prevention released its findings from the 1995 YRBS (USDHHS, 1996). Smoking among high school students had risen from 27.5% in 1991 to 34.8% in 1995. That report attributed factors contributing to this increase as market-
50 ing practices and mass media exposure to tobacco use (e.g., glamorous portrayals in movies as well as commercial exposure).

Previous research has indicated that there are several factors that consistently are found to be associated
55 with uptake of tobacco. These include the presence of other smokers in the environment, adolescents' overestimations of smoking prevalence, perceptions that adolescents have of smokers as mature and independent, low expectations of success in life, risk-taking, and
60 physiological pleasure (Camp, Klesges, & Relyea, 1993; Dinh, Sarason, Peterson, & Onstad, 1995; Simons-Morton et al., 1999; Weinstein, 1998). Some attribute weight control as a reason for smoking, despite the fact that no difference in weight has been
65 shown between smoking and nonsmoking adults (Klesges et al., 1998). Camp et al. (1993) found that use of smoking as a weight control device differentiated between experimenters and regular smokers, but not between regular and never-smokers. Thus, we *do*
70 understand some of the contributing conditions for tobacco use. But given the troubling statistics on continuation and increase of tobacco uptake by adolescents, and given the important role of educational insti-

tutions in the lives of adolescents, there are additional
75 contextual factors that should be addressed by communication scholars. The focus here is on the messages,
often unintentional, that are communicated by our public schools.

Theoretical Rationale

The overarching question we confront here is,
80 "What messages are school systems sending to adolescents regarding tobacco use?" We are not focusing
upon the formal, educational messages regarding
smoking that are taught in classes or evident in official
policy statements. Rather, we examine the informal,
85 "between-the-lines" messages that students decode. As
is evident from other instructional communication research, multiple messages influence student behavior.

In the instructional communication literature, reasons why students choose or do not choose to enact
90 "educationally healthy," productive behaviors have
been explained in a broad cost-benefit model. For example, Gorham and Millette (1997) and Gorham and
Christophel (1992) examined motivators (perceived
rewards) and demotivators (perceived costs) to educa-
95 tional achievement. If we assume that we want adolescents to believe and comply with no-smoking rules, we
can also examine the instructional compliance literature. Richmond (1990) and Frymier (1994), among
many others, studied how teachers provide benefits or
100 extract costs in the classroom. Others such as Kearney,
Plax, and other instructional communication colleagues
have studied not only how teachers gain compliance of
students, but also how students engage in compliance
resistance (e.g., Burroughs, Kearney, & Plax, 1989;
105 Kearney, Plax, Richmond, & McCroskey, 1985; Kearney, Plax, Smith, & Sorensen, 1988).

A recent study of occasional adult smokers showed
that they were more likely to become daily smokers
within two years if there had been relational turmoil
110 such as the loss of a spouse through death, divorce, or
separation in their lives (Hennrikus, Jeffery, & Lando,
1996). Given the tumultuous nature of most adolescents' relationships, similar difficulties may contribute
to tobacco use. Tobacco may be viewed as a constant
115 in their lives, which are otherwise filled with relational
and/or emotional distress.

Hennrikus, Jeffery, and Lando (1996) found that
perceptions of boredom on the job and monotonous,
repetitious tasks significantly contributed to changing
120 occasional smokers to daily smokers. It is likely that
many adolescents who perceive school or their lives to
be boring may look for the answer in smoking as well.
Given the difficulties teen smokers often have with
school (Hu, Lin, & Keeler, 1998), they may be particu-
125 larly likely to feel bored or stressed and perceive negative messages in instructional settings. But how do our
schools counteract such forces? Clearly the "just say
no" technique does not work with tobacco (Reardon,
Sussman, & Flay, 1989). So we investigated what stu-

130 dents (both users and nonusers of tobacco) believe their
schools communicate to them regarding tobacco.

Method

A qualitative research design was selected for this
study. We felt it important to be able to describe the
135 problem from the *emic* perspective, that is, the "native's point of view" (Vidich & Lyman, 1994). In this
case, tobacco-using 14-year-olds may have a very different perception of their lives than do middle-aged
social science researchers. Were a quantitative ap-
140 proach taken, we would have developed a questionnaire with closed-ended questions that reflected our
conceptualization of possible reasons for the behavior
at issue. However, such an *etic* or "world-view" perspective (Vidich & Lyman, 1994) would have led to
145 findings based on our expected reasons for the behavior. Such an approach would be justified had there been
certainty and agreement on the most common responses to our questions we could expect our subjects
to provide. But clearly, despite years of study, and in
150 the face of our educational values that teach that tobacco use is negative, we do not fully understand why
adolescents choose to engage in a behavior that entails
such great costs. Therefore, a qualitative approach was
deemed more appropriate.

Focus group methodology is particularly appropri-
155 ate for these exploratory questions about the informal
institutional messages regarding tobacco (Morse &
Field, 1995). Conducting focus groups of adolescents
enabled us to ask more general questions of participants than closed-format interviews or surveys. These
160 interview questions led to follow-up questions that
were based on participants' responses to the general
questions. In addition, the focus group approach provided opportunities for the discussants to respond to
statements made by their peers, in their own words, and
165 from perspectives not anticipated by the researchers.
Hence, all aspects of the issue raised by the interviewees were able to be explored and extended.

Interviews with Adolescents Regarding Tobacco
and Relationships

This study was a part of a larger project investigat-
170 ing adolescent tobacco use funded by the Centers for
Disease Control and Prevention. The current investigation focused upon informal messages from school systems that may be interpreted to support and maintain
tobacco use.

Procedures and measures for this research were pi-
175 lot tested on two focus groups of smoking and nonsmoking college freshmen. It was reasoned that given
their age, these students would be the closest in perspective to the adolescents of the main study, and being
18 years of age were available for pretesting proce-
180 dures. Pretesting was necessary to examine and refine
discussion procedures, to train moderators, to assess
the timing of components, and test the technical capabilities of the audio equipment to be used. Pilot groups

were videotaped for study of procedures, but were not included in the research analyses. All research groups were adolescents from public school systems.

Participants and Procedures

Participants were recruited with the cooperation of several public middle and high schools. These were in communities in the state at a distance from the university to minimize overrepresentation of academic families. Students whose parents signed and returned consent forms were administered questionnaires that determined their gender and tobacco-use status: nonuser, smoker, or smokeless tobacco user.[1] Tobacco use was liberally defined as having smoked cigarettes or used smokeless tobacco during the past 30 days. Focus group participants were then selected based on these questionnaires.

The main study's 13 focus groups were conducted in the instructional sites by four different facilitators working from a common script. The script questions differed slightly for smoking, nonsmoking, and smokeless tobacco using groups. Separate groups were conducted for 8th- and 12th-grade students and for males and females to avoid conversational dominance effects due to age or gender. The size of the groups was from 5 to 9 participants, with one group only having three. Participants were mostly white, were segregated by smoking status, and in most cases the sex of the interviewer was matched with the participants.

Group discussions began with getting acquainted/oriented, making name tags, and then proceeded into questions about general activities before initiating talk about tobacco. Each group interaction lasted approximately one hour. At the end of the time period, participants were asked to complete a brief demographic questionnaire, and then were debriefed and thanked. Approximately half were paid for their participation.

Data Coding and Analysis

Audiotapes were professionally transcribed and the texts coded and analyzed using Q.S.R. NUD*IST software (Non-numerical Unstructured Data Indexing Searching and Theorizing). This software is designed for the organization, examination, and analysis of qualitative data. Because this study was coordinated with 10 other federally funded prevention centers from across the U.S., the primary coding scheme was developed collaboratively across centers. However, NUD*IST allows creation of new nodes of information

to be coded as the interpretative process proceeds and throughout the analysis. Thus, the codebook included several categories unique to this center's investigation.

Three researchers independently coded the adolescents' text units from one focus group following extensive multiteam collaborative work on development of the coding scheme. Text units were defined as any complete utterance or thought by one participant. Thus, units could be single words (e.g., "yes," which would have to be interpreted in the context of surrounding units, or units could include several sentences as participants explained an experience). This resulted in multiple layers/categories of codes being applied to those extended units. Transcripts were read and reread, providing practice and reliability checks. This resulted in a rate of over 80% agreement across all coders.

Each transcript was subsequently cross-coded by two researchers with disagreements resolved through discussion. Because NUD*IST allows for multiple codes per conversational unit (e.g., unit referenced family, home context, and reasons not to smoke), we opted to "cast the broadest net" to enhance descriptive potential and add codes if the statement seemed to reference additional ideas. Discussion and repeated examination of the data were necessary to contextualize the statements by the adolescents and to avoid attaching too much importance to a specific statement that might have been made by only one participant.

Results

For this study, repeated themes related to perceived messages from schools were scrutinized. Themes consisted of message patterns that were communicated in numerous groups and were voiced by several participants, thus avoiding idiosyncratic, nonrepresentative statements. Specific questions asked in these areas related to what schools said about use or nonuse of tobacco, norms within schools, and messages from teachers. Specific questions from participants illustrate messages individual students perceived, but they also represent patterns of responses in that area.

Two major findings from these students' interviews stand out. First, there were consistent patterns of interpretation that emphasized the "hypocritical" nature of anti-tobacco messages received from school systems. Second, the incentive–punishment procedures used by schools to discourage tobacco use appear to be ineffective.

Hypocritical Messages

Messages from educational institutions often seemed paradoxical to the students. On one hand, schools are designated drug-free zones. But tobacco use clearly occurs regularly on the grounds (both outdoors and indoors), with little deterrent. Thus, schools and teachers were perceived particularly by smoking students as "hypocritical." The adolescents knew the school officials didn't want them to use tobacco. But the authority figures were aware that smoking was oc-

---

[1] We recognize that these selection procedures may result in a not-fully-representative sample of adolescent tobacco users. For a variety of reasons, parents of tobacco-using students may be less likely to return parental forms, or tobacco-using students may be less likely to complete the forms and take them home for signatures. However, this is the system of human subject protection that we work within, realizing that our sample may not include some of the most entrenched tobacco users.

285 curring and did little or nothing to deter it. One young woman's response to the issue of smoking in the schools included, "...they get mad when they [students] smoke in there. Well the teachers can't go all day without smoking so why should we? They go out-
290 side and as soon as they get in their car they want to smoke a cigarette. If someone saw me smoking a cigarette in my car every day, they'd probably yell at me."

Although students are aware that schools are smoke-free zones by law, there are certain areas where
295 it is understood, widely recognized across the organization, and even tolerated, that students smoke. These include parking lots, bus stops, specific outdoor areas, and ubiquitous references to school restrooms.

Regarding the restrooms: "(In the) high school,
300 they don't do nothing about it. You can go in there any time of the day, and like, a lot of those teachers smoke so they don't care. You can go in there any time of the day and there's people in there smoking. There's cigarettes laying all over the bathroom. Ashes on the toilet
305 seats."

Regarding bus stops: "At our bus garage, when I get off my bus there's kids that go behind the bus and smoke and the bus drivers know about it. They just don't care." Clearly, bus drivers are viewed as potential
310 discipline agents within the school system, and are perceived to be remiss if they do nothing in the face of overt tobacco use.

In every school, there were commonly known outdoor areas where smokers gathered. These appeared to
315 serve a group function, were visible and accessible, and yet were typically overlooked by the organization.

Athletic coaches were often seen as hypocritical in their own behavior and in disciplining student athletes. A few representative quotes describe common beliefs:
320 "The track coach doesn't want you to do it, but he's pretty much a hypocrite because he does it himself (smoke)." Another student claimed, "Coaches I know don't care one bit. They ask if the kids have any (snuff) because the coaches do it too." "The basketball coach
325 won't let you do it (smoke), but he may do it himself." One student was more sympathetic, "Like if you play sports or something, I don't think the football coach or his assistants, they might say something to you, but I don't think they would force anything on you."
330 Teachers are particularly vulnerable to negative perceptions of rule enforcement if they smoke themselves. "Some teachers, they tell you they can't punish you for something they do themselves." "Like the teachers here—some of them don't care if you have
335 one in (dip) or not because they do it themselves."

Punishment Procedures Are Ineffective

Students viewed school systems as hypocritical with punishment for smoking either neglected or applied unevenly. This, in turn, makes the students less likely to comply with the rules. The inconsistency of
340 punishment for breaking tobacco use rules was viewed

as a function of a) who the student was, and b) which teacher was the referent. A common theme was that some students appeared to be able to get away with using tobacco. One student put it expansively, "I think
345 a lot of it depends on who you know in the upper staff, because some people seem to get away with it while others get caught. And everyone knows they smoke and even knows what time they smoke. They never seem to get caught."
350 "It seems like if you play sports and stuff, you never get caught for smoking or snuff or anything unless you get caught by the wrong teacher. Most teachers will let you get away with it as long as you're well known and you're liked by most of the teachers. If
355 you're not liked, then the student gets in trouble all the time."

Some nonsmoking female teens put the issue of getting caught smoking another way. After being in a restroom where some people were smoking, those girls
360 received scrutiny. "(The teachers) think that we're the ones smoking and they don't say nothing to the ones they know who *are* smoking." This appears to be either a matter of student perspective, or vigilance on the part of teachers who want to warn the "good students" away
365 from tobacco use.

Along those same lines, teachers are viewed as extremely idiosyncratic in their concern and actions regarding tobacco use. At one extreme are vigilant teachers. All focus groups could name two or three teachers
370 in their schools who were more aggressive in curtailing tobacco, "like Mr. Lang, he's always on the hunt." As another example of idiosyncratic punishment, one boy spoke of a teacher who would make students eat hot peppers or swallow the snuff if he caught them using
375 tobacco in the area. Even some coaches were perceived as stringent in their enforcement of snuff regulations on the baseball field, "Now like you get kicked out of that game and you get suspended for like two games."

But more commonly, students viewed teachers as
380 tolerant, not because of empathy with the student, but because they "didn't care." Most said the schools "wouldn't do nothing to you" if caught, or "it depends on who you are if you get punished or not." Again, even if punishment was meted out, it seemed to have
385 negligible deterring value. At the very least, such patterns would be perceived in Gorham and Millette's terms as "demotivators" to changing tobacco behavior. As one student put it, "The only thing I think you get penalized for is smoking dope."
390 Some students were aware of enforcement, because they had received punishment. "A couple of years ago, I used to get kicked out of school all the time because I'd get caught smoking everywhere." Another referenced difficulties and conflicts with tobacco as occur-
395 ring during the time when he was flunking 6th grade. Tobacco-using students appear to feel unjustly selected for punishment.

Enforcement appears to be more consistent regarding the wearing of apparel with tobacco logos (e.g., Marlboro gear, Camel shirts). Those rules were perceived to be strictly enforced. "First you know, you get like three or four warnings, you know, 'turn the shirt inside out.' As long as it's not day-after-day." It may be that rules about apparel are easier to enforce due to the concrete observation of the gear.

There is recognition among some students of the difficulty of enforcement of anti-tobacco regulation in schools because the problem is so widespread. "Well, you can't stop every person. Like if you stop Tim, then you have to go get Joe, and then Bob over there, and it's an endless process."

Discussion and Educational Implications

It is evident that adolescent tobacco users interpret a variety of messages from schools in ways that are not productive for tobacco cessation. It is not clear whether these messages are real or a result of biased processing. While adolescents acknowledged "costs" of tobacco use at school (e.g., potential punishment, negative image from others, physiological complaints, etc.), these tended to be discounted, and were not sufficiently detrimental to make up for the rewards obtained by tobacco use (see also Weinstein, 1998).

Sometimes the attribution for why adolescents engage in life-threatening behavior is that the perceived "costs" are distal. They are far in the future and are not perceived to be likely to happen to the individual. The tobacco-using adolescents in our groups appeared to recognize risks at school, but minimized the impact and/or probability of enforcement. These explanations are consistent with social learning models in that the anticipated consequences, or outcome expectations, of smoking were generally more positive than negative (e.g., Bandura, 1986; Simons-Morton et al., 1999).

Bui, Peplau, and Hill (1996) found that when predicting commitment and satisfaction in relationships, costs were less compelling than rewards. It may be that adolescent tobacco users are more motivated by the positive, if short-term, outcomes afforded by tobacco use, than by the costs it admittedly extracts. Further, a recent study showed that people often chose short-term benefits even knowing those choices would result in long-term costs when they experienced negative emotional states (Gray, 1998). Many tobacco-using teens experience a great deal of negative affect in their lives and appear to view smoking as a necessary evil in coping (See also Booth-Butterfield, Anderson, & Williams, 1997; Brandon, 1994). Hence, educators may need to address increasing alternative and immediate rewards for at-risk students. Interestingly, not one of our adolescents mentioned any type of school incentive for not using tobacco.

Educators could address the problem of teen smoking by attempting to provide alternate rewards for potential tobacco users. More than one of our interviewees mentioned beginning or increasing their smoking at the same time they were failing a grade in school or having significant family problems. Adolescents who are at risk for tobacco uptake find few rewards in the traditional school setting (whether academic or co-curricular). We need to examine how tobacco users could attain a sense of individual achievement and/or goal attainment leading to perceived rewards for them in avenues other than tobacco usage.

Another major direction for school systems is to make sure that tobacco policy and enforcement of the rules are aligned. This is not an easy task. However, the inconsistency with which the rules are enforced, both dependent upon the identity of the student-rule-breaker and the teacher-enforcer, undermines efforts to eradicate tobacco use from school property.

Regardless of the freedom they *say* they want, adolescents need consistent structure and guidelines from authority figures. Recent studies have reported that tobacco-using adolescents are less internal in their locus of control than are nontobacco-using adolescents (Booth-Butterfield, Anderson, & Booth-Butterfield, in press; Eiser, Eiser, Gammage, & Morgan, 1989). This suggests that credible external rules may assist in deterring tobacco use. One young man who was in a GED/work program stated that the firm rules in the program helped him to cut down on smoking. "Before I came to the program I was (smoking) like almost 2 packs a day. And since I've been here for a year, and they only have breaks at certain times, so you can't smoke in the building, you're limited to how many cigarettes you can smoke here. So that's helped me cut down a lot." As another young man speculated. "I might not do it if they made us sign a contract, like Prom Promise or something." Thus, the rules against smoking themselves may not be aversive if they are evenly applied. But perceived inequity and inconsistency is clearly detrimental.

Admittedly, there are limitations to the qualitative research design employed here. We are able to describe how these teens perceive explicit/implicit messages about tobacco use and rule enforcement, but it is less clear how overt and widespread those patterns of messages actually were. However, we must recognize that we are examining what adolescents *believe* occurs in their school environment, and they respond to those stimuli.

A second limitation is in the use of group interviews. Focus groups may not be representative of all adolescents or all school systems, and findings cannot necessarily be generalized to a larger population. Some schools may have policies of enforcement that are entirely consistent and equitable. However, these descriptive accounts are congruent with other, more empirical, studies of tobacco use and adolescents.

Conclusion

One young woman summed the issue of anti-

510 tobacco regulation in schools up this way: "If they wanted to enforce it, they could do it., but they must not want to do it very bad because you know, they come out and they catch someone about once every three days or so. If they really wanted to enforce it,
515 they could do it, because they've done everything else that they wanted to." From an adult, professional perspective, this may seem like an overly simplistic viewpoint. Nevertheless, adolescents often perceive adults as all-powerful, and when adults do not use their power
520 appropriately, other efforts are undermined.

If schools are to have substantial impact on adolescents' uptake of tobacco, there is a need to examine and recognize what messages the institution and its representatives are sending. To adolescents, the mes-
525 sages seem contradictory. Numerous educational sources stress the need for consistency of reinforcement. It seems advisable for public school systems to review both their policies and their actions to ascertain whether they are communicating mixed messages to a
530 vulnerable audience.

References

Bandura, A. (1986). *Social foundations of thought and action: A social cognitive theory*. Englewood Cliffs, NJ: Prentice Hall.

Barker, D. (1994). Changes in the cigarette brand preferences of adolescent smokers–United States, 1989–1993. *MMWR Morbidity and Mortality Weekly Report, 43*, 577–581.

Booth-Butterfield, M., Anderson, R., & Booth-Butterfield, S. (in press). Health locus of control, self-monitoring, and tobacco use among adolescents. *Health Communication*.

Booth-Butterfield, M., Anderson, R., & Williams, K. (1997). *"If you're smoking, you don't have to talk,"* Interpersonal Applications of Tobacco Use Among Adolescents. Paper presented at the annual conference of the National Communication Association, Chicago.

Brandon, T. (1994). Negative affect as motivation to smoke. *Current Directions in Psychological Science, 3*, 33–37.

Breslau, N., &. Peterson, E. (1996). Smoking cessation in young adults: Age at initiation of cigarette smoking and other suspected influences. *American Journal of Public Health, 86*, 214–220.

Brownson, R., Smith, C., Pratt, M., Mack, N., Jackson-Thompson, J., Dean, C., Dabney, S., & Wilkerson, J. (1996). Preventing cardiovascular disease through community-based risk reduction: The Bootheel Heart Health Project. *American Journal of Public Health, 86*, 206–213.

Bui, K., Peplau, L., & Hill, C. (1996). Testing the Rusbult model of relationships commitment and stability in a 15-year study of heterosexual couples. *Personality and Social Psychology Bulletin, 22*, 1244–1257.

Burroughs, N., Kearney, P., & Plax, T. (1989). Compliance-resistance in the college classroom. *Communication Education, 38*, 214–229.

Camp, D., Klesges, R., & Relyea, G. (1993). The relationship between body weight concerns and adolescent smoking. *Health Psychology, 12*, 24–33.

Connor, M., & Norman, P. (1998). *Predicting health behavior*. Philadelphia: Open University Press.

Dinh, K., Sarason, I., Peterson, A., & Onstad, L. (1995). Children's perception of smokers and nonsmokers: A longitudinal study. *Health Psychology, 14*, 32–40.

Eiser, J., Eiser, C., Gammage, P., & Morgan, M. (1989). Health locus of control and health beliefs in relation to adolescent smoking. *British Journal of Addiction, 84*, 1059–1065.

Frymier, A. (1994). A model of immediacy in the classroom. *Communication Quarterly, 42*, 133–144.

Gold, D., Wang, X., Wypij, D., Speizer, F., Ware, J., & Dockery, D. (1996). Effects of cigarette smoking on lung function in adolescent boys and girls. *New England Journal of Medicine, 335*, 931–937.

Gorham, J., & Christophel, D. (1992). Students' perceptions of teacher behavior as motivating and demotivating factors in college classes. *Communication Quarterly, 40*, 239–252.

Gorham, J., & Millette, D. (1997). A comparative analysis of teacher and student perceptions of sources of motivation and demotivation in college classes. *Communication Education, 46*, 245–261.

Gray, J. (1998). A bias toward short-term thinking in threat-related negative emotional states. *Personality and Social Psychology Bulletin, 25*, 65–75.

Hennrikus, D., Jeffery, R., & Lando, H. (1996). Occasional smoking in a Minnesota working population. *American Journal of Public Health, 86*, 1260–1266.

Hu, T., Lin, Z., & Keeler, T. (1998), Teenage smoking, attempts to quit, and school performance. *American Journal of Public Health, 88*, 940–943.

Kearney, P., Plax, T., Richmond, V., & McCroskey, J. (1985). Power in the classroom III: Teacher communication techniques and messages. *Communication Education, 34*, 19–28.

Kearney, P., Plax, T., Smith, V., & Sorensen, G. (1988). Effects of teacher immediacy and strategy type on college student resistance. *Communication Education, 37*, 54–67.

Klesges, R., Zbikowski, S., Lando, H., Haddock, C. K., Talcott, G. W., & Robinson, L. (1998). The relationship between smoking and body weight in a population of young military personnel. *Health Psychology, 17*, 454–458.

Lerman, C., Gold, K., Orleans, C., Boyd, N., Wilfond, B., Louben, G., & Caporaso, N. (1997). Incorporating biomarkers of exposure and genetic susceptibility into smoking cessation treatment: Effects on smoking-related cognitions, emotions, and behavior change. *Health Psychology, 16*, 87–99.

Morse, J., & Field, P. (1995). *Qualitative research methods for health professionals*. Thousand Oaks: Sage.

Nelson, D., Giovino, G., Shopland, D., Mowery, P., Mills, L., & Erikson, M. (1995). Trends in cigarette smoking among U.S. adolescents, 1974–1991. *American Journal of Public Health, 85*, 34–40.

Pierce, J., & Gilpin, E. (1995). A historical analysis of tobacco marketing and the uptake of smoking by youth in the United States: 1890–1977. *Health Psychology, 14*, 500–508.

Reardon, K., Sussman, S., & Flay, B. (1989). Are we marketing the right message: Can kids "just say no" to smoking? *Communication Monographs, 56*, 307–324.

Richmond, V. (1990). Communication in the classroom: Power and motivation. *Communication Education, 39*, 181–195.

Simons-Morton, B., Crump, A., Haynie, D., Saylor, K., Eitel, P., & Yu, K. (1999). Psychosocial, school, and parent factors associated with recent smoking among early-adolescent boys and girls. *Preventive Medicine, 28*, 138–148.

U.S. Department of Health and Human Services. (1996). Tobacco use and usual sources of cigarettes among high school students—United States, 1995. *Morbidity and Mortality Weekly Report, 45*, 413–418.

Vidich, A., & Lyman, S. (1994). Qualitative methods: Their history in sociology and anthropology. In N. Denzin & Y. Lincoln (Eds.) *Handbook of qualitative research* (pp. 23–59). (2nd ed.) Thousand Oaks, CA: Sage.

Weinstein, N. (1998). Accuracy of smokers' risk perceptions. *Annals of Behavioral Medicine, 20*, 135–140.

About the authors: Melanie Booth-Butterfield, Department of Communication Studies, West Virginia University, Morgantown, WV 26506; Robert Anderson, Associate Director Prevention Research Center, West Virginia University; Kimberly Williams, Research Associate, Department of Community Medicine, West Virginia University.

Acknowledgments: This research project was supported by Grant #U48/CCU310821 from the Centers for Disease Control and Prevention.

Exercise for Article 1

Factual Questions

1. The researchers state that they confronted what "overarching question"?

2. What do the researchers mean by *emic* perspective?

3. Were the responses of the pilot groups included in the research analysis?

4. Were the males and females placed in separate focus groups *or* were they placed in mixed-gender groups?

5. Each transcript was subsequently cross-coded by two researchers. How were any disagreements resolved?

6. The themes the researchers developed in their analysis consisted of message patterns that were communicated in numerous groups and were voiced by several participants. They did this in order to avoid what?

7. According to the students, some teachers were vigilant in curtailing tobacco. However, the researchers state that more commonly teachers were tolerant. Was this tolerance attributed to empathy with the students *or* was it attributed to not caring?

Questions for Discussion

8. The researchers describe their reasons for selecting a qualitative approach rather than a quantitative approach in lines 132–153. Have they convinced you that a qualitative approach is better? Explain.

9. The researchers state "Tobacco use was liberally defined as having smoked cigarettes or used smokeless tobacco during the past 30 days." What is your opinion of this definition? If you had conducted this study, would you have used this definition? Explain.

10. In footnote number 1 in the article, the researchers mention that their selection procedures might have resulted in a "not-fully-representative sample." In your opinion, is this an important limitation of this research? Explain.

11. Do you think that focus groups (discussion groups of students with an adult moderator) are a good way to collect information on this topic? If you had conducted this study, would you have used focus groups or interviews with individuals? Explain.

12. The researchers acknowledge that their methodology does not permit them to determine whether the messages from the schools are "real" or are a result of biased processing by the students. Do you think that it would be worthwhile to conduct an additional study in which the behavior of teachers regarding tobacco was directly observed in order to determine their "reality"? Explain. (See lines 414–415.)

Quality Ratings

Directions: Indicate your level of agreement with each of the following statements by circling a number from 5 for strongly agree (SA) to 1 for strongly disagree (SD). If you believe an item is not applicable to this research article, leave it blank. Be prepared to explain your ratings.

A. The introduction establishes the importance of the study.

   SA   5   4   3   2   1   SD

B. The literature review establishes the context for the study.

   SA   5   4   3   2   1   SD

C. The research purpose, question, or hypothesis is clearly stated.

   SA   5   4   3   2   1   SD

D. The method of sampling is sound.

   SA   5   4   3   2   1   SD

E. Relevant demographics (for example, age, gender, and ethnicity) are described.

   SA   5   4   3   2   1   SD

F. Measurement procedures are adequate.

   SA   5   4   3   2   1   SD

G. All procedures have been described in sufficient detail to permit a replication of the study.

   SA   5   4   3   2   1   SD

H. The participants have been adequately protected from potential harm.

   SA   5   4   3   2   1   SD

I. The results are clearly described.

   SA   5   4   3   2   1   SD

J. The discussion/conclusion is appropriate.

   SA   5   4   3   2   1   SD

K. Despite any flaws, the report is worthy of publication.

   SA   5   4   3   2   1   SD

Article 2

Cooperative Learning: Listening to How Children Work at School

Andrea Mueller
Queen's University, Ontario, Canada

Thomas Fleming
Queen's University, Ontario, Canada

ABSTRACT. Cooperative and collaborative learning are recognized as valuable components of classroom learning. However, many questions remain regarding how teachers might structure and guide children's group-learning experiences. An ethnographic case study of 29 Grade 6 and Grade 7 students who worked in groups over 5 weeks was examined to determine what was learned. Data included audiotape recordings of 6 groups of children working together across 11 work sessions, student interviews, children's self-evaluations and drawings, and research reports. Findings revealed that when working in groups, children require periods of unstructured time to organize themselves and to learn how to work together toward a mutual goal.

From *The Journal of Educational Research*, *94*, 259–265. Copyright © 2001 by Heldref Publications. Reprinted with permission.

Research into children's behavior in groups and their productivity was pioneered at the University of Iowa's Child Welfare Research Station toward the end of the 1930s. Working under the direction of Kurt
5 Lewin, an acclaimed experimental psychologist, graduate students Ronald Lippitt and Ralph White undertook a series of experiments in 1938 to investigate how children worked together in groups (Marrow, 1965). Participants chosen for the studies were 20 children who
10 met after school to make papier maché masks and to engage in other play activities. The children were divided into three groups, two of which were directed by an adult; each child was rotated through each of the three groups. The results of the experiments proved
15 remarkable. Researchers found that children in an autocratically led group seemed discontented, often aggressive, and lacking in initiative. Youngsters in groups without a leader experienced similar problems: members appeared frustrated, and much of the work
20 remained unfinished. In marked contrast, children in groups organized with a democratic leader—someone who allowed the group to set its own agendas and priorities—appeared far more productive, socially satisfied, and demonstrated greater originality and inde-
25 pendence in the work they completed.
   Although the Iowa studies excited the educational community, the advent of World War II—and its af-termath—greatly interrupted research into how children behaved and learned in groups. Scholarly atten-
30 tion did not again turn toward efforts to understand children's behavior and learning in groups until the 1970s (Slavin, 1991). Since that time, researchers have come to agree that cooperative and collaborative learning are valuable components of classroom learning
35 (Blumenfeld, Marx, Soloway, & Krajcik, 1996; Gamson, 1994; Kohn, 1991; Webb, Troper, & Fall, 1995), and children are often instructed to "work together" at school (Gamson, 1994; Patrick, 1994; Wood & Jones, 1994). Slavin (1991, p. 71) stated that cooperative
40 learning has been promoted as a solution to "an astonishing array of educational problems" and has been endorsed as a learning strategy by numerous researchers (Burron, James, & Ambrosio, 1993; Wood & Jones, 1994) who have investigated its effects on student
45 achievement (Slavin), as well as on the contexts and ways in which children work together in classrooms (Keedy & Drmacich, 1994).
   Definitions for cooperative and collaborative learning, however, are contrary for different researchers and
50 theorists. Vygotsky (1978), for example, viewed collaborative learning as part of a process leading to the social construction of knowledge. Other scholars (Kohn, 1992; Sapon-Shevin & Schniedewand, 1992) considered cooperative learning to be a form of critical
55 pedagogy that moves classrooms and societies closer toward the ideal of social justice. Caplow and Kardash (1995) characterized collaborative learning as a process in which "knowledge is not transferred from expert to learner, but created and located in the learning envi-
60 ronment" (p. 209). Others such as Burron, James, and Ambrosio (1993) and Ossont (1993) envisioned cooperative learning as a strategy to help students improve intellectual and social skills.

Context and Task

   Despite publication of such studies, many questions
65 remain unanswered about what children do and what they discuss when they are directed by teachers to work together in classroom groups. The purpose of the following study was to examine what was learned from a small, ethnographic case study of 29 elementary school
70 students who were observed working together in a

Vancouver school over a period of 5 weeks. The case study constituted part of a yearlong research study (Mueller, 1998) in which a former elementary teacher and a university teacher–researcher (the author) collaborated to create opportunities for children to engage in scientific inquiry. Specifically, the case study was composed of observations made when a mixed class of Grade 6 and Grade 7 children were organized into six work groups for a 5-week science project and were asked to design an amusement park ride for a class exhibition that was outlined in the following terms:

Assignment

The Pacific National Exhibition (PNE) will be closing permanently at the end of the season. The exhibition has decided to relocate on a parcel of land in the Fraser Valley. The board of executives is seeking innovative ideas from the public to help plan their new facility.

Your class has been selected to participate in this unique opportunity. We would like teams of students to create a new innovative ride or redesign an existing structure.

Each submission should include research, detailed drawings, and a simple mechanical model of your design. Please remember that space is limited and your group will have one-half of a tabletop to present your model.

Timeline

1. Research and Sketches (May 14)—one page of research on the mechanics of your model; a clear sketch on 8.5 x 11 paper;

2. Final Drawings (May 17)—a detailed drawing of your design on 11 x 17 paper; diagram should include a title, labels, and scale; this drawing will be used in your final presentation;

3. Models (May 28)—a simple model that demonstrates how the mechanical system works; the model should be displayed on cardboard no larger than half a tabletop; and

4. Presentation (May 29)—each group will be required to pitch its design to an audience (2–3 minutes); each member of the group should be prepared to respond to questions from the audience related to the mechanics of their selected systems.

Both the classroom and the instructional format were structured to allow children to participate in small-group inquiry for an extended period of time. Projects were outlined to provide opportunities for children to develop portfolios of information and knowledge about science (including research reports, scale drawings, and models) and to provide children with opportunities to make informal and formal presentations.

Research Framework

The theoretical framework that bounded this study consisted of two parts. In the first part, results of the Iowa study showed conclusively that children in democratically led groups were far more productive in completing tasks than were children in groups that were tightly controlled or leaderless (Marrow, 1965). Moreover, groups that determined their own work methods were characterized by a better spirit among members and were far less susceptible to quarreling and discontent. Both of those findings suggested that groups of children working together in classrooms should be allowed to organize themselves with a minimum of teacher interference. In other words, children should be allowed to work in a self-directed manner. That premise determined that both the teacher and teacher–researcher would assume a supportive but nondirective role in monitoring the science project— and that assistance to students would be provided only at their request.

The second part of the theoretical foundation underlying this research was an ethnographic approach (Britzman, 1991; Denzin, 1997; Ellis & Bochner, 1996). Because prominent writings on cooperative learning are long on prescription (Kohn, 1992; Sapon-Shevin & Schniedewand, 1992; Vygotsky, 1978) but generally short on description, I adopted an ethnographic approach to enlarge the existing state of knowledge about (a) the context in which children learn cooperatively, (b) how they structure their work, (c) how they develop ideas and plans, and (d) how they communicate with each other. Recording and transcribing children's conversations about the science project, in effect, provided an "on the ground" and detailed view of how children organized themselves to learn and to accomplish a task that they defined for themselves.

That approach to the study emerged over 2 years as the university-based principal researcher (and the former elementary school teacher) worked with a Grade 6/7 teacher in central Vancouver as part of a school-wide project to improve children's performance in mathematics and science. Following the successful completion of a small trial project the first year, the teacher and teacher–researcher agreed to undertake a second, longer science project the following year to increase children's involvement in their own science learning, to bring together elements of technology and science, and to allow for a maximum of children's expression. The second study furnishes the basis for this article.

Data Collection

During the 11 sessions of the 5-week study, I used audiotapes to record six groups of children at work. A Walkman-sized tape recorder and microphone were placed on tables where each group worked to record the six groups simultaneously. I also used that method to make audio recordings of conversations with children individually, in pairs, and in groups. Altogether, 36 audiotapes, each 90 min in length, were used to re-

180 cord approximately 54 hrs of children speaking about the project. The tapes were later transcribed verbatim into a written record of 99 pages, which was then analyzed. A coding system identified teacher visits to the groups and the language each group of children used

185 when they (a) generated ideas to accomplish the task at hand and (b) organized themselves socially. The number of teacher visits to each group across the life of the project reflected the different needs of the six groups and their demands for teacher assistance.

190   I obtained additional data from the researcher's field notes, children's drawings and research reports, audiotaped conversations with the teacher, audio and videotape recordings of large-class discussions, videotapes of children in group work, and photographs of

195 children participating in the project. Written self-evaluations about what children learned in undertaking the project provided an additional data source for analysis.

    At the study's outset, several students indicated to

200 the teacher or researcher that they were uncomfortable or annoyed with the recording device. The researcher reminded the teacher and children several times that if the tape recorders were too distracting, they would be removed. After the first day, however, only 2 children

205 mentioned the tape recording again over the 5-week project. Some children perceived that audiotaping their ideas was beneficial and, therefore, requested opportunities to re-listen to their discussions. Tape recorders were removed only during the final days of the project,

210 when students were working full time on their models and when materials were scattered around the classroom.

Purpose of Discussion

    In the following discussion, I examined what children learned from a case study in which Grade 6 and

215 Grade 7 youngsters were asked to work together to create an amusement park ride. The first part of the discussion explores the ways that children used language to define their ideas and activities and to organize themselves in completing the design they proposed.

220 The second part of the discussion reports the responses that children made on the basis of their experience working together in groups, especially as it pertains to learning science and, more generally, to the value of cooperative learning.

Work-Group Composition and Dynamics

225   The class participating in this study was composed of 29 students—16 girls and 13 boys. Nine students in Grade 6 and 18 students in Grade 7 were divided by the teacher into six groups (three groups of 5 students; three groups of 4 students). Data analysis included an

230 examination of the transcript story line, group file folders with sketches, drawings and research notes, as well as the researcher's field notes and observations. From those sources, I constructed the following portraits of the six groups.

235   *Group 1*: Two Grade 7 girls and 2 boys, 1 in Grade 7 and 1 in Grade 6, formed Group 1. Because of frequent absences by 1 Grade 7 girl early in the project, most critical decisions about the project were made by the group's other 3 members. The transcript of group

240 discussions across 11 group work sessions indicates that members expressed diverse ideas and worked diligently to complete the project. Occasionally, sounds of tension and disagreement among group members were evident. A Grade 7 girl, present for all work sessions,

245 took command as the leader of the group, often directing both the discussion and organization of work. The group was successful in their design and modeling of a playground ride, as well as in their presentations, and in the scientific explanations they offered in support of

250 their project.

    Group 2: Three Grade 7 girls and 2 Grade 7 boys (one boy received learning assistance weekly and the other boy had identified behavioral problems) formed Group 2. The transcript reveals that group discussion

255 was frequently distracted by social talk, although diverse ideas were expressed when their attention turned to the task at hand. A Grade 7 girl emerged as the leader in her frustration to keep the group on track, apart from contributing the largest number of ideas.

260 Two boys rarely expressed their thinking throughout the 11 work sessions. The group appeared incapable of making a decision until the last day. Although the ride they designed was creative, and although they gave a lively presentation, they were unable as a group to ex-

265 hibit a clear understanding about the science involved.

    Group 3: Three boys, 2 in Grade 7 and 1 in Grade 6 (received learning assistance weekly) and 2 girls, 1 in Grade 7 and 1 in Grade 6 (English-as-a-second-language [ESL] program) formed Group 3. A Grade 7

270 girl emerged as a gentle leader from the outset, encouraging group members to voice their thoughts and to remain on task. The transcript indicates that the group explored a wide range of ideas and that all members contributed ideas to discussions, although 1 Grade 6

275 girl and 1 Grade 6 boy said relatively little during the 11 work sessions. The transcript shows that some tensions were voiced, but under the direction of the leader, the group quickly dispelled points of disagreement. Overall, the group worked together in a coherent man-

280 ner and helped one another throughout the project. They created a wonderful ride, gave an excellent presentation, and clearly identified the science concepts they addressed.

    Group 4: Two girls, 1 in Grade 7 and 1 in Grade 6,

285 and 2 boys, 1 in Grade 7 (ESL) and 1 in Grade 6, formed Group 4. The Grade 7 boy was absent for many work sessions, and the Grade 6 boy, who was on medication for Attention Deficit Hyperactivity Disorder, contributed infrequently to group discussions and work

290 sessions. The 2 girls often expressed exasperation that they were left to do much of the work in this group. However, the 2 girls expressed a constant flurry of

ideas, and the Grade 6 girl emerged as the leader, directing the flow of conversation and work tasks. It was unclear which design plan this group would pursue until the final work session. Nevertheless, the design for their ride was completed on time, they were well prepared for the presentation, and they furnished a clear scientific explanation about how the proposed ride would operate.

Group 5: Three Grade 6 girls and 2 Grade 7 girls (both ESL) formed Group 5. This was the only all-girls group, and its composition was a function of a larger ratio of girls to boys in the classroom. One Grade 6 girl emerged as the group leader, and, overall, this group functioned smoothly. The transcript indicated that diverse ideas were expressed and debated. One Grade 7 ESL student remained mostly silent throughout all 11 work sessions. Group 5 designed and created a wonderful ride, gave a spirited presentation, and focused on a few key variables in offering scientific support for their amusement park ride.

Group 6: Two Grade 7 girls (1 ESL) and 2 boys, 1 in Grade 7 and 1 in Grade 6, formed Group 6. From the outset, 1 Grade 7 girl assumed the role of group leader, organizing ideas and encouraging participation. Another Grade 7 girl generally remained silent, which meant that the ideas expressed originated with the other 3 group members. Although a wide range of ideas were expressed, work sessions were marked by argumentation and tension. The transcript indicated that the leader frequently experienced difficulty in keeping the group on task, and, in effect, became responsible for making most decisions. Nevertheless, this group created an incredible ride, offered a well-prepared presentation, and thoroughly explained in scientific terms how their ride worked.

Role of Teacher and Teacher–Researcher

During small-group work, both the classroom teacher and the teacher–researcher moved around the classroom listening, asking questions, and supporting group ideas. The total number of combined visits by the teacher and teacher–researcher to each group were recorded as follows: Group 1, 26 visits; Group 2, 36 visits; Group 3, 39 visits; Group 4, 63 visits; Group 5, 46 visits; and Group 6, 30 visits.

In an audiotaped conversation after the amusement park project, the teacher and teacher–researcher comment about the roles they perceived themselves to be playing in the classroom. The teacher recollected as follows:

> Well, we were facilitators in the fact that we designed the problem—the challenge. I think in the sense that we were in some ways observers, but observers that had a vested interest in making sure that these projects were successful. So, we offered any kind of assistance or advice or knowledge that we could lend the groups. In some ways...I don't think we steered them, I really think...I don't know...it's hard to define, isn't it?

The teacher–researcher recalled:

> Yeah, I mean we listened to the groups. Sometimes they just asked us to come look to see what we think. And sometimes they just wanted to show us what they found out. But we were there. And in some way,...I think we also orchestrated—you know, we had a sense of what was going on in all the groups and knew when to...stop. Let's just reevaluate. And some of the kids also mentioned that it was really important the way we set it up and got them thinking and then the discussions that we had with them sometimes—the short ones. Got them thinking in a different way. But if I had to honestly tell somebody how I did it, or how we did it....

It's "really difficult," the teacher observed. "Yeah, because it is evolving," the teacher–researcher added.

In retrospect, both the teacher and the teacher–researcher acknowledged the difficulty of defining their roles as teachers within the experimental setting, perhaps because of their diverse actions and the fact that many of their activities were reactive in nature, that is, prompted by students' needs. In comparison with many instructional settings that are inclined to be teacher or curriculum centered, the emphasis in these work groups was centered on students and their approaches toward solving a science problem. The roles of the teacher and teacher–researcher generally remained those of facilitators, observers, and providers of assistance, advice, and knowledge. The teacher and teacher–researcher listened, orchestrated students' activities, evaluated and reevaluated students' learning opportunities, and, when deemed necessary, redirected students' thinking and activities. Overall, the nature of the roles of the teacher and teacher–researcher were more supportive than directive.

Purposes and Language of Work

Analysis of the transcript revealed that students working together used language for two central purposes. First, they used language to express or propose ideas related to the task at hand. Illustrations of this usage included: "You know Bonny had this idea where we could use magnets" "Like bring it up" and "That would be too hard wouldn't it?" Children's high level of interest in this project, as well as their high level of motivation, was evident both in the volume and range of ideas they advanced using language this way. Opportunities for students to work in small groups during science activities and to develop a discourse of scientific inquiry appear to be critical for student learning in science. Listening to such discourse also may advance educators' understandings about how students build knowledge in a group (Tobin, 1990; Wells & Wells, 1992).

Children also used language in a second way to effect social and organizational agreement. To illustrate: "So is that what we are going to do?" "Do you agree?" "Okay, we agree" and "Write that down on paper." Such comments demonstrated some of the ways that

405 children "operationalized" their ideas and how they obtained sufficient closure to move forward as a group. Listening to students' discourse and inquiry in science is important, but it is equally critical to be aware of what we are listening for in science. Careful attention
410 to student discussion is necessary to first understand the nature of language used among students in groups (Haussling & Mueller, 1995; Mueller, 1997). Then teachers can begin to encourage students to voice their initial thoughts and to continue their discourse of in-
415 quiry. However, it is also necessary to remember that students have learned to use particular language structures in schools. In other words, students have learned that correct answers are desirable and that incomplete or tentative answers are not acceptable. Therefore, cre-
420 ating learning opportunities in science that encourage and require discussion in groups may be an important first step toward fostering student discourse in science.

When an analysis of children's comments was tabulated (each comment was coded and assigned a cate-
425 gory), I found that the language used by the groups to propose ideas accounted for 61% of the children's expression, and the language used to advance social and organizational consensus accounted for 39% of their expression. Transcript analysis showed that all six
430 groups used language more frequently to propose ideas than to secure social and organizational agreement. Across groups, however, the language used by youngsters varied considerably; certain groups proposed greater numbers of ideas than others did.

435 Closer analysis of the proposed ideas category provides some indication about how the language of work was used and changed within and across the six groups. Each group had the opportunity to work together in class for 11 work sessions, coded as Day 1 through
440 Day 11. Across all groups, the first three sessions accounted for 87% of all ideas proposed; 49% of the total number of ideas was proposed during the second session. Similarly, data analysis of language used for social and organizational purposes showed similarly that
445 51% of usage occurred during the first three sessions. Again, Day 2 accounted for the largest single usage of language for those purposes; 29% of the total entries were during this session. Groups varied in the frequency with which they used language for social and
450 organizational objectives throughout the remainder of the work sessions. However, as the project moved toward closure, the use of social and organizational language increased for all groups during the final three work sessions.

455 Analysis of language also revealed that, not surprisingly, each group organized itself differently—a finding already reported in the literature (Ossont, 1993). However, in proposing various ideas for the design of the project—mostly during the initial 3 days—each of
460 the six groups used a coincident social and organizational use of language to explore how these ideas would be implemented into activities that would allow

the project to move toward completion. It is a central notion of the Iowa Studies that social and educational
465 research should take as its scope the full range of human organizations and that such organizations should be examined from interpersonal, group, and intergroup perspectives. The Iowa Studies also were based on the premise that group work should provide individuals
470 with opportunities for personal growth (Marrow, 1965). In other words, acting democratically in a group provides an education in itself (Lewin, 1944).

In retrospect, the fact that Day 2 emerged as the session of highest language usage for all groups was
475 likely conditioned by the teacher's request for information about "what each group is thinking about." Particularly, the teacher's instruction that each group was expected to present their "ideas in progress" in written form by the conclusion of Day 2 clearly spurred the
480 groups to entertain numerous ideas about the nature of their projects during the second work session.

Children's Reflections During the Project

At the end of the first week, the researcher met briefly with four of the six groups to determine how they felt about the project and how they thought it
485 would turn out. Three of the four groups expressed excitement regarding the amusement park challenge, whereas a fourth group indicated that the project would be too difficult to complete. All four groups reflected on their ability to work together. One student re-
490 marked: "I learned a lot about working with an idea and building on to it when a problem comes along." Group 5 reported feeling "very comfortable with their group members" because they had worked together earlier in the year. Group 2, in contrast, reported that
495 they were unsure about how cooperatively the group would function because they had not worked together previously. One Group 4 member clearly stated a desire "to be in a different group" and expressed a fear of ending up doing all the work. Group 6 members ex-
500 pressed the difficulty they were encountering in talking things out and listening to one another because they all talked at once.

Acting on an observation from the first interviews that 2 children from each group voiced their ideas
505 while the others remained silent, the researcher changed the interview strategy at the end of the second week by interviewing pairs of students from each group. During the second round of interviews, group members generally reported they had a better idea of
510 what they were doing. In some instances, children offered a sketch to explain how their amusement ride would work and to describe the materials they required to assemble the models. Discussion during the second interview sessions suggested that group members were
515 thinking through their scientific explanations. When asked about how their particular group was working together, members in each group intimated that they were working things out and declared a genuine inter-

est in their projects. Nevertheless, children from all groups generally reported that certain group members did not participate as much as others.

Children's Reflections After the Project

On completion of the project, self-evaluation and interview data also were collected to gauge children's reflections on the nature of what they had learned. Children completed written self-evaluations on the same day as their final presentations. Ten days later, 2 children from each group were reinterviewed in pairs.

The self-evaluation component asked children to "describe what you learned while working through this project." Their responses to the request generally fell within four categories: (a) acquisition of scientific knowledge or content, (b) acquisition of practical skills, (c) acquisition of group cooperation skills, and (d) learning to enjoy the challenge of science. Fourteen of 26 youngsters, or 54% of participants, reported improvements in their knowledge of science. To illustrate, 1 child wrote: "I learned about the steam engine and how it works." Similarly, 14 out of 26 children, or 54% of participants, also reported learning how to apply science in practical ways through the use of project materials. In this regard, one student observed: "I learned how to make strong enough supports." Eleven out of 26 participants, or 42% of the children, reported learning about group cooperation. "I learned if you don't get the perfect group—and some people slack off—to keep going," one child wrote. Finally, 9 of 26 children, or 35% of participants, observed that their learning was linked directly to the enjoyment they found in taking part in the project. One participant remarked: "I really enjoyed this project because it was fun and challenging."

The postproject interviews likewise proved revealing. During those sessions, the researcher interviewed 2 children from each group using their self-evaluations as a guide to the questions posed. Much of the postproject discussion focused on children's responses to questions about group learning in science and about their experiences with project work in general.

Children reported emphatically that they learned better when they were able to "do something" in contrast to "just reading the textbook" and "answering questions at the end of each chapter." From their responses to interview questions, it was apparent that although the students were only in Grade 6 or Grade 7, they were already dissatisfied with the predominant instructional pattern that centers on textbook learning and answering chapter questions or worksheets. One Grade 7 girl explained, "We're not using textbooks and doing dumb experiments. We are really doing something, and we are learning from our mistakes. It's not like reading about stuff and memorizing it. We actually do research and have to really find out stuff."

In comparison, the children said that "hands-on" project learning was far more exciting and real. Chil-

dren's comments were especially illustrative in this regard. One child observed: "I really learned a lot—I didn't think I could figure it out, like I could know that much information, learn or understand that much about it—but I do." Another offered: "When you do it, you remember it" because "it's not like just reading about it." One girl remarked: "We learned by going through the process" and "I would say not everything works the way it's supposed to." One boy said: "It was like a scavenger hunt and we needed to figure it out." Overall, in their solidly positive responses to activity work, children also appeared to recognize that they were not only learning science "but some math and other things."

No less favorable were children's responses to the advantages of group learning. One child explained: "I think learning to work in a group is really good; I don't always like it but it's a good skill to have; like when you get older, you'll have to work with groups and it's more fun." Others spoke about the benefits of learning "how to cooperate and work with other people." Several acknowledged that they learned more because of their audiences as "the presentations really forced us to know our stuff." "When you learn stuff without help, you are really proud of it," another reported. Still others noted the importance of "doing it ourselves and learning from our mistakes." Such comments, when taken as a whole, suggest the rich diversity of learning opportunities that children see attached to projects in which they work together.

In identifying what they learned, youngsters also identified three criteria for effective group work, notably that (a) sufficient time should be allowed to participants in cooperative learning projects to talk and work their ideas out, (b) to listen and to exchange ideas with others, and (c) to present what they have learned to each other and to an outside audience. At the end of the amusement park project, the teacher asked youngsters to comment about their learning experiences. Some of their spontaneous responses are recorded as follows:

Jade: "I really enjoyed working this way. We didn't have like tests at the end, but really it was tougher than a test 'cuz every day we had to find out something new and be able to explain it. We really learned a lot."

Celia: "The whole thing was like a test with no right or wrong answers. We learned along the way. It was really fun this way. Sometimes it was hard because groups didn't work out that well. But we learned how to work."

Darren: "I think the projects were really neat. It will be a total shock for the Grade 7s because we've heard that in high school all you do is write tests and memorize textbooks. We won't get to do anything anymore that is fun."

Sina: "We're really lucky. People always say to me you're really lucky 'cuz you get to do things in your class. In high school we don't get to do anything. People say your class is so lucky—even people in elementary say that from other schools."

Diva: "I think this is the best class in science I've ever had. We actually got to do things ourselves. We have to figure out how then."

635 **Ria**: "You have more fun when you learn this way. This way you learn every time you do a little part."

Sina: "When I'm actually into doing something I really want to understand it. When I'm reading a textbook it's really boring and I don't want to understand it."

640 Without a doubt, "listening to students communicate about their science adventures provided important insights to Ross and I about the nature of students' learning" (Mueller, 1998, p. 95).

Several other findings from this case study are also 645 worthy of note. First, a girl emerged as group leader in all six groups, a finding which in itself prompts far-reaching questions about gender and subject material, social leadership, and the role that language competency may play in classroom relationships between 650 boys and girls. Second, despite obvious problems that some groups encountered in working together, all the groups found ways to cooperate to the point where they could complete the requirements of the project. Third, self-evaluations provided by the children were valuable 655 to the teacher and sufficiently accurate to be used later—and in conjunction with other sources—as a reliable source of information for assessment purposes.

Finally, observations from this study suggest that the teacher plays a central role in setting up the condi-660 tions for collaborative learning, even though it appears on the basis of other studies (Martens, 1990; Rodrigue & Tingle, 1994) that many teachers feel uncomfortable with this approach despite documented positive effects of cooperative learning. Part of the discomfort has been 665 attributed to the fact that some teachers require support in learning how to become facilitators and how to allow students to work and learn together (Barclay & Breheny, 1994; Caplow & Kardash, 1995; Keedy & Drmacich, 1994; Martin-Kneip, Sussmann, & Meltzer, 670 1995). Welch (1998) recommended that teacher education programs should develop courses and field experiences to introduce prospective teachers to cooperative and collaborative classroom methods. In this study, observations on the teacher's instrumentality in shap-675 ing the learning environment for children in science classes strongly support Welch's recommendation.

References

Barclay, K., & Breheny, C. (1994). Letting the children take over more of their own learning: Collaborative research in the kindergarten classroom. *Young Children, 49*(6), 33–39.

Blumenfeld, P., Marx, R., Soloway, E., & Krajcik, J. (1996). Learning with peers: From small group cooperation to collaborative communities. *Educational Researcher, 25*(8), 37–40.

Britzman, D. (1991). *Practice makes practice:* A *critical study of learning to teach*. New York: SUNY.

Bruffee, K. (1995). Sharing our toys: Cooperative learning versus collaborative learning. *Change, 27*, 12–18.

Burron, B., James, M., & Ambrosio, A. (1993). The effects of cooperative learning in a physical science course for elementary/middle level preservice teachers. *Journal of Research in Science Teaching, 30*(7), 697-707.

Caplow, J., & Kardash, C. (1995). Collaborative learning activities in graduate courses. *Innovative Higher Education, 19*(3), 207–221.

Denzin, N. (Ed.) (1997). *Interpretive ethnography: Ethnographic practices for the 21st century*. California: Sage.

Ellis, C., & Bochner, A. (Eds.) (1996). *Composing ethnography: Alternative forms of qualitative writing*. Walnut Creek, CA: AltaMira.

Gamson, Z. (1994). Collaborative learning comes of age. *Change, 26*, 44–49.

Haussling, A., & Mueller, A. (1995). Lernen durch Hypothesenbilden: Eine praxisbezogene Untersuchung. *Sachunterricht und Mathematik in der Primarstufe, 11*, 476–482.

Keedy, J., & Drmacich, D. (1994). The collaborative curriculum at the school without walls: Empowering students for classroom learning. *The Urban Review, 26*(2), 121–135.

Kohn, A. (1991). Group grade grubbing versus cooperative learning. *Educational Leadership, 48*(5), 83–87.

Kohn, A. (1992). Resistance to cooperative learning: Making sense of its deletion and dilution. *Journal of Education, 174*(2), 38–56.

Lewin, K. (1944). Dynamics of group activity. *Educational Leadership, 1*, 199.

Marrow, A. J. (1965). *The practical theorist: The life and work of Kurt Lewin*. New York: Basic Books.

Martens, M. (1990). Getting a grip on groups. *Science and Children, 27*(5), 18–19.

Martin-Kneip, G., Sussmann, E., & Meltzer, E. (1995). The North Shore collaborative inquiry project: A reflective study of assessment and learning. *Journal of Staff Development, 16*(4), 46–51.

Mueller, A. (1997). Discourse of scientific inquiry in the classroom. *Journal of Elementary Science Education, 9*(1), 15–33.

Mueller, A. (1998). A *desire to inquire: Children experience science as adventure*. Unpublished doctoral dissertation, University of British Columbia, Vancouver.

Ossont, D. (1993). How I use cooperative learning. *Science Scope, 16*(8), 28–31.

Patrick, J. (1994). Direct teaching of collaborative skills in a cooperative learning environment. *Teaching and Change, 1*(2), 170–181.

Rodrigue, P., & Tingle, J. (1994). The extra step: Linking inservice and preservice teachers. *Science and Children, 31*(4), 34–36.

Sapon-Shevin, M., & Schniedewand, N. (1992). If cooperative learning's the answer, what are the questions? *Journal of Education, 174*(2), 10–37.

Simmons, P., & Wylie, C. (1993). Exploring Jurassic Park. *The Science Teacher, 60*(8), 50–53.

Slavin, R. (1991). Synthesis of research on cooperative learning. *Educational Leadership, 48*(5), 71–82.

Tobin, K. (1990). Research on science laboratory activities: In pursuit of better questions and answers to improve learning. *School Science and Mathematics, 90*(5), 403–418.

Vygotsky, L. (1978). *Thought and Language*. Cambridge: MIT Press.

Webb, N., Troper, J., & Fall, R. (1995). Constructive activity and learning in collaborative small groups. *Journal of Educational Psychology, 87*(3), 406–423.

Welch, M. (1998). Collaboration: Staying on the bandwagon. *Journal of Teacher Education, 49*(1), 26–37.

Well, G., & Chang-Wells, G. L. (1992). *Constructing knowledge together: Classrooms as centers of inquiry and literacy*. Portsmouth, NH: Heinemann.

Address correspondence to: Andrea Mueller, Queen's University, Faculty of Education, Kingston, Ontario, Canada K7L 3N6. E-mail: muellera@educ.queensu.ca

Exercise for Article 2

Factual Questions

1. This case study involved how many elementary school students?

2. The students in this study were in what grades?

3. Did the teacher and teacher–researcher assume a highly directive role in supervising the groups?

4. There were how many sessions during the 5-week study?

5. For Group 4, what was the total number of com-

bined visits by the teacher and teacher–researcher?

6. Analysis of the transcript revealed that the students working together used language for how many central purposes?

7. After the project, the children were asked to engage in reflection. The self-evaluation component asked children to describe what?

Questions for Discussion

8. This research is classified in the contents of this book as an example of qualitative research. As such, it contains few statistics and no statistical tests. In light of this, do you consider this study to be "real research"? Explain.

9. The authors discuss their "Research Framework." In your opinion, are the two parts of the framework described in sufficient detail? Explain.

10. Some students were uncomfortable with the tape recording device. Does this surprise you? Could it affect the outcomes of this study? Explain.

11. The six groups in this study varied considerably. For example, Group 5 consisted of all girls, but all the other groups had boys and girls, some groups had English-As-a-Second Language students (ESL) and some did not, and so on. In your opinion, is this diversity across the groups a strength or weakness of the study? Explain.

12. The cooperative project in this study was a science project. Would you be willing to generalize the results of this study to other types of projects? Explain.

13. If you were conducting a study on the same topic, what changes in the research methodology, if any, would you make?

Quality Ratings

Directions: Indicate your level of agreement with each of the following statements by circling a number from 5 for strongly agree (SA) to 1 for strongly disagree (SD). If you believe an item is not applicable to this research article, leave it blank. Be prepared to explain your ratings.

A. The introduction establishes the importance of the study.

   SA   5   4   3   2   1   SD

B. The literature review establishes the context for the study.

   SA   5   4   3   2   1   SD

C. The research purpose, question, or hypothesis is clearly stated.

   SA   5   4   3   2   1   SD

D. The method of sampling is sound.

   SA   5   4   3   2   1   SD

E. Relevant demographics (for example, age, gender, and ethnicity) are described.

   SA   5   4   3   2   1   SD

F. Measurement procedures are adequate.

   SA   5   4   3   2   1   SD

G. All procedures have been described in sufficient detail to permit a replication of the study.

   SA   5   4   3   2   1   SD

H. The participants have been adequately protected from potential harm.

   SA   5   4   3   2   1   SD

I. The results are clearly described.

   SA   5   4   3   2   1   SD

J. The discussion/conclusion is appropriate.

   SA   5   4   3   2   1   SD

K. Despite any flaws, the report is worthy of publication.

   SA   5   4   3   2   1   SD

Article 3

Psychological Parameters of Students' Social and Work Avoidance Goals: A Qualitative Investigation

Martin Dowson
University of Western Sydney

Dennis M. McInerney
University of Western Sydney

ABSTRACT. The study identifies and describes the psychological parameters of middle school students' social and work avoidance goals. Data were collected from 86 students during 114 interviews and 24 structured observation periods. Inductive content analyses of the interview and observation data identified 8 distinct motivational goals (purposes) that the sample of middle school students espoused for their academic achievement. However, this analysis focuses on social and work avoidance goals that have not been widely explored in the literature to date. The analysis also identifies the structure of these goals in terms of their component academic behaviors, affect, and cognitions. The study is significant because it extends and deepens descriptions of the distinct social and work avoidance goals that students may espouse and identifies key psychological components of these goals.

From *Journal of Educational Psychology*, 93, 35–42. Copyright © 2001 by the American Psychological Association. Reprinted with permission.

Apart from some examples (e.g., Allen, 1986; Lee & Anderson, 1993), much of the literature addressing students' motivational goals has used an a priori approach to identify students' goals. Typically, this has meant that researchers have postulated, in advance, the existence of certain goals (usually mastery and performance goals) and then attempted to validate these goals through the use of psychometric research techniques. Such an approach to investigating students' motivational goals, however, may (a) artificially limit the range of goals investigated by researchers and (b) artificially limit descriptions of the content of these goals. In other words, such quantitative investigations of students' goals may misrepresent both the range and complexity of students' motivational goals.

There is a need, therefore, for further studies that investigate students' goals from an inductive perspective. Such an approach would start with students' perspectives regarding their motivational goals rather than with researchers' preconceived categories. Students' perspectives concerning their purposes for achievement may be used to inductively generate a range of salient motivational goals that may or may not be currently represented in the research literature. They may also help clarify both the theoretical and practical implications of aspects of student motivation.

Several authors (e.g., Blumenfeld, 1992; Lemos, 1996; Nicholls, 1984) have identified this need to more systematically address the salience and content of students' goals, particularly in real-life school and classroom contexts. Studies addressing this need, as Lemos (1996) pointed out, should focus particularly on the operation of students' goals in classroom contexts. Such a focus will, in turn, promote the conceptual clarity of achievement goal theory.

Given this, the central purpose of this study was to identify and describe goals middle school students might espouse for their schooling. In doing so, the study builds on recent research that has begun to explore the multiple characteristics of students' motivational goals (e.g., Lemos, 1996; McInerney, Roche, McInerney, & Marsh, 1997; Urdan & Maehr, 1995; Wentzel, 1991a, 1991b , 1994). The present study specifically concerns students' perceptions of their goals and deliberately attempts not to limit either the range or complexity of students' reported goals. Thus, the study focuses on identifying the goals students may hold with respect to their academic achievement and the particular components, or parameters, of these goals. These components include the behavioral, affective, and cognitive components of students' goals suggested by previous authors (e.g., Lee & Anderson, 1993).

Goal Theory

Goal theory, or achievement goal theory (Urdan & Maehr, 1995), is one of a number of social–cognitive theories of motivation that have emerged since the "cognitive revolution" of the late 1960s (Pervin, 1992). In achievement goal theory, goals are defined as cognitive representations of the different purposes students may adopt for their learning in achievement situations (Pintrich, Marx, & Boyle, 1993; Urdan & Maehr, 1995). Thus, students' goals answer the basic question "Why am I doing this [academic] task?" (Pintrich & Schrauben, 1992). In answering this question, students' achievement goals guide and direct students' cognition and behavior as they engage in academic tasks (Dweck & Elliot, 1983; Weiner, 1986).

Recent research has focused on two particular answers to the aforementioned "why" question. These answers represent two goal orientations. Students who engage in a task primarily to improve their level of competence and understanding are said to hold a mastery goal orientation (Ames & Archer, 1988). Within this orientation, learning is valued for its own sake, and success is defined by improved competence and understanding (Butler, 1989). In contrast, performance goals are referenced against the performance of others or against external standards such as grades. As such, rather than focusing on effort, performance goals focus particularly on evaluations of relative ability (Ames, 1992; Dweck, 1986), self-worth (Covington, 1984), and gaining favorable judgments from others (Meece, 1994). Success is defined by beating others or surpassing normative standards (Ames, 1992).

The performance orientation has, in recent literature (Elliot, 1997; Middleton & Midgley, 1997; Urdan, 1997), been partitioned into two independent, but related, orientations: (a) the performance approach and (b) performance avoidance orientations. This dichotomy was incorporated into earlier achievement motivation conceptualizations by researchers such as Lewin, Dembo, Festinger, and Sears (1944) and McClelland (1951). However, it later received little theoretical and empirical attention and was eventually disregarded (Elliot & Harackiewicz, 1996), only to again become the focus of research during the last 5 years.

Despite the emphasis in recent research on performance and mastery goals, students may hold other goals that may potentially affect their academic cognition and performance (Blumenfeld, 1992). For example, work avoidance goals (Ainley, 1993; Lee & Anderson, 1993; Meece & Holt, 1993; Nicholls, Patashnick, & Nolen, 1985) represent a type of goal orientation where students deliberately avoid engaging in academic tasks or attempt to minimize the effort required to complete academic tasks. This orientation, although distinct from both performance and mastery orientations (Meece & Holt, 1993), may nevertheless combine with these orientations to affect students' cognitive engagement and academic achievement (Ainley, 1993).

Social Goals

The previously mentioned goal orientations (performance, mastery, and work avoidance) may be characterized primarily as academic goal orientations. This means that they are concerned with the academic reasons (motives, purposes) students may espouse for learning in academic achievement situations (Urdan & Maehr, 1995). Another important class of goals, however, is students' social goals (Blumenfeld, 1992; Urdan & Maehr, 1995). In contrast to academic goals, students' social goals are concerned with the social reasons for trying to achieve (or not trying to achieve) in academic situations (Urdan & Maehr, 1995). This definition of social goals differs from other definitions that have been used to examine students' social reasons for wanting to achieve (or not wanting to achieve) in social situations (e.g., Eder, 1985; Lochman, Wayland, & White, 1993; Pietrucha & Erdley, 1996; Wentzel, 1989, 1991b) or simply to refer to students' desire to socialize in academic situations (e.g., Allen, 1986).

Although not as extensively researched, students' social goals are nevertheless represented in the literature. Maehr's (1984) formulation, for example, includes social solidarity goals (such as social concern and affiliation goals) in addition to performance, mastery, and extrinsic reward goals (see also McInerney et al., 1997; McInerney, Hinkley, Dowson, & Van Etten, 1998). Pintrich et al.'s (1993) formulation also includes social goals alongside performance, mastery, and epistemic goals. Dodge, Asher, and Parkhurst (1989) emphasized the multiple (and sometimes conflicting) social goals students' may hold with respect to their schooling. Finally, Urdan and Maehr (1995) included social approval, social compliance, social solidarity, and social concern goals in their list of potential social goals students may hold.

The summary mentioned earlier indicates that there is a lack of unanimity in the literature concerning precisely which social goals are of most relevance to include in any given formulation and, indeed, whether the current listing of these in the literature is comprehensive. This provides further reason to investigate which social goals may be of most importance to students in schooling contexts. Moreover, despite the previously mentioned studies, what is generally missing in the literature (for some recent exceptions, see McInerney, 1992 ; McInerney, Hinkley et al., 1998; McInerney, McInerney, Bazely, & Ardington, 1998; Van Etten, Pressley, Freebern, & Eschevarria, 1998) is an inductive approach to the identification of students' social goals. In other words, students' social goals, similar to their academic goals, have been specified by researchers prior to research. As a result, it is unclear whether previous studies have fully explored both the range and complexity of students' social goals in particular.

In summary, even where a variety of motivational goals have been explored, descriptions of these goals have been almost exclusively research driven rather than participant driven. As a result, it is unclear whether descriptions of students' goals in the literature are accurate representations of students' motivational orientations or, indeed, whether they represent all salient goal possibilities. As Lyn Corno, acting as a discussant at a meeting of the American Educational Research Association (1998) put it, "Some of the descriptions of students' goals in the literature just don't sound like the students I know." The present research directly addresses this deficit in the literature by using the actual words of students to develop descriptions of students' social and work avoidance goals, including their behavioral, affective, and cognitive components.

In summary, there is little solid information on the nature and characteristics of work avoidance goals. Furthermore, there is little evidence that the range of social goals discussed in the literature is comprehensive, given the potential complexity of social interactions vis-à-vis the complexity of mastery and performance (which potentially are more simple, uni- or bidimensional constructs). There is an underdeveloped understanding of work and social avoidance goals and their relationship to academic achievement. For example, it is commonly thought that social and work avoidance goals are likely to be maladaptive. However, there is little empirical evidence to support this belief. Indeed, social and work avoidance goals could be adaptive, maladaptive, or neutral, depending on circumstances. For example, work avoidance goals may be adaptive to the student who perceives particular work as too hard or meaningless. The phenomenological approach taken in the present research allows an examination of this issue.

Method

The present study incorporates two types of data collection: interviews and observations. Each of these was composed of more specific forms of data collection. The interviews included conversational (open-ended), semistructured, and structured interviews, which cumulatively focused the study as it proceeded. The observations included structured classroom schedules and unstructured field notes.

Participants

Eighty-six middle school students (ages 12 to 15 years) participated in the study. The students attended six schools (two elementary schools and four secondary schools) in the Sydney, Australia, metropolitan area. Approximately equal numbers of students from each school participated in the research. The average age of the students was approximately 13 ($M = 12.87$) years. More female ($n = 48$) than male ($n = 38$) students participated in the research. Similar numbers of students from grades 6 ($n = 27$), 7 ($n = 36$), and 8 ($n = 23$) participated in the research. Most of the participants ($n = 49$) were Anglo-Australian, with the most significant minority group being Northeast and Southeast Asian students ($n = 17$).

Interviews Conversational Interviews

Sixty-four of the 86 students participated in the conversational interviews, which were conducted on an individual basis. The purpose of the conversational interviews was to establish the range of achievement goals students held. As such, the conversational interviews were deliberately designed to be as open-ended and flexible as possible. They typically involved questions such as "Do you want to do well at school? Why?" "Why do (or don't) you try hard at school?" and "What reasons do you have for wanting to do well in school?"

Semistructured Interviews

Thirty-two students participated in the semistructured interviews. These students included the remaining 22 students who were not interviewed in the conversational interviews as well as 10 students who were interviewed in the conversational interviews. The aim of the semistructured interviews was to more directly explore social and work avoidance goals and to link these with feelings, behaviors, and cognitions (strategies and metacognitive strategies), which have not been extensively explored in the literature.

Structured Interviews

Eighteen students participated in the structured interviews. Twelve of these students were selected for participation in the structured interviews on the basis of particular responses they had given in the semistructured interviews. Usually, these responses had been particularly detailed or insightful. Moreover, 8 of these 12 students had also participated in the conversational interviews. Thus, there was a core group of 8 students who participated in all three types of interviews.

The structured interviews deliberately converged on specific aspects of the research identified in the semistructured and conversational interviews. Examples of questions used in the structured interviews include "Do you agree that students who are motivated to do well at school because they want to please their parents do better than others at school? Why?" and "Some students say that they have to want to beat other students before they can do good work at school. Do you need to be motivated in this way, or can you still do good school work even if you don't want to beat other students? Why?"

Observational Studies

Observational studies were conducted concurrently with the interviews described earlier. Two types of observational methods were used: structured classroom schedules and field notes.

Structured Classroom Schedules

Twenty-four classroom schedules were completed in 12 classes from which students participating in the interviews were drawn. Two observation periods (typically lasting between 30 and 40 min) were completed for each class. The structured classroom schedules were developed, as the interviews progressed, to focus on key ideas identified in the interviews. This meant that each structured classroom schedule used a series of interview responses (up to eight) that acted as focus points for the observations.

The specific content of these observations focused on students' actual social and work avoidance behavior in various learning situations with respect to various learning tasks. These behaviors included students' conversations with each other (and, on occasion, with themselves) as they worked on specific tasks; any questions, answers, or other interactions students had with their teachers; and observations of the apparent intensity (or otherwise) with which students engaged in their work (i.e., whether they appeared distracted from, or focused on, academic tasks at hand and in what circumstances).

Field Notes

Field notes were recorded concurrently with the interviews and classroom observations. The field notes were a more unstructured method of observation and were used in a more open-ended fashion. Thirty-seven field note entries were made. Entries typically included notations concerning students' social and work avoidance behaviors and reactions to various learning situations and the research processes themselves (e.g., whether a student appeared to be comfortable and open in an interview or observation situation).

Coding Processes

The interviews were taped and transcribed. After they were transcribed, the interviews (along with the structured classroom observations and field notes, which were already available in transcript form) were numbered by transcript, page, and line. A coding system was developed so that participants' responses and researchers' observations could be easily located. For example, the code *CO:01:02:33* referred to Conversational Interview 1, page 2, line 33, and *FN:18:01:02–3* referred to Field Note 18, page 1, lines 2 and 3. These codes formed the basic content of the categorization process described later.

Analyses

The interviews were analyzed using inductive content analysis (also known as "protocol analysis"; Ericsson & Simon, 1984; Krippendorf, 1980). This approach upheld both the inductive nature and holistic perspective of the research (Jacob, 1987; Patton & Westby, 1992). Essentially, the protocol analyses involved inducing coherent operational categories from students' coded responses and from researchers' coded observations. This meant initially assessing the "plain meaning" of students' statements (with reference to their related observations) and then examining the contexts in which these statements were made. The contexts of interview statements included both their vertical context (i.e., their location within interviews) and their horizontal context (i.e., their relationship to other statements made in the current, and other, interviews).

As an example of the processes mentioned earlier, the student's comment "I want to do well in school to please my parents" (CO:11:03:14) was first assessed for its plain meaning. This assessment included reference to the structured observation (SO:13:03:23), which noted the content of a relevant classroom conversation between the student and one of his teachers. This conversation included a reference to "trying to pass this subject because my parents really want me to." Second, the initial statement was assessed with reference to other comments within the interview (e.g., "My parents are always at me to do well in school" [line 27] and "When I think of how well my parents want me to do, I really try hard to do good work" [line 38]). Third, the initial response was assessed on the basis of its relationship to comments made in other interviews by (a) the present student; for example, "Even though they're hard on me to do well at school, my parents still help me a lot with my work" (SS [semistructured interview]:12:04:17) and (b) other students; for example, "I really hate it when my parents give me a hard time over my work. I wish they'd just leave me alone" (ST [structured interview]:12:02:43). In this way, the initial response was triangulated against several data sources to assess its overall meaning.

Results

The Appendix [at the end of this article] provides brief descriptions of the social and work avoidance goals identified in the study. The interviews provided new information concerning the structure and operation of students' work avoidance, social affiliation, social responsibility, and social concern goals in academic achievement situations. Specific examples of the parameters of these goals are included throughout this article, and where appropriate, specific interview statements explicating these parameters are also included. For the most part, these statements are presented immediately after the relevant example.

Work Avoidance Goal Orientation Behavioral Components

Students' work avoidance goal orientations emerged as an important aspect of their academic motivation. Specifically, students' work avoidance orientations were associated with a variety of effort minimization strategies, with respect to academic tasks. These became particularly evident during the observations and included copying; asking the teacher to help complete a problem for students, especially as work became more difficult; frequently asking the teacher for assistance on relatively easy tasks; and engaging in off-task behavior (e.g., talking to friends and organizing and reorganizing basic materials such as pens, paper, and rulers; trying to negotiate less demanding alternatives to assessment or general classroom tasks; "tuning out" on all but the simplest or most urgent classroom tasks; and feigning incompetence or misunderstanding, even when understanding or competence on a given task had been demonstrated).

Affective Components

Affectively, students' work avoidance orientations were associated with feelings of laziness, boredom, inertia, and even anger (e.g., "I don't like teachers who give you too much work to do"). These feelings distracted students from engaging, and sustaining effective involvement, in academic work (e.g., "I don't like homework. It takes too much time and you have to think about it too much"). Specific examples of these effects include feeling lazy or lethargic when attempting difficult work (e.g., "If I'm tired or something, then I don't want to do it [school work], even if I can. But if it's [the work] really hard, then I definitely don't feel like doing it"); feeling anger toward the teacher for assigning what is perceived to be difficult or demanding work (e.g., "I don't want to do lots of hard work because I can't handle it"); feeling psychologically inert ("wasted," in the words of one student) when attempting to begin difficult work; feeling relieved when a choice of less taxing academic tasks was available (e.g., "Everyone wants to do the easy work. Well, not everyone but a lot"); wishing to be somewhere other than the present academic situation (e.g., "I don't like subjects that are too hard. I'd rather be somewhere else"); and not caring if "I can do something or not."

Cognitive Components

Cognitively, students' work avoidance orientations were associated with limited engagement in learning. Alternatively, students' work avoidance orientations were associated with patterns of engagement that were not necessarily appropriate to given tasks but that were seen to minimize the effort required for completion of those tasks. Examples of these processes include trying to find ways to get other students to do the work for them; trying to find ways to enlist teacher help so that work could be learned quickly and easily; avoiding planning or organizing work (e.g., "I try not to think about it [schoolwork] until I really have to do it"); not attempting, or attempting only in an ad hoc fashion, to monitor or clarify misunderstandings or difficulties with schoolwork (e.g., "If I really have to ask a question, then I will, but most of the time, I just try to do as little as possible"); when alternatives are available, trying to identify what are the easiest, rather than the most interesting or even the most valuable (in terms of assigned marks), tasks; and not using effective approaches to studying, even when they have worked in the past (e.g., "I know reading over my notes helps me, but I couldn't be bothered").

Social Affiliation Goal Orientation Behavioral Components

Students' social affiliation orientations, particularly working together with other students in productive or cooperative ways, were associated with engagement in, and preference for, affiliative academic behaviors. Moreover, these affiliative behaviors occurred in both formal (in-school) and informal (out-of-school) academic situations. Examples include working with other students in class (including choosing to work with a particular group of students), especially in preference to individual academic work; assisting other students when working together (e.g., "My friends and I help each other so that the teacher will let us stay together"); interacting academically with groups of students beyond the immediate class situation (e.g., in study groups and group homework sessions); and suggesting to teachers group-based academic activities (e.g., "Me and my friends try to get the teacher to let us work together, but then we have to show her that we're doing the work, or she won't let us be together next time").

Affective Components

Affectively, students' social affiliation orientations were associated with wanting to engender feelings of belonging or solidarity within academic groups (e.g., "Well, just say you're in a study group after school. Well, you try real hard to keep up or else you won't feel really good in the group") or, negatively, with strong feelings of isolation or rejection if affiliative desires were not met. Other examples include feeling a strong sense of academic efficacy with a particular academic group of friends in class (e.g., "I feel smarter when I'm working with other people"); wanting to help other students so that "the group can stay together"; being very upset when rejected by a particular person or peer group in class; and even desiring to be involved in academic activities in which a certain group of students are participating, despite a personal dislike for the activities themselves (e.g., "I want to do well in history, even though I don't like it much, because if I don't, then I might have to move to a lower class and then I wouldn't be with my friends").

Cognitive Components

Cognitively, students' social affiliation orientations were associated with a variety of adaptive approaches to learning that manifested themselves particularly in academic group situations. Thus, for students with social affiliation orientations, working in academic groups may either enhance effective approaches already used individually or act to initiate the use of effective approaches not typically used individually. Examples include planning ahead when working with other people but not necessarily when working individually (e.g., "I think about what I'm going to do next if I'm with my friends, but when I'm by myself, my brain doesn't work as well"); "thinking through" schoolwork in conversation with other students; voluntarily testing self-understanding and others' understanding when working in class groups (e.g., "We like to try and see if we've learned what we're trying to"); trying to get the teacher to set group assignments and then "showing the teacher that we're [the group is] working hard on what she wants us to do"; framing clarifying questions for the teacher in collaboration with others; and working harder at solving problems in the group than alone (e.g., "I work really well, even on hard stuff, when I'm with my friends because it's easier when you have other people doing it with you").

Social Responsibility Goal Orientation Behavioral Components

Students' social responsibility orientations were associated with academic behaviors such as involvement in extracurricular academic activities, participation in academically supportive classroom roles, and increased academic effort as a result of perceived role expectations. Specific examples of these include being involved in extracurricular academic activities (e.g., debating) especially when participation in these was expected of students; volunteering for classroom jobs or roles (e.g., board monitoring) because they assisted the class to learn to work more effectively (e.g., "I like to do things to help in my class because then we learn things better"); working hard academically as a result of role expectations associated with involvement in student government or other "senior" roles (e.g., "Now that I'm school captain, I really want to work hard at school to give a good example to other students"); behaving responsibly and making other students aware of school rules and conventions that promote their responsible behavior; and being especially diligent in schoolwork when holding responsible academic positions (e.g., peer tutor).

Affective Components

Affectively, within this orientation, feelings of pride, satisfaction, and excitement, with regard to academic work, were engendered when the progress or completion of academic work was associated with the fulfillment of personal or communal role expectations. Specific examples include feeling personal pride at having contributed to class or school academic activities; feeling an enhanced sense of worth at having participated in an academically supportive activity or role (e.g., "It's a good feeling when you help someone in peer tutoring. You feel like you've done the right thing"); enjoying being involved in activities that were perceived to "make a difference" to personal, class, or even schoolwide academic performance; feeling anxious when other students "don't do the right thing" in class; and looking forward to opportunities to be involved in academically based school projects that involved responsible participation (e.g., in one case, the construction of a native garden as part of a science project).

Cognitive Components

Cognitively, students motivated by social responsibility considerations not only used effective approaches to learning but did so in socially responsible ways. For example, question asking was completed in such a way that role expectations were not violated (i.e., questions were asked at appropriate times and framed politely, and answers were received attentively). Other examples include increasing cognitive effort when holding responsible roles within the class or school (e.g., "I want to understand my work because it's what my teachers expect of me now that I'm a tutor"); planning and organizing schoolwork to meet submission dates and other deadlines (e.g., "I think that I should be on time with my work at school because you're meant to do it"); mentally rehearsing and following established procedures or rules for completing schoolwork; self-monitoring academic progress and understanding against standards established by teachers or parents (e.g., "If I don't do my best at school, then my parents will be disappointed in me because I didn't do what I should have").

Social Concern Goal Orientation Behavioral Components

Students' social concern orientations were associated particularly with substantial academic effort such that students were, at least potentially, involved in "helping" situations or appointed to helping roles. These, for example, include seeking to understand schoolwork to have the ability to help others (e.g., "If I know my work well, then I can help my friends if they need it. I like to help when I can"; working hard at school to be appointed to academic helping positions (e.g., student concern coordinator or peer tutor); and assisting other students academically in out-of-class contexts (e.g., in the library, playground, or in homework situations). It should be noted, however, that students' concern orientations occasionally conflicted with their teachers' expectations of students' classroom behavior (e.g., "Sometimes I get into trouble for talking to my friends, but I'm only trying to help them with their work").

Affective Components

Affectively, students' social concern orientations were associated with a variety of positive feelings (directed toward self or others) when helping roles or situations were salient. For example, this orientation includes feeling concerned when others were experiencing significant difficulty with academic work; feeling excited about the possibility of being able to help other students; enjoying assisting other students with their schoolwork in formal and informal situations (e.g., "If I know my work well, then I like to explain it to my friends so that they will know it as well"); wanting others to understand schoolwork, especially when the work is well understood by the "teaching" student; enjoying responding to requests for assistance (e.g., "If my friends don't understand what they have to do, they ask me what to do because they know I like to help them").

Cognitive Components

Cognitively, social concern orientations appeared to promote a variety of adaptive approaches to learning that enhance both academic understanding and the ability to transfer that understanding to others. These approaches include mentally rehearsing ways in which academic material could be explained to others (e.g., "I try to think how I'd explain things if people ask me, especially if the teacher isn't doing it very well"); monitoring difficulties with personal learning so that similar difficulties may be explained to others (e.g., "I always try to fix up my own mistakes so that my friends won't make them too"); and planning and organizing work so that time was available to assist others.

Discussion

One of the most significant features of the present study is that it has been able to identify salient social and work avoidance goals that a selection of middle school students espoused for their academic achievement. These goals were not specified prior to the research but were inductively generated within the research from the statements of participants and from their observed behavior in classroom contexts. This means that the goals identified in the study may be appropriately labeled *students' goals*.

In addition, the study has identified specific components of students' social and work avoidance goals (viz., their behavioral, affective, and cognitive components) and begins to indicate how these components may be related to each other.

With these points in mind, the next paragraphs discuss some important features of these students' goals with reference, where appropriate, to specific contextual features that further enhance an understanding of the operation of these goals in school contexts.

Work Avoidance

The work avoidance orientation has yet to be extensively explored in the literature. As such, few, if any, of the specific behaviors, affective reactions, and cognitions reported by participants in the present study are noted in the literature. It appears from the present data that the work avoidance orientation had many "faces" that varied according to specific classroom features. Thus, the orientation itself may be consistent across situations, but its actual manifestation in any given situation was dependent on specific classroom features such as, for example, the availability of a computer or other classroom technology, to use as a work-avoiding tool. Some forms of work avoidance behavior may, however, be an exception to this generalization. For example, negotiating easier tasks, feigning incompetence, and needlessly questioning teachers are perhaps more widespread forms of work avoidance. Further research is necessary to ascertain which types of work avoidance behavior identified in this study (if any) are common to other contexts and which are not. Such research would also involve identifying as wide a range of work avoidance tactics used by students as possible. It appears from the comments made in the interviews, and through the observation data, that work avoidance goals are maladaptive in most circumstances, leading to limited engagement in learning. Further research should examine the genesis of work avoidance goals to ascertain the importance of perceived lack of relevance, or difficulty level, of material to the development of this orientation.

Social Affiliation

A particular feature of the present description is that although teachers have often viewed the social affiliation orientation primarily in negative terms (e.g., Ashman & Gillies, 1997), students in this study described the social affiliation orientation in positive terms with respect to school learning (i.e., holding a social affiliation orientation promoted positive approaches to learning rather than the opposite). Hence, social affiliation was seen primarily in adaptive terms, facilitating both effective engagement in learning and positive feelings toward learning. Moreover, students held these views despite the fact that they also identified the potentially detrimental effects that pursuing this goal may have on their ongoing motivation and achievement (e.g., "I really want to work with my friends, and sometimes we get lots done, but sometimes we just muck around and don't get anything done at all. Then I feel like I haven't really tried and it makes it harder to get started on it [work] again").

Social Responsibility

Again, social responsibility was seen primarily in adaptive terms, with it facilitating effective engagement in learning and associated extracurricular activities as well as generating feelings of pride, self-worth, satisfaction, and excitement through fulfilling responsibilities and satisfying communal role expectations. A feature of the social responsibility orientation was that it included references to those in authority over students as well as substantial references to peers. Thus, students felt responsible toward each other, as well as to their parents and teachers, to achieve in academic situations. As one student put it, "I want to do well for my friends' sake too because we all feel like we've done the right thing if the school is going well [academically]."

Social Concern

The parameters of the social concern orientation, despite some recent literature (e.g., McInerney, Hinkley, et al., 1998), have not been widely researched. However, Ford (1992), Wentzel (1991a), and McInerney et al. (1997), for example, have recognized that students may act in academic situations to enhance the welfare of other students. Despite this, the recognition that students may see their own academic achievement as a means of assisting others is a new perspective on the social concern orientation and one that is more consistent with the theoretical orientation of the present research. In other words, there is a relationship between social concern, responsibility, and cognition (i.e., being responsible and concerned is perceived by many students as enhancing their use of cognitive strategies). Previously, studies have focused on academic achievement as an outcome of what Wentzel calls "prosocial" behavior. In the present study, however, academic achievement, from within a social concern orientation, was conceptualized by participants as a means of displaying prosocial behavior. Thus, academic achievement may be conceptualized as both an outcome and an antecedent of prosocial behavior. This perspective is consistent with some goal theory studies, especially those in cross-cultural settings, which, similarly, see academic achievement as both a product and precursor of prosocial, concern-oriented behavior (McInerney, McInerney, et al., 1998).

Implications and Future Research

Perhaps the most important implication of the present study is that a range of social goal orientations has been identified as being important and adaptive to students' engagement in learning and their desire to learn. This stands in stark contrast to the work avoidance goal that appears consistently maladaptive. These social orientations represent a range of social purposes that students may espouse for their achievement in academic situations. Moreover, each of these social orientations comprises important aspects of students' behavior, affect, and cognition in achievement settings. Thus, it is reasonable to suggest that students' social orientations are not peripheral to their academic performance and achievement. Rather, these orientations may directly influence students' psychological processes as they strive toward academic achievement. For this reason, both practitioners and researchers need to take seriously the possibility that diverse social orientations to learning may impact students' achievement. Social goals may actually be more salient and predictive of students' global motivation and achievement than either mastery or performance goals. In other words, it is possible that researchers have got it wrong in putting the emphasis on mastery and performance goals and that either of these will work well only when the social goals of the students are effectively being met. Social motivation is still backstage; it may need to be moved front stage in researchers' thinking about what really motivates students. This is particularly plausible given the age of the students considered in this study, an age when social networking is a major drive for personal development.

Future research should address the ways in which differing social goals interact with each other and with students' academic goals (such as performance, mastery, and work avoidance goals) to influence students' academic performance and achievement. Pintrich et al. (1993), for example, suggested that "there is a need for an examination of how students' social goals could complement, compensate, or conflict with mastery and performance motivation goals" (p. 181). Whether complementary, compensatory, or conflicting, however, a key aspect of future research will be to assess interactions between students' social and academic goals and

their relations to students' cognitive engagement and academic achievement.

Conclusion

The present study is important because it describes, in greater detail than has been the case to date, the structure of students' work avoidance, social affiliation, social responsibility, and social concern goals. The study also explores how the various behavioral, affective, and cognitive components of these goals may be associated with each other in academic achievement situations and whether they are adaptive, maladaptive, or neutral.

In addition, the study is important because it is grounded in the reported perceptions and related observations of students. Moreover, these perceptions and observations are integrated within a theoretical framework (goal theory) that has proven useful for examining students' motivation in both the present and related studies. Thus, the present research clarifies further the content and operation of students' goals, both theoretically and as they operate in real-life classroom situations.

References

Ainley, M. D. (1993). Styles of engagement with learning: Multidimensional assessment of their relationship with strategy use and school achievement. *Journal of Educational Psychology, 85*, 395–405.

Allen, J. D. (1986). Classroom management: Students' perspectives, goals, and strategies. *American Educational Research Journal, 23*, 437–459.

Ames, C. (1992). Classrooms: Goals, structures, and student motivation. *Journal of Educational Psychology, 84*, 261–271.

Ames, C., & Archer, J. (1988). Achievement goals in the classroom: Student learning strategies and achievement motivation. *Journal of Educational Psychology, 18*, 409–414.

Ashman, A. F., & Gillies, R. M. (1997). Children's cooperative behaviors and interactions in trained and untrained work groups in regular classrooms. *Journal of School Psychology, 35*, 261–279.

Blumenfeld, P. C. (1992). Classroom learning and motivation: Clarifying and expanding goal theory. *Journal of Educational Psychology, 84*, 272–281.

Butler, R. (1989). Interest in the task and interest in peers' work in competitive and non-competitive conditions: A developmental study. *Child Development, 60*, 562–570.

Covington, M. V. (1984). The motive for self-worth. (In R. Ames & C. Ames (Eds.), *Research on motivation in education: Vol. 1. Student motivation* (pp. 77–113). San Diego: CA: Academic Press.)

Dodge, K. A., Asher, S. R., & Parkhurst, J. T. (1989). Social life as a goal coordination task. (In C. Ames & R. Ames (Eds.), *Research on motivation in education: Vol. 3. Goals and cognitions* (pp. 107–135). New York: Academic Press.)

Dweck, C. S. (1986). Motivational processes affecting learning. *American Psychologist, 41*, 1040–1048.

Dweck, C. S., & Elliot, E. S. (1983). Achievement motivation. (In E. M. Heatherington (Ed.), *Handbook of child psychology: Vol. 4. Socialization, personality, and social development* (pp. 643–691). New York: Wiley.)

Eder, D. (1985). The cycle of popularity: Interpersonal relations among female adolescents. *Sociology of Education, 58*, 154–165.

Elliot, A. J. (1997). Integrating the "classic" and "contemporary" approaches to achievement motivation: A hierarchical model of approach and avoidance achievement motivation. (In M. L. Maehr & P. R. Pintrich (Eds.), *Advances in motivation and achievement (Vol. 10, pp. 143–180)*. Greenwich, CT: JAI Press.)

Elliot, A., & Harackiewicz, J. (1996). Approach and avoidance achievement goals and intrinsic motivation: A mediational analysis. *Journal of Personality and Social Psychology, 70*, 461–475.

Ericsson, K. A., & Simon, H. A. (1984). *Protocol analysis: Verbal reports as data.* (Cambridge, MA: MIT Press)

Feshbach, N. D., & Feshbach, S. (1987). Affective processes and academic achievement. *Child Development, 58*, 1335–1347.

Ford, M. E. (1992). *Motivating humans: Goals, emotions, and personal agency.* (Newbury Park, CA: Sage)

Jacob, E. (1987). Qualitative research traditions: A review. *Review of Educational Research, 57*, 1–50.

Krippendorf, K. (1980). *Content analysis: An introduction to its methodology.* (London: Sag)

Lebow, D. (1993). Constructivist values for instructional systems design: Five principles toward a new mindset. *Educational Technology Research and Development, 41,* 4–16.

Lee, O., & Anderson, C. W. (1993). Task engagement and conceptual change in middle school science classrooms. *American Educational Research Journal, 30,* 585–610.

Lemos, M. S. (1996). Students' and teachers' goals in the classroom. *Learning and Instruction, 6,* 151–171.

Lewin, K., Dembo, T., Festinger, L., & Sears, P. S. (1944). Level of aspiration. (In J. McHunt (Ed.), *Personality and the behavior disorders* (Vol. 3, pp. 229–315). New York: Academic Press.)

Lochman, J. E., Wayland, K. K., & White, K. J. (1993). Social goals: Relationship to adolescent adjustment and to social problem solving. *Journal of Abnormal Child Psychology, 21,* 135–151.

Maehr, M. (1984). Meaning and Motivation.(In R. Ames & C. Ames (Eds.), *Research on motivation in education: Vol. 1. Student motivation* (pp. 115–144). San Diego, CA: Academic Press.)

McClelland, D. C. (1951). Measuring motivation in phantasy: The achievement motive. (In H. Guetzkow (Ed.), *Groups, leadership, and men* (pp. 191–205). Pittsburgh, PA: Carnegie Press.)

McInerney, D. M. (1992). Cross-cultural insights into school motivation and decision making. *Journal of Intercultural Studies, 13,* 57–74.

McInerney, D. M., Hinkley, J., Dowson, M., & Van Etten, S. (1998). Aboriginal, Anglo, and immigrant Australian students' motivational beliefs about personal academic success: Are there cultural differences? *Journal of Educational Psychology, 90,* 621–629.

McInerney, D. M., McInerney, V., Bazely, P., & Ardington, A. (1998, April). *Parents, peers, cultural values, and school processes: What has most influence on motivating indigenous minority students' school achievement? A qualitative study.* (Paper presented at the annual meeting of the American Educational Research Association, San Diego, CA.)

McInerney, D. M., Roche, L., McInerney, V., & Marsh, H. W. (1997). Cultural perspectives on school motivation. The relevance and application of goal theory. *American Educational Research Journal, 34,* 207–236.

Meece, J. L. (1994). The role of motivation in self-regulated learning. (In D. H. Schunk & B. J. Zimmerman (Eds.), *Self-regulation of learning and performance: Issues and educational applications.* Hillsdale, NJ: Erlbaum.)

Meece, J. L., & Holt, K. (1993). A pattern analysis of students' achievement goals. *Journal of Educational Psychology, 85,* 582–590.

Middleton, M., & Midgley, C. (1997). Avoiding the demonstration of lack of ability: An underexplored aspect of goal theory. *Journal of Educational Psychology, 89,* 710–718.

Nicholls, J. G. (1984). Achievement motivation: Conceptions of ability, subjective experience, task choice, and performance. *Psychological Review, 91,* 328–346.

Nicholls, J. G., Patashnick, M., & Nolen, S. B. (1985). Adolescents' theories of education. *Journal of Educational Psychology, 77,* 683–692.

Patton, M., & Westby, C. (1992). Ethnography and research: A qualitative view. *Topics in Language Disorders, 12,* 1–14.

Pervin, L. A. (1992). The rational mind and the problem of volition. *Psychological Science, 3,* 162–164.

Pietrucha, C. A., & Erdley, C. A. (1996, April). *Sources of influence on children's social goals.* (Paper presented at the annual meeting of the American Educational Research Association, New York.)

Pintrich, P. R., Marx, R. W., & Boyle, R. A. (1993). Beyond cold conceptual change: The role of motivational beliefs and classroom contextual factors in the process of conceptual change. *Review of Educational Research, 63,* 167–199.

Pintrich, P. R., & Schrauben, B. (1992). Students' motivational beliefs and their cognitive engagement in classroom academic tasks. (In D. Schunk & J. Meece (Eds.), *Student perceptions in the classroom: Causes and consequences* (pp. 149–183). Hillsdale, NJ: Erlbaum.)

Urdan, T. C. (1997). Achievement goal theory: Past results, future directions. (In M. L. Maehr & P. R. Pintrich (Eds.), *Advances in motivation and achievement* (Vol. 10, pp. 99–141). Greenwich, CT: JAI Press.)

Urdan, T. C., & Maehr, M. L. (1995). Beyond a two goal theory of motivation and achievement: A case for social goals. *Review of Educational Research, 65,* 213–243.

Van Etten, S., Pressley, M., Freebern, G., & Eschevarria, M. (1998). An interview study of college freshmen's beliefs about their academic motivation. *European Journal of Education, 13,* 105–130.

Weiner, B. (1986). *An attributional theory of motivation and emotion.* (New York: Springer-Verlag)

Wentzel, K. R. (1989). Adolescent classroom goals, standards for performance, and academic achievement: An interactionist perspective. *Journal of Educational Psychology, 81,* 131–142.

Wentzel, K. R. (1991a). Social and academic goals at school: Motivation and achievement in context. (In M. L. Maehr & P. R. Pintrich (Eds.), *Advances in motivation and achievement: A research annual* (Vol. 7, pp. 185–212). Greenwich, CT: JAI Press.)

Wentzel, K. R. (1991b). Social competence at school: Relation between social responsibility and academic achievement. *Review of Educational Research, 61,* 1–24.

Wentzel, K. R. (1994). Relations of social goal pursuit to social acceptance, classroom behavior, and perceived social support. *Journal of Educational Psychology, 2,* 173–182.

Address correspondence to: Dennis M. McInerney, School of Psychology, University of Western Sydney, Penrith South, New South Wales, Australia, 1797. E-mail: d.mcinerney@uws.edu.au

Acknowledgments: We thank all the participants involved in this study.

Appendix A

Table 1
Brief Definitions of Goals

Goal	Definition
Work avoidance	Wanting to achieve academically with as little effort as possible. Conversely, avoiding demanding achievement situations to minimize expended effort.
Social affiliation	Wanting to achieve academically to enhance a sense of belonging to a group or groups and/or to build or maintain interpersonal relationships. Conversely, wanting to achieve to avoid feelings of separateness or isolation.
Social responsibility	Wanting to achieve academically out of a sense of responsibility to others to meet social role obligations, or to follow social and moral "rules." Conversely, wanting to achieve to avoid social transgressions and/or unethical conduct.
Social concern	Wanting to achieve academically to be able to assist others in their academic or personal development. Conversely, avoiding academic achievement situations where the concern of other students is at risk.

Exercise for Article 3

Factual Questions

1. Near the beginning of their research article, the researchers state their "central purpose" in a sentence. What was their central purpose?

2. How many of the 86 students participated in the conversational interviews?

3. A core group of students participated in all three types of interviews. How many students were in their core group?

4. The researchers state that they examined the con-

texts in which the students' statements were made. What do they mean by "vertical context"?

5. Were the work avoidance goals particularly evident during the interviews *or* were they particularly evident during the observations?

6. In the Discussion section of their report, the researchers note that teachers have often viewed the social affiliation orientation in what kind of terms?

7. According to the researchers, what is "perhaps the most important implication" of their study?

Questions for Discussion

8. In the first two paragraphs, the researchers state their reasons for using a qualitative approach to their research topic. Does the material in these paragraphs convince you of the need for a qualitative study? Explain.

9. The researchers point out that they "triangulated" the data by using several different data sources. To what extent does this triangulation (e.g., using several types of interviews and several types of observations) increase your confidence in the results of this study? (See lines 330–355.)

10. Throughout the Results section of this article, the researchers provide numerous quotations of the students' responses. To what extent did these help you understand the results? Did they give you more confidence in the accuracy of the results? Explain.

11. The researchers describe their results in lines 356–607. Which one aspect of the results do you find the most striking (e.g., unusual, unexpected, surprising)? Explain your choice.

12. To what extent do you agree with the points the researchers make in the Conclusion section of their report? (See lines 766–784.)

Quality Ratings

Directions: Indicate your level of agreement with each of the following statements by circling a number from 5 for strongly agree (SA) to 1 for strongly disagree (SD). If you believe an item is not applicable to this research article, leave it blank. Be prepared to explain your ratings.

A. The introduction establishes the importance of the study.

SA   5   4   3   2   1   SD

B. The literature review establishes the context for the study.

SA   5   4   3   2   1   SD

C. The research purpose, question, or hypothesis is clearly stated.

SA   5   4   3   2   1   SD

D. The method of sampling is sound.

SA   5   4   3   2   1   SD

E. Relevant demographics (for example, age, gender, and ethnicity) are described.

SA   5   4   3   2   1   SD

F. Measurement procedures are adequate.

SA   5   4   3   2   1   SD

G. All procedures have been described in sufficient detail to permit a replication of the study.

SA   5   4   3   2   1   SD

H. The participants have been adequately protected from potential harm.

SA   5   4   3   2   1   SD

I. The results are clearly described.

SA   5   4   3   2   1   SD

J. The discussion/conclusion is appropriate.

SA   5   4   3   2   1   SD

K. Despite any flaws, the report is worthy of publication.

SA   5   4   3   2   1   SD

Article 4

Mother-Daughter Communication About Sex Among Urban African American and Latino Families

Lucia F. O'Sullivan
Columbia University

Heino F. L. Meyer-Bahlburg
Columbia University

Beverly X. Watkins
Columbia University

ABSTRACT. Urban minority girls are at considerable risk for the negative health consequences of early sexual activity. Yet few researchers have explored the sources of information about sexual issues for these adolescents, particularly parent-child communication. As part of a larger qualitative study examining social cognitions about sexuality among urban girls, 72 African American and Latina mothers and 72 daughters representing two age groups (6–9 and 10–13) participated in focus group sessions. Both mothers and daughters addressed the cues associated with the timing of these conversations in the course of the daughters' development; the content of their conversations, including the messages mothers used to influence girls' decision making; and the approaches or strategies both employed. The authors' analyses indicate that beneficial communication may be preempted by the antagonistic positions adopted by daughters and mothers as daughters advance sexually. Daughters may in fact benefit more from receiving sex education from other close sources.

From *Journal of Adolescent Research*, *16*, 269-292. Copyright © 2001 by Sage Publications, Inc. Reprinted with permission.

Adolescent girls residing in urban neighborhoods characterized by poverty and crime are at considerable risk for sexually transmitted diseases (STDs) and pregnancy (Westhoff, McDermott, & Holcomb, 1996). On average, urban girls engage in first intercourse approximately 2 years earlier (Rotheram-Borus & Gwadz, 1993), and higher proportions have experienced sexual intercourse at each age during adolescence (Overby & Kegeles, 1994). Furthermore, urban girls are more likely to use poor methods or no methods of protection during sexual intercourse compared with national samples (Ford, Rubinstein, & Norris, 1994; Kirby, Korpi, Adivi, & Weissman, 1997), report expecting to get pregnant during adolescence (Trent, 1994), give birth once pregnant (Alan Guttmacher Institute, 1996), and acquire an STD (Ellen, Aral, & Madger, 1998). Their considerable risk for experiencing the negative health consequences of unprotected sexual activity emphasizes the growing need to explore how urban adolescent girls acquire sexual knowledge and come to understand sexual behavior and relationships.

Past research has generally focused on three main sources of sex information for adolescents: formal sex education programs, peers, and parent-child communication. In a review of formal sex and HIV education programs, Kirby (1997) concluded that most programs produce some desirable consequences, such as increased knowledge, although few produced changes in sexual risk-taking behavior, such as reducing numbers of sexual partners or increasing use of contraception. A similar conclusion was reached in a comprehensive review commissioned by the World Health Organization's Global Programme on AIDS (Grunseit, Kippax, Aggleton, Baldo, & Slutkin, 1997).

Research addressing the extent to which peers contribute to the acquisition of sexual information tends to focus on peers as models of sexual behavior and, less directly, models of sexual attitudes or values (Gibson & Kempf, 1990). Few researchers have investigated whether peers act as more direct sources of sexual information, although there is some evidence to suggest that they play a primary role in this regard (Buysse, 1996; Jaccard & Dittus, 1993).

Parent-Child Communication About Sex

Data from the National Longitudinal Study on Adolescent Health (ADD Health), the most comprehensive study of adolescent health to date, indicate that a large majority of mothers have talked a moderate amount or a great deal about sex with their children (Miller, 1998). This finding is particularly true of communication between mothers and daughters. The findings from large-scale national samples and most smaller research efforts, however, are generally equivocal with regard to the impact of parent-child communication (Miller, 1998; Rodgers, 1999). Some researchers find that adolescents whose parents had openly discussed sexual matters with them were more likely to delay first sexual intercourse, have fewer sexual intercourse partners, and engage in responsible contraceptive behavior (McBride, 1996; Mueller & Powers, 1990). Other researchers were unable to find such associations in their investigations (Fisher, 1993; Newcomer & Udry, 1985).

There may be a number of reasons for the inconsistency in findings. A review of the literature in this area reveals a lack of standard measurement of parent-child communication, with many researchers using single-item indices of either communication or sexual behavior (Christopher, Johnson, & Roosa, 1993; Fisher, 1993). Researchers frequently measure reports of communication, at times in dichotomous form (yes/no), without assessing the content or context of these exchanges (Moore, Peterson, & Furstenberg, 1986). Parents are considered integral components in many prevention programs for adolescents (Hutchinson & Cooney, 1998), yet research has generally failed to clarify whether parents are, or can be, an effective source of information and influence in their children's sexual lives.

Parent-Child Communication About Sex in Urban Minority Families

Past research addressing parent-child communication about sex has, for the most part, employed White, middle-class samples of college students, and at times, their parents (Shoop & Davidson, 1994; Whalen, Henker, Hollingshead, & Burgess, 1996). Still relatively few in number, recent efforts to examine parent-child communication within African American and Latino families have been spurred by the growing concern about the high rates of adolescent pregnancy and growing risk for HIV infection that adolescents from urban epicenters represent. African American and Latino adolescents are at particular risk compared with White adolescents (Diaz, Buehler, Castro, & Ward, 1993), in part because they are more likely to reside in low-income, urban communities.

There are at least four important parallels that can be drawn from the research involving urban minority families and the research involving national or primarily White samples. First, urban minority parents typically speak to their children about sex or sex-related matters (Dusenbury, Diaz, Epstein, Botvin, & Caton, 1994). Second, urban adolescents are more likely to discuss sexual matters with their mothers than with their fathers (Kotchick, Dorsey, Miller, & Forehand, 1999). Third, parents may not be the primary source of sex information for adolescents (Ford & Norris, 1991). Fourth, it is again unclear to what extent the data support urban minority parents' influence as a source of sexual information for their children.

Among a representative sample of Latina girls (ages 12-19) living in a large urban center, more frequent communication with mothers about sex was related to lower sexual activity and pregnancy rates and greater use of contraceptives (Pick & Palos, 1995). Similarly, greater extent of parent-child communication about sex was reported among girls (ages 13-19) in Mexico City who had never been pregnant compared with girls who had been pregnant, attesting to the potential "protective influence" (Baumeister, Flores, & Marin, 1995) of parent-child communication about sex.

These findings contrast with the findings of other studies. Content of sexual communication based on mothers' or adolescents' reports was not associated with adolescents' sexual risk-taking behavior in a sample of African American and Hispanic families participating in the Family Adolescent Risk Behavior and Communication Study (Kotchick et al. 1999). Using a broader perspective of parent-child communication (rather than sex communication specifically), no associations were found between reported sexual involvement and a number of family communication variables, including parental warmth, open communication with parents, and problem parent-child communication in a sample of urban Latino adolescents (sixth through eighth grade) residing in a large southwestern city (Christopher et al., 1993). In fact, attitudes toward premarital sex and peer sexual norms were more useful predictors of sexual involvement than were any of the family variables examined. In a clinical sample of urban adolescent Latina girls (13–18 years), adolescents' subjective ratings of the quality of parent-child general communication were related to reported sexual behavior, although their ratings of the quality of parent-child communication about sexual issues specifically were not (O'Sullivan, Jaramillo, Moreau, & Meyer-Bahlburg, 1999). Without in-depth research on parent-child communication in urban minority families, it is difficult to draw conclusions about the extent to which such communication is a useful and meaningful source of information about sex for urban minority adolescents.

The Current Study

This study employs qualitative methods to permit in-depth exploration of outcomes that may be important to identify as key variables to be later operationalized quantitatively (Berg, 1998). These methods were considered most appropriate given the dearth of information about sexuality-related parent-child communication in urban minority families. The data presented here are part of a larger study examining social cognitions of urban girls with regard to sexual behaviors and relationships.

Girls were the focus of this study because of the heightened risk they represent both in terms of STDs generally, HIV particularly (Centers for Disease Control and Prevention, 1999), and because of their risk for adolescent pregnancy. Although there is a great deal of information with regard to the sexual behavior of older adolescent girls (Leigh, Morrison, Trocki, & Temple, 1994), comparatively little is known about the sexual behavior and perspectives of younger adolescent girls. Therefore, our sample is composed of girls between the ages of 10 and 13 years, and a smaller sample of younger girls (6–9 years). Mothers were also included because they are typically the primary communicators in the family arena (Hutchinson & Cooney, 1998), and because of the value of data collection methods involving multiple informants (Parker, Herdt, & Carballo, 1991).

To gather detailed information about parent-child sex communication in urban minority families, the following areas were addressed: (a) cues and timing of parent-child communication about sex in the course of the child's development to assess situations or events in the family life that prompt conversations about sex or constitute significant starting points for mothers and daughters; (b) content of communication, specifically the types of messages mothers use to influence their daughters' sexual decision making, as well as their daughters' responses to these messages; and (c) approaches adopted by girls and their mothers when discussing sexuality issues together to understand how sex messages were exchanged.

Method

Participants

A convenience sample consisting primarily of African American and Latina mothers and daughters was recruited from the inner-city neighborhoods of Washington Heights and Upper Harlem in New York City. Women were invited to participate in focus groups about dating, sex, and parent-child communication, and agreed to their daughters' participation. Participants were recruited using a variety of methods, including one-to-one contact, flier distribution, posters, and referrals from study contacts or members of previous focus groups. They took part in one of 22 focus groups involving a total of 72 girls and 72 mothers. Sixteen groups were conducted with girls or mothers of girls ages 10–13 years, and 6 were conducted with girls or mothers of girls ages 6–9 years. Ten of the focus groups were conducted with primarily Latina participants, and the remaining involved primarily African American participants. (Additional focus groups were conducted with girls ages 14-17 years but these data are not relevant here.)

Measures

Focus group protocol. Based on gaps noted in our previous research and the existing literature, we developed appropriate questions and probes relating to the age groups (i.e., ages 6–9 and 10–13) in consultation with members of a psychosocial/qualitative assessment core at our research center. All questions were open-ended and designed to be neutral in content and tone to minimize the extent to which the facilitator might influence participants' responses.

Focus groups were conducted separately with daughters and mothers. The protocols employed in their respective sessions were designed to correspond substantively so that they would yield data on both mothers' and daughters' perspectives on the same issues. For the girls' focus group sessions, the facilitator initiated discussions about (a) whether someone had talked to the girls about physical changes they could expect when reaching puberty and whether they felt free to approach someone about these issues; (b) whether someone had talked to the girls about relationships, romance, and sex and whether they felt free to approach someone about these issues; and (c) who (if anyone) had provided the girls with this sexual information. Girls were then prompted to describe the topics discussed with others, the reactions of family members when approached for information, and the contexts associated with these conversations.

For the mothers' focus group sessions, the facilitator was instructed to inquire about (a) whether and how mothers dealt with (or planned to deal with) puberty-related physical changes in their daughter, preparation for menarche, and "boy-girl issues"; (b) their reasons for discussing or not discussing these issues with their daughters; and (c) the ease or difficulty experienced when talking to their daughters about these topics. Mothers were asked to describe which topics (if any) they discussed, the factors or cues that prompted these conversations, and their perceptions of other sex information sources available to their daughters. In addition, mothers and daughters described the ways in which they approached these sex-related conversations.

Background questionnaire. Mothers completed a background questionnaire assessing demographic information. The items assessed age, ethnicity, place of birth, educational background, marital status, and number and ages of children.

Procedure

All procedures were approved in full by the Institutional Review Board prior to implementation. Mothers and daughters took part in separate focus groups organized according to the age group of their daughters (i.e., 6–9, 10–13 years) with approximately 7 participants per group (range 4–10). All mothers provided informed consent for their own and their daughters' participation, and all girls provided assent for their own participation. Mothers also completed the background questionnaire while food and refreshments were served. Focus group sessions took place in a room free of outside distractions with participants and the facilitator seated together around a table. Participants were informed that the discussion would be audiotaped and that the tape would be heard only by the project staff before being transcribed, then erased. Girls were assured that their mothers, in particular, would never hear the audiotapes. No identifying information was used during the sessions, and participants were asked to maintain the privacy of the others after the session was completed.

Focus groups were conducted in Spanish or English by graduate-level female facilitators matched in terms of ethnicity to participants. Following guidelines for conducting focus groups (Berg, 1998), facilitators used the list of topics to guide the discussions, while allowing participants to explore in-depth those issues they found most interesting. Facilitators phrased the open-ended questions in terms that were consistent with those used by participants during the session, and questions were presented in ways congruent with the flow of the conversation. Sessions took approximately 90 minutes to complete. Mothers and daughters each received 30 dollars for their participation and were reimbursed for any travel expenses incurred. Immediately following the session, each focus group was reviewed with the facilitator, including an evaluation of the flow of the conversation and participants' verbal and non-verbal reactions to issues presented. Audiotapes of the focus group sessions were transcribed in their original language and checked for accuracy. Spanish transcripts were translated into English and proofed again by bilingual members of the project staff.

Qualitative Data Analysis

Grounded theory was chosen as an appropriate method to guide our identification of concepts in the session data. Grounded theory is based on the premise that concepts (theory) can be developed and provisionally verified through systematic data collection and analysis of data relevant to the phenomenon (Strauss, 1987; Strauss & Corbin, 1990). Inquiry is conducted bidirectionally with concepts derived from earlier data analysis tested against subsequent data. After conducting a close review of excerpts from the transcribed sessions, initial analytic categories were developed by identifying recurrent themes in the participants' responses. Based on extensive discussions between the two analysts for this study, a template was drafted that identified and defined the analytic categories. After making the first provisional definition of a category, additional excerpts were sought to help refine the category and outline the various dimensions within it. Most of the categories described below comprise a range of dimensions, permitting examination of a wide variety of individual responses along specific themes.

To establish the reliability of the coding, a graduate-level research assistant was trained by the first author to code the excerpts using a small sample of randomly selected excerpts. The first author and the trained rater then coded separately an additional 20% of the excerpts. The interrater reliability was calculated and indicated consistency in rating of excerpts between the two raters (Kappa = 0.81; N = 72 excerpts). Rating errors were typically attributed to oversights of detail in the text rather than disagreements between raters in the criteria applied to a particular excerpt. All disagreements were resolved by discussing the coding decisions and refining the coding instructions when necessary. The first author then completed the thematic coding for the remaining parent-child communication excerpts, checking regularly for consistency and accuracy in ratings by comparing earlier and later coded excerpts.

Results

Sample Characteristics

Descriptive data on mothers participating in the focus groups can be found in Table 1. Most mothers were between the ages of 31 and 35 years (29.2%) and 36 and 40 years (23.6%). The majority of African American mothers (97.3%) were born in the United States, but only 2 (6.1 %) of the Latina mothers were born in this country. The country of origin for most of the Latina mothers was the Dominican Republic (63.6%), reflecting the ethnic makeup of the local community. The remaining Latina mothers originated from El Salvador (6.1%), Nicaragua (6.1%), and Puerto Rico (3.0%). Five Latina women (15.2%) did not report their country of origin. More than two-thirds of the African American (67.6%) mothers reported never being married, whereas the reported marital status of the Latina mothers was fairly evenly distributed across four of the five categories. Most of the mothers in our sample had two children. Both African American and Latina mothers reported a range of educational achievements.

Cues Associated with Timing of Parent-Child Communication About Sexuality

Facilitators asked daughters and mothers to describe when discussions about sexuality occurred, which cues prompted these conversations (if any), and which topics were addressed. A number of categories emerged from the data: Discussions are initiated at puberty, discussions are initiated when mothers become aware of their daughters' sexual interest, discussions are paced throughout the daughters' childhood, and discussions are postponed indefinitely.

Discussions initiated at puberty. The conspicuous physical changes that daughters undergo during puberty, such as breast and hip development, were common cues for mothers to discuss sexual matters with their daughters. These physical changes signaled their daughters' changing sexual status and impending onset of sexual activity. One mother told her group:

I have to prepare her 'cause every day she's growing up. She's developing. I notice she's developed pubic hair at the age of 10, her bust was....I said, "Hey! The change is gonna come soon." And so I used to send her for the napkin, and she used to say, "What's it for?" and I used to explain it to her. (African American mother of girl, 10-13 age group.)

The importance of menarche, in particular, as a signal of girls' developing sexual status, was illustrated by both the mothers and daughters. One girl told her group,

The first day I got my period, I was like, "Mommy, I peed blood!" And then she was like, "'Cause you have your period." And I was like, "Oh." And then she was

Table 1
Demographic Information on African American and Latina Mothers

	African American		Latina	
	N	Percentage	*n*	Percentage
Age (years)				
Younger than 30	5	13.5	4	12.1
31-35	15	40.5	5	15.2
36-40	6	16.2	11	33.3
41-45	7	18.9	7	21.2
Older than 46	4	10.8	6	18.2
Born in the United States	36	97.3	2	6.1
Marital Status				
Never Married	25	67.7	6	18.2
Married	3	8.1	10	30.3
Divorced	3	8.1	6	18.2
Separated	4	10.8	11	33.3
Widowed	2	5.4	0	0.0
Number of Children	Mode = 4		Mode = 2	
	Range = 1–6		Range = 1–10	
Highest level of education				
Fewer than 12 years, without diploma or GED	0	0.0	5	15.2
High school diploma or GED	14	37.8	11	33.4
Trade/technical school	10	27.0	8	24.2
Four-year college	8	21.6	8	24.2
Graduate school	5	13.5	1	3.0

Note. Two women indicated that their ethnicity was "other" and so are not represented in the data. GED = general equivalency diploma.

like, "Well, we'll have a talk at home." And then we got home…that's when she started talking about sex and everything. (African American girl, 10-13 age group.)

Many mothers reported anticipating this discussion. For instance, one mother said, "'Cause when they start menstruating, that's their eggs and their ovaries opening up, so you know you gotta tell them about the boys and, you know, sex. That's automatic." (African American mother of girl, 10–13 age group.) These participants noted that mothers relied on their daughters to approach them for help, comfort, or advice at this time. However, waiting for their daughters to approach them for information was a strategy that failed for a number of mothers as girls did not necessarily inform their mothers that they had begun menstruating (much to these mothers' considerable anguish). These mothers believed that a critical opportunity to caution their daughter about the dangers of sexual involvement had passed.

Discussions initiated when aware of daughters' interest in boys. A somewhat less common starting point than girls' physical development was noting changes in daughters' or her peers' behavior in relation to boys and men. These changes included wearing makeup or sexy clothing and jewelry, talking secretly to boys on the phone or spending time alone with a boy, or commenting on their attraction to particular boys and men (e.g., men in the neighborhood, male television charac-

ters). Some mothers described feeling motivated to talk to their daughters because this interest possibly indicated their daughters were being distracted by boys and losing sight of important educational goals. One mother explained to her group,

Well, my daughter is 12 years old. I notice she already had several boys interested in her, you see? She's never told me, but I notice it. I know one of the boys. He comes to my house since he feels at home. But from this trust is where you find danger. So I advise her, "Don't lose control because he won't be the first and only boy interested in you. You'll have many, many boyfriends. So don't go crazy on me. He won't be the first and only." (Latina mother of girl, 10-13 age group.)

Discussions initiated as opportunities arise. Other mothers addressed their daughters' questions about sexual matters as these questions arose. No singular event marked the beginning of these discussions and, as such, did not seem to involve an assessment of their daughters' "readiness" or new sexual status. In fact, most of these mothers reported having talked openly about sex since their daughters' earliest questions about reproduction and body parts. One mother told her group,

I can't remember a specific age when I first talked, but I mean I always talk to her about, you know, different things, you know. You can be walking down the street and something happens—"Oh, why is he kissing her?"

30

445 You know, in the street or whatever and you just talk about it. I'm real open with my daughter as far as sex and things like that. I guess she was about 11 when I really, you know, when she really came up with questions about it. (African American mother of girl, 10-13 age group.)

450 Another mother said,

Well, my discussion with my daughter about sex has been a progress. When she was small, we took it one level. I taught her, you know, all about my body, you know, "Where did I come from?" And so that's what she
455 needed to know then, and then each year we added more and more. (African American mother of girl, 10-13 age group.)

Frequently, these mothers reported initiating conversations after watching sexual scenes in movies or
460 television shows. Interestingly, 4 mothers took a particularly direct approach and demonstrated on themselves how to use a tampon or sanitary napkin.

Discussions postponed indefinitely. Although the general ethos of the focus groups was typically charac-
465 terized by a belief in the need to communicate openly with daughters about sex and relationships, other participants indicated that this did not occur in their families. This was particularly true for Latina families. Some mothers reported being unable to approach sex-
470 ual topics or else waiting until they believed their daughters were ready or soon to be married. Daughters seemed well aware of the extent to which their mothers were reluctant to discuss sexual matters, particularly issues not directly related to reproduction or hygiene.
475 When asked why they did not approach their mothers with questions about boys or sex, 2 girls responded as follows:

R1: If I asked my mother, she might say to me I shouldn't be speaking that way. I have no reason to
480 be speaking that way.
R2: Anyway, when we're young, our mothers don't like us to be talking about boyfriends or things like this.
R1: Of babies—yes.
R2: Sometimes, yes. Well, at least until you're older.
485 (Latina girls, 6-9 age group.)

Mothers frequently explained that they had left the task of informing their daughters about sexual matters to others, such as counselors, teachers, or other family members. One mother told her group,

490 With my oldest, I started having the talks about sex when she was 13. I haven't spoken to my second daughter 'cause my oldest one is the one who talks to her. She tells her everything and my youngest listens to everything. (Latina mother of girl, 10-13 age group.)

495 In these cases, mothers described other people as being better-prepared to discuss sexual matters or better-informed. One mother explained,

I think those trained and qualified people should find the smoother and gentler way to tell our daughters about it.
500 To teach our daughters those scientific terms for our bodies so our daughters avoid the street slang and vulgarities used instead of those terms. Most of us mothers don't even know the exact terms. (Latina mother of girl, 10-13 age group.)

505 A few Latina mothers expressed the belief that sexual knowledge somehow "comes to her when she gets married" (Latina mother of girl, 6–9 age group), presumably as a result of sexual experience.

On occasion, mothers and daughters told their re-
510 spective groups that the girls knew or thought they already knew everything about sex, thus dismissing their mothers' attempts to address these issues. This belief essentially absolved the mothers from further attempts at communicating about sex. This was noted
515 more often in Latina than African American interactions. One girl reported, "I said, 'Okay, Mom, it's all right. You know I know more than you do.'" (Latina girl, 10–13 age group.) In another case, a girl explained to her group, "I told her to stop talking about all that. I
520 already knew all that from J's mother....She told me everything already I wanted to know." (Latina girl, 10-13 age group.)

Content of Parent-Child Communication About Sex

Our analyses of the transcripts revealed three main thematic categories associated with the content of
525 mothers' and daughters' communication about sex. These were (a) mothers communicate dire consequences associated with sexual participation, (b) mothers emphasize girls' responsibility in avoiding or controlling sexual encounters, and (c) girls reassure moth-
530 ers of their intentions to avoid sexual relations and to continue their pursuit of educational and career goals.

Dire consequences associated with sexual participation. The facilitators asked participants to describe what mothers talked about with their daughters when
535 they discussed sex. One girl said, "When I got my first period, I was 12. And she didn't really tell me nothing about sex. She just told me how to keep myself clean from it because you can have a smell from it and stuff." (African American girl, 10–13 age group.) Mothers and
540 daughters agreed that discussions typically centered on biological factors, such as reproduction, hygiene, and health issues, with little coverage of romantic, interpersonal, or arousal issues. In particular, Latina participants reported that mothers emphasized the extreme,
545 detrimental aspects of sexual and romantic involvement with boys and men, including pain, shame, and humiliation. Their discourse also revealed a common perception that sexual involvement or interest inevitably leads to pregnancy and subsequent abandonment by
550 male partners, and ultimately, a preemption of life goals. One girl explained how her mother told her about how girls get pregnant:

A boy tells her how much he really likes her and, in return, she likes him. Then she gets pregnant and he says
555 "I'll never leave you. I love you." But after they have sex, he tells her, "I'll be right back, honey. I promise I'll

be back. I'll never leave you." But he never comes back and leaves her all by herself to care for their child. And to survive, she has to rely on Welfare and all that stuff. (Latina girl, 10–13 age group.)

They tended to stress how loss of virginity and sexual involvement were equated with dirtiness, shame, and immorality. One girl said,

My mom tells me that I shouldn't let anyone touch me. And when I have a boyfriend how I should take it slow with him, take my time with him. And how special my wedding day is going to be. Otherwise, if I'm 17 or 18 years old and I have a baby, my man will cheat on me because men's hormones rule them and they only think of a hundred different ways to have sex. (Latina girl, 10–13 age group.)

African American mothers were more likely to communicate to their daughters that sexual involvement, and hence pregnancy, is associated with the loss of important resources, such as money, time, and educational opportunities, as well as the future capacity to attract other men interested in a relationship. For example, one mother said, "I explain it to them…The babies start coming…I mean, you don't get the nice clothes no more because you got to give it to your baby. Not my baby—your baby. And I made it very clear: I'm not taking no babies." Similarly, one girl said, "She told me that I couldn't go to the movies anymore or hang out with my friends. I'd have to be at home all the time cleaning and feeding the baby" (African American mother of girl, 10–13 age group).

According to our participants, both African American and Latina mothers exaggerate the pain associated with loss of virginity and with childbirth in their attempts to deter their daughters. Mothers freely disclosed that their motive behind this strategy was to scare their daughters into maintaining sexual abstinence indefinitely. They believed that stressing the detrimental consequences associated with sex was the most likely and direct route to this goal. Of particular importance, the motive behind this strategy is apparently to communicate that there are no alternative outcomes for these girls if they became sexually active. In fact, some of the mothers told their daughters that all methods of contraception were unreliable and could not be trusted to prevent pregnancy.

Also important to note is that very rarely participants indicated that mothers would acknowledge to their daughters the rewarding aspects of sexual activity. Four of our participants described these positive aspects, although mothers appeared to have made them in the context of a conversation about the harmful consequences that were likely to follow. For instance, one mother told her group,

Like I told my children, "This is the other end of the orgasm. The one that you just couldn't wait to have and you thought when you was in the thick of it and it felt so good. Don't let child support wait for you at the other end of the orgasm. I'm still experiencing it (laughter) but I don't like this part…Secondly you are sleeping with everybody he has slept with. And everybody that they have slept with." And I tell them, "Put it in your mind that girl he used to go with that you can't stand? I mean that they think that's wiggling in you making you feel good wiggled in her." My God. Isn't that enough to turn your stomach? (African American mother of girl, 10-13 age group.)

However, many mothers also recognized the likely futility of their attempts to obstruct their daughters' sexual advancement (frequently referring to their own mothers' failed attempts with them). In fact, most girls were aware of their mothers' motives to scare them and seemed to find these efforts pathetic, even humorous. When asked what their mothers had told them about sex, one girl told her group, "All that my mother said was that if you got the guts to open your legs, you got the guts to have a baby…But I'm opening all the way!" (Latina girl, 10–13 age group), to which her group responded by laughing. Another said, "She told me that it was like a knife stabbing into you down there! But she's crazy…I don't know why she bothers saying stuff like that." (African American girl, 10-13 age group.)

Girls' responsibility to avoid or control sexual encounters. Many participants said that mothers emphasized their daughters' duty to assume a restrictive, limit-setting role in their interactions with boys and men and, according to many participants, to avoid all sexual contact. One girl told her group, "She said, 'At a certain age, your period will start bleeding and you can't let boys touch you or else, or else, you get pregnant.'" (African American girl, 6–9 age group.) They frequently described teaching their daughter to recognize lines that boys and men could use to entice girls sexually.

Latina mothers, in particular, tended to impart extremely harsh views about men, especially the belief that men were indiscriminate in their search for sexual opportunities with girls, and that girls should be forever on guard in the presence of boys and men. One girl explained, "My mom said that I should never let a boy touch me. If a boy touches me, I should defend myself, kick him with anything I can." (Latina girl, 10-13 age group.) These views clearly reinforce the traditional standard that it is women's responsibility to avoid exploitation and victimization. Latina participants also frequently described mothers forbidding their daughters to have any type of physical contact with men or to be alone around men. For instance, one mother told her daughter,

"Your father shouldn't even touch you. If he does, you should come and tell me." I give my daughter my full trust to be open with me. I tell her, "No one should be touching you. No one. You can talk to boys to be polite, but no one can touch you. If they do, tell me immediately." (Latina mother of girl, 10-13 age group.)

Conferring an expectation that girls should avoid all sexual encounters at times appeared to contradict other expectations that mothers communicated less directly to their daughters. For example, in African American families, girls' interest in boys seemed to be connected to a belief that the negative consequences associated with sexual interactions, such as early childbearing, could not be prevented despite the pressure placed on girls to avoid such outcomes. "I said, 'You'll be getting it soon. Your body's gonna change.' And I said, 'Once you get this, you start talking to the boys—here comes a baby!'" (African American mother of girl, 10-13 age group.) Unfortunately, the expectation that girls will fail to maintain their responsibilities in this regard is also clearly communicated to girls. For instance, one mother described a conversation she had with her daughter like this:

> I said to [her], "I see you talk to guys and I don't get an attitude, I just teach you how to maintain yourself as a young lady." I said, "We'll sit down and I'll teach you about what life is about 'cause when you get to my age, you gonna go through the same situations or the same problems, you know, sexual encounters." And every now and then, I still say, "Sit down." I still say, "Did you get your period?" I look for it every month and if she misses [a day], I say, "Come here. You got a problem? I want to see some blood." (African American mother of girl, 10-13 age group.)

Another contradictory message from mothers to their daughters noted in these sessions was that men and boys sought to exploit girls and women sexually, yet girls were expected to find a nice boyfriend who wanted to marry her and that marriage was an important and valuable goal in life. One mother said, "I tell my daughter that all men are irresponsible. She has to find a responsible man." This was more common in reports from Latina participants than African American participants.

Reassurance of intentions to avoid sexual relations. In response to their mothers' injunctions to avoid sexual contact with boys, many participants reported that girls vowed to their mothers that they would first complete their studies or have a career. Despite these reassurances, however, mothers reported distrusting their daughters' pledges, citing suspicions that their daughters had already become sexually involved or would be unlikely to resist personal or social pressures to become sexually active. Girls did not admit in the focus group sessions to being insincere in these reassurances, even though clearly many girls were romantically and sexually involved with boys.

Mothers' and Daughters' Approaches to Communication About Sexuality

Our analyses revealed how mothers and daughters viewed their respective approaches to parent-child discussions about sex. Mothers typically sought information about their daughters' sexual experiences, and approached these interactions as a means of obtaining details and practical advantage in their efforts to prohibit sexual experimentation. Daughters, on the other hand, typically withheld personal information from their mothers, thus avoiding conversations about sex when disclosure was expected.

Mothers urge daughters' disclosure of sexual participation. Many mothers in our focus groups reported believing strongly that knowledge about their daughters' activities was key to affecting their daughters' behavior and potential outcomes. Although they encouraged openness in their conversations with their daughters, both mothers and daughters were aware that in many cases, rather than provide information, mothers were seeking information about the girls' personal experiences. Several participants reported that the girls had to mark their periods on a calendar or show their mothers used napkins each month to help their mothers monitor. Some mothers followed their daughters when leaving the house to meet with friends, searched through personal belongings, such as book bags, diaries, and closets, or listened to private conversations in their efforts to obtain information.

Our analyses indicated that African American mothers focused their efforts on preventing pregnancy and disease and thus sought information about sexual activity, whereas Latina mothers tended to focus their efforts on preventing all sexual contact and thus sought information about relationship development. The two following excerpts illustrate this apparent difference in mothers' approaches.

> You can go around with your head in the sand but, let's face it, they're going to have sex. That's just fact. It's up to me to convince her to take her pill each day or think to use a condom. He's not going to look out for her. (African American mother, girl 10–13 age group.)

In contrast, a Latina mother expressed her approach in this way:

> I've told my daughter, "If you like a boy, please trust me and tell me that you like him 'cause I'm your mother. I'm your mother. I am everything for you. I have to know which boy you like. When you are older and become a professional, you'll have a boyfriend, and get married. But for the time being, if you have a boyfriend, you have to tell me because I'm your friend. I won't hit you or insult you or nothing like that." No. My daughter doesn't even go to the restroom by herself. In everything she's involved—I'm involved. (Latina mother of girl, 10–13 age group.)

Girls avoid disclosure of sex-related information. Many girls tried to avoid discussions with their mothers or withhold information, in particular, their involvement in romantic or sexual relationships with boys. As most of the mothers' discussions about sex took the form of moralistic and prohibitive lectures, many of these girls reacted against being told what they could and could not do. Girls' lack of cooperation was clearly a source of great frustration for many mothers.

785 In one case, a mother reported having the following conversation with her daughter when she eventually learned that her daughter had reached menarche:

"Did you start your menstrual cycle?" You know? And she said, "Yes." So I said, "How long ago did it start?"
790 (She said,) "Um, I forgot." I said, "Well, I thought we all been through all of this and we were here, you know, we were seeing eye to eye, that you were gonna tell me. What happened?" She's embarrassed. Embarrassed! I said, "Would you be this embarrassed to tell me about a
795 boy, if somebody touched you? What was the purpose of me doing all this talking all along?" And that's when I had another rude awakening: No matter how much you talk and no matter how much you tell them to come to you, the little things are gonna go ahead and do what they
800 want to do. (African American mother of girl, 10-13 age group.)

In other cases, girls were apparently avoiding conversations about sex in response to cues from their mothers that such talk is uncomfortable or embarrass-
805 ing. When asked by the facilitator to explain why they did not ask such questions, girls often reported feeling too ashamed, guilty, or fearing ridicule. In addition, the girls occasionally reported doubting the veracity of their mothers' responses. One mother told her group,
810 "According to what she says, I answer her question. But I never reveal more information than what I have to. I'm not lying to her, but I'm also not encouraging her to ask me further questions." (Latina mother of girl, 6-9 age group.)
815 On occasion, a girl would describe responding positively to her mother's appeals for openness:

My mother didn't have a problem 'cause she asked those questions to my grandmother. My mother likes it when I ask her 'cause she knows I'm growing up. I need to know
820 things. So my mother acts very well when I ask her. (Latina girl, 10-13 age group.)

More frequently, however, girls explained how they turned to others for information about sex or advice on relationships with boys. Typically, they turned to
825 friends, cousins, older siblings, or friends' mothers. One girl explained,

Like my best friend, she talks to my mother about her problems. And, like, I can talk to her mother about problems…but we tell them to keep it inside, so we don't let
830 each other's mothers know about it. (African American girl, 10-13 age group.)

It was striking how willingly these girls approached others, even adults, for this information, especially in contrast to their general reluctance to discuss these
835 issues with their own mothers.

Discussion

The current study represents a qualitative investigation of mother-daughter communication about sex for families residing in impoverished urban communities of New York City. African American and Latina moth-
840 ers and daughters participated in separate focus groups designed to obtain a range of perspectives about issues pertinent to parent-child communication in urban minority families, including the cues and content of their conversations. Our analyses yielded a wealth of infor-
845 mation about the extent to which mothers may be a useful and meaningful source of sexual information for their adolescent daughters.

Of particular note, most mothers and daughters reported discussing sexual issues together in both the
850 African American and Latino families. However, our analyses revealed that mothers and daughters adopt relatively antagonistic positions that may functionally preclude effective communication. Given our focus on girls in the pubertal years, difficulties in parent-child
855 communication may actually be a function of relationship tension associated with girls' autonomy transitions at this age (Collins, Laursen, Mortensen, Luebker, & Ferreira, 1997). Most communication about sex first occurs at this time and, as such, may account to some
860 extent for their strained discourse. A limitation of the current study is that it is not clear to what extent our data can be generalized to other samples of urban, low-income, African American, and Latino families. However, representativeness is not an objective guiding
865 qualitative investigations. Qualitative studies typically employ purposive sampling, as we did, to ensure adequate inclusion of particular known groups (Berg, 1998).

Participants described mothers' initiation of con-
870 versations about sex as a means of learning more about their daughters' sex-related experiences and of potentially controlling their daughters' sexual outcomes. Mothers revealed considerable ambivalence about accepting their daughters' developing sexual maturity,
875 although this appeared more true of Latino families. Many postponed discussions about sex indefinitely. They often expressed reluctance to educate their children in an open manner, fearing discomfort, or unintentionally encouraging their daughters' sexual involve-
880 ment. Moreover, many felt torn between the desire to maintain their daughters' childhood "innocence" and the need to counteract the social influences promoting girls' sexual involvement.

Girls were also reluctant to participate in these con-
885 versations. Mothers' messages about sex, typically restrictive and moralistic in tone and content, were not well received by their daughters. Girls reacted by withholding information and secretly becoming involved with boys in sexual and/or romantic relationships. They
890 often dismissed these mothers' admonitions as pathetic attempts to scare them into abstinence. Unfortunately, mothers rarely acknowledged the positive aspects of sexuality outside the context of harm. It appears that their communication efforts ultimately deter their
895 daughters from confiding in them about their sexual interest or participation, or later informing them of unintended consequences of their sexual involvement, such as pregnancy or contraction of STDs.

Given the strain between mothers and daughters in their communication about sex, it is perhaps not surprising that many girls turn to others for sexual information, particularly aunts, sisters, friends of the family, or other friends' mothers. Some mothers indicated that they willingly left it to others to answer their daughters' questions. Moreover, those mothers who discussed sexual matters with their daughters typically restricted their focus to reproduction and hygiene. Psychosexual issues, such as commitment, love, jealousy, and desire were not broached even though these are the topics girls most want mothers to address (Mueller & Powers, 1990) and are central to making healthy sexual choices. Mothers may prefer to be the primary source of information for girls (Mueller & Powers, 1990). However, our data suggest that the best source of sexual information for adolescent girls may, in fact, be a source other than a parent.

Because a critical developmental stage of adolescence is becoming independent and making one's own decisions (Collins et al., 1997), it would be worthwhile for an intervention to include components that help girls develop sexual agency. Only in this context can girls feel enabled and motivated to take an active role in ensuring healthy choices for themselves. It would be counterproductive to endorse a message that sexual behavior and relationships make you feel bad about yourself. Therefore, rather than intervening with mothers, the target of an intervention could be adult women trusted by mothers within a community or a community sector, such as faith institutions, health and social agencies, or other civil institutions. Our study indicates that mothers would certainly feel strongly about maintaining their involvement in this communication process, but many would consider working with others to share this responsibility.

In terms of policy, those adults that girls already turn to, including family relatives and adult friends, could be encouraged to make themselves available to girls for information about sex. Concepts of agency rather than reactivity should be reinforced in communication with girls. Promoting parents' consistent communication of disapproval (Jaccard, Dittus, & Gordon, 1998) will be a harmful strategy in the long run. Pervasive concepts in this study were the notions of inevitability and exploitation in girls' understanding of their sexuality. Krueger (1996) maintains that female sexuality is rarely construed in terms other than reactivity, victimization, and restraint. As such, girls may implicitly learn that they should not acknowledge to themselves or others their experiences of sexual desire and interest. Moreover, teaching girls that their sexuality is defined by boys' or men's actions toward them possibly hinders girls' ability to acquire agency. It is unreasonable to expect girls to assume effective decision-making skills related to contraceptive or condom use if they have learned that they are to avoid sexual encounters at all costs.

In summary, our findings indicate that urban minority mothers and daughters discuss sexual matters. However, similar to other samples of parents and puberty-age children (Shoop & Davidson, 1994; Whalen et al., 1996), they experience considerable difficulty in doing so. Involving others in the communication process might remedy problems associated with strain in parent-child relationships during the pubertal years. Girls appear to benefit already by the provision of information from other adults. Interventions could target adult women trusted by mothers within a community or a community sector.

References

Alan Guttmacher Institute. (1996, September 13) Teen sex and pregnancy. Facts in Brief. Available: http://www.agi-usa.org/index.html.

Baumeister, L. M., Flores, E., & Marin, B. V. (1995). Sex information given to Latina adolescents by parents. *Health Education Research, 10*, 233-239.

Berg, B. L. (1998). *Qualitative research methods.* Needham, MA: Allyn & Bacon.

Buysse, A. (1996). Adolescents, young adults and AIDS: A study of actual knowledge vs. perceived need for additional information. *Journal of Youth & Adolescence, 25*, 259-271.

Centers for Disease Control and Prevention. (1999). *HIV/AIDS Surveillance Report, 1998, 10*(2).

Christopher, F. S., Johnson, D. C., & Roosa, M. W. (1993). Family, individual, and social correlates of early Hispanic adolescent sexual expression. *The Journal of Sex Research, 30*, 54-61.

Collins, W. A., Laursen, B., Mortensen, N., Luebker, C., & Ferreira, M. (1997). Conflict processes and transitions in parent and peer relationships: Implications for autonomy and regulation. *Journal of Adolescent Research, 12*, 178-198.

Diaz, T., Buehler, J. W., Castro, K. G., & Ward, J. W. (1993). AIDS trends among Hispanics in the United States. *American Journal of Public Health, 83*, 504-509.

Dusenbury, L., Diaz, T., Epstein, J. A., Botvin, G. J., & Caton, M. (1994). Attitudes toward AIDS and AIDS education among multiethnic participants of school-aged children in New York City. *AIDS Education and Prevention, 6*, 237-248.

Ellen, J. M., Aral, S. O., & Madger, L. S. (1998). Do differences in sexual behavior account for the racial/ethnic differences in adolescents' self-reported history of a sexually transmitted disease? *Sexually Transmitted Diseases, 25*, 130-131.

Fisher, T. D. (1993). A comparison of various measures of family sexual communication: Psychometric properties, validity and behavioral correlates. *The Journal of Sex Research, 30*, 229-238.

Ford, K., & Norris, A. (1991). Urban African-American and Hispanic adolescents and young adults: Who do they talk to about AIDS and condoms? What are they learning? *AIDS Education and Prevention, 3*, 197-206.

Ford, K., Rubinstein, S., & Norris, A. (1994). Sexual behavior and condom use among urban, low-income African-American and Hispanic youth. *AIDS Education and Prevention, 6*, 219-229.

Gibson, J. W., & Kempf, J. (1990). Attitudinal predictors of sexual activity in Hispanic adolescent females. *Journal of Adolescent Research, 5*, 414-430.

Grunseit, A., Kippax, S., Aggleton, P., Baldo, M., & Slutkin, G. (1997). Sexuality education and young people's sexual behavior: A review of studies. *Journal of Adolescent Research, 12*, 421-453.

Hutchinson, M. K., & Cooney, T. M. (1998). Patterns of parent-teen sexual risk communication: Implications for intervention. *Family Relations, 47*, 185-194.

Jaccard, J., & Dittus, P. (1993). Parent-adolescent communication about premarital pregnancy. *Families in Society, 74*, 329-343.

Jaccard, J., Dittus, P. J., & Gordon, V. V. (1998). Parent-adolescent congruency in reports of adolescent sexual behavior and in the communications about sexual behavior. *Child Development, 69*, 247-261.

Kirby, D. (1997). *No easy answers: Research findings on programs to reduce teen pregnancy (Summary).* Washington, DC: The National Campaign to Prevent Teen Pregnancy.

Kirby, D., Korpi, M., Adivi, C., & Weissman, J. (1997). An impact evaluation of Project SNAPP: An AIDS and pregnancy prevention middle school program. *AIDS Education and Prevention, 9* (Suppl. A), 44-61.

Kotchick, B. A., Dorsey, S., Miller, K. S., & Forehand, R. (1999). Adolescent sexual risk-taking behavior in single-parent ethnic minority families. *Journal of Family Psychology, 13*, 93-102.

Krueger, M. (1996). Sexism, erotophobia, and the illusory "no": Implications for acquaintance rape awareness. *Journal of Psychology and Human Sexuality, 8*, 107-116.

Leigh, B. C., Morrison, D. M., Trocki, K., & Temple, M. T. (1994). Sexual behavior of American adolescents: Results from a U.S. national survey. *Journal of Adolescent Health, 15*, 117-125.

McBride, V. M. (1996). An ecological analysis of coital timing among middle-class African American adolescent females. *Journal of Adolescent Research, 11*, 261-279.

Miller, B. (1998). *Families matter: A research synthesis of family influences on adolescent pregnancy.* Washington, DC: National Campaign to Prevent Teen Pregnancy.

Moore, K. A., Peterson, J. L., & Furstenberg, F. F. (1986). Parental attitudes and the occurrence of early sexual activity. *Journal of Marriage and the Family, 48*, 777-782.

Mueller, K. E., & Powers, W. G. (1990). Parent-child sexual discussion: Perceived communicator style and subsequent behavior. *Adolescence, 25*, 469-482.

Newcomer, S. R., & Udry, J. R. (1985). Parent-child communication and adolescent sexual behavior. *Family Planning Perspectives, 17*, 169-174.

O'Sullivan, L. F., Jaramillo, B. M. S., Moreau, D., & Meyer-Bahlburg, H. F. L. (1999). Mother-daughter communication about sexuality in a clinical sample of Hispanic adolescent girls. *Hispanic Journal of Behavioral Sciences, 21*, 447-469.

Overby, K. J., & Kegeles, S. M. (1994). The impact of AIDS on an urban population of high-risk female minority adolescents: Implications for intervention. *Journal of Adolescent Health, 15*, 216-227.

Parker, R.. P, Herdt, G., & Carballo, M. (1991). Sexual culture, HIV transmission, and AIDS research. *The Journal of Sex Research, 28*, 77-98.

Pick, S., & Palos, P. A. (1995). Impact of the family on the sex lives of adolescents. *Adolescence, 30*, 667-675.

Rodgers, K. B. (1999). Parenting processes related to sexual risk-taking behaviors of adolescent males and females. *Journal of Marriage and the Family, 61*, 99-109.

Rotheram-Borus, M. J., & Gwadz, M. (1993). Sexuality among youths at risk. *Child and Adolescent Psychiatric Clinics of North America, 2*, 415-429.

Shoop, D. M., & Davidson, P. M. (1994). AIDS and adolescents: The relation of parent and partner communication to adolescent condom use. *Journal of Adolescence, 17*, 137-148.

Strauss, A. (1987). *Qualitative analysis for social scientists.* New York: Cambridge University Press.

Strauss, A., & Corbin, J. (1990). *Basics of qualitative research: Grounded theory, procedures, and techniques.* Newbury Park, CA: Sage.

Trent, K. (1994). Family context and adolescents' fertility expectations. *Youth and Society, 26*, 118-127.

Westhoff, W. W., McDermott, R. J., & Holcomb, D. R. (1996). HIV risk behaviors: A comparison of U.S. Hispanic and Dominican Republic youth. *AIDS Education and Prevention, 8*, 106-114.

Whalen, C. K., Henker, B., Hollingshead, J., & Burgess, S. (1996). Parent-adolescent dialogues about AIDS. *Journal of Family Psychology, 10*, 343-357.

About the authors: Lucia F. O'Sullivan, Ph.D., is an assistant professor of clinical psychology (in psychiatry) at Columbia University. Her research has focused on sexual dating relationships, particularly gender differences in communication and influence, and adolescent sexual risk behavior. She is currently the principal investigator on a comprehensive study investigating the role of social cognitions in the development of sexual risk behavior on urban adolescent girls.

Heino F. L. Meyer-Bahlburg, Dr rer nat., is a professor of clinical psychology (in psychiatry) at Columbia University. He heads a research program in developmental psychoendocrinology with a focus on the developmental psychobiology of gender and sexuality. In addition, he is an associate director of the HIV Center for Clinical and Behavioral Studies and the principal investigator of its Psychosexual Core, with special emphasis on the development of sexual risk behavior.

Beverly X. Watkins received a Ph.D. in history from Columbia University. She has conducted research addressing minority health issues at the Division of Sociomedical Sciences, Columbia University School of Public Health, and was recently awarded a pilot investigator grant from the Columbia Center for Active Life of Minority Elders.

Address correspondence to: Lucia F. O'Sullivan, Ph.D., HIV Center for Clinical and Behavioral Studies, College of Physicians and Surgeons of Columbia University, 1051 Riverside Drive, Unit 15, New York, NY 10032-2695.

Acknowledgments: This research was supported in part by National Institute of Mental Health (NIMH) Center Grant 2-P50-MH43520 to Anke A. Ehrhardt, a NIMH Fellowship Training Grant T32-MH19139 (Program Director Zena Stein), and a Sexuality Research Fellowship from the Social Science Research Council to Lucia F. O'Sullivan. The authors thank the mothers and daughters for their participation in this study, the Psychosocial/Qualitative Assessment Core (PI Susan Tross) for consultation on qualitative methodology, and Dinah Gay, Leopoldina Cairo, Carmen Navarro, and Elena Mojica for their help with recruitment of participants, data collection, and coding.

Exercise for Article 4

Factual Questions

1. The researchers cite a review of formal sex and HIV education programs. They stated that most programs produce some desirable consequences. What desirable consequence do they name as an example?

2. The researchers state that they employed qualitative methods to "permit" what?

3. What were the ages of the "smaller sample" of girls?

4. The mothers provided informed consent. Did the girls also assent for their own participation?

5. How do the researchers explain what they mean by "inquiry is conducted bidirectionally"?

6. What was the country of origin for most of the Latina mothers?

7. Were mothers more likely to initiate communication about sexuality when they noticed girls' physical development *or* when they became aware of the girls' interest in boys?

8. According to the researchers, what was some mothers' motive for exaggerating the pain associated with loss of virginity and with childbirth?

Questions for Discussion

9. In your opinion, how useful is this research in furthering our understanding of parent-child communication about sex?

10. The researchers state that they used a "convenience sample." Is this important? Why? Why not? (See lines 192–195 and lines 860–863.)

11. Focus groups were conducted separately for daughters and their mothers. In your opinion, would there be advantages to having both the mothers and daughters in the same focus groups?

Disadvantages?

12. How helpful were the quotations in helping you understand the results of this study? Would you like to have seen more of them? Less? Why?

13. The researchers make general references to numbers with phrases such as "many mothers" (line 392) and "frequently, these mothers" (line 458). Would you have preferred to have exact numbers? Would exact numbers distract from the qualitative nature of this study? Explain.

Quality Ratings

Directions: Indicate your level of agreement with each of the following statements by circling a number from 5 for strongly agree (SA) to 1 for strongly disagree (SD). If you believe an item is not applicable to this research article, leave it blank. Be prepared to explain your ratings.

A. The introduction establishes the importance of the study.

   SA   5   4   3   2   1   SD

B. The literature review establishes the context for the study.

   SA   5   4   3   2   1   SD

C. The research purpose, question, or hypothesis is clearly stated.

   SA   5   4   3   2   1   SD

D. The method of sampling is sound.

   SA   5   4   3   2   1   SD

E. Relevant demographics (for example, age, gender, and ethnicity) are described.

   SA   5   4   3   2   1   SD

F. Measurement procedures are adequate.

   SA   5   4   3   2   1   SD

G. All procedures have been described in sufficient detail to permit a replication of the study.

   SA   5   4   3   2   1   SD

H. The participants have been adequately protected from potential harm.

   SA   5   4   3   2   1   SD

I. The results are clearly described.

   SA   5   4   3   2   1   SD

J. The discussion/conclusion is appropriate.

   SA   5   4   3   2   1   SD

K. Despite any flaws, the report is worthy of publication.

   SA   5   4   3   2   1   SD

Article 5

The Interconnection of Childhood Poverty and Homelessness: Negative Impact/Points of Access

Cathryne L. Schmitz
University of Southern Maine

Janet D. Wagner
Columbus State Community College

Edna M. Menke
Ohio State University

ABSTRACT. Child poverty negatively impacts the development of children; family homelessness compounds the issues. Both have dramatically increased over the last two decades with far-reaching, poorly understood consequences. The impact of the instability of poverty and homelessness on children is often hidden or difficult to comprehend. Few studies critically examine the impact on a child's sense of safety and security. Using mixed method inquiry, this research sought to examine the effects of poverty and homelessness on children 8 to 12 years of age. The voices of the children illuminate the underlying strengths and vulnerabilities. Results indicate that homelessness leaves children feeling a decreased sense of support and an increased sense of isolation.

From *Families in Society: The Journal of Comtemporary Human Services, 82*, 69–77. Copyright © 2001 by Families International, Inc. Reprinted with permission.

The high level of poverty among children of all ethnic groups in the United States negatively impacts their development and the nation's future. Poverty places families at risk (Belle, 1990), frequently nega-
5   tively impacting the development and emotional status of children (Committee for Economic Development, 1987; Elmer, 1977; Tuma, 1989). As a result of structural changes (Center on Human Poverty and Nutrition Policy, 1995), the level of poverty facing children in
10   the U.S. is the highest in the industrial world (Children's Defense Fund [CDF], 1991). Child poverty is currently 20.5% (CDF, 1998), with children in minority and female-headed single-parent families experiencing the highest rates (CDF, 1991).
15   While the impact of homelessness cannot be separated from poverty, homelessness is a life event having traumatic effects beyond poverty. It is a systemic problem (McChesney, 1990), increasing as the shortage of affordable housing decreases and the level of poverty
20   increases (Gulati, 1992; Martin, 1991; McChesney, 1990; Shinn & Gillespie, 1994). Family homelessness increased dramatically in the 1980s. It is still rising as "attacks on the social welfare system" continue (Gulati, 1992; Lindsey, 1998), pushing the number of children

25   (CDF, 1995) and female-headed households (Lindsey, 1997) experiencing homelessness steadily upward. The issues arising from this attack are also personal (Gulati, 1992). Homelessness is a condition that compounds the issues faced by families in poverty—frequently involv-
30   ing the loss of friends, belongings, neighborhood, school (Boxill & Beaty, 1990), and a place to "be."
Studies have shown mixed results in understanding the impact of homelessness beyond poverty. A study by Bassuk and Rosenberg (1988) suggests homeless
35   children are different from poor, domiciled children. Other studies, however, conclude children who have been homeless may not be dramatically different from other very poor children (Masten, 1992; Ziesemer, Marcoux., & Marwell, 1994). Ziesemer, Marcoux, and
40   Marwell (1994) found no significant differences between homeless and domiciled low-income children (Ziesemer et al., p. 658); and Martagon, Ramirez, and Masten (1991) found that children who are homeless "did not differ from other children in how far they are
45   expected to go in school or general hopes for the future" (p. 1). In spite of the stress of homelessness in children's lives, it may be the long-term poverty that places children at greatest risk (Ziesemer et al.).
Missing in the literature is the child's perception of
50   the situation of self and environment (Epps, 1998). Children's voices have the potential to give rise to a picture of their lives, dreams, aspirations, and needs. In listening, we may find ways to understand their experiences as a basis for designing empowering programs
55   and policies (Chalhub de Oliveira, 1997). Mixed method inquiry was used in this study to add to our understanding of the impact of poverty and homelessness on latency age children in poverty (domiciled and homeless). Both a priori and grounded theory guided
60   the design. The use of qualitative and quantitative methods increased the richness (Mitchell, 1986; Patton, 1990) adding voice to the data, clarifying the differential impact. The implications for practice are identified with a discussion of the strengths as a basis for inter-
65   vention and remediation.

Table 1
Instruments and Interview Schedules

Instrument	Citations
Reynolds Manifest Anxiety Scale	Test description—Reynolds & Richmond, 1979, 1985
	Construct validity—Reynolds, 1980; Reynolds & Richmond, 1979
	Use with homeless populations—Bassuk & Rubin, 1987
	Reliability—Wisniewski, Mulick, Genshaft, & Coury, 1987
Achenbach Child Behavior Checklist	Description—Achenbach & Edelbrock, 1981, 1983; Kessler, 1988
	Reliability—Achenbach & Edelbrock, 1981
	Comparison mental health vs. normed populations—Achenbach, Edelbrock, & Howell, 1987
Kovacs Child Depression Inventory	Description—Kovacs, 1985
	Reliability—Kovacs, 1985
Children's Nowicki-Strickland Internal–External Locus of Control (CNSIE)	Description, reliability, construct validity, discriminative validity—Nowicki & Strickland, 1973
Child Interview Schedule	A semistructured questionnaire administered verbally; based similar instrument (Wagner & Menke, 1992). Measured child attitude including: (a) beliefs about the future, (b) attitudes toward parents, (c) beliefs about own ability to control present and future environment(s), (d) attitudes toward poverty and housing circumstances, and (e) belief in the potential for change.
Mother Interview Schedule	Minor revisions of an interview used in a previous study of homeless families by Wagner & Menke (1992) and the Homeless Survey developed by Roth, Dean, Lust, and Saveanu (1985); contained questions regarding education, demographic information, health history, obstetrical history, social history, general well-being, social network, and health care practices.

Defining Home and Stability

"Every child needs a place to call home…a place of belonging and a place to keep one's things" (CDF, 1989, p. 108). Home, however, represents much more, implying "layers of meaning" (McCollum, 1990, p.
70 226). "A home provides far more than just a physical shelter against the elements" (CDF, p. 108). "It is a milieu that is safe, above all, but also strong, warm, enfolding, and reliable" (McCollum, p. 226); involving an expression of self, a place of belonging, and the
75 embodiment of personal and family history.

Home and place intertwine as a complex concept moving beyond the immediate family household. "Attachment to place is not holistic but multidimensional" (Gerson, Stueve, & Fischer, 1977, p. 156). Home "an-
80 chors a family in the community and provides children with the stability they need to develop and grow" (CDF, 1989, p. 108). The physical neighborhood, the people, and the actual dwelling all influence attachment. Families surviving amidst poverty in an inner-
85 city environment often do not live in neighborhoods that offer the safety and security implied in "home." Further, low-income families live precariously, frequently spending up to 70% of their income on rent. They have no cushion for changes in income or hous-
90 ing costs. Therefore, all families living in poverty are at risk of homelessness at transition points (Mihaly, 1989).

Methodology

This analysis emerged from a comprehensive study of families living in poverty in Columbus, Ohio. Data
95 were gathered by an interdisciplinary team (social work and nursing) on the physical and emotional well being of children and families living in poverty, many of whom have experienced homelessness. Data were collected on the health, mental health, support, and stabil-
100 ity issues of the families in poverty. The health and mental health of domiciled and homeless children living in poverty were analyzed and compared.

Subjects

A purposive sample was drawn of 133 families with children living in extreme poverty—families hav-
105 ing an income below the federal poverty line and receiving assistance from public services or entitlements. The female caretaker in each family (the mother or custodial grandmother) and one of the children between 8 and 12 years of age were interviewed. By de-
110 sign, half of the families involved in the study were homeless at the time of the interview using the definition outlined by Roth, Bean, Lust, & Saveanu (1985). A family was considered homeless if it was living in: (a) a shelter or transitional housing for the homeless,
115 (b) a residence with an actual or intended stay of less than 45 days, (c) a cheap motel, (d) a car, or (e) the street. (Children living with their mother in a shelter for battered women were not included in this study.) The homeless families were solicited primarily from
120 transitional housing facilities working with homeless families, cheap motels, and soup kitchens. The domiciled families living in poverty environments were solicited primarily from soup kitchens, food pantries, human service agencies, and health clinics.

Data Collection

125 The mother and child participated in a face-to-face interview and completed a number of standardized inst-

Table 2
Family and Child Characteristics

Variable	Frequency	Percent
Income Source		
Entitlement	120	90.2
Other	13	9.8
Domicile Status (*n* = 133)		
Domiciled	63	47.4
Homeless	70	52.6
Times Homeless (*n* = 132)		
0	39	29.5
1	58	43.9
2	26	19.7
3–9	9	6.9
Mother's Age		
22–29	47	35.4
30–39	76	57.1
40–50	10	7.7
Mother's Education		
Grades 4–8	8	6.1
Some High School	56	42.1
High School Graduate	49	36.8
Some College	19	14.4
College Graduate	1	0.8
Mother's Description		
Negative	9	6.8
Neutral	26	19.5
Positive	98	73.7
Child's Gender		
Female	67	50.4
Male	66	49.6
Child's Ethnicity		
African American	80	60.2
Euro American	39	29.3
Other (9 biracial, 3 Native American, 2 Latino/a)	14	10.5
Child's Age		
8	30	22.6
9	24	18.0
10	34	25.6
11	26	19.5
12	19	14.3
Child's GPA		
0–1.9	25	18.9
2–2.9	47	35.3
3–3.9	44	33.1
4	17	12.8

Note. *n* = 133

ruments. Standardized instruments previously used with similar populations were selected to gather data on the child's anxiety, depression, behavior, and locus of control (see Table 1). Interview schedules based on formats previously tested by Wagner and Menke (1992) were used to gather data on attitudes and beliefs. The mother provided demographic and background information about the child. The following questions guided this analysis:

1. Did poverty affect child anxiety, depression, behavior, and locus of control?
2. What were the children's career goals? Did they understand the path to those goals?
3. How did the children—homeless and domiciled—view family finances?
4. Who did the children—homeless and domiciled—turn to with problems?
5. What were the major concerns of the children?

The semistructured questionnaires/interview schedules used with the mother and child were designed to be administered verbally. Content validity was addressed by using a panel of experts (faculty knowledgeable about child development and/or the conditions for poor families) and conducting a field test. The field test also addressed the face validity. Reliability/credibility was assessed by having an independent

Table 3
Indicators of Child Mental Health

Variable	N	Range	Mean	SD	%PastClin.Cut*
Anxiety	133	26–79	51.95	10.5	20.0
Problem Behavior	132	26–93	53.05	10.5	19.7
Social Competence	133	19–70	42.62	8.9	36.6
Depression	131	0–27	8.40	6.2	18.3
Locus of Control	127	4–25	17.28	4.1	NA

*Percent past clinical cutoff

observer review the transcribed answers for confirmation of the interpretation and analysis using the methods of Kirk & Miller (1986) and Lincoln & Guba (1985).

Data Analysis

Qualitative and quantitative data provided a basis for this analysis. Themes were identified and then coded using a combination of the methods described by Bogdan & Biklen (1992), Miles & Huberman (1984), and Strauss & Corbin (1990). Statistical analysis involved primarily descriptive statistics with minimal use of inferential statistics. Relationships between this sample and large, national samples for anxiety, depression, and behavior were examined using *t* tests (see Schmitz, Wagner, & Menke (1995) for review of inferential analysis).

Results and Findings

Descriptive Data

All the families participating in the study faced multiple risk factors due to poverty and instability. The families interviewed lived in extreme poverty, with 90% relying on entitlement programs as their primary source of income (see Table 2). As a result, 53% were homeless at the time of the interview and 71% had been homeless at least once; only a quarter (26%) of the children had been homeless more than once. Many of the children had experienced instability beyond homelessness. The average family had moved 1-1/3 times in the previous 2.5 yrs with a third (33.9%) moving 2–5 times.

The mean age of the mothers was 32 years with 77% ranging from 27 to 37 years of age. The mother's educational level placed many of the families at risk. In line with national data, which indicate that 50% of poor single mothers have not graduated from high school, approximately half (48%) of the mothers in this study had not graduated from high school. This is more than twice the rate (17%) for nonpoor single mothers (Human Resources, 1991) and twice (23%) that of all adults (U.S. Bureau of the Census, 1991). A direct relationship existed between the mother's education and the child's reported academic performance, with the child's performance increasing as the mother's education increased (Schmitz, 1993).

The mothers' view of their children was assessed qualitatively. When asked to describe their children, almost three-quarters (73.4%) viewed the child positively (interrater reliability = 82%). The mothers described their children with words such as "loving," "sensitive," "concerned," "caring," "bright," "energetic," "wonderful," "understanding," "helpful," "considerate," and "affectionate." As one mother, who was homeless when interviewed, stated about her 11-year-old son, "He's charming, sweet, easy to get along with. He's inquisitive, understanding and lovable. He's the kind of child you would like to have. The All-American boy. He's not bad 'cause he don't like to be."

The children were evenly divided in gender and dispersed across age. Children of color were overrepresented, with almost three-quarters (70%) African American, Native American, Asian American, or biracial. African American children constituted three-fifths of the sample. Life events and health problems increased the risk for many. Almost half (46%) of the children had experienced a significant life crisis involving violence, and a tenth (10.5%) had a significant health problem.

In spite of the risks, the children exhibited much strength. They were frequently performing above average academically (as reported by the mothers) and generally scored within the normal range on the standardized tests (see Table 3). In comparisons between the homeless and domiciled children on the standardized tests, the only significant difference occurred in anxiety. Children homeless at the time of the interview exhibited ($p < .05$) higher anxiety levels ($M = 55.06$) than domiciled children ($M = 51.37$).

Qualitative Findings

The qualitative data added depth in identifying the common struggles of the children and families, as well as the added emotional costs of homelessness. Strengths and vulnerabilities, similarities and differences (see Table 4) were uncovered. When asked if anything bothered them about their current living environment, there was little difference between the responses of the homeless and domiciled children. A quarter (25%) of the domiciled children and 23% of the homeless children said yes, while 73% of the domiciled children and 61% of the homeless children said no. They had difficulty, however, expressing what bothered them. In addition, the children viewed homelessness negatively, with only six children saying it would be okay to be without a home. Many reported they thought homelessness was "sad," "hard," "lonely,"

Table 4
Children's Goals, Concerns, and Perceptions of Support and Resources

Variable	Percent		
Career Goals			
Professional	35		
Skilled	16		
Sports	16		
Artist	13		
Other	20		
Path to Success			
Education	59		
Study/Good Grades	19		
Work Hard	7		
Other	15		
Neighborhood/Community Concerns	% Worried		
Violence	23		
School	8		
Losing Home	5		
Family Has Enough Money	Yes	No	Unsure/DK
All Children	57	23	31
Domiciled	78	14	8
Homeless	39	31	31
How Can You Handle Your Problems?	Withdraw	Tell Someone	Work it Out
Domiciled	25	57	10
Homeless	47	30	3
Who Can Help with Child's Problems?	Parents	Family	School	Friends
Domiciled	88	94	21	19
Homeless	51	64	6	13

"embarrassing," "bad," or "scary" for children. When asked how children could handle being without a
245 home, they gave responses such as "be brave," "be mad," "be sad," "be nice," "talk to someone," "don't tell anyone," and "don't give up."

Although 67% of the children said their living environment didn't bother them, a third of the children
250 (30%) across environments were concerned about safety in their neighborhoods. Almost a third (30%) of the children—homeless and domiciled—were concerned about concrete housing and environmental/neighborhood safety and crime issues. The chil-
255 dren mentioned issues such as "gun shots," "the streets," "school," "detention," "bad people," "getting hurt," "dying," "stealing," "moving," and "not having a home."

The majority of the children interviewed had con-
260 crete goals for their future and a vision of how to reach those goals (see Table 4). They believed that they and/or their parents could impact that vision. More than two-thirds (64%) aspired to professional, skilled, or artistic goals. The children interested in a professional
265 career talked about being a doctor, lawyer, teacher, judge, or nurse, while those aspiring to a skilled profession mentioned careers in law enforcement, the fire department, the armed services, computer operation, airplane piloting, or trucking. The children understood
270 the avenues to those goals. Fifty-nine percent of the children mentioned school, college, and/or education as the vehicle to reach their goal. More than a third (36%) discussed the need to "work hard," "get good grades,"

"study," "get a degree," "save money," "respect the
275 teacher," or "get a job." Only one child responded with "marriage" as her only goal.

The major differences between the homeless children and those who were domiciled occurred in perceptions of money and support. When asked if their family
280 had enough money, more than half (57%) said yes while almost a quarter (23%) said no. The two groups diverged in perception. Twice as many domiciled children (78%) as homeless children (39%) said their families had enough money. On the other hand, twice as
285 many homeless children (32%) compared to domiciled children (14%) said their families did not have enough money.

The children were also asked who could help them with their problems or things that bother them. Again,
290 differences between the homeless and domiciled children surfaced. Homeless children were less likely to view members of their family as people who could help with their problems. While 94% of the domiciled children saw family members as people who could help,
295 only 64% of the homeless children did. Half of the children mentioned parents. Parents were mentioned as people who could help them with things that bother them by 88% of the domiciled and 51% of the homeless children. In addition, withdrawal and denial were
300 reported as ways to deal with issues that bother them by 47% of the homeless children but only 25% of the domiciled children. The domiciled children were more likely to tell someone about their problems while homeless children were more likely to withdraw. Fi-

305 nally, only 10% of the homeless children said they would try to work out their problems.

Summary of Findings

The children and families faced multiple barriers. They were at risk due to income, housing instability, and mother's education. There were many similarities.
310 Both groups were equally concerned about neighborhood safety; the levels of depression did not vary; there was no practical difference in behavior; and locus of control did not differ (Schmitz, 1993). Further, in spite of the risks, many strengths emerged. The mothers
315 were overwhelmingly positive in their description of the children, the majority of the children were performing passably in school, and most had positive goals for the future.

Analysis of the relationships between the child's
320 current domicile status and their emotional status and perceptions of safety, security, and stability revealed significant differences in anxiety and different perceptions about money, support, and safety. The children who were homeless expressed heightened awareness of
325 financial and emotional vulnerability. They were more likely to feel like their families did not have enough money. Even though both sets of families were surviving on minimal income, twice as many domiciled children said their families had enough money. On the
330 other hand, twice as many homeless children said their families did not have enough money. In addition, the homeless children were more likely to feel their parents could help them with their difficulties.

Conclusion and Implications

Understanding the goals and aspirations, as well as
335 the concerns, of children living in poverty is vital to building support programs. The findings indicate the need for both preventive and remedial programs targeting multiple levels—individuals, families, neighborhoods, and communities. There were a number of fac-
340 tors supporting the importance of individualizing intervention. Although most of the children were functioning within the normal range on scales measuring anxiety, depression, and behavior, a significant percentage scored in the range beyond the clinical cutoff point.
345 Approximately a fifth of the children scored in ranges indicating the need for remedial intervention for anxiety, depression, and behavior. When we look at social competence, the percent operating outside normal ranges leaps to over a third, indicating the importance
350 of social skill training, which could be incorporated into neighborhood, school, and after-school programs. The fact that few of the children would try to work out their problems underscores the importance of integrating programs teaching children surviving amid poverty
355 to problem-solve and deal with conflict.

The needs of the children who were homeless and those who were not were similar in many respects. The major differences occurred in the higher levels of anxiety, increased sense of economic instability, and de-
360 creased perception of vulnerability among homeless children. An apparent sense of isolation also arises from the data, with the children who were homeless reporting an increased tendency to withdraw with problems and a decreased likelihood to view members of
365 their family as people who can help with problems. These attitudes and concerns could easily interfere with the child's ability to perform academically, form supportive relationships, and develop emotionally and behaviorally.

370 The outcome of this analysis supports and extends beyond previous studies in uncovering the additive impact of homelessness on children and families. A review of the major findings and their implications intertwined with the conclusions and observations of
375 related research provides guidance in designing intervention models. Multilevel program development is suggested.

Families entering homelessness (often due to a crisis) arise from those families already at risk due to
380 poverty (Masten, 1992). Low parenting stress and fewer major life concerns have been connected to better outcomes for homeless children in a study by Danseco and Holden (1998) supporting the importance of strengthening and supporting parents and families.
385 Shelters and transitional housing are not well suited to meeting the needs of families (Huttman & Redmond, 1992). Both fail to address the underlying need for safe, stable housing and employment; and there is a contradiction between transitional housing rules and
390 "the goal of self-sufficiency" (Fogel, 1997, p. 131). While these data indicate that the children need assistance viewing their parents as people who can provide support, shelters often undermine parental authority with rigid rules and staff control. This study, however,
395 supports the potential mediating effect of shelter (Rafferty & Shinn, 1991), which seems to buffer some of the most negative consequences reported in many studies (Bassuk & Rosenberg, 1988; Feitel, Margetson, Chamas, & Lipman, 1992; Polakow, 1998). Giving
400 families control for "organizing their lives in the shelter" (Thrasher & Mowbray, 1995, p. 100) supports and strengthens the mother as the "head of the family."

Frequently, children living in poverty are considered high risk and approached from a deficit model.
405 While the potential negative consequences of poverty and homelessness are well established (Bassuk & Rosenberg, 1988; Bassuk & Rubin, 1987; Danzig, 1997; Feitel, Margetson, Chamas, & Lipman, 1992; Polakow, 1998; Rafferty & Shinn, 1991), this study
410 identified strengths that also exist in the families (homeless and domiciled). Supporting areas of positive functioning recognizes competencies (Thrasher & Mowbray, 1995), which can be built upon to empower children and families as they work toward the future.
415 Supportive, family centered services provide the opportunity and context for families to rebuild their lives (Bruder, 1997).

The strengths identified form a basis for remedial and preventive programs. Hope provides a building block for coping and positive outcomes (Farran, Herth, & Popovich, 1995). The hopes of the children framed within the context of goals for the future provide a basis for intervention. The children had strong career goals and were able to discuss the steps to their goals. These children had positive hopes and goals with a realistic understanding of the work needed to reach those goals. "Good schools and good teachers can and do make a significant difference" (Polakow, 1998, p. 17). School social workers can be pivotal in providing or facilitating the services and resources, which strengthen the children and families. They can take the lead in developing collaborative efforts, which respond on institutional and community as well as the individual and family levels (Wall, 1996).

For the vast majority of the children and mothers, their overall emotional status was good. The positive attitudes of the mothers toward the child, even under frequently stressful conditions, provide a basis for engaging the mother as a part of the team to help a child experiencing difficulties. The children's career goals in combination with the fact that four-fifths of the children were receiving passing grades and half were performing above average also indicate avenues for engaging the children remedially and preventively. The grades for the oldest children did show signs of slippage, however, emphasizing the importance of intensive intervention and support for latency age children.

Neighborhood, school, and after school programs provide ideal sites for preventive and remedial services. The preferences of the local residents provide an important source of information on program design (Goering, Durbin, Trainor, & Paduchak, 1990). Programs could build on the children's strengths while providing the services to address the needs and concerns of the children and families. The mothers' positive attitudes could be used by outreach workers to engage them in supporting their children. The children's goals could and should be nurtured and supported. Academic support and social skills training could help with long-term success. These programs could also incorporate methods designed to help the children learn to work out problems.

Staff in shelters and other social service agencies play a significant role in assisting mothers emotionally and instrumentally (Lindsey, 1996), filling a gap resulting from the inadequate social supports available to homeless families (Khanna, Singh, Nemil, Best, & Ellis, 1992). A study by Lindsey found that mothers who have restabilized from homelessness have personal strengths and resources "describing themselves as independent, persistent, strong-willed, and tough" (p. 212). Looking back at their experience of themselves while they were homeless, they "described themselves as desperate, lost, confused, and uncertain.... Many were not able to attend adequately to their children's needs" (p. 212). Shelter staff impacted the mother's development of skills and internal resources, helping them recognize inner strengths and abilities as well as develop skills and abilities (Lindsey). Involving the mother as an "expert" who is the most knowledgeable about her child provides a significant role. She becomes a member of the team in the design of a family plan and an active participant in the implementation.

The concern of many of the children with neighborhood safety points to the need for programs enhancing both the child's sense of safety and neighborhood safety. Many of the families have experienced significant life crises and major health problems, pointing to the importance of multidisciplinary neighborhood programs. Easy access is imperative since low-income families have few resources for transportation. Finally, the fact that only half the mothers completed high school is significant. This is twice the 23% national average (U.S. Bureau of the Census, 1991) and a major risk factor with changing welfare policies emphasizing parental employment. Neighborhood programs are ideal sites for adult education and training programs.

With high levels of poverty and increasing homelessness, the issues must be dealt with at multiple levels. While working at the community level to help families stabilize as they emerge from homelessness, we must also address the problems structurally (Lindsey, 1998). Both homeless and poor domiciled children are at high risk for developmental, health, and educational difficulties, which require a public-policy agenda addressing housing, services, health care, and child poverty (Danzig, 1997; Rafferty & Shinn, 1991). Long term, the structural factors responsible for high rates of family poverty, inadequate housing, and homelessness must be addressed through major attitudinal and policy changes. Structural racism and sexism are responsible for high rates of poverty among families of color and female-headed single-parent families, placing our children and our country at risk. Policies must attack the root causes—poverty and lack of adequate, safe housing that low-income families can afford (McChesney, 1990; Shinn & Gillespie, 1994).

Social work professionals and students need to be educated in the importance of multilevel assessment and intervention. The practice and policy implications are clear and interwoven. Poverty, safety/stability, and homelessness impact the level of stress facing families and neighborhoods, which in turn impacts the development of our children. Individual, family, neighborhood, and community programs can address the issues remedially and preventively.

References

Achenbach, T. M., & Edelbrock, C. (1981). Behavioral problems and competencies reported by parents of normal and disturbed children. *Monograph Social Research Child Development, 46*, 188.

Achenbach, T. M., & Edelbrock, C. (1983). *Manual for the Child Behavior Checklists and Revised Child Behavior Profile*. Vermont: University of Vermont.

Achenbach, T. M., Edelbrock, C., & Howell, C. (1987). Empirically based assessment of the behavioral/emotional problems of two- and three-year-old children. *Journal of Abnormal Child Psychology*, 15, 629–640.

Bassuk, E., & Rosenberg, L. (1988). Why does family homelessness occur? A case-control study. *American Journal of Public Health, 78*, 783–788.

Bassuk, E., & Rubin, L. (1987). Homeless children: A neglected population. *American Journal of Orthopsychiatry, 57*, 279–286.

Belle, D. (1990). Poverty and women's mental health. *American Psychologist, 45*, 385–389.

Bogdan, R. C., & Biklen, S. K. (1992). *Qualitative research for education: An introduction to theory and methods*. Boston: Allyn and Bacon.

Boxill, N., & Beaty, A. (1990). An exploration of mother/child interaction among homeless women and their children in a public night shelter in Atlanta, Georgia. In N. Boxill & A. Beaty, *The waiters and the watchers: American homeless children* (pp. 49–64). New York: Hawthorne.

Bruder, M. B. (1997). Children who are homeless: A growing challenge for early care and education. *Advances in Early Education and Day Care, 9*, 223–246.

Center on Hunger, Poverty and Nutrition Policy. (1995). *Statement on key welfare reform issues: The empirical evidence*. Medford, MA: Author.

Chalhub de Oliveira, T. (1997). Homeless children in Rio de Janeiro: Exploring the meanings of street life. *Child and Youth Care Forum, 26*(3), 163–174.

Children's Defense Fund. (1991). *Child poverty in America*, Washington, DC: Author.

Children's Defense Fund. (1995). Children's hardships intensify. *CDF Reports, 16*(6), p. 1–2, 12.

Children's Defense Fund. (1998). *The state of America's children: Yearbook 1998*. DC: Author.

Committee for Economic Development. (1987). *Children in need: Investment strategies for the educationally disadvantaged*. New York: Author.

Danseco, E. R., & Holden, E. W. (1998). Are there different types of homeless families? A typology of homeless families based on cluster analysis. *Family Relations, 47*, 159–165.

Elmer, E. (1977). A follow-up of traumatized children. *Pediatrics, 59*, 273–279.

Epps, A. M. (1998). *Children living in temporary shelter: How homelessness affects their perception of home*. New York: Garland Publishing, Inc.

Farran, C. J., Herth, K. A., & Popovich, J. M. (1995). *Hope and hopelessness: Critical clinical constructs*. Thousand Oaks, CA: Sage Publications.

Feitel, B., Margetson, N., Chamas, J., & Lipman, C. (1992). Psychosocial background and behavioral and emotional disorders of homeless and runaway youth. *Hospital and Community Psychiatry, 43*(2), 155–159.

Fogel, S. J. (1997). Moving along: An exploratory study of homeless women with children using a transitional housing program. *Journal of Sociology and Social Welfare, 24*(3), 113–133.

Gerson, K., Stueve, C. A., & Fischer, C. S. (1977). Attachment to place. In C. S. Fischer, R. M. Jackson, C. A. Stueve, K. Gerson, L. M. Jones, & M. Baldessare (Eds.), *Networks and places: Social relations in the urban setting* (pp. 139–161). New York: Free Press.

Goering, P., Durbin, J., Trainor, J., & Paduchak, D. (1990). Developing housing for the homeless. *Psychosocial Rehabilitation Journal, 13*(4), 33–42.

Gulati, P. (1992). Ideology, public policy, and homeless families. *Journal of Sociology and Social Welfare, 19*(4), 113–128.

Human Resources Division. (1991). *Mother-only families: Low earnings will keep children in poverty* (GAO/HRD-91-62). Washington, DC: U.S. Government Printing Office.

Huttman, E., & Redmond, S. (1992). Women and homelessness: Evidence of need to look beyond shelters to long term social service assistance and permanent housing. *Journal of Sociology and Social Welfare, 19*(4), 89–111.

Kessler, J., (1988). *Psychopathology of childhood*. Englewood Cliffs, NJ: Prentice-Hall, Inc.

Khanna, M., Singh, N. N., Nemil, M., Best, A., & Ellis, C. R. (1992). Homeless women and their families: Characteristics, life circumstances, and needs. *Journal of Child and Family Studies, 1*(2), 155–165.

Kirk, J., & Miller, M. L. (1986). *Reliability and validity in qualitative research*. Beverly Hills, CA: Sage Publications.

Kovacs, M. (1985). The children's depression inventory. *Psychopharmacology Bulletin, 21*, 995–999.

Lincoln, Y. S., & Guba, E. G. (1985). *Naturalistic inquiry*. Newbury Park, CA: Sage Publications.

Lindsey, E. W. (1996). Mothers' perceptions of factors influencing the restabilization of homeless families. *Families in Society, 77*(4), 203–215.

Lindsey, E. W. (1997). The process of restabilization for mother-headed homeless families: How social workers can help. *Journal of Family Social Work, 2*(3), 49–72.

Lindsey, E. W. (1998). Service providers' perception of factors that help or hinder homeless families. *Families in Society, 79*, 160–172.

Martagon, M., Ramirez, M., & Masten, A. S. (1991, April) *Future aspirations of homeless children*. Paper presented at the Society for Research in Child Development.

Masten, A. S. (1992). Homeless children in the United States: Mark of a nation at risk. *Current Directions in Psychological Science, 1*(2), 41–44.

McChesney, K. Y. (1990). Family homelessness: A systemic problem. *Journal of Social Issues, 46*(4), 191–205.

McCollum, A. T. (1990). *The trauma of moving: Psychological issues for women*. Newbury Park, CA: Sage Publications, Inc.

Mihaly, L. (1989, April). *Beyond the numbers: Homeless families with children*. Paper presented at Homeless Children and Youth: Coping with a National Tragedy. Washington, DC.

Miles, M. B., & Huberman, A. M. (1984). *Qualitative data analysis: A sourcebook of new methods*. Beverly Hills, CA: Sage Publications.

Mitchell, E. S. (1986). Multiple triangulation: A methodology for nursing science. *Advances in Nursing Science, 8*, 18–26.

Nowicki, S., & Strickland, B. R. (1973). A locus of control scale for children. *Journal of Consulting and Clinical Psychology, 40*, 148–154.

Patton, M. Q. (1990). *Qualitative evaluation and research methods* (2nd ed.). Newbury Park, CA: Sage Publications.

Polakow, V. (1998). Homeless children and their families: The discards of the postmodern 1990s. In S. Books (Ed.), *Invisible children in society and its schools* (pp. 3–22). Mahwah, NJ: Lawrence Erlbaum Associates.

Rafferty, Y., & Shinn, M. (1991). The impact of homelessness on children. *American Psychologist, 46*, 1170–1179.

Reynolds, C. R. (1980). Concurrent validity of What I Think and Feel: The Revised Children's Manifest Anxiety Scale. *Journal of Consulting and Clinical Psychology, 48*, 774–775.

Reynolds, C. R., & Richmond, B. O. (1979). Factor structure and construct validity of "What I Think and Feel": The revised Children's Manifest Anxiety Scale. *Journal of a Personality Assessment, 43*, 281–283.

Reynolds, C. R., & Richmond, B. O. (1985). *The Revised Children's Manifest Anxiety Scale*. Los Angeles, CA: Western Psychological Services.

Roth, D., Dean, J., Lust, N., & Saveanu, T. (1985). *Homelessness in Ohio: A study of people in need*. Columbus, OH: Ohio Department of Mental Health.

Schmitz, C. L. (1993). Children at risk: Ex post facto research examining relationships among poverty, housing stability, anxiety, attitudes, locus of control, academic performance, and behavior. (Doctoral dissertation, The Ohio State University, 1993). *Dissertation Abstracts International, 54*, 1097A.

Schmitz, C. L., Wagner, J. D., & Menke, E. M. (1995). Homelessness as one component of housing stability and its impact on the development of children in poverty. *Journal of Social Distress and the Homeless, 4*, 301–318.

Shinn, M., & Gillespie, C. (1994). The roles of housing and poverty in the origins of homelessness. *American Behavioral Scientist, 37*(4), 505–521.

Strauss, A., & Corbin, J. (1990). *Basics of qualitative research*. Newbury Park, CA: Sage Publications.

Thrasher, S. P., & Mowbray, C. T. (1995). A strengths perspective: An ethnographic study of homeless women with children. *Health & Social Work, 20*(2), 93–101.

Tuma, J. M. (1989). Mental health services for children: The state of the art. *American Psychologist, 44*, 188–199.

U.S. Bureau of the Census (1991). *Statistical Abstract of the United States* (111th ed.). Washington, DC: U.S. Government Printing Office.

Wagner, J. D., & Menke, E. M. (1992). Case management of homeless families. *The Journal for Professional Nursing Practice, 6*(2), 65–70.

Wagner, J., Schmitz, C. L., & Menke, E. (1995). Homelessness and depression in children: Implication for interventions. In *Directions in Child & Adolescent Therapy, 2*(3)

Wall, J. C. (1996). Homeless children and their families: Delivery of educational social services through school systems. *Social Work in Education, 18*(3), 135–144.

Wisniewski, J. J., Mulick, J. A., Genshaft, J. L., & Coury, D. L. (1987). Testretest reliability of the Revised Children's Manifest Anxiety Scale. *Perceptual and Motor Skills, 65*, 67–70.

Ziesemer, C., Marcoux, L., & Marwell, B. E. (1994). Homeless children: Are they different from other low-income children? *Social Work, 39*, 658–668.

About the authors: Cathryne L Schmitz is associate professor and Director, Social Work Program, University of Southern Maine, 96 Falmouth Street, P.O. Box 9300, Portland, ME 04104. Janet D. Wagner is dean, Department of Community Education and Workforce Development, Columbus State Community College, 550 E. Spring Street, Columbus, OH 43216. Edna M. Menke is an associate professor, College of Nursing, Department of Community, Parent-Child and Psychiatric Nursing, Ohio State University, 1585 Neil Avenue, Columbus, OH 43210-1289.

Note: Based on a paper presented at Public Policy Challenges for Social Work Education, the 42nd Annual Program Meeting of the Council of Social Work Education, Washington, DC, February 1996.

Acknowledgments: The authors would like to thank the Ohio Department of Mental Health for financial support of this project through grant number 92.1051, and the National Institutes of Health for their support through grant number 1R15NR02462 from the National Center for Nursing Research.

Exercise for Article 5

Factual Questions

1. The sample included how many famililes?

2. If a family lived in a cheap motel, was it considered "homeless"?

3. How did the researchers address the issue of content validity?

4. What percentage of the children in this study were children of color?

5. On what variable were the two groups statistically significant? Which group had a significantly higher mean?

6. What percentage of homeless children said their families had enough money?

7. The researchers state that other researchers have approached the study of poverty from a "deficit model." Do the researchers believe that their results fully support a deficit model in which poor families lack any strengths or strong points?

Questions for Discussion

8. These researchers included both domiciled and homeless families. In your opinion, how important was it to include domiciled families in a study of homeless families? Explain.

9. In addition to the children, only female caretakers were interviewed. Do you think that it would be fruitful to include male caretakers in future studies? Explain.

10. The researchers report an interrater reliability of 82% for coding the mothers' responses when they were asked to describe their children. In your opinion, is this high enough? Are you surprised that it is not 100%? Explain.

11. This research article presents both quantitative and qualitative results. Are both of equal interest to you? Do both contribute equally to your understanding of the sample the researchers studied? Explain.

12. If you were to conduct a study on the same topic, what changes, if any, would you make in the research methodology?

Quality Ratings

Directions: Indicate your level of agreement with each of the following statements by circling a number from 5 for strongly agree (SA) to 1 for strongly disagree (SD). If you believe an item is not applicable to this research article, leave it blank. Be prepared to explain your ratings.

A. The introduction establishes the importance of the study.

SA   5   4   3   2   1   SD

B. The literature review establishes the context for the study.

SA   5   4   3   2   1   SD

C. The research purpose, question, or hypothesis is clearly stated.

SA   5   4   3   2   1   SD

D. The method of sampling is sound.

SA   5   4   3   2   1   SD

E. Relevant demographics (for example, age, gender, and ethnicity) are described.

SA   5   4   3   2   1   SD

F. Measurement procedures are adequate.

SA   5   4   3   2   1   SD

G. All procedures have been described in sufficient detail to permit a replication of the study.

SA   5   4   3   2   1   SD

H. The participants have been adequately protected from potential harm.

SA   5   4   3   2   1   SD

I. The results are clearly described.

SA   5   4   3   2   1   SD

J. The discussion/conclusion is appropriate.

SA   5   4   3   2   1   SD

K. Despite any flaws, the report is worthy of publication.

SA   5   4   3   2   1   SD

Article 6

Passionately Committed Psychotherapists: A Qualitative Study of Their Experiences

Raymond F. Dlugos
University at Albany, State University of New York

Myrna L. Friedlander
University at Albany, State University of New York

ABSTRACT. Twelve peer-nominated psychotherapists were interviewed to provide a rich understanding of their sustained high levels of work commitment. Common themes included creating boundaries between professional and nonprofessional life, using leisure activities to provide relief, turning obstacles into challenges, finding diverse activities to provide freshness and energy, continually seeking feedback and supervision, taking on social responsibilities, and experiencing a strong sense of spirituality. Whereas participants did not differ significantly from norm groups on measures of work salience, job satisfaction, emotional exhaustion, and depersonalization, they reported high levels of personal accomplishment and scored in the 99th percentile on openness to experience.

From *Professional Psychology: Research and Practice, 32,* 298–304. Copyright © 2000 by the American Psychological Association. Reprinted with permission.

The stress of working as a psychotherapist in the current economic and social climate has negatively affected the career satisfaction of many individuals who entered the field with commitment, enthusiasm, and idealism. In spite of experiencing the same pressures, demands, and conflicts that confront all psychotherapists, some have managed not only to survive, but also to thrive, experiencing a joy, love, and passion in their work that enhance rather than detract from their passion for other important life commitments. The present qualitative study was designed to uncover common and distinctive themes about the personal experiences of therapists who impressed their peers as being passionately committed to their work over a long period of time.

On the basis of the literature on optimal experience (Csikszentmihalyi, 1990), burnout and burnout prevention (Cherniss, 1995; Grosch & Olsen, 1994), and commitment (Marks, 1979), we formulated a working definition of *passionate commitment* as (a) a sense of being energized and invigorated by work rather than drained and exhausted by it; (b) the ability to continue to thrive and love one's work in spite of the personal and environmental obstacles one might face in it; (c) a demonstrable sense of balance and harmony with other aspects of one's life; and (d) a sense of energizing and

invigorating those with whom one works. We used this definition to solicit peer nominations (cf. Luborsky, McClellan, Woody, O'Brien, & Auerbach, 1985) from our local professional community. Nominees were then interviewed extensively about their personal experiences of work in the context of the rest of their lives.

Owing to the emotional nature of the work, psychotherapists are not reinforced by clear and unambiguous indicators of success like other professionals— attorneys or business executives, for example. Indeed, therapists are at great risk for burnout. In one sample of licensed psychologists, 40% were in the high burnout range with regard to emotional exhaustion, and 34% were in this range with regard to depersonalization (Ackerley, Burnell, Holder, & Kurdek, 1988). Grosch and Olsen (1994) proposed that burnout reflects the failure of work to fill the void of incompletion that first motivated the individual to choose the career of psychotherapist. This failure occurs either because the person seeks satisfaction only through work or because his or her work satisfaction is thwarted by internal or professional pressures.

In our view, sustaining passionate commitment to work as a psychotherapist reflects passionate commitment in other areas of life. Recently, Zeddies (1999) noted, "Because therapists draw on their personal emotional resources in attempting to understand clients, being emotionally available in clinical work may be predicated on being alive more generally" (p. 231). Indeed, the theoretical sources on which we based this study suggest a reciprocal relationship between passion for life and passion for work. Csikszentmihalyi (1990) developed the concept of *flow*, which Jackson & Marsh (1996) described as "an intrinsically enjoyable state...accompanied by an order of consciousness whereby the person experiences clarity of goals and knowledge of performance, complete concentration, feelings of control, and feelings of being totally in tune with performance" (p. 18). According to Csikszentmihalyi, all life can be transformed into a continuous flow experience by cultivating purpose, forging resolution, and discovering harmony.

From a more cognitive perspective, Marks (1979) observed that energy is fully available for activities to which a person is highly committed. Whereas one feels

75 energized to do these things, engaging in activities to which one is not committed leaves the person feeling spent, drained, and exhausted. Marks posited a sacralized system of commitment, one in which the individual is able and willing to expend energy on activities that are both important and unimportant, so that the energy spent on taxing activities is replenished by enjoyable, nurturing ones.

80 Cherniss (1995) described professionals who prevailed over burnout after having experienced it early in their careers. These individuals proactively sought ways to overcome difficulties and were willing to risk leaving an environment when they could not find the

85 necessary nurturance for their commitment. Although they had a high need for achievement, they set realistic goals and expectations. In contrast to those who succumbed to burnout, they had better negotiation skills, viewing systemic problems in more sophisticated and

90 analytical ways, avoiding and resolving conflicts, generating organizational support for their own initiatives, and having fun solving organizational problems. They took advantage of informal as well as formal avenues to develop themselves professionally. Achieving a bal-

95 ance between work, family, and leisure allowed them to maintain a strong commitment to their work.

By interviewing a sample of seasoned therapists viewed by their peers as exemplifying passionate commitment to their work, we sought a rich under-

100 standing of how such individuals structure their lives to achieve a continual sense of fulfillment and personal meaning. Allowing the stories of passionately committed psychotherapists to be told from within the lived context of their personal experiences, we were inter-

105 ested in identifying behavioral, existential, interpersonal, and personality factors that might be common to such individuals. Our goal was to shed light on lifestyle features that might guide present and future psychologists to achieve a measure of optimal career develop-

110 ment.

The Study of Passionately Committed Psychotherapists

Peer nomination was used to identify participants because no measures of passionate commitment exist. To ensure that a nominee's commitment was indeed longstanding, he or she had to have worked in the field

115 for at least 10 years and spend at least 50% of the work week engaged in psychotherapy or psychotherapy-related activities. Written nominations were sought from local psychologists, psychiatrists, clinical social workers, and counselors ($N = 548$) who were identified

120 from telephone directories, professional organization lists, and provider panels in a northeastern urban community.

All those who received three nominations or more ($N = 15$) were invited to participate in the study.

125 Among the 12 who agreed to be interviewed, 1 person had 10 nominations, 1 person had 6 nominations, 1 person had 5 nominations, 3 people had 4 nominations, and 6 people had 3 nominations. Participants ranged in age from 38 to 76 years, ($M = 51.83$; $SD = 10.35$). Ten

130 (83%) were married (including 3 of whom were remarried), 1 (8%) was cohabiting, and 1 (8%) was a Roman Catholic priest. Nine therapists were men and 3 were women; 11 were European American, and 1 was African American. Ten were psychologists, 1 was a psy-

135 chiatrist, and 1 was a clinical social worker. Nine (75%) participants indicated their primary work setting as independent practice, 2 worked in outpatient clinics, and 1 worked at a Veterans Administration hospital. They reported working an average of 43.92 hr/week

140 ($SD = 9.75$), and they devoted a mean of 85% ($SD = 10.44$) of those hours to psychotherapy (including case management, training, and supervision).

We developed a semistructured interview protocol based on the guiding theoretical models. Questions

145 included, for example, "Can you describe or illustrate with an example how your commitment to being a psychotherapist has changed over the course of your career?" and "What is the most serious obstacle in your way of doing what you believe would be your best

150 work as a therapist?" To minimize bias, we formulated some questions so as to provide participants with the opportunity to offer disconfirming evidence, such as, "Can you describe or illustrate what makes you hate or dislike your work as a psychotherapist?" and "In what

155 ways does the term 'passionate commitment' not apply to you?" (A copy of the interview protocol is available from Raymond F. Dlugos.) Participants were also asked to describe their reactions to having been nominated for the study by their peers.

160 To develop common and distinctive themes, we followed the method of Consensual Qualitative Research (CQR; Hill, Thompson, & Williams, 1997). A trained panel of four judges (with 3–9 years of clinical experience) assigned codes to the transcribed narratives using

165 a "start list" (Miles & Huberman, 1994, p. 58) that was revised as the data accumulated. After receiving feedback on the codes from an auditor, the panel summarized the codes for each participant and then clustered and synthesized the data into categories and themes. To

170 assess testimonial validity, we sought feedback on these themes from the participants (Stiles, 1993). We also presented the results to the research panel to assess coherence (Hill et al., 1997).

To obtain information about the sample from an-

175 other perspective, we asked participants to complete four self-report measures: the Openness scale of the NEO Personality Inventory—Revised (NEO-PI—R; Costa & McCrae, 1992), the Salience Inventory (Super & Nevill, 1985), the Job in General Scale (Balzer et al.,

180 1997), and the Maslach Burnout Inventory—Human Services Survey (Maslach & Jackson, 1986; Maslach,

Table 1
Qualitative Themes and Categories

Theme and categories	% of therapists[a]
Balance	100
Maintaining physical and psychological boundaries between work and personal life	92
Passionate engagement in at least one nonwork activity as a key to maintaining passionate commitment to work	92
Deliberately seeking diversity within work activities to maintain freshness and excitement about work	92
Recognition of the power of economic motivation to diminish passion for work as a psychotherapist	83
Adaptiveness/openness	100
Meeting obstacles as challenges to be faced with persistence or creativity	100
Hunger for feedback about work through supervision	92
Transcendence/humility	100
Acknowledgment of the spiritual nature of therapy	83
Locating the significance of therapy within communal and social responsibility	33
Intentional learning	100
Recognition of the complementarity of personal and professional development	100
Understanding that work as a therapist allows for congruent self-expression	92
Continual fascination with human development and change	83

[a]This column of data reflects the percentage of participants whose narratives reflected each theme or category.

Jackson, & Leiter, 1996).[1] A comparison of participants' data with the normative data for each measure provided a means of triangulation (Hill et al., 1997; Stiles, 1993).

Results and Discussion

As shown in Table 1, the narrative accounts showed remarkable consistency across participants. Four general themes emerged that were salient features in all 12 narratives. Within each of these themes were found more specific categories. Among the categories, two were found in all cases, five were found in 11 cases (92%), three were found in 10 cases (83%), and one was found in 4 cases (33%).

Balance

Every therapist in the sample expressed that attending to his or her nonprofessional life is essential to maintaining passion and avoiding burnout. Within this general theme, 10 therapists mentioned that they were

prone to overextension at work and needed to make conscious efforts to provide time for nonwork activities. All but 1 participant expressed the belief that insufficient attention to nonprofessional life negatively affects their performance as a therapist.

Maintaining Boundaries Between Work and Personal Life

The first typical category under the general theme of balance is taking direct action to create physical and psychological boundaries between professional and nonprofessional life. Five therapists placed great value on taking vacations and, more specifically, scheduling vacations so that they are optimally effective. Two participants pointed out that their need for time and space is as legitimate as the demands made on them by patients and clients. As one participant put it:

> It's taken me a lot of years to figure out what's right for my biochemistry and my mood and everything else, but it's better than taking two weeks off and then going six or eight months before taking another vacation. That doesn't work for me; I've tried that. Every four months or so, I'm ready for a full week off. (Participant 5)

[1] One participant chose not to complete the self-report measures.

The 3 youngest participants were the only ones with young children. Each expressed a simultaneous love for work and a desire to provide the time, attention, and care necessary to maintain a healthy family life. They made it clear that they have made, and would continue to make, whatever professional sacrifices are necessary to care for their families in the most responsible way. One of these (the only woman in this subgroup) changed work settings (from a hospital to a group practice) to have the flexibility to be both parent and professional. She indicated carefully planning both family and professional life so that each can flourish, realizing that she has made some professional concessions to maintain this balance.

Nonprofessional Activities to Maintain Balance and Passion

As uniform as the need to create physical and psychological boundaries between professional and nonprofessional life was the tendency of the participants to speak about at least one nonprofessional activity with as much, if not more, passion as they spoke about work. Only 1 participant failed to mention such an activity. Two participants belong to clubs in which no one knows what they do for a living. Participants run marathons and enjoy the theater, photography, painting, playing the stock market, coaching, hiking, auto racing, and meditation. Several participants stated that sports allow them to express dimensions of their personalities that are not expressed in the therapy room.

Seeking Diversity Within Work Activities

All but 1 therapist viewed having multiple work roles as an important means of growing personally and professionally. In this typical category, some therapists viewed new cases as a way to avoid staleness, and another indicated doing so by seeing clients of diverse backgrounds. Two people spoke about continual professional renewal as a result of serving diverse clinical populations. One individual put it this way:

> I've been working in this since '75, and I think there was a period of time where I really was more energized working with adolescents.... But in the last 10 years I have found that my interests, while not necessarily devoid of that, have really gotten more focused in issues of trauma recovery with people, with adults, and subsequently I've been working with a lot of folks, females in recovery, that I would never expect that I as a male therapist would be doing. (Participant 5)

Other participants use teaching, studying, supervising, and consulting to keep themselves critically attuned to new ways of thinking about their work.

Recognizing the Power of Economic Forces to Diminish Passion

Ten therapists expressly pointed out the power of the fiscal, economic, or business aspects of psychotherapy to drain and enervate them. One participant said, "Probably the only drawback is that it's my living.

Sometimes I wish it wasn't my living because you've got to think about the aspects of it that are a business, even though it's not totally a business" (Participant 10).

One participant noted that the increasing emphasis on economics throughout the health care system is moving the profession out of touch with those it is meant to serve, and other participants simply noted that if one is to be passionate about being a therapist, one cannot do it for the money.

Adaptiveness and Openness

It is not the presence or absence of obstacles that set these therapists apart from their peers. Rather, it may be how they respond to difficult and challenging distractions. Adaptiveness/openness was chosen as the title of this general theme because it seemed to capture the attitude that all of these therapists expressed in response to these obstacles.

Obstacles Become Challenges

Each therapist was asked, "What is the most serious obstacle in your way of doing your best work?" Ten of the 12 therapists included managed care in their responses. Managed care was described as an obstacle because it places limits on creativity and autonomy, it creates another entity in the therapeutic relationship, and it detracts from time for professional development, thinking about clients, and leisure activities. In addition to managed care, obstacles included physical problems, dealing with nontherapist administrators, and the pressure against doing psychotherapy as a psychiatrist. Several participants also acknowledged that they saw themselves as their own greatest obstacle to their best work.

All 12 participants described transforming obstacles into challenges. Each of the 10 therapists who named the reality of managed care as a serious obstacle had a different approach to the problem, including organizing time and tasks so as not to be overwhelmed by paperwork, learning the rules of managed care thoroughly to find ways to work around them, developing good relationships with representatives of managed care organizations, and using peer support as well as practical organizational solutions. One participant consistently does pro bono work to fulfill an ethical obligation and to provide an opportunity to work without outside interference. One participant simply tries to construe the problem of managed care differently:

> At first, I was like just angry, or trying to avoid it, and then said, "O.K. this is something you just have got to learn how to deal with." Just spending some time about learning whatever the language is, making appointments in advance rather than waiting on the telephone line for people forever. Knowing that I can't go around it but trying to do it in the most efficient way and making it Caesar, not God. I put as little energy into it as possible. (Participant 11)

The only participants who said nothing about managed care were those whose lifestyle (priesthood) and work setting (VA hospital) allowed them not to be as concerned with the financial aspects of the profession as their peers ($n = 2$).

The other major obstacle mentioned by some therapists was a physical disability. One participant must follow a strict regime to maintain his energy level and be alert and attentive. Other participants have chronic pain, to which they respond with regular exercise during the work day.

Hunger for Feedback and Supervision

After managed care, the second most frequent obstacle to work as a therapist was "myself." Indeed, 9 therapists named themselves as an obstacle. Several have sought personal therapy to face intrapersonal barriers and all but 1 participant mentioned making use of supervision, either formal or informal. One participant acknowledged the difficulty, as well as the necessity, of finding appropriate feedback as an independent practitioner:

> Well, for the first 10 years, I was supervised once a week, sometimes twice a week, which was with a very good therapist. That was much more valuable than anything I ever learned academically. When you work privately it's much more difficult and, therefore, potentially lethal because supervision is not structured into your day. You've got to make it happen. You've got to make sure. It is lonely. You don't have meetings; you don't see people walking the halls. You have to structure time, where lunch is a chance to talk over an issue that's coming up for you or what a case is about. I have lunch every week with my partners, and I walk usually about 3 hours a week with another partner and we talk about it. (Participant 4)

Transcendence and Humility

Eleven participants either introduced the topic of spirituality as it relates to their work or described their experiences as a therapist in unambiguously spiritual terms.

Acknowledgment of the Spiritual Dimension of Being a Therapist

Without being asked, the participants shared the following descriptive information about their religious or spiritual lives. One participant is an ordained Roman Catholic priest, and another is an ordained Protestant minister. Several participants named their religious affiliations, and others actively practice forms of Eastern spiritual disciplines. One participant expressed the kind of transcendent awareness and humility that seemed to characterize the sample:

> To the extent that you feel inflated as a beginning therapist, you float a bit above ground. I think the origin of "humility" is *humus*, which is "ground." You are pulled back to the ground and you are less than what you wished for but more than you feared.... And to have some appreciation of that, some sense of something larger and basically about becoming less of a god over time. Becoming more human and so trying to be open and appreciative of

those moments where you see some kind of grace, some kind of blessing happening and it may be something that happened here, it may be something else. (Participant 4)

Locating the Significance of Therapy Within Social and Communal Responsibility

Four participants (33%) expressed experiencing a connection with humanity beyond therapeutic relationships. One participant offered these reflections on social justice:

> I think there is a need for our field to just get more involved in what is happening in this country, not only just with issues of violence, but how people are being destroyed, issues of abuse and trauma, and what it's doing. Our field has a particular responsibility because this is what we do, and this is our profession. Like the medical profession is saying, "Look, you better get your blood pressure down or you're going to have a heart attack," I think we need to be saying, "Look, if you don't deal with helping families be together, and spend time together, and address issues—hey folks, forget it...you think it's bad now." (Participant 10)

Intentional Learning

On the basis of the volume of material collected under this general theme, we concluded that these therapists had more to say about this aspect of their experience than about any other. This theme expresses the characteristic of passionately committed therapists as open to experience and their disposition to receive energy and wisdom from as many sources as possible.

Complementarity of Personal and Professional Development

In one way or another, all 12 therapists indicated that their work has enabled them to live better, fuller, and more complete lives. Five participants discussed the importance of failure and discovering their own human inadequacies through their work as being profoundly enriching. One participant said:

> Once, I made a grave mistake where the person was suicidal....I rebuked myself severely. It's one of my discouraging moments....I recall one of my teachers saying, "Your blackest, most discouraging moments have the potential of being your best moments. Hang in with it. Stay with it. Lean into it. Don't run away from it....Make it an experience that really has the potential to move you forward." I hung in for about three days, but I stayed with that directive, or that insight, or that approach, and I began to realize that part of it comes with strength inside me, you know, that I will make mistakes and I can still be a very effective therapist.

Work As a Therapist Facilitates Congruent Self-Expression

Eleven participants indicated continuing to work as therapists in spite of obstacles that make it difficult because it is somehow an innate part of their identity. One participant could not have been more succinct: "I guess it's just who I am" (Participant 3). Five of these

Table 2
Participants' Scores on the Salience Inventory as Compared with Norms

Group	Study			Work			Community Service			Home			Leisure		
	M	SD	z	M	SD	z	M	SD	z	M	SD	z	M	SD	z
							Participation								
Norm	24.5	7.3		30.4	5.6		18.2	6.7		27.0	6.2		25.2	6.4	
Participants	25.6	6.3	0.2	31.8	4.2	0.1	21.2	5.6	0.4	29.6*	6.2	0.4	27.6*	5.6	−.08
							Commitment								
Norm	27.7	8.0		34.2	5.6		23.6	7.9		35.0	6.1		28.2	7.0	
Participants	29.6	7.0	0.2	35.0	5.0	0.1	27.7*	6.7	0.5	38.5**	2.8	0.6	32.8*	5.5	0.7
							Values expectation								
Norm	35.6	10.2		43.7	7.8		31.3	10.7		43.6	8.7		37.6	9.7	
Participants	38.9	11.4	0.3	47.4	6.5	0.5	39.2	10.2	0.7	48.8	6.9	0.6	44.2	8.6	0.7

Note. Norm group refers to the general adult sample in the Work Importance Study (Super & Sverko, 1995). $N = 11$, z-scores indicate the mean rank of a given life role relative to the other four. The norm group data are from *Life Roles, Values and Careers: International Findings of the Work Importance Study* (p. 373) by D. E. Super and B. Sverko (Eds.), 1995, San Francisco: Jossey-Bass, Copyright 1995 by Jossey-Bass, a subsidiary of John Wiley & Sons. Reprinted with permission.

* $p = .05$, ** $p = .01$

11 therapists further acknowledged that this sense of self that is allowed to be expressed in therapy is both an innate desire to help as well as awareness of personal woundedness. The other 6 therapists who talked about finding a goodness of fit between themselves and their work discovered it in the process of career exploration. Through other work or academic experiences, they found themselves drawn to the kind of work that psychotherapists do.

Continued Fascination with Human Development and Change

Ten therapists indicated that a major motivating factor comes from the privilege and honor of witnessing human beings evolve, heal, develop, and change. This includes work with individuals with specific issues and problems as well as more global concerns about human evolution. One participant stated that this privilege more than compensates for the lack of external reinforcers. Another expressed incompleteness:

> I like doing this because I'm constantly coming up against myself. And there are everyday opportunities for me to grow and dealing with countertransference, dealing with my own distractibility, you know, and really I see it as a mindfulness practice for me to be present and to really be able to concentrate and to be there for people, to always review my own values and to come to grips with my own values and what I am promoting as values of people, explicitly or implicitly just by how I conduct myself. (Participant 7)

Quantitative Results

Responses to the Openness Scale (Costa & McCrae, 1992) indicated that, compared with the general population, participants reported being much more prone to seek new knowledge and experiences and to appreciate ordinary experience as potentially extraordinary. All raw scores ($M = 195.2$, $SD = 17.3$) were at least 3 standard deviations above the normative mean ($M = 110.6$, $SD = 17.3$), and all T scores were greater than or equal to 80 and at the 99th percentile for a normative adult sample (Costa & McCrae, 1992).

The Salience Inventory (Nevill & Super, 1986) measures the relative importance that an individual assigns to each of five life roles (study, work, community service, home and family, and leisure) across three dimensions (Participation, Commitment, and Values Expectations). As Table 2 indicates, only the group means for home and family and leisure on the Commitment scale, and community service, home and family, and leisure on the Participation scale were significantly greater than the normative means. This indicates that this group of psychotherapists is not more committed to multiple roles than the general population. However, when individuals' scores were converted to z-scores to examine the importance of each life role relative to the other life roles for this group of individuals, we found that these participants ranked work third among the five life roles for participation, fifth for commitment, and fourth for expectation of satisfaction (individual scores are not shown in Table 2). This indicates that work is not the primary commitment in the lives of therapists considered to be passionately committed to their work.

On the Job in General Scale (Balzer et al., 1997), 10 participants' job satisfaction scores were above the median ($Mdn = 48$) of a comparable sample of professionals (range = 42–54, $Mdn = 52$). These results were not statistically significant, contrary to our expectation that passionate commitment to work would be reflected in exceptionally high levels of job satisfaction. It is interesting to note that items like *ideal*, *superior*, and *excellent* were not regularly endorsed by participants.

On the Maslach Burnout Inventory—Human Services Survey (Maslach et al., 1996), a high degree of burnout is inferred when a respondent has high scores on the Emotional Exhaustion and Depersonalization scales and a low score on the Personal Accomplish-

Table 3
MBI (Maslach et al., 1996) Raw Scores and Categories of Burnout

	EE		DP		PA	
Participant	Score	Category	Score	Category	Score	Category
1	1	Low	6	Low	46	High
2	0	Low	31	High	47	High
3	0	Low	4	Low	48	High
4	9	Moderate	33	High	43	High
5	2	Low	17	Moderate	43	High
6	6	Moderate	14	Low	46	High
7	7	Moderate	15	Low	45	High
8	6	Moderate	19	Moderate	45	High
9	6	Moderate	17	Moderate	42	High
10	0	Low	13	Low	45	High
11	2	Low	4	Low	48	High

Note. In this inventory, high burnout is characterized by high EE and DP scores and low PA scores; MBI = Maslach Burnout Inventory—Human Services Survey; EE = Emotional Exhaustion scale; DP = Depersonalization scale; PA = Personal Accomplishment scale.

ment scale. As shown in Table 3, few participants obtained moderate to high scores on the Emotional Exhaustion and Depersonalization scales, but all participants had high scores on the Personal Accomplishment scale (range = 42–48), suggesting that they viewed themselves as competent and successful in their work. Only for the Personal Accomplishment scale did the categorical distribution of participants' scores differ significantly from those in the normative sample of helping professionals, χ^2 (2, $N = 11$) = 22.22, $p < .01$.

In general, our findings were consistent with the theoretical models guiding the study. In their interviews, the therapists expressed a continuous state of flow (Csikszentmihalyi, 1990; Jackson & Marsh, 1996) in their professional activities, they described behaviors characteristic of people who avoid burnout, and they reported engaging in other commitments that supply them with reciprocal sources of energy. On the other hand, the high level of spiritual commitment and practice reported by the present participants is not evident in the writings of Csikszentmihalyi (1990), Cherniss (1995), Grosch and Olsen (1994), or Marks (1979). Our other findings that passionately committed therapists find creative ways to maintain their autonomy and are passionately involved in nonwork activities adds to theory in this area.

Although our working definition of passionate commitment was based on four theoretical models, its validity has not been established. It may be that those who nominated peers as "passionately committed to their work" chose individuals who seem confident, optimistic, warm, who are highly visible in the community, or who possess positive qualities other than passionate commitment. Furthermore, the nominees may not necessarily be highly skillful therapists.

On the other hand, the peer nomination process provided a window through which to glimpse the attitudes and behaviors that psychotherapists value in their peers, and the qualitative themes shed light on the behavior, personality factors, and spiritual and existential beliefs and attitudes that contribute to professional careers that are deeply satisfying, life giving, and energizing. It is our hope that these themes will be useful guides for students preparing for careers as psychotherapists as well as for those struggling to maintain their passion for a career chosen long ago.

Implications for Practice and Training

Taken together, the qualitative and quantitative data suggest that passionately committed psychotherapists create work situations in which they experience personal autonomy while maintaining meaningful relationships in their work, balancing roles and responsibilities, and being open to new ideas and learning. These individuals experience a pervasive sense of meaning and significance in their work by integrating and locating it within a larger, more transcendent perspective. They do not close themselves off from experiences that are potential sources of energy. Rather, they display an openness to all experience as well as a flexibility to attend to multiple activities that supply them with a continually renewed source of energy for their work.

The interview data further suggest that passionate commitment to work does not mean overcommitment to work. Indeed, the participants in this study expressed the belief that their passion and effectiveness would be compromised if they did not make deliberate efforts to prevent work from encroaching on their personal lives. They described investing energy in activities that give them pleasure even if doing so prevents them from reaping the maximum possible economic rewards. This theme was consistent with the quantitative findings that (a) work was not ranked as participants' most significant life role, and (b) participants did not differ significantly from the average worker on a measure of job

53

satisfaction or from the average mental health professional in terms of reported emotional exhaustion and depersonalization.

565 On a practical level, our results suggest that maintaining passion for work as a therapist requires the discipline of balancing one's life with other meaningful activities even if it means reducing work hours, passing up opportunities for formal professional development, and changing work environments. Developing interests
570 in activities unrelated to work as a therapist and paying attention to one's spiritual discipline and development are as crucial, if not more crucial, than pursuing professional avenues of achievement. Current programs of training and continuing education encourage the use of
575 supervision directed at continued self-knowledge and growth from one's work. The results of this study show that such efforts are associated with sustaining one's passion over a long career. Training and education programs that emphasize balance, integration of work with
580 the rest of life, and the spiritual and transcendent nature of therapy may be essential for the field to retain passionate, competent professionals.

The current economic climate is frequently blamed for the waning of passion among helping professionals.
585 The present therapists acknowledged that the material benefits of being a therapist are not enough to sustain their passion and that an overemphasis on these benefits detracts from the positive elements that attracted them to the profession. The ways they have found to
590 respond to the intrusion of managed care into their work may be particularly helpful to therapists who feel overwhelmed by this obstacle. Using time management, organizational skills, and good interpersonal skills to influence managed care decisions and doing
595 pro bono work in order to enjoy some measure of therapeutic autonomy seem to allow therapists to bring their strengths to this battle.

References

Ackerley, G. D., Burnell, J., Holder, D. C., & Kurdek, L. A. (1988). Burnout among licensed psychologists. *Professional Psychology: Research and Practice, 19,* 624–631.

Balzer, W. K., Kihm, J. A., Smith, P. C., Irwin, J. L., Bachiochi, P. D., Robie, C., Sinar, E. F., & Parra, L. F. (1997). *Users manual for the Job Descriptive Index (JDI; 1997 Revision) and the Job in General (JIG) Scales.* (Bowling Green, OH: Bowling Green State University Press)

Cherniss, C. (1995). *Beyond burnout.* (New York: Routledge)

Costa, P. T., & McCrae, R. R. (1992). *Revised NEO Personality Inventory (NEO-PI—R) and NEO Five Factor Inventory (NEO-FFI) professional manual.* (Odessa, FL: Psychological Assessment Resources)

Csikszentmihalyi, M. (1990). *Flow: The psychology of optimal experience.* (New York: Harper & Row)

Grosch, W. N., & Olsen, D. C. (1994). *When helping starts to hurt: A new look at burnout among psychotherapists.* (New York: Norton)

Hill, C. E., Thompson, B. J., & Williams, E. N. (1997). A guide to conducting consensual qualitative research. *The Counseling Psychologist, 25,* 517–572.

Jackson, S. A., & Marsh, H. W. (1996). Development and validation of a scale to measure optimal experience: The Flow State Scale. *Journal of Sport and Exercise Psychology, 18,* 17–33.

Luborsky, L., McClellan, T. A., Woody, G. E., O'Brien, C. P., & Auerbach, A. (1985). Therapist success and its determinants. *Archive of General Psychiatry, 42,* 602–611.

Marks, S. (1979). Culture, human energy, and self-actualization: A sociological offering to humanistic psychology. *Journal of Humanistic Psychology, 19,* 27–42.

Maslach, C., & Jackson, S. E. (1986). *Maslach Burnout Inventory manual* ((2nd ed.). Palo Alto, CA: Consulting Psychologists Press)

Maslach, C., Jackson, S. E., & Leiter, M. P. (1996). *Maslach Burnout Inventory manual* ((3rd ed.). Palo Alto, CA: Consulting Psychologists Press)

Miles, M. B., & Huberman, A. M. (1994). *Qualitative data analysis: An expanded sourcebook* ((2nd ed.). Thousand Oaks, CA: Sage)

Nevill, D. D., & Super, D. E. (1986). *The Salience Inventory: Theory, application, and research.* (Palo Alto, CA: Consulting Psychologists Press)

Stiles, W. B. (1993). Quality control in qualitative research. *Clinical Psychology Review, 13,* 593–618.

Super, D. E., & Nevill, D. D. (1985). *The Salience Inventory.* (Palo Alto, CA: Consulting Psychologists Press)

Super, D. E., & Sverko, B. (Eds.) (1995). *Life roles, values and careers: International findings of the Work Importance Study.* (San Francisco: Jossey-Bass)

Zeddies, T. J. (1999). Becoming a psychotherapist: The personal nature of clinical work, emotional availability, and personal allegiances. *Psychotherapy, 36,* 229–235.

Acknowledgments: This article is based on a dissertation by Raymond F. Dlugos under the direction of Myrna L. Friedlander. An earlier version of this article was presented at the 107th Annual Convention of the American Psychological Association, Boston, August 1999. The contributions of the other committee members, David L. Blustein, Richard F. Haase, and William N. Grosch, are gratefully acknowledged as well as the research assistance provided by Carol Carlson, Rachel Kiehle, Bonnie McIntosh-Saelens, Brian Saelens, Joyce DeWitt-Parker, and Michelle Schwam. Finally, we are appreciative of the time and effort offered by the participants.

Address correspondence to: Raymond F. Dlugos, the Southdown Institute, 1335 St. John's Sideroad East, Aurora, Ontario, Canada, L4G 3G8. E-mail: raydlugos@aol.com

Exercise for Article 6

Factual Questions

1. The researchers present four characteristics [(a) through (d)] in their working definition of "passionate commitment." What is the first characteristic they mention?

2. Written nominations were sought from 548 local psychologists, psychiatrists, clinical social workers, and counselors. How were these 548 identified?

3. What was the minimum number of nominations required to be invited to participate in the study?

4. To minimize bias, the researchers formulated some questions to provide participants with the opportunity to offer disconfirming evidence. They give two sample questions of this type. What is the first question they give?

5. What did the researchers do to assess testimonial validity?

6. When therapists were asked about the most serious obstacle in their way of doing their best, how many mentioned managed care?

7. What was the mean score of the norm group on commitment to community service? What was the

corresponding mean for the participants?

8. The researchers expected to find that the participants would have exceptionally high levels of job satisfaction. Were the researchers' results consistent with this expectation?

Questions for Discussion

9. Twelve of the 15 who were invited to participate in this study agreed to be interviewed. Could the fact that three declined to be interviewed have affected the results of this study? Explain.

10. Peer nomination (nomination by others in the same and related fields) was used to identify the participants. An alternative would be to use self-nomination in which therapists are asked how committed they are and those who answer highly committed would be invited to participate. In your opinion, are there advantages and disadvantages of each method? Which method would you prefer if you were conducting research on this topic? Explain.

11. The qualitative results are illustrated with quotations from the participants. Which of the quotations did you find most interesting? Why?

12. The results are divided into two main sections. First, the qualitative results from the interviews are presented followed by a presentation of the quantitative results. Are both types of results of equal interest to you? Explain.

13. The researchers point out limitations of their work in lines 513–521. In your opinion, how important are these to the validity of the study? Explain.

Quality Ratings

Directions: Indicate your level of agreement with each of the following statements by circling a number from 5 for strongly agree (SA) to 1 for strongly disagree (SD). If you believe an item is not applicable to this research article, leave it blank. Be prepared to explain your ratings.

A. The introduction establishes the importance of the study.

   SA   5   4   3   2   1   SD

B. The literature review establishes the context for the study.

   SA   5   4   3   2   1   SD

C. The research purpose, question, or hypothesis is clearly stated.

   SA   5   4   3   2   1   SD

D. The method of sampling is sound.

   SA   5   4   3   2   1   SD

E. Relevant demographics (for example, age, gender, and ethnicity) are described.

   SA   5   4   3   2   1   SD

F. Measurement procedures are adequate.

   SA   5   4   3   2   1   SD

G. All procedures have been described in sufficient detail to permit a replication of the study.

   SA   5   4   3   2   1   SD

H. The participants have been adequately protected from potential harm.

   SA   5   4   3   2   1   SD

I. The results are clearly described.

   SA   5   4   3   2   1   SD

J. The discussion/conclusion is appropriate.

   SA   5   4   3   2   1   SD

K. Despite any flaws, the report is worthy of publication.

   SA   5   4   3   2   1   SD

Article 7

Parental Involvement During the Transition to High School

Toni Falbo
University of Texas at Austin

Laura Lein
University of Texas at Austin

Nicole A. Amador
The California Commission on
Teacher Credentialing

ABSTRACT. In this article, the authors conducted a study to discover what types of parent involvement are effective as students make the transition to high school. This study also aimed to elaborate on the role parents play in connecting their children to desirable peer networks during this transition. In-home interviews were conducted with 26 students as well as their parents before and after entering high school. The successfulness of the students' transition was evaluated in terms of their final grades as well as the number of credits earned and their school attendance. They identified five forms of parental involvement that helped students succeed: monitoring the teen's academic and social life, evaluating the information obtained about the teen, helping the teen with schoolwork, creating positive peer networks for the teen, and participating directly in the school.

From *Journal of Adolescent Research*, *16*, 511–529. Copyright © 2001 by Sage Publications. Reprinted with permission.

Many studies have examined the relationship between parent involvement and student success (Epstein, 1987; Muller, 1993, 1995). These studies have concluded that parent involvement is a
5 multidimensional construct that both directly and indirectly promotes school success (Grolnick & Slowiaczek, 1994; Muller, 1995; Sui-Chi & Willms, 1996). Parent involvement has evolved into a complex array of parental actions, including parental
10 participation in school activities, parental discussion of school with their child at home, and parental help with homework (Epstein, 1987; Grolnick & Slowiaczek, 1994; Muller, 1995; Sui-Chi & Willms, 1996). This large and growing body of literature suggests that
15 different kinds of parent involvement are effective at different times during the student's life (Muller, 1995). Notably, the type of parental involvement changes when the student enters high school (Baker & Stevenson, 1986; Muller, 1995).
20 The purpose of this study was to examine more fully what types of parent involvement are effective as the student enters high school. The transition from eighth to ninth grade is regarded as a crucial time in a student's educational career, determining whether the

25 student becomes trained for postsecondary education or leaves the formal education system without a diploma (Romo & Falbo, 1996; Schiller, 1999). This transition is difficult not only because the students must enter a different school with a larger enrollment but also
30 because the teachers expect students to take much more responsibility for their own performance in high school (Schiller, 1999). At this time, parents tend to give high school students greater autonomy (Romo & Falbo, 1996; Schiller, 1999; Steinberg, 1996).
35 Most of the studies of parent involvement in the secondary education of their children have been based on surveys in which students describe their parents or parents describe themselves using statements followed by a series of forced-choice responses. For example,
40 the National Educational Longitudinal Study (NELS) (National Center for Education Statistics, 1992) contains information about the actions of parents relevant to the schooling of thousands of students throughout the United States. Sui-Chi and Willms
45 (1996) examined NELS data from eighth-grade students and their parents and found their responses to many items could be grouped in terms of four parent-involvement factors. These measured the extent to which the parents discussed school at home,
50 communicated with the school about the student, supervised the student's life outside of school, and participated in school events.
Sui-Chi and Willms (1996) found that three of these parent involvement factors were positively
55 related to the academic achievement of students, whereas one factor was negatively related to academic achievement. Specifically, parents' discussion of school at home had the most positive association with the achievement of students; parents' supervision and
60 participation had smaller yet positive correlations with achievement, whereas communications with the school had a negative and significant association with school achievement. The positive associations were consistent with the general view that parental involvement is good
65 for student success. However, Sui-Chi and Willms explained the negative correlation as caused by the parents of students with learning or behavioral difficulties. Such parents received more

70 communications from the school, and their children were more likely to score poorly on achievement tests; consequently, the correlation between communications from the school and student achievement was negative.

75 Although surveys using structured response items are efficient, this approach to research limits the kinds of information we can obtain about parent involvement. There may be whole domains of activity that we have missed about what parents do to assist their adolescent children with the transition to high school. To test this possibility, we asked parents open-
80 ended questions during interviews in their homes. We asked them to identify positive and negative events their teen had experienced in school and to explain what caused these events.

In this way, we were trying to uncover not only
85 what action parents took to help their children during the transition to high school but also what events prompted their actions and whether the parents perceived their efforts as efficacious. We asked the students the same questions to ascertain their
90 involvement in solving school problems. We interviewed both parent and student when the student was in eighth grade and again after the first grading period in high school.

When delving into the causes of student success,
95 researchers often dichotomize them into school versus family characteristics. We stepped beyond this dichotomy to consider the possible influence of peer networks on the transition to high school. Researchers examining the determinants of high school success
100 have identified peers as an influential force (Brown, Mounts, Lamborn, & Steinberg, 1993; Fletcher, Darling, Steinberg, & Dornbusch, 1995). In fact, the influence of peers has been portrayed recently as outweighing the influence of parents (Harris, 1995,
105 1998). Peer influences reflect a third source of help or hindrance for students making the transition to high school. Early views of peers portrayed them as outside the control of parents (Parsons, 1942; Riesman, 1961), although there has been speculation that parents
110 attempt to control peer influences by selecting neighborhoods to live in and schools for their children to attend (Harris, 1995, 1998; Steinberg, 1996). Schools also play a role in defining peer networks for students. They are responsible for putting students
115 together, although schools generally assume no responsibility for the social networks that develop among students (Romo & Falbo, 1996). The present study was poised to discover what role parents play in connecting students to peer networks during the
120 transition to high school.

Method

Sample and Procedure

We selected a public middle school that offered a range of student characteristics in a suburban school district. This middle school enrolled about 700 students

125 (Grades 6 through 8), with 29% eligible for free or reduced-price lunch and an ethnic/racial mix consisting of 72% non-Hispanic Whites, 10% Blacks, and 18% Hispanics. All of the students were expected to attend the same high school, which enrolled approximately 3,300 students, about 30% more than the facility had
130 been originally designed for. The high school provided free or reduced-price lunches to 14% of the students. The ethnic composition of the high school was 70% non-Hispanic White, 7% Black, and 19% Hispanic.

After issuing an invitation to all families with
135 children in the eighth grade, we selected randomly from the volunteers to obtain a sample that reflected the ethnic/racial diversity of the eighth-grade class. We were able to schedule and complete interviews with the families of 26 students during the last half of eighth
140 grade. We sent pairs of interviewers to the homes; one interviewed the eighth grader in one room while the other interviewed the parent(s) in another room. Although most (72%) of the parent interviews involved one parent (all mothers), the remaining parents chose to
145 be interviewed as couples. After the first grading period of ninth grade (6 weeks after the start of school), the interviewers returned to the homes of the participants and reinterviewed them. Of the original 26 students participating in the eighth-grade interview, we
150 did not obtain ninth-grade information for three. One of these had become home schooled, and the other two had moved out of state.

After the end of their ninth-grade school year, we obtained information about each student's school
155 performance from the school district, including the final grades for each class taken, the number of credits earned, and the percentage of absences.

Instruments

The first two authors of this article created interview instruments to elicit

160 1. parental actions, particularly focusing on helping the student with schoolwork, solving problems at school, and monitoring the student's social and school life;

2. the family's resources, which was not just a
165 listing of assets but an assessment of the parents' responsibilities and/or other family characteristics that enriched or depleted these assets;

3. social network involvement, which encompassed a variety of networks, including neighborhood,
170 school, recreational organizations, and religious communities; and

4. the adolescent's characteristics, which included strengths and weaknesses of the specific target student, such as special needs or talents.

175 The interviewers asked parents and students a series of open-ended questions that were almost identical in content but differed in perspective. For example,

students were asked, "What was your biggest accomplishment in high school so far?" Parents were asked, "What was your child's biggest accomplishment in high school so far?" The open-ended interview instrument consisted of 27 questions for eighth graders and their parents, and the instrument used to interview ninth graders and their parents consisted of 40 questions.

In addition, the parents were asked to describe family resources, such as income, parental education, employment, hours of employment, and health problems within the family. The parents were given a list of income levels and asked to check the level that best represented the family income. These levels were based on 1990 census information about family incomes found in the zip code where all our research subjects lived.

Data Coding and Analysis Plan

Our plan was to categorize students first in terms of the success of their transition to high school and then return to the transcripts of the interviews to determine what parental actions differentiated these students. To illustrate our findings, we selected two cases that contrasted the relationship between high school success and parental involvement.

Results

Demographic Characteristics of the Sample

The participating students were 46% male, 54% female, 68% non-Hispanic White, 8% African American, and 24% Hispanic. The sampled families ranged widely in the resources available to them. In terms of income, about 75% of our families earned yearly incomes within the $25,000 to $75,000 range. Two of our families earned less than $15,000 a year, 2 earned $15,000 to $25,000 a year, 5 earned $25,000 to $35,000 a year, 5 earned $35,000 to $50,000 a year, 8 earned $50,000 to $75,000 a year, 2 earned $75,000 to $100,000 a year, but no family reported earning more than $100,000 a year. In our sample, the mothers' educational attainment ranged from possessing a GED to a master's degree, with all but three mothers having at least a high school diploma. The fathers' educational attainment ranged from a high school diploma to a master's degree, with all but three of the fathers having at least some college experience. In terms of hours worked outside the home, the employed mothers (77%) worked from 2 to 55 hours a week. The fathers typically spent more hours a week in employment than did mothers, with all fathers employed at least full time. Also relevant to family resources is the number and type of parents in the sample. All but one of the students lived with his mother, and 73% of the students lived with their father (or a father substitute).

Indices of Transition Success

We considered three indices of transition success. The first one was grade point average (GPA),

calculated by averaging the student's final grades received for all courses taken during the freshman year. This score ranged from 0, assigned to the student who dropped out of school before earning a passing final grade in any course, to 95. Unlike the GPA used by the school to calculate class rank, the GPA score used here was not adjusted for the difficulty level of the course. The second index of transition success was the number of credits earned during the freshman year, which ranged from 0 to 8.5. To be promoted to the next grade (i.e., 10th), students needed to have five credits. The third index was percentage of absences, which ranged from 0% to 99%. Although some of our students (25%) had perfect attendance, one attended very little of the first weeks of ninth grade and was given a 99% absent score.

At minimum, we considered a student as making the transition to high school successfully if he or she passed all coursework, earned enough credits, and attended school often enough to be promoted to the next grade level. Only three students failed to meet this minimum standard of success. Otherwise, students varied in their degree of success in making the transition, and we also considered this degree of success when differentiating parental behaviors.

Parental Actions

We identified three interrelated parental activities that were common among parents whose teens made the transition to high school successfully. We summarize these three kinds of parental activities in terms of monitoring, evaluating, and intervening.

Monitoring. We found that parents who closely monitored their teens every day during the transition to high school were more likely to discover difficulties their children were experiencing before these issues became significant problems. By monitoring their teen every day, the parents learned if their teen was doing homework, going to school, and interacting positively with peers. Most monitoring was overt; however, some monitoring had to be covert or indirect, using the eyes and ears of other adults or teens to provide important information. These observations were not mindless invasions of the teen's privacy but strategically aimed for the purpose of evaluating the teen's well-being.

Evaluating. We found that some parents were more able to identify possible problems than were others. Some parents obtained information during monitoring that suggested possible problems but failed to appreciate the significance of this information. While parents were evaluating the information they obtained from monitoring, they usually compared what they observed their teens thinking, feeling, and doing with what they thought the teen should be thinking, feeling, and doing. As a guide during evaluation, many parents used their experiences with their older children, their memory of their own high school experiences, or their interpretation of what experts advised.

Table 1
Parents' Characteristics in the Two Case Studies

Parents' Characteristic	Adam	Fran
Family income	$50,000 to $75,000	$35,000 to $50,000
Father's education	Master's degree	Associate's degree
Father's job	Planner, state agency	Technician, industry
Hours worked—father	40 hours/week	40 hours/week
Hours worked—mother	40 hours/week	40 hours/week
Mother's education	Master's degree	Bachelor's degree
Mother's job	Social worker	Hospital nurse
Number of children	2	3

Intervening. The point of monitoring the teen and evaluating the information obtained from monitoring was to motivate and inform the parents' actions to help the teen make the transition to high school successfully. We found that three kinds of parental interventions assisted the teen in making the transition to high school successfully: (a) active involvement in schoolwork, (b) nesting the teen in a desirable peer network, and (c) direct participation in the school. For a student to be successful, parents had to engage in at least two of these three kinds of interventions. We found that parents of successful students actively involved themselves in their children's completion of schoolwork. Sometimes, this intervention involved tutoring the teen or helping the teen find the necessary information for a project. Sometimes, parents provided continuous encouragement while overseeing homework sessions every night. Occasionally, we found that supporting homework came in the form of helping the teen overcome the emotional distress associated with being overwhelmed by schoolwork.

The second type of parental intervention concerned parental involvement in nesting the teen within social networks that promoted participation in high school. We found that parents of successful students prepared their children for success in high school by enrolling them in appropriate middle school coursework and extracurricular activities that led to participation in specific high school organizations, such as band, sports teams, or academic clubs. In advance of high school, parents often paid for and pressed their children to participate in private sports leagues, music lessons, or other types of community organizations, such as church groups, designed to help the student be accepted into various high school peer groups. Thus, these parents prepared their children for acceptance into a peer group that was supportive of school participation. The consequence of this network participation was that the student entered high school with an array of peers who fulfilled the student's needs for affiliation and did so in a way that was consistent with a serious commitment to meeting the demands of high school.

The third type of intervention in which parents engaged involved direct participation in the school. Parents whose children made the transition to high school successfully were more likely to participate in the teen's course selection and extracurricular activities than were parents of less successful students. Some of these parents were actively communicating with teachers, counselors, and administrators about their children before the child had problems. In some cases, these parents participated in booster clubs, raised funds for the school, and chaperoned the students off campus. Consequently, school personnel regarded them as an asset. This allowed these parents to establish positive relationships with teachers who funneled information to the parents about their children. Furthermore, through their presence on campus, these parents were able to monitor their children more closely.

Case Studies

To illustrate the power of these parental actions, we have selected two case studies. Adam earned straight As as his final grades for his freshman year, with an average of 94.3 in his core classes all of which were designed to be as challenging as possible. In contrast, Fran took courses of average difficulty but failed three courses, and her final average in core courses was 68.0, just below the passing score of 70.

The parents of Adam and Fran are described in Table 1. Both students lived with both of their biological parents. The two sets of parents earned adequate income to support their families financially, and they were educated enough to understand the academic demands of high school.

Adam

When we first interviewed Adam's mother, she was a frequent visitor at his middle school. She described herself as a very hands-on parent who sought involvement in every aspect of her son's education. She realized that Adam was not always appreciative of her efforts on his behalf. She told us of a time in eighth grade when he asked her to back off:

> It was just eating lunch with him and just asking me not to do it. And it hurts my feelings, you know, but I try to understand that in the eighth grade, he probably doesn't want me coming and sitting at lunch with him.

Her monitoring of her son did not diminish when he first entered high school, although her methods of monitoring did. Attending a parent orientation meeting one night early in the school year, she explained,

> I was sitting in his theater arts class, and his teacher was talking about this wonderful assignment that they had just turned in, this mask that everyone had turned in. And I was sitting there going, "I don't remember Adam doing a mask!" And I came home and said, "Adam, did you make a mask?" "No, I forgot to do it." So, then we went out that night, and we went to go get a planner, and that's much better because he writes, he doesn't try to commit everything to memory. Adam used the planner every day, telling us how much he liked checking off assignments when he had finished them.

Both of Adam's parents were highly productive people who emphasized the importance of time management, organizational skills, and hard work to their son. His mother was particularly concerned about her son's procrastination. Because he was bright, he could get away with waiting until the last minute to work on his homework in middle school. His mother told us that she hoped that by signing him up for difficult classes and challenging sports training in high school, he would be forced to get organized and stay focused on his schoolwork.

Adam's mother was a social worker who provided services to teens in trouble. She was familiar with all the things that could go wrong in a teenager's life, and this intensified her vigilance about her children. Adam understood this about his mother. He said,

> I think my mom just worries about it a lot because as a social worker, she deals with the pregnant 13- and 14-year-olds and the drunk 15-year-olds and the crack babies and all of that, so I think she thinks kind of like a police officer. Some of her view of the general public is kind of warped in that way because she deals with those types of people every day.

Adam's mother had no qualms about intervening in her son's life. As an eighth grader, Adam stated, "It's everything. If I don't follow the little manual, the thick manual that she has in her head, then we're going to be disagreeing." During both interviews, Adam described his mother as engaging in "marathon hounding" to get him to do what she wanted. "My mom controls me so much. Like she'll ask if I have homework like five times after school, and then she'll bother me about doing it."

Adam's mother did not slack off when he entered high school. Not only did she help him stay organized, she helped him cope with the stress of heavy homework demands. She explained,

> The school expects a lot...We had to deal with work at 11:00 at night, he's so stressed out. He had this big cell organelle that he had to design, and he was really clueless as to how to do it. First, we have to have the 45 minutes where he talks about how much he hates his teacher and venting.

After listening to her son, Adam's mother said, "And so I got on the Internet and was pulling things off just to kind of show him. And once he settled down about it, everything was fine."

When Adam was in eighth grade, his mother disapproved of one of his close friends even though this boy had won national awards in mathematics. Although Adam thought this boy was funny, his mother thought of him as a "rising Unabomber." She said,

> He's one of these kids that goes out of his way to be as obnoxious as he can possibly be. He says things for shock value...But Adam is figuring out, and this is one of the reasons that I'm excited about high school, that I want him to have more kids to choose from.

She wanted him to have more wholesome friends so she pressured her son to enter a competitive swimming league in eighth grade. His active training schedule that continued through the summer left little time for him to spend with his old friend. Describing his new friends, Adam said,

> There was a lot of bonding over the summer because they are mostly on the summer league that was coached by the head coach of the swim team. The high school head coach was coaching this recreational thing, and everybody was part of it so we were like going to each other's houses, and that was like the first time I really did that type of thing and I really connected fast.

His training paid off when he earned a spot on the varsity swim team in high school. Describing his new friends, he said, "My closest friends are all swimmers." Unlike his old friends, who were bright but did not like doing schoolwork, his new friends "appreciate school because they know what it will do for them." Most of his teammates were older, "When I'm hanging out with people who are like older, that a lot of them are more focused on college, they understand what is going to be. They need to make good grades now for college later." But these new friends were not just grinds. Adam explained,

> Like Sunday night, I'll be just so depressed because of all this work that I am seeing that I have to do and the next day, going to swimming, you know, everybody is just laughing and having a good time and it just puts everything into perspective.

Although Adam's mother approved of his new friends, she maintained her control of his social life. The older teens on the swim team had different curfews than Adam. Nonetheless, his mother insisted that he meet her curfew of midnight. If not, she said,

> We do embarrassing things. Like, if he can't manage to come in before 12:00, then the next round, I'll be going to get him and knocking on the door of this house where all these people are having a good time and there I am, his mother, picking him up. Believe me, the threat of that...He doesn't want that!

Adam's mother was as proactive in his schools as the school personnel would permit. In middle school, Adam's mother had lobbied the principal to provide challenging classes for talented students like her son. He did. She also made certain that Adam was enrolled in courses in high school that were designed for talented and gifted children. She was in frequent communication with the swim coach and with all of his teachers in high school.

Assessing her son's development during ninth grade, she concluded, "It's still hard for me when he says, 'I can handle it.' It's still hard for me, as a parent, to step back." She was pleased with his success at high school, "Of course, as a parent, I'd like to think that we had some influence on that."

Fran

When we first interviewed Fran's mother, she had difficulty answering our questions. She tried to explain,

> Maybe I'm just thinking too hard, I…I'm not quite sure, uh, (pause) I just don't feel right, I…it's just something nagging at the back of me to say there's not, there hasn't been a time 'cause that's not true, uh…but I can't think of anything that sticks out of my mind. So…what was the question?

As Fran entered adolescence, she and her family were suffering from a series of losses. It started before middle school. Fran said,

> When I was in fifth grade, I stopped doing my work and everything like that because my uncle was sick. Then he died that year. And so I wouldn't do my work. I sometimes would do it, but then I would get low grades. And then my parents had to talk to me about that because I wouldn't do anything. I would just sit there, and I wouldn't care that much.

Then, when Fran was in middle school, her brother dropped out of high school. At this time, her family moved from North Texas to Central Texas, and Fran had to adjust to a new social environment. When Fran was in eighth grade, her brother had become a teen father, and his wife and infant son came to live with Fran and her parents. Then, Fran's father became ill, and helping him recover took a lot of her mother's time. As he recovered, her mother was hit again with another tragedy. Her sister died, and this event led to several legal issues that her mother had to deal with in court.

Even though Fran's mother had trouble thinking of answers to our questions, she was able to explain that Fran had some general problems. As her mother saw it, Fran seemed to be attracted to girls who had problems. Referring to Fran, she said, "She kind of tends, you know, if you're kind of on the social outcast side, she will kind of take you in."

She also had noticed that her daughter did not have any discipline when it came to doing work. She explained,

> I mean, just even at home she's very, uh, by her being the only girl, I think we all have catered to her. And so, since she [was] little, she was very lazy. A lot of things have been handed to her, you know, so now when you really want to see it, you don't because that's…it's a failure, not only, you know, hers but ours, too.

Although Fran's mother believed that she needed to set firmer limits on Fran so that her daughter would develop good work habits, she found doing this difficult. She explained, "I'm very lenient, my husband's probably not. What happens is I forget and end up giving in. So remembering that she's being punished becomes a big problem with me sometimes, so I try not to make long-range punishments anymore."

If her parents weren't disciplinarians, they were warm and helpful toward her. Fran described them as follows:

> My family has always been there for me. Doesn't matter what it was. If it had to do with me not doing my work or if I did do it but didn't understand it, they would sit down and talk to me and ask me, "What's going on?" and "Why am I not doing this?" and "Why didn't I come to them before?"

In eighth grade, Fran described the strong support she received from her mother:

> My mom will sit there all night long, if she has to, to get me to understand one thing. My mom helped me with my math before when I didn't get it. And she stayed up, like we stayed up until 1:00 trying to figure it out. Then, after I got it, she sat there and waited for me to finish the rest of my paper, and then she checked it.

Fran's mother explained that she didn't always intervene when she saw an issue coming up, "You know, I sometimes foresee a problem…I wonder if it is my avoidance or her avoidance. I know she had one of her friends actually skip school, and it was really strange that she told me about it." Fran's mother continued,

> I am not foolish enough to think she doesn't have any problems, but what they are are not well defined to me in terms of what is happening. We will talk about school in general, and she is pretty free in talking about school and what happened, but it is never "me." What happened here or this is what "I" saw today. I don't know if she is telling me indirectly that this happened to "me" and "What would you do if this happened?"

After the first 6 weeks of high school, Fran told us that she was skipping classes and telling her father about it:

> Like one day I did skip for lunch and instead of going to class, I went to all four lunches. And after that, I felt totally guilty, and I told my dad. And my friends were like, "What? What kid in their right mind would tell their dad?" But I had to. I felt so guilty that I had to tell somebody, and my dad was just there. He just told me that "Well, you have to do what you do. Even though you can't turn back the clock, you're gonna have to go to class now." He told me that he doesn't want to hear that I'm skipping any classes because he says that that's a bad way to start high school. He says, "Just go for it! There's no problem big enough that you have to run away. If you

don't understand something, don't run away, go to class and talk to your teacher and tell her what's going on."

Her parents had tried to induce responsibility by giving her household chores, but Fran would either avoid the chore or make the parents wish they had not given it to her. For example, her parents assigned her the job of making dinner one night, and she did it, but during the meal, she sobbed and refused to eat. Her mother described the scene:

I mean, it is upsetting that she actually cries through a whole meal that I made her make. I mean, she just thought it was horrible that I was making her cook. She actually cried and I was looking at her and she was serious. I mean, her whole thing is "Why do I have to do it? I don't care! I won't eat if I have to cook it."

Fran told us that her parents were easy targets. "I'll usually pout when they don't want to do something I want to do. It really works for my dad, but for my mom, I'll lay on her and go, 'Mommy' (in a pleading tone of voice)."

Her parents did continue to encourage her completion of homework at home. As Fran described it,

All the time my dad will get me psyched up to do my homework. He turns the TV off and grabs my book bag, and we sit there and he says like, "OK, you don't understand this?" and I'd be like, "No, I don't get this problem." He'd explain it to me and break it down for me to different levels. We'd get the answer together, and he'd check to see if that was the answer and he'd check it and he'd be like, "You got it!" And we'd go on to the next one, and he would get so pumped up and get me pumped up for having homework!

Fran's mother had lost her contact with Fran's school because she had stopped attending PTA meetings and volunteering at the school, something she had done when Fran entered middle school. She no longer had the time to participate because she was employed full time and trying to overcome all of her family's setbacks.

Fran always had a lot of friends. When she was in middle school, they tended to be girls who lived in her neighborhood. Reflecting back on them, Fran's mother described them: "They are very friendly; they are very sweet. I know all of their parents, so they think it is a conspiracy."

When she entered high school, Fran made additional friends with new kids that her mother did not know. Fran told us that her new friends were obstacles to her success in high school:

I have a bunch of friends that like to go crazy. They like to skip school and go smoke pot and stuff. I met them before, when they were good kids. When I first got into middle school, I didn't know anybody and that was when I was in seventh grade and they helped me out. They helped me adjust and get my work done. Now, they're just totally changed. I hope that I can get at least one of

my friends back into class because she goes to class with me and I want her to go back.

In addition to her concern about her friends, she was worried about her brother. When Fran entered high school, her brother left home for drug rehabilitation. "It's sort of like a rehab, where they deal with different issues of self-esteem and stuff like that. Because he used to take drugs and the police sent him there. And I don't know exactly where he is."

Discussion

This study yielded significant information about what types of parent involvement were effective in supporting teens' successful transition to high school. Some types of parent involvement we found have also been discovered by other researchers to be associated with school success. Notably, parental monitoring of children has been found to have a powerful effect on the academic achievement of high school students (Dornbusch, Ritter, Leiderman, Roberts, & Fraleigh, 1987). We found that parents who consistently made daily observations of their teens were more likely to detect problems, and this gave parents the opportunity to intervene before the problem became serious. All of the parents in our sample engaged in some monitoring. The teens that avoided problems were ones whose parents consistently spent time every day in direct and indirect monitoring. The teens that failed had parents who were much more inconsistent in their monitoring.

Likewise, previous studies have found that parental support for homework has positive effects on high school grades and standardized test scores (Cooper, Lindsay, Nye, & Greathouse, 1998). We found that for high school freshmen, parental help with homework involved not only tutoring but also overseeing homework every night, helping them complete projects, and calming them when distressed by the demands of high school. While parents were helping their kids with schoolwork, they had the opportunity to determine if their kids were completing assignments on time. Parental participation in homework also informed parents about whether the teen's skills were at a level appropriate for completing schoolwork. Thus, this type of intervention helped the parent maintain continuous monitoring and evaluation of the child's academic progress. These parents used the information they obtained from their homework sessions with their children to justify further interventions, such as professional tutoring or changing course schedules.

We also identified new forms of parent involvement. In particular, we found that the parents' skill at evaluating information about their teen was critical in making the teen's transition to high school successful. In our sample, parents ranged from hypervigilant to dismissive when they encountered information that reflected potential problems. Our case studies shed some light on what caused some parents to evaluate information more skillfully than others.

Adam's mother was a social worker whose job involved solving the problems of teenagers. She had professional expertise to devote to her son's transition to high school. For example, when Adam's mother discovered that her son had missed an assignment at the beginning of his freshman year, she realized that this was a serious problem that needed immediate attention. She drove him to an office supply store to buy a daily planner so that he could record all of his assignments.

In contrast, Fran's parents failed to react to clear signs of problems. When Fran told her parents that she had skipped school, they explained to Fran why skipping was bad and how to get back into school. But they did not evaluate Fran's confession as important enough to justify monitoring her school attendance more closely. Furthermore, they knew that she was attracted to kids with problems, but they took no action to place her into another peer group. Thus, Fran's parents were not able to evaluate the information that they obtained from monitoring their daughter in a way that prompted appropriate action.

We also uncovered a high degree of parental involvement in creating social networks for their children. We were surprised by the degree to which most parents in our sample purposely nested their teen in specific social networks before the teen entered high school to facilitate the student's transition. For some students, the social networks were sports teams, music groups (i.e., choir or band), or drill or dance teams. For a few of our subjects, the families were involved in religious communities that functioned to provide a network of peers within the school that promoted school participation. We found that parents who did not nest their teen in a positive peer network within high school ran the risk of their child acquiring undesirable friends.

For example, Adam's mother created a niche for her son in high school by pressuring him to participate in a competitive swimming league in middle school. This experience qualified Adam for a position on the high school team, where he became nested in a network of older students who were very serious about their grades and their athletic performance. This network of swimmers became his friendship network as well, providing him with male and female friends whose parents were all in communication with one another.

In contrast, Fran's parents had relied on the school and the neighborhood to provide Fran with girlfriends. During middle school, this arrangement had worked. But when Fran went to high school, she had the opportunity to interact with many new students, and she gravitated to kids with problems. This tendency might have been caused by her own set of negative experiences, leading her to feel sympathy for kids with problems. Fran's parents knew what was happening, but they did not attempt to create a different social

network for her, something that other parents in our sample did. Instead, they tried to talk her into backing off her commitment to some of these students rather than providing her with alternative social networks. Fran's involvement with students who were skipping school, or had stopped attending school, did not help her keep up with her studies and distracted her from the everyday life of the school.

By nesting the teen in a social network supported by or at least compatible with the school, parents retained control of their teen's social life. They also acquired a network of adults who helped the parents monitor their teen. The other parents within a network coordinated social schedules and set expectations about curfews so that the teens within a network shared similar limits.

Finally, another type of parent involvement we found in our sample concerned the parents' direct participation in the life of the high school. Students who made the transition successfully were more likely to have parents who came to the school from time to time to participate in an activity designed for parents. Steinberg (1996) has speculated that the presence of parents in the school signals to teachers and other school personnel that the parents value the education of their children. The presence of parents on campus encourages teachers to direct information about opportunities to the student and his or her parents, increasing the likelihood that the freshman becomes involved in special classes and school activities.

Direct participation in the school provided the parents with additional sources of information about their children. It provided parents with comparable children to observe other teens whose behavior they could use to evaluate the behavior of their own child. How much homework did these other teens have? What kind of grades were they getting? Who was skipping school? What were the signs of trouble?

Adam's mother was extremely active in the school. She was in frequent communication with administration, teachers, and coaches. Fran's mother had been more active in her middle school, but the series of family crises and her full-time job forced her to pull out of participation in high school activities.

It is worth noting that the parental involvement of Adam's parents had instilled in him a strong work ethic. Their "marathon hounding" at home, coupled with a peer group that valued school success, motivated him to work hard in school and sports. Fran's parents understood that they had failed to instill in Fran a strong work ethic. They even understood what they could have done to instill such a work ethic in Fran. Yet, the burden of setting expectations and enforcing limits was more than they could bear. Their inability to involve themselves in her day-to-day life, coupled with their inability to nest her in a peer group that promoted school achievement, led to Fran's failure to pass three courses. Nonetheless, it is likely that Fran's school

825 failure would have been worse if her parents had not been as emotionally supportive as they were.

Although it is easy to blame Fran's parents for their lack of involvement, this may not be fair. Fran's family had suffered from a series of serious problems, and it is
830 likely that these setbacks had stressed the parents to such an extent that they could no longer respond effectively. Research suggests that experiencing repeated stress over long periods of time reduces the capacity of individuals to respond to challenges
835 (Folkman, Lazarus, Dunkel-Schetter, DeLongis, & Gruen, 1986). Future research should be aimed at determining what causes some parents to be more skilled at evaluating school-related information than others and what can be done in schools and
840 communities for students like Fran, who are subject to stress and whose parents are not able to involve themselves sufficiently in their high school experiences.

References

Baker, D., & Stevenson, D. (1986). Mothers' strategies for school achievement: Managing the transition to high school. *Sociology of Education, 59*, 156–167.

Brown, B. B., Mounts, N., Lamborn, S. D., & Steinberg, L. (1993). Parenting practices and peer group affiliation in adolescence. *Child Development, 64*, 467–482.

Cooper, H. M., Lindsay, J. J., Nye, B., & Greathouse, S. (1998). Relationships among attitudes toward homework, amount of homework assigned and completed, and student achievement. *Journal of Educational Psychology, 90*, 70–84.

Dornbusch, S. M., Ritter, P. L., Leiderman, P. H., Roberts, D. F., & Fraleigh, M. J. (1987). The relation of parenting style to adolescent school performance. *Child Development, 58*, 1244–1257.

Epstein, J. L. (1987). Parent involvement: What research says to administrators. *Education and Urban Society, 19*, 119–136.

Fletcher, A. C., Darling, N. E., Steinberg, L., & Dornbusch, S. M. (1995). The company they keep: Relation of adolescents' adjustment and behavior to their friends' perceptions of authoritative parenting in the social network. *Developmental Psychology, 31*, 300–310.

Folkman, S., Lazarus, R. S., Dunkey-Schetter, C., DeLongis, A., & Gruen, R. J. (1986). Dynamics of a stressful encounter: Cognitive appraisal, coping, and encounter outcomes. *Journal of Personality and Social Psychology, 50*, 992–1003.

Grolnick, W. S., & Slowiaczek, M. L. (1994). Parents' involvement in children's schooling: A multidimensional conceptualization and motivational model. *Child Development, 65*, 237–252.

Harris, J. R. (1995). Where is the child's environment? A group socialization theory of development. *Psychological Review, 102*, 458–490.

Harris, J. R. (1998). *The nurture assumption: Why children turn out the way they do.* New York: Free Press.

Muller, C. (1993). Parent involvement and academic achievement. In B.S. & J.S. Coleman (Eds.), *Parents, their children, and schools* (pp. 77–113). Boulder, CO: Westview.

Muller, C. (1995). Maternal employment, parent involvement, and mathematics achievement among adolescents. *Journal of Marriage and the Family, 57*, 85–100.

National Center for Education Statistics. (1992). *National Educational Longitudinal Study of 1988 first follow-up: Data file user's manual* (NCES 92-030). Washington, DC: U.S. Department of Education.

Parsons, T. (1942). Age and sex in the social structure of the United States. *American Sociological Review, 7*, 604–616.

Riesman, D. (1961). *The lonely crowd.* New Haven, CT: Yale University Press.

Romo, H. D., & Falbo, T. (1996). *Latino high school graduation: Defying the odds.* Austin: University of Texas Press.

Schiller, K.S. (1999). Effects of feed patterns on students' transition to high school. *Sociology of Education, 72*, 216–233.

Steinberg, L. (1996). *Beyond the classroom: Why school reform has failed and what parents need to do.* New York: Simon & Schuster.

Sui-Chi, E. H., & Willms, J. D. (1996). Effects of parental involvement on eighth-grade achievement. *Sociology of Education, 69*, 126–141.

About the authors: Toni Falbo is a professor of educational psychology and sociology at the University of Texas at Austin. For over 25 years, she has studied the influence of family characteristics on children's outcomes. In 1996 she co-authored *Latino High School Graduation*, a longitudinal and qualitative study of "at risk" Latino youth. She is continuing her research on the relations between families, high school experiences, and health and educational outcomes. Laura Lein is a professor in the Department of Anthropology and the School of Social Work at the University of Texas at Austin. Her research has concentrated on the study of low-income families and the institutions that serve them. In 1997 she co-authored *Making Ends Meet*, a study of the strategies used by low-income, single-parent mothers. Nicole A. Amador is an educational psychologist and consultant at The California Commission on Teacher Credentialing. She has studied the effects of different parenting styles on adolescent personality and social behavioral outcomes as well as student achievement and retention. Her current research is in teaching and learning.

Acknowledgments: We wish to thank the Hogg Foundation for Mental Health for support of this project.

Address correspondence to: Toni Falbo, Department of Educational Psychology, University of Texas at Austin, Austin, TX 78712. E-mail: toni@prc.utexas.edu

Exercise for Article 7

Factual Questions

1. The researchers state that "the purpose of this study" was what?

2. The researchers were unable to obtain ninth-grade information for how many of the original 26 participants?

3. Were the open-ended questions posed to the students very different from those posed to the parents?

4. The interview instrument for ninth graders consisted of how many questions?

5. The researchers used how many indices of transition success?

6. Adam's father held what educational degree?

7. Did Adam's mother *or* did Fran's mother describe herself as a very hands-on parent?

Questions for Discussion

8. The outcome measures of transition success were quantitative, while the parental involvement variables are described qualitatively (i.e., narrative describing themes and trends illustrated with case studies). Do you consider this study to be primarily quantitative *or* primarily qualitative? Explain.

9. Of the families that volunteered to participate, a

random sample was drawn. Is this an ideal procedure for obtaining participants? Explain. (See lines 134–137.)

10. Most of the parent interviews involved only one parent—all of them mothers. Does this affect your interpretation of the results? Explain. (See lines 143–145.)

11. Based on the information in Table 1, are the parents of Adam and Fran reasonably similar in terms of their backgrounds (i.e., demographics)? Is it important that they be similar? Explain.

12. Of the quotations that are presented to illustrate the two case studies, which one(s), if any, are the most interesting? The most surprising? The most revealing? Explain.

13. Do you agree with the researchers' suggestion for future research that they state at the end of the article? Explain. (See lines 836–843.)

Quality Ratings

Directions: Indicate your level of agreement with each of the following statements by circling a number from 5 for strongly agree (SA) to 1 for strongly disagree (SD). If you believe an item is not applicable to this research article, leave it blank. Be prepared to explain your ratings.

A. The introduction establishes the importance of the study.

    SA   5   4   3   2   1   SD

B. The literature review establishes the context for the study.

    SA   5   4   3   2   1   SD

C. The research purpose, question, or hypothesis is clearly stated.

    SA   5   4   3   2   1   SD

D. The method of sampling is sound.

    SA   5   4   3   2   1   SD

E. Relevant demographics (for example, age, gender, and ethnicity) are described.

    SA   5   4   3   2   1   SD

F. Measurement procedures are adequate.

    SA   5   4   3   2   1   SD

G. All procedures have been described in sufficient detail to permit a replication of the study.

    SA   5   4   3   2   1   SD

H. The participants have been adequately protected from potential harm.

    SA   5   4   3   2   1   SD

I. The results are clearly described.

    SA   5   4   3   2   1   SD

J. The discussion/conclusion is appropriate.

    SA   5   4   3   2   1   SD

K. Despite any flaws, the report is worthy of publication.

    SA   5   4   3   2   1   SD

Article 8

Gender Stereotyping and Intended Audience Age: An Analysis of Children's Educational/Informational TV Programming

Mark R. Barner
Niagara University

ABSTRACT. This study examined sex-role stereotyping within FCC-mandated children's educational programming. A content analysis compared stereotyping across program age ranges and revealed that programs intended for young children present a more traditional view of sex roles than programs intended for teens. Male characters in old programs were stereotyped to a lesser extent than their young program counterparts, while female characters remained equally stereotyped across age ranges. These results suggest that children are being exposed to consistently gender stereotyped television role models at precisely the age when they are forming their own sex-role identities.

From *Communication Research Reports*, 16, 193–202. Copyright © 1999 by Eastern Communication Association. Reprinted with permission.

While there has been a great deal of research examining gender stereotyping in children's television, very little has compared the levels of such stereotyping across programs with different intended audience ages.
5 The age of children viewers not only determines what and how much they understand, but also what they seek out in order to better understand themselves and the world around them. Most child development theorists suggest that children develop their sex roles at
10 different stages throughout childhood. What then are the different messages concerning sex-roles that are presented in television programs designed for different-aged children viewers? This study attempted to answer that question by examining gender stereotyping in a
15 new category of children's television: FCC-mandated educational/informational (E/I) programming. This category consists of a designated three-hour group of shows that every broadcast station must air weekly in order to qualify for license renewal from the FCC. E/I
20 programming represents the culmination of a nearly four-decade-long debate among the government, broadcasters, the FCC, and community groups to establish definable educational programming. A major step in this debate occurred in 1990 when Congress enacted
25 the Children's Television Act, part of which was to

both define and recommend the airing of educational programming for children. While these goals were considered a step in the right direction by children's television activists, there remained loopholes in exactly what
30 was meant by "educational" and how many hours of programming broadcasters were responsible for airing. In an effort to clear up these ambiguities, the FCC adopted in August 1996 a proposal from the Clinton Administration and the National Association of Broad-
35 casters that further defined educational programming and mandated a three-hour programming standard required for broadcasters to renew their FCC licenses.

The 1996 regulations kept the FCC's 1990 definition of educational programming (with a minor reword-
40 ing) as, "any television programming that furthers the educational and informational needs of children 16 years of age and under in any respect, including children's intellectual/cognitive and social/emotional needs" (FCC, 1996, para. 79). To notify viewers of the
45 categorization, E/I programs are identified as educational/informational in television program listings and carry a notice at the beginning of the show. While evaluation of stations' compliance with the new regulations did not begin until September 1, 1997, broad-
50 casters were required to begin identifying their core educational programs on January 2, 1997.

E/I programming presents an ideal way to examine the question of age-related gender stereotyping for two reasons: First, in addressing children's "social/emo-
55 tional needs," it attempts to teach lessons about many social attributes—not the least of which is gender. Second, because it is neatly separated into two audience age brackets (roughly 6–11 and 12–16), E/I programming offers an ideal way to study gender representation
60 across intended audience age. Before using these two characteristics of E/I programming to explore age-related gender stereotyping, a brief review of relevant child development and gender stereotyping literature is presented.
65 Child development theorists have suggested that one of the primary ways that children learn sex-role-related behavior is through observational learning from

models (Kohlberg, 1966; Mischel, 1966) and that a primary source for such models is television (Bandura, 1967, 1977, 1986; Huesman, Lagerspetz, & Eron, 1984). More specifically, studies have found that children attend to and imitate same-sex models more than opposite-sex models (Grusec & Brinker, 1972; Hoffner, 1996; Slaby & Frey, 1975; Sprafkin & Liebert, 1978), name same-sex characters as people they want to be like (Miller & Reeves, 1976), and select gender-typed toys when they have seen them modeled on television by same-sex children (Ruble, Balaban, & Cooper, 1981). Given the potential impact that television characters play in the sex-role development of children, it is important to examine how these characters are presented in terms of gender stereotyping.

Despite slight improvements over the past several decades, television programming in general remains highly sex-role stereotyped. Women are consistently underrepresented, given a narrower set of roles to play, and presented in more unimportant and limited ways (Signorielli, 1989). This picture holds true for children's educational programming as well (Barner, 1998; Cantor, 1977; De Vaney & Elenes, 1991; Dohrman, 1975; Jones, 1994).

Several studies (Beuf, 1974; McGhee & Frueh, 1980; Williams, 1986) have suggested that exposure to consistently gender-stereotyped images has an influence on children's sex-role acquisition; however, they do not address the influence of the child's age on this development. Research into children's developmental stages suggests that age is an important factor in the appropriate consciousness of gender stereotypes; they also become more open to variations and exceptions to them. They begin to learn that stereotypes are arbitrary social definitions, not fixed universal rules.

Based on the above information, two questions arise: First, does the gender stereotyping in children's educational television mirror the age-related sex-role development of the children who watch it? Second, what impact might such a separation have on children's development of sex-roles? To address these questions, the following hypothesis is presented.

Hypothesis

The proposed hypothesis is based on the information presented above, which suggests that young children are more open to and even seek out gender-stereotyped information, while older children are more flexible in their beliefs. It would logically follow that children's television programming would mirror this difference with programs for younger children being more highly stereotyped than those for older children and teens. Based on this information, the hypothesis states:

H1: Characters in E/I programs intended for young children (in the 6–11 age range) will be more gender-stereotyped than characters in programs intended for teens.

Specifically, it is hypothesized that males and females in child-oriented programs will exhibit traditional stereotypical social behaviors (as defined by previous research) at a greater rate than those in teen-oriented programs.

Method

Content analysis was used to compare recurrent patterns in characters' gender-related social behaviors in different age categories of E/I programming.

Sample

A sample of programs airing in summer 1997 was selected from the mandatory three-hour educational core from five broadcast networks airing in the Metropolitan Buffalo, New York, market. In its quarterly report to the FCC, each station must specify those programs that make up the required three-hour educational core. Because individual stations have control over what shows they select as E/I, educational core programming may vary from affiliate to affiliate. However, all the shows in this sample were either network programs or available nationally through syndication. Therefore, these same programs are labeled as educational by many network affiliates across the nation.

Given the objectives of the study, only those programs that featured narrative story lines and included social interaction as a vital plot element were analyzed. Taking this into consideration, eleven programs remained from the original 23 E/I programs. Three consecutive weeks of these programs were analyzed, resulting in 33 episodes. The specific programs making up the sample were: *Saved by the Bell–The New Class, Hang Time, California Dreams, Sweet Valley High, Bailey Kipper's P. O. V., C-Bear and Jamal, Bobby's World, The New Adventures of Doug, The New Captain Planet, Life with Louie,* and *Ghostwriter.*

Coding

Each program was analyzed at the level of the individual scene (defined as a sequence of related shots in which there was no change in location or break in continuity of time). Specifically, for each scene, each foreground character (defined as a character whose speech or action served an important plot function) was coded for their gender, social behaviors, and whether they appeared in a "child-oriented" or "teen-oriented" program. Child-oriented shows were those with an intended age range of 6 to 11 (as specified by the broadcast station in each program's FCC-required quarterly report). Teen-oriented shows were those with an intended age range of 12 to 16. Of the eleven programs in the study, 7 were child-oriented, 4 were teen-oriented.

Eight categories of social behavior (adapted from Sternglanz & Serbin, 1974) were scored. These were:

Construction: To plan and carry out one's own plans. To build, to overcome an obstacle.

Table 1
Aggregated Social Behaviors Compared Across Gender

| | Mean Behaviors per Scene | | | | |
	Males	Females	t value	p	df
Behavior in Child-Oriented Shows					
Stereotypic Male Behavior	1.4	.8	4.1	<.001	98
Stereotypic Female Behavior	.4	1.0	5.1	<.001	98
Behavior in Teen-Oriented Shows					
Stereotypic Male Behavior	1.0	.6	2.7	<.01	59
Stereotypic Female Behavior	.5	.9	5.1	Not Significant	59

Dominance: To influence or control others. To persuade, prohibit, dictate. To lead, direct, restrain. To organize the behavior of a group.

Aggression: To assault or injure purposely. To harm,
180 blame, ridicule, threat, use sarcasm.

Autonomy: To resist influence or coercion. To defy an authority or seek freedom. To strive for independence.

Deference: To follow directions or example (imitate) of leader. To admire or compliment.

185 *Harm Avoidance*: Tendency to avoid physical pain. To withdraw or flee from injury. Includes "startle" or "fear" reactions.

Dependence: To seek aid, protection, sympathy, or information to carry out a project. To cry for help. To
190 be dependent.

Nurturance: To nourish, aid, or protect another. To express sympathy.

Each behavior was categorized as "male" or "female" using Bakan's (1966) dualistic view of mascu-
195 line and feminine stereotyping. Bakan suggested that personality attributes can be clustered into two dimensions using the concepts of agency and communion. Agency is directed toward the self and includes those traits that emphasize accomplishment, achievement,
200 and assertiveness, while communion is directed toward others and includes traits that emphasize sensitivity and a desire to get along with others. Bakan associated agency with male-stereotyped behavior and communion with female-stereotyped behavior.

205 Studies of popular conceptions of gender stereotyping reveal that the agency/communion dichotomy is widely held and relatively consistent. In separate studies conducted 15 years apart, Rosenkrantz, Vogel, Bee, Broverman, and Broverman (1968) and Ruble (1983)
210 found that college students consistently identified agency-related characteristics with men and communion-related characteristics with women. Williams and Best (1982) found similar findings in a cross-cultural study on respondents from 30 nations.

215 Using the consistency of these findings as a guide for gender stereotyping, the above behaviors were categorized as either male stereotypical or female stereotypical. Therefore, construction, dominance, ag-

gression, and autonomy were aggregated under the
220 concept of agency and were labeled "male" behaviors, while deference, harm avoidance, dependence, and nurturance were aggregated under the concept of communion and were labeled "female" behaviors.

Two trained coders coded the programs. Eight ran-
225 domly chosen episodes were used to determine a measure of intercoder reliability. On the behavior variables for each character in the sub-sample, intercoder agreement ranged from 92% to 95%.

Results

To reveal differences in stereotyping of males and
230 females, their social behaviors (calculated as average behaviors per scene [bps]) were compared in two different ways: across gender for both child-oriented and teen-oriented shows, and across program age range for both males and females.

235 In the child-oriented shows, both males and females exhibited significantly more stereotypic behavior than the other gender. On average, males exhibited almost twice as many "male" behaviors as females, and females exhibited more than twice as many "female"
240 behaviors as males. In the teen-oriented shows, females exhibited significantly more "female" behaviors than males; however, males did not exhibit significantly more "male" behaviors than females.

Among female characters, there was no significant
245 difference between child-oriented and teen-oriented shows. Females in both age categories exhibited female stereotypic behaviors at roughly the same rate. Among male characters, however, those in child-oriented shows exhibited significantly more male stereotypic
250 behavior than those in teen-oriented shows.

Results of the comparisons of social behavior across both gender and program age range suggest that males are the only characters to escape gender stereotyping, and then only in the teen-oriented shows. Males
255 in child-oriented shows and females in all shows remain stereotyped in their social behaviors.

Individual Social Behaviors Compared Across Program Age Range

To add detail regarding the differences between

Table 2
Aggregated Social Behaviors Compared Across Show Age

| | Mean Behaviors Per Scene | | | | |
	Child-Oriented Shows	Teen-Oriented Shows	t value	p	df
Male Characters					
Stereotypic Male Behavior	1.4	1.0	2.2	<.05	93
Stereotypic Female Behavior	.4	.5	1.4	Not Significant	93
Female Characters					
Stereotypic Male Behavior	.8	.6	.9	Not Significant	64
Stereotypic Female Behavior	1.0	.9	.6	Not Significant	64

males and females across child-oriented and teen-oriented shows, individual social behaviors were also compared. To do this, each character's rate of a given behavior was expressed as a percentage derived from the following formula:

$$\frac{\text{number of occurrences of a given behavior for character "X"}}{\text{total number of all character "X's" behaviors}} \times 100$$

There was no significant difference between child-oriented and teen-oriented program females on any of the social behaviors. Among males, however, there were several significant differences. Males in teen-oriented shows were more likely to exhibit deference and less likely to exhibit construction, aggression, and harm avoidance than males in child-oriented shows.

Discussion

The analysis of gender-related behaviors yielded different results for males and females. Using the aggregated "male" and "female" behaviors as a measure of gender stereotyping, it was found that both genders were stereotyped in both child-oriented and teen-oriented programs; however, males in teen-oriented programs were stereotyped to a lesser extent than their child-oriented program counterparts. Child-oriented program males exhibited significantly more "male" behavior than those in teen-oriented programs. Among female characters, however, there was no significant difference between child-oriented and teen-oriented programs. Females in both age-range shows exhibited female stereotypic behavior at roughly the same rate.

These results partially support the proposed hypothesis, which suggested that E/I programs intended for young children would be more gender stereotyped than programs intended for teens. This hypothesis was supported for the male characters but was not supported for female characters who remained stereotyped equally in child-oriented and teen-oriented programs.

Analysis of individual behaviors revealed a more detailed picture of how males in teen-oriented programs differed from males in child-oriented programs: Males in teen-oriented programs exhibited less construction and aggression (two stereotypical male behaviors) and more deference (a stereotypical female behavior). These differences suggest that male characters in the teen-oriented programs were able to break out of the traditional male stereotype to a certain extent. They became less traditional in terms of gender stereotyping. Males in teen-oriented programs also exhibited less of one stereotypic female behavior—harm avoidance, an attribute that would initially appear to make them more traditional in terms of gender stereotyping. An explanation for this apparent exception to the above findings may lie in an examination of the structures and plots of the programs themselves.

Most of the child-oriented programs featured a single male central character—typically, a young boy of elementary school age. The plots of the shows tended to focus on the experiences of these boys in and around their schools. Typical plots dealt with run-ins with school bullies, parents, and teachers—all confrontational situations in which characters were placed in positions of "harm" (as defined in this study). On the other hand, teen-oriented programs, set primarily in high schools and featuring ensemble casts of males and females, dealt primarily with romance and relationship problems. There were fewer situations in which characters were placed in "harm" in these programs. It only makes sense, then, that males in the teen-oriented shows exhibited less harm avoidance simply because they had less of an opportunity or need to avoid "harm."

The differences in plot lines, as noted above, also offer an explanation as to why males in teen-oriented programs exhibited significantly less "male" behavior. Because the stories of these programs dealt with romance and relationship issues, characters had to use cooperation to a greater extent in resolving plots. Female characters, who in child-oriented programs were already equipped with behaviors such as deference to others and nurturance toward others, could operate effectively in these types of stories. Males, on the other hand, who were equipped with attributes such as aggression, influencing others, and overcoming obstacles in child-oriented programs, were forced to change in

Table 3
Individual Male Social Behaviors Compared Across Show Age

Behaviors for Male Characters	Mean Rate (%) of Behavior In Child-Oriented Shows	In Teen-Oriented Shows	t value	p
Construction	21.0	9.7	4.6	<.001
Dominance	25.0	33.9	1.7	Not Significant
Aggression	21.8	15.0	2.2	<.05
Deference	9.1	20.8	2.8	<.01
Autonomy	6.5	3.6	1.6	Not Significant
Harm Avoidance	6.2	3.1	2.0	<.05
Succorance	4.5	8.4	1.5	Not Significant
Nurturance	5.9	5.5	0.2	Not Significant

Note. df = 93

order to become effective elements in the teen-oriented program plots. Males in teen-oriented programs were forced to exhibit more "female" and less "male" behaviors in order to function and take part in the resolution of these plots, whereas females could retain their traditional social behavior patterns.

Considering this difference from a television producer's standpoint, it makes sense, then, to allow male characters to break from traditional stereotyping while keeping females locked in to their more traditional roles. Such an arrangement works well in the types of plots typically offered in teenage programs. However, taken from a child development viewpoint, this difference is quite alarming. As discussed in the first half of this paper, child development theorists suggest that children first become aware of their own gender at an early age and develop their sex-roles throughout early childhood. This time period corresponds to the intended age range of the child-oriented E/I programs. Given the potential importance that television role models play in children's sex-role development, it is alarming that children are consistently exposed to highly gender-stereotyped television characters at arguably the most important point in their own sex-role development. It is at this young age when children are learning what is socially accepted of and expected from them as girls and boys, and the television characters they watch are certainly very powerful role models for these attributes.

While teenage males are given slightly less stereotyped role models in the teen-oriented E/I programs, teenage girls are stuck with the same old thing. They are consistently presented with the same gender-stereotyped female characters who were present in the shows they watched as young children. They also witness a gender inequity between how males and females are allowed to act. As the male characters "grow up" from child-oriented to teen-oriented programs, they become more fully developed and are given more latitude in their social behaviors. Female characters, on the other hand, remain equally stereotyped, regardless of the age range of the intended audience.

It was not the goal of this study to question whether E/I programs are educational; the goal was to suggest that they are, in fact, more educational than we realize. Children learn many more lessons from television than are proposed in an educational program's written objectives. Unfortunately, one of these lessons is a reinforcement of conventional gender stereotypes. Even more unfortunate is the fact that this message seems to be strongest at precisely the time in a child's life when he or she is actively seeking sex-role information and forming attitudes that may influence behavior later in life.

While gender stereotyping is very complex and there are many ways that it is presented through television messages, this study examined only one: gender-related social behavior. While it may seem to present a limited window for examining such a diverse issue, the study of characters' behavior in relation to one another presents a unique opportunity. Gender stereotyping at this level is very subtle. As opposed to obvious character traits such as occupation, family role, and physical appearance, social behaviors occur very inconspicuously. The majority of viewers, whether children or not, probably do not take notice of them. This kind of latent information could be the most harmful because it is impossible to be critical of that which we do not consciously notice. It is hoped that results from this study will make clear the importance of examining television programming at a very subtle level, and will emphasize the point that often the most inconspicuous and seemingly unimportant information can convey very powerful messages. It is also hoped that this study will encourage parents to take an active role in examining the programming that they allow and encourage their children to watch, regardless of how it is labeled.

References

Bakan, D. (1966). *The duality of human existence*. Chicago: Rand McNally.
Bandura, A. (1967). The role of modeling processes in personality development. In W. W. Hartup & N. L. Smothergill (Eds.), *The young child: Re-*

views of research (pp. 42–58). Washington, DC: National Association for the Education of Young Children.

Bandura, A. (1977). *Social learning theory.* Englewood Cliffs, NJ: Prentice-Hall.

Bandura, A. (1986). *Social foundations of thought and action: A social cognitive theory.* Englewood Cliffs, NJ: Prentice-Hall.

Barner, M. R. (1998). *Sex-role stereotyping in FCC-approved children's educational television.* Paper presented at the Broadcast Education Association Convention, Las Vegas, NV.

Berk, L. E. (1994). *Child development,* 3rd ed. Boston: Allyn and Bacon.

Beuf, A. (1974). Doctor, lawyer, household drudge. *Journal of Communication, 24,*142–145.

Cantor, M. G. (1977). Women and public broadcasting. *Journal of Communication, 27,* 14–19.

Carter, D. B., & Patterson, C. J. (1982). Sex roles as social conventions: The development of children's conceptions of sex role stereotypes. *Developmental Psychology, 18,* 812–824.

De Vaney, A., & Elenes, A. (1991). Square One Television and gender. *Proceedings of Selected Research Presentations at the Annual Convention of the Association for Educational Communications and Technology,* IR 015 132.

Dohrman, R. (1974). A gender profile of children's educational TV. *Journal of Communication, 25*(4), 56–65

Federal Communications Commission. (1996). *Policies and rules concerning children's television programming report and order.* [On-line]. Available: http://www.fcc.gov/Bureaus/Mass_Media/Orders/fcc96335.txt.

Grusec, J. F., & Brinker, D. B., (1972). Reinforcement for imitation as a social learning determinant with implications for sex-role development. *Journal of Social Psychology, 21,* 149–158.

Hoffner, C. (1996). Children's wishful identification and parasocial interaction with favorite television characters. *Journal of Broadcasting and Electronic Media, 40*(3), 389–402.

Huesman. L. R., Lagerspetz, K., & Eron, L. D. (1984). Intervening variables in the TV violence-aggression relation: Evidence from two countries. *Developmental Psychology, 20,* 746–775.

Jones, R. W. (1994). *Ratio of female:male characters and stereotyping in educational programming.* Paper presented at the Annual Meeting of the American Psychological Association, Los Angeles, CA.

Kohlberg, L. (1966). A cognitive-developmental analysis of children's sex-role concepts and attitudes. In E. E. Maccoby (Ed.), *The development of sex-differences* (pp. 82–173). Palo Alto, CA: Stanford University Press.

Levin, D. E., & Carlsson-Paige, N. (1994). Developmentally appropriate television: Putting children first. *Young Children, 49,* 38–44.

Masters, J. C., & Wilkinson, A. (1976). Consensual and discriminative stereotypes of sex-type judgments by parents and children. *Child Development, 47,* 208–217.

McGhee, P. E., & Frueh, T. (1980). Television viewing and the learning of sex-role stereotypes. *Sex Roles, 6,* 179–188.

Miller, M. M., & Reeves, B. (1976). Dramatic TV content and children's sex-role stereotypes. *Journal of Broadcasting, 20,* 35–50.

Mischel, W. (1966). A social learning view of sex differences in behavior. In E. E. Maccoby (Ed.), *The development of sex differences* (pp. 56–81). Palo Alto, CA: Stanford University Press.

Rosenkrantz, P., Vogel, S., Bee, H., Broverman, I., & Broverman, D. (1968). Sex-role stereotypes and self-concepts in college students. *Journal of Consulting and Clinical Psychology, 32,* 287–295.

Ruble, D.N., Balaban, T., & Cooper, J. (1981). Gender constancy and the effects of sex-typed television toy commercials. *Child Development, 52,* 667–673.

Ruble, T.L. (1983). Sex stereotypes: Issues of change in the 1970s. *Sex Roles, 9,* 397–402.

Serbin, L.A., Powlishta, K. K., & Gulko, J. (1993). The development of sex typing in middle childhood. *Monographs of the Society for Research in Child Development, 58* (2, Serial No. 232).

Serbin, L.A., & Sprafkin, C. (1986). The salience of gender and the process of sex-typing in three- to seven-year-old children. *Child Development, 57,* 1188–1199.

Signorielli, N. (1989). Television and conceptions about sex roles: Maintaining conventionality and the status quo. *Sex Roles, 21,* 341–360

Address correspondence to: Mark R. Barner, Ph.D., Department of Communication Studies, Niagara University, NY 14109.

study? Note that the researcher identifies it as "H1," which stands for "hypothesis 1."

2. After eliminating programs that did not have narrative story lines nor include social interaction as a vital plot element, how many of the 23 E/I programs remained in the study?

3. Coding was done at the level of the individual scene. How was "individual scene" defined for this study?

4. Was "deference" labeled as a male behavior *or* as a female behavior?

5. For behavior in child-oriented shows, what was the mean (average) number of stereotypic male behaviors exhibited by the male characters? (Hint: The answer is in one of the three tables.)

6. In child-oriented shows, the percentage of behavior that exhibited aggression for males was 21.8%. Is this higher or lower than the corresponding percentage in teen-oriented shows? Explain.

7. Is the difference referred to in question 6 statistically significant? If yes, at what probability level?

Questions for Discussion

8. Before reading this article, would you have hypothesized that programs intended for young children are more gender stereotyped than those for teens? Explain.

9. This study is based on an analysis of 33 episodes from 11 programs. In your opinion, is this an adequate number in order to test the hypothesis? Explain.

10. The coding in this study was based on a "dualistic" view of masculine and feminine stereotyping. In your opinion, was this reasonable? Explain. (See lines 193–214.)

11. How important is the information on intercoder agreement presented in lines 224–228? How credible would the study be without this information?

Exercise for Article 8

Factual Questions

1. What is the explicitly stated hypothesis for this

Quality Ratings

Directions: Indicate your level of agreement with each of the following statements by circling a number from 5 for strongly agree (SA) to 1 for strongly disagree (SD). If you believe an item is not applicable to this research article, leave it blank. Be prepared to explain your ratings.

A. The introduction establishes the importance of the study.

SA   5   4   3   2   1   SD

B. The literature review establishes the context for the study.

SA   5   4   3   2   1   SD

C. The research purpose, question, or hypothesis is clearly stated.

SA   5   4   3   2   1   SD

D. The method of sampling is sound.

SA   5   4   3   2   1   SD

E. Relevant demographics (for example, age, gender, and ethnicity) are described.

SA   5   4   3   2   1   SD

F. Measurement procedures are adequate.

SA   5   4   3   2   1   SD

G. All procedures have been described in sufficient detail to permit a replication of the study.

SA   5   4   3   2   1   SD

H. The participants have been adequately protected from potential harm.

SA   5   4   3   2   1   SD

I. The results are clearly described.

SA   5   4   3   2   1   SD

J. The discussion/conclusion is appropriate.

SA   5   4   3   2   1   SD

K. Despite any flaws, the report is worthy of publication.

SA   5   4   3   2   1   SD

Article 9

Poverty As We Know It:
Media Portrayals of the Poor

Rosalee A. Clawson
Purdue University

Rakuya Trice
Indiana University

Introduction

On the campaign trail during the 1992 presidential election, Bill Clinton's stump speech included a pledge to "end welfare as we know it" to the delight of most audiences. Two years later during the 1994 congres-
5 sional election, one of the most popular planks of the Republicans' Contract with America was the "Personal Responsibility Act," which called for a major overhaul of the welfare system. The election of this Republican Congress initiated a great deal of legislative activity and
10 presidential maneuvering on the issue of welfare reform. The culmination of those efforts occurred in August of 1996 when President Clinton signed into law sweeping welfare reform legislation. By ending the federal guarantee of support for the poor and turning
15 control of welfare programs over to the states, this legislation reversed 6 decades of social policy and begot a new era of welfare politics. Throughout this period of intense political activity, the media focused a significant amount of attention on poverty and welfare reform.
20 In this research, we analyze media portrayals of the poor during this time when welfare reform was high on the nation's agenda. We investigate whether the media perpetuate inaccurate and stereotypical images of the poor. Specifically, we examine the photographs that
25 accompany stories on poverty in five U.S. news magazines between January 1, 1993, and December 31, 1998.

Portrayals of the Poor

In a study of news magazines between 1988 and 1992, Gilens (1996a) investigated the accuracy of the
30 media in their portrayals of the poor. Gilens (1996a) found that poverty was disproportionately portrayed as a "black" problem. Blacks make up less than one-third of the poor, but the media would lead citizens to believe that two out of every three poor people are black.
35 Moreover, Gilens (1996a) found that the "deserving" poor, especially the black deserving poor, were underrepresented in news magazines. For example, the black

elderly poor and black working poor were rarely portrayed. In addition, Gilens examined media depictions
40 of the poor between 1950 and 1992 and found that blacks were "comparatively absent from media coverage of poverty during times of heightened sympathy for the poor" (1999, p. 132). In this research, we pick up where Gilens left off by analyzing media portrayals of
45 the demographics of poverty between 1993 and 1998.

In addition, we extend Gilens's work by investigating whether common stereotypical traits or behaviors associated with the poor are portrayed in the media. In our society, citizens believe poor people have many
50 undesirable qualities that violate mainstream American ideals. For example, many citizens say people are poor due to their own "lack of effort" and "loose morals and drunkenness" (Kluegel and Smith, 1986, p. 79). A majority of Americans believe that "most people who re-
55 ceive welfare benefits are taking advantage of the system" (Ladd 1993, p. 86). Another piece of conventional wisdom is that poor mothers on public assistance have additional babies to receive greater welfare benefits. People also believe that poor families are much
60 larger than middle-class families (Sidel, 1996).

Several media studies have found such stereotypical representations of poverty (Golding and Middleton, 1982; Martindale, 1996). The media often describe the underclass in behavioral terms as criminals, alcoholics,
65 and drug addicts, and the underclass is linked with pathological behavior in urban areas (Gans, 1995). Parisi's (1998) in-depth analysis of a *Washington Post* series on poverty demonstrated that the media perpetuate stereotypes of the poor as lazy, sexually irresponsi-
70 ble, and criminally deviant. Coughlin (1989) discussed the media's emphasis on "welfare queens" – a phrase that invokes images of poor women living the high life by defrauding and taking advantage of the welfare system. These studies focused on how the poor were de-
75 scribed in the text of news stories; in this study, we analyze whether stereotypical traits of the poor are presented in magazine photographs.

Why is it important to study the visual images surrounding the issue of poverty? The visual representa-
80 tion of a political issue is an integral part of the definition of that issue.[1] Visual images (along with

Table 1
Representations of Poverty by Magazine, 1993-98

	Business Week	Newsweek	New York Times Magazine	Time	U.S. News & World Report	Total
Number of Stories	18	13	8	13	22	74
Number of Pictures	21	24	18	30	56	149
Number of Poor People	40	64	35	78	140	357

metaphors, exemplars, and catch phrases) define and illustrate particular issue frames (Gamson and Lasch, 1983). For example, Nelson and Kinder (1996) demonstrate that visual frames have a significant impact on public attitudes toward affirmative action. People and events that appear in photographs accompanying news stories are not simply indicative of isolated individuals and occurrences; rather, the photographs are symbolic of "the whole mosaic" (Epstein, 1973, p. 5). The pictures provide texture, drama, and detail, and they illustrate the implicit, the latent, the "taken for granted," and the "goes without saying." Furthermore, scholars should pay attention to visual images because journalists and editors perceive them to be a central part of a news story. In his classic study of how journalists select stories, Gans argues that magazine "editors consider still pictures as important as text" (1979, p. 159).

Research Design

In this research, we test the hypothesis that the media portray poor people inaccurately and stereotypically. The data were collected by examining every story on the topics of poverty, welfare, and the poor between January 1, 1993, and December 31, 1998, in five news magazines: *Business Week, Newsweek, New York Times Magazine, Time,* and *U.S. News & World Report.*[2] We used the *Reader's Guide to Periodical Literature* to locate the stories and to identify other cross-referenced topics (e.g., income inequality). Seventy-four stories were identified as relevant for a total of 149 pictures of 357 poor people.[3] See Table 1 for the distribution of stories, pictures, and people by magazine.

The photographs were analyzed in two ways. First, we scrutinized each picture as a whole. For those pictures that included a mother with children, we noted the size and race of the family. Second, we examined the demographic characteristics of each poor individual in the pictures. For coding race, we departed from Gilens's coding procedure. Gilens (1996a, 1999) coded whether the poor person was black, nonblack, or undeterminable. In contrast, we used a more detailed classification scheme and coded whether the poor person was white, black, Hispanic, Asian American, or undeterminable.

We coded each person's gender (male or female), age (young: under 18; middle-aged: 18–64; or old: 65 and over), residence (urban or rural), and work status (working/job training or not working).[4] We also analyzed whether each individual was depicted in stereo-typical ways, such as pregnant, engaging in criminal behavior, taking or selling drugs, drinking alcohol, smoking cigarettes, or wearing expensive clothing or jewelry.[5] For many of our variables, we were able to compare the portrayal of poverty in news magazines to the reality of poverty as measured by the Current Population Survey (CPS) conducted by the U.S. Census Bureau or as reported by the U.S. House of Representatives Committee on Ways and Means.[6]

Research Findings

Many citizens greatly overestimate the number of black people among the poor (Gilens, 1996a). Do news magazines perpetuate and reinforce that belief? According to the 1996 CPS, African Americans make up 27 percent of the poor, but these five magazines would lead citizens to believe that blacks are 49 percent of the poor ($p < .001$; see Table 2). Whites, on the other hand, are depicted as 33 percent of the poor, when they really make up 45 percent of those in poverty ($p < .001$). There were no magazine portrayals of Asian Americans in poverty, and Hispanics were underrepresented by 5 percent.

This underrepresentation of poor Hispanics and Asian Americans may be part of a larger phenomenon in which these groups are ignored by the media in general. For example, Hispanics and Asian Americans are rarely found in mass media advertising (Bowen and Schmid, 1997; Wilkes and Valencia, 1989). Similarly, Dixon (1998) documented the invisibility of Hispanics in local news; however, there is evidence that in particular regions, Hispanics are represented in accordance with their proportion in the population (Greenberg and Brand, 1998; Turk et al., 1989). Unlike blacks, Asian Americans are associated with intelligence, not welfare dependency (Gilbert and Hixon, 1991; Gilens, 1999). Thus, their absence may reflect a positive stereotype, but a stereotype nonetheless. Clearly, these comments regarding Hispanics and Asian Americans are speculative. Further research is needed on media representations of these two groups.

Focusing on just the three magazines Gilens included in his study (i.e., *Newsweek, Time,* and *U.S. News & World Report*), whites make up 33 percent, blacks make up 45 percent, and Hispanics are 22 percent of the magazine poor (see Table 2). In comparison, Gilens (1996a) found that 62 percent of the poor were African American in these magazines between 1988 and 1992. Although at first glance our statistics may

Table 2

The Percent of True Poor and the Percent of Magazine Poor by Race, 1993-1998

	Whites	African Americans	Hispanics	Asian Americans
True Poor	45	27	24	4
Magazine Poor	33[***]	49[***]	19[*]	0[**]
Poor in *Newsweek*, *Time*, and *U.S. News & World Report*	33[***]	45[***]	22	0[**]

Source: "March Current Population Survey" (U.S. Bureau of the Census, 1996)

Note. We conducted difference of proportion tests in which the proportion observed in the magazine is compared to the true proportion as reported by the Current Population Survey for each racial category (Blalock, 1979). A statistically significant result indicates that the magazine portrayal of a particular racial group is not representative of the true poor. Due to rounding, the percentages may sum to more than 100 percent. The sample size is 347 for the analysis based on all five magazines. The sample size is 272 for the analysis based on *Newsweek*, *Time*, and *U.S. News & World Report*.

[*]$p < .05$.
[**]$p < .01$.
[***]$p < .001$.

suggest that the magazines have become less likely to put a black face on poverty, we hesitate to draw that conclusion given the coding difference mentioned earlier. Recall that Gilens coded whether the poor person was black, nonblack, or undeterminable. Since Gilens (1996a) reports a higher percentage of poor people for which race was not identified (12 percent compared to our 4 percent), it seems likely that many of the poor people we coded as Hispanic, Gilens would have coded as undeterminable. If we treat Hispanics in that fashion and therefore exclude them from our analysis, blacks make up 58 percent of the poor and whites make up 42 percent—figures that mirror Gilens's data quite closely. Regardless of the exact proportion, it is clear these news magazines continue to race code the issue of poverty.[7]

Table 3

The Percent of AFDC Parents and the Percent of Magazine Adult Poor by Race, 1993-1998

	Whites	African Americans	Hispanics	Native Americans, Asian Americans, and Other
AFDC parents	36	37	21	7
Magazine adult poor	34	48[**]	18	0[***]

Source: *Overview of Entitlement Programs* (U.S. House of Representatives, Committee on Ways and Means, 1998)

Note. N = 159.

[**]$p<.01$.
[***]$p<.001$.

Since we are examining portrayals of the poor during a period of intense debate over welfare reform, perhaps the racial characteristics of the magazine poor mirror welfare recipients more closely than they represent poor people in general. The House Ways and Means Committee provides the racial breakdown for

parents on Aid to Families with Dependent Children (AFDC). Therefore, in Table 3 we compare the racial composition of AFDC parents to the magazine portrayal of poor adults. Indeed, the portrayal of poor whites and Hispanics matches more closely the true racial characteristics of welfare recipients; however, blacks are still heavily overrepresented (48 percent) among the magazine poor. Moreover, blacks make up 52 percent of the poor adults who are portrayed in stories that focus specifically on welfare (rather than on poverty in general).

Gilens (1996a, 1999) found that blacks were even more prominent in stories on poverty topics that were not very popular with the public. Between 1993 and 1998, there were several stories on unpopular issues, such as welfare reform and pregnancy, public housing, and welfare and the cycle of dependency.[8] We examined the proportion of blacks among the poor in these stories and found that it jumped to 63 percent, whereas whites made up only 19 percent and Hispanics were 18 percent. In contrast, blacks were associated less often with sympathetic topics. In stories on welfare reform and children, welfare recipients and day care, and job training, 46 percent of the poor were black, while 32 percent were white and 22 percent were Hispanic.[9] We also analyzed two stories that focused on various "myths" surrounding welfare reform. Ironically, 16 of the 22 poor people depicted in these two stories were black.

The news magazines exaggerated the feminization of poverty by about 14 percent. According to the CPS, 62 percent of the adult poor are women, whereas 76 percent of the magazine poor are women ($N = 161$).[10] Again, though, since most of these stories discuss poverty specifically in the context of welfare reform, it is important to compare the magazine poor to people on welfare. The vast majority of adult AFDC recipients are female, so the predominance of women among the poor is fairly accurate (U.S. House of Representatives, Committee on Ways and Means, 1998).

In terms of the age of the poor people, we found that children were overrepresented among the magazine poor (see Table 4).[11] Children are usually thought of as a fairly deserving group of poor people (Cook and Barrett, 1992); however, the large proportion of black children among the magazine poor may undermine that belief. In Iyengar's (1990) experimental research on attributions of responsibility for poverty, subjects indicated that black children should take responsibility for their own plight, whereas white children were not expected to solve their own problems.

Table 4

The Percent of True Poor and the Percent of Magazine Poor by Age, 1993-1998

	Under 18	18-64	65 and Over
True Poor	40	51	9
Magazine Poor	53***	43**	4**

Source: "March Current Population Survey" (U.S. Bureau of the Census, 1996)

Note. N = 347.

**$p < .01$.

***$p < .001$.

In contrast, the elderly, who are the most sympathetic group of poor people, were rarely portrayed. Most people believe the elderly really need their benefits and that they use them wisely (Cook and Barrett, 1992). Iyengar (1990) found that people thought society should aid (both black and white) poor elderly widows. This sympathetic group makes up 9 percent of the true poor, but only 4 percent of the magazine poor (see Table 4).

We also examined whether poor people were portrayed in urban or rural settings. The magazine depictions implied that poverty is almost completely an urban problem. Ninety-six percent of the poor were shown in urban areas.[12] According to the CPS, most poor people (77 percent) do reside in metropolitan areas; however, the magazine portrayals greatly exaggerate the true proportion ($p < .001$).[13] According to Gans (1995), the urban underclass is often linked with various pathologies and antisocial behavior. Thus, this emphasis on the urban poor does not promote a positive image of those in poverty.

The media leave the impression that most poor people do not work: Only 30 percent of poor adults were shown working or participating in job training programs ($N = 198$). In reality, 50 percent of the poor work in full- or part-time jobs, according to the CPS ($p < .001$).[14] When we focus solely on those stories that specifically discuss welfare, 35 percent of the poor are shown either working or in job training. According to the House Ways and Means Committee, 23 percent of AFDC recipients worked or participated in education or job training programs in 1995. These photographs reflect the emphasis of many contemporary welfare reformers, liberal and conservative, on "workfare" rather than welfare. Since many citizens support work requirements for welfare recipients (Weaver, Shapiro, and Jacobs, 1995), these images are positive ones. Not surprisingly, whites were more likely to be shown in these pictures than blacks.

Next, we analyzed the extent to which the news magazines relied on stereotypical traits in their depictions of the poor. We examined whether the media perpetuate the notion that women on welfare have lots of children. When a mother was portrayed with her children in these magazines, the average family size was 2.80. This is virtually identical to the figure of 2.78 reported by the House Ways and Means Committee for the average AFDC family size in 1996. In the magazines, the representation of poor women and their children differed by race. The average family size for whites was 2.44, whereas the average size for blacks was 3.05 and 2.92 for Hispanics. Although these differences are not statistically significant, the direction suggests that citizens received a less flattering view of poor minority families. The Ways and Means Committee does not report the true figure by race; however, the U.S. Census Bureau (1995) provides data on the average number of children ever had (rather than the average number of children currently receiving benefits) by AFDC mothers by race.[15] These data show that black AFDC women have only slightly (and nonsignificantly) more children than white AFDC women. Hispanic AFDC mothers, on the other hand, do have more children than non-Hispanic AFDC women.

To our surprise, the media did not overly emphasize other stereotypical characteristics associated with the poor. Of the 357 people coded, only three were shown engaging in criminal behavior, and another three were shown with drugs. No alcoholics were presented, and only one person was smoking a cigarette. However, of those seven stereotypical portrayals, only the person smoking was white—the others were either black or Hispanic. Only one poor woman was pregnant, so the media were not providing images suggesting that poor women simply have babies to obtain larger welfare checks. Again, though, this stereotypical portrayal is of a Hispanic woman. We also examined whether the media presented images consistent with the "welfare queen" stereotype. We felt that poor people who were shown wearing expensive jewelry or clothing would fit this stereotype. Thirty-nine individuals were shown with flashy jewelry or fancy clothes; blacks and Hispanics were somewhat more likely to be portrayed this way than whites.

In sum, the magazines often portrayed an inaccurate picture of the demographic characteristics of poor people. These magazines overrepresented the black, urban, and nonworking poor. Blacks were especially prominent in stories on unpopular poverty topics, and black women were portrayed with the most children. Other stereotypical traits linked with poor people were not common in the magazine portrayals. Nevertheless, in those instances when the media depicted poor people with stereotypical characteristics, they tended to be black or Hispanic. The most sympathetic group of poor people, the elderly, was underrepresented among the magazine poor. The media were most accurate in mirroring the predominance of women among welfare recipients.

Discussion

These portrayals of poverty are important because they have an impact on public opinion. A variety of experimental research demonstrates that negative images of blacks influence public opinion (Gilliam et al., 1996; Iyengar, 1990; Johnson et al., 1997; Mendelberg, 1997; Peffley, Shields, and Williams, 1996). Furthermore, white citizens' stereotypical beliefs about blacks decrease their support for welfare (Gilens 1995, 1996b).

In turn, public opinion has an impact on public policy (Page and Shapiro, 1983). Thus, if attitudes on poverty-related issues are driven by inaccurate and stereotypical portrayals of the poor, then the policies favored by the public (and political elites) may not adequately address the true problems of poverty. Furthermore, these inaccurate portrayals of the racial characteristics of the poor may prime the white public to favor political candidates who make racially coded arguments a linchpin of their campaign strategies. When these candidates are elected, they favor welfare (and other) policies that are in keeping with their racialized rhetoric.

It is possible that the text of these stories on poverty contains data describing the true demographic characteristics of the poor. It is unclear what impact a story that dispels stereotypes in its text but perpetuates stereotypes in its photographs would have on public opinion. Graber's research on television suggests that audiovisual themes are more memorable than verbal information (Graber, 1990, 1991). Although news magazines are a very different medium than television, it is certainly possible that magazine photos capture the audience's attention in the same way as television visuals. Psychological research suggests that vivid images of particular cases are more memorable and influential than dry statistical data (Fischhoff and Bar-Hillel, 1984). Indeed, Hamill, Wilson, and Nisbett's (1980) experimental research shows that a vivid, detailed description of a poor woman on welfare has a larger impact on subjects' opinions about welfare recipients than statistical information about women on welfare.

Gilens (1996a, 1999) investigated several explanations for why blacks are overrepresented among the poor and concluded that, at least in part, it is due to journalists' stereotypes. Gilens's research received considerable attention from media elites, including being the lead topic of discussion on CNN's *Reliable Sources* on August 24, 1997. Unfortunately, our data illustrate that journalists and editors have continued the practice of race coding the issue of poverty even after it was brought to their attention.

We must also point out that this race coding of poverty in news magazines is not an isolated incident; rather, the racial bias reported here is a widespread phenomenon. For example, Clawson and Kegler (in press) conducted a comparable analysis on the portrayal of poverty in introductory textbooks on American government and found that blacks were disproportionately represented. In addition, several scholars have documented the negative images of blacks in news coverage of crime (Delgado, 1994; Dixon, 1998; Entman, 1990, 1992, 1994; Johnson, 1987). And it does not end there: Whether it is children's programs, "reality-based" programs, sitcoms, or advertising, blacks are often portrayed in a stereotypical fashion (Graves, 1996; Humphrey and Schuman, 1984; Oliver, 1994; Poindexter and Stroman, 1981). These images are pervasive in our society.

Conclusion

In conclusion, blacks were disproportionately portrayed among magazine portrayals of the poor between 1993 and 1998. Blacks were especially overrepresented in negative stories on poverty and in those instances when the poor were presented with stereotypical traits. In addition, the "deserving" poor were underrepresented in the magazines. Overall, the photographic images of poor people in these five news magazines do not capture the reality of poverty; instead, they provide a stereotypical and inaccurate picture of poverty which results in negative beliefs about the poor, antipathy toward blacks, and a lack of support for welfare programs.

References

Blalock, Hubert M., Jr. 1979. *Social Statistics*. 2d ed. New York: McGraw-Hill.

Bowen, Lawrence, and Jill Schmid. 1997. "Minority Presence and Portrayal in Mainstream Magazine Advertising: An Update." *Journalism and Mass Communication Quarterly* 74(1):134–146.

Clawson, Rosalee A., and Elizabeth R. Kegler. In press. "The 'Race Coding' of Poverty in American Government Textbooks." *Howard Journal of Communications*.

Cook, Fay Lomax, and Edith Barrett. 1992. *Support for the American Welfare State*. New York: Columbia University Press.

Coughlin, Richard M. 1989. "Welfare Myths and Stereotypes." In *Reforming Welfare: Lessons, Limits, and Choices*, ed. Richard M. Coughlin. Albuquerque: University of New Mexico.

Delgado, Richard. 1994. "Rodrigo's Eighth Chronicle: Black Crime, White Fears—on the Social Construction of Threat." *Virginia Law Review* 80:503-48.

Dixon, Travis L. 1998. "Race and Crime on Local Television News." Paper presented at the annual meeting of the National Communication Association, New York.

Entman, Robert M. 1990. "Modern Racism and the Images of Blacks in Local Television News." *Critical Studies in Mass Communication* 7:332-45.

1992. "Blacks in the News: Television, Modern Racism and Cultural Change." *Journalism Quarterly* 69(2):341-61.

1994. "Representation and Reality in the Portrayal of Blacks on Network Television News." *Journalism Quarterly* 71(3):509-20.

1995. "Television, Democratic Theory and the Visual Construction of Poverty." *Research in Political Sociology* 7:139-59.

Epstein, Edward Jay. 1973. *News from Nowhere*. New York: Random House.

Fischhoff, Baruch B., and Maya Bar-Hillel. 1984. "Diagnosticity and the Base Rate Effect." *Memory and Cognition* 12:402-10.

Gamson, William A., and Kathryn E. Lasch. 1983. "The Political Culture of Social Welfare Policy." In *Evaluating the Welfare State*, ed. Shimon E. Spiro and Ephraim Yuchtman-Yaar. New York: Academic Press.

Gans, Herbert J. 1979. *Deciding What's News*. New York: Pantheon Books.

1995. *The War against the Poor*. New York: Basic Books.

Gilbert, Daniel T., and J. Gregory Hixon. 1991. "The Trouble of Thinking: Activation and Application of Stereotypic Beliefs." *Journal of Personality and Social Psychology* 60(4):509-17.

Gilens, Martin. 1995. "Racial Attitudes and Oppositions to Welfare." *Journal of Politics* 57(4):994-1014.

1996a. "Race and Poverty in America." *Public Opinion Quarterly* 60(4):515-41.

1996b. "'Race Coding' and White Opposition to Welfare." *American Political Science Review* 90(3):593-604.

1999. *Why Americans Hate Welfare*. Chicago: University of Chicago Press.

Gilliam, Franklin D., Jr., Shanto Iyengar, Adam Simon, and Oliver Wright. 1996. "Crime in Black and White." *Harvard International Journal of Press/Politics* 1(3):6-23.

Golding, Peter, and Sue Middleton. 1982. *Images of Welfare*. Oxford: Martin Robertson.

Graber, Doris A. 1990. "Seeing Is Remembering: How Visuals Contribute to Learning from Television News." *Journal of Communication* 40:134-55.

1991. "What You See Is What You Get." Paper presented at the annual meeting of the American Political Science Association, Washington, DC.

Graves, Sherryl Browne. 1996. "Diversity on Television." In *Tuning In to Young Viewers*, ed. Tannis M. MacBeth. Thousand Oaks, CA: Sage Publications.

Greenberg, Bradley S., and Jeffrey E. Brand. 1998. "U.S. Minorities and the News." In *Cultural Diversity and the U.S. Media*, ed. Yahya R. Kamalipour and Theres Carilli. Albany, NY: SUNY Press.

Hamill, Ruth, Timothy DeCamp Wilson, and Richard E. Nisbett. 1980. "Insensitivity to Sample Bias: Generalizing from Atypical Cases." *Journal of Personality and Social Psychology* 39:578-89.

Humphrey, Ronald, and Howard Schuman. 1984. "The Portrayal of Blacks in Magazine Advertisements: 1950-1982." *Public Opinion Quarterly* 48:551-63.

Iyengar, Shanto. 1990. "Framing Responsibility for Political Issues: The Case of Poverty." *Political Behavior* 12(1):19-40.

Johnson, James D., Mike S. Adams, William Hall, and Leslie Ashburn. 1997. "Race, Media, and Violence: Differential Racial Effects of Exposure to Violent News Stories." *Basic and Applied Social Psychology* 19(1):81-90.

Johnson, Kirk A. 1987. "Black and White in Boston." *Columbia Journalism Review* 26 (May/June): 50-52.

Kluegel, James R., and Eliot R. Smith. 1986. *Beliefs about Inequality*. New York: Aldine de Gruyter.

Ladd, Everett Carll, ed. 1993. "Public Opinion and Demographic Report: Reforming Welfare." *Public Perspective* 4(6):86-87.

Martindale, Carolyn. 1996. "Newspaper Stereotypes of African Americans." In *Images That Injure*, ed. Paul Martin Lester. Westport, CT: Praeger.

Mendelberg, Tali. 1997. "Executing Hortons." *Public Opinion Quarterly* 61(1):134-57.

Nelson, Thomas E., and Donald R. Kinder. 1996. "Issue Frames and Group-Centrism in American Public Opinion." *Journal of Politics* 58(4):1055-78.

Oliver, Mary Beth. 1994. "Portrayals of Crime, Race, and Aggression in 'Reality-Based' Police Shows: A Content Analysis." *Journal of Broadcasting and Electronic Media* 38(2):179-92.

Page, Benjamin I., and Robert Y. Shapiro. 1983. "Effects of Public Opinion on Policy." *American Political Science Review* 77:175-90.

Parisi, Peter. 1998. "A Sort of Compassion: The *Washington Post* Explains the 'Crisis in Urban America.'" *Howard Journal of Communications* 9:187-203.

Peffley, Mark, Todd Shields, and Bruce Williams. 1996. "The Intersection of Race and Crime in Television News Stories: An Experimental Study." *Political Communication* 13:309-27.

Poindexter, Paula M., and Carolyn A. Stroman. 1981. "Blacks and Television: A Review of the Research Literature." *Journal of Broadcasting* 25:103-22.

Sidel, Ruth. 1996. *Keeping Women and Children Last*. New York: Penguin Books.

Turk, Judy VanSlyke, Jim Richstad, Robert L. Bryson, Jr., and Sammye M. Johnson. 1989. "Hispanic Americans in the News in Two Southwestern Cities." *Journalism Quarterly* 66(1):107-13.

U.S. Bureau of the Census. 1995. "Statistical Brief: Mothers Who Receive AFDC Payments—Fertility and Socioeconomic Characteristics." *Census Bureau Web Page*. http://www.census.gov

1996. "March Current Population Survey." *Census Bureau Web Page*. http://www.census.gov/ftp/pub/income/histpov

U.S. House of Representatives, Committee on Ways and Means. 1998. *Overview of Entitlement Programs*. Washington, DC: U.S. Government Printing Office.

Weaver, R. Kent, Robert Y. Shapiro, and Lawrence R. Jacobs. 1995. "The Polls—Trends: Welfare." *Public Opinion Quarterly* 59(4):606-27.

Wilkes, Robert E., and Humberto Valencia. 1989. "Hispanics and Blacks in Television Commercials." *Journal of Advertising* 18(1):19-25.

Acknowledgments: We would like to thank the Purdue University MARC/AIM Summer Research Program for providing summer support for Rakuya Trice, the Purdue Research Foundation for providing a Summer Faculty Grant for Rosalee Clawson, and the Purdue University Library Scholars Grant Program. We greatly appreciate the efforts of Jill Clawson and Chris Salisbury, who were instrumental in obtaining information from the Census Bureau Web site. We would also like to thank the editor and anonymous reviewers for their helpful comments.

Endnotes

[1] See Entman (1995) for a discussion of how poverty is implicitly linked to other issues such as crime, drugs, and gangs through visual images on television news.

[2] Taken as a whole, these five magazines have a circulation of over 12 million: *Business Week* reaches 1,000,000 people; the *New York Times Magazine* has a circulation of 1,650,179; *Newsweek* has an audience of 3,100,000; *U.S. News & World Report* has a distribution of 2,351,313; and *Time* has the largest readership with 4,083,105 subscribers.

[3] There were several stories on poverty we did not include in our sample because: (1) the story did not include any pictures; (2) the story was an editorial or opinion column that only included a picture of the author; (3) the story was found to be irrelevant to our research topic (e.g., one story was cross-listed as income inequality and poor, but actually focused on Democratic and Republican party efforts to win working-class votes); (4) the pictures in the story did not pertain to contemporary poverty in the United States; (5) the story itself was missing from its bound volume ($n = 6$); or (6) the story was in a magazine that was at the binders ($n = 1$).

[4] A "Do Not Know" category was included for these variables.

[5] To ensure the integrity of our data, we conducted a test of intercoder reliability. A second person, who was unaware of the hypotheses, coded a subset of our sample of photographs. Across the variables of interest, there was an average intercoder reliability of .90.

[6] Although we are analyzing media portrayals of poverty between 1993 and 1998, for ease of presentation we use CPS data from March 1996 or Ways and Means Committee data from 1996 to establish the true characteristics of the poor. The 1996 data represent a reasonable midpoint. Moreover, the relevant numbers do not vary much across the time period of interest; in no instance would the minor fluctuations change the substantive or statistical interpretation of our results.

[7] Unfortunately, we faced a trade-off between providing a more detailed analysis of the racial portrayal of the poor and making exact comparisons with Gilens's research.

[8] These stories on unpopular issues included 75 poor individuals.

[9] These stories on sympathetic topics included 100 poor individuals.

[10] There was no race by gender interaction.

[11] There was no race by age interaction.

[12] Please note these statistics are based on a reduced sample size ($N = 205$), because many (43 percent) of the poor individuals were coded as "Don't Know" for their residency. In many cases it was difficult to ascertain whether the setting was a rural or urban one, so we decided to err on the conservative side and code only the unambiguous settings.

[13] There was no race by residence interaction.

[14] The data on the working poor from the Current Population Survey include people who are 16 and over, whereas the data on the magazine working poor include people who are 13 and over.

[15] These data are from the Survey of Income and Program Participation conducted between June and September of 1993 (U.S. Bureau of the Census, 1995).

Exercise for Article 9

Factual Questions

1. According to the researchers, the visual representation of a political issue is an "integral" part of what?

2. A person was coded as being "young" if he or she appeared to be what age?

3. According to the CPS, African Americans make up what percentage of the poor?

4. For Hispanics, was the difference between the percentage of "True Poor" Hispanics and "Magazine Poor" Hispanics statistically significant?

5. According to the researchers, who constitutes the most sympathetic group of poor people?

6. When mothers were portrayed with their children in the magazines (without regard to race), was there a substantial difference between the average family size in the magazines and the figure cited by Congress? Explain.

7. Were any alcoholics represented in the magazines?

Questions for Discussion

8. The five magazines are listed in lines 104–105. Would you be interested in knowing the basis for their selection (i.e., how and why they were selected)?

9. Each person in a photograph was coded as either being white, black, Hispanic, Asian American or undeterminable. In addition, they were also coded for other characteristics such as their age. In your opinion, might it be difficult to make some of these judgments? Explain. (See Endnote 5 at the end of the article.)

10. Does it surprise you that the researchers found it difficult to ascertain whether the setting in a photograph was rural or urban? Explain. (See Endnote 12.)

11. In Endnote 3, the researchers note that some stories on poverty were omitted for a variety of reasons. In your opinion, could these omissions have affected the validity of the study? Explain.

12. The researchers mentioned that they were surprised by some of the findings. Were you surprised by any of them? (See lines 313–332.) Explain.

Quality Ratings

Directions: Indicate your level of agreement with each of the following statements by circling a number from 5 for strongly agree (SA) to 1 for strongly disagree (SD). If you believe an item is not applicable to this research article, leave it blank. Be prepared to explain your ratings.

A. The introduction establishes the importance of the study.

SA   5   4   3   2   1   SD

B. The literature review establishes the context for the study.

SA   5   4   3   2   1   SD

C. The research purpose, question, or hypothesis is clearly stated.

SA   5   4   3   2   1   SD

D. The method of sampling is sound.

SA   5   4   3   2   1   SD

E. Relevant demographics (for example, age, gender, and ethnicity) are described.

SA   5   4   3   2   1   SD

F. Measurement procedures are adequate.

SA   5   4   3   2   1   SD

G. All procedures have been described in sufficient detail to permit a replication of the study.

SA   5   4   3   2   1   SD

H. The participants have been adequately protected from potential harm.

SA   5   4   3   2   1   SD

I.   The results are clearly described.

       SA   5   4   3   2   1   SD

J.   The discussion/conclusion is appropriate.

       SA   5   4   3   2   1   SD

K.   Despite any flaws, the report is worthy of publication.

       SA   5   4   3   2   1   SD

Article 10

Ethnic Representation in a Sample of the Literature of Applied Psychology

Leslie Case
University of South Dakota

Timothy B. Smith
Brigham Young University

ABSTRACT. A number of authors have raised concerns over the external validity of psychological research. This study examined the extent to which empirical articles include human participants from diverse ethnic backgrounds. Articles published over a 5-year period in 14 selected journals representing 3 applied subdisciplines of psychology were examined. Of the 2,536 articles coded, only 61% indicated the ethnicity of the participants. For those articles, the ethnic compositions approximated U.S. Census estimates, with the exception of an overrepresentation of African Americans and an underrepresentation of Hispanic Americans. The results imply that although the field is apparently adequately recruiting English speakers, representation of non-English speakers should be increased. To further enhance the external validity of psychological research, ethnicity of participants should be not only specified but also analyzed in relation to the results of a study.

From *Journal of Consulting and Clinical Psychology*, *68*, 1107–1110. Copyright © 2000 by the American Psychological Association. Reprinted with permission.

In his parting editorial, former *Journal of Consulting and Clinical Psychology* editor Larry Beutler (1996) emphasized the importance of detailed reporting of demographic information of human participants. He encouraged efforts to reliably measure and analyze demographic constructs, and he cited a statement developed by the National Institute of Mental Health's Editor's Consortium that clearly spells out the need to do so:

Not only is the complete description of a study sample central to the scientific goals of sound and replicable research, but also these variables may affect the generalizability of the research findings. This information is necessary for the meaningful interpretation of findings from a particular study. Moreover, the availability of this information provides the methodological basis for determining the extent to which findings depend upon individual and sociodemographic characteristics of the sample. (Beutler, 1996, pp. 846–847)

Reporting and analyzing sample composition is "good science," a standard to be met in the interest of external validity. Of course, representative sampling is essential to external validity (Babbie, 1998). Because psychological research must be relevant and appropriate for individuals from diverse ethnic backgrounds (S. Sue, 1999), researchers must use samples that adequately represent diverse populations. Published research often determines what is taught and which mental health interventions are used. However, if the results of research are not examined in relation to the ethnic composition of the participants, the value of such research is limited, and what it advocates may even prove harmful (D. W. Sue & Sue, 1999).

The majority of psychotherapy research has been conducted with predominantly middle-class White Americans (Alvidrez, Azocar, & Miranda, 1996; Graham, 1992). As a result, limited data are available to help researchers and practitioners ensure that appropriate services are provided to clients from different backgrounds (Miranda, 1996). Few psychotherapy studies include representative numbers of people of color in their samples, despite the fact that the proportion of people of color is increasing in the United States (Alvidrez et al., 1996). Such traditional patterns reflect cultural biases within the field, and some observers imply that underrepresentation of people of color in psychological research may be a product of institutionalized racism (D. W. Sue & Sue, 1999). Although likely unintentional, such misrepresentation clearly compromises the quality of the field.

Multicultural Publication Content

Previous studies on the inclusiveness of psychological research have noted the lack of journal articles focused specifically on people of color. For example, Graham (1992) found that only 3.6% of the articles in 6 journals published by the American Psychological Association (APA) between 1970 and 1989 had content specific to African Americans. Furthermore, she noted a decline in such articles over time, from 5.2% during the period 1970–1974 to 2.0% during the period 1985–1989. Similarly, Santos de Barona (1993) reported an average annual decline of 1.5 articles on people of color in 11 APA journals over 21 years. Proportions of journal content specific to people of color as low as 1.3% have been reported by reviewers (Iwamasa & Smith, 1996).

Table 1
Reporting Rates of Psychology Journals Reviewed

Journal	%
Clinical psychology	
Journal of Abnormal Psychology	60.0
Journal of Clinical Child Psychology	78.6
Journal of Clinical Psychology	59.8
Journal of Consulting and Clinical Psychology	69.4
Professional Psychology: Research and Practice	37.0
Counseling psychology	
Counseling Psychologist	65.0
Counselor Education and Supervision	54.0
Journal of Counseling and Development	56.8
Journal of Counseling Psychology	82.1
School psychology	
Journal of Instructional Psychology	33.3
Journal of School Psychology	59.5
Psychology in the Schools	61.9
School Psychology Review	57.6
The School Counselor	37.0

Note. % = percentage of research articles reporting participant ethnicity.

Because a disproportionately small percentage of the research literature focuses on concerns specific to people of color, an implicit (albeit incorrect) assumption may be that such a focus is not necessary: As long as people of color are adequately represented in the research samples, then the results should generalize to those populations. However, although several studies have examined the content of research with respect to its focus on people of color, no examination has scrutinized the degree to which people of color are actually represented in research samples.

Difficulties Achieving Representative Samples

Researchers have given varied reasons for not including people of color in their studies. For some, the unwillingness to investigate topics that are socially relevant but not "politically correct" is problematic (Beutler, Brown, Crothers, Booker, & Seabrook, 1996). For others, the practical difficulties and higher expenses incurred in gaining access to certain populations serve as deterrents (S. Sue, 1999), because people of color are underrepresented in the university and mental health settings from which researchers typically recruit participants (Hough et al., 1987; Santos de Barona, 1993; Snowden & Cheung, 1990; Wells, Hough, Golding, Burnam, & Karno, 1987). Distrust of research among some people of color is another factor to consider, because research has often been misused in regard to these groups (Maultsby, 1982; D. W. Sue & Sue, 1999). For example, research has historically been used as a justification for slavery, as a "scientific" rationale for segregation, and as support for the concept of racial inferiority and superiority (Williams, 1986). Additionally, the stigma that some people of color attach to concepts of mental health and illness may reduce their willingness to become involved in psychological research (Griffith & Baker, 1993).

Despite the number of reasons given for noninclusive research, strategies to overcome these difficulties have also been detailed in the literature. For example, techniques that have been used to successfully recruit participants of Hispanic origin for psychological research include incorporating social networking strategies, using face-to-face recruitment, forming professional relationships with community agencies and offering free training to agency personnel, advertising in both English and Spanish, providing transportation and childcare, and placing reminder phone calls (e.g., Hooks, Tsong, Henske, Baranowski, & Levin, 1986). Furthermore, retention can be enhanced through culturally sensitive treatment and by incorporating family members, assessing level of acculturation, and using bilingual staff (Mezzich, Ruiz, & Munoz, 1999; Miranda, Azocar, Organista, Munoz, & Lieberman, 1996).

Recent Multicultural Emphases

The recommendations for inclusive recruitment strategies we have just listed are part of the larger context of the contemporary emphasis on multiculturalism. For example, the APA's training standards have been revised to include provisions for integrating multicultural themes into the curricula of psychology training programs (e.g., Yutrzenka, 1995). Similarly, revisions of ethical codes of the APA (1992), the National Association of School Psychologists (NASP; 1997), and the American Counseling Association (ACA; 1995) address multicultural issues for researchers and practitioners.

Concerns over the issue of adequate sample representation have also led to changes in the policies of

Table 2

Percentages of Ethnic Groups in Psychology Research Samples Compared with U.S. Census Data

Ethnic Group	Research Samples (%)	U.S. Census (%)
People of color	25.9	26.3
African American	16.4	12.0
Hispanic origin	5.7	10.3
Asian American or Pacific Islander	2.8	3.3
American Indian	1.1	0.7
European American (White)	74.1	73.6

Note. Percentages for research sample composition are those with "other" and "international" participants eliminated from analyses. Census data are from the U.S. Bureau of Census (1996).

research-funding institutions. For example, the National Institutes of Health (NIH) has mandated that women and minority group members be included in all NIH-supported research (NIH, 1994). Neither the cost of including diverse populations nor the geographic area of the investigator can be used to rationalize inadequate representation. Such changes are being adopted throughout the field to correct the underrepresentation of minorities in clinical research and to aid the scientific community in producing generalizable research (Miranda, 1996).

A Needed Self-Examination: Scrutinizing Psychology

Although the field of psychology is certainly "talking the talk" about multiculturalism, is it also "walking the walk"? It is hoped that the recent discourse on multiculturalism in the literature of psychology has initiated action. To determine whether efforts have been made to adequately represent people of color in empirical research samples, this study examines a sample of literature produced over a recent 5-year period. We then compare data from a recent census of the United States with the percentages of people of color included in the research samples. On the basis of the research cited previously in this article, we hypothesized that the overall percentage of people of color among research participants would be less than the percentage represented in census population estimates and that this underrepresentation would be found for all ethnic minority groups.

Method

We chose journals from 1993 to 1997 to represent the applied subdisciplines of clinical, counseling, and school psychology on the basis of their classification in the most recent edition of APA's *Journals in Psychology* (APA, 1997). Journals were not included in this study if they did not focus on service provision, if they had an explicitly international focus, if they represented specific subspecialties, if they were explicitly theoretical, or if they specifically focused on people of color. Table 1 lists the resulting 14 journals selected by subdiscipline.

Within the selected journals, we reviewed each empirical article with human participants. Theoretical articles, program descriptions, book reviews, rebuttals, editorial statements, literature reviews, meta-analyses, film reviews, commemorative award speeches, tributes, and brief reports of 2 pages or less were not considered in the analyses.

For each article, we recorded the ethnic composition of the research sample reported by the authors. Researchers used various descriptions of the ethnicity of their sample, with most being compatible with the categories of the U. S. Bureau of the Census (1996). However, some authors used a nondescriptive "other," and some studies involved participants from outside the United States. Thus, eight categories of participants were coded in this study: African American, Hispanic American, Asian American or Pacific Islander, Native American, European American, international, other, and not reported. Studies in which content focused on a specific ethnic group were also noted following examination of the abstract and the *Method* section of the article.

Results

After the data were coded, a reliability check of the articles was performed by an independent, trained coder. The number of agreements divided by the number of agreements and disagreements yielded a reliability estimate of 99.7%. Of the 2,536 empirical articles coded, 1,552 (61.2%) reported the ethnicity of their participant pools. The average reporting rates differed substantially between the individual journals, ranging from 82% to 33% (see Table 1).

Across all articles, 54.4% of the research participants were European American, 12.3% were African American, 4.4% were Hispanic American, 2.1% were Asian American, 0.8% were Native American, 22.5% were international, and 3.4% were other. To facilitate accurate comparison with U.S. Census data, we subsequently removed the other and international categories

from the analyses (Table 2). When the resulting percentages from all studies were compared with those of the 1996 U.S. Census data, significant differences were found, χ^2 (4, $N = 1180$) = 46.91, $p < .001$. Specifically,
215 the research samples typically overrepresented African Americans ($z = 4.68$, $p < .001$) but underrepresented Hispanic Americans ($z = 5.21$, $p < .001$) in comparison with their representation in the general population.

We also examined the content of the research stud-
220 ies to see how many of the studies focused specifically on issues pertinent to people of color. Overall, 7.2% of the articles focused on a specific racial or ethnic group, with 5.2% focused solely on one group of interest, and 2.0% comparing that group with a Caucasian sample.

Discussion

225 In light of recent concerns about the external validity of psychotherapy research (e.g., S. Sue, 1999; D. W. Sue & Sue, 1999), the purpose of this study is to investigate the current state of participation of people of color in psychological research. Although previous
230 critiques have focused on content relevant to specific ethnic groups (Alvidrez et al., 1996) or on the report rates of demographic variables (Beutler et al., 1996), this article is the first to examine a broad range of applied research to determine ethnic-specific content,
235 reporting rates, and representation of ethnic groups compared with population estimates.

Contrary to expectations (Graham, 1992), African American participants were actually overrepresented in comparison with population estimates. This finding
240 seems to indicate that some researchers emphasize recruitment among this group. Research samples also included Asian Americans and Native Americans in proportions similar to population estimates. However, research samples underrepresented Hispanic Ameri-
245 cans by about 44% in comparison with population estimates.

Although these data do not identify causative factors, the related estimate that about 39% of the people of Hispanic origin living in the United States are not
250 fluent in English (U.S. Bureau of the Census, 1996) may indicate that researchers fail to use the Spanish language in their recruitment procedures. The field of psychology seems to be talking the talk about multiculturalism, but apparently in English only. Because His-
255 panic Americans constitute the fastest growing ethnic group in the nation (U.S. Bureau of the Census, 1996) and because monolingual Spanish speakers may have greater needs for clinical services than English speakers do (Schur & Albers, 1996), the results of this study
260 should serve as a wake up call (or *llamada urgente*) to the field. Recommendations for adaptations of mental health care (e.g., Mezzich et al., 1999) and for successful research recruitment and retention (e.g., Hooks et al., 1986) should be seriously considered.
265 Because we recognize the need for enhanced external validity in psychological research (S. Sue, 1999), it

270 is encouraging to note that 7.2% of the studies had content specific to an ethnic group. This estimate is notably higher than the proportions found in previous studies, which have ranged between 1% and 5% (e.g., Graham, 1992; Iwamasa & Smith, 1996). Support for increasing the quantity of such ethnic research comes from Triandis (1996), who has argued that work with specific groups is the key to a universal psychology,
275 wherein cultural variants to theory are identified and cultural biases are appropriately minimized.

It should be recognized, however, that the results of this study are subject to a major limitation. Similar to the findings of Beutler et al. (1996), we found that
280 nearly 40% of the studies we reviewed failed to report the ethnicity of the participants. Hence, the results of this study suffer from problems related to external validity (we note the irony of this). It is possible that ethnicity was not reported in many studies because the
285 samples were predominantly or exclusively Caucasian. However, because so much data are missing, this interpretation is speculative.

Given the wide variability across the journals in the reporting of ethnic information (see Table 1), efforts to
290 enhance external validity are perhaps best made at the level of manuscript review. Although it is encouraging that the editors of APA journals have begun to address this issue (Azar, 1999), the discourse must initiate widespread change in editorial practice. In this regard,
295 Beutler et al.'s (1996) recommendations remain the standard to which the field should adhere: If we are to substantially increase our knowledge about "what works with whom," ethnicity should consistently be treated like any other construct in the social sciences.
300 To report detailed information regarding ethnicity is therefore only the bare minimum standard. Strength of ethnic identification and variables that have been found to mediate the effects of ethnicity, such as individualism-collectivism (Triandis, 1996), can be analyzed in
305 relation to the results of a study. The burden of proof of external validity therefore shifts from those conducting ethnic minority research to all professionals publishing their work (S. Sue, 1999). Such burden is not a politically correct subjugation of scientific practice to the
310 tenets of multiculturalism; it is simply "walking the talk" of good science.

References

Alvidrez, J., Azocar, F., & Miranda, J. (1996). Demystifying the concept of ethnicity for psychotherapy researchers. *Journal of Consulting and Clinical Psychology*, 64, 903–908.

American Counseling Association (1995). *ACA code of ethics and standards of practice.* (Baltimore, MD: American Counseling Association.)

American Psychological Association. (1992). Ethical principles of psychologists and code of conduct. *American Psychologist*, 47, 1597–1611.

American Psychological Association. (1997). *Journals in psychology: A resource listing for authors.* (Washington, DC: Author)

Azar, B. (1999, February). Journal editors find consortium helps researchers shape goals. *APA Monitor*, 20

Babbie, E. (1998). *The practice of social research* ((8th ed.). Boston: Wadsworth.)

Beutler, L. E. (1996). The view from the rear: An editorial. *Journal of Consulting and Clinical Psychology*, 64, 845–847.

Beutler, L. E., Brown, M. T., Crothers, L., Booker, K., & Seabrook, M. K. (1996). The dilemma of factitious demographic distinctions in psychological research. *Journal of Consulting and Clinical Psychology, 64*, 892–902.

Graham, S. (1992). "Most of the subjects were White and middle class": Trends in published research on African Americans in selected APA journals, 1970–1989. *American Psychologist, 47*, 629–639.

Griffith, E. H., & Baker, F. M. (1993). Psychiatric care of African Americans. (In A. C. Gaw (Ed.), *Culture, ethnicity and mental illness* (pp. 147–173). Washington, DC: American Psychiatric Press.)

Hooks, P. C., Tsong, Y., Henske, J. C., Baranowski, T., & Levin, J. S. (1986). Social networking as a recruitment strategy for Mexican American families in community health research. *Hispanic Journal of Behavioral Sciences, 8*, 345–355.

Hough, R. L., Landsverk, J. A., Karno, M., Burnam, M. A., Timbers, D. M., Escobar, J. I., & Regier, D. A. (1987). Utilization of health and mental health services by Los Angeles Mexican Americans and non-Hispanic Whites. *Archives of General Psychiatry, 44*, 702–709.

Iwamasa, G. Y., & Smith, S. K. (1996). Ethnic diversity in behavioral psychology: A review of the literature. *Behavior Modification, 20*, 45–59.

Maultsby, M. C. (1982). A historical view of Blacks' distrust of psychiatry. (In S. M. Turner & R. T. Jones (Eds.), *Behavior modification in Black populations: Psychosocial issues and empirical findings.* (New York: Plenum.)

Mezzich, J. E., Ruiz, P., & Munoz, R. A. (1999). Mental health care for Hispanic Americans: A current perspective. *Cultural Diversity and Ethnic Minority Psychology, 5*, 91–102.

Miranda, J. (1996). Introduction to the special section on recruiting and retaining minorities in psychotherapy research. *Journal of Consulting and Clinical Psychology, 64*, 848–850.

Miranda, J., Azocar, F., Organista, K. C., Munoz, R. F., & Lieberman, A. (1996). Recruiting and retaining low-income Latinos in psychotherapy research. *Journal of Consulting and Clinical Psychology, 64*, 868–874.

National Association of School Psychologists. (1997). *Principles for professional ethics.* (Bethesda, MD: NASP Publications)

National Institutes of Health. (1994). *NIH guidelines on the inclusion of women and minorities as subjects in clinical research.* (59, Fed. Reg. 14, 508 (Document No. 94–5435, National Archives and Records Administration, Washington, DC).)

Santos de Barona, M. (1993). The availability of ethnic materials in psychology journals: A review of 20 years of journal publication. *Contemporary Educational Psychology, 18*, 391–400.

Schur, C. L., & Albers, L. A. (1995). Language, sociodemographics, and health care use of Hispanic adults. *Journal of Health Care for the Poor and Underserved, 7*, 140–158.

Snowden, L. R., & Cheung, F. K. (1990). Use of inpatient mental health services by members of ethnic minority groups. *American Psychologist, 45*, 347–355.

Sue, D. W., & Sue, D. (1999). *Counseling the culturally different: Theory and practice* ((3rd ed.). New York: Wiley.)

Sue, S. (1999). Science, ethnicity, and bias: Where have we gone wrong? *American Psychologist, 54*, 1070–1077.

Triandis, H. C. (1996). The psychological measurement of cultural syndromes. *American Psychologist, 51*, 407–415.

U. S. Bureau of the Census. (1996). *Statistical abstracts of the United States* ((116th ed.). Washington, DC: U. S. Government Printing Office.)

Wells, K. B., Hough, R. L., Golding, J. M., Burnam, M. A., & Karno, M. (1987). Which Mexican Americans underutilize health services? *American Journal of Psychiatry, 144*, 918–922.

Williams, D. H. (1986). The epidemiology of mental illness in Afro-Americans. *Hospital and Community Psychiatry, 37*, 42–49.

Yutrzenka, B. A. (1995). Making a case for training in ethnic and cultural diversity in increasing treatment efficacy. *Journal of Consulting and Clinical Psychology, 63*, 197–206.

Address correspondence to: Timothy B. Smith, Department of Counseling Psychology and Special Education, Brigham Young University, 328 MCKB, Provo, UT 84602.

Exercise for Article 10

Factual Questions

1. What percentage of the research articles in the *Journal of Instructional Psychology* reported participant ethnicity?

2. Which journal had the highest percentage of articles that reported participant ethnicity?

3. Did the researchers hypothesize that there would be underrepresentation for all ethnic minorities?

4. What was the reliability estimate (expressed as a percentage) for the coding in this study?

5. According to U.S. Census data, what percentage of the population is African American?

6. What percentage of the participants in the research articles examined in this study were African American?

7. The researchers speculate that a large percentage of the studies reviewed failed to report the ethnicity of the participants for what reason?

Questions for Discussion

8. In lines 104–119, the researchers name some techniques that have been used successfully to recruit participants of Hispanic origin. In your opinion, could some of these be used successfully to recruit participants from other minority ethnic groups? Explain.

9. What is your opinion on the researchers' decision to exclude journals that specifically focused on people of color?

10. The researchers note that their study has a major limitation because 40% of the studies they reviewed failed to report the ethnicity of the participants. In your opinion, is this "a major limitation"?

11. If you were to conduct a study on the same topic, what changes in the research methodology, if any, would you make?

Quality Ratings

Directions: Indicate your level of agreement with each of the following statements by circling a number from 5 for strongly agree (SA) to 1 for strongly disagree (SD). If you believe an item is not applicable to this research article, leave it blank. Be prepared to explain your ratings.

A. The introduction establishes the importance of the study.

SA   5   4   3   2   1   SD

B. The literature review establishes the context for the study.

SA   5   4   3   2   1   SD

C. The research purpose, question, or hypothesis is clearly stated.

SA   5   4   3   2   1   SD

D. The method of sampling is sound.

SA   5   4   3   2   1   SD

E. Relevant demographics (for example, age, gender, and ethnicity) are described.

SA   5   4   3   2   1   SD

F. Measurement procedures are adequate.

SA   5   4   3   2   1   SD

G. All procedures have been described in sufficient detail to permit a replication of the study.

SA   5   4   3   2   1   SD

H. The participants have been adequately protected from potential harm.

SA   5   4   3   2   1   SD

I. The results are clearly described.

SA   5   4   3   2   1   SD

J. The discussion/conclusion is appropriate.

SA   5   4   3   2   1   SD

K. Despite any flaws, the report is worthy of publication.

SA   5   4   3   2   1   SD

Article 11

I'm Lonely and Apprehensive: The Presentation of Stigmatizing Information in Personal Ads

Robert Lemieux
Western Maryland College

Roxanne Parrott
Pennsylvania State University

Karen Ogata Jones
University of Georgia

ABSTRACT. The present study attempted to extend previous personal ad research by contacting ad writers directly. Previous research has suggested that personal ad writers may differ from the general population along certain personality characteristics and that certain types of information they present may be perceived as stigmatizing. This study's specific intentions were to explore the types of information presented, assess loneliness via the UCLA Loneliness Scale, and communication apprehension via the Personal Report of Communication Apprehension. Results indicated that personal ad writers who divulge stigmatizing information experience a greater degree of loneliness and communication apprehension than ad writers presenting nonstigmatizing information.

From *Communication Research Reports*, *16*, 353–359. Copyright © 1999 by Communication Research Reports. Reprinted with permission.

The use of print media as a means of establishing interpersonal relationships represents a unique approach to relational development. Although the practice of advertising one's wants and desires is as old as the nation itself, it has only been within the last 20 years that researchers have focused on what is commonly known as the personal ad (Parrott et al., 1997) Within that 20-year span, most of the research has explored personal ads using the matching hypothesis perspective (Harrison & Saeed, 1977; Hirschman, 1987), implicit theories of attraction (Lynn & Shurgot, 1984; Koestner & Wheeler, 1988), and gender role expectation (Deaux & Hanna, 1984).

Each research approach has been used to explain and predict the differences and similarities within personal ads. Specifically, the matching hypothesis approach implies that personal ad writers select dating partners of the same or similar level of social desirability as defined by physical attractiveness or wealth. The implicit theories of attraction approach implies that men and women offer the attributes that are sought by the opposite sex, thus demonstrating an understanding of implicit theories of attraction. Emphasis of the ad is on the strategic use of communication to manage one's impression and to promote the most positive view of self. The gender role approach focuses on the use of gender role expectations to explain the content in personal ads.

Although each approach has increased the understanding of personal ad use, Lynn and Bolig (1985) assert that more personal ad research should be undertaken because the ads provide researchers with naïve subjects who are participating in consequential behavior. Additionally, they represent a broad spectrum of the population (e.g., they vary in social economic status, race, sexual orientation, etc.).

Lynn and Bolig (1985) further suggest that researchers go beyond content analysis, which has been the methodology of choice. Specifically, they suggest that researchers should consider placing ads and evaluating the responses, and they should consider acquiring additional information by directly contacting the ad writers. Of the two suggestions, direct contact is the most intriguing.

Much of the past content analyses of personal ads have elaborated on why an ad was placed. In their analysis of personal ads, Parrott et al. (1997) posited that media modes of self-presentation are less immediate and less threatening than face-to-face meetings. This may be particularly true if the ad contains stigmatizing information. Such information could range from Goffman's (1963) notion of tribal stigmas (race, ethnicity, religion) to Parrott et al.'s (1997) mentioning of health conditions (overweight, smoker, herpes, AIDS). By presenting information via print, an ad writer is spared the discomfort associated with determining how and when to disclose the information in a face-to-face setting.

Associated with the reasons why an ad is placed are the attributes of ad writers. Specifically, there may be certain personality variables that lead a person to use personal ads as a way of initiating a relationship. One of the most common explanations for the use of personal ads, and one most cited by researchers (e.g., Austrom & Hanel, 1983; Lynn & Bolig, 1985; Parrott et al., 1997), is loneliness. Perlman and Peplau (1981) describe loneliness as a situation that represents an unpleasant or unacceptable discrepancy between an individual's actual social relationships and their desired ones. Gove and Hughes (1980) assert that individuals in satisfying, intimate relationships are "protected" from loneliness and unhappiness. Individuals without a partner or whose partner is incapable of providing intimacy are more susceptible to loneliness. Further, it is plausible that lonely individuals may seek alternative ways of meeting people (e.g., personal ads).

If an ad writer is experiencing loneliness or feels stigmatized, it may be reasonable to assume that an ad writer may have a "fear or anxiety associated with...communication with another person" (McCroskey, 1977, p.78). Specifically, they may suffer from communication apprehension (CA). Results from previous research (e.g., Bell & Daly, 1985; Downs et al., 1988; Sadava & Matejcic, 1987) support the link between loneliness and CA by providing evidence of positive and significant relationships between the two variables.

Although most of the CA research examines total apprehension, the current study will examine only the dyadic and group dimensions. These two dimensions are perhaps most applicable when initiating a dating relationship. The activities associated with dating obviously involve a dyadic encounter. Additionally, there may be dating activities associated with a group type of activity (e.g., double dating, small party, etc.). Having to divulge a latent stigma, as may be the case in a dyadic setting, or having a manifest stigma (e.g., being overweight), as may be evident to others in a group setting, may explain the anxiety associated with dyadic and group encounters.

A plethora of CA research has shown that CA can have negative consequences in one's social life (McCroskey, Richmond, & Stewart, 1986). When one considers the social skill and assertiveness needed to pursue a potential dating partner, it becomes conceivable that apprehensive individuals might resort to other strategies such as personal ads.

In short, personal ads could be a comfortable way of initiating a relationship for lonely and apprehensive individuals. The ad writer has a certain degree of control over the type of information divulged. Depending on how the personal ad is written, a good degree of uncertainty about the initial interaction could be greatly reduced (Parrott et al., 1997). This might help lonely and apprehensive individuals to be more comfortable initiating an initial interaction. Further, this may be particularly true if the individual perceives himself or herself to possess a stigmatizing attribute.

In an attempt to combine these issues with Lynn & Bolig's (1985) suggestions, the current study seeks to contact personal ad writers to determine whether stigmatizing information is presented and to measure the degree of loneliness and communication apprehension. Since this is perhaps the first study to undertake this task, it can best be viewed as exploratory. As such, the following research questions and hypothesis are posited:

RQ1: Do personal ad writers present stigmatizing information?

RQ2: What is the relationship between stigmatizing information and loneliness?

RQ3: What is the relationship between stigmatizing information and communication apprehension?

H1: As communication apprehension increases, loneliness increases.

Method

Procedures

The sample consisted of 338 personal advertisements published over a four-month period in a southeastern U.S. newspaper. All of the selected ads had voice mail capability, which, for a small fee, enables a potential respondent to answer the ad via telephone. The researchers were granted permission to access, free of charge, all ads attached to the voice mail system. Once accessed, a short verbal message was left, which identified the researchers, indicated that the study was a follow-up to a larger personal ad study, and provided a university address to send for the questionnaire.

All ad writers that wrote to request a questionnaire were provided with one. The questionnaire was accompanied by a cover letter and a self-addressed, stamped, return envelope bearing the university's address. Participants were asked to complete the questionnaire and return it in the return envelope.

Measures

The questionnaire consisted of two sections. The first section included open-ended questions that focused on why they wrote the ad. There was also a question that asked whether their ad contained information that was more comfortable to disclose in an ad than in a face-to-face situation.

The second section of the questionnaire consisted of randomly ordered questions from the revised version of the UCLA Loneliness Scale (Russell et al., 1980) and the Personal Report of Communication Apprehension (PRCA) (McCroskey, 1982). All questions in section two used five-point Likert type responses with "1" equaling strongly disagree and "5" equaling strongly agree. The UCLA Loneliness Scale (alpha = .92) is used to assess an individual's level of loneliness by asking questions that focus on one's lack of companionship and isolation.

As discussed by Richmond and McCroskey (1992), PRCA (alpha = .95), responses should be transformed to create four submeasures of communication apprehension that range from "no apprehension" (6) to "extreme apprehension" (30). The four apprehension submeasures are public, dyad, meeting, and group. As noted earlier, the current study focused solely on dyadic apprehension and group apprehension.

Table 1
Means for Loneliness and Communication Apprehension

	Comfortable Information ($n = 55$)	Uncomfortable Information ($n = 27$)	$F(1,80)$	Eta^2
Loneliness	2.22	2.69	8.42*	.10
Dyadic Apprehension	13.53	15.52	3.99**	.05
Group Apprehension	13.82	17.52	10.24*	.11

* means are significantly different at $p < .01$
** means are significantly different at $p < .05$

Results

A total of 91 questionnaires were requested and returned, which represented 27% of the total number of ads contacted. This is a similar number of responses received by Austrom and Hamel (1983) in their attempt to contact ad writers. Forty-six of the respondents were male and 43 were female.

Research question one was addressed via the question, "Does your ad contain information that was more comfortable for you to disclose in the ad than it would be face-to-face?" Frequency analysis indicated that of the 87 participants that responded to the question, 27 (31%) indicated that their ad contained uncomfortable information. Of the 27, eight were female and 19 were male.

Research questions two and three were analyzed via multivariate analysis of variance (MANOVA). The presence of comfortable or uncomfortable information served as the independent variable. Loneliness, dyadic apprehension, and group apprehension served as the dependent variables. The overall MANOVA revealed a significant multivariate effect of information type, $F(3,78) = 3.92$, $p < .05$, $eta^2 = .13$. Group means and univariate tests are presented in Table 1.

As noted earlier, previous research (e.g., Bell & Daly, 1985; Downs et al., 1988; Sadava & Matejcic, 1987) indicated a positive relationship between loneliness and apprehension. Correlations within those studies ranged from .31 to .42. In an attempt to address this relationship, hypothesis one was tested via Pearson correlation analyses of loneliness and dyadic apprehension and group apprehension. Results indicated significant correlations between loneliness and dyadic apprehension ($r = .55$) and group apprehension ($r = .56$). This lends support for hypothesis one, and indicates a positive relationship between communication apprehension and loneliness.

Discussion

Personal ad research offers a unique opportunity to blend interpersonal and mass communication. The current study was an exploratory attempt at furthering personal ad research. Most of the previous research on personal ads employed content analysis and was limited to information provided by the ad writer. The current study made an effort to contact ad writers and assess the presence of stigmatizing information within the ad and the relationship between this information and two variables—loneliness and communication apprehension.

Results indicated that almost one-third of the current sample reported the presentation of uncomfortable information within their ad. Unfortunately, the researchers had no way of matching each questionnaire with its respective personal ad. This could have led to an analysis of the participant's presentation of the uncomfortable information. However, a review of the initial 338 personal ads provided hints as to the presentation of potentially stigmatizing information. Specifically, certain ad writers described themselves as having herpes, being very overweight, having a criminal record, and being HIV+, to name a few. In short, it seems clear that some ad writers use personal ads to divulge stigma information in their personal ads.

Although the current data do not specifically address the contention, it is possible that the personal ad provided a less threatening and more controlled way of presenting the stigma information. Anyone responding to the ad would seemingly be accepting of the information. This could possibly reduce any anxiety and uncertainty associated with having to divulge the information during interaction and ease the beginning of relational development.

It is also possible that the stigmatizing information offers an explanation as to the significantly higher levels of loneliness and communication apprehension reported by the stigmatized ad writers. Perhaps the thought of having to divulge the stigma information may deter them from initiating relationships and lead to a greater feeling of loneliness. Interestingly, many loneliness researchers (e.g., Lau & Gruen, 1992; Rotenberg & Kmill, 1992) indicate that loneliness itself is a stigma. Specifically, a number of studies indicate that adults stigmatize loneliness by viewing it as a negative attribute (Rotenberg, 1998).

Collectively, the findings imply that using personal ads may be an important means of initiating a relationship for certain individuals. Thus, it would be imperative that the information within the ad be presented in a manner that enhances their opportunities to receive responses.

Although the current study extends current personal ad research, it is important to note a few limitations. First is the possibility of a biased sample. The data collection procedures allowed the participants to self-
270 select themselves into the study. Second, the modest sample size limits the ability to generalize the results to a greater population. Third, although there were a relatively equal number of male and female respondents, the majority of ad writers were male. Thus, the dispro-
275 portionate gender representation in the total sample may limit the ability to generalize the results.

Even with the above concerns, the current study was able to reliably address issues relevant to personal ad research. Further, the procedures and measures used
280 in the study provide evidence that it is possible to contact personal ad writers and investigate personality variables. Future personal ad research should explore additional variables and issues that are associated with personality and relationship initiation.

References

Austrom, D., & Hanel, K. (1983). *Looking for companionship in the classified section*. Unpublished manuscript, York University.

Bell, R.A., & Daly, J.A. (1985). Some communicator correlates of loneliness. *The Southern Speech Communication Journal, 50*, 121–142.

Deaux, K., & Hanna, R. (1984). Courtship in the personals column: The influence of gender and sexual orientation. *Sex Roles, 11*, 363–375.

Downs, V. C., Manoochehr, J., & Nussbaum, J.F. (1988). A comparative analysis of the relationship between communication and apprehension and loneliness for elderly nursing home and non-nursing home residents. *Western Journal of Speech Communication, 52*, 308–320.

Goffman, E. (1963). *Stigma: Notes on the management of spoiled identity*. Englewood Cliffs, NJ: Prentice-Hall.

Gove, W. R., & Hughes, M. (1980). Reexamining the ecological fallacy: A study in which aggregate data are critical in investigating the pathological effects of living alone. *Social Forces, 57*, 1157–1177.

Harrison A. A., & Saeed, L. (1977). Let's make a deal: An analysis of revelations and stipulations in lonely hearts advertisements. *Journal of Personality and Social Psychology, 35*, 257–264.

Hirschman, E. C. (1987). People as products: Analysis of a complex marketing exchange. *Journal of Marketing, 51*, 98–108.

Koestner, R., & Wheeler, L. (1988). Self-presentation in personal advertisements: The influence of implicit notions of attraction and role expectations. *Journal of Social and Personal Relationships, 5*, 149–160.

Lau, S., & Gruen, B. E. (1992). The social stigma of loneliness: Effect of target person's and perceiver's sex. *Personality and Social Psychology Bulletin, 18*,182–189.

Lynn, M., & Bolig, R. (1985). Personal advertisements: Sources of data about relationships. *Journal of Social and Personal Relationships, 2*, 377–383.

Lynn, M., & Shurgot, B. A. (1984). Responses to lonely hearts advertisements: Effects of reported physical attractiveness, physique, and coloration. *Personality and Social Psychology Bulletin, 10*, 349–357.

McCroskey, J. C. (1977). Oral communication apprehension: A summary of recent theory and research. *Human Communication Research, 4*, 78–96.

McCroskey, J. C. (1982). Oral communication apprehension: A reconceptualization. In M. Burgoon (Ed.), *Communication Yearbook, 6*, (pp. 136–170). Beverly Hills, CA: Sage.

McCroskey, J. C., Richmond, V. P., & Stewart, R. (1986). *One on one: Foundations of interpersonal communication*. Englewood Cliffs, NJ: Prentice Hall.

Parrott, R., Lemieux, R., Harris, T., & Travillion, L. (1997). Interfacing interpersonal and mediated communication in personal ads: Active and strategic self-disclosure. *The Southern Communication Journal, 62*, 319–332.

Perlman, D., & Peplau, L. A. (1981). Towards a social psychology of loneliness. In S.W. Duck & R. Gilmour (Eds.), *Personal Relationships in Disorder*, (pp. 31–56). London: Academic.

Richmond, V. P., & McCroskey, J. C. (1992). *Communication: Apprehension, Avoidance, and Effectiveness* (3rd ed.). Scottsdale, AZ: Gorsuch Scarisbrick.

Rotenberg, K. J. (1998). Stigmatization of transitions in loneliness. *Journal of Personal and Social Relationships, 15*, 565–576.

Rotenberg, K. J., & Kmill, J. (1992). Perception of lonely and nonlonely persons as a function of individual differences in loneliness. *Journal of Personal and Social Relationships, 9*, 325–330.

Russell, D., Peplau, L., & Curtona, C. (1980). The revised UCLA Loneliness Scale. *Journal of Personality and Social Psychology, 39*, 472–480.

Sadava, S.W., & Matejcic, C. (1987). Generalized and specific loneliness in early marriage. *Journal of Behavioral Science, 19*, 56–66.

About the authors: Robert Lemieux (Ph.D., University of Georgia, 1996) is an assistant professor in the Department of Communication, Western Maryland College, Westminster, MD 21157. Roxanne Parrott (Ph.D., University of Arizona, 1990) is a professor in the Department of Speech Communication, Pennsylvania State University, University Park, PA 16802. Karen Ogata Jones (M.A., University of Georgia, 1994) is a doctoral candidate in the Department of Mass Communication, University of Georgia, Athens, GA 30602.

Acknowledgments: The authors wish to thank Yvonne Pomerleau for her valuable comments.

Exercise for Article 11

Factual Questions

1. According to earlier researchers, what do "personal ads provide researchers with"?

2. The letters "CA" stand for what words?

3. In the second section of the questionnaire, a response of "5" equaled what?

4. According to the researchers, what was the independent variable?

5. Those who said they presented uncomfortable information in their ads had a mean loneliness score of 2.69. Was this significantly higher than the mean for those who presented only comfortable information? If yes, at what probability level was the difference significant?

6. What was the value of the correlation coefficient (r) for the relationship between loneliness and group apprehension?

7. The researchers state that a number of studies indicate that adults stigmatize loneliness by viewing it as what?

Questions for Discussion

8. Having read this article, do you think that research on personal ads is important? Explain.

9. Speculate on what "H1" means. (See lines 125–135.)

10. The researchers contacted only those whose ads were attached to a voice mail system. In your opinion, could this affect the generalizability of the results? Explain. (See lines 138–142.)

11. The researchers had no way to match the information they collected with the ad placed by a participant. Would it be important to try to do this in future studies? Explain. (See lines 227–231.)

12. In the next to last paragraph, the researchers mention "a few limitations." In your opinion, are these important limitations? Might they be avoided in future research? Explain.

Quality Ratings

Directions: Indicate your level of agreement with each of the following statements by circling a number from 5 for strongly agree (SA) to 1 for strongly disagree (SD). If you believe an item is not applicable to this research article, leave it blank. Be prepared to explain your ratings.

A. The introduction establishes the importance of the study.

   SA   5   4   3   2   1   SD

B. The literature review establishes the context for the study.

   SA   5   4   3   2   1   SD

C. The research purpose, question, or hypothesis is clearly stated.

   SA   5   4   3   2   1   SD

D. The method of sampling is sound.

   SA   5   4   3   2   1   SD

E. Relevant demographics (for example, age, gender, and ethnicity) are described.

   SA   5   4   3   2   1   SD

F. Measurement procedures are adequate.

   SA   5   4   3   2   1   SD

G. All procedures have been described in sufficient detail to permit a replication of the study.

   SA   5   4   3   2   1   SD

H. The participants have been adequately protected from potential harm.

   SA   5   4   3   2   1   SD

I. The results are clearly described.

   SA   5   4   3   2   1   SD

J. The discussion/conclusion is appropriate.

   SA   5   4   3   2   1   SD

K. Despite any flaws, the report is worthy of publication.

   SA   5   4   3   2   1   SD

Article 12

Young Children's Perceptions of Time Out

Christine A. Readdick
Florida State University

Paula L. Chapman
Florida State University

ABSTRACT. Preschoolers' perceptions of, and feelings about, time out were assessed. Observations were conducted in 11 child care centers by pairs of trained child study students. Forty-two young children were interviewed subsequent to a time-out experience. More children were observed to be isolated for reasons of noncompliance than for aggression. The largely negative self-attributions expressed by most—feeling alone, disliked by one's teacher, and ignored by one's peers—as well as the feelings of sadness and fear expressed by many, suggest that time out is perceived as a punishment by the very young child. Furthermore, the inability of many young children to say why they were in time out (or to recall an adult telling them why) reduces the likelihood that the specific time-out event, as a punishment, will inhibit future occurrence of the same aggressive or noncompliant behavior

From *Journal of Research in Childhood Education, 15*, 81–87. Copyright © 2000 by the Association for Childhood Education International. Reprinted with permission.

Time out, a brief social isolation and temporary suspension of usual activity, is a discipline technique frequently employed to decrease young children's undesirable behavior in early childhood settings. Origi-
5 nally designed as a technique for the modification of deviant behavior in clinical populations (Wolf, Risley, & Mees, 1964), time out has been embraced by many as a means of quelling an array of undesirable behaviors in noncompliant children, from thumb sucking to
10 crying to hitting others (Clark, Rowbury, Baer, & Baer, 1973).

While a vast literature details with whom and for what behavior the technique has been successfully or unsuccessfully employed (e.g., Harris, 1985; Sachs,
15 1973), no one has tapped the perceptions of time out as constructed and held by children themselves. Certainly, young children's understandings of time out and perceptions of self and others vis-à-vis the time-out event are interesting and worthy of investigation. More im-
20 portant, however, children's perceptions may provide insights for adults trying to determine the developmental appropriateness of using time out as a guidance technique.

The utility of time out first was demonstrated as a
25 means to reduce tantrums and self-destructive behavior in an autistic child (Wolf et al., 1964). Each time a de-

viant behavior occurred, the child was placed alone in a room and allowed to leave only after the tantrum or self-destructive behavior subsided. Applied immedi-
30 ately and consistently, time out has been determined to be most useful in the reduction of aggressive behavior, both verbal and physical (Zabel, 1986).

Proponents of using time out with young children extol its virtues, at least for children 2 or 3 years of age
35 and older (e.g., Dobson, 1978; Twiford, 1984). Time out is viewed as an efficient means of providing space and time for the young child to mull over wrongdoings, refresh feelings of guilt, and ponder socially desirable responses in similar circumstances. Consequently, time
40 out appears to remain a popular technique because of the positive reinforcement received by the adult when administering time out to a misbehaving child (Webber & Scheuermann, 1991).

Critics of time out acknowledge that the practice
45 can reduce undesirable behavior; they lament, however, that time out fails to teach desirable behavior (e.g., Betz, 1994). Time out, say these critics, should be reserved for use only when a child is wildly out of control or is a threat to other children. Under these extreme
50 circumstances (for example, when the young child is engaged in flagrant hitting or biting), the adult is advised to approach the child physically, get down to the child's level, look him in the eye and tell him calmly what the offense is, and then escort the child to the
55 time-out site; the rule of thumb for the length of time out is one minute per year of the child's age (Betz, 1994). Others recommend selecting a boring location for time out, setting a timer to prevent forgetting the child in time out, announcing "time out is over," and
60 seeking the next available opportunity to praise the child for a good behavior (Saarni, as cited in Israeloff, 1994).

There is speculation that time out may be hurtful in a number of ways. If the child perceives it as a pun-
65 ishment, time out can have serious side effects that are commonly associated with punishment, including increases of other maladaptive behaviors and withdrawal from or avoidance of the adults administering time out (Miller, 1986). Furthermore, when escape is impossi-
70 ble, some young children are apt to withdraw and become passive (Parke, 1969).

Because of the young child's limited knowledge and experience, he or she may ultimately feel anxious,

rejected, hurt, and humiliated as a result of time out
(Clewett, 1988). Gartrell (1995) suggests that, given
their social inexperience, young children tend to inter-
nalize negative labels, see themselves as they are labeled, and react accordingly. Stone (1993) declares
time out a "dead end" for young children at the threshold of social development. Instead, the preschool-age
child, who is wrestling with egocentrism and with limited knowledge of social relations, would probably
benefit from social skill modeling and instruction.

Because no one has paused to ask children their
perceptions of time out and their feelings about being
placed in time out, there is no known support, other
than suppositional, for these expectations. Therefore,
this exploratory study was designed to flesh out young
children's views of time out, subsequent to the experience of a time-out event in an early childhood education setting.

The following research questions were asked:

1. What feelings about time out do young children express?
2. What perceptions of time out do young children express?
3. What behavioral events are resulting in preschool
   children being placed in time out by their teachers?
4. What differences in feelings about time out can be
   identified between children who perceive themselves to be frequently in time out and those who
   perceive themselves to be infrequently in time out?
5. What is the correspondence of the child's stated reason for being in time out and the observer's view of
   the reason for the child being in time out?

Method

Participants

Subjects included 42 two-, three-, and four-year-old
children. Twenty-three of the children were boys, 19
were girls.

Setting

Observations were conducted in 11 child care centers in a north Florida community that serves primarily
working and fee-paying families (60% Caucasian, 35%
African American, and 5% other ethnic backgrounds,
including Hispanic and Asian American). The centers
constituted a convenience sample of sites at which di-
rectors reported the use of time out as a disciplinary
technique. Observations were performed both in indoor
and outdoor classroom environments.

Measure

An interview targeting children's perceptions and
feelings about time out was constructed by the first
author. The 17-question interview, revised from a 14-
item interview employed in a pilot study, was designed
to gauge children's views of school, ability to recount
the specific event that led to the time out incident, specific feelings about being in time out, and perceptions
of time out in general.

Procedure

After receiving parental and teacher permission,
observations were conducted at local child care centers
by students enrolled in a child study class at a local
university. These students had been trained in observation techniques and interviewing skills for a minimum
of 30 hours prior to data collection. To minimize bias,
the social desirability of time out as a disciplinary
technique was not addressed, and the exploratory nature of the investigation was emphasized. Each of 40
pairs of observers observed a minimum of 6 hours over
a 30-day period and recorded time-out events using an
anecdotal format.

Each anecdote included a description of the precipitating event (what the child was doing that led to
placement in time out), adult direction of the child to
time out, location of time out, child behavior in time
out, adult release of child from time out, and duration
of the time-out incident. *Time out* was defined as an
occasion in which the child is removed from an activity
or group for performing an act deemed unacceptable or
undesirable by an adult, and spends time in a designated spot isolated from others at the request of the
adult.

Precipitating events expected to lead to time out
were aggressive and noncompliant behaviors. *Physical
aggression* was defined as the act of striking, slapping,
kicking, pushing, biting, or pulling others, or throwing
objects at others; *verbal aggression* was described as
aiming offensive words at others with the intent to
harm another person. *Noncompliance* was designated
as refusal to initiate or complete a request made by an
adult.

At the conclusion of a time-out episode, one researcher would approach the affected child and invite
him or her to talk about being in time out. If a child did
not want to participate, that name was deleted and the
child was excluded from the study. If the child responded favorably to the invitation to talk about time
out, one researcher asked each of the questions, while
the other recorded the child's answers. Upon completion of the interview, the child was thanked and encouraged to rejoin the class.

In anticipation of this research project, a pilot study
was conducted at a similar child care center. The purpose of the pilot study was to assess the usefulness of
an interview measure and develop procedures for training undergraduate students in techniques for accurately
recording anecdotal records of noncompliant and aggressive behavior and subsequent time-out events, as
well as teaching the students interviewing skills. In this
pilot study, five students observed and interviewed 15
young children placed in time out. It was determined
that the clarity of the operational definition of *time out*
assured 100% interobserver agreement. Subsequent
modifications to the interview included simplification
of wording, omission of two items, and development of

Table 1
Preschoolers' Feelings About and Perceptions of Time Out

	f	%	χ^2	p
Children's View of School				
Do you like school?				
Yes	37	93	28.90	< .001
No	3	7		
Do you have friends at school?				
Yes	39	93	30.86	< .001
No	3	7		
Children's Feelings About Time Out				
When you are in time out, do you feel…				
alone or	24	75	8.00	.005
part of the group?	8	25		
scared or	8	29	5.14	.023
safe?	20	71		
happy or	20	54	.24	.622
sad?	17	46		
that the teacher liked you or	9	27	6.82	.009
disliked you?	24	73		
that everyone was looking at you or	7	21	10.94	.001
was not looking at you?	26	79		
that the other kids like you or	13	43	.53	.465
dislike you?	17	57		
that you like time out or	5	13	20.63	< .001
don't like time out?	33	87		
Children's Perceptions of Time Out				
Can you tell me what just happened?				
Yes	29	81	13.44	< .001
No	7	19		
Did the teacher tell you why you were in time out?				
Yes	23	66	3.46	.063
No	12	34		
Are you in time out a little or	24	71	5.76	.016
a lot?	10	29		
Do you think you needed to be in time out?				
Yes	21	54	.23	.630
No	18	46		
Do you think you will do (the act) again?				
Yes	6	16	17.79	< .001
No	32	84		
What do you have to do to get out of time out?				
Be quiet	6	17		
Be good	6	17		
Do what I'm told	3	9		
Other	12	34		
Don't know	8	23	6.286	.179

five items to better tap into young children's perceptions of time out.

Results

Analyses were made up of cross-tabulations and nonparametric chi-square tests. The results are presented as answers to the following research questions:

Question #1: What feelings about time out do young children express?

Children's recountings of their feelings during the incident of time out were measured using seven questions (see Table 1). Significantly more children than not reported feeling all alone, yet safe; disliked by their teacher; and ignored by their peers while in time out. Significantly more children reported disliking, as opposed to liking, being in time out. About as many chil-

Table 2
Feelings About Time Out Expressed by Children Perceiving Themselves to be in Time Out Frequently and Infrequently

Feelings About Time Out	Frequently (n = 10)		Infrequently (n = 24)	
	f	%	f	%
alone or	7	1.00	14	.64
part of the group	-	-	8	.36
scared or	3	.38	4	.24
safe	5	.62	13	.76
happy or	2	.33	15	.63
sad	6	.66	9	.37
others liked you or	1	.11	10	.56
disliked you	8	.89	8	.44
like time out or	-	-	5	.21
dislike time out	10	1.00	19	.79

Note. Of the 42 subjects, only 34 answered the query regarding their perceptions of frequency of being in time out. Of these 34 children, only the answers of children responding to each question about feelings are presented.

dren declared themselves to be happy in time out as admitted to being sad. Similarly, almost as many children felt liked by their peers during time out as felt disliked.

200 *Question #2: What perceptions about time out do young children express?*

Children's perceptions of time out were ascertained by six questions. Significantly more children than not were able to describe a precipitating event of some 205 nature, such as "I wasn't playing the right way," or "I was standing on the bookshelves," when asked to tell what had just happened. Significantly more children reported being in time out "a little" than "a lot"; and more declared they would not repeat the behavior that 210 led to the time-out incident. Regarding their other perceptions of time out, almost two-thirds of the children reported that an adult told them why they were put in time out. More admitted that they deserved to be in time out than not. Finally, most children expressed 215 some notion about what they needed to do to be released from time out, from "be quiet" to "be good" to "do what I'm told."

Question #3: What behaviors result in preschool children being placed in time out by their preschool 220 *teachers?*

Most children were placed in time out for noncompliance (n = 27). Fewer still were placed in time out for physical aggression (n = 16) or verbal aggression (n = 3) toward others.

225 *Question #4: What differences in feelings and knowledge about time out can be identified between children who perceive themselves to be frequently or infrequently in time out?*

Eight children admitted being in time out a lot, 230 while 22 said they were in time out a little. Children who perceived themselves to be frequently in time out differed from their peers who believed themselves to be infrequently in time out on five of seven expressions of feelings (see Table 2). They liked being in time out 235 less, and while in time out, they declared they felt more alone, scared, sad, and disliked by their peers.

Question #5: What is the correspondence of the child's stated reason for being in time out and the observer's view of the reason for the child being in time 240 *out?*

While almost three-quarters of the children acknowledged that they knew why they were put into time out, only a little more than half of those children gave answers that actually corresponded with the ob- 245 servers' anecdotal records.

Discussion

Despite their rosy accounts of liking preschool and having friends at preschool, the young children queried in this study upon release from a time-out event expressed largely negative feelings about time out and 250 about themselves in time out. Not only did they not like being in time out, many said they felt sad and scared while in time out. Such negative self-attributions confirm Clewett's (1988) and Gartrell's (1995) expectations regarding the feelings likely to be generated in the 255 very young, socially inexperienced child in time out. The negative impressions of self, vis-à-vis the larger social group expressed here—feeling alone and disliked by one's teachers and disliked and ignored by one's peers—suggest that time out may indeed be per- 260 ceived as punishment by the very young child, as cautioned by Parke (1969).

The inability of many children to tell why they were in time out or to recall an adult telling them why they were in time out makes it less likely that the specific time-out event will be effective in inhibiting future occurrences of the same aggressive or noncompliant behavior. Punishment is more effective when accompanied by a rationale that is understood (Parke, 1969).

Children in this study were placed in time out for a variety of reasons (e.g., biting, spitting, splashing water out of the sink, not sitting in circle for story time), yet most were isolated for nonaggressive, noncompliant behavior. Clearly, in these preschool settings, time out is not being reserved consistently for use when a child is wildly out of control or a threat to other children, contrary to the recommendations of Betz (1994). Indeed, many children are receiving time out for trivial reasons that are a far cry from the behavior that the technique was initially meant to address (e.g., Wolfe et al., 1964), thus confirming Webber and Scheuermann's (1991) observation that time out is a seductively easy reinforcing technique for harried caregivers, who may be eager to get a noncompliant child "out of their hair" for a few moments.

Intuitively, one might expect differences in feelings about and perceptions of time out to be expressed by young children who believe themselves to be in time out "a lot" as compared to those who believe themselves to be in time out "a little"; indeed, such was the case. The responses of two subjects are indicative of even these young children's ability to describe their perceptions of time spent in time out. In response to the question, "Do you think you are in time out a lot or a little?" one child volunteered, "Lots, maybe a hundred," while another said, "Just a little. Sometimes I have good days." Clearly, those children who perceived themselves to be in time out often liked time out less and felt more isolated, sad, scared, and disliked by their peers. These harshly negative self-attributions again appear to confirm the punitive effects of time out when employed with the preschool child, especially the child who is frequently in time out.

The fact that fewer than half of the young children queried could accurately recall what they had done that resulted in their placement in time out, or refused to recall their misbehavior, despite most declaring that someone had told them why they were in time out, raises doubts that *these* preschoolers, at least, were mulling over their misbehavior, generating feelings of guilt, or pondering alternative desirable responses in similar circumstances, contrary to the expectations of Dobson (1978) and Twiford (1984). What is more likely is that these children are withdrawing or acting out in other, even more undesirable, ways (Parke, 1969). With little direct tuition provided by adults to children regarding the specific misbehavior to correct, it is hard to imagine that the children in this sample, despite their earnest protestations to the contrary, will not misbehave again.

In this sample, at least, the observations of young children in a variety of child care centers appear to indicate that time out can have unintended consequences. Miller (1986) cautioned that time out could lead to increases in other maladaptive behaviors, here evidenced by one boy calling his caregiver "Meany" upon being placed in time out. One girl's response, crying, "I want my mommy. I want my mommy," throughout the entire episode of time out, suggests that some young children may indeed feel anxious and hurt by the practice (Clewett, 1988).

Finally, what is clear is the discomfort of many young children on the heels of being released from a time out. When asked at the end of the interview, "Is there anything else you want to tell me about time out?," one subject offered, "I want to go play," while another implored, "I want to say something good—about my family and toys."

Several limitations of the current study, as conducted, must be acknowledged. First and foremost, use of a convenience sample limits generalization of the findings to other children in other settings. Furthermore, many more incidents of time out were observed among children whose parents had not granted permission for their participation in this investigation. It is possible that the findings of this study may not be applicable to these other young children. Finally, as with any observational study, there is the possibility that the observers alone may have influenced the findings by affecting the behavior of the adults administering time out, the behavior of the children, or both. Observer effect may have been amplified to the extent that observation and interview were performed by the same pair of researchers.

Summary

In this investigation, young children in selected group child care settings were queried individually about their time out experiences and feelings. Despite recommendations that time out be reserved for occasions when the child is wildly out of control or an imminent threat to other children, it appears that time out is being used largely for reasons of noncompliance that give immediate irritation to caregivers. Furthermore, it appears that the consequences of time out, for many young children, may be punitive rather than instructional. Systematic, fine-grained observations of caregiver application of time out procedures over time, and documentation of children's attendant responses to, and feelings about, time out are needed to confirm these preliminary and potentially disturbing findings.

References

Betz, C. (1994). Beyond time-out: Tips from a teacher. *Young Children, 49,* 10–14.

Clark, H. B., Rowbury, T., Bear, A. M., & Baer, D. M. (1973). Timeout as a punishing stimulus in continuous and intermittent schedules. *Journal of Applied Behavior Analysis, 6,* 413–455.

Clewett, A. S. (1988). Guidance and discipline: Teaching young children appropriate behavior. *Young Children, 43*, 27–31.

Dobson, F. (1978). *How to discipline—with love: From crib to college.* New York: Rawson Associates Publishers.

Gartrell, D. (1995). Misbehavior or mistaken behavior? *Young Children, 50*, 27–35.

Harris, K. R. (1985). Definitional, parametric, and procedural considerations in timeout interventions and research. *Exceptional Children, 51*, 279–288.

Israeloff, R. (1994). Meltdown. *Parents, 69*, 76.

Miller, D. E. (1986). The management of misbehavior by seclusion. *Residential Treatment for Children and Youth, 4*, 63–73.

Parke, R. D. (1969). Social effects of punishment on children's behavior. *Young Children, 24*, 225–240.

Sachs, D. A. (1973). The efficacy of time-out procedures in a variety of behavior problems. *Journal of Behavior Therapy and Experimental Psychology, 4*, 237–242.

Stone, S. J. (1993). Taking time to teach social skills. *Childhood Education, 69*, 194–195.

Twiford, J. R. (1984). *Managing children's behavior.* Englewood Cliffs, NJ: Prentice-Hall.

Webber, J., & Scheuermann, B. (1991). Managing behavior problems: Accentuate the positive...eliminate the negative! *Teaching Exceptional Children, 24*, 13–19.

Wolf, M., Risley, T., & Mees, H. (1964). Application of operant conditioning procedures to the behaviour problems of an autistic child. *Behaviour Research and Therapy, 1*, 305–312.

Zabel, M. K. (1986). Time out with behaviorally disabled students. *Behavioral Disorders, 21*, 15–20.

Exercise for Article 12

Factual Questions

1. In their literature review, the researchers cite a reference that suggests that time out "appears to remain a popular technique" because of what?

2. How many of the participants (i.e., subjects) were boys?

3. Students enrolled in a child study class collected the data. These students were trained in observational techniques and interviewing skills for a minimum of how many hours?

4. In the pilot study, the operational definition of time out obtained what percentage agreement (i.e., interobserver reliability)?

5. The researchers state, "About as many children declared themselves to be happy in time out as admitted to being sad." According to Table 1, how many said they were happy?

6. How many children were placed in time out for physical aggression?

7. According to the researchers, the inability of many children to tell why they were in time out or to recall an adult telling them why they were in time out makes what less likely?

Questions for Discussion

8. In lines 87–91, the researchers refer to their study as "exploratory." In your opinion, is their research topic worthy of more definitive research in the future? Explain.

9. Often educational research is conducted in a single setting (such as a single school). The observations for this research were conducted in 11 child care centers. To what extent does this increase your confidence in the generalizability of the results? Explain.

10. The children were not required to participate in the interviews. (See lines 160–162.) Do you think that the refusal of some children might have an important impact on the results of this study? If you were conducting this research, would you require their participation (assuming that you had permission of the parents and teachers to do so)? Explain.

11. The researchers state several limitations of their study in lines 339–354. In your opinion, how important are these limitations? Do you think that this study provides valuable information in spite of the limitations? Explain.

12. Were any of the results especially interesting or surprising to you? Explain.

Quality Ratings

Directions: Indicate your level of agreement with each of the following statements by circling a number from 5 for strongly agree (SA) to 1 for strongly disagree (SD). If you believe an item is not applicable to this research article, leave it blank. Be prepared to explain your ratings.

A. The introduction establishes the importance of the study.

SA   5   4   3   2   1   SD

B. The literature review establishes the context for the study.

SA   5   4   3   2   1   SD

C. The research purpose, question, or hypothesis is clearly stated.

SA   5   4   3   2   1   SD

D. The method of sampling is sound.

SA   5   4   3   2   1   SD

E. Relevant demographics (for example, age, gender, and ethnicity) are described.

      SA   5   4   3   2   1   SD

F. Measurement procedures are adequate.

      SA   5   4   3   2   1   SD

G. All procedures have been described in sufficient detail to permit a replication of the study.

      SA   5   4   3   2   1   SD

H. The participants have been adequately protected from potential harm.

      SA   5   4   3   2   1   SD

I. The results are clearly described.

      SA   5   4   3   2   1   SD

J. The discussion/conclusion is appropriate.

      SA   5   4   3   2   1   SD

K. Despite any flaws, the report is worthy of publication.

      SA   5   4   3   2   1   SD

Article 13

Black and White Girls' Racial Preferences in Media and Peer Choices and the Role of Socialization for Black Girls

Lisa O'Connor
Teachers College, Columbia University

Jeanne Brooks-Gunn
Teachers College, Columbia University

Julia Graber
Teachers College, Columbia University

ABSTRACT. This exploratory research compared Black and White girls' racial preferences as exhibited through their media (music and television) and peer choices. The sample included 140 8- and 9-year-old Black and White girls of various socioeconomic levels. Findings suggested that both Black and White girls have more Black music preferences than White or no-race music preferences. Also, both Black and White girls made more White television program choices than Black or no-race choices. In their peer selections, all girls preferred same-race peers. Black mothers who engaged in racial socialization practices had girls who were more likely to prefer Black music and television to the other categories. Further, Black mothers who promoted more cultural distance and mothers who were poor had girls with more same-race peer preferences.

From *Journal of Family Psychology, 14*, 510–521. Copyright © 2000 by the American Psychological Association. Reprinted with permission.

All children in our society become aware at some point of the existence of racial prejudice that is directed against either their own or other groups (Shils, 1948). However, the extent and the intensity of children's
5 attitudes and the nature of their responses vary with the social-structural features of their environment, especially those that create differences among subgroups of the population in the extent and intensity with which those attitudes are held (e.g., poor vs. nonpoor fami-
10 lies). The process of social comparison emerges in the early school years, at which time children begin to describe themselves in reference to other individuals (Butler, 1989; Ruble, 1987). They focus on salient characteristics, such as skin color, to make social com-
15 parisons (Asher & Allen, 1969; Harter, 1983; Spencer, 1983) and to classify people systematically into groups (Aboud, 1988; Wilder, 1986).

Many researchers have attempted to understand the way in which children acquire and process knowledge
20 about racial differences and racial attitudes (see review articles by Banks, 1976, Brand, Ruiz, & Padilla, 1974,

and Proshansky, 1966). A growing body of research suggests that in the course of development, children experience the notion of race through racial awareness,
25 racial constancy, and racial preferences (Gopaul-McNichol, 1995; Gunthrope, 1978; Semaj, 1980). Racial awareness occurs fairly early (at about age 3), when children are able to distinguish among different races and are therefore aware that individuals are
30 categorized into different racial groups (Gunthrope, 1978). The second process, racial constancy, or the understanding that one's race does not change, is cognitively constrained, but is usually attained by age 6 or 7. The third process, the development of racial prefer-
35 ences, is characterized by the differentiation and integration of the child's beliefs, feelings, and behavioral tendencies regarding different racial groups (which are themselves based on prevailing social attitudes and values; Gopaul-McNichol, 1995). This article focuses
40 on racial preferences, specifically the media and peer choices of Black and White girls in middle childhood, to determine the pervasiveness of same-race choices versus mixed- or other-race preferences.

Racial preference has been measured through some
45 expression of likes and dislikes of objects that are either representative or symbolic of race (Gunthrope; 1978). Historically, racial preferences in Black and White children for dolls and drawings or pictures of Black or White children are often discussed as a pref-
50 erence for either White or Black racial groups (Clark & Clark, 1939; Hraba & Grant, 1970; Stevenson & Stewart, 1958). Procedures in most studies focused on whether a child's or a group's average score was in the pro-White or pro-Black range. However, Morland
55 (1962) suggested that some children do not express any preference for one group over another. Although many studies have indicated that young Black children are predominantly represented in the pro-White category when only the dichotomous categories are available,
60 Cross (1981) found that a significant percentage of Black children have no preference when choosing

among pictures and drawings of Black and White children if three categories (Black, White, and no preference) are used. Doyle and Aboud (1995), who used a sample of kindergarten and third-grade children, found that only 7% of kindergarten children had pro-Black doll choices, 44% were unbiased, and 49% exhibited very low pro-Black doll choices. Banks (1976) also suggests that Black children do not show any preference but are equally favorable to both racial groups on account of their bicultural status, that is, being simultaneously a member of a predominantly White society and a member of the Black ethnic group (Boykin & Toms, 1985). Prior to the inclusion of the no-race or mixed-preference categories, investigators repeatedly encountered high frequencies of no responding in participants, ranging from 1% of the sample in some studies (e.g., Clark & Clark, 1947) to up to 91% in others (Gregor & McPherson, 1966). Thus, the inclusion of the no-preference category (no race or mixed race) is a necessary addition to the literature.

Research on dolls or drawings is limited, as the findings are not related to actual day-to-day activities of children. Although limited research exists on the association between peer preferences and race, much less is known about preferences as expressed by media choices. Hence, this present article focused on the aspect of racial preferences as indicated by girls' day-to-day preferences in music and television. Adolescents use music listening and television watching to explore numerous possible selves, including those that are desired and feared (Larson, 1995). Both music and television exposure influence adolescents' character evaluation of different races. For example, White male and female college students evaluated the personality of Black women more negatively after being exposed to music videos featuring songs of devoted love or rap music designed to be sexually titillating (Gan, Zillmann, & Mitrook, 1997). Music and television preferences also influenced early adolescents' expressed preferences for Black and White social encounters (McCrary, 1991). For elementary-school-aged children (ages 6–8 and 9–11), the proportion of same-race mutual friendships increased with age (Graham, Cohen, Zbikowski, & Secrist, 1998). There are racial differences in the association between race and peer preferences. Although older Black children (age 9–11) have more same-race than cross-race mutual friends, Black children are more accepting of White children as friends than White children are of Black friends (Graham & Cohen, 1997). Interracial friendships in both school and nonschool settings are significantly more common among Black children than among White children (ages 12–14) (Dubois & Hirsch, 1990).

How are racial preferences formed? The atmosphere in which children live and the values passed on to them in school and the media may all be powerful influences (Gopaul-McNichol, 1995; Hallinan & Teixeira, 1987a; 1987b; Johnson, 1992). The structural and organizational characteristics of a child's environment influence the likelihood of interracial friendliness. Likewise, interracial friendliness is affected primarily by the number of opportunities students have for cross-race interaction (Hallinan & Smith, 1985; Hallinan & Teixeira, 1987b).

The formation of racial attitudes may be influenced directly and indirectly by parents according to the manner in which they socialize their children (Goodman, 1964). The direct transmission of racial attitudes from parents to children may be exhibited in discussions about race or discrimination. Indirect transmission may also occur (e.g., in overheard conversations between adults, parents' own preferences for peers and media, or subtle behavioral cues such as a White mother pressing down the locks on her car door as she drives through a predominantly Black residential neighborhood; Coles, 1964). Likewise, where a child lives and the actual interchanges between Blacks and Whites may influence choices for both Black and White children.

Racial socialization refers to the process by which Black parents equip their children with the skills and strategies necessary to cope with the knowledge that in this society, being Black may have detrimental consequences and negative outcomes (Hughes & Chen, 1997; Peters, 1981; Spencer, 1983). This process entails providing children with information on race and race relations.

Little research has focused on the content of parental racial socialization practices. Thornton, Chatters, and Taylor (1990) indicated that parents' socialization practices have emphasized areas of achievement, moral values, racial pride, racial history, self-image, racism, equality, religion, and peaceful coexistence as well as verbal behavior (direct statements regarding race) and modeling behavior. Within the racial socialization literature, a varying percentage of Black parents engage in racial socialization practices; the range may be from 38% to 64% of sampled parents who engaged in any racial socialization (Spencer, 1983; Thornton et al., 1990). These estimates suggest that at least one-third of Black parents do not provide racial socialization experiences for their children (Spencer, 1983). Some Black parents choose not to make their children aware of issues about racism and discrimination because they believe it may make their children bitter. Some believe it is not important until the child has experienced racism because the concept of racism is too difficult for children to understand unless they have experienced it. Still others believe such socialization is not necessary because racism is not as prevalent as it used to be (Stevenson & Renard, 1993). The fact that parents do different things in terms of educating their child about race and racism leads us to ask whether these different practices (telling or not telling children about race and racism) have different effects on children and children's choices. However, until recently, research did not provide extensive descriptions of possible racial socialization dimensions.

Boykin and Toms (1985) outlined themes that guide the content of what parents incorporate in their racial socialization practices. These themes are based on aspects of the social dynamics of African Americans in a discriminatory society and are (a) cultural experience (e.g., styles, traditions, and motifs), (b) minority experience (social, economic, and political forces impinging on racial minorities and social outlook), and (c) mainstream experience (influences of White culture). Research indicates that the elements of the cultural experience of Blacks are primarily limited to recounts of historical events and famous historical figures as the extent of Black racial socialization (Spencer, 1983; Tatum, 1987). In the minority experience, the primary goal of racial socialization is to prepare children for life in an oppressive environment (Richardson, 1981). Parents stress learning to survive and deal with prejudice, having self-respect, and understanding the importance of good education. The mainstream experience focuses on instilling human values and minimizing the importance of race.

As indicated, Black girls' racial preferences are likely influenced by their parents' socialization practices, as race is such a salient issue in the rearing of Black children (Garcia Coll et al., 1996). Likewise, for all children, racial preferences are likely influenced by their parents' own experiences of race in society. For example, in the United States, negative connotations of race are often associated with negative attitudes individuals may have toward poverty or the poor (Spencer, 1983). The history of discrimination practices in the United States has also led to disproportionate rates of Black families living in poverty (Massey & Eggers, 1990). As such, children growing up in poverty or at lower income levels may experience more negative interactions with mainstream society, that is, the predominantly White middle-class culture. Parents of these children may feel more disconnected from other groups in society and hence may be more likely to socialize their children in ways that are more isolating. Educational experiences of parents, separate from income, may also influence the home environment of children through parents' exposure to different people and cultures in educational institutions. Moreover, higher education may potentially mean more professional level occupations (those usually dominated by White middle-class workers). Mothers operating in professional settings may have more interactions with members outside their own racial group from which to draw attitudes and beliefs about different races of people.

The current investigation explored the racial socialization practices of Black mothers toward their preadolescent daughters. The transition into and the period of adolescence pose unique challenges for the mother-daughter relationship. These challenges are sources of increased conflict between mothers and daughters; however, the closeness and affection of these relationships are not necessarily diminished (Graber & Brooks-Gunn, 1999). In fact, the strength of these relationships plays a significant role, for both mother and daughter, in the navigation of this period of adjustment (Paikoff & Brooks-Gunn, 1991). It is during this period of early adolescence that the watching of television and listening to music peaks (Adams, Gullotta, & Markstrom-Adams, 1994). This increase in television viewing and music is important not only in relation to academic performance, but also in relation to the social transitions made in adolescence. Television and music strongly shape adolescents' attitudes toward people, places, and things (Adams et al., 1994). Hence, the racial socialization teachings that parents (in this case, mothers) use prior to this transition may be important as early adolescents begin making choices about the types of friends they keep, the music they listen to, and the television shows they watch.

To further understand the racial preferences of young children, we set out to accomplish two goals: (a) to study the pervasiveness of same-race versus other-race preferences and (b) to investigate the influence of Black mothers' racial socialization on Black girls' racial choices. Hence, this investigation compared Black and White girls' racial preferences as exhibited through media choices (television shows and music); Black and White girls' racial preferences as indicated by their peer selections; and the association between family characteristics, such as the experience of poverty and maternal education, and racial preferences in Black and White girls. In the subsample of Black girls, we examined the influence of the three dimensions of Black mothers' socialization (cultural history, cultural emersion, and cultural distance) on Black girls' behaviors. The concurrent association between parental racial socialization practices and child preferences (in media and peer selections) was investigated only for Black girls, as racial socialization is most relevant for Black families. This research went beyond examining the stereotypes of the classic doll studies (Clark & Clark, 1939, 1947) to examining actual behavior and behavioral choices in children.

Method

Participants

The participants were 140 Black and White girls and their families recruited from school districts in the New York, NY, communities of Queens, Brooklyn, and Yonkers. Particular school districts were selected because of their racial breakdown that indicated that schools in those districts would be racially integrated. For example, one of the selected school districts in Brooklyn contained 45% Black and 37% White students; one in Queens, 35% Black and 41% White students; and one in Yonkers, 29% Black and 31% White students (University of the State of New York, 1994).

Teacher reports of the racial distribution of their classrooms indicated a level of integration that mimicked district distributions.

Table 1
Maternal and Familial Characteristics

Characteristic	Overall	Black	White
Maternal age at birth of target child			
M	29	26	30
SD	2	3	2
Mother is high school graduate or above (%)	89	82	84
Family resides at or below the poverty line (%)	42	48	19
Family structure of single, mother-headed household (%)	45	69	27
Mother employed full time (%)	68	75	58
N	140	51	89

Of the 140 girls, 51 were Black (36%). The girls ranged in age between 8 and 9 years, with a mean age of 8.5 years, and were in the third or fourth grade at the onset of data collection (1995–1997; see Table 1 for descriptive information on the sample).[1] These families were drawn from a larger longitudinal study of the ways psychological processes and relationships with peers and parents set girls on various trajectories leading to more or less positive adjustment. Letters describing the project were distributed in class to all third-grade girls in participating schools. Parents sent back cards or called the project office indicating they were interested in participating in the project. Families were contacted and informed that the project was designed to investigate the psychological, emotional, and physiological development of young girls (of middle childhood age) as they make the transition into puberty. Mothers and girls were interviewed during the course of a 2-hr home visit, participated in two parent-child activities, and completed a series of questionnaires and physiological specimen collections on their own over the course of three days. Two female researchers conducted the home visit. One of the researchers was the same race as the child. Families were offered $60 dollars for their participation. The girls were also given a project T-shirt as a gift from the project members.

Measures Media and Peer Preferences

During the home visit interview, the girls were asked the following four questions, which were used to identify preferences (Question 1 is the preface to Question 2): (1) "Who are your favorite people to play with/hang out with?" and (2) "Are these friends [Black/White/Asian/Hispanic/Biracial]?" (Interviewers were instructed to prompt for the race of each friend listed in Question 1.); (3) "What is your favorite televi-

sion show?"; and (4) "Who is your favorite singer/singing group/band?" The racial preference for friend was originally coded into five categories: all same-race as self, more same-race as self, mixed races, more different race than self, all different race than self. These categories were collapsed into three groups: in-group preference (all and more same-race as self), out-group preference (all and more different race as self), and mixed preference. For favorite television show and musical group, children were encouraged to give one choice. If a girl indicated two choices for either television show or musical group, the interviewers prompted her to choose her favorite of the two.

Television shows were coded into three groups: Black preference, White preference, or no-race preference (indicating no preference for one group over another but for mixed races). We watched the television shows named by the participants at the Museum of Television and Radio, New York, NY, to ensure that shows that were coded were episodes that originally aired during the time the original data were collected (1995–1997). Lisa A. O'Connor arbitrarily selected three episodes of each show mentioned by the participants, rather than a single episode, as television shows geared toward children and teenagers often have special episodes that deal with larger societal issues (e.g., underage drinking, race relations, or eating disorders). This was done to avoid selecting the one episode whose story line was about race relations and would include a higher-than-usual proportion of time that a Black character was present.

The three selected episodes aired within the three months prior to the date of the home visit. Each episode was watched three times: first, to identify the main characters; second, to time the presence of a Black main character; and third, to time the presence of a White main character. Categorization into the three preference groups was made on the basis of the proportion of time each character was present averaged over the three episodes. After the initial times were recorded, a subsample (every third show listed) of the television shows were retimed by a different researcher to test for the reliability of the first recorded time. Coders' times were always within 4 s of each other ($M = 2.34$ s).

Shows categorized as Black preference were shows that had very high proportions of Black character time to White character time. These shows, in general, had all Black characters, both primary and secondary (98% to 100% of the time). Similarly, shows in the White preference category had mainly all White primary and secondary characters, although sometimes out of a group of four or five main characters only one character was Black. Shows in the no-race preference category ranged from cartoons (which have few racial undertones) to television talk shows (e.g., Ricki Lake or

---

[1] Because of the high demand on scheduling and limited data collectors, some girls originally contacted in the third grade to participate were not seen until the beginning of the fourth grade.

Table 2
Children's Preferences Across Media and Peer Choices by Race (Percentages)

	Music			Television			Friend		
Child race	No race	Black	White	No race	Black	White	Mixed	Black	White
Black	21	76	8	20	56	25	29	56	15
White	16	32	47	9	7	83	15	16	69

385 Jenny Jones), which on any given day would have a milieu of different racial groups present.

Music choices were also coded into three groups: Black, White, and no-race preference. Categorizations were based on Billboard's (http://www.billboard.com) music categories. The White preference category in-
390 cludes artists from the pop, rock, alternative, country, and heavy metal categories—categories traditionally dominated by White performers. The Black preference category includes artists from music categories such as rhythm and blues, hip-hop, rap, soul, and gospel—
395 categories traditionally dominated by Black perform-ers. The no-race preference choice included music from the dance and light sounds musical categories—categories that usually include both Black and White artists.

Child Race, Maternal Education, and Family Income

400 During the interview with mother, mothers reported the race of their daughter. Additionally, mothers indi-cated the highest level of education that they had achieved. Responses were then grouped into 3 catego-ries: less than high school education, high school
405 graduate, and some college or more.

The United States government sets the poverty threshold, the official measurement of poverty. This poverty level is a needs-adjusted income line that is adjusted for family size and the number of children
410 under the age of 18 living in the household. This in-come is an estimated cost of a shopping cart of food multiplied by three (assuming that a family's food cost is one-third of their budget). Adjustments to this pov-erty threshold are made annually and are based on the
415 consumer price index (Citro & Michael, 1995; Duncan & Brooks-Gunn, 1997). For this project, poverty status was calculated from maternal reports of household size and family income and compared with national levels of the poverty threshold for 1996. For example, in a
420 family of three (one parent and two children), the pov-erty threshold is $12,980 as an annual income.

Maternal Socialization

Maternal racial socialization was measured using a 19-item scale designed to assess parental socialization practices (Racial Socialization Scale; Hughes, 1995). It
425 is scored on a 5-point Likert scale ranging from 1 (*never*) to 5 (*very often*). Socialization practices were categorized into three subscales: Cultural History ($M =$ 2.6, $SD = .29$, $\alpha = .84$), Cultural Distance ($M = 1.45$, $SD = .49$, $\alpha = .60$), and Cultural Emersion ($M = 2.78$,

430 $SD = .29$, $\alpha = .87$). The Cultural History dimension relates to providing children with information about racial discrimination and the historical background of Black culture, emphasizing the minority experience (e.g., "Do you ever talk to your daughter about racism
435 and discrimination against Black people in this coun-try?"). Cultural Distance relates to sharing personal feelings about race and race relations in this society reflecting the mainstream experience (e.g., "Do you ever tell her that she should not trust White people?").
440 Cultural Emersion refers to exposing children to Black culture by taking part in activities important to the cul-ture (e.g., "Have you ever taken your daughter to a Black cultural event like Kwanza celebrations, Black expo, or a play about Black Americans or Africans?").

Results

Black and White Girls' Media Preferences

445 As indicated, this study first examined girls' media and peer preferences. When "no-race" or "mixed-race" was an option for preferences, more Black than White girls named no-race preferences for music and televi-sion and mixed preference peer choices (see Table 2).
450 Across music, television, and peer choices, approxi-mately 20% to 30% of Black girls were in the no-race and mixed-race preference categories. For White girls, across all categories, approximately 10% to 15% were in the no-race and mixed-race preference categories.
455 Analyses also indicate that both Black and White girls had more no-race or mixed-race preferences than the literature suggests (see Table 2).

Results indicated that Black girls had more same-race preferences in the music category than did White
460 girls, $\chi^2 (2, N = 138) = 28.63, p < .001$. As expected, analyses also indicated that White girls had more same-race preferences in their television choices than did Black girls, $\chi^2 (2, N = 138) = 49.19, p < .001$. Partition-ing chi-square analysis indicated that Black girls chose
465 the Black music preference category more often than the White music and no-race preference categories, $\chi^2 (1, N = 138) = 26.23, p < .001$, whereas White girls chose the White music category as often as they chose the Black or no-race preference, $\chi^2 (1, N = 138) =$
470 25.89, *ns*. These analyses also indicated that for televi-sion choices, White girls chose White shows over Black and no-race shows, $\chi^2 (1, N = 138) = 45.93, p < .001$, whereas Black girls, as hypothesized, chose the Black television category as often as they chose the
475 White or no-race preference category, $\chi^2 (1, N = 138) =$

Table 3
Racial Socialization and Children's Media and Peer Choices

Measure	Music choices				Television choices				Friend choices			
	No race	Black preference	White preference	p	No race	Black preference	White preference	p	Mixed preference	Black preference	White preference	p
Cultural Emersion												
M	1.50	1.55	1.00	.10	2.08	3.12	2.84	.004	1.45	1.49	1.41	ns
SD	0.53	0.50	0.0		0.43	0.49	0.52		0.52	0.52	0.51	
Cultural History												
M	1.63	1.44	1.00	.07	1.10	1.57	1.38	.03	1.45	1.43	1.33	ns
SD	0.52	0.50	0.0		0.32	0.50	0.51		0.52	0.51	0.50	
Cultural Distance												
M	1.55	1.75	1.50	.04	1.20	1.69	1.59	.04	1.54	1.67	1.16	.05
SD	0.46	0.51	0.58		0.42	0.48	0.50		0.52	0.52	0.37	

40.22, ns. Examination of the association between peer and media choices indicated that Black girls who had more mixed-race or out-group peer preferences had more no-race preferences in music and television choices than did White girls who had more mixed-race or out-group peer preferences, $\chi^2 (2, N = 138) = 13.26$, $p < .05$.

We also conducted partitioning chi-square analyses to examine the correlates of girls' media and peer preference. There was little association between poverty status and girls' music choices. However, poverty status was associated with Black girls' television choices such that, for Black girls living at or below the poverty line, Black television shows were more popular than White ones. For Black girls living above the poverty line, White and no-race shows were more popular than Black television shows, $\chi^2 (2, N = 76) = 10.02$, $p < .05$. For White girls, these analyses revealed no significant associations. White girls chose White television shows over Black and no-race shows regardless of poverty status. Girls' media choices were not significantly associated with mother's education level in either group.

Black Girls' Media Preferences and Maternal Socialization

For the subsample of Black girls, we conducted analyses of variance (ANOVAs) to test the association of media preference choices (Black, White, and mixed) with Black mothers' racial socialization practices (see Table 3 for means and standard deviations by group). Girls' music choices were somewhat related to parental socialization practices such that Black mothers who engaged in cultural emersion had girls who were somewhat more likely to prefer Black music over White and no-race music, $F (2, 47) = 2.28$, $p < .10$. Black mothers who engaged in more cultural history socialization had girls who were more likely to have mixed-preference music choices over Black or White music choices, $F (2, 48) = 2.19$, $p < .05$. Mothers who engaged in more cultural distance socialization had

girls who had more Black music choices, $F (2, 47) = 2.81$, $p < .05$.

ANOVA analyses also indicated that Black mothers with higher scores on the Cultural Emersion, Cultural History, and Cultural Distance subscales had girls with more Black preferences in television show selections, $F (2, 49) = 2.90$, $p = .05$; $F (2, 48) = 3.70$, $p < .05$; $F (2, 47) = 3.30$, $p < .05$, respectively, over no-race or White television show preferences (see Table 3 for means and standard deviations).

Black and White Girls' Peer Preferences

Both Black and White girls had more same-race peer preferences than mixed-race or out-group preferences, $\chi^2 (2, N = 82) = 11.31$, $p < .05$. Across race, girls preferred same-race peers (64%) over out-group peers (17%) or mixed-group peers (19%). Black girls had a mixed-race peer group more often than did White girls, partitioning $\chi^2 (2, N = 82) = 2.06$, $p < .05$, with 29% and 15%, respectively (see Table 2).

Black girls living at and below the poverty line had more in-group preferences than mixed group or out-group preferences, $\chi^2 (2, N = 82) = 6.10$, $p < .05$. However, for Black girls living above the poverty line, peer choices shifted to include more mixed-race and out-group preferences than in-group preferences, $\chi^2 (2, N = 82) = 2.55$, $p < .05$. No significant associations between poverty status and peer choices were found for White girls. Maternal educational level was not associated with girls' peer selections.

Black Girls' Peer Preferences and Maternal Socialization

Again, for the subsample of Black girls, we conducted ANOVAs to assess the association of parental racial socialization and daughters' peer choices (see Table 3 for means and standard deviations). Black girls whose mothers engaged in more cultural distance socialization practices had more in-group peer preferences, $F (4, 45) = 2.24$, $p = .05$. No links were found between girls' peer preferences and the cultural emersion and cultural history racial socialization practices.

Discussion

Our findings are comparable to other more recent studies of children's preferences. In particular, both Black and White girls in the late 1990s (at least in our small sample from New York, NY) were having interracial experiences. Although our society is not free of racism and discrimination, it may be that girls are taking advantage of the new (yet still limited) diversity in their lives. Children have access to multiple media through which they have out-group exposure. This premise is corroborated through the high levels of White television preferences in Black girls and the high levels of Black music preferences in White girls. Currently, Black music, most notably hip-hop and rhythm and blues, has permeated the American pop culture so much that we see the influence of the urban culture in commercials (e.g., for Coca Cola™ and Burger King™) and in adolescent fashion (e.g., baggy jeans and oversized shirts).

The high preference for White or no-race in the television category may be because at the time of data collection (1995) there were few "Black" television shows from which girls could choose, reflecting a certain level of discrimination in television show production. Since these data were collected, two television networks have targeted marketing for Black audiences by introducing a wave of new Black television situation comedies. Thus, it may be that, with more options available, children would now report more Black television show preferences. It could also be argued that the preferences for shows in the no-race category reflect successful marketing and packaging of these shows by producers and not necessarily children's attitudes. However, the success of these kinds of shows, whether through conscious racial choices by children or successful marketing strategies, indicates that children are making choices that include interracial contact. Hence, television can highlight interracial contact because children are open to alternatives to the all-White norm of television as long as the marketing and packaging of shows grab their attention.

Although peer preferences are primarily same-race, a portion of Black and White girls (29% and 15%, respectively) chose mixed-race peer groups. These findings suggest that girls are participating in more diverse settings than when earlier preference research was conducted. Considering that the United States is as segregated today as it was in the 1950s, this is a promising finding. A review of national conditions shows that economic and racial segregation persists in the United States (Powell et al., 1997). Notably, the girls in this project were living in a city (New York, NY) that is relatively less racially segregated than are most urban areas (Massey & Eggers, 1990).

For all measures, girls were not forced to choose between favoring their own group and favoring the other group. Nevertheless, the girls in this study demonstrated clear signs of in-group preferences. Although these girls were having interracial interactions, their primary relationships were within their same-race groups. The higher levels of in-group peer preferences might be expected given the voluntary nature of friendships. Similarity and common ground are necessities in both friendship formation and maintenance (Gottman, 1983). Racial similarity may be important in friendships throughout the school years (Aboud & Mendelson, 1996). Children from preschool onward tend to like, and play with, classmates of their own race to a greater extent than those of another race (Aboud, 1988). Yet, compared with White children, Black and other minority children show greater attraction and friendship toward other-race peers (Hallinan & Teixeira, 1987a). It may be that in terms of other-race peer selections, Black girls sharing a minority status with other racial groups is a common ground. Thus, we may see, for example, more Black-Hispanic racial-ethnic peer friendships developing in communities that are not highly segregated. (This sample was too small to test this hypothesis.)

Prior research on racial preferences has shown that between the ages of 4 and 7 years, White children become more strongly biased against others in favor of their own ethnic members (Bigler & Liben, 1993). Minority children remain split over which is negative and which is the favored group up to age 7. After 7 years of age, ethnic minority children express negative attitudes toward out-group members less frequently. The usual pattern is either bias against other groups in favor of their own group or a more neutral attitude toward their own group and others (Brand et al., 1974). In contrast, White children either show no change or show little decline in prejudice while maintaining a less intense bias for their own group. At age 8, children use their perceptions of racial similarity and differences to make judgments about others; by ages 11 or 12, they abandon these perceptions in favor of perceptions of individual features (Doyle & Aboud, 1995). Thus, the present findings that girls have some group preferences for peers is not surprising although many girls in this sample of 8- and 9-year-olds already appeared to be making decisions that were not based solely on race.

The strong in-group preference for girls' peer selections could be due to the de facto racial segregation in children's neighborhoods and schools. Thus, it is not surprising that poor Black girls had more same-race friendships than did Black girls above the poverty line. It is possible that in poorer communities, there is limited exposure to members of the dominant race. The reality is that a life in poverty often results in a life of segregation as well (Massey & Eggers, 1990).

Moreover, as relatively more Black families become middle class, many often move out of a poor neighborhood to a more middle class, usually more White, neighborhood (Wilson, 1987, 1991). Consequently, the possibilities for new mixed-race friendships for their girls are likely to increase; however, little research addresses this issue. More interracial friendships also may influence girls' media choices. As friendships call for the sharing of interests, one's favorite television show or musical group or singer may become part of that common ground.

The findings on links between Black girls' preferences and maternal racial socialization practices are intriguing. The most striking finding is the association between the cultural distance socialization practice and girls' preferences. The cultural distance socialization scale stresses more negative relations between Blacks and Whites. This form of socialization was significantly related to Black girls' in-group preference in music, television, and peers. An emphasis on cultural distance may in fact have led to more segregated lifestyles for these girls; alternatively, leading more segregated lifestyles may have increased a parent's practice of cultural distance. With cross-sectional data, an exploration of the directionality of this association is impossible. We suspect that the pathways are multidetermined. For example, it is possible that being poor and residing in a poor neighborhood (which is likely to comprise a large proportion of minorities, at least in urban areas) leads to actual cultural distance as well as more same-race lifestyles. Thus, maternal racial socialization strategies may reinforce the likelihood that their daughters will have same-race preferences (the girl herself being influenced by the racial composition of the neighborhood, school, and peer group).

These three categories of parental socialization have been linked to parental characteristics. First, Black mothers of elementary school girls below the poverty level are less likely to engage in racial socialization practices than are mothers at or above the poverty level (O'Connor, Gyamfi, & Brooks-Gunn, 1997). This research has also found that particular aspects of maternal characteristics influence parents' level of engaging in racial socialization, such that mothers' temperament, positive affect, and social support were significantly associated with mothers' engagement in racial socialization.

There are some limitations to this study. First, the sample size does not allow for the examination of some issues that are clearly important, such as the specific pattern of mixed-race friendships (e.g., Black/Hispanic versus Black/White). We see this investigation as exploratory given the small sample size. Also, the findings on friendships are all based on self-report rather than observation. Additionally, the data presented here are indicative of only one point in time. The girls were also drawn from a unique context in that they lived in more integrated environments than most girls (by study design). Thus, generalizability of these findings is constrained. Finally, we have limited information on the context in which these preferences were made and in which friendships were formed. Thus, future research should explore the influence of neighborhood and school characteristics (e.g., concentration of poverty, level of neighborhood and school integration, and neighborhood unemployment rate) on children's experiences and choices.

Implications for Application and Public Policy

This research suggests that children are open to interracial experiences, including friendships and entertainment. As a society, we could benefit from this openness and encourage more integration, especially in our media productions. In a time when the National Association for the Advancement of Colored People is chastising major television networks about their lack of Black characters, either as main characters or in supporting roles, our children are indicating that they are interested in and comfortable with integration. Media, both music and television, have become such a vital source of information and are such important resources for adolescents (indicated by their increased television watching and music listening; Adams et al., 1994) that they should be used as significant venues designed to reach young people. The topography of entertainment is changing such that Black music, notably hip-hop and rap music, has become the mainstream. Although this trend is not overwhelmingly evident in television, the potential for positive effects is there. Television shows like "Moesha" (Spears, 2000) have spawned a large following among both Black and White adolescent girls such that the show's star, Brandy, has become a role model for Black and White girls alike, and is continually being featured in teen magazines (e.g., *YM* magazine).

This research has suggested that maternal racial socialization is associated with Black girls' racial preferences. Racial socialization is part of family processes and should be assessed when examining interactions between parents and children. Notably, the aspect of cultural distance is an important one. Black parents' perception and experience of inequality probably encourages the practice of cultural distance. Income inequality and housing and neighborhood segregation also promote interpersonal segregation. It is likely that an increase in mixed-race peer friendships and media choices will be constrained by inequality and segregation. Efforts to reduce cultural distance in the absence of more integration in housing and schools will be difficult. Hence, encouraging interracial contact (in all venues) in young children is paramount in the struggle toward reducing cultural distance between the races.

References

Aboud, F. E. (1988). Children and prejudice. (New York: Basil Blackwell).

Aboud, F. E., & Mendelson, M. J. (1996). Determinants of friendship selection and quality: Developmental perspectives. (In W. M. Bukowski, A. F. Newcomb, & W. W. Hartup (Eds.), *The company they keep: Friendship in childhood and adolescence* (pp. 87—112). New York: Cambridge University Press.)

Adams, G. R., Gullotta, T. P., & Markstrom-Adams, C. (1994). Adolescent life experiences. (Pacific Grove, CA: Brooks/Cole)

Asher, S., & Allen, V. (1969). Racial preference and social comparison processes. *Journal of Social Issues, 25,* 157-166.

Banks, W. C. (1976). White preference in Black children: A paradigm in search of a phenomenon. *Psychological Bulletin, 83,* 1179-1186.

Bigler, R., & Liben, L. (1993). A cognitive-developmental approach to racial stereotyping and reconstructive memory in Euro-American children. *Child Development, 64*, 1507-1519.

Boykin, A. W., & Toms, F. (1985). Black child socialization: A conceptual framework. (In H. P. McAdoo & J. L. McAdoo [Eds.], *Black children: Social, educational, and parental environments*. Beverly Hills, CA: Sage.)

Brand, E. S., Ruiz, R. A., & Padilla, A. M. (1974). Ethnic identification and preference behavior: A review. *Psychological Bulletin, 81*, 860-890.

Butler, R. (1989). Mastery versus ability appraisal: A developmental study of children's observations of peers' work. *Child Development, 60*, 1350-1361.

Citro, C., & Michael, R. (1995). Measuring poverty: A new approach. (Washington, DC: National Academy of Sciences Press)

Clark, K. B., & Clark, M. P. (1939). The development of consciousness of self and the emergence of racial identification in Negro preschool children. *Journal of Social Psychology, 10*, 591-599.

Clark, K. B., & Clark, M. P. (1947). Racial identification and preference in Negro children. (In Society for the Psychological Study of Social Issues [Ed.], *Readings in social psychology* (pp. 157-185). New York: Holt.)

Coles, R. (1964). Children of crisis. (Boston: Little, Brown)

Cross, W. E. (1981). Black families and Black identity development. *Journal of Comparative Family Studies, 19*, 341-350.

Doyle, A. B., & Aboud, F. E. (1995). A longitudinal study of White children's racial prejudice as a social-cognitive development. *Merrill-Palmer Quarterly, 41*, 209-228.

DuBois, D. L., & Hirsch, B. J. (1990). School and neighborhood friendship patterns of Blacks and Whites in early adolescence. *Child Development, 61*, 524-536.

Duncan, G. J., & Brooks-Gunn, J. (1997). Income effects across the life span: Integration and interpretation. (In G. J. Duncan & J. Brooks-Gunn [Eds.], *Consequences of growing up poor* (pp. 596-610). New York: Russell Sage Foundation.)

Gan, S., Zillmann, D., & Mitrook, M. (1997). Stereotyping effect of Black women's rap on White audiences. *Basic and Applied Social Psychology, 19*, 381-399.

Garcia Coll, C., Crnic, K., Lamberty, G., Wasik, B. H., Jenkins, R., Garcia, H. V., & McAdoo, H. P. (1996). An integrative model for the study of developmental competencies in minority children. *Child Development, 67*, 1891-1914.

Goodman, M. E. (1964). Race awareness in young children.(New York: Collier)

Gopaul-McNichol, S. (1995). A cross-cultural examination of racial identity and racial preference of preschool children in the West Indies. *Journal of Cross-Cultural Psychology, 26*, 141-152.

Gottman, J. M. (1983). How children become friends. (*Monographs of the Society for Research in Child Development, 78* (3, Serial No. 201).

Graber, J. A., & Brooks-Gunn, J. (1999). "Sometimes I think that you don't like me": How mothers and daughters negotiate the transition to adolescence. (In M. Cox & J. Brooks-Gunn [Eds.], *Conflict and cohesion in families: Causes and consequences* (pp. 207-242). Mahwah, NJ: Erlbaum.)

Graham, J. A., & Cohen, R. (1997). Race and sex as factors in children's sociometric ratings and friendship choices. *Social Development, 6*, 355-372.

Graham, J. A., Cohen, R., Zbikowski, S. M., & Secrist, M. E. (1998). A longitudinal investigation of race and sex as factors in children's classroom friendship choices. *Child Study Journal, 28*, 245-266.

Gregor, A. J., & McPherson, D. A. (1966). Racial attitudes among White and Negro children in a deep south standard metropolitan area. *Journal of Social Psychology, 68*, 95-106.

Gunthrope, W. W. (1978). Skin color recognition, preference, and identification in interracial children: A comparative study (Doctoral dissertation, Rutgers University, 1978.) Dissertation Abstract International, 38, (B-3468)

Hallinan, M. T., & Smith, S. S. (1985). The effects of classroom racial composition on students' interracial friendliness. *Social Psychology Quarterly, 48*, 3-16.

Hallinan, M. T., & Teixeira, R. A. (1987a). Opportunities and constraints: Black-White differences in the formation of interracial friendships. *Child Development, 58*, 1358-1371.

Hallinan, M. T., & Teixeira, R. A. (1987b). Students' interracial friendships: Individual characteristics, structural effects, and racial difference. *American Journal of Education, 95*, 563-583.

Harter, S. (1983). To smile or not to smile. Issues in the examination of cross-cultural differences and similarities. *Monographs of the Society for Research on Child Development, 48*, 80-87.

Hraba, J., & Grant, G. (1970). Black is beautiful: A reexamination of racial preference and identification. *Journal of Personality and Social Psychology, 16*, 398-402.

Hughes, D. (1995, June). Dimensions of occupational racism as predictors of racial socialization in African American families. (Paper presented at the 5th Biennial Conference of the Society for Community Research and Action, Chicago, IL.)

Hughes, D., & Chen, L. (1997). When and what parents tell children about race: An examination of race-related socialization among African American families. *Applied Developmental Science, 1*, 200-214.

Johnson, D. J. (1992). Racial preferences and biculturality in biracial preschoolers. *Merrill-Palmer Quarterly, 38*, 233-244.

Larson, R. (1995). Secrets in the bedroom: Adolescents' private use of media. *Journal of Youth and Adolescence, 24*, 535-550.

Massey, D. S., & Eggers, M. L. (1990). The ecology of inequality: Minorities and the concentration of poverty, 1970-1980. *American Journal of Sociology, 95*, 1153-1188.

McCrary, J. H. (1991). The effects of listeners' and performers' race on music preferences and the relationship between listeners' expressed music preference and expressed preferences for Black and White social encounters. *Dissertation Abstracts International, 52*, 1-A 107

Morland, J. K. (1962). Racial acceptance and preference of nursery school children in a southern city. *Merrill Palmer Quarterly of Behavior and Development, 8*, 271-280.

O'Connor, L. A., Gyamfi, P., & Brooks-Gunn, J. (1997). Antecedents and consequences: Racial socialization in Black girls' families. (Poster presented at the biennial meeting of the Society for Research in Child Development, Washington, DC).

Paikoff, R., & Brooks-Gunn, J. (1991). Do parent-child relationships change during puberty? *Psychological Bulletin, 110*, 47-66.

Peters, M. F. (1981). Parenting in Black families with young children: A historical perspective. (In H. McAdoo [Ed.], *Black families* [pp. 228-241] Newbury Park, CA: Sage.)

Powell, J., Kay, V., Cleary, S., Cooper, K., Lydell, L., & Myall, H. (1997). Examining the relationship between housing, education, and persistent segregation. (Minneapolis, MN: Center for Urban and Regional Affairs)

Proshansky, H. (1966). The development of intergroup attitudes. (In L. W. Hoffman & M. L. Hoffman [Eds.], *Review of child development research: Vol. 2* [pp. 295-305]. New York: Russell Sage Foundation.)

Richardson, B. (1981). Racism and child rearing: A study of Black mothers (doctoral dissertation, Claremont Graduate School, 1981). *Dissertation Abstracts International, 42*, 125A.

Ruble, D. (1987). The acquisition of self-knowledge: A self-socialization process. (In N. Eisenberg [Ed.], *Contemporary topics in developmental psychology* [pp. 243-270]. New York: Wiley.)

Semaj, L. (1980). The development of racial evaluation and preference: A cognitive approach. *Journal of Black Psychology, 6*, 59-79.

Shils, E. A. (1948). The present state of American sociology. (Glencoe, IL: Free Press)

Spears, V. (2000). Moesha. (New York: WWOR-TV)

Spencer, M. B. (1983). Children's cultural values and parental child rearing strategies. *Developmental Review, 3*, 351-370.

Stevenson, H. C., & Renard, G. (1993). Trusting ole' wise owls: Therapeutic use of cultural strengths of African American families. (*Professional Psychology: Research and Practice, 24*, 433-442.)

Stevenson, H. W., & Stewart, E. C. (1958). A developmental study of racial awareness in young children. *Child Development, 29*, 399-409.

Tatum, B. (1987). Assimilation blues. (Westport, CT: Greenwood)

Thornton, M. C., Chatters, L. M., & Taylor, R. J. (1990). Sociodemographic and environmental correlates of racial socialization by Black parents. *Child Development, 61*, 401-409.

University of the State of New York. (1994). Racial/ethnic distribution of public school students and staff. (Albany, NY: The State Education Department)

Wilder, D. (1986). Social categorization: Implication for creation and reduction of intergroup bias. (In L. Berkowitz [Ed.], *Advances in experimental social psychology* [pp. 157-189]. New York: Academic Press.)

Wilson, W. J. (1987). The truly disadvantaged: The inner city, the underclass, and public policy. (Chicago: University of Chicago Press)

Wilson, W. J. (1991). Public policy research and the truly disadvantaged. (In C. Jencks & P. E. Peterson [Eds.], *The urban underclass* [pp. 460-481]. Washington, DC: Brookings Institution.)

Acknowledgments: Funding from the National Institute of Child Health and Development (NICHD; Grant No. HD32376) supported the research in this article. We thank the girls and parents who participated in this investigation, the members of the Center for Children and Families who worked on the Girls' Health and Development Project, and Michelle Warren and her laboratory staff. We also thank Diane Hughes for the use of her socialization measure and Margaret Spencer for her assistance in the selection of measures and for serving as a consultant on this project. Portions of this article were presented at the biennial meeting of the Society for Research in Child Development, 1999, Albuquerque, New Mexico.

Address correspondence to: Lisa O'Connor, Teachers College, Columbia University, 525 West 120th Street, New York, NY 10027. E-mail: lao10@columbia.edu

Exercise for Article 13

Factual Questions

1. According to Richardson (1981), what is the "primary goal" of racial socialization in the minority experience?

2. The researchers selected particular school districts because they had what characteristics?

3. How much money were the families offered for their participation in this study?

4. The original five categories for "racial preference for friend" were collapsed into how many categories?

5. What percentage of White children was classified as having a preference for Black music?

6. For girls living above the poverty line, were Black television shows more popular than the other types of shows?

7. According to the researchers, encouraging interracial contact (in all venues) in young children is paramount in what "struggle"?

Questions for Discussion

8. In their literature review, the researchers point out that historically, other researchers have used dolls, drawings, and pictures to study racial preferences. In your opinion, are there any advantages to using this technique? Disadvantages?

9. In your opinion, does the examination of media choices yield valid information about racial preferences? Does it yield interesting information? Explain.

10. How important are the sample questions for Cultural History, Cultural Distance, and Cultural Emersion in helping you understand what was measured? Would you like to see more of the questions? Explain. (See lines 430–444.)

11. The researchers point out that the findings on friendships in this study are based on self-reports rather than direct observations of the children. In your opinion, is this a serious limitation? Explain. (See lines 712–714.)

12. Do you agree with the researchers that the generalizability of these findings is constrained? Explain. (See lines 718–719.)

Quality Ratings

Directions: Indicate your level of agreement with each of the following statements by circling a number from 5 for strongly agree (SA) to 1 for strongly disagree (SD). If you believe an item is not applicable to this research article, leave it blank. Be prepared to explain your ratings.

A. The introduction establishes the importance of the study.

SA   5   4   3   2   1   SD

B. The literature review establishes the context for the study.

SA   5   4   3   2   1   SD

C. The research purpose, question, or hypothesis is clearly stated.

SA   5   4   3   2   1   SD

D. The method of sampling is sound.

SA   5   4   3   2   1   SD

E. Relevant demographics (for example, age, gender, and ethnicity) are described.

SA   5   4   3   2   1   SD

F. Measurement procedures are adequate.

SA   5   4   3   2   1   SD

G. All procedures have been described in sufficient detail to permit a replication of the study.

SA   5   4   3   2   1   SD

H. The participants have been adequately protected from potential harm.

SA   5   4   3   2   1   SD

I. The results are clearly described.

SA   5   4   3   2   1   SD

J. The discussion/conclusion is appropriate.

SA   5   4   3   2   1   SD

K. Despite any flaws, the report is worthy of publication.

SA   5   4   3   2   1   SD

Article 14

Most Working Women Deny Gender Discrimination in Their Pay

Lydia Saad
The Gallup Poll

EDITOR'S NOTE: The material in lines 1 through 56 appears at the beginning of each issue of *The Gallup Poll Monthly*. It describes general issues in the conduct and interpretation of the telephone surveys reported in the journal. The report on the survey on working women's views on pay discrimination begins with line 57.

From *The Gallup Poll Monthly* (Number 413: February 2000), 35–36.

The Gallup Poll gathers public opinion data primarily through surveys conducted by telephone, which are designed to provide representative samples of adults living in the continental United States.

5 The standard methods used to conduct telephone surveys and the sampling tolerances for interpreting results collected by telephone are detailed below.

Design of the Sample for Telephone Surveys

The samples of telephone numbers used in telephone interview surveys are based on a random digit
10 stratified probability design. The sampling procedure involves stratifying the continental U.S. into 4 time zones and 3 city-size strata within each time zone to yield a total of 12 unique strata.

In order to avoid possible bias if only listed tele-
15 phone numbers are used, the Gallup Poll uses a random digit procedure designed to provide representation of both listed and unlisted (including not-yet-listed) numbers. Samples are drawn within each stratum only from "active blocks," where an "active block" is defined as
20 100 contiguous telephone numbers containing three or more residential telephone listings. By eliminating nonworking blocks of numbers from the sample, the likelihood that any sampled telephone number will be associated with a residence increases from only 20%
25 (where numbers are sampled from all banks) to approximately 55%. Since most banks of telephone numbers are either substantially filled (i.e., assigned) or empty, this practical efficiency is purchased at a negligible cost in terms of possible coverage bias.
30 The sample of telephone numbers drawn by this method is designed to produce, with proper adjustments for differential sampling rates, an unbiased random sample of telephone households in the continental United States.

35 The standard size for national Gallup Poll telephone surveys is 1,000 interviews. More interviews are conducted in specific instances where greater survey accuracy is desired. Fewer interviews are conducted in specific instances where speed in collecting data and
40 reporting the results is required.

Telephone Survey Weighting Procedures

After the survey data have been collected and processed, each respondent is assigned a weight so that the demographic characteristics of the total weighted sample of respondents matches the latest U.S. Census Bu-
45 reau estimates of the demographic characteristics of the adult population living in households with access to a telephone.

The procedures described above are designed to produce samples approximating the adult civilian
50 population (18 and older) living in private households (that is, excluding those in prisons, hospitals, hotels, religious and educational institutions, and those living on reservations or military bases), with access to a telephone. Survey percentages may be applied to Cen-
55 sus estimates of the size of these populations to project percentages into numbers of people.

The Report on Pay Discrimination

A new Gallup Poll finds that 30 percent of working women in the U.S. believe they are paid less than they would be if they were a man, while more than two in
60 three, 70 percent, do not. On the other hand, with just 13 percent saying women at their workplace get paid less than men who perform the same job, working men are even less likely to perceive that women are victims of gender discrimination in their pay.
65 "Pay equity," a longtime goal of the feminist movement, resurfaced in the news when former President Clinton proposed increased federal funding for programs aimed at closing the wage gap between working men and women in this country. Clinton did
70 so touting statistics showing that the average salary for full-time working women is only 75 cents on the dollar of what full-time working men earn.

The Gallup survey, conducted January 25-26, asked respondents about their employment status. Roughly
75 two-thirds of men and just under half of women indicated they are employed full time. Among these groups, only slight differences in attitudes about women's pay were found along age, educational status, income, and other dimensions. The largest difference
80 among full-time employed women is seen by education. Those with a college degree are less likely to feel discriminated against in this way than are women with less formal education, by a 22 percent to 35 percent margin.

Clinton's Plan

85 Critics of President Clinton's initiative say that the "75 cents" indicator is misleading, and cite other statistics showing that men and women of equal educational and work experience are actually virtually equal when it comes to pay. Nevertheless, Gallup finds the Ameri-
90 can people widely supportive of Clinton's proposal to spend $27 million on additional pay equity efforts. Seventy-nine percent favor the proposed spending, including 70 percent of men and 86 percent of women. Just 18 percent are opposed to the plan.

Table 1

Question: As you may know, President Clinton proposed that Congress allocate $27 million to increase enforcement of equal pay laws relating to women in the workplace. Do you favor or oppose this proposal?

	Favor	Oppose	No Opinion
2000 Jan 25-26	79%	18	3

Table 2

Question: Which of the following best describes your current situation—employed full time, employed part time, retired, a homemaker, a student, unemployed but looking for work, or unemployed and not looking for work?

	Men	Women
Employed full time	65%	45
Employed part time	5%	12
Retired	19%	20
Homemaker	0%	15
Student	5%	4
Unemployed, looking for work	3%	2
Unemployed, not looking for work	1%	2
Disabled (vol.)	2%	*
No answer	*	*

* Less than 0.5%

Methodology

95 The results are based on telephone interviews with a randomly selected national sample of 1,044 adults, 18 years and older, conducted January 25–26, 2000. For results based on this sample, one can say with 95 per-
100 cent confidence that the maximum error attributable to sampling and other random effects is plus or minus 3 percentage points. In addition to sampling error, question wording and practical difficulties in conducting surveys can introduce error or bias into the findings of public opinion polls.

Table 3

[Based on 265 women employed full time; ± 7 Pct Pts]
Question: Do you personally feel that because you are a woman, you get paid less than a man would in your same job, or is this not the case?

	Yes, get paid less	No, not the case	No opinion
2000 Jan 25–26	30%	70	0

Table 4

[Based on 331 men employed full time; ± 6 Pct Pts]
Question: From what you know or just your impression—do women at your workplace get paid less than men who do the same job, or is this not the case?

	Yes, get paid less	No, not the case	No opinion
2000 Jan 25–26	13%	78	9

Exercise for Article 14

Factual Questions

1. The 12 strata are based on which two variables?

2. What is done to avoid a possible bias if only listed telephone numbers are used?

3. What is the standard sample size for Gallup telephone surveys?

4. What is the purpose of assigning "weights" to the respondents?

5. For the full sample of 1,044 respondents used in this poll, how many percentage points should be allowed for sampling and other random effects (based on 95% confidence)?

6. What percentage of the women were homemakers?

7. A separate question was asked of men who were employed full time. What percentage of these men had no opinion on the question?

Questions for Discussion

8. This poll was conducted via telephone. In your opinion, are there advantages to polling via telephone over polling via direct face-to-face interviews? Explain.

9. The researcher uses procedures to approximate the adult civilian population, excluding certain groups. Do you think that the exclusions affect the validity of the poll? (See lines 48–54.)

10. The researcher notes that question wording can introduce error or bias into the findings of public opinion polls. Do you think that the wording of the four questions used in this poll is adequate? Explain. (See lines 101–104.)

Quality Ratings

Directions: Indicate your level of agreement with each of the following statements by circling a number from 5 for strongly agree (SA) to 1 for strongly disagree (SD). If you believe an item is not applicable to this research article, leave it blank. Be prepared to explain your ratings.

A. The introduction establishes the importance of the study.

SA   5   4   3   2   1   SD

B. The literature review establishes the context for the study.

SA   5   4   3   2   1   SD

C. The research purpose, question, or hypothesis is clearly stated.

SA   5   4   3   2   1   SD

D. The method of sampling is sound.

SA   5   4   3   2   1   SD

E. Relevant demographics (for example, age, gender, and ethnicity) are described.

SA   5   4   3   2   1   SD

F. Measurement procedures are adequate.

SA   5   4   3   2   1   SD

G. All procedures have been described in sufficient detail to permit a replication of the study.

SA   5   4   3   2   1   SD

H. The participants have been adequately protected from potential harm.

SA   5   4   3   2   1   SD

I. The results are clearly described.

SA   5   4   3   2   1   SD

J. The discussion/conclusion is appropriate.

SA   5   4   3   2   1   SD

K. Despite any flaws, the report is worthy of publication.

SA   5   4   3   2   1   SD

Article 15

The Feasibility of a Web-Based Surveillance System to Collect Health Risk Behavior Data from College Students

Lisa N. Pealer
University of Florida, Gainesville

Robert M. Weiler
University of Florida, Gainesville

R. Morgan Pigg, Jr.
University of Florida, Gainesville

David Miller
University of Florida, Gainesville

Steve M. Dorman
University of Florida, Gainesville

ABSTRACT. This study examined the feasibility of collecting health risk behavior data from undergraduate students using a Web-based survey. Undergraduates were randomly selected and assigned randomly to a mail survey group and a Web survey group. There were no statistically significant differences between the two groups for demographics, response rates, item completion, and item completion errors. Yet differences were found for response time and sensitive item completion. This is the first study to demonstrate the feasibility of collecting health risk behavior data from undergraduates using the Web. Undergraduates are just as likely to respond to a Web survey compared with a mail survey and more likely to answer socially threatening items using this method. Also, the Web format and protocol required less time to administer. Researchers and practitioners conducting health survey research with college students or other homogeneous populations who have access to e-mail and the Web should consider using a Web-based survey design as an alternative to a mail, self-administered survey. In such a population, a Web-based survey should not discourage participation, particularly if participants are interested in the questionnaire content.

From *Health Education & Behavior*, 28, 547-559. Copyright © 2001 by SOPHE. Reprinted with permission.

Society is witnessing and engaging in rapid and widespread use of the World Wide Web for a variety of reasons. Searches for health information rank among the most popular activities on the Web. For example, the proactive search for personal health information so individuals can be better equipped in the health care decision-making process represents one motivating factor behind the intense interest in Web-based health.

The Web is emerging as a new tool for researchers, as well. Traditionally used to exchange research data, rather than for collecting data,[1] survey researchers have begun to take advantage of its sweeping presence and are experiencing positive results. Although the Web currently supports many online surveys, few examine its effectiveness as a method for collecting data, particularly when compared with traditional survey methods. Yet, the Web recently has been acknowledged for providing access to a growing and widespread population of research participants.[2] Consequently, the Web is now recognized as an important medium not only for education and collaboration but also for conducting research.[3]

Both the Internet and Web have been used previously in survey research. Most studies compared mailed, self-administered questionnaires; personal interviews; and e-mail surveys for differences in response rates and response effects.[4-7] Few studies determined the feasibility of using Web-based surveys as a tool for collecting actual data of any type,[8] particularly health survey data.[1,3,9] However, results from the few published studies appear promising. Web-based surveys offer distinct design elements such as check boxes, radio buttons, and text-entry boxes that limit data entry errors because the data entry is completed by the survey participant.[3,10,11] Bell and Kahn,[3] in a study collecting health status information about medical outcomes, found participants had little difficulty in completing a Web-based survey. Ninety-seven percent of their participants (n = 4,876) completed the 36-item survey in less than 10 minutes, with an item completion rate of 99.28%. In the same study, Bell and Kahn[3] reported values of Cronbach's alpha of 0.76 to 0.90 for the scored scales. These values show a high degree of internal consistency and are similar to results found in the more traditional Medical Outcomes Study. The design elements and technology behind Web-based surveys show potential to overcome shortcomings of the traditional modes of survey research.

Traditional survey research poses numerous methodological problems. Personal interviews often prove too costly and time-consuming, and they may cause overreporting of socially desirable responses, especially if sensitive information is being collected. Telephone interviews, while less costly than personal inter-

55 views, are often seen as intrusive and exclude persons in a population without telephones.[12] Similar to personal interviews, telephone interviews can involve participants needing to please the interviewer, therefore providing socially desirable responses and creating a

60 response effect.[4] Self-administered questionnaires are relatively anonymous, and participants are less likely to overreport socially desirable responses.[4,13] However, self-administered questionnaires produce lower response rates and more mistakes in item completion.[12,13]

65 Electronic surveys, whether computer-assisted questionnaires or electronic mail, require less time and are less expensive compared with personal interviewing, telephone interviewing, and mailed, self-administered questionnaires. Electronic surveys are

70 limited nevertheless in the sampling frame available. As first noted 13 years ago by Kiesler and Sproull,[4] until computers and networks are as ubiquitous as telephones, the electronic survey will probably not be feasible for population surveys.

75 In 1996, Hewson, Laurent, and Vogel[14] estimated the existence of more than 9.5 million hosts, 1.8 million U.S. academic domains, and 2.43 million commercial domains creating an extensive computer networking infrastructure. Estimating the number of Internet

80 users is more difficult, and the reported number of users varies. In 1995, the American Internet Survey estimated that 9.5 million Americans, including 8.4 million adults and 1.1 million children younger than age 18, were using the Internet.[15] CommerceNet Research

85 Center[16] and Nielsen Media Research[17] released numbers in spring 1997, estimating that 220 million people older than age 16 in the United States and Canada were using the Internet. In May 1998, Relevant Knowledge®,[18] a company founded at the Advanced Tech-

90 nology Development Center at the Georgia Institute of Technology, reported 57 million users on the Internet's World Wide Web alone.

To date, no Web-based survey research has been conducted soliciting health risk behavior data. This

95 study assessed the feasibility of collecting health risk behavior data from a random sample of undergraduates using a Web-based survey. Consistent with the study's purpose, our research questions focused on the following: Do differences exist for response rates, response

100 times, number of items completed, item completion errors, and number of sensitive items answered between a mailed, self-administered survey and a Web-based survey? Findings from this investigation can be used by survey researchers in public health searching

105 for alternative data collection techniques, which may circumvent common methodological problems associated with collecting health survey research. Specifically, the Centers for Disease Control and Prevention (CDC) may weigh these findings when planning for the

110 next National College Health Risk Behavior Survey (NCHRBS) and consider a Web-based version as a viable alternative to the mailed, self-administered pro-

cedures used in the past.

Method

Design

We designed a true experimental study that ran-
115 domly assigned members of a probability-based sample to one of two groups that served as the independent variable for the investigation: (1) the mailed, self-administered survey group (mail group) and (2) the Web-based survey group (Web group). Dependent
120 variables included response rate, response time, item completion, item completion errors, and number of sensitive items completed.

Sample

The sample ($n = 600$) was randomly drawn from the enrolled population of University of Florida (UF)
125 undergraduates (30,866) who were 18 years of age or older and holding a free computing account ($N = 22,623$) in spring 1999, the latter representing 73% of the total undergraduate student body. To secure the best sample based on enrollment, the sample was not
130 drawn until week 5 of the semester. Simple random sampling procedures created a database that included student names, current mailing addresses, and current e-mail addresses. Because other population characteristics were not considered relevant to the research ques-
135 tions for this preliminary investigation, we chose not to draw a stratified random sample. Sample members were randomly assigned either to the mail group ($n = 300$) or to the Web group ($n = 300$).

Students who attend UF are eligible to receive a
140 free computing account. This account, known as GatorLink, gives students access to computer centers on campus and services that allow students with computing hardware to use the UF's computer network connected to the Internet. In June 1998, UF instituted a
145 student computer requirement, requiring all students to have access to and ongoing use of a computer. Thus, given the availability and accessibility of computing resources on campus and the student computer requirement, we assumed minimal technical barriers for
150 student participation.

Instrumentation

In 1995, the NCHRBS served as the model for the two forms of the independent variable. This survey was developed to monitor nine categories of priority health risk behaviors: (1) personal safety and violence; (2)
155 suicide ideation and attempts; (3) tobacco use; (4) alcohol use; (5) marijuana, cocaine, and other drug use; (6) sexual behaviors; (7) body weight; (8) dietary behaviors; and (9) physical activity.[19] A national panel of experts reviewed the instrument for sensitive items and
160 identified 13 questions as possibly sensitive to the study population (e.g., "During your life, have you ever been forced to have sexual intercourse against your will?" and "During the past 12 months, how many times did you attempt suicide?"). Moreover, the mail

Figure 1. Investigation procedures.

165 form included one item asking participants if they were
willing to complete the questionnaire in a Web-based
format. The Web form included one item designed to
identify the location where participants completed the
questionnaire.

170 The mail form of the NCHRBS was mailed to
members of the mail group using the U.S. Postal Service. The second form of the questionnaire was developed for Web-based administration using the software
program *Perseus Survey Solutions for the Web.*[20] Both
175 forms of the questionnaire contained 99 items, and the
content sections were presented in the same order.

Data Collection

Data collection began in March 1999. Members of
both groups were mailed a prenotification postcard by
standard U.S. mail and an electronically mailed preno-
180 tification message about the forthcoming survey. The
prenotification postcard and e-mail explained to the
entire sample that if they participated in the study, they
would receive a $2 bill as compensation for participa-
tion. (The decision to use an incentive was based on the
185 1995 NCHRBS methodology, which offered a chance
to win a $100 U.S. savings bond.[21]) Sample members
were asked to watch their regular postal mail and their
GatorLink e-mail for further information about the
survey. Participants were not told whether they would
190 be asked to participate in a mail survey or a Web-based
survey.

The self-administered questionnaire was sent via

first-class mail to the mail survey group 5 days following the prenotification postcard and e-mail. Most par-
195 ticipant addresses were local, so participants received a
questionnaire the day after they were mailed. Web
group participants were sent an e-mail requesting participation in the Web-based survey 6 days after the
prenotification phase. If participants in the Web group
200 chose to participate, they were instructed to click the
link for the Web survey cover letter, and then from the
cover letter they linked to the Web-based survey.
Therefore, participants in both groups received information about the survey on the same day.

205 Approximately 1 week following the initial mail-
out of both surveys, participants in the mail group were
sent a reminder postcard, and participants in the Web
group were sent a reminder e-mail message. After 4
weeks, a computation of the initial response rate was
210 calculated for both groups. Consequently, we decided
to mail participants in both groups who had not yet
responded a personalized, second follow-up letter by
standard U.S. mail and a personalized e-mail message.
Figure 1 illustrates the data collection procedures used
215 during the investigation.

Informed Consent

A description of the informed consent process for
the mail group was included in the questionnaire's
General Instructions section. The informed consent
statement described the research procedures and ex-

Table 1
A Comparison of Study Sample and University Population (in percentages)

Demographic	Mail Group (*n* = 186)	Web Group (*n* = 175)	Sample[a] (*n* = 361)	University[b] (*n* = 30,866)
Gender				
Male	43.5	45.1	44.3	48.5
Female	56.5	54.9	55.7	51.5
Year in school				
Freshman	20.0	19.4	19.7	14.3
Sophomore	22.2	28.6	25.2	20.2
Junior	26.6	27.3	26.9	27.3
Senior	28.6	25.7	27.1	33.3
Race				
Asian	6.5	11.4	8.9	6.1
Black	5.4	8.0	6.6	6.6
Hispanic	10.8	7.4	9.1	10.0
White	73.1	70.9	72.0	73.8
Other	4.3	1.7	3.0	1.6

a.   Sample includes overall response from both study groups.
University estimates are based on spring 1999 undergraduate enrollment.

220 plained the steps used to protect participants' privacy. For participants in the Web group, an identical informed consent statement was included in the cover letter. After reading the recruitment e-mail message, partici-
225 pants were instructed to go to the cover letter by clicking the referent link. Participants who read the cover letter containing the informed consent statement and voluntarily agreed to participate in the research procedures were instructed to continue by clicking the link for the Web survey.

Data Processing

230 Data collected from the mail survey group were transferred from the paper questionnaire to electronic answer sheets. The answer sheets were then scanned and saved in ASCII format to be read and analyzed using the Statistical Analysis System (SAS). Data col-
235 lected from the Web-based survey were automatically formatted, e-mailed to us, and transferred to the Web-based survey database created by the Web survey software.

Results

A total of 365 of the 600 questionnaires were re-
240 turned, and 361 were usable, yielding a response rate of 60.2%. Of the total usable responses, 55.7% were from females (*n* = 201) and 44.3% from males (*n* = 159), with a mean age of 20.39. Close to three-fourths of the participants were White (*n* = 260, 72.0%), most (*n* =
245 353, 97.8%) were full-time students, and the majority (*n* = 285, 78.9%) lived with roommates or friends, residing in an off-campus house or apartment (*n* = 121, 61.2%). Table 1 provides a comparison of the demographics and profile characteristics of each group, the
250 study sample, and the UF population. Chi-square analysis of the demographic variables (age, gender,

race, and marital status) showed no significant difference between the mail group and the Web group, confirming the two groups' homogeneity.
255 No statistically significant difference existed between response rates for the mail group (*n* = 186, 62%) and the Web group (*n* = 175, 58.3%), χ^2 = .6954, *p* = .3590. Yet, a *t* test for independent means found a statistically significant difference between the two groups
260 in the mean number of days required to complete and return the survey questionnaire *t*(354) = 3.12, *p* = .002. In the mail survey group (*n* = 184), the number of days fell between 2 and 25 days, with a mean of 9.75 (*SD* = 7.12). In the Web survey group (*n* = 172), the number
265 of days fell between 1 and 24 days, with a mean of 7.34 (*SD* = 7.52). On average, the Web-based survey method required 2.42 fewer days to complete and return the questionnaire.

With respect to item completion, no statistically
270 significant differences were detected between the two groups on the mean number of items not completed (Web: *M* = 14.05, *SD* = 6.43; mail: *M* = 14.07, *SD* = 7.45) or the mean number of item completion errors (Web: *M* = .37, *SD* = 1.31; mail: *M* = .50, *SD* = 1.46).
275 However, a statistically significant difference was found between the Web group and the mail group on the number of sensitive items completed *t*(359) = 2.83, *p* = .005. Web group participants on average skipped fewer sensitive questions than participants in the mail
280 group (*M* = .314, *SD* = .605 vs. *M* = .511, *SD* = .707, respectively).

Finally, no statistically significant differences were found between the two groups with respect to profile characteristics (e.g., class standing, full-time student
285 status, fraternity membership, parental education, health care coverage, and employment) and the inci-

dence and prevalence of health risk behaviors assessed by the NCHRBS. These findings further confirm the two groups' homogeneity.

Discussion

290   These results demonstrate the feasibility of using a Web-based survey for collecting health behavior data from undergraduates who attend UF. Based on these results, we drew two main conclusions. First, a response rate of 60.2% ($n = 361$) reflected the popula-
295   tion's willingness to participate in a health behavior survey. Several participants from both groups requested results from the survey or asked where they might obtain the results, suggesting an interest in the health content of the survey. Comments from partici-
300   pants in the Web group were overwhelmingly positive about all aspects of the survey process. Second, the demographics and profile characteristics of both study groups were similar to each other and to the larger population, suggesting that the Web-based survey
305   method did not discourage participation. UF undergraduates seemed interested in both the questionnaire content (health risk behaviors) and in the survey process (Web based).

Evidence of Feasibility

Statistically, no difference existed between the re-
310   sponse rate between the two survey groups, suggesting that the survey method did not influence participation or affect the decision of prospective respondents to participate in the survey.

Response time, defined as the number of days re-
315   quired for participants to complete and return the questionnaire used in this study, may serve as a criterion for selecting a particular survey method. Web-based survey research on average requires less time for participants to complete and return a questionnaire. Partici-
320   pants in the Web group responded to Web-based survey requests quicker than did participants in the mail group. The modified version of the NCHRBS developed and used in this investigation was lengthy; both questionnaires contained 99 items. However, the aver-
325   age number of questionnaire items completed in the Web group was similar to the mail group. Participants in the Web group were as likely as their mailed, self-administered counterparts to complete most items on the survey questionnaire. Thus, length of the question-
330   naires did not appear to affect overall participation.

When completing the questionnaires, participants in the Web group and the mail group made a comparable number of errors. No participant exceeded nine errors. Likewise, participants in both groups made similar
335   types of errors typically associated with a contingency question format (skip patterns). Participants in the Web group experienced no more difficulty in completing the questionnaire than did participants in the mail group.

An expert panel identified 13 items on the
340   NCHRBS as "sensitive." Participants in the Web group answered, on average, more sensitive items than did participants in the mail group. Therefore, Web group participants were more inclined to reveal potentially embarrassing or sensitive information than were par-
345   ticipants in the mail survey group.

Implications for University Populations

Researchers and practitioners conducting health survey research with a university population having unimpeded access to the Internet and World Wide Web should consider Web-based survey research as an al-
350   ternative to mailed, self-administered survey research. While findings from the study are limited to similar student populations attending colleges and universities with equivalent computing infrastructure and Internet access, the results should prove useful in research with
355   other populations with access to the Internet and World Wide Web.

The academic literature contains little information regarding the use of sampling techniques in Web-based survey research. Most recent studies used convenience
360   samples relying on open enrollment and passive recruitment strategies such as survey announcements on electronic mailing lists or listed in search engines. For example, Bell and Kahn[3] passively recruited 4,876 survey participants for a Web-based survey on health
365   status about medical outcomes. Likewise, Stones and Perry[9] recruited 300 respondents within 5 weeks. Soetikno, Provenzale, and Lenert[22] reported 582 visitors to an open enrollment Web site with approximately 30% ($n = 170$) completing the posted question-
370   naire.

The research design for this study incorporated randomization at all levels, including a randomly selected sample randomly placed into research groups. The Web group recorded 238 visitors to the Web-based
375   survey cover letter and 214 visitors to the Web-based questionnaire. However, the response rate was 58% ($n = 175$) for the Web group and an overall response rate of 60.2% ($n = 361$) for both groups. This response rate is acceptable and similar to other survey research re-
380   sponse rates among college populations. Response rates fluctuate greatly for mailed, self-administered surveys among college populations no matter what the topic is.

Most Web group participants (66.3%) completed
385   the survey with private access to a computer (college dorm/residence hall, off-campus house or apartment, parent's/guardian's home). Only 27.5% of Web group participants used a computer provided in a UF computer center. When participants in the mail group were
390   asked if they had been willing to complete the survey on the Web, 71.2% responded yes.

It appears that college students are comfortable with Internet communication technology. Participants in the study seemed willing, interested, and eager to
395   incorporate this technology into their daily lives. This response supports findings from previous computer-based survey research,[23,24] which found younger popu-

lations more comfortable with, or even preferring, computers to traditional paper-and-pencil question-
400   naires.

Implications for Practitioners

Just as telephone surveys must contend with services and devices to screen telephone calls that can lower response rates,[25] Web surveys face similar cir-
405   cumstances. Web-based survey research incorporating a design similar to the current study may encounter several obstacles: (1) participants not attending to e-mail regularly; (2) participant computer systems purging old e-mail messages; (3) participants intentionally or unintentionally deleting a survey participation re-
410   quest and URL; and (4) participants initially reading a request then forgetting to return later for response. Besides e-mail, the current study design offered other types of reminders to participants in both groups. Participants received postcards, personal letters, and e-
415   mail messages as reminders.

Incentives and questionnaire length also influence response rates. The most effective monetary incentives are those incentives enclosed with the first mailing rather than approaches promising payment on receipt
420   of a completed questionnaire.[26] However, Web-based surveys do not allow mailing an up-front, tangible incentive as do mailed survey packets. Currently, Web marketers are using approaches such as online coupons for online or offline products with Web surveys. Re-
425   searchers using the Web should consider using such creative approaches to provide an up-front incentive that will encourage participation in Web-based surveys while maintaining research parity between study groups. In this study, the amount of the incentive (U.S.
430   $2.00) may not have been sufficiently attractive to this population, or they may not have trusted that the incentive would be mailed on completion of the survey, influencing the response rate.

Questionnaire length, while possibly influencing a
435   response rate, also may influence the number of items completed. Research suggests that lengthy questionnaires are better suited for personal interviews in which interviewers can prevent a premature end, deal with participant boredom, and counter decreased motiva-
440   tion.[25] Such strategies cannot be used with self-administered questionnaires, mailed or Web-based; therefore, they should be kept brief to encourage participant response. However, evidence suggests that content interest and the ease by which the question-
445   naire can be completed are more important to a response rate than length, and questionnaire length itself does not dramatically affect response rates.[27] Findings from this study supported that conclusion.

Of the total usable questionnaires returned in this
450   study, 99.4% of participants read the entire questionnaire and answered the final question on their respective questionnaires. Statistically, the two groups did not differ on the number of items completed per question-

naire, suggesting participants were not discouraged by
455   the number of questionnaire items. This commitment to the survey process by the participants could be due, at least in part, to genuine interest in the health topics addressed.

Other Web-based survey research also reported
460   high item completion rates. Bell and Kahn[3] reported an overall item completion rate of 99.28% for a 36-item, multiple-choice, Web-based questionnaire. Soetikno et al.[1] also reported a high item completion rate for an 80-item multiple-choice questionnaire. In a review of tra-
465   ditional survey methodologies, response rate, and questionnaire length, Aday[25] found that the content of health surveys, particularly in telephone interviews, influences survey "success." Participants are more interested in discussing their health than in consumer
470   product marketing or politics.

Beyond high item completion, Web-based surveys simplify data entry, thereby decreasing the chance for error. In this study, the average number of item completion errors between the study groups was not sig-
475   nificant, suggesting that participants in the Web group experienced no more difficulty in questionnaire completion than expected in a paper-and-pencil survey format. Ease of completing Web-based surveys has been reported in the literature,[2,10] and the approach is
480   supported by similar findings in computer-based and other electronic forms of survey research.[4,28]

The most common type of error found in this study, across groups, involved errors associated with contingency format. Both groups required the close attention
485   of participants in correctly following the contingency question format. While rudimentary skip patterns were incorporated into the Web survey for contingency questions, errors were still possible. More sophisticated Web survey programming can control such errors,
490   eliminating most possibilities of participant error. This is an advantage already realized by other electronic survey data collection procedures such as computer-assisted telephone interviewing (CATI).

While Web-based surveys are easy to complete,
495   they also provide a faster overall response time. In this study, most (51%) Web-based questionnaires were received within 3 days of the initial mail-out. The remaining questionnaires were received in clusters immediately after the follow-up e-mail and the second
500   reminder e-mail. Little activity occurred between these times. Web group participants seemed to complete the survey either immediately or not at all. Some participants may have intended to complete it later but did not remember until the follow-up e-mails. Several partici-
505   pants sent an apology, by e-mail, for not responding to the survey sooner.

Unlike regular mail, the e-mail medium does not allow for visual reminders. As a result, the mailed surveys were returned at a more uniform rate. The visual
510   cue provided by the oversized green and white envelope and the gray questionnaire booklet on the desk

helped to maintain interest and remind participants to respond. Even so, a difference occurred in the average number of days required to complete and return the questionnaire. Participants in the Web group, on average, required 2.42 fewer days to complete and return their questionnaires than did participants in the mail group.

While no Web-based survey research has yet reported findings on time estimates and comparisons between survey type, these study results were similar to findings from e-mail surveys. E-mail survey research has reported a faster response time from their participants[4,6,7] when compared with mailed, self-administered surveys. As for efficiency, the Web group required less researcher time for preparation, publication, and data entry than did the mail group.

Houston and Fiore[2] proposed that participants may be more revealing on Web-based surveys compared with more traditional mailed, self-administered surveys because of an increased perception of anonymity. This study found participants more willing to answer sensitive items or those items identified as subject to contamination from social desirability. Previous computer-based survey research[4,28–32] found that the impersonal or nonsocial nature of the computer setting reduces the tendency toward social desirability and allows participants to admit to socially undesirable behaviors.

While participants in the Web group answered more sensitive items, researchers should be careful if a research design relies solely on the use of campus computer centers. The proximity of computers in the centers and the presence of other students waiting for the computers might discourage participants from answering candidly. Few participants in the Web group reported a concern in the Web-based survey comment section. However, Beebe, Harrison, McRae, Anderson, and Fulkerson,[33] in a study of computer-administered surveys, found that students were more likely to report various types of sensitive information in the paper-and-pencil questionnaire than in the computer form. Beebe et al.[33] concluded that their study design, which relied on school computer laboratories where computers and students were in close proximity, may have influenced the findings.

Implications for Future Research

Web surveys easily could be applied to a variety of questionnaires regularly used in health survey research. Future Web-based survey research should examine elements associated with the traditional survey research methods to learn if they affect response rates of Web-based surveys. Elements to consider include number and type of follow-ups, monetary incentive amounts, varying types of incentives, and questionnaire length. In addition, researchers need to explore, identify, and clarify those features of Web-based survey research unique to the medium—for example, Web survey layout (e.g., a single scrolling page vs. a series of linked pages), skip patterns, and the use of multimedia. Research that examines collecting sensitive data should be conducted to confirm that Web surveys solicit more responses to sensitive items than other survey methods. In collegiate settings, additional research might address undergraduate characteristics believed to affect response rates such as academic major and hours completed. Similarly, future Web-based survey research should include graduate and professional students. Finally, to advance the knowledge about the effectiveness of collecting health risk behavior data and Web-based survey research in general, a true experimental study designed to compare the response rates from a Web-based survey; a mailed, self-administered survey; and a telephone survey using random-digit dialing that concurrently examines several of the above elements is needed.

Conclusion

College populations represent one of the most convenient samples to recruit for Web surveys and, for the purposes of this study, presented an ideal situation to test the feasibility of a Web-based data collection method. Sampling, however, will remain a serious limitation to Web survey research until access to the Internet is as ubiquitous as its technological cousin, the telephone. Presently, attempts to use Web-based surveys for general population studies may be futile.

Additional Web-based research will help increase the external validity of present findings and advance the method for collecting health risk behavior data. The demographics of Web users are increasing in diversity, which "increases availability of samples whose diversity approximates that of the entire population, and it also makes distinct groups directly accessible for research specific to group definitions" (p. 186).[14] Until Web users represent the population at large, targeting specific populations can strengthen the external validity of the research design.

Findings from this study confirmed Web-based surveys as a feasible method and an alternative to traditional mailed, self-administered surveys in an undergraduate population with open access to the Internet and World Wide Web for collecting college health risk behavior data. As colleges and universities make computer requirements, and as students develop a greater trust and reliance on computers for courses and daily campus activities (e.g., register, check grades, pay fees), Web-based surveys may eventually replace traditional campus data collection methods. Web-based surveys will not supplant traditional survey methodologies but, given their feasibility, will likely play a valuable role in mixed-mode data collection. Just as some survey research designs currently use telephone surveys to enhance mail surveys, it appears that Web surveys, at least in the near future, will find their greatest utility complementing traditional approaches.

References

[1] Soetikno RM, Mrad R, Pao V, Lenert LA: Quality-of-life research on the Internet: Feasibility and potential biases in patients with ulcerative colitis. *Journal of the American Medical Informatics Association* 4(6):426-435, 1997.

[2] Houston JD, Fiore DC: Online medical surveys: Using the Internet as a research tool. *MD Comput* 15(2):116-120, 1998.

[3] Bell DS, Kahn CE: Health status assessment via the World Wide Web. Proceedings from the American Medical Informatics Association Annual Fall Symposium:338-342, 1996.

[4] Kiesler S, Sproull LS: Response effects in the electronic survey. *Public Opinion Quarterly* 50:402-413, 1986.

[5] Good KP: A study of factors affecting responses in electronic mail surveys (Ph.D. dissertation, Western Michigan University). *Dissertation Abstracts International* 58(10):AAT 9813581, 1997.

[6] Kittleson MJ: An assessment of the response rate via the postal service and e-mail. *Health Values* 18(2):27-29, 1995.

[7] Schuldt BA, Totten JW: Electronic mail vs. mail survey response rates. *Marketing Research* 6(1):36-39, 1994.

[8] Wu HFM: Use of Web-based survey instrument to collect, analyze and present course evaluation data (Ph.D. dissertation, George Washington University). *Dissertation Abstracts International* 58(10):AAT 9817201, 1997.

[9] Stones A, Perry D: Survey questionnaire data on panic attacks gathered using the World Wide Web. *Depression and Anxiety* 6(2):86-87, 1997.

[10] Schmidt WC: World Wide Web survey research: Benefits, potential problems, and solutions. *Behavior Research Methods, Instruments, & Computers* 29(2):274-279, 1997.

[11] Turner JL, Turner DB: Using the Internet to perform survey research. *Syllabus* 12(4):58-61, 1998.

[12] Isaac S, Michael WB: Handbook in Research and Evaluation (3rd ed.). San Diego, CA, EdITS/Educational and Industrial Testing Services, 1995.

[13] Rossi PH, Wright JD, Anderson AB (eds.): *Handbook of Survey Research.* Orlando, FL, Academic Press, 1983.

[14] Hewson CM, Laurent D, Vogel CM: Proper methodologies for psychological and sociological studies conducted via the Internet. *Behavior Research Methods, Instruments, & Computers* 28(2):186-191, 1996.

[15] Emerging Technologies Research Group: *The American Internet User Survey* [Online]. Available: http://etrg.findsvp.com/Internet/highlights.html (1995).

[16] CommerceNet Research Center: *World Wide Internet Statistics* [Online]. Available: http://www.commercenet.net/research/stats/wwwstats.html (1998).

[17] Nielsen Media Research: *CommerceNet/Nielsen Internet Demographics Survey* [Online]. Available: http://www.commercenet.com/work/pilot/nielsen_96/index.html (1997).

[18] Relevant Knowledge®: *RelevantKnowledge's Most Recent Enumeration Study* [Online]. Available: http://www.relevantknowlege.com/Press/release/05_04_98.html (1998).

[19] Division of Adolescent and School Health, National Center for Chronic Disease Prevention and Health Promotion: Youth risk behavior surveillance: National college health risk behavior survey—United States, 1995. *Morb Mortal Wkly Rep* 46(SS-6):1-56, 1997.

[20] Truppin A, Benson D, Nelson P, Washburn S, Henning J: *Perseus Survey Solutions for the Web: User Guide.* Braintree, MA, Perseus Development, 1997.

[21] Douglas KA, Collins JL, Warren C, Kann L, Gold R, Clayton S, Ross JG, Kolbe LJ: Results from the 1995 National College Health Risk Behavior Survey. *J Am Coll Health* 46(2):55-66, 1997.

[22] Soetikno RM, Provenzale D, Lenert LA: Studying ulcerative colitis over the World Wide Web. *Am J Gastroenterology* 92(3):457-460, 1997.

[23] Johnston J, Walton C: Reducing response effects for sensitive questions: A computer-assisted self interview with audio. *Soc Sci Comput Review* 13(3):304-319, 1995.

[24] Paperny DM, Aono JY, Lehman RM, Hammar SL, Risser J: Computer-assisted detection and intervention in adolescent high-risk health behaviors. *J Pediatrics* 116(3):456-462, 1990.

[25] Aday LA: *Designing and Conducting Health Surveys* (2nd ed.). San Francisco, Jossey-Bass, 1996.

[26] Denton JJ, Tsai CT, Chevrette P: Effects on survey responses of subjects, incentives, and multiple mailings. *J Experimental Education* 56(2):77-82, 1988.

[27] O'Rourke DP, O'Rourke TW: Improving response rates to health surveys using mail questionnaires. *The Eta Sigma Gamman* (15)1:12-16, 1983.

[28] Booth-Kewley S, Edwards JE, Rosenfeld P: Impression management, social desirability, and computer administration of attitude questionnaires: Does the computer make a difference? *J Applied Psychology* 77(4):562-266, 1992.

[29] Finegan JE, Allen NJ: Computerized and written questionnaires: Are they equivalent? *Computers in Human Behavior* 10(4):483-496, 1994.

[30] Martin CL, Nagao DH: Some effects of computerized interviewing on job applicant responses. *J Applied Psychology* 74:72-80, 1989.

[31] Skinner HA, Allen BA: Does the computer make a difference? Computerized versus face-to-face versus self-report assessment of alcohol, drug, and tobacco use. *J Consult Clin Psychol* 51(2):267-275, 1983.

[32] Tourangeau R, Smith TW: Asking sensitive questions: The impact of data collection mode, question format, and question context. *Public Opinion Quarterly* 60:275-304, 1996.

[33] Beebe TJ, Harrison, PA, McRae JA, Anderson RE, Fulkerson JA: An evaluation of computer-assisted self-interviews in a school setting. *Public Opinion Quarterly* 62(4):623-624, 1998.

About the authors: Lisa N. Pealer, Robert M. Weiler, R. Morgan Pigg, Jr., and Steve M. Dorman, Department of Health Science Education, University of Florida, Gainesville. David Miller, Foundations of Education, University of Florida, Gainesville. Lisa N. Pealer is currently with the Centers for Disease Control and Prevention. Steve M. Dorman is currently with Texas A&M University.

Address correspondence to: Lisa N. Pealer, Ph.D., Prevention Services Research Branch, Division of HIV/AIDS Prevention, Centers for Disease Control and Prevention, 1600 Clifton Road NE, Mailstop E-46, Atlanta, GA 30333. Phone: (404) 639-2090; e-mail: lnp2@cdc.gov

Exercise for Article 15

Factual Questions

1. According to the researchers, personal interviews are often costly and time-consuming. In addition, what undesirable outcome might they cause?

2. The researchers identify which variables as their "dependent variables"?

3. How were members of the Web Group contacted for the second follow-up?

4. How many of the 600 questionnaires were returned? How many were usable?

5. Were the differences on demographic variables between the mail group and the Web group statistically significant?

6. Of the 13 sensitive items, what was the mean number skipped by the Web group?

7. Do the researchers regard their response rate of 60.2% as "acceptable"?

Questions for Discussion

8. The researchers assigned students to the two groups at random. Is this important information? Does it affect the validity of their study? Explain.

9. The students in this study were offered a $2 bill as compensation for participation. Would such an offer increase the odds that you would respond to a survey? Explain.

10. Participants in both groups received information on the same day. Is this important information? Does it affect the validity of the study? (See lines 194–204.)

11. The researchers do not provide data on whether the two groups differ in terms of how they answered the questions. For example, one of the questions was, "During the past 12 months, how many times did you attempt suicide?" This research report does not indicate whether the two groups differed in their response to this question. Would you like to see a follow-up study that provides such information? Explain.

Quality Ratings

Directions: Indicate your level of agreement with each of the following statements by circling a number from 5 for strongly agree (SA) to 1 for strongly disagree (SD). If you believe an item is not applicable to this research article, leave it blank. Be prepared to explain your ratings.

A. The introduction establishes the importance of the study.

SA   5   4   3   2   1   SD

B. The literature review establishes the context for the study.

SA   5   4   3   2   1   SD

C. The research purpose, question, or hypothesis is clearly stated.

SA   5   4   3   2   1   SD

D. The method of sampling is sound.

SA   5   4   3   2   1   SD

E. Relevant demographics (for example, age, gender, and ethnicity) are described.

SA   5   4   3   2   1   SD

F. Measurement procedures are adequate.

SA   5   4   3   2   1   SD

G. All procedures have been described in sufficient detail to permit a replication of the study.

SA   5   4   3   2   1   SD

H. The participants have been adequately protected from potential harm.

SA   5   4   3   2   1   SD

I. The results are clearly described.

SA   5   4   3   2   1   SD

J. The discussion/conclusion is appropriate.

SA   5   4   3   2   1   SD

K. Despite any flaws, the report is worthy of publication.

SA   5   4   3   2   1   SD

Article 16

Drinking Glucose Improves Listening Span in Students Who Miss Breakfast

Neil Morris
University of Wolverhampton

Peter Sarll
University of Wolverhampton

ABSTRACT. Low blood sugar level resulting from fasting has been shown to reduce performance on a number of cognitive tasks. In this study, 80 nondiabetic A-level students missed breakfast. They completed a version of Daneman and Carpenter's *Listening Span Test* at 9.00 A.M. Half were then given a drink containing glucose, while the other half received a saccharine drink matched for taste. After 20 minutes, both groups completed another form of the *Listening Span Test*. A subset of the sample had their blood glucose levels determined immediately before the drink and again before the second application of the test. Blood glucose levels did not change, but listening span performance significantly improved after a glucose drink, yet not after a saccharine drink. It is concluded that missing breakfast does not seriously affect blood sugar levels in healthy young students, but listening span performance, which is a good predictor of listening comprehension, is improved when fasting individuals imbibe a glucose-rich drink, although not when a saccharine drink is drunk. Ideally students should eat breakfast, but if this is omitted, then a glucose snack or drink before the first class may reverse any adverse effects.

From *Educational Research*, 43, 201–207. Copyright © 2001 by National Foundation for Educational Research in England and Wales. Reprinted with permission.

Failure to eat breakfast before commencing a day of study is probably a fairly common occurrence. Although students may "self-medicate" by drinking sugar-laden drinks during the break between classes, it is likely that many young scholars attend a 9:00 A.M. class without having taken in a significant number of calories since the previous day. This study addresses the consequences of this for listening comprehension by examining the effects of a glucose drink on performance. It addresses the possibility that a "snack," consisting of glucose-rich material, may ameliorate any adverse effects of short-term fasting.

In healthy young individuals, blood glucose levels are maintained at around 5 mmol/l. This control is attained via a negative feedback loop. Insulin is released from the pancreas when blood sugar begins to rise above 5 mmol/l, and it results in glucose being removed from the circulation and immobilized, as glycogen, in the liver and in muscles. When blood sugar levels drop much below 5 mmol/l, the pancreas releases glucagon that releases glycogen from the liver. Glycogen is broken down into glucose and released into the bloodstream, increasing blood sugar until insulin release is triggered. In fact, insulin and glucagon are mutually inhibiting, so deviations from the "set point" for blood sugar occur largely because of absorption of glucose, mainly from the gut, and this is then rapidly regulated. Thus, even in early starvation, blood sugar is maintained because glycogen can be mobilized. Tight control of blood sugar is essential because the brain uses glucose as its "fuel" but it cannot store it—brain processes rely on glucose delivered by the bloodstream.

It is clear that blood glucose level is crucial to brain metabolism. Positron emission tomography studies, which can directly quantify the use of radioactively labeled glucose in the brain, show that different brain areas "light up" depending on the cognitive task being performed (Raichle, 1998). Nevertheless, a clear picture of the relationship between blood sugar level and cognitive capacity has not emerged. For example, Benton and Sargent (1992) found that memory for spatial material and lists of words was better after eating breakfast. However, although Lapp (1981) also found that lists of words were better recalled when blood sugar was high, Azari (1991) found no improvement. Benton and Sargent suggest that one generality that can be made is that tasks that require the participant to remember new information may be sensitive to consumption of breakfast. If this contention is valid, then this has clear implications for the efficiency of study.

Short-term, or working, memory capacity has been implicated in most intellectual tasks (see Baddeley, 1997, for a detailed account of this), and in particular, deficiencies in reading ability and comprehension, especially when listening, have often been associated with reduced working memory capacity (Gathercole and Baddeley, 1993). It is hardly surprising, then, that a test designed by Daneman and Carpenter (1980) to measure individual differences in working memory capacity has considerable predictive power with respect to standards of comprehension (Gathercole and Baddeley, 1993; King and Just, 1991). However, despite its usefulness as a psychometric instrument, Wa-

65   ters and Caplan (1996) have argued that although the Daneman and Carpenter (1980) tasks measure several components of working memory, they do not allow the individual components to be isolated, that is, the measures cannot separate comprehension from memory re-

70   tention. Thus, a fine-grained analysis of sub-components is not possible with this instrument. Notwithstanding this, the test remains useful as a slightly "blunt" instrument with considerable predictive power.

In this study, we employ the *Listening Span Test* of

75   Daneman and Carpenter (1980) as oral presentation of verbal material is still a predominant mode of delivery in the educational setting. Although Waters and Caplan (1996) did not examine this version of the task, it is likely that the same caveats apply. The *Listening Span*

80   *Test* provides a measure of verbal memory capacity for *spoken* material, presented in sentences, with comprehension required. It is formally equivalent to the *written* reading comprehension test and addresses a fundamental aspect of the learning situation, the ability to

85   process lecture material, and, thus, provides an educationally significant measure.

It is predicted that listening span will be sensitive to glucose consumption. This experiment compares two groups of A-level students who have fasted overnight

90   and then twice completed the listening span task with a glucose or saccharine-laden drink being consumed between the two tests. Specifically, it is predicted that students who have fasted overnight will improve on this task after receiving a glucose-rich drink, whereas

95   an almost calorie-free drink will not improve performance after fasting.

Method

Participants

Eighty A-level students from two colleges in the West Midlands participated in this study: 44 were male and 36 were female. The mean age was 21.15 years

100   (s.d. = 4.35). None of these participants was under the age of 17, and none suffered from diabetes mellitus or had a known family history of diabetes mellitus. All had English as a first language.

Procedure

Students at two colleges in the West Midlands were

105   approached, during classes, with a request that they volunteer to take part in a study of the effects of missing breakfast on intellectual performance. Those who were willing to participate signed informed consent forms, which included consenting to providing blood

110   samples. All participants believed that they might have to give a blood sample to verify their abstinence. This strategy was used to ensure honesty of report when questioned about compliance with the fasting instructions.

115   Students were briefed on the day before testing and advised that they must not eat anything after midnight and must only drink water. No non-fasting group was included, as standardized calorie intake could not be

120   meaningfully imposed because of differences in body weight, choice of food items consumed, etc. Clearly, there are likely to be individual differences in physiology within a fasting sample, but these should be minimized by using a young sample (who have very efficient blood sugar control, which deteriorates with age).

125   Each participant was requested to report to a specified room for group testing at 9:00 a.m. Groups were never larger than 10, and several assistants ran sessions concurrently in a series of rooms within a particular college. Participants confirmed that they had fasted in the

130   manner requested and were then randomly assigned to either the glucose or placebo group (they were not aware that there was a distinction) within a room.

They were administered a version of the Daneman–Carpenter (1980) *Listening Span Test,* which requires

135   the student to listen to a series of sentences presented via a tape recorder. On response sheets provided, students recorded whether the proposition in each sentence was true or false. After a series of sentences had been presented, a different voice on the tape requested

140   "recall." The students were then required to write down, in forward serial order, the last word in each sentence they had heard. For example, the sequence: (1) "Karl Marx was an Irish composer"; (2) "Tony Blair is a politician" would require "false," "true" to be

145   ticked and "composer, politician" to be written on the recall sheet. The number of sentences in a sequence was incremented by one every two sequences, with the result that the longest sequence of sentences from which a student could recall all the last words in the

150   order presented provided a measure of their listening span.

The decisions about the propositions were not scored for analysis; they were required to ensure that students actively listened to the whole of each sen-

155   tence. (It was decided, before the study commenced, that students scoring less than 90 percent would be excluded from the analysis as they may have sacrificed comprehension for memory performance.) The study began with several practice and demonstration trials

160   followed by trials with, initially, two sentences. The longest trials were six sentences. Two sets of trials were prepared for the study. Half the students in each condition experienced version 1 first, and the remainder experienced version 2 first. All sentences had a

165   spoken duration of 2–2.5 seconds.

After completion of the *Listening Span Test*, there was an interval of 20 minutes. Students were given a 300 ml glass of orange juice to drink at the beginning of this interval, and they were requested to drink it rap-

170   idly. The students in the glucose condition received a drink consisting of 50 g glucose in 250 ml of water plus 40 ml sugar-free Robinson's "Whole-orange quash" and 10 ml of lemon juice (to reduce the sweetness). Those students who were assigned to the placebo

175   condition drank orange juice that was identical, except that 2 g of "Sweetex" replaced the glucose. A pilot

Table 1

Means and Standard Deviations (in Parentheses) for Scores on the Daneman and Carpenter *Listening Span Test* Before and After Either a Glucose-Rich Drink or Drink with Saccharine Substituted for Glucose (Maximum Score Possible, 6; *n* = 80)

	Listening span before drink	Listening span after drink
Group receiving a glucose drink (*n* = 40)	2.4 (0.7)	3.1 (0.7)
Group receiving a saccharine drink (*n* =40)	2.5 (0.7)	2.6 (0.6)

study at the University of Wolverhampton indicated that students could not distinguish between these two drinks.

180 During the 20-min interval between tests, the experimenters engaged in a question-and-answer session with the students about studying at the university. At the end of this time, a different version of the *Listening Span Test* was administered. Following this, the pur-
185 pose of the study was explained and all students were advised to eat before attending their first class of the day.

The study was carried out in the classrooms that students studied in to maximize the realistic nature of
190 the environment. Unfortunately, such environments are ill-suited to carrying out biologically hazardous procedures. The taking of blood samples within classrooms was deemed to be a biologically hazardous procedure by the University of Wolverhampton safety committee,
195 with the result that restrictions were placed on the procedure, and only one room was designated for blood sampling. A clinically trained member of staff was present throughout sampling and handled disposal of sharps and other blood-contaminated material. As a
200 result of this, blood samples were taken only from 10 participants (five from the placebo, and five from the glucose group). These participants provided three blood samples prior to ingestion of the drink and three further samples 20 min later, just prior to the second
205 administration of the *Listening Span Test*. Blood glucose level was tested using BM–Test 1–44 blood glucose test strips, following the manufacturer's procedure and then measured with a Prestige Medical Healthcare Ltd. HC1 digital Blood Glucometer. The average of the
210 three measures was recorded at each testing. It should be stressed that the selection of students to give blood samples was based purely on the room attended. All participants in the study had consented to provide blood prior to volunteering for the study.

Results

Blood Glucose Levels

215 Before administration of the drink, both groups who had their blood glucose levels measured had blood glucose levels of 4.60 mmol/l (glucose group s.d. = 0.16 and placebo group s.d. = 0.14). Twenty min after administration of drinks, the glucose group had a blood
220 sugar level of 4.68 mmol/l (s.d. = 0.17, not significantly different from the first administration—*t*(4) =

2.24, *p* > 0.05), and the placebo group had a blood sugar level of 4.62 mmol/l (s.d. = 0.15, *t*(4) = 0.01, *p* > 0.05—no significant change). Thus, blood glucose lev-
225 els were not significantly changed within 20 min by administration of a glucose-rich drink, and they remained at physiologically acceptable levels throughout the study. The two groups did not significantly differ in blood sugar levels across the study.

Listening Span Test

230 All participants scored at least 90 percent correct on the true/false decisions, so none was excluded from the analysis. The listening span data were subjected to a two-way mixed-design analysis of variance with Group (glucose/placebo) as the between-subject factor and
235 Test (first test vs. second test) as the within-subject factor. There was no main effect of group (F(1,78) = 2.62, *p* > 0.05), but performance was significantly better after consuming the drink (F(1,78) = 28.15, *p* < 0.001). This effect was modified by an interaction
240 (F(1,78) = 17.38, *p* < 0.001). Simple effects analysis (Kirk, 1968) revealed no performance differences before the drink was consumed (*p* > 0.05), but a large improvement in the glucose group after receiving the drink (*p* < 0.01). The means and standard deviations
245 are shown in Table 1.

In summary, there were no reliable changes in blood glucose level within 20 min of receiving a drink containing glucose. However, performance on the Daneman–Carpenter *Listening Span Test* significantly
250 improved in the group that had received a glucose drink but not in the group that received the saccharine drink. These two groups did not differ in their listening span performance before receiving the drink.

Discussion

These data show a modest increase—about a half
255 sentence, on average—in listening span. If this recall of a half-item simply represented recalling an additional half-word, then, in practical terms, the increase would be trivial. Clearly, however, considerable working memory capacity is required. One might expect A-level
260 students to recall seven or more items (Miller, 1956), but only three are recalled in the optimal condition. For simple word recall, this level of performance would be pathological. However, an average of a half-word recall improvement on the *Listening Span Test* represents
265 a considerably larger increase in available capacity. It would be more accurate, given the nature of the test, to

view this increase as being better represented as about a half-sentence increment in retention. Such an increase would allow comprehension of sentences with more clauses. Evidently, then, a half-item increment constitutes a useful improvement in listening comprehension/memory capacity and may lead to better comprehension of complex, educationally relevant material.

The literature suggests that this improvement occurs because blood sugar levels are elevated, and this glucose is available as "brain fuel." The failure to find any significant change in blood sugar level but a sugar-administration-related improvement in performance suggests a more complex relationship. One can only speculate on what this might be, and it should be borne in mind that the trend is in the right direction and might be more marked in a study with greater statistical power. One possible explanation is that reduced glucose availability results in release of stored glycogen to compensate and that this has physiological costs that impair cognitive processing. For example, neurotransmitter systems may be very sensitive to the pulses of glucose that they received. 5-HT (a.k.a. serotonin—an important transmitter in the brain) release, for example, is modified by glucose levels (Wurtman and Wurtman, 1986). Absorption of glucose from the gut may maintain levels more smoothly than the "crisis" release from the liver when levels suddenly start to fall.

Whatever the mechanism by which glucose ameliorates fasting effects, the rapidity with which it improves performance, without creating any hazard, suggests that most students can be advised to consume a convenient form of glucose if they have missed breakfast. One caveat, derived from Thayer (1989), is that "sugar-snacking" can rebound. It appears to be energizing initially but induces later fatigue. This is unlikely to occur following fasting. However, it would be preferable for students to eat a nutritious breakfast with abstinence from sugar snacks *unless* the student has missed breakfast.

References

Azari, N. P. (1991). Effects of glucose on memory processing in young adults, *Psychopharmacology, 105*, 521–4.

Baddeley, A. D. (1997). *Human memory: Theory and practice.* (2nd ed.). Hove: Psychology Press.

Benton, D., & Sargent, J. (1992). Breakfast, blood glucose and memory, *Biological Psychology, 24*, 95–100.

Daneman, M., & Carpenter, P. (1980). Individual differences in working memory and reading, *Journal of Verbal Learning and Verbal Memory, 19*, 450–66.

Gathercole, S. E., & Baddeley, A. D. (1993). *Working memory and language.* Hove: Lawrence Erlbaum.

King, J., & Just, M. A. (1991). Individual differences in syntactic processing: The role of working memory, *Journal of Memory and Language, 30*, 580–602.

Kirk, R. E. (1968). *Experimental design: Procedures for the behavioural sciences.* Belmont, Calif.: Brooks/Cole.

Lapp, J. E. (1981). Effects of glycaemic alterations and noun imagery on the learning of paired associates, *Journal of Learning Disorders, 14*, 35–8.

Miller, G. A. (1956). The magical number seven, plus or minus two: Some limits on our capacity for processing information, *Psychological Review, 63*, 81–97.

Raichle, M. E. (1998). Behind the scenes of functional brain imaging: A historical and physiological perspective, *Proceedings of the National Academy of Science, USA, 95*, 765–72.

Thayer, R. E. (1989). *The biopsychology of mood and arousal.* Oxford: Oxford University Press.

Waters, G. S., & Caplan, D. (1996). The measurement of verbal working memory capacity and its relation to reading comprehension, *Quarterly Journal of Experimental Psychology, 49A*, 51–79.

Wurtman, R. J., & Wurtman, J. J. (1986). *Nutrition and the brain: Food constituents affecting normal and abnormal behaviours.* New York: Ravens, Vol. 7.

Address correspondence to: Neil Morris, School of Health Sciences, Psychology Division, University of Wolverhampton, 62–68 Lichfield Street, Wolverhampton WV1 1DJ, UK.
E-mail: n.g.morris@wlv.ac.uk

Exercise for Article 16

Factual Questions

1. Does the *Listening Span Test* present sentences *or* does it present isolated words?

2. Was a nonfasting control group (i.e., a group that did not fast the night before) included in this study?

3. Were the participants randomly assigned to the two groups?

4. Blood samples were taken from how many participants in the placebo group?

5. What was the mean score for the glucose group after they received the drink (i.e., what was the posttest score for the glucose group)?

6. Do the researchers characterize the increase in listening span for the glucose group as "very large"?

7. Do the researchers interpret these results to suggest that students should be advised to eat sugar snacks in the morning?

Questions for Discussion

8. Half the participants were administered version 1 of the *Listening Span Test* first, and the other half were administered version 2 first. This is an example of what researchers call "counterbalancing." Speculate on why the researchers counterbalanced the two versions of the test.

9. This research report is identified as an example of "true experimental research" in the table of contents of this book. Do you agree with the classification? Why? Why not?

10. The blood tests failed to reveal elevated blood

sugar levels in the glucose group. In your opinion, does this fact make it difficult to interpret the results of this study? Does it decrease your confidence in the results of this study? Explain. (See lines 276–293.)

11. In your opinion, does this study provide definitive evidence that students should eat breakfast in the morning? Explain.

12. To what population(s) of students, if any, would you be willing to generalize the results of this study?

Quality Ratings

Directions: Indicate your level of agreement with each of the following statements by circling a number from 5 for strongly agree (SA) to 1 for strongly disagree (SD). If you believe an item is not applicable to this research article, leave it blank. Be prepared to explain your ratings.

A. The introduction establishes the importance of the study.

SA   5   4   3   2   1   SD

B. The literature review establishes the context for the study.

SA   5   4   3   2   1   SD

C. The research purpose, question, or hypothesis is clearly stated.

SA   5   4   3   2   1   SD

D. The method of sampling is sound.

SA   5   4   3   2   1   SD

E. Relevant demographics (for example, age, gender, and ethnicity) are described.

SA   5   4   3   2   1   SD

F. Measurement procedures are adequate.

SA   5   4   3   2   1   SD

G. All procedures have been described in sufficient detail to permit a replication of the study.

SA   5   4   3   2   1   SD

H. The participants have been adequately protected from potential harm.

SA   5   4   3   2   1   SD

I. The results are clearly described.

SA   5   4   3   2   1   SD

J. The discussion/conclusion is appropriate.

SA   5   4   3   2   1   SD

K. Despite any flaws, the report is worthy of publication.

SA   5   4   3   2   1   SD

Article 17

The San Diego Navy Experiment:
An Assessment of Interventions
for Men Who Assault Their Wives

Franklyn W. Dunford
University of Colorado at Boulder

ABSTRACT. Three different 12-month interventions for servicemen who had been substantiated as having physically assaulted their wives were used and the outcomes examined. The 861 couples of the study were randomly assigned to 4 groups: a men's group, a conjoint group, a rigorously monitored group, and a control group. Cognitive–behavioral interventions were implemented for the men's and conjoint groups, and outcome data were gathered from male perpetrators and female victims at roughly 6-month intervals over the approximately 18-month experimental period. Data analyses revealed nonsignificant differences between the experimental groups over a variety of outcome measures.

From *Journal of Consulting and Clinical Psychology*, 68, 468–476.

Reviews of treatment services for men who abuse their wives or cohabitant partners reveal that the majority of group interventions for men who batter have been based on a cognitive–behavioral model (Eisikovits & Edleson, 1989; Hamberger & Hastings, 1993; Rosenfeld, 1992; Tolman & Bennett, 1990), that evaluations have routinely failed to use rigorous experimental designs (Chalk & King, 1998; Fagan, 1996), and that little evidence exists that the prevailing interventions for men who batter are efficacious (Crowell & Burgess, 1996; Healey, Smith, & O'Sullivan, 1998). The ability to rule out alternative explanations for what appear to be positive findings regarding the cessation of spouse or partner abuse has been notably absent in almost all evaluations of domestic violence programs. The net effect is a lack of reliable information about how to best treat men who abuse their wives or cohabitant partners (Boruch, 1994; Fagan, 1996).

A literature search conducted before the San Diego Navy Experiment was initiated in 1991 found only one evaluation of an intervention conducted in a military setting for wife abuse. In that evaluation of the Domestic Conflict Containment Program (Neidig, 1985) implemented with Marine Corps men, Neidig (1986) indicated that postintervention measures showed significant and positive changes on the Dyadic Adjustment Scale subscales, consensus and cohesion measures, and the Norwicki Strickland Locus of Control Scale. In 1992, Mollerstrom, Patchner, and Milner referred to an evaluation of programs for batterers in the Air Force, but no published results have been found in the literature for that or for any other evaluation of military batterer treatment programs. Neither of these evaluations used an experimental research design.

A much larger number of evaluations have been conducted on programs for male batterers in civilian settings, but with few exceptions (Davis & Taylor, 1997; Feder, 1998; Palmer, Brown, & Barrera, 1992) the evaluations were no more rigorous than those found for the military. According to Rosenfeld (1992), as of 1992 only three research projects for spouse or partner abuse had randomly assigned participants to different treatment conditions, and only one of those used what could be conceptualized as a control group.

The present study, the San Diego Navy Experiment, was designed to experimentally evaluate the effectiveness of cognitive–behavioral interventions implemented in different treatment settings for men who batter. This intervention model was selected for evaluation for several reasons. As noted earlier, it was the most prevalent group intervention for men who batter their cohabitant partners used at the time the San Diego project was initiated (Tolman & Bennett, 1990). In addition, a relatively large number of uncontrolled evaluations suggested, at that time, that interventions based on the cognitive–behavioral model effectively addressed the problem of the continued abuse of cohabitant partners. Finally, it was the treatment model most frequently used by the Navy. (For a brief description of the cognitive–behavioral model, see Saunders, 1999.)

The decision to evaluate the effectiveness of a cognitive–behavioral intervention in both men's and conjoint groups was based primarily on existing Navy practice. In addition, at the Navy's request, the study evaluated a third intervention that used a "stake in conformity" strategy (Toby, 1957). The objective was to determine if male perpetrators held accountable for their abusiveness toward their wives, using systema-

70 tized and official monitoring procedures, would stop the continued abuse. This intervention was called *rigorous monitoring*.

Method

Participants

The experimental sample consisted of 861 married
125 U.S. Navy couples in which active-duty husbands were
75 substantiated as having physically assaulted their wives. The sample was young (mean age = 27 years, mode = 24 years), newly married (mean length of marriage = 47 months, mode = 24 months), with children (83%, mean number of children = 1.7), moderately
80 educated (mean number of school years = 12.6), mostly White (men = 48%, women = 40%) or Black (men = 35%, women = 28%), and low in rank (mean = Petty Officer Third and Fourth Class, the equivalent of Private First Class and Corporal, respectively, in the
85 Army), with low to moderate incomes (M = $2,594 total family income per month before taxes).

Interventions

The study participants were randomly assigned to a men's group, conjoint group, rigorous monitoring group, or control group.

Men's Group

90 The men's group, which used a cognitive–behavioral model of change, met weekly for 6 months and then monthly for another 6 months, for a total 1-year treatment period. The curriculum for this intervention was developed by Daniel Saunders and David
95 Wexler based on their work in domestic violence (Saunders, 1996; Wexler, 1999). The weekly meetings included both didactic and process activities.

In the didactic portion of the weekly sessions, group leaders addressed perpetrator attitudes and val-
100 ues regarding women and violence toward women and taught the men a wide variety of skills thought to be important to the successful elimination of the continued abuse of women (e.g., cognitive restructuring, empathy enhancement, communication skills, anger modifica-
105 tion, and jealousy). All of the skills taught were derived from the cognitive–behavioral model. Each session involved a set of tasks that group leaders were obliged to complete. Session 2, for example, specified the following eight tasks: review weekly check-in form, re-
110 view the nine commandments (statements ranging from "We are all 100% responsible for our behavior" to "Counselors and case managers cannot make people change—they can only set the stage for change to occur"), explain the need for a responsibility plan, iden-
115 tify warning signals, explain "time-out," review each step of a responsibility plan, guide all members in developing individual responsibility plans, and assign time-out homework. The process portion of the weekly sessions involved dealing with issues raised in the
120 didactic segments of the sessions as well as with other

issues that emerged. The six monthly sessions that followed consisted of review and process activities.

Conjoint Group

Despite the controversy associated with treating victims and perpetrators of spouse abuse together (Ed-
125 leson & Tolman, 1992), the Navy was interested in assessing a conjoint group treatment approach because of the long-standing use of couples–group approaches. The conjoint group was organized in much the same way as the men's group, with 26 weekly sessions that
130 included both didactic and process activities followed by 6 monthly sessions. The curriculum for this intervention was also based on the cognitive–behavioral model and was developed by Geffner (2000). The interventions were similar to those used in the men's
135 group, with the major difference being that the presence of wives was expected to alter the dynamics of the conjoint group interventions. The presence of wives in the conjoint group was expected, for example, to promote realistic and personalized role-playing, reduce
140 "women bashing," personalize violence (including intimidation and emotional abuse), and enhance empathy in ways more poignant than were evident in the men's group. In addition, the ability of wives to witness authority figures confronting the offensive and oppressive
145 nature of spouse abuse, as well as address constructive ways to deal with conflict, were proposed as sources of empowerment and confidence not available to women whose husbands were assigned to the other interventions. These kinds of contextual differences were ex-
150 pected to increase the effectiveness of the cognitive–behavioral treatment model. As in the men's group, the 6 monthly sessions consisted of review and process activities.[1]

Rigorous Monitoring Group

The rigorous monitoring intervention represents the
155 formalization and systematization of the Navy's attempts to hold perpetrators accountable for their abusiveness toward their wives. The goal of the interventions was to inhibit continued abuse by making new instances of abuse more visible to those having control
160 over the lives of service members (i.e., their commanding officers). Perpetrators were seen monthly for individual counseling for 12 months by a case manager at the Family Advocacy Center (FAC), the Navy agency responsible for the treatment of men who abuse their
165 wives. Every 6 weeks a record search was completed to determine if perpetrators had been arrested or referred to court anywhere in San Diego County. Wives were called monthly and asked about new instances of

---

[1] The details of the curricula for the men's and conjoint groups are too lengthy to describe in this report. Manuals that specify the content and stated objectives for all of the group sessions for each of these approaches (U.S. Navy, 1993a, 1993b) are available from Franklyn W. Dunford.

abuse. They were advised during the calls that they were not obliged to reveal anything to the FAC representative about their husbands' behavior if doing so would place them in jeopardy (which may have reduced the effectiveness of this intervention). Case managers delivered individual counseling at each session as they thought appropriate. Case managers were required, as a part of the rigorous monitoring treatment intervention, to inform clients that their behavior was being monitored and that their commanding officers would be advised monthly of all new instances of abuse. At the end of each treatment session, case managers sent progress reports to perpetrators and their commanding officers specifying the presence or absence of new instances of abuse. In this manner, an attempt was made to create a "fishbowl" effect for the male participants of the rigorous monitoring group.

Control Group

Men assigned to the control group were to receive no FAC treatment. However, their wives, like the wives of the men assigned to the other treatment groups, did receive preliminary assistance called *stabilization and safety planning*. That is, the FAC contacted victimized wives as soon as possible after the presenting incident to ensure that they were not in immediate danger of continued abuse. Once their safety was assured, the FAC provided them with safety planning information.

Random Assignment

Sample selection took 46 months. The majority of the sample came from referrals from the ships or stations to which servicemen were assigned, the Family Service Centers (Navy agencies tasked to provide support and educational services to Navy families), and Navy medical facilities. Once a serviceman was determined to be eligible for the research, the case was given to the research staff and subsequently entered into a computer programmed to randomize cases to one of the four experimental treatments. For a serviceman to be deemed eligible for the research, the Navy Case Review Committee had to substantiate that he had physically assaulted his wife, that divorce procedures were not officially in process, that he had more than 6 months left to serve in the area, that he was not alcoholically impaired, and that he was devoid of significant pathology (i.e., he did not present with active psychosis, antisocial personality disorder, pathological jealousy, or suicidal ideation). Servicemen suspected of alcoholic impairment were required to go through an official assessment for alcoholism called a *Counseling and Assistance Center (CAAC) screen*. These screens resulted in three outcomes: Level I (no ongoing treatment required), Level II (4 weeks of outpatient counseling), and Level III (4 to 6 weeks of in-patient treatment conducted in a Navy hospital). Twenty percent of the eligible cases were referred for CAAC screens. Fifty-three percent of those cases were subsequently returned to the FAC for treatment when identified as nonalcoholic or when they had completed treatment for their alcoholism.

Measures

Two major types of measures were used in the analyses for this report: demographic and outcome assessments. The demographic measures assessed such standard variables as ethnicity, income, education, age, rank, and family size. Four types of outcome measures were used. A self-reported episodic measure assessed the number of incidents or episodes in which a victim or perpetrator reported being abused across three different levels of abuse. Female victims were asked, for example, to indicate how many incidents had occurred in which they (a) felt like they were in danger of being hurt by their husbands; (b) they were pushed, hit, or had hands laid on them, or were beaten up by their husbands; and (c) were physically injured by their husbands (e.g., knocked down, bruised, scratched, cut, choked, had bones broken, had eyes or teeth injured, or were still hurting the next day).

The second outcome measure, the Modified Conflict Tactics Scale (MCTS; Straus, 1979), focused on types of abusive behaviors as reported by respondents. The items of the MCTS differed from the original CTS in two ways. The "double-barreled" items of the original scale were divided into separate questions, and a few items were added to gather additional information about what can best be described as psychological abuse. For each of the 42 items of the MCTS, respondents were asked to indicate the frequency with which they engaged in or were subject to a specific behavior. For scoring, the items were combined into eight subscales, two of which (All Violence and Severe Violence) were patterned after traditional CTS measures (Straus, 1979). The following is a brief description of the subscales, with their attendant reliability (standardized item alpha) levels for both men and women reports: Passive Abuse consisted of such items as "Treated her as if she was inferior" and "Ignored her requests or feelings" (for women, $\alpha = .89$; for men, $\alpha = .88$); Control Abuse consisted of items like "Controlled money against her will" and "Refused to let her get or keep a job" (for women, $\alpha = .77$; for men, $\alpha = .38$); Menacing Abuse consisted of such items as "Looked at her in ways that she knew he meant to hurt her" and "Destroyed furniture, walls, objects, and things because he was mad at her" (for women, $\alpha = .70$; for men, $\alpha = .61$); Misdemeanor Abuse consisted of items like "Grabbed, restrained, held on to her against her will" and "Pushed, shoved, or slapped her" (for women, $\alpha = .78$; for men, $\alpha = .75$); Felony Abuse consisted of such items as "Hit her with a fist" and "Threatened her with a knife or gun" (for women, $\alpha = .81$; for men, $\alpha = .73$); Sexual Abuse consisted of the items "Verbally pressured her to have sex" and "Forced her to have sex against her will" (for women, $\alpha = .50$, for men, $\alpha =$

280 .87). The All Violence (for women, α = .86; for men, α = .80) and Severe Violence (for women, α = .84; for men, α = .76) subscales were aggregates of items from the Misdemeanor Abuse and Felony Abuse subscales. In all of these measures, high scores indicated high 285 levels of abuse. The measures were developed as theoretical, rather than empirically derived, constructs.

The third outcome measure consisted of official police and court records for all respondents (both victims and perpetrators) living within the boundaries of San 290 Diego County. The fourth outcome measure focused on the date of the first instance in which a repeat case of spouse assault occurred as indicated by both official arrest records and victim reports of new physical injuries.

Interviews with Victims and Perpetrators

295 The research design called for the University of Colorado research team (not FAC/Navy staff) to interview victims and perpetrators separately, typically in their homes, four times over the course of the experiment at approximately 6-month intervals. A baseline 300 measure was taken before treatment began, a second interview was conducted at the conclusion of the first 6 months of treatment, and two more interviews were conducted at subsequent 6-month intervals. The interviews were designed to measure the outcome effects of 305 the interventions. Extensive provisions were made to ensure that respondents knew that the interviewers were employees of the University of Colorado, that the information they shared with the interviewers would be sent directly to the University of Colorado, and that 310 neither the Navy nor spouses would ever have access to individual responses to the interviews. For example, participants were given a letter from the admiral of the San Diego Naval Base assuring them that the information given to university interviewers would be sent 315 directly to the University of Colorado, that the Navy would never have access to it, and that their answers could in no way adversely affect them. Further, respondents were given a certificate of confidentiality issued by the Department of Health and Human Ser-320 vices that protects survey data from subpoena. Each participant also received an incentive payment of $50 for a completed interview.

Not all the participants agreed to be interviewed by the research staff. The cumulative completion rate was 325 as follows: first interview, 86%; second interview, 82%; third interview, 78%; and fourth interview, 75%. Refusals accounted for the majority of cases that did not complete the first interview, and the inability to find or contact people accounted for the majority of 330 later losses (individuals and couples moved away from the area; were no longer in the Navy; were no longer living together [separated or divorced]; or, as was often the case, took steps to avoid being found). Comparing cases lost and not lost by the fourth interview, using the 335 baseline measures of episodic and MCTS abuse, a ten-dency was found for those who failed to be interviewed to be slightly more involved in prior abusiveness as reported by wives than those who agreed to be interviewed, although only 2 of the 11 comparisons be-340 tween the groups (Misdemeanor Abuse and Sexual Abuse) yielded results that were statistically significant. No statistically significant differences or trends were found for the same comparisons for men.

Results

Equivalency

Comparisons of the experimental groups on the 345 prevalence and frequency of episodic abuse during the 6-month period prior to the presenting incident revealed no statistically significant differences. Similarly, comparisons using the MCTS subscales for abuses occurring during the 6-month period prior to the pre-350 senting incident and for abuses occurring during the presenting incident showed fewer differences than would be expected to occur by chance. Furthermore, nonsignificant differences were found between the groups for a set of mediator/predictor variables used in 355 the research; for the prevalence or frequency of prior arrests for spouse abuse; and for the demographic variables of ethnicity, age, education, income, rank, injury in prior relationships, witnessing of parental violence, number of children in the family, victim employment 360 status, alcohol use, and drunkenness. The results suggest that random assignment was effective.

Treatment Integrity

The curricula for each of the 26 sessions for the men's groups, conjoint groups, and the rigorous monitoring sessions specified the tasks that were to be com-365 pleted for each session. Each group session lasted 1.5 hr and was conducted by a male cotherapist and a female cotherapist. To ensure uniformity of services over time and across therapists, all of the group leaders conducted both men's and conjoint groups, thus control-370 ling, in part, the effects of therapist characteristics. The rigorous monitoring sessions were typically 1-hr sessions conducted by individual case managers. All of the sessions (men's, conjoint, and rigorous monitoring) were audiotaped.

375 Sample audiotapes for each therapist and case manager were evaluated monthly over the course of the experiment. Research staff listened to each of the tapes in its entirety to determine the extent to which appointed tasks were completed (adherence) and to 380 evaluate the performance skills of the group leaders. Adherence to treatment protocols was relatively high for all three treatments (for the men's group, 78% thoroughly addressed, 7% moderately addressed, 5% introduced, and 3% mentioned; for the conjoint group, 72% 385 thoroughly addressed, 9% moderately addressed, 5% introduced, and 3% mentioned; for the rigorous monitoring group, 82% thoroughly addressed and 7% introduced). Findings from the reviews of the audiotapes were reported to the group leaders and case managers

390 as the data were collected. The between-coders correlation (Pearson's r) was .93.

With regard to performance skills, the audiotapes were evaluated to determine, for example, how well the group leaders integrated process and didactic material, 395 used appropriate confrontation skills with clients, and provided suitable feedback. Less than 5% of the group therapists were rated below an "at-standard" level of performance for any of the performance dimensions assessed over the course of the study.

Dropouts

400 At the conclusion of prescribed treatment periods, the Navy's FAC formally closes all cases for which treatment has been assigned. FAC records indicated that 71% of the cases involved in the analyses for the 1-year follow-up period were closed as successfully 405 completing treatment. Another 15% of the men were discharged from the Navy during treatment; and although not dropouts in the traditional sense, they did not complete treatment. The remainder of the cases (14%) were not closed as completing treatment because 410 the men were transferred out of the area, recidivated and received another treatment, or failed to attend the required treatment sessions.

The proportion of men who failed to complete treatment was larger than expected. Discharges from 415 the Navy, transfers, deployments, and a lack of support from commanding officers had negative effects on completion rates. Although space limitation prevents the presentation of detailed findings in this report, one finding is especially noteworthy. Analyses of atten-420 dance data indicated that the continued abuse of wives was inconsistently and only limitedly affected by the amount of treatment received, a finding that is consistent with data reported elsewhere (Palmer et al., 1992).

Crossovers

A crossover occurred when a case was randomly 425 assigned to one group but received an alternative treatment. Twenty-three cases (3% of the sample) were crossovers. Crossovers occurred for a variety of reasons, the most common being deployment schedules, which required men to be in and out of port on a regu-430 lar basis over relatively long periods of time. Such cases were often moved from a group treatment approach, which required meeting at preset and regularly scheduled times, to individualized treatment, where services could be delivered on an ad hoc basis. Also, 435 the local courts would occasionally require that a case referred to the FAC and assigned to the experiment be reassigned to a specific type of treatment. Unique and relatively uncommon circumstances were responsible for other types of crossovers. Among those circum-440 stances were mistakes in the assignment process, seriously sick or terminally ill clients, and reassignment to groups outside of the experiment following the emergence of new information. When analyses were conducted on the basis of treatments as delivered or when

445 the 23 crossover cases were eliminated from the analyses, outcome findings did not differ from those obtained from analyses based on treatment as assigned. All of the analyses presented in this article are based on treatment as assigned, which is the protocol suggested 450 by Weinstein and Levin (1989) and used by others (Davis & Taylor, 1997).

Conjoint Group Attendance

Notwithstanding efforts to increase the attendance of wives in the conjoint group, including the provision of funds for child care and the use of victim advocates, 455 the average number of wives attending the conjoint group sessions was relatively low. The average ratio of attendance of women to men was 2:5. Given the role that women were hypothesized as playing in the conjoint group and the variability in the attendance ratios 460 across time (from a low of 1:10 to a high of 7:10), analyses were conducted to assess the effects that the attendance of varying numbers of women may have had on outcome.

Three different measures of female victim atten-465 dance at conjoint group sessions were assessed: (a) the average number of women attending the sessions; (b) the number of sessions attended by men when there were 1, 2, 3, or more women in attendance; and (c) the average number of sessions in which a woman attended 470 with her husband. Analyses were completed using the total sample, restricting the sample to men who attended 20 or more sessions, and restricting the sample to men attending 10 or more sessions. When simple correlations were calculated between the various 475 women's attendance variables and the frequency of episodic abuse reported at the fourth interview for all versions of the samples, no statistically significant correlations were found. Similarly, when multivariate regression models were used that added prior abuse, liv-480 ing together, and men's attendance records as independent variables, no statistically significant relationships between victim attendance and continued abuse were found. These data suggest that victim attendance, as operationalized and measured here, did not have the 485 impact envisioned for the conjoint group intervention, although the findings might have been different had the attendance ratio of women to men been higher.

Victim- and Perpetrator-Reported Outcome

Results of comparisons of the four experimental groups on all of the outcome variables assessed at the 490 third and fourth interviews (combined) using a variety of prevalence and frequency measures are shown in Tables 1–4. Third- and fourth-interview outcome data were combined for several reasons. First, second-interview data (collected at the end of the first 6 495 months of treatment) could not be used as a primary measure for treatment effects because of the time–order confound between the number of sessions attended and participant-reported recidivism during the second interview period. Since the dates of all new abuses were

Table 1
Wives' Reports of Husbands' Spouse Abuse by Treatment Group at 1-Year Follow-Up and for 6 Months Prior to FAC Referral

	Victim felt endangered?										Victim pushed or hit?										Victim physically injured?									
	Men's group		Conjoint group		RM group		Control group		Total		Men's group		Conjoint group		RM group		Control group		Total		Men's group		Conjoint group		RM group		Control group		Total	
Outcome	n	%	n	%	n	%	n	%	n	%	n	%	n	%	n	%	n	%	n	%	n	%	n	%	n	%	n	%	n	%
Yes	60	37	59	37	51	33	61	42	231	37	48	29	47	30	41	27	50	35	186	30	31	19	25	16	26	17	31	21	113	18
No	104	63	99	63	104	67	84	58	391	63	116	71	111	70	114	74	95	66	436	70	133	81	133	84	129	83	114	79	509	82
Yes prior 6 months		56		43		50		58	728			61		56		58		58	730			48		40		42		39	730	
Frequency of victimization 1-year follow-up	2.732		4.165		10.245		1.766				0.884		1.614		8.555		1.228				0.470		0.633		1.452		0.414			
Prior 6 months	9.132		6.585		7.330		9.034				6.577		5.148		5.033		7.910				3.332		3.623		2.804		2.551			

500 not recorded, new instances of abuse could have occurred early in the second measurement period before many of the weekly treatments had been delivered, midway through the measurement period, or late in the 505 measurement period after most of the weekly treatment had been delivered, obscuring the relationship between the amount of treatment received and new instances of abuse. To avoid the confound, the decision was made to measure outcome after the weekly sessions had ended. Second, because the men's and conjoint groups 510 were the two major interventions of the experiment, and because the effects of treatment for these two groups were expected to be greatest at the end of the first 6 months of weekly sessions, third- and fourth-interview data were expected to most accurately cap- 515 ture the outcome data for these two groups. Third, when experimental analyses were conducted separately for data obtained from second, third, and fourth interviews, the results produced the same findings as those found when third- and fourth-interview data were com- 520 bined, thus supporting the use of the combined data and facilitating a more parsimonious presentation of the findings. Thus, all of the outcome measures used in this report involve the 1-year follow-up period following the first 6 months of treatment.

525 Table 1 shows victim reports of episodic spouse abuse, using the combined third- and fourth-interview outcome data. No statistically significant differences ($p < = .05$) were found between the four experimental groups for the prevalence of continued abuse using 530 these measures. The frequency with which women were victimized is also reported in Table 1. Although the results were not statistically significant, women from the rigorous monitoring group reported that their husbands recidivated at much higher frequencies on all 535 three of the episodic measures than did the husbands from the other experimental groups. These high numbers are primarily the result of extreme scores reported by a few women in the rigorous monitoring group (1 of the women, for example, reported over 1,000 incidents 540 of abuse). When a log transformation of the frequency of reoffending was used to reduce the influence of the extreme scores, the differences between the groups disappeared.

Table 2 summarizes male perpetrator reports of the 545 abuse of their wives. No statistically significant differences between the groups were found for any of the comparisons for the prevalence or frequency measures. Differences were less when log transformations were used to eliminate the influence of extreme scores.

550 Comparisons of data for the episodic measures, for both victim and perpetrator reports of new abuse (see Tables 1 and 2), produced no evidence that membership in any of the three experimental treatment groups was any more effective in reducing continued abuse 555 than was membership in the control group.

Comparisons of the frequency of continued abusive behaviors for the different groups using the MCTS are shown in Table 3. None of the differences between groups for either the women's or the men's reports of 560 the continued abuse of wives were found to be statistically significant. The apparent substantive differences between the means of some of the subscales of Table 3 were due, once again, to the extreme scores reported by a few respondents.

565 To further assess the effects of treatment, the men's and conjoint groups were collapsed to form one treatment group to be compared with the control group using the same comparative techniques and outcome variables represented in Tables 1–3. Similar analyses 570 were completed by collapsing the men's, conjoint, and rigorous monitoring groups into one group and comparing it with the control group. None of these assessments altered any of the findings presented earlier. Further, pairwise t tests conducted on all possible com- 575 binations of treatment groups showed no statistically significant differences for any of the comparisons.

Abuse reported by victimized wives/partners is almost always found in the literature to be greater than that reported by perpetrating husbands/partners (Szi- 580 novacz, 1983), a finding clearly reflected in Tables 1–3. To address this disparity, victim and perpetrator reports of abuse were combined and assessed. The results did not alter any of the findings.

Table 2
Husbands' Reports of Husbands' Spouse Abuse by Treatment Group at 1-Year Follow-Up and for 6 Months Prior to FAC Referral

	Victim felt endangered?										Victim pushed or hit?										Victim physically injured?									
	Men's group		Conjoint group		RM group		Control group		Total		Men's group		Conjoint group		RM group		Control group		Total		Men's group		Conjoint group		RM group		Control group		Total	
Outcome	n	%	n	%	n	%	n	%	n	%	n	%	n	%	n	%	n	%	n	%	n	%	n	%	n	%	n	%	n	%
Yes	30	19	26	18	32	19	37	26	125	20	22	14	21	14	25	15	27	19	95	15	8	5	3	2	9	5	9	6	29	5
No	130	81	120	82	136	81	107	74	493	80	138	86	125	86	143	85	117	81	523	85	152	95	143	98	159	96	135	94	589	95
Yes prior 6 months		41		37		37		37	731			51		50		46		47	741			21		19		23		17	737	
Frequency of victimization 1-year follow-up	0.475		3.294		0.506		0.792				0.256		0.308		0.607		0.396				0.075		0.062		0.149		0.083			
Prior 6 months	2.571		2.978		2.628		2.520				2.462		2.303		1.873		1.672				0.538		0.903		0.835		0.559			

Official Outcome Data

The data in Table 4 represent all arrests in which the same perpetrating husband revictimized the same victimized wife during the 12-month period following the first 6 months of treatment. No statistically significant difference was found between the groups for the prevalence of new arrests.

Survival Analyses

Survival analyses were applied to data from two sources to determine if time to recidivism varied for the different experimental groups. First, wives were asked to indicate the date of the first incident in which they had been physically injured by their husbands following the first 6 months of treatment, and second, official police arrest records were used to determine the date of the first arrest for spouse abuse for the same period of time. The time between the end of treatment and the first incident of physical injury as reported by victimized wives, or the time between the end of treatment and the first arrest for spouse abuse as found in official records, was considered the survival time. When both sets of data were analyzed using the Kaplan-Meier technique (Norusis, 1993), differences in survivorship profiles across groups were not significant. The log-rank (Mantel-Cox) test for group differences was 1.35 ($p = .72$) for victim reports and 3.48 ($p = .32$) for arrest records.

Military Setting

It is possible that the military setting in which the experiment was conducted could, in and of itself, explain the no-difference findings if men in the Navy referred to the FAC for assaulting their wives perceived that their Navy careers would be put at risk if they continued to abuse their wives. The effects of such a perception may have overwhelmed the deterrent effects of the interventions. This point of view is consistent with a "stake in conformity" interpretation of the findings (Toby, 1957).

Two sets of analyses were completed to assess this hypothesis. One assessment compared the frequency of continued spouse abuse for men in the control group who reported that their Navy careers were or were not important to them. The assessment found no statistically significant differences for wife reports of episodic abuse and just one significant difference when the MCTS was used. Likewise, no statistically significant differences were found for assessments that compared outcome data for men who reported that their Navy careers would or would not be damaged if their superiors were to learn that they were continuing to abuse their wives. These findings suggest that a referral to the FAC and the associated visibility to commanding officers may not have been the overwhelming deterrent to continued abuse hypothesized earlier.

Prior Abuse

When the data on offending for the 6-month period prior to referral to the FAC (which did not include the presenting incident) were compared with the same data for the 1-year period following the first 6 months of treatment (see Tables 1 and 2), significant reductions in both the prevalence and frequency of violence were found for men assigned to all four of the experimental groups. These reductions were recorded irrespective of the treatment group to which men were randomized and irrespective of whether husbands or wives reported the violence. Although not noted in Table 3, the MCTS subscale scores for the 6-month period prior to the referral to the FAC paralleled those reported for the episodic measures.

These findings may be explained, in part, by an occurrence known as "telescoping." With this phenomenon, which is often associated with retrospective measures, old events are recalled as occurring more recently than they actually occurred, thus artificially inflating the baseline scores. The findings could also be a consequence of conducting four consecutive interviews over an 18-month period. If the interviews associated with the research are conceptualized as treatment interventions, they could explain the reductions in violence noted for men irrespective of the experimental treat-

Table 3
The Frequency of Continued Abuse by Treatment Group at 1-Year Follow-Up Using the Modified Conflict Tactics Scale (MCTS)

MCTS subscale	Men's group	Conjoint group	RM group	Control group	F	p
			Wives' reports			
Passive Abuse	144.97	197.85	141.21	159.67	0.818	.48
Control Abuse	54.68	48.71	30.64	33.42	1.184	.31
Menacing Abuse	13.44	16.68	29.33	13.69	0.973	.40
Misdemeanor Abuse	8.88	6.45	20.37	6.34	0.904	.44
Felony Abuse	6.49	1.60	4.11	.64	0.893	.44
Sexual Abuse	3.49	4.15	3.87	1.77	0.333	.80
All Violence	9.48	4.79	13.29	3.51	0.746	.52
Severe Violence	6.20	1.82	3.74	1.10	0.657	.58
			Husbands' reports			
Passive Abuse	15.87	27.04	52.90	33.07	1.997	.11
Control Abuse	2.91	9.42	6.81	9.45	1.300	.27
Menacing Abuse	1.08	2.16	2.83	1.34	0.770	.51
Misdemeanor Abuse	0.60	0.86	2.96	1.01	1.030	.38
Felony Abuse	0.04	0.08	0.11	0.01	0.788	.50
Sexual Abuse	0.00	0.04	0.92	0.04	1.223	.30
All Violence	0.35	0.62	2.60	0.40	1.050	.37
Severe Violence	0.08	0.21	0.19	0.06	0.880	.45

660 ment group to which they were assigned. That is, men were required, as a result of the interviews, to think periodically about violence-related issues in a way in which they may not have thought if the interviews had not been conducted. The interviews may have become,
665 in this manner, interventions. Whatever the explanation, these reductions do not appear to be the results of the treatment interventions of the experiment.

Discussion

Findings from this study indicate that the cognitive–behavioral model, as implemented, demonstrated
670 little power to foster change in men receiving treatment for spouse abuse. All of the assessments made, including comparisons of victim reports of continued abuse, perpetrator reports of continued abuse, official arrest records, and survival analyses, point to the same con-
675 clusion: The interventions of the cognitive–behavioral model failed to produce meaningful changes in the behavior they were designed to impact.

Although the effects of a military setting may play some role in deterring Navy personnel who abuse their
680 wives, the Navy cannot assume that a referral to the FAC represents a treatment in and of itself or that interventions administered by the Navy will not add to the deterrent effect of such a referral.

Further, it would not be unreasonable to argue that
685 a military setting is an optimal place in which to evaluate the efficacy of batterer treatment programs. All of the men were required to attend treatment, most men with serious mental health problems had been screened out of the population, all the participants were literate
690 and reasonably competent, all were married and gainfully employed, and alcoholism and drug addiction were closely monitored and addressed. These circumstances may lend credence to the findings of this ex-

periment and foster consideration among practitioners
695 and others from nonmilitary settings.

Finally, the results of this experiment underscore the need to use experimental designs to evaluate all interventions for domestic violence. As noted at the outset, although the results of dozens of evaluations of
700 batterer treatment programs indicate that the majority of men referred for treatment for spouse abuse discontinue their physical abuse of their wives or cohabitant partners, almost none of the studies used experimental research designs to evaluate what appear to be treat-
705 ment successes. This limitation seriously compromises the validity of their conclusions. When the wife-reported data of the present experiment, for example, are examined independent of the control group, the findings indicate that 83% of the men in treatment
710 (men's, conjoint, and rigorous monitoring) did not reinjure their wives during a 1-year outcome period. This finding ranks among the best of the evaluations found in the literature. However, when these results are examined in the context of the behavior of the men as-
715 signed to the control group, it is apparent that the treatment interventions were not responsible for the relatively low recidivism rates. The use of strong research designs is imperative if interventions for men who batter are ever to be validated as effective.
720 Perhaps the greatest limitation of the San Diego Navy Experiment is the fact that it stands alone. The results of the five replications of the Minneapolis Experiment (Garner, Fagan, & Maxwell, 1995; Sherman, 1992) demonstrate, if nothing else, that the results from
725 a single experiment cannot be generalized to the world. The results of the San Diego Navy Experiment could also be questioned because of the use of a one-size-fits-all approach to the treatment of men who batter. It is generally believed that men abuse their wives/partners

730 for a variety of reasons and that interventions must be tailored to their differential motivations/needs. A one-size-fits-all approach to the treatment of batterers may not be expected to address the different treatment needs of all batterers.

Table 4
Arrest Recidivism by Treatment Group at 1-Year Follow-Up

No. of arrests	Men's group (n = 168)		Conjoint group (n = 153)		RM group (n = 173)		Control group (n = 150)		Total (N = 644)	
	n	%	n	%	n	%	n	%	n	%
0	162	96	149	97	163	94	144	96	618	96
1	6	4	4	3	10	6	6	4	26	4
Frequency	0.036		0.026		0.058		0.040		0.040	

735   The results of this experiment suggest at least three priorities for future research. First, replication is needed. Second, the call throughout the past decade for the use of rigorous experimental designs to assess treatment interventions for men who batter should be
740 taken seriously. The risks of conducting randomized experiments to assess interventions for men who batter are likely to be fewer than the consequences of failing to do so. Finally, the possibility that a one-size-fits-all approach to the treatment of men who abuse their
745 wives/partners is responsible for the ineffectiveness of treatment should receive full and preferential attention. Offender types should be identified and matched to intervention approaches to be followed by rigorous experimental evaluation.

References

Boruch, R. F. (1994). The future of controlled randomization experiments: A briefing. *Evaluation Practices, 15*, 265–274.

Chalk, R., & King, A. (1998). *Violence in families: Assessing prevention and treatment programs.* (Washington, DC: National Academy Press)

Crowell, N. A., & Burgess, A. W. (1996). *Understanding violence against women.* (Washington, DC: National Academy Press)

Davis, R. C., & Taylor, B. G. (1997). A proactive response to family violence: The results of a randomized experiment. *Criminology, 2*, 307–333.

Edleson, J. L., & Tolman, R. M. (1992). *Intervention for men who batter: An ecological approach.* (Newbury Park, CA: Sage)

Eisikovits, Z. C., & Edleson, J. L. (1989). Intervening with men who batter: A critical review of the literature. *Social Service Review, 63*, 385–414.

Fagan, J. (1996). *The criminalization of domestic violence: Promises and limits* (NIJ Research Report). Washington, DC: U.S. Department of Justice, National Institute of Justice)

Feder, L. (1998, July). *A test of the efficacy of court mandated counseling for domestic violence offenders: Preliminary results from the Broward County experiment.* (Paper presented at the international conference Program Evaluation and Family Violence Research, Durham, NH)

Garner, J., Fagan, J., & Maxwell, C. (1995). Published findings from the Spouse Assault Replication Program: A critical review. *Journal of Quantitative Criminology, 11*, 3–28.

Geffner, R., & Mantooth, C. (2000). *Ending spouse/partner abuse: A psychoeducational approach for individuals and couples.* (New York: Springer)

Hamberger, L. K., & Hastings, J. E. (1993). Court-mandated treatment of men who assault their partners.(In N. Z. Hilton (Ed.), *Legal responses to wife assault* (pp. 188–229). Newbury Park, CA: Sage.)

Healey, K., Smith, C., & O'Sullivan, C. (1998). *Batterer intervention: Program approaches and criminal justice strategies.* (Washington, DC: U.S. Department of Justice, Office of Justice Programs, National Institute of Justice)

Mollerstrom, W. W., Patchner, M. A., & Milner, J. S. (1992). Family violence in the Air Force: A look at offenders and the role of the Family Advocacy Program. *Military Medicine, 157*, 371–374.

Neidig, P. H. (1985). *Domestic Conflict Containment Program workbook.* (Beaufort, SC: Behavioral Science Associates)

Neidig, P. H. (1986). The development and evaluation of a spouse abuse treatment program in a military setting. *Evaluation and Program Planning, 9*, 275–280.

Norusis, M. (1993). SPSS for Windows: Advanced statistics (Release 6.0) [Computer software manual]. (Chicago: SPSS)

Palmer, S. E., Brown, R. A., & Barrera, M. E. (1992). Group treatment program for abusive husbands: Long-term evaluation. *American Journal of Orthopsychiatry, 62*, 276–283.

Rosenfeld, B. D. (1992). Court-ordered treatment of spouse abuse. *Clinical Psychology Review, 12*, 205–226.

Saunders, D. G. (1996). Feminist–cognitive–behavioral and process–psychodynamic treatments for men who batter: Interaction of abuser traits and treatment models. *Violence and Victims, 11*, 393–414.

Saunders, D. G. (1999). Feminist, cognitive, and behavioral group interventions for men who batter: An overview of rationale and methods.(In D. Wexler (Ed.), *Domestic violence 2000: An integrated skills program for men* (pp. 21–31). New York: Norton.)

Sherman, L. W. (1992). *Policing domestic violence: Experiments and dilemmas.* (New York: Free Press)

Straus, M. A. (1979). Measuring intrafamily conflict and violence: The Conflict Tactics (CT) scales. *Journal of Marriage and the Family, 41*, 75–88.

Szinovacz, M. E. (1983). Using couple data as a methodological tool: The case of marital violence. *Journal of Marriage and the Family, 45*, 633–644.

Toby, J. (1957). Social disorganization and stake in conformity: Complementary factors in the predatory behavior of hoodlums. *Journal of Criminal Law, Criminology and Police Science, 48*, 12–17.

Tolman, R. M., & Bennett, L. W. (1990). A review of quantitative research on men who batter. *Journal of Interpersonal Violence, 5*, 87–118.

U.S. Navy (1993a). *Domestic violence conjoint groups—A combined treatment program: Group leader's manual.* (San Diego, CA: San Diego Naval Base, Family Advocacy Center)

U.S. Navy (1993b). *Domestic violence men's group: Group leader's manual.* (San Diego, CA: San Diego Naval Base, Family Advocacy Center)

Weinstein, G. S., & Levin, B. (1989). Effect of crossover on the statistical power of randomized studies. *The Society of Thoracic Surgeons, 48*, 490–495.

Wexler, D. (Ed.) (1999). *Domestic violence 2000: An integrated skills program for men.* (New York: Norton)

Address correspondence to: Franklyn W. Dunford, Institute of Behavioral Science, University of Colorado, Boulder, CO 80309.

Note: The grant (2 RO1MH4508) supporting this research was awarded and administered by the National Institute of Mental Health (NIMH). All funds were provided by the U.S. Navy through an interagency agreement with NIMH. The contents of this report reflect the views of the author and not necessarily the position of either the U.S. Navy or NIMH.

Acknowledgments: I am indebted to the officials of the U.S. Navy, who, contrary to common research practice in this area, supported a strong experimental research design to determine if the interventions provided to Navy men who abuse their wives were effective. I am indebted, as well, to Sandra Rosswork, U.S. Navy, and James Breiling, NIMH, for the major contributions they made to this experiment. I thank the staff of the Family Advocacy Center, San Diego Naval Base, and the Colorado University research team for their loyal support, as well as the scholars who so thoroughly and thoughtfully reviewed an earlier version of this article.

Exercise for Article 17

Factual Questions

1. According to the literature review, is there much evidence that prevailing interventions for men who batter are efficacious?

2. Nine commandments were used in the Men's Group. What is the first commandment that is given as an example in this report?

3. How did the researcher attempt to create a "fishbowl" effect in the Rigorous Monitoring Group?

4. For the subscale for Felony Abuse of the MCTS, what is the first sample item that the researcher provides?

5. The researcher evaluated sample audiotapes for each therapist and case manager in order to determine the extent to which they were conducting the treatments in the way that the researcher had prescribed (i.e., adherence to the treatment protocols). Did the evaluations indicate a relatively high level of adherence?

6. Table 1 shows that 39% of the wives whose husbands were in the Control Group reported being physically injured in the prior six months. What is the corresponding percentage for wives whose husbands were in the Men's Group?

7. The first part of Table 3 is based on wives' reports. For which condition (Men's Group, Conjoint Group, RM Group, *or* Control Group) was there the highest frequency of reporting Severe Violence? What was the frequency for this group?

8. In the Discussion, the researcher states that all of the assessments he made "point to the same conclusion." What is the conclusion?

Questions for Discussion

9. The researcher discusses random assignment of participants to treatment conditions throughout their article. In your opinion, why is random assignment important?

10. The researcher gave incentive payments of $50.00 each for a completed interview. For the first interview, the completion rate was 86%. Would you have expected a higher completion rate given the fact that they were offered the incentive payments? Explain. (See lines 320–322.)

11. If you had been planning this study, would you have expected the number of wives attending the Conjoint Group would be low? (See lines 452–457.)

12. The researcher cites a source for this statement: "Abuse reported by victimized wives/partners is almost always found in the literature to be greater than that reported by perpetrating husbands/partners." Does this surprise you? In your opinion, could this affect the validity of the self-reports

used as an outcome measure in this study? Explain. (See lines 577–583.)

13. Do you think that the Official Outcome Data was an important measure for this study? Would you like more information on it? Explain. (See lines 584–589 and Table 4.)

14. Would you be willing to generalize the results of this study to the general (nonmilitary) population? Why? Why not?

Quality Ratings

Directions: Indicate your level of agreement with each of the following statements by circling a number from 5 for strongly agree (SA) to 1 for strongly disagree (SD). If you believe an item is not applicable to this research article, leave it blank. Be prepared to explain your ratings.

A. The introduction establishes the importance of the study.
   SA   5   4   3   2   1   SD

B. The literature review establishes the context for the study.
   SA   5   4   3   2   1   SD

C. The research purpose, question, or hypothesis is clearly stated.
   SA   5   4   3   2   1   SD

D. The method of sampling is sound.
   SA   5   4   3   2   1   SD

E. Relevant demographics (for example, age, gender, and ethnicity) are described.
   SA   5   4   3   2   1   SD

F. Measurement procedures are adequate.
   SA   5   4   3   2   1   SD

G. All procedures have been described in sufficient detail to permit a replication of the study.
   SA   5   4   3   2   1   SD

H. The participants have been adequately protected from potential harm.
   SA   5   4   3   2   1   SD

I. The results are clearly described.
   SA   5   4   3   2   1   SD

J. The discussion/conclusion is appropriate.
   SA   5   4   3   2   1   SD

K. Despite any flaws, the report is worthy of publication.
   SA   5   4   3   2   1   SD

Article 18

Evaluation of a Brief Intervention for Increasing Seat Belt Use on a College Campus

Luigi Pastò
Defence and Civil Institute of Environmental Medicine

Andrew G. Baker
McGill University

ABSTRACT. The authors evaluated a brief intervention for increasing seat belt use among the front seat occupants of cars at a junior college in a jurisdiction with a mandatory belt use law. The intervention included public posting of performance feedback and distribution of an informational flyer to cars in a target parking lot. Feedback was the display of the proportion of drivers observed wearing seat belts on the previous observation day. Seat belt use among drivers increased from 64% during the baseline phase to 71% during the intervention phase. Seat belt use among front passengers increased from 49% during the baseline phase to 67% during the intervention phase. In both cases, seat belt use at follow-up was comparable to seat belt use during the intervention phase, although a trend toward decreasing belt use was noted. Also found was higher seat belt use among females as compared with males irrespective of their front seat occupant status (driver or passenger). Effects of the intervention are discussed in the context of increasing seat belt use in a hardcore nonuser population of predominantly young adults.

From *Behavior Modification*, 25, 471–486. Copyright © 2001 by Sage Publications. Reprinted with permission.

A large proportion of car occupants does not use seat belts, despite their proven effectiveness in reducing the likelihood of injury and death in traffic accidents (Conn, Chorba, Peterson, Rhodes, & Annest,
5 1993; Smith-Seemiller, Lovell, Franzen, Smith, & Townsend, 1997) and the enforcement of mandatory belt use laws (Dee, 1998; Thyer & Geller, 1990). There is evidence that resistance to mandatory belt use laws reflects a hardcore nonuser population also character-
10 ized by a greater frequency of other risk behaviors (Foss, Beirness, & Sprattler, 1994; Hunter, Stutts, Stewart, & Rodgman, 1990). Among this presumably hardcore nonuser population are young adults who are both least likely to wear seat belts (Clark, 1993; Rein-
15 furt, Williams, Wells, & Rodgman, 1996; Wilson, 1990) and more likely than older adults to be involved in traffic accidents (Hunter et al., 1990; Miller, Lestina, & Spicer, 1998). In this article, we evaluate the effectiveness of a brief intervention to increase seat belt use
20 among predominantly young adults above that achieved with a mandatory belt use law.

Behavioral interventions for increasing seat belt use may include extrinsic or intrinsic incentives. Extrinsic incentives emphasize external, tangible inducements
25 and include stepped-up enforcement of mandatory belt use laws or monetary incentives (Hagenzieker, Buleveld, & Davidse, 1997; Johnston, Hendricks, & Fike, 1994). Monetary incentives may involve immediate rewards, such as cash, and delayed rewards, such as
30 sport tickets or chances to win a lottery (Hagenzieker et al., 1997). Interventions for increasing seat belt use that include extrinsic incentives are effective across a broad range of populations and contexts (Hagenzieker et al., 1997; Johnston et al., 1994). Interventions that promote
35 the acquisition of internal justifications for performing a target behavior are typically characterized as involving intrinsic incentives (Thyer & Geller, 1990). Examples of interventions with primarily internal incentives are participative goal setting (e.g., Ludwig & Geller,
40 1997), awareness and consensus building sessions (e.g., Kelo, Geller, Rice, & Bryant, 1988; Ludwig & Geller, 1991), public information and education (e.g., Hunter, Stewart, Stutts, & Marchetti, 1993), and posting of group performance feedback (e.g., Malenfant,
45 Wells, Van Houten, & Williams, 1996). These interventions differ from those involving primarily extrinsic incentives as behavior change is presumed to occur as a consequence of the internalization of behavior-consistent attitudes and standards of conduct. For ex-
50 ample, group performance feedback may invoke social comparison processes through which behavior-consistent attitudes and standards of conduct are internalized and consequently modify behavior. Conformity pressure in the direction of seat belt use emerges from
55 the social comparison process itself rather than from any external incentive such as a threat of punishment or a monetary reward.

Despite the effectiveness of interventions with extrinsic incentives, there are reasons why researchers
60 and policy makers alike may wish to focus on intrinsically based programs. First, in a review of seat belt promotion programs, Geller, Rudd, Kalsher, Streff, and Lehman (1987) reported that interventions with and without extrinsic incentives have similar immediate
65 impacts on seat belt use but that the maintenance of behavior change appears to be greater following inter-

ventions without extrinsic incentives (Cope, Grossnickle, & Geller, 1986). Second, interventions for increasing driving-related safety behaviors with intrinsic
70 incentives often result in the generalization of behavior changes to other driving-related behaviors (e.g., Ludwig & Geller, 1991; Streff, Kalsher, & Geller, 1993). For example, Ludwig and Geller (1997) reported that a participative goal setting intervention for
75 car stops increased the target behavior, as well as turn signal and seat belt use. Finally, those who are at a relatively high risk of car accidents, such as younger drivers, appear to be more responsive to interventions with intrinsic incentives as compared to interventions
80 with extrinsic incentives. For example, mandatory belt use laws appear to be least effective among younger drivers (Dee, 1998; Tipton, Camp, & Hsu, 1990). Ludwig and Geller (1991) assessed the effectiveness of an intervention that consisted of the participation in a
85 seat belt awareness session, as well as the signing of a buckle-up promise card. Postintervention seat belt use among drivers younger than 25 years of age increased by about 50% as compared to baseline use. In contrast, seat belt use among drivers older than 25 years of age
90 was unaffected by the intervention (Ludwig & Geller, 1991).

Intervention and Rationale

The objective of this report is to evaluate the effectiveness of a two-component intervention for increasing seat belt use among front seat occupants of cars
95 using one target parking lot on the campus of a junior college. The intervention included both the public posting of performance feedback and the distribution of an informational flyer among a sample of predominantly young adults and adolescents. Although the separate
100 and combined effects of performance feedback and public information on seat belt use have been evaluated in previous reports, their effect on the seat belt use of younger car occupants is unknown.

Public posting of performance feedback typically
105 includes display of the proportion of drivers observed performing a target behavior in a previous observation period (e.g., Van Houten & Nau, 1981). Performance feedback has been shown to promote a number of safety behaviors including the following: seat belt use
110 (Grant, Jonah, Wilde, & Ackersville-Monte, 1983), slower driving (Van Houten & Nau, 1981; Van Houten, Nau, & Marini, 1980), and greater compliance with workplace safety guidelines (Sulzer-Azaroff & De Santamaria, 1980). Malenfant et al. (1996) assessed the
115 effect of a roadside sign providing belt use rates to car occupants in two cities where a belt use law was in force. Seat belt use in both cities increased reliably above an already high baseline use rate of more than 70%. Grant (1990) evaluated a seat belt promotion
120 program that included both feedback and education components in a jurisdiction with a belt use law. Seat belt use at the intervention site increased by 26% for

drivers and by 65% for passengers as compared to the seat belt use at a control site (Grant, 1990). The effect
125 of performance feedback on seat belt use appears to be greatest in jurisdictions with a mandatory belt use law and where the majority of car occupants wear seat belts (Grant et al., 1983).

It remains unclear if public posting can increase
130 belt use among younger adults above that achieved with a mandatory belt use law. Previous reports on the effect of performance feedback on seat belt use have been conducted among predominantly older drivers. For example, in the report by Grant (1990), 95% of the
135 participants targeted by the public posting intervention were older than 25 years of age. As younger car occupants are more likely to be involved in traffic accidents and less likely to wear seat belts as compared to older occupants (Miller et al., 1998; Reinfurt et al., 1996),
140 evaluating the effect of seat belt promotion interventions among this presumably hardcore nonuser population is desirable. Accordingly, the current intervention occurred among participants who were predominantly younger than 25 years of age.

145 The performance feedback component of the intervention was supplemented by the distribution of an informational flyer to cars in the target parking lot. The flyer informed car occupants about the nature and goal of the investigation under way and also provided feed-
150 back on the change in seat belt use that occurred between the baseline and the intervention phases. Although information is typically considered to be insufficient on its own to motivate behavior change, it may be a necessary prerequisite (Grant et al., 1983). Conse-
155 quently, providing information is often one of several components of a seat belt promotion program that also includes incentives or enhanced enforcement of mandatory belt use laws (e.g., Decina, Temple, & Dorer, 1994; Hunter et al., 1993; Kay, Sapolsky, & Montgom-
160 ery, 1995; Williams, Hall, Tolbert, & Wells, 1994).

Information approaches to reducing risk behaviors are predicated on the assumption that people will behave in a fashion to increase the likelihood of personal safety if provided with the appropriate information and
165 behavioral options (Thyer & Geller, 1990). When assessed independently of incentives or enforcement, public information interventions result in only very modest increases in seat belt use (Johnston et al., 1994). The effectiveness of public information appears
170 related to the frequency of exposure to the informational sources. For example, the modest effects of mass media campaigns on the frequency of risk behaviors is often attributed to limited exposure (Gantz, Fitzmaurice, & Yoo, 1990). To maximize any direct behavioral
175 response, the informational flyer was distributed to every car in the target parking lot three times during a 5-day intervention phase, each time during peak hours of parking lot use.

Table 1
Number and Percentage of Observations by Occupant Status (Driver, Front Passenger), Gender, and Estimated Age

| | Estimated Age (years) | | | | | | | |
| | < 25 | | 24–45 | | > 45 | | Total | |
	#	%	#	%	#	%	#	%
Driver								
Female	817	36	153	7	59	3	1029	45
Male	915	40	209	9	132	6	1256	55
Total	1732	76	362	16	191	8	2285	100
Front Passenger								
Female	309	47	24	4	8	1	341	51
Male	289	44	18	3	12	2	319	49
Total	598	91	42	6	20	3	660	100

Note. Percentages are calculated relative to front seat occupant status. Percentage totals may not sum accurately due to rounding.

Method

Participants and Setting

The participants in this study included drivers and front passengers of cars that used one parking lot on the campus of Vanier College in Montreal during a 4-week period of the winter academic term. The parking lot could accommodate approximately 300 cars and had only one access point. An attendant was stationed in a booth at the entrance of the parking lot during business hours, and cars entering or exiting the lot first came to a full stop at the attendant's booth before proceeding. At the time of this study, a belt use law was in effect in the province of Quebec, with a $25 fine for violators. No comparable seat belt promotion program was ever attempted at the college.

The front seat occupants of 2,285 cars were observed during the course of the study, resulting in 2,285 observations of driver belt use and 660 observations of front passenger belt use. Consistent with previous reports (Williams et al., 1994), the age of front seat occupants was estimated according to broad criteria to minimize error (i.e., < 25, 25–45, > 45). Table 1 lists the number and percentage of participants by occupant status (driver, front passenger), gender, and estimated age. The age distribution of participants is consistent with the status of Vanier as a junior college, which provides preuniversity degrees as well as professional diplomas primarily to recent high school graduates.

Observation Procedures and Data Collection

One observer recorded shoulder belt use, gender, and estimated age of front seat occupants on a portable tape recorder from within the parking lot attendant's booth. A pilot study demonstrated that data obtained with this procedure are reliable, which also ensured unobtrusive observations.

Eighteen observation sessions were conducted during the 4-week duration of the study. Cars were observed exiting the parking lot from 15:30 to 17:30 during each day of the study. These observation times represented the period of greatest traffic flow from the parking lot. In addition, probe observation sessions were conducted of cars entering the parking lot from 07:00 to 09:00 on two occasions: one on the last day of the first week and the other on the last day of the second week of the study. These sessions were to ensure that the seat belt use observed between 15:30 and 17:30 accurately represented the use rate of people using the parking lot throughout the day. Observations during the probe sessions were obtained at an intersection of a public street and the private road leading to the target parking lot. The entrance of the parking lot and the feedback sign were not visible from this location. Observations were not taken on weekends.

Weather and road conditions were noted throughout the 4-week duration of the study. The pavement was wet, due to a light drizzle, on 4 of the 6 observation periods during the first week of the study (i.e., baseline phase). Wet road conditions, without precipitation, were noted on 2 of 12 observation periods conducted from the 2nd to the 4th week of the study, one in each of the intervention and follow-up phases.

Experimental Phases

Baseline. During baseline, shoulder belt use, gender, and estimated age of the front seat occupants of cars were recorded during the observation sessions for 5 consecutive days (i.e., Monday to Friday) according to the procedure outlined above. Five daily observation sessions were conducted from 15:30 to 17:30, and a probe observation session was conducted from 07:00 to 09:00 on the Friday of this week. Only administrative personnel, who granted permission to conduct this study, and the parking lot attendant were aware of the data collection under way.

Intervention. During the intervention, the sampling of shoulder belt use, gender, and estimated age of front seat occupants proceeded as during baseline for 5 consecutive days of the 2nd week of the study (i.e., Monday to Friday). During this period, two different intervention components were implemented simultaneously: a) public posting of the seat belt use rate of drivers using the lot on the previous observation day, and

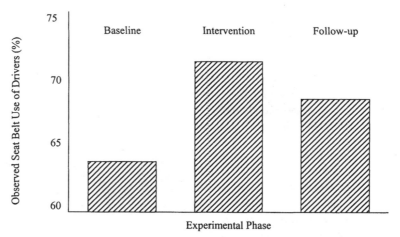

Figure 1. Rate of driver belt use in each of the three experimental phases (number of observations: Baseline = 739, Intervention = 869, Follow-up = 677).

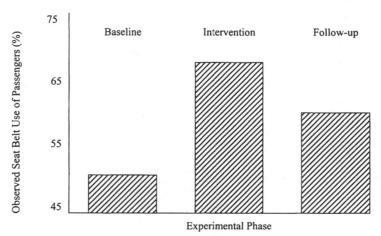

Figure 2. Rate of front passenger belt use in each of the three experimental phases (number of observations: Baseline = 222, Intervention = 236, Follow-up = 202).

b) distribution of an informational flyer to all the cars within the parking lot at prescribed times.

260 A feedback sign, placed adjacent to the entrance of the parking lot, indicated the percentage of drivers wearing a seat belt on the previous observation day. Cars entering the parking lot came to a full stop at the attendant's booth approximately 6 meters away from the sign. The sign measured 46 cm wide and 91 cm high, and was fastened to a stand approximately 2 me-265 ters above the ground. The reflective lettering on the sign measured approximately 6 cm wide and 9 cm high, and the message read "DRIVERS WEARING SEAT BELTS YESTERDAY, XX%." The actual rate indicated on the sign was changed daily to reflect the 270 percentage of drivers observed to be wearing seat belts on the previous observation day. The sign was erected on the 2nd day of the intervention phase and remained there for 4 consecutive days until the end of this phase.

Flyers were distributed to all cars in the parking lot 275 on the 1st, 3rd, and 5th days of the intervention phase (Monday, Wednesday, and Friday). A total of 284 flyers was distributed on Monday, 102 flyers on Wednesday, and 261 flyers on Friday. The distribution oc-280 curred at 11:30 on each of the 3 days, when the parking lot contained the greatest number of cars. Flyers were placed under the driver's side windshield wiper of the cars, ensuring both visibility and accessibility by the driver.

The flyer was divided into four different content ar-285 eas. The first area presented a message in bold print stating "SEAT BELTS SAVE LIVES. BUCKLE UP PLEASE." The second area presented fatality and injury rates due to car accidents in Quebec and a statement of the effectiveness of seat belts in reducing fa-290 talities and injuries in car accidents. The third content area contained the message "Whether or not you wear a seat belt may be your own business, but tell that to the family and friends of someone who has been injured in a car accident." The content of the fourth area of the flyer was changed between the first 2 days of distribution and the 3rd day. During the first 2 distribution days, the fourth content area advised the reader that the safety belt use of people using the parking lot was being monitored and explained the purpose of the feedback sign. On the 3rd day of distribution, the fourth content area provided feedback on the actual change in seat belt use that occurred between the baseline phase and the intervention phase.

Follow-up. During this phase, the sampling of shoulder belt use, gender, and estimated age of front seat occupants proceeded as before on the 3rd and 4th weeks of the study, with the exception that a probe observation session was not conducted. Observations during this phase were interrupted by school holidays. Consequently, observations for the follow-up phase were conducted on the first 2 days of the 3rd week of the study (Monday and Tuesday) and the last 4 days of the 4th week (Tuesday, Wednesday, Thursday, and Friday). During this phase, the feedback sign was not present and no flyers were distributed.

Results

On the 2 days that included probe sessions, observations were made from 07:00 to 09:00 and from 15:30 to 17:30. Belt use during these two different observation periods was equivalent. Consequently, data for these two observation periods were pooled for the subsequent discussion.

Results from the seat belt observations are considered separately for the data that included all the cars (*n* = 2,285) and for the subset of the data that included cars with both a driver and a front passenger (*n* = 660).

Driver Belt Use

The overall rate of seat belt use among drivers across experimental phases was 68%, and more female drivers wore seat belts than did male drivers (female drivers' belt use = 75%, male drivers' belt use = 63%). Figure 1 displays the rate of driver belt use in each of the three experimental phases. Inspection of this figure reveals that driver belt use was higher during the intervention phase of the experiment (71%) relative to driver belt use during the baseline phase (64%), representing a relative increase in seat belt use of about 11%. Although driver belt use remained higher during the follow-up phase (68%) relative to the baseline phase, there appeared a tendency for driver belt use to decline between intervention and follow-up phases.

Front Passenger Belt Use

The overall rate of seat belt use among front passengers across experimental phases was 59%, and more female front passengers wore seat belts than did male front passengers (female passengers' belt use = 66%, male passengers' belt use = 52%). Figure 2 displays the rate of front passenger belt use in each of the three experimental phases. Inspection of this figure reveals a similar pattern of observed seat belt use as described above for drivers. Passenger belt use was higher during the intervention phase of the experiment (67%) relative to passenger belt use during the baseline phase (49%), representing a relative increase of about 37%. Passenger belt use during the follow-up phase (61%) was lower than passenger belt use during the intervention phase, but remained about 25% higher relative to the baseline phase.

Discussion

In this article, we evaluated a brief intervention for increasing seat belt use among front seat occupants of cars on the campus of a junior college. The combination of public posting of performance feedback and the distribution of an informational flyer effectively increased the seat belt use both of drivers and of front passengers. The belt use rate of drivers increased by about 11% following the intervention phase, whereas the belt use of front passengers increased by about 37%, relative to the baseline phase. In both cases, belt use at follow-up was comparable to belt use during the intervention phase, although a trend toward decreasing belt use was noted.

These findings are important in light of two predominant considerations. First, the observed increases in seat belt use were obtained among participants who were not previously complying with a mandatory belt use law. The minority of car occupants who do not comply with belt use laws are thought to be part of a hardcore nonuser population also characterized by other risk behaviors. For example, nonuse of seat belts is related with poorer driving records, larger consumption of alcohol, and increased likelihood of having an arrest record (Dee, 1998; Foss et al., 1994; Hunter et al., 1993; Hunter et al., 1990; Reinfurt et al., 1996; Wilson, 1990). Second, the participants in this study were predominantly young adults who are among the least likely to wear seat belts (Clark, 1993; Schootman, Fuortes, Zwerling, Albanese, & Watson, 1993; Wilson, 1990). It was estimated that 76% of drivers and 91% of front passengers observed in this study were younger than 25 years of age. Consequently, increases in seat belt use observed with the current intervention occurred among predominantly younger drivers and front passengers whose behavior is most resistant to change (Dee, 1998; Reinfurt et al., 1996).

The positive effects of the intervention, however, are tempered by one other finding. The seat belt use of drivers during the follow-up phase (68%) was between their belt use rate during the intervention (71%) and baseline (64%) phases. Gains in seat belt use were clearly maintained at follow-up relative to the baseline phase only among front passengers. However, this finding may be more striking because of a much lower baseline belt use among front passengers as compared to drivers. Driver belt use at baseline was already 64%. In comparison, belt use among front passengers was only 49% during the baseline phase. In general, significantly less baseline belt use among passengers than drivers is consistent with previous reports (e.g., Grant, 1990; Malenfant et al., 1996).

Also consistent with previous reports is that seat belt use was greater among females than among males irrespective of their front seat occupant status. Among drivers, seat belt use for females was 75% as compared with 63% for males. Among passengers, 66% of females and only 52% of males wore seat belts. Females are typically reported to have higher belt use rates than males during both baseline and follow-up phases of intervention programs (Johnston et al., 1994). As this intervention occurred in a jurisdiction with a mandatory belt use law, this finding is also consistent with reports that males are less responsive to belt use laws than are females (Dee, 1998; Hunter et al., 1990; Tipton et al., 1990).

The effect of performance feedback on seat belt use may have been mediated by at least two separate processes (Grant et al., 1983). As already considered in the introduction to this article, performance feedback may present car occupants with a group standard against which their own behavior is compared. According to social comparison theory (Festinger, 1954), people tend to compare themselves with their peers and to bring their behavior more in line with the group standard or norm. In the face of evidence that a majority of drivers use seat belts, nonusers may change their behavior to conform with the majority. In the current report, driver belt use was consistently higher than 60%, and any conformity pressure was in the direction of belt use from the outset of the intervention phase. The effect of the performance feedback on seat belt use may also be extrinsically motivated. The mere presence of performance feedback implies that individual behavior is monitored. Implied surveillance may motivate seat belt use particularly in a jurisdiction with a belt use law, where police officers are the most likely surveillants. Car occupants, then, may wear seat belts to avoid receiving a traffic fine. Consequently, the context in which the current intervention was implemented provided the two conditions that are most favorable to the effective use of performance feedback: (a) initial belt use rate greater than 50%, and (b) enforced mandatory belt use law. In this context, both social comparison and implied surveillance may have contributed to increasing the observed seat belt use.

The effect of the current intervention among participants estimated to be predominantly younger than 25 years of age is consistent with evidence that feedback of seat belt use may be selectively effective among younger drivers. Grant et al. (1983, Experiment 1) reported that a feedback sign increased seat belt use only among younger drivers (i.e., younger than 25 years of age). However, as seat belt use among the participants in Grant et al.'s experiment was consistently less than 50%, the extent to which social comparison

mediated the effect of their intervention is unclear. More generally, age differences in the effect of performance feedback may be consistent with the notion that social comparison is implicated. This is because younger persons may be more likely to conform than older persons when faced with conformity pressure (e.g., Pasupathi, 1999), and the use of social comparison itself may decline with age (Gibbons & Gerrard, 1997). To the extent that the effect of performance feedback is at least partly mediated by social comparison, this intervention may be selectively targeted at younger drivers who have the greatest to benefit from increased seat belt use.

Although the current findings suggest that posting of performance feedback is an effective method of increasing seat belt use among younger adults, these findings must be considered in light of a major methodological consideration. The two components of the intervention described in this article (i.e., posting of performance feedback, and distribution of an informational flyer) were implemented simultaneously. Consequently, the differential effect of each component on the observed seat belt use could not be assessed. The assumption in the previous discussion is that the posting of performance feedback was the primary active component in the intervention package. This assumption is based on the finding that public information interventions result in only very modest increases in seat belt use when assessed independently of other treatment components (Johnston et al., 1994). As the resources and effort required to implement each of the two components of the current intervention package differed greatly, future investigations could be designed to directly assess their relative effectiveness.

In sum, an intervention with performance feedback increased seat belt use among predominantly young adults (i.e., younger than 25 years of age), who are both less likely to wear seat belts and more likely to be involved in traffic accidents as compared to older adults (Dee, 1998; Miller et al., 1998). Although the absolute increase in driver seat belt use following the intervention was modest, it occurred in a presumably hardcore nonuser population who would benefit most from increased seat belt use. Brief interventions with performance feedback may be a cost-effective method for promoting seat belt use in institutional settings and with younger persons whose behavior is refractory to mandatory belt use laws and who are at greater risk of traffic accidents.

References

Clark, M. J. (1993). Seat belt use on a university campus. *College Health, 41*, 169–171.

Conn, J. M., Chorba, T. L., Peterson, T. D., Rhodes, P., & Annest, J. L. (1993). Effectiveness of safety-belt use: A study using hospital-based data for nonfatal motor-vehicle crashes. *Journal of Safety Research, 24*, 223–232.

Cope, J. G., Grossnickle, W. F., & Geller, E. S. (1986). An evaluation of three corporate strategies for safety belt use promotion. *Accident Analysis and Prevention, 18*, 243–251.

Decina, L. E., Temple, M. G., & Dorer, H. S. (1994). Increasing child safety-seat use and proper use among toddlers. *Accident Analysis and Prevention*, *26*, 667–673.

Dee, T. S. (1998). Reconsidering the effects of seat belt laws and their enforcement status. *Accident Analysis and Prevention*, *30*, 1–10.

Festinger, L. (1954). A theory of social comparison processes. *Human Relations*, *7*, 117–140.

Foss, R. D., Beirness, D. J., & Sprattler, K. (1994). Seat belt use among drinking drivers in Minnesota. *American Journal of Public Health*, *84*, 1732–1737.

Gantz, W., Fitzmaurice, M., & Yoo, E. (1990). Seat belt campaigns and buckling up: Do the media make a difference? *Health Communication*, *2*, 1–12.

Geller, E. S., Rudd, J. R., Kalsher, M. J., Streff, F. M., & Lehman, G. R. (1987). Employer-based programs to motivate safety belt use: A review of short- and long-term effects. *Journal of Safety Research*, *18*, 1–17.

Gibbons, F. X., & Gerrard, M. (1997). Health images and their effects on health behavior. In B. P. Buunk & F. X. Gibbons (Eds.), *Health, coping, and well-being: Perspectives from social comparison theory* (pp. 63–94). Mahwah, NJ: Erlbaum.

Grant, B. A. (1990). Effectiveness of feedback and education in an employment based seat belt program. *Health Education Research: Theory and Practice*, *5*, 197–205.

Grant, B. A., Jonah, B. A., Wilde, G.J.S., & Ackersville-Monte, M. (1983). *The use of feedback to encourage seat belt wearing* (TMRU 8301). Road Safety and Motor Vehicle Regulation Directorate, Transport Canada, Ottawa, Canada.

Hagenzieker, M. P., Buleveld, F. D., & Davidse, R. J. (1997). Effects of incentive programs to stimulate safety-belt use: A meta-analysis. *Accident Analysis and Prevention*, *29*, 759–777.

Hunter, W. W., Stewart, J. R., Stutts, J. C., & Marchetti, L. M. (1993). Nonsanction seat belt law enforcement: A modern day tale of two cities. *Accident Analysis and Prevention*, *25*, 511–520.

Hunter, W. W., Stutts, J. C., Stewart, J. R., & Rodgman, E. A. (1990). Characteristics of seat belt users and nonusers in a state with a mandatory belt use law. *Health Education Research: Theory and Practice*, *5*, 161–173.

Johnston, J. J., Hendricks, S. A., & Fike, J. M. (1994). Effectiveness of behavioral safety belt interventions. *Accident Analysis and Prevention*, *26*, 315–323.

Kay, B. K., Sapolsky, B. S., & Montgomery, D. J. (1995). Increasing seat belt use through PI & E and enforcement: The thumbs up campaign. *Journal of Safety Research*, *26*, 235-245.

Kelo, J. E., Geller, E. S., Rice, J. C., & Bryant, S. L. (1988). Motivating auto safety belt wearing in industrial settings: From awareness to behavior change. *Journal of Organizational Behavior Management*, *9*, 7–21.

Ludwig, T. D., & Geller, E. S. (1991). Improving the driving practices of pizza deliverers: Response generalization and moderating effects of driving history. *Journal of Applied Behavior Analysis*, *24*, 31–44.

Ludwig, T. D., & Geller, E. S. (1997). Assigned versus participative goal setting and response generalization: Managing injury control among professional pizza deliverers. *Journal of Applied Psychology*, *82*, 253–261.

Malenfant, L., Wells, J. K., Van Houten, R., & Williams, A. F. (1996). The use of feedback signs to increase daytime seat belt use in two cities in North Carolina. *Accident Analysis and Prevention*, *28*, 771–777.

Miller, T. R., Lestina, D. C., & Spicer, R. S. (1998). Highway crash costs in the United States by driver age, blood alcohol level, victim age, and restraint use. *Accident Analysis and Prevention*, *30*, 137–150.

Pasupathi, M. (1999). Age differences in response to conformity pressure for emotional and nonemotional material. *Psychology and Aging*, *14*, 170–174.

Reinfurt, D., Williams, A., Wells, J., & Rodgman, E. (1996). Characteristics of drivers not using seat belts in a high belt use state. *Journal of Safety Research*, *27*, 209–215.

Schootman, M., Fuortes, L. J., Zwerling, C., Albanese, M. A., & Watson, C. A. (1993). Safety behavior among Iowa junior high and high school students. *American Journal of Public Health*, *83*, 1628–1630.

Smith-Seemiller, L., Lovell, M. R., Franzen, M. D., Smith, S. S., & Townsend, R. N. (1997). Neuropsychological function in restrained versus unrestrained motor vehicle occupants who suffer closed head injury. *Brain Injury*, *11*, 735–742.

Streff, F. M., Kalsher, M. J., & Geller, E. S. (1993). Developing efficient workplace safety programs: Observations of response covariation. *Journal of Organizational Behavior Management*, *13*, 3–14.

Sulzer-Azaroff, B., & De Santamaria, M. (1980). Industrial safety hazard reduction through performance feedback. *Journal of Applied Behavior Analysis*, *13*, 287–295.

Thyer, B. A., & Geller, E. S. (1990). Behavior analysis in the promotion of safety belt use: A review. In M. Hersen, R. M. Eisler, & P. Miller (Eds.), *Progress in behavior modification* (vol. 26, pp. 150–172). Newbury Park, CA: Sage.

Tipton, R. M., Camp, C. C., & Hsu, K. (1990). The effects of mandatory seat belt legislation on self-reported seat belt use among male and female college students. *Accident Analysis and Prevention*, *22*, 543–548.

Van Houten, R., & Nau, P. A. (1981). A comparison of the effects of posted feedback and increased police surveillance on highway speeding. *Journal of Applied Behavior Analysis*, *14*, 261–271.

Van Houten, R., Nau, P. A., & Marini, Z. (1980). An analysis of public posting in reducing speeding behavior on an urban highway. *Journal of Applied Behavior Analysis*, *13*, 383–395.

Williams, A. F., Hall, W. L., Tolbert, W. G., & Wells, J. K. (1994). Development and evaluation of pilot programs to increase seat belt use in North Carolina. *Journal of Safety Research*, *25*, 167–175.

Wilson, R. J. (1990). The relationship of seat belt nonuse to personality, lifestyle and driving record. *Health Education Research: Theory and Practice*, *5*, 175–185.

About the authors: Luigi Pastò is an experimental psychologist at the Defence and Civil Institute of Environmental Medicine in Toronto, Canada. He received a B.A. and an M.A. in psychology from McGill University and a Ph.D. in clinical psychology from the University of Ottawa. His research interests include large-scale modification of health-related behaviors, stress management, and judgment and decision-making processes. Andrew G. Baker is a professor in the Department of Psychology at McGill University.

Note: This project was partially supported by scholarships from the Fonds pour la Formations de Chercheurs et l' aide à la Recherché du Québec and the Ontario Graduate Scholarships Program to Luigi Pastò.

Acknowledgments: We thank the students, faculty, and staff of Vanier College in Montreal, Canada, for their participation. We also thank Megan Thompson, Valérie Gil, Pierre Mercier, Ross Pigeau, Joe Baranski, and two anonymous reviewers for helpful comments on earlier drafts of this article.

Address correspondence to: Luigi Pastò, Defence and Civil Institute of Environmental Medicine, 1133 Sheppard Avenue West, P.O. Box 2000, Toronto, Ontario, Canada, M3M 3B9. E-mail: lpasto@dciem.dnd.ca

Exercise for Article 18

Factual Questions

1. According to the literature review, are those who are at high risk of car accidents more likely to be responsive to interventions with intrinsic incentives *or* are they more likely to be responsive to interventions with extrinsic interventions?

2. Across all age groups combined (i.e., total group) of front passengers, what percentage was female?

3. The baseline period lasted how many consecutive days?

4. Where was the feedback sign placed?

5. Were flyers distributed during the follow-up phase?

6. According to the researchers, was there a "similar pattern" of observed seat belt use for drivers and passengers?

7. The researchers refer to Festinger's theory, which suggests that people tend to compare themselves with their peers and to bring their behavior more

in line with the group standard or norm. What is the name of the theory?

Questions for Discussion

8. The informational flyers were distributed only during peak hours of parking lot use. Is this an important consideration? Is it a limitation of the study? Explain. (See lines 174–178 and lines 214–216.)

9. The researchers used only three age categories. Was this a good idea? Explain. (See lines 195–198.)

10. The researchers report on weather and road conditions. Is this important information? Explain. (See lines 229–236.)

11. Posting performance feedback and distribution of the informational flyers were done at the same time (i.e., during the intervention phase). Hence, they cannot isolate the effects of each of these interventions separately. Do you think it would be a good idea to present the interventions separately in a future study? Why? Why not? (See lines 474–494.)

12. To what populations, if any, would you be willing to generalize the results of this study?

Quality Ratings

Directions: Indicate your level of agreement with each of the following statements by circling a number from 5 for strongly agree (SA) to 1 for strongly disagree (SD). If you believe an item is not applicable to this research article, leave it blank. Be prepared to explain your ratings.

A. The introduction establishes the importance of the study.

   SA   5   4   3   2   1   SD

B. The literature review establishes the context for the study.

   SA   5   4   3   2   1   SD

C. The research purpose, question, or hypothesis is clearly stated.

   SA   5   4   3   2   1   SD

D. The method of sampling is sound.

   SA   5   4   3   2   1   SD

E. Relevant demographics (for example, age, gender, and ethnicity) are described.

   SA   5   4   3   2   1   SD

F. Measurement procedures are adequate.

   SA   5   4   3   2   1   SD

G. All procedures have been described in sufficient detail to permit a replication of the study.

   SA   5   4   3   2   1   SD

H. The participants have been adequately protected from potential harm.

   SA   5   4   3   2   1   SD

I. The results are clearly described.

   SA   5   4   3   2   1   SD

J. The discussion/conclusion is appropriate.

   SA   5   4   3   2   1   SD

K. Despite any flaws, the report is worthy of publication.

   SA   5   4   3   2   1   SD

Article 19

Comparison of Health Promotion and Deterrent Prompts in Increasing Use of Stairs Over Escalators

William D. Russell
Eastern Illinois University

Jasmin Hutchinson
Florida State University

ABSTRACT. This study compared the effectiveness of two point-of-decision prompts within the same environmental setting. The effects of a health promotion sign were compared with activity change resulting from a deterrent sign. Individuals were observed using the upward stairs or upward escalator at a Midwest regional airport during a 5-week period in which intervention signs were compared with no-sign conditions on activity choice. During Weeks 1, 3, and 5, behaviors were assessed without any prompts. During Week 2, a health promotion sign was posted at the behavioral choice point, which read "Keep your heart healthy, use the stairs." During Week 4, a deterrent sign, which read "Please limit escalator use to staff and those unable to use the stairs" was posted at the same behavioral choice point. Younger (<40) women (14.8%) and men (10.8%) used the stairs more frequently, followed by older women (9.3%) and older men (6.9%). A hierarchical log linear analysis showed that stair use increased during both interventions, which was significantly moderated by age. Point-of-decision prompts appear to be effective environmental interventions for promoting increases in physical activity.

From *Perceptual and Motor Skills*, *91*, 55–61. Copyright © 2000 by Perceptual and Motor Skills. Reprinted with permission.

The benefits of increasing daily amounts of physical activity are now well established within the various disciplines in exercise science (U.S. Department of Health and Human Services, 1996). For example, sed-
5 entary individuals have higher risk for hypertension, coronary heart disease, elevated serum cholesterol, and mortality than active individuals. It has also been documented that as many as one in three adults reports no leisure time physical activity (USDHHS, 1996).
10 Such statistics have prompted the Centers for Disease Control and Prevention and the American College of Sports Medicine to revise their exercise recommendations, suggesting that Americans accumulate 30 minutes or more of moderate intensity activity on most, if
15 not all, days of the week (Pate, Pratt, & Blair, 1995). One noted means for apparently healthy sedentary in-

dividuals to become more active is walking and taking the stairs instead of using elevators and escalators.

Point-of-decision prompts in the environment have
20 been examined for their utility as a low-cost intervention for increasing lifestyle activity. Brownell, Stunkard, and Albaum (1980) examined a health-promotion sign placed adjacent to stairs and escalators in an urban mall, train station, and bus terminal, and reported that
25 stair use more than doubled (6.3% to 14.4%) and remained elevated above baseline even one month after the sign was removed. Blamey, Mutrie, and Aitchinson (1995) recently showed the effects for encouraging stair use for health benefits in a Scottish train station as
30 a low-cost sign significantly increased stair use.

Recently, Andersen, Franckowiak, Snyder, Barlett, and Fontaine (1998) compared both prompts with different messages, comparing a health benefits sign and a weight-control sign in the same setting. Both signs
35 significantly increased the proportion of people taking the stairs across different subgroups; however, they did note that for African Americans, stair use decreased for the health benefits sign and did not significantly increase following a weight-control sign. Boutelle,
40 Jeffery, and Schmitz (1999) recently evaluated the frequency of stair and elevator use, perceived barriers to using the stairs, and assessed the effect of highlighting attractiveness and attention to a stairwell on stair use. Their results indicated that both an intervention prompt
45 and a prompt combined with stairwell music and artwork significantly increased stair use compared to the baseline condition. In addition, participants were asked about conditions perceived to increase physical activity. Subjects responded that they would take the stairs
50 more often if access to the stairs was easier, if friends took the stairs, if traveling one or two flights of stairs, and if the stairwell was more attractive.

Finally, Russell, Dzewaltowski, and Ryan (1999) examined the effects of a deterrent prompt, designed
55 exclusively to decrease the value of a more sedentary behavioral option and found stair use in a university library increased significantly during the intervention. The effects of this intervention appeared to be moder-

ated by day of week, sex, and age of the subject. Equivocal findings have been noted for various subgroups in response to different types of prompts. For example, Russell et al. (1999) found that younger individuals responded with greater increases in stair use than older individuals using a deterrent sign. Yet Andersen et al. (1998) found older shoppers as compared to younger shoppers were more likely to take the stairs in response to both the health benefits sign and weight-control sign.

Point-of-decision prompts designed to decrease perceived accessibility and attractiveness of a sedentary option show promise as valuable environmental interventions. Epstein and colleagues have shown that by manipulating access (Epstein, Smith, Vara, & Rodofer, 1991) and proximity (Raynor, Coleman, & Epstein, 1998) of sedentary and active behaviors, children were more physically active when sedentary options were less available. To date, there are no published investigations directly comparing the effectiveness of a health promotion message to a deterrent message in the same setting. It may be argued that differential effects of health promotion signs may reflect their perception as less salient and less restrictive of behavior than deterrent messages, which may be more salient because they are specifically aimed at decreasing the perceived accessibility to the target sedentary behavior. In addition, perceived accessibility may play an important role in people's activity choices, as individuals may choose a less reinforcing physically active behavior (stair use) when the preferred sedentary alternative behavior (escalator use) is perceived as less accessible (Epstein et al., 1991; Vara & Epstein, 1993; Epstein, Saelens, & O'Brien, 1995).

The present study examined if both a health promotion sign designed to increase attractiveness of the physically active choice and a deterrent sign designed to decrease accessibility and attractiveness of the physically sedentary choice would increase stair use in a natural setting. We hypothesized that both signs would increase stair use above baseline and that the deterrent sign would increase stair use significantly more than the health promotion sign.

Method

Setting and Design

Participants had the choice of traveling up an escalator or a flight of stairs (two sets of 10 stairs separated by a landing) to flight arrival and departure gates at a regional Midwest airport. Two signs were used in this study. Both signs (11 in. x 17 in.) were located at eye level on the ground floor directly between the stairs and escalator. Data were collected for five weeks in which baseline data were collected for the first week, followed by the health promotion sign (one week), sign removal (one week), deterrent sign (one week), and sign removal (one week).

Sample

Trained observers watched 3,369 individuals elect to take the stairs or escalator and categorized them by sex and age (under 40 years/over 40). The trained observers did not include any observation of individuals who were physically challenged, traveling with young children, or carrying more than one piece of travel luggage, as these conditions biased travelers to use the escalator. Racial or ethnic background was not measured as a variable given the inherent lack of reliability in such an observational measure.

Measure

Data were collected on Thursdays and Fridays from 9:00 a.m. to 2:00 p.m. for five weeks during the summer. These days were chosen because the airport management informed the researchers that these days would yield the most daily air travel during the week. The observer sat on a bench, at an inconspicuous location, within direct view of the stairs and escalators. The observer was trained for two weeks prior to data collection. Training included learning to categorize individuals according to activity choice (stairs or escalator), sex (male or female), and age category (over 40 years or under 40). This age cutoff was chosen because pilot testing indicated that the older age category would have been overrepresented if a younger cutoff had been used. Pilot data also showed reliable observations between individuals over and under 40 years. To provide further evidence of reliability, at selected unannounced occasions across the study, one of the authors also collected data for 14.3% (483) of the overall sample. Interobserver agreement was 98% on sex, age, and activity.

Intervention

Two interventions were compared in this study. The health promotion sign read "Save time, keep your heart healthy, use the stairs," and had a graphic of a fit-looking heart caricature. The deterrent sign read "Please limit escalator use to staff and those individuals unable to use the stairs," and had a graphic of a businessman using the stairs. The intent of the deterrent was to discourage escalator use by more clearly stating the purpose of the sedentary option (Russell et al., 1999). Airport employees were informed of the interventions so signs would not be removed. No other activity promotion occurred.

Analysis

Hierarchical log linear analysis with follow-up chi-squared analyses were used to examine interactions among the variables of sex (male/female), age (< 40/> 40), and week (one through five) on activity choice (stairs/escalator). Trained observers collected data for 5-hr. increments on Thursdays and Fridays for five weeks.

Results

Of the 3,369 observations, overall stair use was

Table 1
Frequency and Percentage of Stair Use by Week for Subjects Over and Under 40 Years of Age

Stair Use	Age, yr.			
	< 40		> 40	
	f	%	f	%
Week 1: No sign				
Men	28	11.3	5	2.7
Women	22	12.8	9	7.1
Week 2: Health				
Men	20	11.2	23	14.0
Women	39	24.8	9	8.1
Week 3: No sign				
Men	19	8.4	10	6.1
Women	21	9.1	11	10.4
Week 4: Deterrent				
Men	25	12.9	15	9.3
Women	37	19.0	16	16.8
Week 5: No sign				
Men	21	9.5	3	2.1
Women	18	10.4	7	5.9

relatively low (10.6%) yet similar to previous studies (Brownell et al., 1980; Blamey et al., 1995). From the hierarchical log linear analysis with activity as the response variable, significant two-way interactions were found ($p < .05$) for sex and age ($\chi_1^2 = 8.21$) and age by week ($\chi_4^2 = 17.66$). There was also a significant main effect for week of study ($\chi_4^2 = 31.62$). Table 1 presents frequency and percentage of stair use for age and sex categories across weeks of the study.

Sex and Age

There was a significant interaction for sex by age ($\chi_3^2 = 8.21$, $p < .004$), indicating that overall stair use differed across sex and age categories regardless of condition. Younger women had the highest stair use (14.8%) followed by younger men (10.8%). Older women used the stairs 9.4% of the time, while older men within the study were least likely to use the stairs (6.9%).

Point-of-decision Prompt Interventions

During both the health promotion and deterrent interventions, there was a significant increase in stair use compared to weeks when no sign was present ($\chi_2^2 = 35.10$, $p < .0001$). Stair use rose from 8.22% when no signs were present to 14.89% with the health promotion sign and 14.40% with the deterrent sign. A chi-square analysis comparing the two point-of-decision prompts yielded no significant differences between the two signs for increasing stair use over baseline ($\chi_1^2 = .06$, ns).

Age and Week

There was also a significant interaction for age by week ($\chi_4^2 = 17.66$, $p < .001$), indicating that stair use differed across point-of-decision prompts for different age groups. For younger individuals, stair use was sig-

nificantly higher during the weeks in which the health promotion sign (17.56%) and the deterrent sign (15.54%) were present, compared to weeks when no sign was present (10.24%; $\chi_4^2 = 21.37$, $p < .001$). For older individuals, stair use was significantly higher during the weeks in which the deterrent sign (12.06%) and health promotion sign (11.64%) were present, compared to weeks when no signs were present (5.37%; $\chi_4^2 = 22.50$, $p < .001$).

Discussion

These results indicate that both health promotion and deterrent point-of-decision prompts may be somewhat effective and low-cost methods by which to promote short-term lifestyle physical activity patterns in a wide age range of sedentary populations. This study contradicted findings from Russell et al. (1999) who found that younger men had the highest stair use. While the overall percentage of stair use was lower for younger (<40) women in this study (14.8%) compared to the Russell et al. (1999) study (45.5%), the higher percentage of stair use in this category may have been due to fewer younger women with travel luggage. This conclusion is tenuous since this condition was not included in the analysis. However, the observation that this category had the highest percent stair use is encouraging based upon previous findings that women are less active (USDHHS, 1996). Both interventions had a significant overall effect on increasing stair use over no signs; however, there were no significant differences between signs in increased stair use. The interventions seemed to differ in their effectiveness depending on whether the individuals were under or over 40 years old.

Although the increases in short-term stair use were modest, they were comparable to previous point-of-

decision prompt studies conducted by Blamey et al.
(1995) 7.0%, Brownell et al. (1980) 8.1%, Andersen et
al. (1998) 2.1%, and Russell et al. (1999) 2.2%. This
study demonstrates the utility of a simple paradigm for
studying physical activity patterns in a natural environment and the effectiveness of various types of environmental prompts. There are several reasons why the
success of the interventions may have differed by age.
Self-efficacy has been shown to be a moderator variable in determining amounts of physical activity (Gill,
Kelley, & Williams, 1994; McAuley, Courneya, Rudolph, & Lox, 1994). Younger individuals may have
higher self-efficacy for stair use than older individuals.
Older individuals may also have read the deterrent sign
and perceived that they themselves were included in
the group "unable to use the stairs," thus perceiving the
escalator to be an accessible behavior option. Since the
perception of intended meaning seems to be an inherent consideration with sedentary deterrent signs (Russell et al., 1999), further study may examine the salience of the prompt in determining perceived inclusiveness into the type of prompt.

It appears that meaningful long-term increases in
physical activity may best be achieved by altering sedentary individuals' perceptions of having more access
to and preference for physically active behavior (Epstein, Saelens, Myers, & Vito, 1997). In natural settings, where no immediate reinforcement contingency
exists for choosing physically active behaviors, deterrent prompts may ultimately be more effective because
their salience places immediate behavioral restrictions
on sedentary activities. Researchers should examine
subjects' perceived preferences for activities after comparing different types of prompts.

Conclusions from these results should be viewed
cautiously regarding the following limitations: While
interobserver agreement was high, observers' judgments were not validated by directly requesting age
and sex. This may have resulted in some inaccuracy in
categorizing observations. In addition, data collection
took place during a period of excessively hot regional
weather conditions and, while the airport was air-
conditioned, the environmental condition may have
contributed to more travelers using the escalators. Finally, the length of this study precludes conclusions
regarding long-term changes in stair use. Subsequent
studies should also examine longer prompt comparisons and whether training staff and establishing a social and environmental climate (Boutelle et al., 1999)
would create stronger effects for a sedentary deterrent
sign.

References

Andersen, R. E., Franckowiak, S. C., Snyder, J., Barlett, S. J., & Fontaine, K. R. (1998). Physical activity promotion by encouraged use of stairs. *Annals of Internal Medicine, 129,* 363–369.

Blamey, A., Mutrie, N., & Aitchinson, T. (1995). Health promotion by encour-aged use of stairs. *British Medical Journal, 311,* 289–290.

Boutelle, K. N., Jeffery, R. W., & Schmitz, K. H. (1999). The use of music and artwork to promote daily physical activity. *Annals of Behavioral Medicine, 10,* S206.

Brownell, K. D., Stunkard, A. J., & Albaum, M. (1980). Evaluation and modi-fication of exercise patterns in the natural environment. *American Journal of Psychiatry, 137,* 1540–1545.

Epstein, L. H., Saelens, B. E., Myers, M. D., & Vito, D. (1997). The effects of decreasing sedentary behaviors on activity choice in obese children. *Health Psychology, 17,* 101–119.

Epstein, L. H., Saelens, B. E., & O'Brien, J. G. (1995). Effects of reinforcing increases in active versus decreases in sedentary behavior for obese children. *International Journal of Behavioral Medicine, 2,* 41–50.

Epstein, L. H., Smith, J. A., Vara, L. S., & Rodofer, J. S. (1991). Behavioral economic analysis on activity choice in obese children. *Health Psychology, 10,* 311–316.

Gill, D. L., Kelley, B. C., & Williams, K. (1994). The relationship of self-efficacy and perceived well-being to physical activity and stair climbing in older adults. *Research Quarterly for Exercise and Sport, 65,* 367–371.

McAuley, E., Courneya, K. S., Rudolph, D. L., & Lox, C. L. (1994). Enhanc-ing exercise adherence in middle-age males and females. *Preventive Medi-cine, 23,* 498–506.

Pate, R. R., Pratt, M., & Blair, S. N. (1995). Physical activity and public health: A recommendation from the Centers for Disease Control and the American College of Sports Medicine. *Journal of the American Medical Association, 273,* 402–407.

Raynor, D. A., Coleman, K. J., & Epstein, L. H. (1998). Effects of proximity on the choice to be physically active or sedentary. *Research Quarterly for Exercise and Sport, 69,* 99–103.

Russell, W D., Dzewaltowski, D. A., & Ryan, G. (1999). The effectiveness of a point-of-decision prompt in deterring sedentary behavior. *American Journal of Health Promotion, 13,* 257–259.

U.S. Department of Health and Human Services. (1996). *Physical activity and health: A report of the Surgeon General.* Atlanta, GA: Department of Health and Human Services, Centers for Disease Control and Prevention, National Center for Chronic Disease Prevention and Health Promotion.

Vara, L. S., & Epstein, L. H. (1993). Laboratory assessment of choice between exercise or sedentary behaviors. *Research Quarterly for Exercise and Sport, 64,* 356–360.

Address correspondence to: William D. Russell, Ph.D., 227A Lantz Gymnasium, Department of Physical Education, Eastern Illinois University, Charleston, IL 61920. E-mail: cfwdr@eiu.edu

Exercise for Article 19

Factual Questions

1. Until this study was conducted, had there been other studies directly comparing the effectiveness of a health promotion message to a deterrent mes-sage in the same setting?

2. Which of the two types of signs did the research-ers hypothesize would be more effective?

3. During which week were baseline data collected?

4. What percentage was reported for the interob-server agreement?

5. What did the deterrent sign say?

6. Overall, which sex/age group had the highest stair use?

7. Overall, stair use rose from 8.22% to what per-centage when the health promotion sign was posted?

Questions for Discussion

8. What is your opinion on the researchers' decision not to include racial or ethnic background as a variable in this study? (See lines 120–122.)

9. The deterrent sign had a graphic of a businessman using the stairs. Do you think this was a good idea? Explain. (See lines 147–150.)

10. The researchers characterize the increases in short-term stair use as "modest." Do you agree with this characterization? Explain. (See lines 227–228.)

11. The first limitation that the researchers mention is the failure to validate observers' judgments by directly requesting age and sex. Do you think this is an important limitation? Explain. (See lines 263–268.)

12. If you were conducting a study on the same topic, what changes in the research methodology, if any, would you make?

Quality Ratings

Directions: Indicate your level of agreement with each of the following statements by circling a number from 5 for strongly agree (SA) to 1 for strongly disagree (SD). If you believe an item is not applicable to this research article, leave it blank. Be prepared to explain your ratings.

A. The introduction establishes the importance of the study.

    SA 5 4 3 2 1 SD

B. The literature review establishes the context for the study.

    SA 5 4 3 2 1 SD

C. The research purpose, question, or hypothesis is clearly stated.

    SA 5 4 3 2 1 SD

D. The method of sampling is sound.

    SA 5 4 3 2 1 SD

E. Relevant demographics (for example, age, gender, and ethnicity) are described.

    SA 5 4 3 2 1 SD

F. Measurement procedures are adequate.

    SA 5 4 3 2 1 SD

G. All procedures have been described in sufficient detail to permit a replication of the study.

    SA 5 4 3 2 1 SD

H. The participants have been adequately protected from potential harm.

    SA 5 4 3 2 1 SD

I. The results are clearly described.

    SA 5 4 3 2 1 SD

J. The discussion/conclusion is appropriate.

    SA 5 4 3 2 1 SD

K. Despite any flaws, the report is worthy of publication.

    SA 5 4 3 2 1 SD

Article 20

Influence of Social Context on Reported Attitudes of Nondisabled Students Toward Students with Disabilities

Linda Meyer
Louisiana State University

Marcus Duke
Louisiana State University

Wm. Drew Gouvier
Louisiana State University

Claire Advokat
Louisiana State University

ABSTRACT. The Attitudes Toward Disabled Persons scale was completed by groups of university students with a disability and their nondisabled peers in the presence of either another student with a disability or a nondisabled student. Results showed that the presence of a person with disabilities improved the reported attitudes of individuals without disabilities.

From *Rehabilitation Counseling Bulletin*, *45*, 50–52. Copyright © 2001 by PRO-ED. Reprinted with permission.

Although earlier results had not been so positive (Anthony, 1972), recent evidence has suggested that negative attitudes of nondisabled individuals toward persons with a disability may be improved through actual contact with the latter (Amsel & Fichten, 1988; Strohmer, Grand, & Purcell, 1984). However, with some exceptions (Bailey, 1991; Gibbons, Stephan, Stephenson, & Petty, 1980; Marinelli & Kelz, 1973), these conclusions have been based on the results of surveys and questionnaires rather than "real world" situations (which may not be as supportive, Anthony, 1972). For this reason, the present study sought to empirically determine whether reported attitudes toward people with disabilities would be affected by the social context in which they were obtained. Specifically, would the mere presence of a student with a disability affect the responses of nondisabled students to a survey that assessed their attitudes toward people with disabilities? It was predicted that individuals would report (a) a more tolerant attitude toward persons with disabilities and (b) less discomfort in a social setting when they were paired with a similar individual rather than with a dissimilar individual (i.e., that just the proximity of a person with disabilities would be insufficient to influence the attitudes of nondisabled individuals).

Method

Thirty undergraduate students at Louisiana State University in Baton Rouge participated in this study. Ten of them were persons with disabilities, operationally defined as an individual who used a wheelchair to perform any daily living activities. There were also two confederates, women between the ages of 20 and 30 who were matched on physical characteristics, with the exception that one was able to ambulate independently, and the other used a wheelchair.

In addition to a demographic questionnaire, data were gathered through the use of two scales—the original Attitudes Toward Disabled People Scale (ATDP-O; maximum score of 120; Millington, Strohmer, Reid, & Spengler, 1996; Yuker, Block, & Campbell, 1960) and a Likert-type general measure of ease (GME) scale (1 = *very comfortable* to 7 = *very uncomfortable*).

Three experimental conditions were employed: ND/ND, D/ND, and D/D. In the ND/ND condition, each nondisabled participant (9 women/1 man; mean age = 22 years, SD = 2.6 years) and the nondisabled confederate were escorted into the testing room by the (nondisabled) experimenter and told to make themselves comfortable. The experimenter explained that the data would be used in a large study analyzing the way individuals viewed themselves and others. After signing the consent form, the participant and confederate completed the ATDP-O, followed by the demographic questionnaire and the GME. The experimenter remained in the room to answer any questions.

In the D/ND condition, the confederate with a disability and each nondisabled participant (9 women/1 man; mean age = 22.5 years, SD = ±4.9 years) were escorted into the testing room by the same experimenter. The confederate was directed to the space cleared for the wheelchair, and the nondisabled participant sat across from the confederate. Procedures were otherwise the same as for the ND/ND condition.

In the D/D condition, the confederate and each participant with a disability (4 women/6 men; mean age = 30.5 years, SD = ±12.6 years) were escorted into the testing room by the same experimenter and directed to the cleared spaces across from each other at the confer-

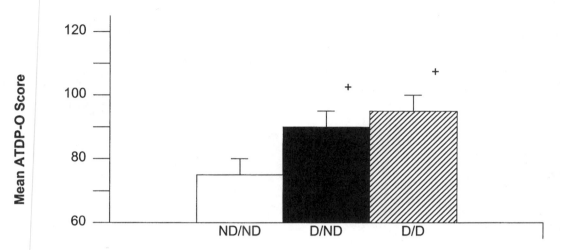

Figure 1. Mean score (± *SEM*) on the Attitudes Toward Disabled Persons Scale of the three experimental groups: Nondisabled participants who completed the survey in the presence of another nondisabled participant (ND/ND, *n* = 10), nondisabled participants who completed the survey in the presence of a person with disabilities (D/ND, *n* = 10), and participants with a disability who completed the survey in the presence of another person with a disability (D/D, *n* = 10). As indicated by the symbols (+), the scores of the ND/ND group were lower than those of the other two groups, indicating less tolerance for persons with a disability.

ence table. Procedures were otherwise identical to those for the ND/ND condition.

Results and Discussion

ATDP-O scores differed significantly among the groups, $F(2, 29) = 9.29$, $p < .001$. Post hoc comparisons (see Figure 1) showed that the ND/ND scores were significantly lower (indicating less tolerance) than those for both the D/ND and the D/D groups ($p < .05$ in each case). However, there was no difference on the GME questionnaire, $p = .062$. Mean scores were 1.90 ($SEM \pm 0.4$), 2.60 ($SEM \pm 0.4$), and 1.40 ($SEM \pm 0.2$), for the ND/ND, D/ND, and D/D groups, respectively, indicating a high level of "comfort" in each case. Although the GME score was larger for the dissimilar pair (D/ND), the Pearson product-moment correlation was not significant ($r = .32$).

The prediction of this study was that nondisabled individuals would be uncomfortable in the presence of a person with a disability (D/ND) such that their ATDP-O scores would be lower than those for the ND/ND group, whereas the ND/ND and D/D scores would be the same. This was not the case. The ND/ND group had the lowest scores, indicating the least tolerance; the other two groups did not differ. Nondisabled individuals reported a more favorable attitude toward persons with disabilities when they were in the presence of such an individual.

It must be emphasized that the basis for this social context effect cannot be determined from these data. There was no difference on the GME assessments and no correlation between the GME and the ATDP-O, suggesting that the reported increase in tolerant attitude was not induced by a sense of social discomfort.

One obvious interpretation is that the nondisabled participants in the D/ND condition faked their responses so as to appear more tolerant. This might be an example of what Antonak and Livneh (1995) referred to as *reactivity*—the distortion of attitudes when one is aware that his or her attitude is being measured, especially in an effort to show either a socially appropriate or open-minded attitude. It has been acknowledged that nearly all items on the ATDP-O could be faked (Yuker, 1986). However, this has previously only been demonstrated in situations where participants were specifically asked to respond in a positive manner (Hagler, Vargo, & Semple, 1987; Yuker, 1986). In the present study, this interpretation would mean that the mere presence of a person with a disability led the nondisabled participants to spontaneously and independently modify their responses, but the presence of a nondisabled person did not lead to this action. This could be tested, perhaps by having a single group of nondisabled individuals participate in both conditions, conducting a posttest debriefing, or using an indirect measure such as the error-choice method described by Antonak and Livneh.

The results might also have been influenced by any past experience the nondisabled participants had with persons with a disability. Although we have no information on this point, there is no reason to expect that one group of nondisabled participants would have had more of these experiences than the other or that such exposure would produce the differential outcome.

The implication of these data is that mere physical proximity of nondisabled individuals and those with a

disability might have a beneficial effect on their social
interactions. With respect to rehabilitation training, one
135 interpretation might be that "less is more"; that is, ha-
bituation between nondisabled persons and those with a
disability may be a cost-effective way to begin to modify negative attitudes.

Because of the study's limitations, this interpreta-
140 tion remains speculative. The result needs replication
with, at a minimum, other types of disabilities (e.g.,
blindness, developmental disabilities), different
amounts of time spent in the presence of the person
with a disability, and the presence or absence of other
145 persons who either have or do not have a disability.
Such variables need to be evaluated in future experiments to determine the generalizability of these findings.

A final comment concerns the fact that the D/ND
150 and D/D scores were the same. Although the values
indicated a high degree of tolerance, they were still
approximately 20% less than the maximum (120). That
the responses of the D/D group were not higher may be
relevant to an observation of Fichten, Robillard,
155 Tagalakis, and Amsel (1991) that "wheelchair-
users…were found to experience significantly greater
ease with able-bodied students than with students who
use a wheelchair" (p. 9).

References

Amsel, R., & Fichten, C. S. (1988). Effects of contact on thoughts about interaction with students who have a physical disability. *Journal of Rehabilitation, 54*, 61–65.

Anthony, W. A. (1972). Societal rehabilitation: Changing society's attitudes
toward the physically and mentally disabled. *Rehabilitation Psychology, 19*,
117–126.

Antonak, R. F., & Livneh, H. (1995). Direct and indirect methods to measure
attitudes toward persons with disabilities, with an exegesis of the error-
choice test method. *Rehabilitation Psychology, 40*, 3–24.

Bailey, J. W. (1991). Evaluation of a task partner who does or does not have a
physical disability: Response amplification or sympathy effect? *Rehabilitation Psychology, 36*, 99–110.

Fichten, C. S., Robillard, K., Tagalakis, V., & Amsel, R., (1991). Casual interaction between college students with various disabilities and their nondisabled peers: The internal dialogue. *Rehabilitation Psychology, 36*, 3–19.

Gibbons, F. X., Stephan, W. G., Stephenson, B., & Petty, C. R. (1980). Reactions to stigmatized others: Response amplification vs sympathy. *Journal of
Experimental Social Psychology, 16*, 591–605.

Hagler, P., Vargo, J., & Semple, J. (1987). The potential for faking on the
Attitudes Toward Disabled Persons Scale. *Rehabilitation Counseling Bulletin, 31*, 72–76.

Marinelli, R. P., & Kelz, J. W. (1973). Anxiety and attitudes toward visibly
disabled persons. *Rehabilitation Counseling Bulletin, 16*, 198–205.

Millington, M. J., Strohmer, D. C., Reid, C. A., & Spengler, P. M. (1996). A
preliminary investigation of the role of differential complexity and response
style in measuring attitudes toward people with disabilities. *Rehabilitation
Psychology, 41*, 243–254.

Strohmer, D. C., Grand, S. A., & Purcell, M. J. (1984). Attitudes toward persons with a disability: An examination of demographic factors, social context, and specific disability. *Rehabilitation Psychology, 29*, 131–145.

Yuker, H. E. (1986). The Attitudes Toward Disabled Persons Scale: Susceptibility to faking. *Rehabilitation Counseling Bulletin, 29*, 200–204.

Yuker, H. E., Block, J. R., & Campbell, W J. (1960). *A scale to measure attitudes toward disabled persons: Human Resources Study No. 5.* Albertson,
NY: Human Resources Center.

About the authors: Linda Meyer, BS, is a graduate student in community counseling in the College of Education at Louisiana State
University. Wm Drew Gouvier, Ph.D., is an associate professor of
psychology with a specialty in neuropsychology. Marcus Duke, MS,
was conducting research in spinal cord injury while a graduate student in the psychology department during the course of this study.
Claire Advokat, Ph.D., is a professor of psychology, with research
interests in the neurobiology of analgesia, spasticity, and psychiatric
disorders.

Address correspondence to: Claire Advokat, Ph.D., Louisiana State
University, 236 Audobon Hall, Baton Rouge, LA 70803.

Exercise for Article 20

Factual Questions

1. How was "persons with disabilities" operationally
defined in this study?

2. The two confederates were matched on physical
characteristics with what exception?

3. In the ND/ND condition, was the confederate disabled or nondisabled?

4. What was the average of the participants in the
Disabled/Nondisabled (D/ND) condition?

5. For which group (ND/ND, D/ND, *or* D/D) were
the scores significantly lower on the ATDP-O?

6. The difference referred to in question 5 was statistically significant at what probability level?

7. What is the technical term used by the researchers
to refer to the "distortion of attitudes when one is
aware that his or her attitude is being measured"?

Questions for Discussion

8. Nondisabled participants were assigned to the
three groups. The researchers do not say whether
this assignment was done at random. Is this an
important omission? Explain.

9. What is your opinion on the possibility that the
mere presence of a person with a disability led the
nondisabled participants to spontaneously and
independently modify their responses? (See lines
113–118.)

10. The researchers discuss the need for replication.
Do you agree? (See lines 140–148.)

11. If you were conducting a study on the same topic,
what changes, if any, would you make in the
methodology?

Quality Ratings

Directions: Indicate your level of agreement with each of the following statements by circling a number from 5 for strongly agree (SA) to 1 for strongly disagree (SD). If you believe an item is not applicable to this research article, leave it blank. Be prepared to explain your ratings.

A. The introduction establishes the importance of the study.

 SA   5   4   3   2   1   SD

B. The literature review establishes the context for the study.

 SA   5   4   3   2   1   SD

C. The research purpose, question, or hypothesis is clearly stated.

 SA   5   4   3   2   1   SD

D. The method of sampling is sound.

 SA   5   4   3   2   1   SD

E. Relevant demographics (for example, age, gender, and ethnicity) are described.

 SA   5   4   3   2   1   SD

F. Measurement procedures are adequate.

 SA   5   4   3   2   1   SD

G. All procedures have been described in sufficient detail to permit a replication of the study.

 SA   5   4   3   2   1   SD

H. The participants have been adequately protected from potential harm.

 SA   5   4   3   2   1   SD

I. The results are clearly described.

 SA   5   4   3   2   1   SD

J. The discussion/conclusion is appropriate.

 SA   5   4   3   2   1   SD

K. Despite any flaws, the report is worthy of publication.

 SA   5   4   3   2   1   SD

Article 21

Preliminary Evaluation of an Abstinence-Based Program for 7th-Grade Students from a Small Rural School District

Shawn M. Fitzgerald
Kent State University

Timothy R. Jordan
Mercy Health Care Center

Raymond Hart
Kent State University

ABSTRACT. The purpose of this study was to investigate the effects of an abstinence-based program designed for 7th-grade students ($n = 59$) from a rural school district. Analysis suggested that after the program more students intended to avoid having sex before marriage, but no change was noted for knowledge, attitudes, and self-efficacy.

From *Psychological Reports*, *88*, 28. Copyright © 2001 by Psychological Reports. Reprinted with permission.

The Responsible Social Values Program is an abstinence-based program developed for adolescents in grades 6–8 for the purpose of reducing early sexual activity and pregnancy. The program presents informa-
5 tion about human sexuality along with goal-oriented activities to effect change in adolescents' behavior and attitudes toward sexual involvement (Thoms, 1985). Although the program has been used for over 20 years, no formal evaluation has been presented.
10 In this study, the program was implemented for six 1-hr sessions in three schools of a rural district with 59 7th graders who voluntarily participated. Their reported mean age was 13.1 years ($SD = .6$), and most lived with both parents (67%), were boys (59%), Euro-
15 American (98%), and did not attend religious services regularly (75%). A one-group pre-experimental design examined pre- to posttest mean differences on five constructs measured on a scale developed by the researchers.

Measure	M$_{Diff.}$	SD	t ($\alpha = .05$)	Scale Reliability (α)
General knowledge	−.51	1.79	2.20, ns	.58
Attitude	−.67	4.26	1.03, ns	.82
Self-efficacy expectation	.59	2.35	1.86, ns	.74
Behavioral intention	−.34	1.60	−.36, ns	.71
Self-efficacy outcome expectation	1.06	2.93	.26, ns	.82

20 Mean differences were not significant for the five measures. At pretest, however, 47% said they planned to avoid having sex until marriage, and at posttest, 57% reported such intentions. These results are consistent with those of other abstinence-based programs of short
25 duration. Evaluations of longer duration, involving a control group and behavioral measures, are required at a minimum.

Reference

Thoms, A. I. (1985). *R.S.V.P.: Responsible Social Values Program.* (Better Choice, Inc., Cuyahoga Falls, OH 44221).

Address correspondence to: S. M. Fitzgerald, Department of Educational Foundations and Special Services, Kent State University, 405 White Hall, P. O. Box 5190, Kent, OH 44242-0001. E-mail: sfitzgerald@emerald.educ.kent.edu

Exercise for Article 21

Factual Questions

1. What was the purpose of the Responsible Social Values Program?

2. What was the average age of the participants?

3. What is the name of the test that was used to determine statistical significance?

4. What probability level was used to determine significance?

5. Which of the scales had the lowest reliability?

Questions for Discussion

6. The researchers state that the program was of "short duration." Given its purpose, do you agree that it was "short"? Explain. (See lines 10–11 and 23–25.)

7. The researchers mention the desirability of using a control group. Do you agree? Explain. (See lines

25–27.)

8. The increase from 47% to 57% is based on "intentions." In your opinion, are "intentions" a good outcome measure? Explain. (See lines 21–23.)

9. If you were to conduct a study on the same topic, what changes, if any, would you make in the research methodology?

Quality Ratings

Directions: Indicate your level of agreement with each of the following statements by circling a number from 5 for strongly agree (SA) to 1 for strongly disagree (SD). If you believe an item is not applicable to this research article, leave it blank. Be prepared to explain your ratings.

A. The introduction establishes the importance of the study.

SA   5   4   3   2   1   SD

B. The literature review establishes the context for the study.

SA   5   4   3   2   1   SD

C. The research purpose, question, or hypothesis is clearly stated.

SA   5   4   3   2   1   SD

D. The method of sampling is sound.

SA   5   4   3   2   1   SD

E. Relevant demographics (for example, age, gender, and ethnicity) are described.

SA   5   4   3   2   1   SD

F. Measurement procedures are adequate.

SA   5   4   3   2   1   SD

G. All procedures have been described in sufficient detail to permit a replication of the study.

SA   5   4   3   2   1   SD

H. The participants have been adequately protected from potential harm.

SA   5   4   3   2   1   SD

I. The results are clearly described.

SA   5   4   3   2   1   SD

J. The discussion/conclusion is appropriate.

SA   5   4   3   2   1   SD

K. Despite any flaws, the report is worthy of publication.

SA   5   4   3   2   1   SD

Article 22

The Effectiveness of a Sexuality Education Newsletter in Influencing Teenagers' Knowledge and Attitudes About Sexual Involvement and Drug Use

Catherine A. Sanderson
Amherst College

ABSTRACT. This study examined the effectiveness of a newsletter written by teenagers on sexual and health issues in changing knowledge and attitudes regarding sexual activity, condom use, and drug use. Four hundred and nineteen high school students completed a pretest, were given a copy of an eight-page newsletter on sexual and health issues to read as homework, and then completed a posttest during the next class period. Findings indicate that reading the newsletter led to more positive attitudes toward postponing sexual involvement and more negative attitudes toward using drugs. Moreover, the newsletter was particularly effective in changing the knowledge and attitudes of Black students. Discussion focuses on the implications of these findings for school-based sexuality education.

From *Journal of Adolescent Research*, *15*, 674–681. Copyright © 2000 by Sage Publications, Inc. Reprinted with permission.

For several reasons, school-based sex education is a particularly important component in reducing the sexual risk-taking behavior of adolescents. First, the vast majority of teenagers are enrolled in school (National Center for Education Statistics, 1993), and, thus, education administered in the classroom has the potential to reach most adolescents. Second, schools are obviously well suited to provide education, and many states even require the provision of education specifically on sexuality (DeMauro, 1990; Gambrell & Haffner, 1993). Finally, research on school-based sexuality education suggests that in-class education can be effective in leading to changes in knowledge, attitudes, and behavior for both junior and senior high school students (Barth, Fetro, Leland, & Volkan, 1992; Brown, Fritz, & Barone, 1989; Eisen, Zellman, & McAllister, 1990; Kirby, 1996; Kirby & Coyle, 1997; Main et al., 1994; Siegel, DiClemente, Durbin, Krasnovsky, & Saliba, 1995). School-based sexuality education therefore has the potential to be one of the most effective methods of preventing teenage pregnancy, STDs, and HIV infection.

Despite the potential effectiveness of such programs, the exposure of students to sex education in school is generally quite limited: The average exposure of students in grades 7 through 12 is a total of 39 hours, or 6½ hours per year (Silverstone, 1992), and fewer than 10% of students receive comprehensive sexuality education in schools (DeMauro, 1990; Dickman, 1982; Gambrell & Haffner, 1993; Haffner & DeMauro, 1991). The reasons for this lack of comprehensive school-based sexuality education are complex. First, some administrators, teachers, and parents are concerned that providing thorough sexuality education (e.g., specific information on birth control methods and strategies for HIV prevention) encourages sexual behavior, and, thus, some districts include only abstinence-focused information. Although the association between sex education and increased sexual activity has been disproven by research (see Kirby & Coyle, 1997, for a review), it remains a widely held misconception. Second, schools often are pressured to increase the time spent teaching academic subjects, which can lead to quantifiable results (e.g., higher rates of graduation, higher mean SAT scores, greater percentage of students attending college), and therefore decrease the amount of time spent on "extraneous" topics, such as sexuality and health. Finally, many teachers are not trained to provide comprehensive instruction on such sensitive and controversial topics and may even lack the comfort necessary to effectively convey such information to adolescents (Kirby, 1996). Therefore, although the potential value of providing school-based sexuality education is clear, the practical constraints of district and school politics, limited classroom time, and teacher competence and comfort suggest that the majority of students may not receive comprehensive and well-taught sexuality education in school.

This research examines one potential and partial solution to these problems by evaluating the effectiveness of a newsletter for teenagers on sexuality and health issues in leading to changes in knowledge and attitudes. Although merely reading a newsletter is obviously not an effective replacement for a thorough in-class discussion of sexual issues, there are several benefits to providing such a supplement to sexuality education in the classroom. First, providing a comprehensive newsletter ensures that students are receiving thorough and accurate information, regardless of possible limitations in the training or comfort of teachers with these topics. Students who receive a sexuality education newsletter in addition to regular classroom materials can also reflect on the information presented for longer periods of time and can refer back to relevant material. Moreover, distributing the newsletter and assigning it to be read as homework does not take up considerable amounts of class time and can be an effective tool in initiating classroom discussions on sexuality issues. Thus, the primary goal of this study is to examine whether providing such a newsletter as a supplement to regular classroom sexuality education can have a significant impact on students' knowledge of and attitudes toward sexual and health issues. Finally, this research will examine both student-based (gender, race) and school-based (location of district) factors that may influence students' responsiveness to the newsletter.

Method

Participants

Four hundred and nineteen students (207 girls and 212 boys) in nine New Jersey high schools served as participants in this study. These students ranged in age from 13 to 18 ($M = 15.3$, $SD = 1.23$). Seventy percent of the students were White ($n = 291$); 18% were African American/Black ($n = 74$); 4% were Asian ($n = 17$); 2% were Hispanic/Latino ($n = 8$); 1% were Native American ($n = 4$); and 6% were "other" ($n = 25$). The high schools that participated in this evaluation represented a variety of geographic areas and socioeconomic levels.

Procedure

As part of a health class, students completed a brief survey assessing knowledge and attitudes about sexual activity, condoms, and drug use. They were then given a copy of the winter 1997 edition of *SEX, etc.* to read for homework. During the next class period, they again completed the same items on knowledge and attitudes, as well as an additional questionnaire assessing reactions to the newsletter. The time interval between the pretest and posttest ranged from 1 day to 1 week, depending on the schedule of class meetings at each school.

Newsletter

SEX, etc. is an eight-page newsletter on health and sexuality issues produced three times a year by the Network for Family Life Education of the Rutgers University School of Social Work. It is produced by an editorial board of high school students from diverse districts in New Jersey, with the assistance of an adult journalist and health professionals. This newsletter has a circulation of more than 580,000 teenagers, including 135,000 in New Jersey and 445,000 in 49 other states and is distributed free to schools, community health departments, libraries, and youth-serving organizations. The particular issue that was used as the stimulus material in this study included 10 articles addressing the following topics: saving sex for marriage, losing one's virginity, buying condoms, effects of chlamydia, effects of HIV, the problems of teenage girls dating older men, the dangers of drug use, and the consequences of unintended pregnancy.

Measures

Knowledge of and Attitudes Toward Sex and Drugs

Participants completed a 34-item scale assessing individuals' knowledge of and attitudes and beliefs of sex, condoms, and drugs. All items were answered based on a 5-point scale (1 = *strongly disagree* to 5 = *strongly agree*). A principal components factor analysis with a varimax rotation was conducted on all of the items in order to group questions into subscales. An inspection of the scree plot and factor loadings revealed that a five-factor solution was the best fit of the data. These factors were as follows: postponing sexual relationships ($\alpha = .74$; e.g., "It is a good idea to wait until you are married to have sex"), the naturalness and "uncontrollability" of sex ($\alpha = .65$; e.g., "Once you are really turned on, it is impossible not to have sex"), myths about sex ($\alpha = .72$; e.g., "There is something wrong with people who date each other for a long time without having sex"), drug use ($\alpha = .80$; e.g., "Smoking pot can lead to addiction to other drugs"), and acid and crack use ($\alpha = .73$; e.g., "Using even a little crack is dangerous"). Participants completed these measures both before and after reading the newsletter.

Reactions to the Newsletter

Using a 5-point scale (1= *strongly disagree* to 5 = *strongly agree*), participants completed seven items assessing their reactions to reading *SEX, etc.* The items were as follows: "*SEX, etc.* was easy to understand"; "I learned new things from reading *SEX, etc.*"; "*SEX etc.* discussed issues that are important to me"; "*SEX etc.* answered some questions I had that I couldn't ask anyone"; "I would like to read more issues of *SEX, etc.*"; "I talked about *SEX, etc.* with my friends"; "I talked about *SEX, etc.* with my parents" ($\alpha = .71$).

Demographics

Participants completed several demographic items, including age, race, and sex. They were also asked to note which of the 10 articles in the issue they had read ($M = 6.05$, $SD = 3.14$).

Table 1
Pretest and Posttest Means and Standard Deviations (in parentheses) in Attitudes and Beliefs

Subscale	Pretest		Posttest	
Postponing sexual relationships	3.21	(0.92)	3.34	(0.88)
The naturalness and "uncontrollability" of sex	2.47	(0.78)	2.48	(0.81)
Myths about sex	2.03	(0.79)	2.07	(0.77)
Drug use	2.43	(1.00)	2.37	(0.99)
Acid and crack use	4.42	(0.93)	4.37	(0.94)

Results

Main Effects

ANCOVAs, controlling for pretest scores, were conducted to examine whether there were overall changes in knowledge and attitudes as a function of reading the newsletter. As shown in Table 1, these analyses revealed significant positive effects of reading *SEX, etc.* on attitudes toward postponing sex, $F(1, 418) = 29.73$, $p = .0001$, and attitudes toward drug use, $F(1, 418) = 5.20$, $p = .02$. There were no significant differences on any of the other subscales.

Changes in Knowledge and Attitudes Based on School and Student Characteristics

Repeated measures ANOVAs were then conducted to determine if there were changes in attitudes and beliefs as a function of various differences in schools and students. Students were classified by gender and race, and schools were classified based on whether they were located in urban (three schools) or nonurban (six schools) districts. First, there were no significant Time x Gender interactions on any of the subscales, and there was a significant Time x School Location interaction only on the subscale measuring the belief that sex is natural and uncontrollable, with urban students decreasing in this belief and nonurban students showing no change, $F(1, 417) = 6.09$, $p < .01$ (urban = 2.74 to 2.63; nonurban = 2.38 to 2.43). There were, however, significant Time x Race interactions on several subscales, including postponing sexual involvement, $F(1, 357) = 9.82$, $p < .002$ (Black students = 3.16 to 3.45; White students = 3.19 to 3.28); acceptance of myths about sex, $F(1, 357) = 5.16$, $p < .02$ (Black students = 2.14 to 2.06; White students = 2.02 to 2.09); and beliefs that sex is natural and uncontrollable, $F(1, 357) = 3.40$, $p < .07$ (Black students = 2.85 to 2.74; White students = 2.39 to 2.41). In all cases, Black students showed more positive changes than White students did.

Differences in Reactions to SEX, etc., Based on School and Student Characteristics

Finally, ANOVAs were conducted to see if differences in schools and students influenced reactions to *SEX, etc.*, using the same three criteria described previously. These analyses revealed significant effects of all three variables: Female students had more positive reactions to *SEX, etc.* than male students did, $F(1, 379) = 13.29$, $p < .0003$ (Ms = 3.20 vs. 2.93); Black students had more positive reactions than White students did, $F(1, 327) = 35.78$, $p < .0001$ (Ms = 3.55 vs. 2.95); and urban students had more positive reactions than nonurban students did, $F(1, 380) = 5.45$, $p < .02$ (Ms = 3.24 vs. 3.02).

Discussion

This study suggests that reading a newsletter on sexual and health issues can have significant positive effects on teenagers' knowledge and attitudes. Specifically, after reading *SEX, etc.*, students had significantly more positive attitudes about postponing sexual involvement and more negative attitudes about drug use. This research is in line with prior work demonstrating the benefits of peer-based sexuality education (Davis, Weener, & Shute, 1977; Howard & McCabe, 1990; Wren, Janz, Carovano, Zimmerman, & Washienko, 1997). These findings are particularly encouraging given the diverse population used in this study (i.e., students from a variety of districts across New Jersey) and the very minimal intervention (i.e., students were merely asked to read an issue of the newsletter at home). In sum, this research suggests that providing peer-written material on sexual and health issues may be a valuable addition to school-based sexuality education classes.

Interestingly, this newsletter was particularly effective in leading to knowledge and attitude change among Black students. Although all students became more positive in their attitudes toward postponing sexual involvement after reading *SEX, etc.*, Black students showed greater attitude change than White students did, and Black students also showed greater decreases than White students in their acceptance of myths about sex and beliefs in the uncontrollability of sex. These differences emerged despite the fact that Black students actually read significantly fewer articles in the newsletter, $t(347) = 4.69$, $p < .0001$ (4.65 vs. 6.51). These findings are in line with those from other research studies showing that sex and AIDS education programs are more effective with African Americans than with other ethnic groups (see Kirby & Coyle, 1997). To our knowledge, this is the first research to demonstrate that race differences can influence reactions to sexual health programs, presumably because many other studies have focused only on students of predominantly one race. These findings suggest that different types of education may be most effective for different students, and, hence, sex education messages may need to be

250 specifically tailored to the particular needs, goals, and concerns of different populations of students (e.g., as a function of race, gender, sexual activity, age, etc.). For example, our findings indicated that certain subgroups of students (i.e., girls, Black students, students in urban
255 districts) had more positive reactions toward *SEX, etc.* than others did.

Although this research suggests that reading a relatively brief newsletter on sexual and health issues may be effective in changing teenagers' attitudes and beliefs
260 toward postponing sexual involvement and using drugs, this work has several limitations that should be addressed by future research. First, this research examined only very short-term effects of *SEX, etc.* on knowledge and attitude change. Future research is
265 needed to examine whether these effects remain over longer periods of time and whether they are associated with corresponding changes in sexual behavior and drug use. Second, the sample of students used in this research may not be generalizable to all students in that
270 it included only those whose teachers and schools were willing to allow such an evaluation. However, this research included a remarkably diverse sample of students and districts and, hence, suggests that the attitude changes observed are not limited only to particular
275 types of schools or students. Finally, although the overall effects found in this study are modest, they are particularly impressive given the very controlled and low-impact experimental manipulation used to test our hypothesis (e.g., students were given only a single copy
280 of the newsletter to read as homework). Future research should examine the effectiveness of this and other newsletters in more effective, and more typical, settings to assess whether the effects observed in this study are even greater when assessed in real-world
285 settings. Given the many limitations of school-based sexuality education (e.g., time, teacher training and comfort, administrative and/or parental pressures), this research provides some encouraging evidence that providing a comprehensive newsletter on sexual health
290 issues as a supplement to in-class education can be effective in leading to changes in teenagers' knowledge and attitudes about sexual involvement and drug use.

References

Barth, R. P., Fetro, J. V., Leland, N., & Volkan, K. (1992). Preventing adolescent pregnancy with social and cognitive skills. *Journal of Adolescent Research, 7,* 208–232.

Brown, L. K., Fritz, G. J., & Barone, V. J. (1989). The impact of AIDS education on junior and senior high school students. *Journal of Adolescent Health Care, 10,* 386–388.

Davis, A. K., Weener, J. M., & Shute, R. E. (1977). Positive peer influence: School-based prevention. *Health Education, 8,* 20–22.

DeMauro, D. (1990). Sexuality education 1990: A review of state sexuality and AIDS curricula. *SIECUS Report, 18,* 1–9.

Dickman, I. R. (1982). *Winning the battle for sex education.* New York: Sex Information Education Council of the United States.

Eisen, M., Zellman, G. L., & McAllister, A. L. (1990). Evaluating the impact of a theory-based sexuality and contraceptive education program. *Family Planning Perspectives, 22,* 261–271.

Gambrell, A. E., & Haffner, D. (1993). *Unfinished business: A SIECUS assessment of state sexuality education programs.* New York: Sex Information Education Council of the United States.

Haffner, D. W., & DeMauro, D. (1991). *Winning the battle: Developing support for sexuality and HIV/AIDS education.* New York: Sex Information Education Council of the United States.

Howard, M., & McCabe, J. B. (1990). Helping teenagers postpone sexual involvement. *Family Planning Perspectives, 22,* 21–26.

Kirby, D. (1996). A review of educational programs designed to reduce sexual risk-taking behaviors among school-aged youth in the United States. In *The Effectiveness of AIDS Prevention Efforts* (pp. 159–235). Washington, DC: American Psychological Association.

Kirby, D., & Coyle, K. (1997). School-based programs to reduce sexual risk-taking behavior. *Children and Youth Services Review, 19,* 415–436.

Main, D. S., Iverson, D. C., McGloin, J., Banspach, S. W., Collins, K., Rugg, D., & Kolbe, L. J. (1994). Preventing HIV infection among adolescents: Evaluation of a school-based education program. *Preventive Medicine, 23,* 409–417.

National Center for Education Statistics. (1993). *Digest of education statistics, 1993.* Washington, DC: U.S. Department of Education, Office of Educational Research and Improvement.

Siegel, D., DiClemente, R., Durbin, M., Krasnovsky, F., & Saliba, P. (1995). Change in junior high school students' AIDS-related knowledge, misconceptions, attitudes and HIV-preventive behaviors: Effects of a school-based intervention. *AIDS Education and Prevention, 7,* 534–543.

Silverstone, R. (1992). Sexuality education in adolescents. *State of Art Reviews: Adolescent Medicine, 3,* 192-205.

Wren, P. A., Janz, N. K., Carovano, K., Zimmerman, M. A., & Washienko, K. M. (1997). Preventing the spread of AIDS in youth: Principles of practice from 11 diverse projects. *Journal of Adolescent Health, 21,* 309–317.

Acknowledgments: This research was supported by the Office of Prevention of Mental Retardation and Developmental Disabilities of the New Jersey Department of Human Services. I gratefully acknowledge the assistance of Susan Wilson, Philip Mackey, and Ann Schurmann in designing and conducting this research; Debra Cohen in providing funding; Darren Yopyk for his assistance in entering and analyzing the data; and the administrators, teachers, and students at the participating schools.

About the author: Catherine A. Sanderson is an assistant professor of psychology at Amherst College. She has published several articles on issues of STD and HIV prevention in college and adult populations. Her research focuses on the role of personal goals and situational factors in predicting safer sex behavior, how the erroneous perception of a "thinness norm" can lead to eating disorders, and the impact of one's intimacy focus on satisfaction in close relationships.

Address correspondence to: Catherine A. Sanderson, Department of Psychology–Box 2236, Amherst College, Amherst, MA 01002. E-mail: casanderson@amherst.edu

Exercise for Article 22

Factual Questions

1. The researcher states that there are "several benefits" to providing a supplement to sexuality education. What is the first benefit she mentions?

2. How many high schools were involved in this study?

3. The factor analysis of the 34-item scale revealed that it measured how many factors?

4. What was the mean number of articles read by the participants?

5. For the subscale called "postponing sexual relationships," the pretest mean is 3.21. What is the posttest mean?

6. The mean score on the reactions to the newsletter for urban students was 5.45, and the mean for nonurban students was 3.24. Was the difference between these two means statistically significant?

7. The researcher briefly describes "several limitations" of her study. What is the first limitation that she mentions?

Questions for Discussion

8. The research states that the high schools that participated represented a variety of geographic areas and socioeconomic levels. Would you be interested in knowing more about this diversity? Why? Why not? (See lines 95–98.)

9. The researcher provides a sample item for each of the five factors in the measure of knowledge of and attitudes toward sex and drugs. In your opinion, how important are these sample items? Would this research article be as understandable without them? Explain.

10. The researcher points out that this study is limited by the fact that only those students whose teachers and schools were willing to allow the evaluation were included. Do you think that this is an important limitation? Explain. (See lines 268–275.)

11. In your opinion, are the results of this study sufficiently encouraging to justify additional studies on this topic? Explain.

12. If you conducted a study on the same topic, what changes in the research methodology, if any, would you make?

Quality Ratings

Directions: Indicate your level of agreement with each of the following statements by circling a number from 5 for strongly agree (SA) to 1 for strongly disagree (SD). If you believe an item is not applicable to this research article, leave it blank. Be prepared to explain your ratings.

A. The introduction establishes the importance of the study.

SA   5   4   3   2   1   SD

B. The literature review establishes the context for the study.

SA   5   4   3   2   1   SD

C. The research purpose, question, or hypothesis is clearly stated.

SA   5   4   3   2   1   SD

D. The method of sampling is sound.

SA   5   4   3   2   1   SD

E. Relevant demographics (for example, age, gender, and ethnicity) are described.

SA   5   4   3   2   1   SD

F. Measurement procedures are adequate.

SA   5   4   3   2   1   SD

G. All procedures have been described in sufficient detail to permit a replication of the study.

SA   5   4   3   2   1   SD

H. The participants have been adequately protected from potential harm.

SA   5   4   3   2   1   SD

I. The results are clearly described.

SA   5   4   3   2   1   SD

J. The discussion/conclusion is appropriate.

SA   5   4   3   2   1   SD

K. Despite any flaws, the report is worthy of publication.

SA   5   4   3   2   1   SD

Article 23

Measurement of Nonverbal Receptive Abilities in Medical Students

A. James Giannini
Chemical Abuse Centers

Rachel K. Bowman
Youngstown State University

Jocelyn D. Giannini
Poland Seminary

ABSTRACT. Physicians have been reported to have difficulty in communicating with their patients. An element of this communication gap is proposed to be related to the educational curriculum and the selection process of medical schools, in particular, with the emphasis on scientific methodology reducing exposure to humanistic values. This hypothesis was tested by measuring nonverbal receptive abilities in two groups. Thirty medical students were compared with 30 college students who were not science majors but were age-, sex- and race-matched. The nonscience majors were better at perceiving nonverbal cues than medical students. Male nonscience majors had higher scores than male medical students, while similar results were seen when female nonscience majors were compared with female medical students. Finally, medical students planning to practice as primary care specialists had higher scores than those interested in specialties that do not involve direct or prolonged patient care.

From *Perceptual and Motor Skills, 90*, 1145–1150. Copyright © 2000 by Perceptual and Motor Skills. Reprinted with permission.

It has been reported that contemporary physicians have difficulty in appropriately responding to their patients' needs. This impairment in communication produces deterioration in the doctor-patient relationship
5 (Hall, Stein, Roter, & Rieser, 1999; Toon, 1999). Surprisingly, such deficient communication skills persist despite evidence that indicates that improved medical outcome is correlated with increased communication with patients (Stewart, Brown, Boon, Galadja, Mere-
10 dith, & Sangster, 1999). Unfortunately, such skills also may create potentially fatal patient-initiated delays in beginning treatment (Zapka, Estabrook, Gilliland, Leviton, Meischke, & Melville, 1999). Given this problem in communication, patients give more trust to phy-
15 sicians' assistants (Assenso-Okyeriere, Osei, Anum, & Adukono, 1999) and other alternative health care providers (Duwrick & Frith, 1999) than to physicians (Shaughnessy, Cincotta, & Adelman, 1999).

This situation is claimed not to have developed in
20 America until the post-World War I era, at which time some medical schools converted to a completely scientific curriculum, while those that did not were closed (Wolberg, 1983; Toon, 1999). Apprenticeship programs were also abolished, and thereafter medical
25 schools emphasized scientific knowledge and skills. Although any college graduate could apply to medical school, regardless of major, the large number of required undergraduate science courses made it difficult to pursue a nonscience baccalaureate major (Stevenson
30 & Multhaef, 1968). Since this postwar era, a progressive dissonance has been noted between physicians and patients (Barbrow, Kasch, & Ford, 1998). This may have generated diminished interpersonal trust between these two groups and even expectations of exploitation
35 by minority patient groups (Corbie-Smith, Thomas, Williams, & Moody-Ayers, 1999).

The focus by medical school admission committees on scientifically oriented individuals at the expense of arts and humanities graduates may have resulted in the
40 selection of physicians with relatively lower interpersonal skills (Hmelo, 1998). This hypothesis was tested by measuring nonverbal receptive skills in medical students.

Method

Subjects

Thirty medical students between the ages of 20 and
45 24 years volunteered for this study. Half were men and half were women. All men and 13 women were Euro-American; one woman was black and one Asian. Thirty age-, race- and sex-matched controls were chosen from volunteers who responded to posted adver-
50 tisements at three local colleges.

The medical students were recruited from four medical schools and had completed a psychiatric course. The first 30 who volunteered were chosen. Of the schools, two were of allopathic medicine, i.e., lead-
55 ing to an M.D. degree, and two were of osteopathic medicine (D.O. degree). Nineteen students were pursuing the M.D. degree and 11 the D.O. All 30 had indicated specialty preferences: 4 were interested in family medicine, 7 in internal medicine, 4 in obstetrics/gyne-
60 cology, 2 in pathology, 3 in pediatrics, 4 in psychiatry, 1 in radiology, and 5 in surgery. All 30 had majored in the sciences as undergraduates or as part of a six-year combined B.S.-M.D. program.

All controls were students between the ages of 20 and 24 years and in undergraduate or graduate courses. Thirteen were majors in arts and humanities, 10 in the social sciences, 2 in the fine arts, 3 in the performing arts, and 2 in business.

All subjects signed consent forms identical to those used in previous similar studies.

Procedure

Videotapes of undergraduates engaged in a sham gambling task were used as a source of nonverbal cues, i.e., "Senders." This method was originally developed with 154 subjects involved in prior work reported previously. These successfully replicated over a 22-yr. period (Miller, Giannini, & Levine, 1977; Giannini, Daood, Giannini, Boniface, & Rhodes, 1978). On these tapes, 10 Senders attempted to win variable amounts of money at a slot machine during 10 trials each. The amount, which was determined by random sequence, was a dime, a quarter, or a dollar. During playing time, their facial expressions were covertly taped. At the end of the study, these Senders signed appropriate release forms.

The medical students and the controls were asked to assess, solely on the basis of nonverbal cues, the money at risk during each Sender's trial. They were seated in a chair that had a control panel mounted on the right arm. On this panel were three buttons labeled $.10, $.25, and $1.00, respectively; the chair faced a television set on which videotapes of the Senders were shown. Above the television was a speaker.

These devices and their functions were explained to each subject. Subjects were to view each of the 10 Senders for 10 6-sec. trials each. These trials were marked by "white noise" from the speaker. These periods corresponded to the interval during which each undergraduate Sender had an opportunity to make a response and win a specific jackpot. These periods, however, ended before the Senders received reinforcement.

Subjects were instructed to judge the amount of money at risk during each Sender's 10 gambling sessions on the basis of the presented nonverbal cues and to press the appropriately marked button to indicate the amount of money at risk. Thus, each subject viewed 10 Senders engaged in 10 gambling tasks. All subjects were told initially that they were evaluating empathy of doctors in training. At the end of their participation, the true nature of the paradigm was explained to them.

Results

An analysis of variance design was used to compare correct responses, with alpha held at .05. Results are presented in Table 1 and Table 2 for between-group comparisons and within-group comparisons. When medical and nonmedical students' scores were compared, controls were more accurate in their interpretation ($F_{1,58} = 9.82$). The mean and standard deviation for

the medical group was 43.3 and 20.7, respectively, and for the control group 56.8 and 11.3.

When scores of male medical students were compared with scores of female medical students, the difference was not significant ($F_{1,28} < 1.00$). The mean and standard deviation for male medical students was 43.9 and 20.4, respectively, and for female medical students 42.7 and 21.6. A similar result was found for controls ($F_{1,28} < 1.00$). However, when scores of female medical students were compared to those of female controls, the controls were significantly more accurate ($F_{1,28} = 5.61$). The mean and standard deviation for female medical students were 42.7 and 21.6, respectively, and for female controls 58.1 and 13.0. Means were not significantly different for male medical students and male controls ($F_{1,28} = 3.92$). The mean and standard deviation for male medical students were 43.9 and 20.4, respectively, and for control males 55.4 and 9.6.

Table 1
Between-Group Comparisons: Means and Standard Deviations of Correct Responses

Group	M	SD	F	p
Medical Students	43.30	20.65	9.82	.002
Control	56.77	11.28		
Male Medical Students	43.87	20.41	3.92	.06
Male Controls	55.40	9.58		
Female Medical Students	42.73	21.59	5.61	.03
Female Controls	58.13	12.96		

Next, scores of medical students indicating a preference for primary care specialties, i.e., family medicine, obstetrics/gynecology, pediatrics, and psychiatry, were compared with those in nondirect-care specialties, i.e., pathology, radiology, internal medicine, and surgery. The F ratio was 10.51 with df of 1,28, indicating that students with preference for primary care were more accurate at judging the facial cues of the subjects.

Table 2
Within-Group Comparisons: Means and Standard Deviations of Correct Responses

Group	M	SD	F	p
Male Medical Students	43.87	20.41	0.02	ns
Female Medical Students	42.73	21.59		
Male Controls	55.40	9.58	0.43	ns
Female Controls	58.13	12.96		
Psych/Ped/OB/GYN/GP	55.67	21.94	16.51	.0004
Surg/Rad/Int Med/Path	30.93	8.64		

Conclusions

In this preliminary study, medical students were less accurate at interpreting nonverbal cues than non-science students. This is in agreement with previously cited studies that show that physicians assess patients' distress inaccurately (Hyuda, Eguchi, & Takiyawa, 1999; Toon, 1999; Zapka et al., 1999). Apparently as a result, they are not perceived as truthful but as exploitative (Akabayashi, Kai, Takamunra, & Okazaki,

1999; Corbie-Smith et al., 1999; Shaughnessy, Cincotta, & Adelman, 1999).

155   This emphasis on scientifically oriented students can produce well-trained diagnosticians with excellent technical skills. There seems, however, to be a concurrent low level of interpersonal skills. This is despite a demand in the medical profession for physicians who
160 possess such skills (Baldwin, Paisley, & Brown, 1999). This communication gap was anticipated soon after the scientific explosion in medicine. An important progenitor of the scientific curriculum, Sir William Osler, recognized this potential danger and proposed remedies
165 (Osler, 1921). He developed a bedside learning technique that focused on the patient rather than the disease. Later, he designed a "great books" library for physicians, which emphasized humanistic values. It was his hope that emphasis on patients and rereading of
170 the library books would be the basis of a lifelong educational process for physicians.

    Unfortunately, the patient-oriented model has been replaced by the "problem-oriented record" and the humanistic library-concept has all but disappeared. The
175 sheer volume of scientific data that must now be mastered has reduced the emphasis and available time allotted to "humanistic electives" (Wolberg, 1983; Toon, 1999). Under the pressure of "scientification," the few humanistic medical school courses, such as community
180 medicine and psychiatry, have metamorphosed into "demographic studies" and psychiatry into neurophysiology (Giannini, 1987).

    The historical development of the scientific medical curriculum seems to be associated with previously
185 cited reports of a growing communication divide between doctor and patient. The results of this limited study indicated that the medical students are less proficient in perceiving and differentiating emotional states (Hermann, Deneken, Van den Eyden, Van Royen, Ver-
190 rupt, & Maes, 1999). This may have produced a situation in which patients' perceptions are markedly different from those of the physician (Prince, Frader, & Busk, 1998; Westert & Groenwegen, 1999).

    Nevertheless, our study has shown that medical
195 students who indicated a preference for primary care specialties achieved higher scores than those who preferred specialties removed from direct and prolonged interaction with patients. This may be related to a finding that general practitioners and primary care special-
200 ists identify patients as a source of learning while nonprimary specialists do not (Rogers, 1999; Westert & Groenwegen, 1999). Nonprimary specialists also have a tendency to rely on structure rather than interpersonal interaction (Hmelo, 1998; Prince et al., 1998). This
205 reliance may reflect the different underlying assumptions of the various medical specialties. In the primary care specialties, a longitudinal-training approach is used. Students are assigned a limited number of patients, some of whom they follow throughout their
210 training. Over time, students come to know their pa-

tients' personal histories and form bonds with them. In the nondirect-care specialties, patients are seen either for short periods of acute care, e.g., surgical specialties, or are seen after death, e.g., pathology, or as the sum of
215 laboratory tests as in pathology and radiology. As students drift towards and eventually choose a specialty, they invariably adopt the assumptions of that specialty and the attitude of the specialist (Hmelo, 1998; Akabayashi et al., 1999).

References

Akabayashi, A., Kai, I., Takamunra, M., & Okazaki, H. (1999). Truth telling in the case of a pessimistic diagnosis. *Lancet, 354*(9186), 1263.

Assenso-Okyeriere, W. K., Osei, A. F., Anum, A., & Adukono, A. (1999). The behavior of health care workers in an era of cost sharing. *Tropical Medicine and International Health, 4*, 586–593.

Baldwin, P. J., Paisley, A. M., & Brown, S. P. (1999). Consultant surgeons' opinions of the skills required of basic surgical trainees. *British Journal of Surgery, 86*, 1078–1082.

Barbrow, A. S., Kasch, C. R., & Ford, L. A. (1998). The many meanings of uncertainty and illness: Towards a systematic accounting. *Health Communication, 10*, 1–23.

Corbie-Smith, G., Thomas, S. B., Williams, M. V., & Moody-Ayers, S. (1999). Attitudes and beliefs of African Americans towards participation in medical research. *Journal of General Internal Medicine, 14*, 537–546.

Duwrick, C., & Frith, L. (1999). *General practice and ethics.* London: Routledge.

Giannini, A. J. (1987). *The biological foundations of clinical psychiatry.* New York: Elsevier.

Giannini, A. J., Daood, J., Giannini, M. C., Boniface, R., & Rhodes, P. G. (1978). The intuition versus intellect: Dichotomy in the reception of nonverbal communication. *Journal of General Psychology, 116*, 241–244.

Hall, J. A., Stein, T S., Roter, D. C., & Rieser, N. (1999). Inaccuracies in physicians' perceptions of their patients. *Medical Care, 37*, 1164–1168.

Hermann, I., Deneken, J., Van Den Eyden, B., Van Royen, P, Verrupt, H., & Maes, R. (1999). General practitioners caring for terminally ill patients in a hospice. *Support Care in Cancer, 7*, 437–438.

Hmelo, C. E. (1998). Cognitive consequences of problem-based learning for the early development of medical expertise. *Technology and Learning in Medicine, 10*, 92–100.

Hyuda, I., Eguchi, K., & Takiyawa, N. (1999). Psychological impact of informed consent in hospitalized cancer patients. *Support Care in Cancer, 7*, 396–399.

Miller, R. S., Giannini, A. J., & Levine, J. (1977). Nonverbal communication in man with a cooperative conditioning task. *Journal of Social Psychology, 103*, 101–113.

Osler, W. (1921). *The evaluation of modern medicine.* New Haven, CT: Yale Univer. Press.

Prince, E. F., Frader, J., & Busk, C. (1998). On healing in physician-physician discourse. In R. J. DiPietro (Ed.), *Linguistics and the professions.* Norwood, Ablex. Pp. 83–97.

Rogers, W. A. (1999). Beneficence in general practice: An empirical investigation. *Journal of Medical Ethics, 25*, 388–393.

Shaughnessy, A. F., Cincotta, J. A., & Adelman, A. (1999). Family practice patients' attitudes towards firearm safety as a preventive medicine issue. *Journal of the American Board of Family Practice, 12*, 354–359.

Stevenson, I. A., & Multhaef, R. P. (1968). *Medicine, science, and culture.* Baltimore, MD: Johns Hopkins Univer. Press.

Stewart, M., Brown, J. B., Boon, M., Galadja, J., Meredith, L., & Sangster, M. (1999). Evidence on patient-doctor communication. *Cancer Prevention and Control, 3*, 25–30.

Toon, P. D. (1999). *Towards a philosophy of general practice: A study of the virtuous practitioner.* London: Royal College of General Practitioners Press.

Westert, G. P., & Groenwegen, P. P. (1999). Medical practice variations: Changing the theoretical approach. *Scandinavian Journal of Public Health, 27*, 173–180.

Wolberg, H. J. (1983). Scientific literacy and economic productivity. *Proceedings of the American Academy of Arts and Sciences, 112*, 1–28.

Zapka, J., Estabrook, B., Gilliland, J., Leviton, L., Meischke, H., & Melville, S. (1999). Health care providers' perspective on patient delay for seeking care for symptoms of acute myocardial infarction. *Health Education and Behavior, 26*, 714–733.

Address correspondence to: A. James Giannini, M.D., 721 Boardman-Poland Rd., Suite 200, Boardman, OH 44512.

Exercise for Article 23

Factual Questions

1. When did some medical schools convert to a completely scientific curriculum?

2. How many of the subjects were pursuing M.D. degrees?

3. While they watched the videotapes, what were the subjects asked to assess?

4. What was the total number of gambling tasks that each subject viewed?

5. The value of p had to be at what level (i.e., alpha level) before a difference was declared to be statistically significant?

6. What was the mean score for female controls?

7. For the difference between the mean for those preferring primary care specialties and the mean for the other medical students, what is the associated probability?

Questions for Discussion

8. The researchers used volunteers as subjects. In your opinion, could this affect the validity of the study?

9. The researchers state that they are interested in "interpersonal skills." In your opinion, how useful is the task of guessing the Senders' jackpots in measuring interpersonal skills? Are there other ways these skills could be measured? Explain.

10. In line 145, the researchers call this study "preliminary." In lines 186–188, they refer to it as "limited." Do you agree with these characterizations of the study? Explain.

11. The students who were studying to be the types of physicians who would have the most contact with patients (see Psych/Ped/OB/GYN/GP in Table 2) had a relatively high mean of 55.67. In your opinion, is this consistent with the researchers' hypothesis? (See lines 37–43.)

12. If you were to conduct another study on the same topic, what changes in the research methodology, if any, would you make?

Quality Ratings

Directions: Indicate your level of agreement with each of the following statements by circling a number from 5 for strongly agree (SA) to 1 for strongly disagree (SD). If you believe an item is not applicable to this research article, leave it blank. Be prepared to explain your ratings.

A. The introduction establishes the importance of the study.

SA   5   4   3   2   1   SD

B. The literature review establishes the context for the study.

SA   5   4   3   2   1   SD

C. The research purpose, question, or hypothesis is clearly stated.

SA   5   4   3   2   1   SD

D. The method of sampling is sound.

SA   5   4   3   2   1   SD

E. Relevant demographics (for example, age, gender, and ethnicity) are described.

SA   5   4   3   2   1   SD

F. Measurement procedures are adequate.

SA   5   4   3   2   1   SD

G. All procedures have been described in sufficient detail to permit a replication of the study.

SA   5   4   3   2   1   SD

H. The participants have been adequately protected from potential harm.

SA   5   4   3   2   1   SD

I. The results are clearly described.

SA   5   4   3   2   1   SD

J. The discussion/conclusion is appropriate.

SA   5   4   3   2   1   SD

K. Despite any flaws, the report is worthy of publication.

SA   5   4   3   2   1   SD

Article 24

Late Adolescents' Perspectives on Marital Rape: The Impact of Gender and Fraternity/Sorority Membership

Carol J. Auster
Franklin and Marshall College

Janel M. Leone
The Pennsylvania State University

ABSTRACT. Although recent studies of marital rape have examined both victims' and perpetrators' social and psychological characteristics, little attention has been directed to the attitudes of others toward marital rape. Using a systematic sample of college students, this study examined attitudes toward marital rape—in particular, the impact of gender and fraternity/sorority membership on respondents' (1) views regarding marital rape compared to rape by a stranger; (2) feelings about possible actions a woman who is a victim of marital rape can take; and (3) attitudes toward legislation pertaining to marital rape. It was found that college women were significantly more likely than college men to say they strongly agree that marital rape and stranger rape should be treated as similar crimes. In addition, nonfraternity men were significantly more likely than fraternity men to indicate that they strongly approve of marital rape legislation and that husbands who perpetrate marital rape should be prosecuted. Sorority membership had little impact on women's responses.

From *Adolescence*, 36, 141-152. Copyright © 2001 by Libra Publishers, Inc. Reprinted with permission.

As individuals make the transition from childhood to adolescence, their behavior and attitudes are increasingly shaped by peer groups. Informal intimate friendship groups as well as more formally organized groups, such as those associated with school-supported extra-curricular activities, have an impact on adolescents' conduct and beliefs. Single-sex social organizations, such as fraternities and sororities, may also affect late adolescents' attitudes and actions.

The purpose of the present analysis was to examine the effects of gender and fraternity/sorority membership on how highly educated late adolescents, namely college students, conceptualize marital rape laws and the legal right of a woman to prosecute her spouse for rape. The findings may reveal not only the degree to which fraternity/sorority membership and gender influence late adolescents' views of several aspects of marital rape, but also how they may influence the level of tolerance for violence against women more generally.

Background

For the past two decades, human rights activists and women's rights advocates have fought to change U.S. legislation prohibiting a wife from pressing criminal charges against her husband for marital rape. As of 1993, "...marital rape became a crime in all fifty states, in at least one section of the sexual offense codes, usually regarding force" (National Clearinghouse on Marital and Date Rape, 1998). However, in thirty-two states, there are still some provisions for exempting husbands from prosecution for rape, and some states identify marital rape as a lesser crime than nonmarital rape or rape by a previously unknown assailant (Brown, 1995; National Clearinghouse on Marital and Date Rape, 1998; Sitton, 1993). Nevertheless, greater public awareness of such issues as domestic violence, child abuse, and incest has led to increased attention to family violence in general, and, more recently, some social scientists have become attentive to the issue of marital rape.

Studies of marital rape have tended to focus on the social and psychological factors associated with this form of spousal abuse, as well as the impact on the victim (Bergen, 1996; Bidwell & White, 1986; DeKeseredy & Schwartz, 1996; Finkelhor & Yllo, 1985; Hanneke & Shields, 1985; Russell, 1990; Shields & Hanneke, 1983). Such examinations of the life experiences of victims have led to a much greater understanding of the dynamics and consequences of marital rape. In addition to research on victims, Jeffords and Dull (1982) studied the effect of demographic variables on Texas residents' attitudes toward a law that would permit a wife to accuse her husband of rape. They found that young, single, educated women expressed more support than others for such a law. More recently, Roberts et al. (1996) surveyed Canadians about rape-reform legislation, particularly the change in legal terminology from rape to sexual assault and the elimination of spousal immunity. However, their study focused on knowledge of the substantive legal changes, rather than attitudes toward the changes. In short, there has been little research on individuals' attitudes regarding either marital rape or a woman's right to have her husband prosecuted for rape.

Although they have not focused on marital rape in particular, a number of studies of young people, mostly college students, have examined the impact of gender and membership in a fraternity or sorority on attitudes toward sexual coercion and rape myths. Typically, these studies have found that men are more likely than women to believe rape myths and to regard sexual coercion as acceptable (Blumberg & Lester, 1991; Davis et al., 1993; Dull & Giacopassi, 1987; Feltey et al., 1991; Garrett-Gooding & Senter, 1987; Giacopassi & Dull, 1986; Gilmartin-Zena, 1988; Holcomb et al., 1991; Proto-Campise et al., 1998). In addition, fraternity membership has often been associated with negative attitudes toward women and acceptance of sexual coercion rape myths (Boeringer et al., 1991; Bohmer & Parrot, 1993; Boswell & Spade, 1996; DiCanio, 1993; Garrett-Gooding & Senter, 1987; Kalof & Cargill, 1991; Martin & Hummer, 1989; Sanday, 1990; Schwartz & DeKeseredy, 1997). Furthermore, some studies have found a high incidence of rape, most notably gang rape, occurring in fraternities (see, for example, Bohmer & Parrot, 1993; DiCanio, 1993; Sanday, 1990). While there are differences between gang rape or stranger rape and spousal rape, the beliefs surrounding these forms of rape may overlap. Regardless of the setting, rape is an act of violence and sexual control. Thus, members of those groups that are more likely to condone one type of rape may, in fact, be more willing to accept rape that occurs in other situations. Again, research has focused little attention on attitudes concerning marital rape, except as one item among many on a list of rape myths (see, for example, Proto-Campise et al., 1998).

Method

The variables used for this analysis were part of a larger study of college life and student attitudes. A face-to-face interview, with over one hundred mostly close-ended questions on a wide variety of topics (ranging from academic life and participation in extracurricular activities to family background and future career plans), was conducted with each of the respondents. As part of this multifaceted survey, respondents were asked questions pertaining to a variety of social issues, including marital rape. The questions about marital rape were intended to shed light on (1) how college students see marital rape in relation to rape by a stranger; (2) their feelings about possible actions a woman who is a victim of marital rape can take; and (3) their willingness to support legislation concerning marital rape.

First, to see whether respondents would conceptualize stranger rape and marital rape similarly or differently, they were asked, "How do you feel about the following? A husband who forces sex upon his wife without her consent should be prosecuted for the same type of crime as a man who forces sex upon a complete stranger." The four response options were: *strongly agree, agree, disagree,* and *strongly disagree.* This question was important because, as the laws concerning marital rape show, this act is sometimes considered to be a "lesser" crime than stranger rape.

A second set of questions asked respondents to consider a wide range of actions a victimized woman could take to stop the abuse against her: "If a woman is continually being forced to have sexual intercourse with her husband against her will, should she (1) seek counseling for herself and her husband? (2) file for divorce? (3) prosecute her husband for rape?" For each of these three actions, the response options were *yes, no,* and *don't know.*

The last question explored how the respondents viewed laws on marital rape. While laws cannot prevent a woman from being the victim of marital rape, they are a crucial step in deterring it. Respondents' answers to this question may reflect not only their beliefs about the legal aspects of this issue, but also how far they believe legislators should go to protect women from being raped by their husbands. The word "felony" was used in an attempt to measure the extent to which respondents thought marital rape should be considered a serious crime. The question was as follows: "Some states have laws about forced marital intercourse and some do not. How would you feel if legislation was passed in your state that made forced marital intercourse a felony?" The four response options were *strongly approve, approve, disapprove,* and *strongly disapprove.*

Gender was used as an independent variable so that differences in how men and women feel about the issue of marital rape could be examined. It was hypothesized that women would be more likely to view forced intercourse within a marital relationship as rape, more supportive of laws that allow husbands to be prosecuted, and more willing to say a woman should take legal action against her husband. This is not to say that men are not sensitive to the issue of rape, or by any means advocate it; rather, because women are more likely to be victims of rape, the issue of marital rape is perhaps more salient for them. In addition, findings from previous studies regarding the effect of gender on attitudes toward sexual coercion, rape myths, and male dominance led to the expectation that women's and men's attitudes would differ on the issue of marital rape.

Since previous studies had indicated that the culture of fraternity life promotes and reinforces negative beliefs about women, including beliefs related to sexual coercion and rape, membership in a sorority or fraternity was also used as an independent variable. Thus, it was expected that men who are fraternity members would be less harsh in their judgments about marital rape than their male counterparts who are not members of a fraternity. Since values associated with the denigration of women have not been shown to be related to

175 sorority membership, no differences were expected between women who are members of a sorority and those who are not.

A systematic sample was selected using an alphabetical list of the approximately 1,800 students enrolled
180 at a private, liberal arts college located in the northeastern United States. The resulting sample of 209 college students, 108 women and 101 men, was distributed relatively evenly among freshmen, sophomores, juniors, and seniors. With regard to race, 83.3% identi-
185 fied themselves as White, 6.2% as Asian, 4.3% as African American, 2.9% as Latino, and 3.4% as other. By religion, 27.8% identified themselves as Catholic, 24.9% as Protestant, 15.6% as Jewish, 20.0% as other, and 11.7% as none. The respondents' parents were
190 relatively well educated, with two-thirds of the respondents reporting that their mothers had a college degree or received some postgraduate education, and more than 70% reporting the same for their fathers. Finally, 28.8% of the women and 35.0% of the men indicated
195 that they belonged to a sorority or fraternity.

Results

When respondents were asked whether marital rape and stranger rape should be treated as similar crimes, 63.9% of the women and 44.4% of the men strongly agreed (see Table 1). This gender difference was statis-
200 tically significant, $\chi^2 = 11.9$, $df = 3$, $p < .01$. Furthermore, 17.1% of the men but only 4.6% of the women disagreed or strongly disagreed.

Table 1
Attitude Toward Marital Rape Being Prosecuted Like Stranger Rape, by Gender and Fraternity/Sorority Membership (%)

			Fraternity		Sorority	
	Men	Women	Yes	No	Yes	No
Strongly Agree	44.4	63.9	31.4	51.6	63.3	65.8
Agree	38.4	31.5	42.9	35.9	30.0	31.6
Disagree	13.1	3.7	14.3	12.5	6.7	1.3
Strongly Disagree	4.0	0.9	11.4	0.0	0.0	1.3

Table 1 also shows that 51.6% of nonfraternity men and 31.4% of fraternity men strongly agreed that the
205 two are equivalent criminal acts. The difference was significant, $\chi^2 = 9.7$, $df = 3$, $p < .05$. In addition, nonfraternity men (12.5%) were somewhat less likely than fraternity men (25.7%) to disagree or strongly disagree. On the other hand, no significant differences were
210 found for the women: 65.8% of the nonsorority women and 63.3% of the sorority women strongly agreed that forced intercourse within marriage should be prosecuted as rape. Likewise, only 2.6% of the nonsorority women and 6.7% of the sorority women disagreed or
215 strongly disagreed.

When asked whether a wife who is continually forced to have sex with her husband against her will should seek counseling for herself and her husband, about 95% of both women and men answered affirma-

220 tively (see Table 2). On the other hand, women (61.1%) were significantly more likely than men (39.4%) to indicate that the wife should have her husband prosecuted for rape, $\chi^2 = 12.5$, $df = 2$, $p < .005$. In fact, 30.3% of the men but only 13.0% of the women
225 said that the wife should not have her husband prosecuted. Moreover, women (76.6%) were significantly more likely than men (61.0%) to say that the wife should divorce her husband, $\chi^2 = 6.2$, $df = 2$, $p < .05$.

Table 2
Attitude Toward Potential Actions Taken by Wife, by Gender and Fraternity/Sorority Membership (%)

			Fraternity		Sorority	
	Men	Women	Yes	No	Yes	No
Seek Counseling						
Yes	93.0	97.2	88.6	95.4	100.0	96.1
No	3.0	0.0	5.7	1.5	0.0	0.0
Don't Know	4.0	2.8	5.7	3.1	0.0	3.9
Prosecute for Rape						
Yes	39.4	61.1	32.4	43.1	63.3	60.5
No	30.3	13.0	47.1	21.5	13.3	11.8
Don't Know	30.3	25.9	20.6	35.4	23.3	27.6
File for Divorce						
Yes	61.0	76.6	60.0	61.5	82.8	73.7
No	12.0	5.6	11.4	12.3	3.4	6.6
Don't Know	27.0	17.8	28.6	26.2	13.8	19.7

Table 2 also shows that nonfraternity men (43.1%)
230 were significantly more likely than fraternity men (32.4%) to say that a wife should have her husband prosecuted for rape, $\chi^2 = 7.1$, $df = 2$, $p < .05$. On the other hand, sorority women (63.3%) and nonsorority women (60.5%) were nearly equally likely to feel that
235 the husband should be prosecuted. Although the difference was not statistically significant, sorority women (82.8%) were more likely than nonsorority women (73.7%) to feel that a wife who is the victim of marital rape should divorce her husband, while the difference
240 between fraternity men (60.0%) and nonfraternity men (61.5%) was negligible.

Finally, respondents were asked whether they approved of legislation making forced sex within marriage a felony (see Table 3). Women (56.5%) were
245 significantly more likely than men (35.0%) to indicate that they strongly approved of such legislation, $\chi^2 = 14.6$, $df = 3$, $p < .005$. Furthermore, 16.0% of the men said they disapproved or strongly disapproved, compared with only 3.7% of the women. Nonfraternity men
250 (44.6%) were significantly more likely than fraternity men (17.1%) to indicate that they strongly approved of the legislation, $\chi^2 = 10.3$, $df = 3$, $p < .05$. The majority of both sorority women (56.7%) and nonsorority women (56.6%) strongly approved.

Discussion

255 One pattern that emerged from the data was that women were consistently more likely than men to see marital rape as a serious act. Thus, the original hy-

pothesis was supported: Women were significantly more likely to define forced intercourse within marriage as rape and, therefore, prosecutable by the state. The fact that 56.5% of the women and only 35.0% of the men strongly supported the notion that marital rape should be a felony illustrates how differently the men and women viewed this issue. It is not surprising that women would be supportive of legislation that could one day protect them. Furthermore, the various feminist groups that have pressured legislators to adopt laws that allow for this type of prosecution have been overwhelmingly made up of women.

Table 3
Attitude Toward Marital Rape Legislation, by Gender and Fraternity/Sorority Membership (%)

| | Men | Women | Fraternity | | Sorority | |
			Yes	No	Yes	No
Strongly Approve	35.0	56.5	17.1	44.6	56.7	56.6
Approve	49.0	39.8	60.0	43.1	40.0	40.8
Disapprove	14.0	2.8	17.1	12.3	3.3	2.6
Strongly Disapprove	2.0	0.9	5.7	0.0	0.0	0.0

On the other hand, it should not be overlooked that only a little more than half of the women strongly approved of the passage of marital rape legislation. This shows that some women hold many of the same views as men concerning the criminalization of marital rape. Thus, women may also be captives of traditional ways of thinking: "One of the legacies of the rape-supportive culture is that it teaches both men and women that women are responsible for preventing sexual assault" (Schwartz & DeKeseredy, 1997, p. 89).

Among the respondents, 23.4% of the women and 39.0% of the men did not think that, or were uncertain whether, a woman who is continually forced to have sex against her will with her husband should file for divorce. Regardless of how sensitive women, compared to men, may be to marital rape, they are not always willing to criminalize it or support a woman who divorces her husband because of it. Women may be viewed as "peace keepers" in marriages, those whose role it is to keep the family together. Thus, marital rape is more complex than other forms of rape in that it challenges normative ideas about marital sexuality and privacy, and religious notions about marriage (Russell, 1990; Bergen, 1996).

The fact that only about a third of the men strongly supported marital rape legislation can be explained. Some male legislators have voiced the concern that women would use this as a tool to humiliate and "ruin" their husbands (Sitton, 1993; Finkelhor & Yllo, 1985). The fear of false accusations made by wives against their husbands has caused some male legislators to delay or refuse changing laws, but there is no empirical support for the argument that wives would suddenly begin falsely charging husbands with this crime if given the chance (Russell, 1990). Despite this fact,

many men are unwilling to support this type of legislation.

Over three-fifths of the women but under two-fifths of the men felt that a wife who is forced to have sexual intercourse with her husband against her will should have her husband prosecuted for rape. In essence, more than half of the men believed that marital rape should not be considered a crime and that the wife should not make any attempt to hold her husband legally responsible for his actions. Thus, forced sex within marriage does not fit the picture of rape held by many men and even a high percentage of women. Some people are unwilling to accept the idea that a husband can be prosecuted for a crime that stereotypically has been thought to be committed by a stranger. However, the fact is that regardless of the relationship between the two people, the act committed is the same: rape.

In addition to the gender analysis, the data were examined according to membership in fraternities and sororities. Several relationships were found between fraternity membership and level of sensitivity to the issue of marital rape. Nonfraternity men were significantly more likely than fraternity men to strongly support marital rape laws and the prosecution of husbands for rape. However, this was not the case for women. We found no significant differences in the responses given by the sorority and the nonsorority women.

Why is fraternity membership such a significant factor in men's beliefs about marital rape? According to DeKeseredy and Schwartz (1996), membership in this type of social organization has a direct impact on beliefs concerning women and violence against them: "They [men] learn the sexual objectification of women...through the actions of more organized groups, such as fraternities, who may use women as 'bait' to bring in new members, as adornments, or as servants at parties" (p. 348). Although the bonding and brotherhood offered by the fraternity can be alluring, pledges are often only accepted into the brotherhood after degrading and emotionally and physically painful initiation rituals. Such rituals promote group loyalty and male bonding by emphasizing male social and sexual domination. This form of male bonding creates a social climate in which women are perceived as the despised "other," and may potentially become the target of male sexual aggression (Sanday, 1990). Thus, "Fraternity initiation rituals provide a forum for adolescent males to solidify an identity...this identity intertwines brotherhood, misogyny and phallocentrism" (Sanday, 1990, p. 155). Further, Bohmer and Parrot (1993) argue that fraternity pledges are more likely to commit rape or sexual assault because they feel strong pressure to conform to these highly masculinist norms and are the least secure about pursuing masculinity through more constructive avenues. In sum, fraternities appear to shape their members' beliefs about women and, consequently, their notions about rape in marriage.

Nevertheless, the fact that the fraternity men in the present study may have answered the way they did for other reasons cannot be discounted. It is possible that self-selection plays a role in fraternity membership, such that men with a history of sexual aggression may seek out like-minded friends and find them among the members of certain fraternities (Kanin, 1967). It could also be that given the stereotypes associated with fraternities, some men may have felt the need to answer this way in order to "live up" to the expectations of their fraternities. For example, because fraternities have been labeled as being highly insensitive to women's issues, fraternity members' lower support for marital rape legislation may simply reflect these expectations.

There are several explanations for the lack of differences between the sorority and nonsorority women. First, gender could be such a salient factor that other variables have little influence. Second, it could be that sororities do not advocate the need for their members to devalue women in order to gain acceptance. This makes intuitive sense, in that it would not seem likely that college women would want to belong to a social organization in which they were the target of violence and sexual objectification.

Conclusion

The purpose of this study was to better understand how two variables—gender and fraternity/sorority membership—affect how one category of late adolescents conceptualizes marital rape. The results make clear that marital rape is not viewed similarly by all groups in society, nor even those on one college campus. In general, men view marital rape differently from women. Moreover, men who are fraternity members view this issue differently from their male counterparts who are not fraternity members.

The generalizability of the findings may be limited because the sample consisted of students at one institution of higher education with a predominantly White, middle-class population. The sample did not include late adolescents who were not attending college. Further research is needed with more diverse samples.

Nevertheless, the findings regarding the respondents' beliefs about marital rape lend further support to the notion that gender and social organizations, such as fraternities, play a role in late adolescents' attitudes. Targeting agents of socialization that condone sexual assault is thus important, because those agents can potentially influence individuals' beliefs and their subsequent conduct during late adolescence and beyond.

References

Bergen, R. K. (1996). *Wife rape: Understanding the response of survivors and service providers*. Thousand Oaks, CA: Sage.

Bidwell, L., & White, P. (1986). The family context of marital rape. *Journal of Family Violence, 1*, 277-287.

Blumberg, M. L., & Lester, D. (1991). High school and college students' attitudes toward rape. *Adolescence, 26*, 727-729.

Boeringer, S. B., Shehan, C. L., & Akers, R. L. (1991). Social contexts and social learning in sexual coercion and aggression: Assessing the contribution of fraternity membership. *Family Relations, 40*, 58-64.

Bohmer, C., & Parrot, A. (1993). *Sexual assault on campus: The problem and the solution*. New York: Lexington.

Boswell, A. A., & Spade, J. Z. (1996). Fraternities and collegiate rape culture: Why are some fraternities more dangerous places for women. *Gender and Society, 10*, 133-147.

Brown, E. R. (1995). Changing the marital rape exemption: I am chattel(?!)—Hear me roar. *American Journal of Trial Advocacy, 18*, 657-671.

Davis, T. C., Peck, G. Q., & Storment, J. M. (1993). Acquaintance rape and the high school student. *Journal of Adolescent Health, 14*, 220-224.

DeKeseredy, W. S. (1990). Male peer support and woman abuse: The current state of knowledge. *Sociological Focus, 23*, 129-139.

DeKeseredy, W. S., & Schwartz, M. D. (1996). Violence against women in intimate relationships. In W. S. DeKeseredy & M. D. Schwartz (Eds.), *Contemporary criminology* (pp. 317-353). Belmont, CA: Wadsworth.

DiCanio, M. (1993). *The encyclopedia of violence: Origins, attitudes, consequences*. New York: Facts on File.

Dull, R. T., & Giacopassi, D. J. (1987). Demographic correlates of sexual and dating attitudes: A study of date rape. *Criminal Justice and Behavior, 14*, 175-193.

Estrich, S. (1987). *Real rape: How the legal system victimizes women who say no*. Cambridge: Harvard University Press.

Feltey, K. M., Ainslie, J. J., & Geib, A. (1991). Sexual coercion attitudes among high school students. *Youth and Society, 23*, 229-250.

Finkelhor, D., & Yllo, K. (1985). *License to rape: Sexual abuse of wives*. New York: Holt, Rinehart and Winston.

Garrett-Gooding, J., & Senter, R. (1987). Attitudes and acts of aggression on a university campus. *Sociological Inquiry, 57*, 348-371.

Giacopassi, D. J., & Dull, R. T. (1986). Gender and racial differences in the acceptance of rape myths within a college population. *Sex Roles, 15*, 63-75.

Gilmartin-Zena, P. (1988). Gender differences in students' attitudes towards rape. *Sociological Focus, 21*, 279-292.

Hanneke, C. R., & Shields, N. M. (1985). Marital rape: Implications for the helping professions. *Social Casework, 66*, 451-458.

Holcomb, D. R., Holcomb, L. C., Sondag, K. A., & Williams, N. W. (1991). Attitudes about date rape: Gender differences among college students. *College Student Journal, 25*, 434-439.

Jeffords, C. R., & Dull, R. T. (1982). Demographic variations in attitudes towards marital rape immunity. *Journal of Marriage and Family, 44*, 755-782.

Kalof, L., & Cargill, T. (1991). Fraternity and sorority membership and gender dominance attitudes. *Sex Roles, 25*, 417-423.

Kanin, E. J. (1967). An examination of sexual aggression as a response to sexual frustration. *Journal of Marriage and the Family, 29*, 428-433.

Martin, P. Y., & Hummer, R. (1989). Fraternities and rape on campus. *Gender and Society, 3*, 457-473.

National Clearinghouse on Marital and Date Rape. (1998). *State Law Chart*. Berkeley, CA: Author.

Parrot, A., & Bechhofer, L. (Eds.). (1991). *Acquaintance rape: The hidden crime*. New York: Wiley.

Proto-Campise, L., Belknap, J., & Wooldredge, J. (1998). High school students' adherence to rape myths and the effectiveness of high school rape-awareness programs. *Violence Against Women, 4*, 308-328.

Roberts, J. V., Grossman, M. G., & Gebotys, R. J. (1996). Rape reform in Canada: Public knowledge and opinion. *Journal of Family Violence, 11*, 113-148.

Russell, D. E. H. (1990). *Rape in marriage*. Bloomington, IN: Indiana University Press.

Russell, D. E. H. (1991). Wife rape. In A. Parrot & L. Bechhofer (Eds.), *Acquaintance rape: The hidden crime* (pp. 129-139). New York: Wiley.

Sanday, P. R. (1990). *Fraternity gang rape: Sex, brotherhood, and privilege on campus*. New York: New York University Press.

Sanday, P. R. (1996). *A woman scorned: Acquaintance rape on trial*. New York: Doubleday.

Schwartz, M. D., & DeKeseredy, W. S. (1997). *Sexual assault on the college campus: The role of male peer support*. Thousand Oaks, CA: Sage.

Shields, N. M., & Hanneke, C. R. (1983). Attribution processes in violent relationships: Perceptions of violent husbands and wives. *Journal of Applied Social Psychology, 13*, 515-527.

Sitton, J. (1993). *Old wine in new bottles: The "marital" rape allowances*. North Carolina Law Review, 72, 261-289.

About the authors: Janel M. Leone, Department of Human Development and Family Studies, The Pennsylvania State University, University Park, Pennsylvania. Reprint requests to Carol J. Auster, Department of Sociology, Franklin and Marshall College, P.O. Box 3003, Lancaster, Pennsylvania 17604. E-mail: c_auster@fandm.edu

Exercise for Article 24

Factual Questions

1. The researchers cite an earlier study of Texas residents' attitudes toward a law that would permit a wife to accuse her husband of rape. Which demographic group was found to be most in favor of such a law?

2. Did the researchers identify "gender" as an independent variable *or* as a dependent variable?

3. What percentage of the sample identified themselves as White?

4. What percentage of nonfraternity men strongly agreed that marital rape should be prosecuted like stranger rape?

5. What percentage of fraternity men strongly agreed that marital rape should be prosecuted like stranger rape?

6. Were fraternity men *or* nonfraternity men significantly more likely to say that a wife should have her husband prosecuted for rape?

7. The researchers discuss two possible reasons for the lack of differences between the sorority and nonsorority women. What is the *second* reason?

Questions for Discussion

8. The authors used face-to-face interviews to collect their data. In your opinion, is this superior to using questionnaires for this type of study? Explain.

9. The second set of questions asked about a woman who is *continually* being forced to have sexual intercourse against her will. In your opinion, could the adverb *continually* affect the results? Would you have used this adverb if you were conducting the study? Explain.

10. In lines 332–362, the researchers discuss the possibility that fraternity membership shapes their members beliefs about rape in marriage. In lines 363–376, they discuss other possible explanations. What is your opinion on the viability of the explanations? Does this study provide data that support one over the other? Explain.

11. The researchers state that further research is needed with more diverse samples. Do you agree? If so, what types of diversity would be desirable?

Quality Ratings

Directions: Indicate your level of agreement with each of the following statements by circling a number from 5 for strongly agree (SA) to 1 for strongly disagree (SD). If you believe an item is not applicable to this research article, leave it blank. Be prepared to explain your ratings.

A. The introduction establishes the importance of the study.

SA 5 4 3 2 1 SD

B. The literature review establishes the context for the study.

SA 5 4 3 2 1 SD

C. The research purpose, question, or hypothesis is clearly stated.

SA 5 4 3 2 1 SD

D. The method of sampling is sound.

SA 5 4 3 2 1 SD

E. Relevant demographics (for example, age, gender, and ethnicity) are described.

SA 5 4 3 2 1 SD

F. Measurement procedures are adequate.

SA 5 4 3 2 1 SD

G. All procedures have been described in sufficient detail to permit a replication of the study.

SA 5 4 3 2 1 SD

H. The participants have been adequately protected from potential harm.

SA 5 4 3 2 1 SD

I. The results are clearly described.

SA 5 4 3 2 1 SD

J. The discussion/conclusion is appropriate.

SA 5 4 3 2 1 SD

K. Despite any flaws, the report is worthy of publication.

SA 5 4 3 2 1 SD

Article 25

Teachers' Perceptions of Principal Effectiveness in Selected Secondary Schools in Tennessee

Henry S. Williams
Central Washington University

ABSTRACT. The purpose of this study was to compare teachers' perceptions of principal effectiveness in secondary schools nominated for the National Secondary School Recognition Program and a randomly selected sample of schools not nominated for the National Secondary School Recognition Program in Tennessee. Evaluation of principal effectiveness was based upon teachers' perceptions as measured by the Audit of Principal Effectiveness (APE).

The data were gathered by mail survey. The Audit of Principal effectiveness was sent to participating secondary schools in the state of Tennessee with enrollment of 1,000 and more. The teachers were asked to participate by answering a questionnaire regarding their principal. Analysis of variance was used to determine whether there was a difference in teachers' perceptions of the principals. The results of this study were as follows:

Scores on organizational development, organizational directions, organizational procedures, student relations, affective processes, educational program, instructional improvement, and curriculum improvement of principals in high schools nominated for the National Secondary School Recognition Program were significantly higher than scores of principals of randomly selected high schools not nominated.

No significant differences were found in organizational linkage, organizational environment, teacher relations, and interactive processes scores of principals in high schools nominated for the National Secondary School Recognition Program when compared to principals of randomly selected high schools not nominated.

From *Education*, *121*, 264–275. Copyright © 2000 by Project Innovation. Reprinted with permission.

The literature on school effectiveness repeatedly refers to the need for strong leadership of the principal. The principal has received extraordinary attention in the literature of educational administration and in the press. The reason for this attention in the scholarly literature stems largely from the intense interest on the part of educators and scholars in achieving better understanding of the dynamics of school effectiveness. Furthermore, the educational reform movement and the accompanying search for conditions and causes in effective schools have fueled broader public interest in the principalship. In discussing the review of literature, I divided it into six sections. The National Secondary School Recognition Program is explained in the first section. The definition of educational leadership is discussed in the second section. Role perception is dealt with in the third section. The domain of organizational development is discussed in the fourth section; organizational environment is summarized in the fifth section, and the sixth section deals with effective instructional leadership.

National Secondary School Recognition Program

For any school to be judged deserving of recognition, there should be strong leadership and an effective working relation among the school, the parents, and others in the community. The school should have an atmosphere that is orderly, purposeful, and conducive to learning and good character. The school should attend to the quality of instruction and the professionalism of its teachers. There must be a strong commitment to educational excellence for all students and a record of progress in sustaining the school's best features and solving its problems (U.S. Department of Education, 1999). The goal of the Secondary School Recognition Program is to give public recognition to outstanding schools across the United States. Schools are identified on the basis of their effectiveness and standards of quality applicable to secondary schools generally. An important consideration is given to schools successful in furthering the intellectual, social, and moral growth of all students (U .S. Department of Education, 1988–89).

Educational Leadership

Educational leadership seems to have as many definitions as there are people willing to define it. Lipman (1974) implied that "leadership" is not all a matter of group maintenance but "the initiation of a new structure or procedure for accomplishing an organization's goals and objectives." To be the leader, one must be concerned with initiating change. According to Fuhr

Table 1
Response from Nominated Secondary Schools

School	Number of teachers	Number of respondents	Percent
1	52	20	38.46
2	49	21	42.85
3	53	17	42.07
4	49	40	81.63
5	42	37	82.22
6	45	31	68.88
7	56	50	89.28
8	38	17	44.73
9	22	16	72.72
10	64	27	42.18
11	52	20	38.46
12	68	26	38.23
13	58	51	87.93
14	42	37	88.09
Total	690	410	59.42

Note. The overall response rate was 59.42 percent.

(1970), the administrator, on the other hand, may be identified as the individual who utilizes existing structures or procedures to achieve an organizational goal or objective. As in the case of the leader, the administrator may bring to bear the authority of his role and the influence of his personality in his relationships with other members in the organization. But the administrator is concerned primarily with maintaining, rather than changing established structure, procedure, or goals (Fuhr, 1970, p. 48). The principal has been recognized as the educational leader by Neagley and Evans (1964) by stating that in any size district, the principal should be recognized as the educational leader of his/her school and immediate community. He/she is responsible for the supervision of instruction as well as for execution of administrative functions (p. 12).

According to Delapp (1988), educational leadership skills can be learned and practiced with some effort and clear vision of what must be accomplished. These skills come from the principal's knowledge of the school or district and what is needed to be done to improve education for all students. As an administrator, the principal has a unique opportunity to lead. Several distinct groups of people depend on him for leadership and direction. The teachers, students, parents, and members of the general public see school administrators as community leaders. School principals must provide leadership in developing liaisons with community members as school volunteers and in maintaining student discipline. The responsibility for school improvement represents an area in which the leadership role of the school administrator is important.

Role Perception

Nakornsri (1977) studied the differences between teachers' perceptions of their principal's administrative performance and the relationship, if any, between teachers' perceptions of their principal's role behavior and administrative performance. Considering the teachers' educational level, there was a difference in their perceptions of the principal's role behavior and his/her administrative performance. It was further reported that principals, by gender, do not differ in their role. However, they do differ as far as their educational leadership ability is concerned. Female principals exemplified higher levels of educational leadership than did male principals.

Role perception study in recent years has been concerned with systematic descriptions of what principals actually do. Research studies using this method have looked at principals' use of time and the nature of the tasks with which they are involved through observations (Gronn, 1982; Willis, 1980). These studies have revealed that principals' working days are characterized by brevity, variety, and fragmentation. Most activities engaged in by principals last for a few minutes and are constantly interrupted by demands from various sources (Martin and Willower, 1981; Willis, 1980). A greater number of the principals spend large portions of the day in their offices or the surrounding vicinity of the school's main office, and spend only about nine percent of their time in classrooms.

The secondary principal is confronted by an often overwhelming myriad of responsibilities, demands, pressures, and expectations (Lyons, 1981). The school principal, as the educational administrator of his school, is expected to fill many roles. He is expected to set the tone and the pace of his institution to see that the school program runs safely, smoothly, and efficiently (Kearney, 1977). The performance of the school principal is cited by Goldhammer and his colleagues. They perceived principals as managers who "…have the ability to work effectively with people to secure their cooperation." They were aggressive in securing recognition of the needs of their schools, and as such,

Table 2
Response from Randomly Selected Secondary Schools

School	Number of Teachers	Number of Respondents	Percent
1	46	22	47.82
2	52	27	51.92
3	80	43	53.75
4	59	45	76.27
5	56	49	87.5
6	59	52	88.14
7	59	53	88.83
8	56	24	42.85
9	45	8	26.66
10	45	12	17.77
11	50	49	98
12	40	30	75
Total	647	414	63.98

Note. The overall response rate was 63.98 percent.

were enthusiastic as principals, accepting their responsibilities as those of a mission rather than as those of a job. Finally, they were committed to education, and were especially capable of distinguishing between long- and short-term educational goals (pp. 18–19).

In a study conducted by Branscum (1983) on Competencies of Rural Oklahoma School Principals, the major findings indicated that the expectations of secondary school principals and those of board members, superintendent, and teachers are similar with respect to competency requirements in several areas. Both the principals and the teachers felt that principals should possess competencies in community relations and service, pupil personnel services, pupil control, and personnel services. The subjects felt that these are areas in which principals devote effective top priority efforts. Similarly, neither the principals nor the role partners felt that competencies in the areas of financial management or school plant operations and auxiliary services were highly important. The findings suggested that both groups view the principalship as a position in which competencies in dealing with the human component of the school (community, teachers, students, and central office personnel), and with the improvement of the educational program, are ideally important.

Organizational Development

The domain of organizational development provides insight into the ability of the principal to work with the personnel inside and outside the school setting to establish processes and relationships that most effectively promote positive growth and change of organization (Valentine, 1987). The factors considered in the organizational domain are organizational direction, organizational linkage, and organizational procedures.

The principal occupies a most strategic position in the school organizational development and change. Blumberg and Greenfield (1980) asserted that in many ways the school principal is the most important and influential individual in any school. He is the person responsible for all of the activities that occur in and around the school building. It is his leadership that sets the tone of the school, the climate for learning, the level of professionalism and morale of teachers and the degree of concern for what students may or may not become. He is the main link between the school and the community, and the way he performs in that capacity largely determines the attitudes of students and parents about the school. If a school is a vibrant, innovative, child-centered place; if it has a reputation for excellence in teaching; and if students are performing to the best of their ability, one can almost always point to the principal's leadership as the key to success (p. 65). In an effective organization, the leader articulates its major purposes and undertakes systematic dissemination (Brandt, 1982). High school principals need to provide eloquent and frequent articulation of the school's goals such that they are transmitted to parent, citizens, staff, and students (Clark et al. 1982).

Organizational Environment

Organizational environment is unstable and unpredictable. Its organic nature is constantly changing and is determined more by prevailing forces, which affect activity, than by mechanical considerations. However, like weather, it too can be predicted, if one examines the seasonal patterns and regularities within the organization.

Organizational environment, from the researcher's point of view, refers to the internal environment of an organization that influences work behavior. These unique and enduring characteristics of each organization's environment is distinctive as a result of having its own tempo, norms, traditions, styles, and values are determinants of behavior. One way to foster change within an organization is to change the organizational climate; that is, the premises on and purposes for which individuals interact and relate to each other. If improved organizational performance is desired, it is as important to change organizational environment as it is

Table 3
Coefficient Alpha Reliability of the APE

Domains and Factors		No. of Items	Coefficient Alpha
Domain:	Organizational Development	27	.9253
Factor:	Organizational Direction	7	.9471
	Organizational Linkage	11	.9037
	Organizational Procedures	9	.9608
Domain:	Organizational Environment	37	.9443
Factor:	Teacher Relations	13	.9747
	Student Relations	8	.9618
	Interactive Processes	9	.9551
	Affective Processes	7	.9430
Domain:	Educational Program	15	.9783
Factor:	Instructional Improvement	8	.8506
	Curriculum Improvement	7	.9698

to enhance individual performance. Individuals within an organization come and go, but the organizational environment and the forces generating collective feelings remain. The extent to which individuals constitute an organizational force is determined by their positions and the leadership they give to the overall direction of an organization.

The domain of organizational environment provides insight into the ability of the principal to nurture the ongoing climate of the school through development of positive interpersonal relationships among members of the organization and effective day-by-day operational procedures for the school. In a study of successful schools, the researchers reported that principals were skilled in providing a structured environment in which teachers could function effectively, and where they felt appreciated and regarded for their effort (Levine and Stark, 1982).

Effective Instructional Leadership

The term effective instructional leadership refers to those practices and activities of a principal that are concerned with the school's central purposes. These are teaching, learning, and the resources that support the activities. Effective principals are often found to be characterized by strong participation in the planning, monitoring, and evaluation of the instructional program (Austin, 1979; Cotton and Savard, 1980; Edmonds, 1979). Schools in which principals feel strongly about the importance of instruction are more likely to show gains in student achievement (Wellisch, MacQueen, Carriere, and Duck, 1978).

The domain of instructional program provides insight into the ability of principals to serve as educational leaders of schools through active involvement in instructional leadership and curriculum development (Valentine, 1987). Principals have a discernible effect on a school's productivity. They appear to exert this influence primarily as instructional leaders (Bossert, Dwyer, Rowan, and Lee, 1982).

Researchers have pointed out that principals believe that they should be totally involved in instruction and curriculum and that a greater portion of their time should be spent in the classroom (Boocock, 1972). Other studies have revealed that principals spend most of their time at school on managerial tasks unrelated to curriculum and instruction (Cuban, 1984), thus pointing to a discrepancy between beliefs and practices. In a study conducted by Peterson (1978), it was concluded that principals spend less than 5% of their time in the classroom and less than 6% of their time planning and coordinating instructional programs, curricula, and materials.

Hannaway and Sproull (1979) stated that 90% of high school principals' activities were concerned with other than curricular and instructional issues. In the findings of Martin and Willower (1981), studies showed a slightly higher percentage. They stated that 17% of the principals' time was devoted to their schools' academic programs. This time was described as passive or supportive rather than active or directive (p. 84). Meyer and Rowan (1978) reported that only 12% of the school principals said they had any real decision power over instructional methods used by teachers, a finding that was corroborated by Deal and Celotti (1980). Furthermore, principals generally perform infrequent evaluations of instruction, and the evaluations are unsystematic, subjective, and replete with generalities and praises (Cohen and Miller, 1980). Even though the principals considered instruction in their schools to be their first priority, in practice they did not appear to exercise much control over the teaching and learning processes in the classrooms.

Effective instructional leaders establish and implement clear goals and specific achievement objectives for the school. They plan, implement, and evaluate instructional programs including learning objectives and instructional strategies for the school. They also provide a purposeful school environment conducive to learning, conduct an effective school program, and evaluate teachers and staff members.

Purpose of the Study

The primary purpose of the study was to compare the effectiveness of principals in Tennessee secondary schools nominated for the National Secondary School Recognition Program and principal effectiveness in randomly selected secondary schools in Tennessee that have not applied for nomination, as perceived by teachers in those schools. This study sought to determine whether teachers in secondary schools in Tennessee hold similar or different perceptions regarding principals' effectiveness.

If characteristics of effective principals can be determined, the selection of effective principals with these characteristics would possibly increase teachers' and students' performance. This study will provide an increase in the knowledge of principal effectiveness, and identify the characteristics that relate to effective schooling in the areas of educational leadership, role perception, organizational development, organizational environment, and effective instructional leadership.

Method

Population

The schools utilized in this study were selected from information supplied by the Tennessee Department of Education. The Tennessee Directory of Public Schools was used to identify 51 randomly selected secondary schools with grades nine to twelve, enrollments of one thousand or more students, and which were not nominated for the Tennessee National Secondary School Recognition Program. The Tennessee National Secondary School Recognition Program record was used to identify 22 secondary schools with grades nine to twelve, with enrollments of one thousand or more students, and which were nominated for membership in this organization.

After the population was identified, a sample was drawn that represented 20 randomly selected secondary schools not nominated to participate in the study. In much the same way, a sample of 20 of the nominated secondary schools that have participated in the National Secondary School Recognition Program was drawn from the population. The population was identified and listed in alphabetical order in two lists. Numbers were assigned to each school in the population, and a sample was drawn using a table of random numbers. After the specified number of schools on each list was identified, alternate schools were identified in case permission to survey a school was denied.

The 20 randomly selected secondary schools not nominated had a teacher population of 1,288. The 20 nominated secondary schools that have participated in the Secondary School Recognition program had a teacher population of 1,221.

The sample surveyed included 14 (70%) nominated secondary schools and 12 (60%) randomly selected secondary schools. Of the 690 survey instruments sent to the teachers of the nominated secondary schools,

410 were returned and were all usable. Data from nominated schools are shown in Table 1.

Six hundred forty-seven survey instruments were sent to teachers in randomly selected secondary schools and 414 were returned. All the returned instruments were usable. Data from randomly selected schools are presented in Table 2.

Instrumentation

The instrument, Audit of Principal Effectiveness, was designed to describe teachers' perceptions of principals' effectiveness. Items for the instrument were generated from an extensive review of literature and research relative to the role of the principal (Valentine and Bowman, 1986). The three domains and factors in Table 3 represent the major areas of focus in the development of the instrument. The factors describe the most significant issues of the instrument.

Research Design

This study was a causal-comparative study, utilizing the questionnaire method of collecting data. The causal-comparative procedure was employed because it identifies possible cause for the phenomenon being studied by comparing subjects in whom a characteristic was present with similar subjects in whom it was absent or present to a lesser degree. The advantage of the causal-comparative method is that it enables researchers to investigate relationships among many variables in a single study (Borg and Gall, 1983).

Data Analysis Procedures

Completed Audit of Principal Effectiveness instruments were received from 824 teachers in both nominated high schools and randomly selected high schools. The Audit of Principal Effectiveness contains 80 items and requests a response rating from 1, for not effective, to 9, for very effective. A high score indicates a more positive view of the effectiveness of the principal. The t test for independent samples was used to test for differences in each of the groups.

The 17 items for which the teachers of nominated high schools reported their principals as being most effective are as follows:

1. The principal is supportive of and operates within the policies of the district (mean = 8.01).
2. The principal establishes a process by which students are made aware of school rules and policies (mean = 7.92).
3. The principal has high, professional expectations and standards for self, faculty, and school (mean = 7.87).
4. The principal maintains good rapport and good working relations with other administrators of the district (mean = 7.81).
5. The principal envisions future goals and directions for the school (mean = 7.68).
6. The principal is committed to instructional improvement (mean = 7.67).

174

7. The principal enjoys working with the students (mean = 7.65).

8. The principal develops and implements school practices and policies that synthesize educational mandates, requirements, and theories (e.g., legal requirements, social expectations) (mean = 7.57).

9. Through effective management of the day-to-day operation of the school, the principal promotes, among staff, parents, and the community, a feeling of confidence in the school (mean = 7.57).

10. The principal positively reinforces students (mean = 7.54).

11. The principal is able to organize activities, tasks, and people (mean = 7.53).

12. The principal develops appropriate rules and procedures (mean = 7.53).

13. The principal promotes the development of educational goals and objectives that reflect social needs and trends (mean = 7.52).

14. The principal encourages changes in school programs that lead to a better school for the students (mean = 7.52).

15. The principal works with other leaders of the school in the implementation of a team approach to managing the school (mean = 7.51).

16. The principal employs new staff that enhances the overall effectiveness of the school and complements the existing staff (mean = 7.57).

17. The principal strives to achieve autonomy for the school (mean =7.50).

The teachers of randomly selected high schools not nominated for recognition reported that the principals were effective on only 4 items. The items are as follows:

1. The principal is supportive of and operates within the policies of the district (mean = 8.00).

2. The principal maintains a good rapport and working relationship with other administrators of the district (mean = 7.87).

3. The principal establishes a process by which students are made aware of school rules and policies (mean = 7.85).

4. The principal has high, professional expectations and standards for self, faculty, and school (mean = 7.57).

Findings

This study sought to determine whether teachers in secondary schools in Tennessee hold similar or different perceptions regarding principals' effectiveness. The results of this study were as follows:

Organizational development, organizational directions, and organizational procedures scores of principals in secondary schools nominated for the National Secondary School Recognition Program were significantly higher than organizational development scores of principals of randomly selected secondary schools not nominated.

No significant differences were found in organizational linkage, organizational environment, teacher relations, and interactive processes scores of principals in secondary schools nominated for the National Secondary School Recognition Program when compared to principals of randomly selected secondary schools not nominated.

However, student relations, affective processes, and educational program scores of principals in secondary schools nominated for the National Secondary School Recognition Program were significantly higher than scores of principals of randomly selected secondary schools not nominated.

The instructional improvement and curriculum improvement scores of principals of schools nominated for the National Secondary School Recognition Program were significantly higher than scores of principals of randomly selected secondary schools not nominated.

Conclusions Based on the Findings

Based upon the findings in this study, the following conclusions were made:

Principals of secondary schools nominated for the National Secondary School Recognition Program provide better leadership in organizational development. They have greater insight into the ability to work with personnel both inside and outside the school setting. They provide better leadership in organizational direction and directions for the school through work with faculty to develop goals, establish expectations, and promote appropriate changes.

Principals of secondary schools nominated for the National Secondary School Recognition Program provide better leadership in organizational procedures and utilize effective procedures for problem solving, decision making, and change. They promote positive working relationships among the school, the community the school serves, and other educators and agencies that work with the school.

On the other hand, all the principals from the secondary schools surveyed nurture the ongoing climate of the school through development of positive interpersonal relationships among members of the organization. They do develop effective working relationships with staff through communication, sensitivity of needs, appropriate support, and reinforcement.

Secondary school principals nominated for the National Recognition Program use their time organizing tasks and personnel for the effective day-to-day management of the school compared to principals of randomly selected high schools. The study shows that secondary school principals are not spending as much time as they should on curriculum development and instructional improvement. Also, principals spend more time on being supportive of and operative with the policies of the district. Role conflict is apparent among principals and conflict is obvious in the actual time that they allocate for selected supervisory activities.

The results of this study suggest that teachers from schools nominated for the National Secondary School Recognition Program and principals of randomly selected schools not nominated do differ to some extent in perceptions of their principals' effectiveness.

References

Austin, G. (1979). Exemplary schools and the search for effectiveness. *Educational Leadership, 37,* 10–14.

Blumberg, A., & Greenfield, W.D. (1980). *The effective principal: Perspectives on school leadership.* Boston: Allyn & Bacon.

Boocock, S. S. (1972). *An introduction to the sociology of learning.* Boston: Houghton-Mufflin.

Borg, W. R., & Gall, M. D. (1983). *Educational research: An introduction.* Longman, Inc.

Bossert, S. T., Dwyer, D. C., Rowan, B., & Lee. V. (1982). The instructional management role of the principal. *Educational Administration Quarterly, 18.*

Branscum, J. D. (1983). Competencies of rural Oklahoma school principals. *High School Journal, 66,* 141–48.

Clark, D. L., Lotto. L. S., & McCarthy, M. M. (1980). Factors associated with success in urban elementary schools. *Phi Delta Kappan, 66,* 467–470.

Cohen. E. G., & Miller, R. H. (1980). Coordination and control of instruction in schools. *Pacific Sociological Review, 23,* 446–472.

Cotton, K., & Savard W. (1980). *Time factors in learning.* Paper prepared for Alaska State Department of Education by the Northwest Regional Laboratory. Portland, OR.

Crowson, R. L., & Porter-Getirie, C. (1981). The urban school principalship: Organizational stability role. *Planning and Changing, 12,* 26–53.

Cuban, L. (1984b). Transforming the frog into a prince: Effective schools research, policy, and practice at the district level. *Harvard Educational Review, 54*(2), 129–151.

Deal, T. E., & Celotti. L. S. (1980). How much influence do (and can) educational administrators have on classrooms? *Phi Delta Kappan, 61*(7), 471–473.

Delapp, T. (1988). Leadership skills required in schools. *Association of California School Administrators, 18*(2), 3.

Edmonds, R. (1979). Effective schools for the urban poor. *Educational Leadership, 37*(1), 15–24.

Fuhr, M. (1970). *Leadership role of principal related to innovative practices in selected schools in Ohio.* Unpublished doctoral dissertation. Wayne State University.

Gronn, P. C. (1982). Neo-Taylorism in educational administration? *Educational Administration Quarterly, 18*(4), 17–35.

Hannaway, J., & Sproull, L. S. (1979). Who's running the show? Coordination and control in educational organizations. *Administrator's Notebook, 27,* 1–4.

Kaerney, J. (1977). The principal: Teacher of teachers. *NASSP Bulletin, 61,* 1–6.

Levine, D. U., & Stark, J. (1982). Instructional and organizational arrangements that improve achievement in inner-city schools. *Educational Leadership, 40*(3), 41–46.

Lipham, J. M., & Hoeh, J. A. (1974). *The principalship: Foundations and functions.* New York: Harper and Row.

Lyon, J. E. (1981). Competencies needed by beginning secondary school principals. *NASSP Bulletin,* 59–66.

Martin, W. J., & Willower, D. J. (1981). The managerial behavior of high school principals. *Educational Administrative Quarterly, 17*(1), 69–90.

Meyer, J. W., & Rowan, B. (1978). *The structure of educational organizations.* San Francisco: Jossey-Bass.

Morris, V. C., Crowson, R. L., Hurwitz, E., & Porter-Gehrie, C. (1981). *The urban principal.* Chicago: University of Chicago Press.

Nakomsri, T. (1977). Principals' role behavior and administrative performance as perceived by selected teachers. *Dissertation Abstracts International, 38,* 7062A.

Neagley, R. L., & Evans, D. N. (1964). *Handbook for effective supervision of instruction.* Englewood Cliffs, New Jersey: Prentice-Hall.

Peterson, K. D. (1978). The principal's tasks. *Administrator's Notebook, 26*(8), 1–14.

Valentine, J. W., & Bowman, M. L. (1987). *Audit of principal effectiveness.* Columbia. Missouri: University of Missouri.

Valentine, J. W., Bowman, M. (1988). *Audit of principal effectiveness: Key behaviors/skills.* Columbia, Missouri: University of Missouri.

Wellisch, J., MacQueen, Q., Carriere, R., & Duck, G. (1978). School organization and management in successful schools. *Sociology of Education, 51,* 211–226.

Willis, Q. (1980). The work activity of school principals: An observational study. *The Journal of Educational Administration, 18*(1), 27–54.

Woods, T. E. (1967). *The administration of educational innovation.* Eugene, Oregon: University of Oregon.

Exercise for Article 25

Factual Questions

1. In the section of the researcher's literature review titled Role Perception, the researcher cites a study that suggests that principals spend large portions of the day in their offices or in the surrounding vicinity of the school's main office. They also spend about what percentage of their time in classrooms?

2. From the researcher's point of view, organizational environment refers to the internal environment of an organization that influences what?

3. The researcher reports the percentage of teachers who responded from each school, with schools being identified by numbers. Which of the nominated secondary schools had the highest rate of response? (Identify it by its school number.)

4. From the population of non-nominated schools, 20 were selected for this study. How were they drawn from the population?

5. The researcher states that the items in the Audit of Principal Effectiveness were generated from what?

6. The researcher states that the causal-comparative method was used for this study because it identifies possible causes by comparing subjects in whom a characteristic was present with what?

7. What was the average score for non-nominated schools for the item that states, "The principal is supportive of and operates within the policies of the district"?

Questions for Discussion

8. In your opinion, does the researcher provide enough information on how schools are selected to be recognized by the National Secondary School Recognition Program? Explain.

9. Examine the footnotes in Tables 1 and 2. Do you think that the overall response rates for the two groups are acceptable? Would you have expected higher or lower response rates? Explain.

10. The researcher limited his research to schools with enrollments of 1,000 or more. By doing this, he has controlled for school size (both groups of schools consisted of only relatively large schools and, thus, were comparable on this variable). If you were conducting the study, would you have done the same thing? Explain.

11. The results of this study are based on *teachers' perceptions*. Do you think that this is a good source of data on the effectiveness of principals? Are there other ways to measure the effectiveness of principals? Explain.

12. In your opinion, has this study made an important contribution to our understanding of the effectiveness of principals in Tennessee? Why? Why not?

Quality Ratings

Directions: Indicate your level of agreement with each of the following statements by circling a number from 5 for strongly agree (SA) to 1 for strongly disagree (SD). If you believe an item is not applicable to this research article, leave it blank. Be prepared to explain your ratings.

A. The introduction establishes the importance of the study.

SA   5   4   3   2   1   SD

B. The literature review establishes the context for the study.

SA   5   4   3   2   1   SD

C. The research purpose, question, or hypothesis is clearly stated.

SA   5   4   3   2   1   SD

D. The method of sampling is sound.

SA   5   4   3   2   1   SD

E. Relevant demographics (for example, age, gender, and ethnicity) are described.

SA   5   4   3   2   1   SD

F. Measurement procedures are adequate.

SA   5   4   3   2   1   SD

G. All procedures have been described in sufficient detail to permit a replication of the study.

SA   5   4   3   2   1   SD

H. The participants have been adequately protected from potential harm.

SA   5   4   3   2   1   SD

I. The results are clearly described.

SA   5   4   3   2   1   SD

J. The discussion/conclusion is appropriate.

SA   5   4   3   2   1   SD

K. Despite any flaws, the report is worthy of publication.

SA   5   4   3   2   1   SD

Article 26

Understanding Shame in Adults: Retrospective Perceptions of Parental Bonding During Childhood

Nita Lutwak
CUNY/Baruch College

Joseph R. Ferrari
DePaul University

ABSTRACT. The association between perceptions of parental-bonding style during childhood and moral affect of shame at young adulthood was examined with 264 women and 140 men (mean age [± *SD*] = 20.4 ± 1.6 years old). Shame affect was significantly positively related to fear of negative evaluation by others and social avoidance, and negatively related to recalled parental care in one's childhood. Multiple regression analyses indicated that maternal protectiveness, paternal care, fear of negative social evaluation, and social avoidance were significant predictors of shame, explaining 41% of the variance. Results support object relations theory, which states that shame is a moral affect associated with social evaluation apprehension and may have developmental implications for one's parental relations.

From *The Journal of Nervous and Mental Disease, 185,* 595–598. Copyright © 1997 by Williams & Wilkins. Reprinted with permission.

In the past decade, the role of shame has been given increased attention in the empirical-clinical literature as a potentially important emotion in a range of psychological disorders (Kohut, 1971; Lewis, 1971, 1987; Nathonson, 1987). Shame is a self-conscious emotion involving negative evaluations not of one's behavior but of one's entire self. When faced with negative events, it is the entire self that is painfully scrutinized and negatively evaluated. Clinical theory suggests that shame-prone individuals typically focus on how they believe others evaluate them negatively, and these apprehensions may promote social avoidance and anxiety (Harder and Zalma, 1990; Lewis, 1987; Lutwak and Ferrari, in press; Tangney et al., 1992). Studies have explored the determinants of shame, including a number of negative behavioral and cognitive tendencies such as anger arousal, depression, self-derogation, shyness, interpersonal anxiety, perfectionism, self-critical cognitions, and a diffuse-oriented self-identity (Harder and Zalma, 1990; Lutwak and Ferrari, 1996, in press; Lutwak et al., 1996; Tangney and Fischer, 1995).

The moral affect of shame has become a major focus of psychodynamically oriented conceptualizations (Tangney and Fischer, 1995). Object relation theory, which stresses the role of internalization of interpersonal experiences in psychopathologies (Greenberg and Mitchell, 1983; Tangney and Fischer, 1995), claims that shame arises from the unique role that parents play in a developing child. Within this framework, mother is considered the primary object of attachment and separation from her is one of the hallmarks of early development. The father is perceived as the first significant other outside the mother-child dyad that represents external reality (Kaywin, 1993). Essentially, this theoretical model states that early parental experiences become internalized in the process of personality formation and that later affective modes (such as shame) may be linked to the quality of these earlier object relations.

Studies demonstrated that individuals who recall early (perceived) negative parental experiences report maladjustments in their later personality styles, coping skills, and interpersonal relationships. As opposed to data recorded on direct, actual parent-child interactions, retrospective accounts of early childhood may involve selective memories, as well as selective reporting of those events. Nevertheless, retrospective studies indicate that adult chronic procrastinators, perfectionists, frequent indecisives, depressives, and substance abusers self-reported perceived poor parental care (Ferrari and Olivette, 1994; Flett et al., 1996; McCown et al., 1991). Negative perceptions of parental care recalled about childhood, in fact, have been associated with adult risk for psychopathology (Bornstein and O'Neil, 1992; Goldney, 1985), therapeutic processes and dynamics (Diamond et al., 1990), and predictive of recovery from maladjustments (Keitner et al., 1987; Vaughn and Leff, 1976).

This study examined the perceptions of parental bonding styles during childhood by individuals who reported the moral emotion of shame at young adulthood. The moral affect of shame was expected to be related to (and predictive of) negative evaluations by others and avoidance of social interactions, as clinical psychodynamic (object relations) theory would predict (Greenberg and Mitchell, 1983; Tangney and Fischer,

1995). To the extent that parental relations affect a person's development (Kaywin, 1993) and that shame is a negative affect concerning one's global perspective of himself or herself (Lewis, 1971), it also was expected that perceived negative parenting styles (e.g., low levels of affection) would predict shame among young adults. Furthermore, because the mother is believed to be the principal agent of affection and nurturance during childhood (Kaywin, 1993; Nathonson, 1987), it was predicted that increases in shame would be related to perceptions of low levels of maternal affection and care.

Methods

Participants

Young adults (264 women, 140 men) enrolled in a lower division psychology course at an urban, public, northeastern university were asked to participate in this study for extra course credit. Participants ranged in age from 18 to 28 (mean age = 20.4 ± 1.6 years old) and represented diverse ethnic identities (43% Asian American, 18% Hispanic American, 18% African American, 15% Caucasian, 5% unidentified) and religious affiliations (29% Roman Catholic, 11% Buddhist, 10% Protestant, 6% Jewish, 3% Hindu, 2% Islamic, 38% unidentified).

Psychometric Measures

Hoblitzelle's (1982) 11 descriptive adjective Adapted Shame Scale (AS) was used to assess the moral affect of shame. Respondents described themselves along 7-point scales (1 = never true; 7 = always true) to each adjective. The shame scale has acceptable internal consistency (alpha $r = .83$) and temporal stability (retest $r = .93$) for a research tool and appropriate construct validity (Harder and Zalma, 1990; Hoblitzelle, 1982). Participants also completed Parker, Tupling, and Brown's (1979) 25-item Parental Bonding Instrument to measure perceptions of care and protection by one's parents received during childhood. Respondents report their perceptions separately for their mother and father during the first 16 years of life. Using 4-point rating scales (1 = very unlike, 4 = very like) to each item, respondents evaluate a "care" dimension (from affectionate, emotionally warm, and empathetic to neglecting, cold, and indifferent) and a "protective" dimension (from controlling, intrusive, and infantile to passive, independence, and autonomy) to yield maternal care (mC) and protectiveness (mP) and paternal care (pC) and protectiveness (pP) dimensions. The scale's authors report good internal consistency (.77) and temporal stability (.80) for the total scale score, and the instrument has been evaluated as a psychometrically valid measure of parental bonding (Gerlsman et al., 1990). Watson and Friend's (1969) 28-item, 5-point Social Avoidance Scale (SA) was used to examine whether individuals reported avoidance of social situations they perceived as potentially or actually distress-

ful. The inventory has acceptable internal consistency (.87) and retest reliability (.82), as well as acceptable validity (Watson and Friend, 1969). Participants also completed Leary's (1983) revised 23-item, 5-point Fear of Negative Evaluation Scale (FNE) to assess apprehension that others would evaluate oneself negatively. The scale's author reported an internal consistency of .79 and retest reliability of .75, as well as good construct and predictive validities.

Procedure

After signing and returning a consent form, participants completed demographic information (age, gender, ethnic identity, and religious preference) and the psychometric measures (in random order). Testing occurred at the beginning of the semester in groups of about 35 persons and took about 75 minutes to complete.

Results

There was no significant gender difference on the self-reported shame scores; therefore, no further gender comparisons were assessed. Scores on the seven self-reported measures were intercorrelated (Table 1). As expected, shame was significantly related to social avoidance and fear of negative social evaluation. Furthermore, although the magnitude of the coefficients was small, shame was significantly negatively related to both maternal and paternal care and affection and positively related to maternal protectiveness and control.

In addition, multiple regression analyses were performed to ascertain predictors of shame from the six other self-reported variables (entered: negative social evaluation, social avoidance, and parental care and protection separately for mother and father). Analyses indicated that the best predictors of shame were fear of negative social evaluation, social avoidance, low paternal care, and maternal protectiveness, $F (7, 382) = 36.67, p < .001$. These variables explained 41% of the variance in shame ($R^2 = .41$).

Discussion

As expected, the results of this study were consistent with clinical models of moral affect (Lewis, 1971, 1987). Lindsay-Hartz (1984) and others (Harder and Zalma, 1990), for instance, claimed that feelings of shame about one's self may be related to self-consciousness over others' evaluations of one's self and experiences of anxiety in social or interpersonal contexts that may, in turn, elicit a social avoidance response. Participants in this study reported an association between shame affect and fear of negative social evaluation as well as social anxiety and interpersonal avoidance. In fact, both social interaction variables were significant predictors of shame. These results, then, support other studies that demonstrate a social interaction component to shame as a moral affect (Lutwak and Ferrari, 1996, in press; Tangney and

Table 1
Zero-order Correlation Coefficients between Self-reported Measures

Measure	AS	SA	FNE	mC	mP	pC	pP
Adaptive shame (AS)	[.83]						
Social avoidance (SA)	.457**	[.88]					
Negative social evaluation (FNE)	.453**	.440**	[.86]				
Maternal care (mC)	−.249*	−.189*	−.067	[.87]			
Maternal protectiveness (mP)	.196*	.084	.102	−.373**	[.83]		
Paternal care (pC)	−.225*	−.042	−.122	.412**	−.146	[.90]	
Paternal protectiveness (pP)	.137	.039	.111	−.163*	.371**	−.210	[.87]

($N = 404$)   *$p \leq > .01$ **$p \leq .001$
Values in brackets are coefficient alpha with this sample.

Fischer, 1995).

Moreover, this study confirmed empirically a link between perceptions of inadequate parental respon-
175 siveness during childhood and self-reported shame affect by adults (Kohut, 1978). The moral affect of shame was associated with memories of one's parents as demanding, overcontrolling, and nonnurturing. Specifically, individuals associated increases in shame
180 with perceptions of their mother as neglectful, controlling, and affectionless and their father also as someone who did not express affection and warmth. These results were consistent with theoretical formulations suggesting that parental perceptions may be central to the
185 formulation of the self and that early parenting experiences dispose one to anomalies in self-perception and psychopathology (Grinker, 1955; Lewinsohn and Rosenbaum, 1987).

Of course, this study does contain several methodo-
190 logical limitations. All participants were college students, raising the possibility that results may not be generalizable to other populations. Also, no questions were asked about blended families, number of siblings, or birth order, and all items were self-reported. Partici-
195 pants were required to recall past experiences with their parents, raising the possibility of selective memories in their retrospective reports. These results may simply reflect the fact that some people were more willing than others to acknowledge negative events and
200 experiences. Future studies should conduct more in-depth, longitudinal assessments into different family structures and with participants from different age levels. Parental influences should be recorded from *actual* parent-child interactions, and measures of social desir-
205 ability should be obtained.

Nevertheless, this study raised some interesting issues concerning social anxiety/avoidance, recollections of perceived parental bonding, and shame affect in adulthood. Clinicians should be attentive to informa-
210 tion regarding client's avoidance of social interactions because social evaluation apprehension and avoidance were predictive of shame. Although nonclinical participants were used in this study, the fact that parental perceptions predicted shame (a negative moral affect)
215 suggested that this information may help ascertain a potential source for the client's internal feelings of

shame about themselves. Further research is needed to clarify further the antecedents and consequences of shame as a negative moral affect with clinical partici-
220 pants.

References

Bornstein RF, O'Neil RM (1992) Parental perceptions and psychopathology. *J Nerv Ment Dis* 180:475–483.

Diamond D, Kaslow N, Coonerty S, Blatt SJ (1990) Changes in separation-individuation and inter-subjectivity in long-term treatment. *Psychoanal Psychol* 7:363–397.

Ferrari JR, Olivette MJ (1994) Parental authority and the development of female dysfunctional procrastination. *J Res Pers* 28:87–100.

Flett G, Hewitt P, Singer A (1996) Perfectionism and parental authority styles. *Individ Psychol* 124:87–111.

Gerlsman C, Emmelkamp PM, Arrindell WA (1990) Anxiety depression and perception of early parenting: A meta-analysis. *Clin Psychol Rev* 10:251–277.

Goldney RD (1985) Parental representations in young women who attempt suicide. *Acta Psychiatr Scand* 72:230–232.

Greenberg JR, Mitchell SA (1983) *Object relations in psychoanalytic theory.* Cambridge, MA: Harvard University Press.

Grinker E (1955) Growth inertia and shame: Their therapeutic implications and dangers. *Int J Psychoanal* 36:242–253.

Harder DW, Zalma AZ (1990) Two promising shame and guilt scales: A construct validity comparison. *J Pers Assess* 55:729–745.

Hoblitzelle W (1982) *Developing a measure of shame and guilt and the role of shame in depression.* Unpublished dissertation, Yale University, New Haven, CT.

Kaywin R (1993) The theoretical contributions of Hans W. Loewald. *Psychoanal Study Child* 48:99–114.

Keitner GI, Miller IW, Epstein NB (1987) Family functioning and the course of major depression. *Compr Psychiatry* 28:54–64.

Kohut H (1971) *The analysis of the self.* New York: International Universities Press.

Kohut H (1978) *The search for the self.* New York: International Universities Press.

Leary MR (1983). A brief version of the Fear of Negative Evaluation Scale. *Pers Soc Psychol Bull* 9:371–376.

Lewinsohn PM, Rosenbaum M (1987) Recall of parental behavior by acute depressives, remitted depressives, and non-depressives. *J Pers Soc Psychol* 52:611–619.

Lewis HB (1971) *Shame and guilt in neurosis.* New York: International Universities Press.

Lewis HB (1987) Shame the "sleeper" in psychopathology. In HB Lewis (Ed), *The role of shame in symptom formation* (pp 1–28). Hillsdale, NJ: Erlbaum.

Lindsay-Hartz J (1984) Contrasting experiences of shame and guilt. *Am Behav Sci* 27:389–404.

Lutwak N, Ferrari JR (1996) Moral affect and cognitive processes. *Pers Individ Differ* 21:891–896.

Lutwak N, Ferrari JR (in press). Shame-related social anxiety: Replicating a link with various social interaction measures. *Anxiety, Stress, and Coping: An International Journal.*

Lutwak N, Ferrari JR, Cheek, JM (1996). *Shame-proneness, guilt-proneness, and self-identity: The role of orientation and processing style in moral affect.* Unpublished manuscript.

McCown W, Carise D, Johnson J (1991) Trait procrastination in adult children of alcohol abusers. *J Soc Behav Pers* 5:121–134.

Nathonson DL (1987) *The many faces of shame.* New York: Guilford.

Parker G, Tupling H, Brown LB (1979) A parental bonding instrument. *Br J Med Psychol* 42:1–10.

Tangney JP, Fischer KW (1995) *Self-conscious emotions: Shame, guilt, embarrassment, and pride.* New York: Guilford.

Tangney JP, Wagner PE, Gramzow R (1992) Proneness to shame, proneness to guilt, and psychopathology. *J Abnorm Psychol* 103:469–478.

Vaughn CE, Leff JP (1976) The influence of family and social factors on the course of psychiatric illness. *Br J Psychiatry* 29:125–137.

Watson D, Friend R (1969) Measurement of social evaluation anxiety. *J Consult Clin Psychol* 33:448–457.

About the authors: Nita Lutwak, Department of Psychology, CUNY/Baruch College, 17 Lexington Avenue, New York, NY 10010. Joseph R. Ferrari, Department of Psychology, DePaul University, 2219 North Kenmore Avenue, Chicago, IL 60614-3504. Send reprint requests to Dr. Ferrari.

Exercise for Article 26

Factual Questions

1. Is "shame" defined as a self-conscious emotion involving one's behavior?

2. What is the reported value of the test-retest reliability coefficient (for temporal stability) for the Adapted Shame Scale?

3. Did the participants sign a consent form?

4. What is the value of the correlation coefficient for the relationship between AS and pC?

5. What is the value of the correlation coefficient for the relationship between maternal care and paternal care?

6. The researchers report that the best predictors of shame were fear of negative social evaluation, social avoidance, low parental care, and maternal protectiveness. These variables explained what percentage of the variance in shame?

7. In Table 1, six different variables are correlated with AS. (See the column labeled AS.) Which one of these correlation coefficients represents the weakest relationship?

Questions for Discussion

8. The researchers mention the limitations of retrospective reports. (See lines 42–46 and lines 194–200.) Do you agree with the researchers? Explain.

9. The AS is described in lines 89–97. In your opinion, is the description adequate? Explain.

10. Speculate on why the researchers administered the psychometric measures "in random order."

11. The researchers do not present averages and measures of variability (such as means and standard deviations). In your opinion, is this an important omission? Explain.

12. Beginning in line 189, the researchers discuss methodological limitations. In your opinion, how serious is the first limitation they discuss? Explain.

Quality Ratings

Directions: Indicate your level of agreement with each of the following statements by circling a number from 5 for strongly agree (SA) to 1 for strongly disagree (SD). If you believe an item is not applicable to this research article, leave it blank. Be prepared to explain your ratings.

A. The introduction establishes the importance of the study.

SA   5   4   3   2   1   SD

B. The literature review establishes the context for the study.

SA   5   4   3   2   1   SD

C. The research purpose, question, or hypothesis is clearly stated.

SA   5   4   3   2   1   SD

D. The method of sampling is sound.

SA   5   4   3   2   1   SD

E. Relevant demographics (for example, age, gender, and ethnicity) are described.

SA   5   4   3   2   1   SD

F. Measurement procedures are adequate.

SA   5   4   3   2   1   SD

G. All procedures have been described in sufficient detail to permit a replication of the study.

SA   5   4   3   2   1   SD

H. The participants have been adequately protected from potential harm.

SA   5   4   3   2   1   SD

I. The results are clearly described.

SA   5   4   3   2   1   SD

J. The discussion/conclusion is appropriate.

SA   5   4   3   2   1   SD

K. Despite any flaws, the report is worthy of publication.

SA   5   4   3   2   1   SD

Article 27

Drug Use and Validity of Substance Use Self-Reports in Veterans Seeking Help for Posttraumatic Stress Disorder

Patrick S. Calhoun
Duke University Medical Center

Hayden B. Bosworth
Duke University Medical Center

Angela C. Kirby
VAMC

Timothy P. Wampler
VAMC

Scott D. Moore
Duke University Medical Center

William S. Sampson
Duke University Medical Center

Michelle E. Feldman
VAMC

Michael A. Hertzberg
Duke University Medical Center

Faye Tate-Williams
VAMC

Jean C. Beckham
Duke University Medical Center

ABSTRACT. The present study assessed drug use and the validity of self-reports of substance use among help-seeking veterans referred to a specialty clinic for the assessment of posttraumatic stress disorder (PTSD). Patients ($n = 341$) were asked to provide a urine sample for use in drug screening as part of an evaluation of PTSD. Self-reports of substance use were compared with same-day supervised urine samples for 317 patients who volunteered to participate in a drug screening. Results suggested that self-reports were generally quite valid. Only 8% of the cases involved patients not reporting substance use detected by urine screens. A total of 42% of the participants were identified as using drugs of abuse (excluding alcohol) through self-report and urine drug screens. Among participants using drugs, PTSD diagnosis was significantly associated with greater marijuana and depressant use as compared with stimulant (cocaine and amphetamines) use.

From *Journal of Consulting and Clinical Psychology*, *68*, 923–927. Copyright © 2000 by the American Psychological Association. Reprinted with permission.

High rates of comorbid substance abuse in participants with posttraumatic stress disorder (PTSD) have been documented in both clinical and community samples (Boudewyns, Woods, Hyer, & Albrecht, 1991;
5 Davidson, Hughes, Blazer, & George, 1991; Keane & Wolfe, 1990; Kessler, Sonnega, Bromet, Hughes, & Nelson, 1995; Kulka et al., 1990; Sierles, Chen, McFarlane, & Taylor, 1983), making accurate evaluation of substance abuse in PTSD patients important for
10 assessment and treatment planning. Patients' potential underreporting or denial of drug use, however, compli-

cates accurate assessment of substance abuse. Widespread underreporting of drug use by patients with mental illness has been reported in studies that com-
15 pared self-report measures with observer reports and laboratory tests (Brady, Casto, Lydiard, Malcolm, & Arana, 1991; Drake, McHugo, & Biesanz, 1995; Fuller, Lee, & Gordis, 1988; Goldfinger et al., 1996; Stone, Greenstein, Gamble, & McLellan, 1993; Shaner
20 et al., 1993). In a study that examined the validity of substance use self-reports by PTSD patients, however, Weiss et al. (1998) demonstrated high validity of self-reports for drug use in a sample of dually diagnosed women with PTSD and substance abuse. These authors
25 noted, however, that aspects of the assessment context might have positively affected the validity of self-reports: Participants were in treatment, knew staff well, had prior knowledge of urine tests, had no negative consequences for reporting substance use, had strong
30 encouragement to be honest, and had repeated data collection (Weiss et al., 1998). It is unknown to what extent the findings from this study (Weiss et al., 1998) can be generalized to other contexts or with patients with different clinical characteristics (e.g., patients with
35 combat-related PTSD).

Given compensation issues that frequently surround a PTSD diagnosis (Lees-Haley, 1989), the validity of self-report data from patients seeking treatment for PTSD has been questioned (Frueh, Gold, &
40 deArellano, 1997; Hyer, Fallon, Harrison, & Boudewyns, 1989). Hyer et al. noted that disability compensation in the Veterans Administration (VA) system often depends on obtaining a PTSD diagnosis,

Table 1
Descriptive Statistics for Study Groups

Sample	n	Age (years) M	Age (years) SD	Education (years) M	Education (years) SD	SES M	SES SD	% African American	CES M	CES SD
PTSD	271	47.60	7.36	13.24	2.12	55.21	12.30	56	25.17	11.40
Non-PTSD	22	47.27	4.66	13.45	2.30	51.00	15.70	59	12.60	13.20
Noncompleters	48	44.29	8.85	12.48	2.05	57.44	9.75	67	21.24	11.82
Combat veterans	293	47.72	6.96	13.05	2.13	55.51	11.82	58	26.75	9.65
Noncombat veterans	48	43.35	9.58	13.68	2.11	53.74	14.51	60		
Vietnam era	263	50.25	3.82	13.11	2.42	55.48	12.39	57	26.91	10.70
Post-Vietnam era	78	36.54	7.32	13.25	1.74	54.54	11.74	60	13.02	9.72
Total Sample	341	47.11	7.52	13.14	2.13	55.26	12.20	58	23.84	11.96

Note. SES = socioeconomic status; CES = Combat Exposure Scale; PTSD = posttraumatic stress disorder.

and they have argued that disability status is likely to be a strong influence on symptom response (cf. Jordon, Nunley, & Cook, 1992; Smith & Frueh, 1996). Validity of substance use self-reports may be significantly lower than found by Weiss et al. (1998) in a population of male help-seeking veterans who may have feared that a substance abuse diagnosis would jeopardize any potential claims for disability compensation. Thus, the first purpose of the present study was to evaluate the validity of self-report of drug use in veterans seeking an evaluation for PTSD as compared with same-day supervised urine samples.

The second purpose of the study was to investigate drug use patterns in veterans seeking help for PTSD. Consistent with a self-medication model of substance use (e.g., Brown & Wolfe, 1994; Khantzian, 1985), Bremner, Southwick, Darnell, and Charney, (1996) have noted that PTSD patients describe a tendency for depressants and marijuana to alleviate symptoms, whereas cocaine exacerbates symptoms (particularly *Diagnostic and Statistical Manual of Mental Disorders* [4th ed.; American Psychiatric Association, 1994] Cluster C PTSD symptoms [viz., avoidance and numbing]). On the basis of these findings, we expected that PTSD participants who used drugs would be more likely to use depressants and marijuana as opposed to stimulants.

Method

The sample was composed of 341 consecutive help-seeking male veterans referred to a VA Medical Center PTSD specialty clinic from January 1997 to September 1998. Patients completed all information as part of their clinic evaluation. Two hundred seventy-one patients were diagnosed with PTSD (97% with combat-related PTSD and 3% with noncombat-related PTSD), and 22 patients were diagnosed as non-PTSD. Forty-eight patients did not complete their evaluation (i.e., did not report for the interview portion of the assessment). Those diagnosed with PTSD were clinician rated as having PTSD on the basis of the Clinician-Administered PTSD Scale (Blake et al., 1995; kappa coefficient among raters = .98). To qualify as a combat veteran, the veteran had to score greater than 0 on the Combat Exposure Scale (Keane et al., 1989). Socioeconomic status (SES) was rated using the Hollingshead index (Hollingshead & Redlich, 1958). Participants also completed the Mississippi Scale for Combat-Related PTSD (Keane, Caddell, & Taylor, 1988) and the Davidson Trauma Scale (DTS; Davidson et al., 1997).

Demographic information for the sample is summarized in Table 1. Veterans diagnosed with PTSD were of similar age, education, and SES as those diagnosed as not having PTSD. Veterans who did not complete the evaluation were somewhat younger than those veterans diagnosed with PTSD, $F (1, 333) = 8.01$, $p < .005$. Veterans with PTSD had a higher mean combat exposure (moderate—heavy) than veterans without PTSD (moderate), $F (1, 333) = 22.97$, $p < .0001$, but did not have a higher mean combat exposure than those veterans who did not complete the evaluation (moderate—heavy).

As part of their clinic evaluation, patients were asked to provide a urine sample. Urine samples were not a mandatory requirement of the evaluation and were provided voluntarily. Patients who agreed to take a drug test completed supervised urine samples, which were analyzed for drugs of abuse at the accredited hospital laboratory using an enzyme-multiplied immunoassay test screen. Urine tests screened for amphetamines, barbiturates, benzodiazepines, cannabinoids, cocaine, opiates, and phencyclidine.

Self-report data were collected through the use of a questionnaire that asked about the frequency of use of specific drugs (i.e., amphetamines, barbiturates, cocaine, marijuana, heroin, Percodan, Tylenol 3, Valium, LSD, psilocybin, and "other") during the past 6 months. There were no negative consequences directly attached to reporting substance use, although patients were instructed that all information collected during

Table 2
Percentage of Patients with Drug Use in Past 6 Months

| | Group | | | | | | | |
| | PTSD ($n = 271$) | | Non-PTSD ($n = 22$) | | Noncompleters ($n = 48$) | | Total Sample ($n = 341$) | |
Drug	%	n	%	n	%	n	%	n
Opiates	23	61	9	2	21	10	21	73
Marijuana	20	55	5	1	25	12	20	68
Benzodiazepines	11	30	9	2	8	4	10	36
Cocaine	8	21	5	1	23	11	10	33
Barbiturates	5	13	9	2	4	2	5	17
Amphetamines	3	8	5	1	8	4	4	15
Psilocybin	3	7	0	0	4	2	3	9
LSD	1	2	0	0	8	4	1	6
PCP	1	3	0	0	0	0	1	3
Any substance use*	44	118	23	5	44	21	42	118

Note. Percentages represent results from self-reports of drug use and urine drug screens. Some individuals reported or tested positive for more than one substance. PTSD = posttraumatic stress disorder.

*Excluding alcohol.

their evaluations would be made part of their medical record.

125 Percentage of agreement between self-report and urine data for drugs that were both tested and queried were calculated to provide an assessment of the validity of self-report. Comparisons of the proportion of individuals underreporting substance use were made 130 between groups for PTSD diagnosis, presence of combat exposure, and service-era status (i.e., Vietnam era vs. post-Vietnam era). The proportion of participants using specific substances (depressants [opiates, benzodiazepines, or barbiturates], marijuana, stimulants [co135 caine or amphetamines], and hallucinogens [LSD, PCP, and psilocybin]) was also examined.

Results

The majority of patients (317/341, or 93%) agreed to participate in drug testing during their evaluation. Fourteen of those who refused testing (14/24, or 58%) 140 admitted using illegal substances. The remaining 10 individuals denied any illegal substance use.

Validity Results

Convergence of self-report with urinalysis results revealed generally valid self-report data. Only 26 individuals (8% of the cases with drug screens, $n = 317$) 145 denied using substances that were detected by a urine screen (hereinafter referred to as *underreporters*). Self-reports and urine results were consistent in 225 (71%) of 317 instances, with 38 instances of positive self-reports and urine tests and 182 matched negative re150 sults. Five instances (2%, $n = 317$) involved positive tests associated with reported prescription drug use that was subsequently confirmed by medical chart review (in subsequent descriptions of drug use patterns, these cases were omitted). Among the 92 inconsistent re155 ports, 66 (72%, $n = 92$) involved overreporting

whereby the participant reported substance use that was not detected by urine testing. Compared with accurate reporters or overreporters, underreporters were of lower SES, $F (1, 333) = 6.05$, $p < .05$ (underreporters 160 were of lower SES vs. lower middle for accurate and overreporters), but did not differ in racial status, age, level of combat exposure, Mississippi Scale scores, DTS scores, PTSD diagnosis, evaluation completion status, or service-era status.

Drug Use Patterns

165 A number of patients (53/341, or 16%) were identified through self-report and drug testing as having used more than one substance over the past 6 months. The percentage of patients using specific drugs (as identified through self-reports or urinalysis) during the study 170 period is summarized in Table 2. Substances with depressant effects were used by the largest number of patients, followed in order by cannabis, stimulants, and hallucinogens.

Among those patients identified as using drugs, un175 derreporters were more likely to use hallucinogens compared with accurate reporters and overreporters, $\chi^2 (1, N = 144) = 4.52$, $p < .05$. The proportion of PTSD patients ($n = 118$) using only depressants or marijuana (79%) was significantly higher than those using stimu180 lants (21%), $\chi^2 (1, N = 118) = 39.20$, $p < .001$. Conversely, among drug-using patients who were diagnosed as non-PTSD or who did not complete the evaluation ($n = 26$), there was no significant difference in the proportion of individuals using only depressants 185 or marijuana (46%) compared with those using stimulants (59%), $\chi^2 (1, N = 26) = 0.15$, $p = .70$. Individuals who did not complete the evaluation were more likely to use cocaine (23%) than both those diagnosed with PTSD (8%) and those without PTSD (5%), $\chi^2 (1, N = 190$ $144) = 11.40$, $p < .01$. Although a definitive diagnosis cannot be made for the individuals in the group who did not complete the evaluation, the majority of these individuals (39/48, or 81%) scored above suggested cutoffs on both the Mississippi Scale (>107) and the DTS (>48).

Discussion

The overwhelming majority of the patients (93%) voluntarily provided a urine sample for use in a drug-screening procedure as part of their clinical evaluation for PTSD. Of those who refused, over half admitted illicit drug use. Results indicated that the self-reports of substance use from help-seeking veterans who consent to drug testing were highly valid. If one conservatively included all those individuals who both refused drug testing and denied using drugs with those individuals who were identified as underreporting substance use through urine drug screens, only 11% of the sample would be considered to be underreporting substance use. This finding is encouraging given previous research, which has suggested that self-report data may be suspect in a help-seeking veteran population (e.g., Frueh et al., 1997; Hyer et al., 1989). These results are consistent with a previous study (Weiss et al., 1998) and extend validity findings to help-seeking male veterans. The many advantages of self-reports (e.g., low cost, ease of administration, and noninvasiveness) are desirable for use in this population.

The low rate of underreporting in our sample is noteworthy given the lack of a number of factors that previous research has shown to encourage truthful responding (e.g., Barbor, Stephens, & Marlatt, 1987; Skinner & Sheu, 1982; Sobell & Sobell, 1975). In our design, unlike Weiss et al.'s (1998), patients were new to the clinic, did not know the clinicians well, and had no prior knowledge that they would be asked to provide a urine sample for drug testing, and drug use data were collected on only one occasion. Although no direct negative consequences were directly linked to reporting substance use, it is unclear whether patients believed that potential claims for PTSD-related disability would be affected by reporting substance use. If so, this belief did not seem to inhibit truthful responding in the majority of cases.

Our finding that marijuana and depressant use appeared more frequently than stimulant use among PTSD patients is consistent with the findings of Bremner et al. (1996). Although these authors did not report the proportion of patients using depressants and marijuana compared with those using stimulants, they described that PTSD patients perceived the use of alcohol, marijuana, heroin, and benzodiazepines (but not cocaine) as beneficial for their symptoms of PTSD (Bremner et al., 1996). However, our observation that PTSD participants were more likely to report depressant or marijuana use is complicated by identifying a significant group of patients (23% of the noncompleters) who used cocaine but did not complete the interview portion of their assessment. Although a definitive diagnosis for these individuals could not be made without the benefit of a clinical interview, psychometric data suggested that a majority of these individuals had PTSD. Although patients may not complete their evaluation for a number of reasons (e.g., stress associated with evaluation or time and travel requirements), our data suggest that cocaine use may be another contributing factor to the abortion of the assessment process. The identification of a significant group of PTSD patients who abuse cocaine and drop out of the assessment process has significant clinical and empirical implications.

There are a number of limitations associated with this study. Although supervised urine sample screenings offer an objective means of detecting or monitoring substance use, they can detect only recent or current use (Carroll, 1995). Indeed, 21% of the participants reported drug use that was not detected by urine tests, presumably because their drug use occurred sufficiently before drug testing for concentrations to fall below screening thresholds. In fact, the large number of false negatives (i.e., overreporting) in the present study likely reflects a methodology that permitted a report of substance use outside the window of expected substance-positive urine results. The clinically relevant outcome (i.e., the number of patients not reporting drug use who were subsequently identified through urine screens), however, was unaffected by this methodology. It is possible that patients may be more or less forthright when reporting recent or current drug use as opposed to reporting frequency of use over a 6-month period. Because a substance-positive urine screen measures only recent drug use, it is unlikely that underreporting of substance use was affected by poor recall (e.g., not reporting an episode of drug use that occurred several weeks or months ago as a result of forgetting).

The validity of self-reported amount or frequency of use could not be adequately assessed with the present design. We used urine screens to detect the presence of illicit substances in conjunction with dichotomous self-reports (i.e., "yes" or "no") of specific substance use. Thus, underreporting of drug use was defined when a patient tested positive for a specific substance on urinalysis after not admitting its use. Determining the validity of the self-reported amount or frequency of use would have required observer monitoring. The study was also limited by the urine drug screen, which did not screen for all potential drugs of abuse (e.g., LSD and alcohol). Given the reported high incidence of alcohol abuse among patients with PTSD (Keane & Wolfe, 1990), determining the validity of self-reported alcohol use among PTSD patients is an important direction for future research.

References

American Psychiatric Association. (1994). *Diagnostic and statistical manual of mental disorders* ((4th ed.). Washington, DC: Author)

Barbor, T. F., Stephens, R. S., & Marlatt, G. A. (1987). Verbal report methods in clinical research on alcoholism: Response bias and its minimization. *Journal of Studies on Alcohol, 48,* 410–424.

Blake, D. D., Weathers, F. W., Nagy, L. M., Kaloupek, D. G., Gusman, F. D., Charney, D. S., & Keane, T. M. (1995). The development of a clinician-administered PTSD scale. *Journal of Traumatic Stress, 8,* 75–80.

Boudewyns, P. A., Woods, M. G., Hyer, L., & Albrecht, J. M. (1991). Chronic combat-related PTSD and concurrent substance abuse: Implications for treatment of this frequent "dual diagnosis." *Journal of Traumatic Stress, 4,* 549–560.

Brady, K., Casto, S., Lydiard, R. B., Malcolm, R., & Arana, G. (1991). Substance abuse in an inpatient psychiatric sample. *American Journal of Drug and Alcohol Abuse, 17,* 389–397.

Bremner, J. D., Southwick, S. M., Darnell, A., & Charney, D. S. (1996). Chronic PTSD in Vietnam combat veterans: Course of illness and substance abuse. *American Journal of Psychiatry, 153,* 369–375.

Brown, P. J., & Wolfe, J. (1994). Substance abuse and post-traumatic stress disorder comorbidity. *Drug and Alcohol Dependence, 35,* 51–59.

Carroll, K. M. (1995). Methodological issues and problems in the assessment of substance use. *Psychological Assessment, 7,* 349–358.

Davidson, J. R. T., Book, S. W., Colket, J. T., Tupler, L. A., Roth, S., David, D., Hertzberg, M., Mellman, T., Beckham, J. C., Smith, R. D., Davison, R. M., Katz, R., & Feldman, M. E. (1997). Assessment of a new self-rating scale for posttraumatic stress disorder: The Davidson Trauma Scale. *Psychological Medicine, 27,* 153–160.

Davidson, J. R. T., Hughes, D., Blazer, D. G., & George, L. K. (1991). Post-traumatic stress disorder in the community: An epidemiological study. *Psychological Medicine, 21,* 713–721.

Drake, R. E., McHugo, G. J., & Biesanz, J. C. (1995). The test-retest reliability of standardized instruments among homeless persons with substance abuse disorders. *Journal of Studies on Alcohol, 56,* 161–167.

Frueh, B. C., Gold, P. B., & deArellano, M. A. (1997). Symptom overreporting in combat veterans evaluated for PTSD: Differentiation on the basis of compensation seeking status. *Journal of Personality Assessment, 68,* 369–384.

Fuller, R. K., Lee, K. K., & Gordis, E. (1988). Validity of self-report in alcoholism research: Results of a Veterans Administration cooperative study. *Alcohol, Clinical, and Experimental Research, 12,* 201-205.

Goldfinger, S. M., Schutt, R. K., Seidman, L. J., Tuner, W. M., Penk, W. E., & Tolomiczenko, G. S. (1996). Self-report and observer measures of substance abuse among homeless mentally ill persons in the cross-section and over time. *Journal of Nervous and Mental Disease, 184,* 667–672.

Hollingshead, A. B. & Redlich, F. L. (1958). *Social class in mental illness* (New York: Wiley)

Hyer, L. F., Fallon, J. H., Harrison, W. R., & Boudewyns, P. A. (1989). MMPI overreporting by Vietnam combat veterans. *Journal of Clinical Psychology, 52,* 475–486.

Jordon, R. G., Nunley, T. V., & Cook, R. R. (1992). Symptom exaggeration in PTSD inpatient population: Response set or claim for compensation. *Journal of Traumatic Stress, 4,* 633–642.

Keane, T. M., Caddell, J. M., & Taylor, K. L. (1988). Mississippi Scale for Combat-Related Posttraumatic Stress Disorder: Three studies in reliability and validity. *Journal of Consulting and Clinical Psychology, 56,* 80–85.

Keane, T. M., Fairbank, J. A., Caddell, J. M., Zimering, R. T., Taylor, K. L., & Mora, C. (1989). Clinical evaluation of a measure to assess combat exposure. *Psychological Assessment: Journal of Consulting and Clinical Psychology, 1,* 53–55.

Keane, T. M., & Wolfe, J. (1990). Comorbidity in post-traumatic stress disorder: An analysis of community and clinical studies. *Journal of Applied Psychology, 20,* 1776–1788.

Kessler, R. C., Sonnega, A., Bromet, E., Hughes, M., & Nelson, C. B. (1995). Posttraumatic stress disorder in the National Comorbidity Survey. *Archives of General Psychiatry, 5,* 1048–1060.

Khantzian, E. J. (1985). The self-medication hypothesis of addictive disorders: Focus on heroin and cocaine dependence. *American Journal of Psychiatry, 142,* 1259–1264.

Kulka, R. A., Schlenger, W. F., Fairbank, J. A., Hough, R. L., Jordon, B. K., Marmar, C. R., & Weiss, D. (1990). *Trauma and the Vietnam War generation: Report of findings from the National Vietnam Veterans Readjustment Study* (New York: Brunner/Mazel).

Lees-Haley, P. R. (1989). Malingering posttraumatic stress disorder on the MMPI. *Forensic Reports, 2,* 89–91.

Shaner, A., Khalsa, M. E., Roberts, L., Wilkins, J., Anglin, D., & Hsieh, S. C. (1993). Unrecognized cocaine use among schizophrenic patients. *American Journal of Psychiatry, 150,* 758–762.

Sierles, F. S., Chen, J. J., McFarlane, R. E., & Taylor, M. A. (1983). Posttraumatic stress disorder and concurrent psychiatric illness: A preliminary report. *American Journal of Psychiatry, 140,* 1177–1179.

Skinner, H. A., & Sheu, W. J. (1982). Reliability of alcohol use indices: The lifetime drinking history and the MAST. *Journal of Studies on Alcohol, 43,* 1157–1170.

Smith, D. W., & Frueh, B. C. (1996). Compensation seeking, comorbidity, and apparent exaggeration of PTSD symptoms among Vietnam combat veterans. *Psychological Assessment, 8,* 3–6.

Sobell, L. C., & Sobell, M. B. (1975). Outpatient alcoholics give valid self-reports. *Journal of Nervous and Mental Disease, 16,* 32–42.

Stone, A. M., Greenstein, R. A., Gamble, G., & McLellan, A. T. (1993). Cocaine use by schizophrenic outpatients who receive depot neuroleptic medication. *Hospital and Community Psychiatry, 44,* 176–177.

Weiss, R. G., Najavits, L. M., Greenfield, S. F., Sotoa, J. A., Shaw, S. R., & Wyner, D. (1998). Validity of substance abuse self-reports in dually diagnosed outpatients. *American Journal of Psychiatry, 155,* 127–128.

Acknowledgments: Preparation of this article was supported in part by a National Research Service Award, Grant T32 HS00079-01 from the Agency for Health Care Policy and Research, Grant RO1 81595-01 from the National Cancer Institute, Grant R29 AA10994-01 from the National Institute on Alcohol Abuse and Alcoholism, and a Veterans Affairs Merit Review award.

Address correspondence to: Patrick S. Calhoun, Health Services Research (152), VAMC, 508 Fulton Street, Durham, NC 27705. E-mail: calho002@mc.duke.edu

Exercise for Article 27

Factual Questions

1. Did the researchers expect PTSD participants who used drugs to be more likely to use stimulants?

2. What was the mean age of the post-Vietnam era participants?

3. How did the researchers define the term "underreporters"?

4. How many of the participants reported substance use that was not detected by urine testing?

5. What percentage of the PTSD participants were identified as using marijuana?

6. Was the proportion of PTSD patients using only depressants/marijuana significantly higher than those using stimulants? If yes, at what probability level was the difference significant?

7. The researchers name three of the "many advantages" of self-reports. What three do they name?

Questions for Discussion

8. The researchers note that in an earlier study, the participants had knowledge that there would be a urine test prior to providing their self-reports. In your opinion, is this a weakness of the earlier study? Explain. (See lines 24–28.)

9. In the present study, submitting to urine testing was voluntary. In your opinion, how important is this fact? Explain. (See lines 105–108 and 137–141.)

10. The researchers note that it was unclear whether patients believed that reporting substance abuse would affect their disability claims. Do you think that this would be an interesting variable to explore in future studies on this topic? Explain. (See lines 226–232.)

11. Based on the results of this study, do you think that self-reports of drug use by male veterans referred to VA Medical Center PTSD specialty clinics (such as the sample in this study) have adequate validity? Do you think that the results should be generalized to other types of samples? Explain.

12. In a subsequent study on the same topic, what changes in the research methodology, if any, would you make?

Quality Ratings

Directions: Indicate your level of agreement with each of the following statements by circling a number from 5 for strongly agree (SA) to 1 for strongly disagree (SD). If you believe an item is not applicable to this research article, leave it blank. Be prepared to explain your ratings.

A. The introduction establishes the importance of the study.

   SA   5   4   3   2   1   SD

B. The literature review establishes the context for the study.

   SA   5   4   3   2   1   SD

C. The research purpose, question, or hypothesis is clearly stated.

   SA   5   4   3   2   1   SD

D. The method of sampling is sound.

   SA   5   4   3   2   1   SD

E. Relevant demographics (for example, age, gender, and ethnicity) are described.

   SA   5   4   3   2   1   SD

F. Measurement procedures are adequate.

   SA   5   4   3   2   1   SD

G. All procedures have been described in sufficient detail to permit a replication of the study.

   SA   5   4   3   2   1   SD

H. The participants have been adequately protected from potential harm.

   SA   5   4   3   2   1   SD

I. The results are clearly described.

   SA   5   4   3   2   1   SD

J. The discussion/conclusion is appropriate.

   SA   5   4   3   2   1   SD

K. Despite any flaws, the report is worthy of publication.

   SA   5   4   3   2   1   SD

Article 28

Chapman-Cook Speed of Reading Test: Performance of College Students

Roee Holtzer
State University of New York, Binghamton

Lynanne M. McGuire
State University of New York, Binghamton

Richard G. Burright
State University of New York, Binghamton

Peter J. Donovick
State University of New York, Binghamton

ABSTRACT. The performance of 116 college students on the Chapman-Cook Speed of Reading Test on three different occasions was investigated. Descriptive statistics, test-retest reliability measures, and correlations with other tests of reading and verbal ability are provided. Analyses suggest that the Chapman-Cook test provides some information not available from tests currently used to assess reading and verbal ability.

From *Perceptual and Motor Skills*, 86, 687–690. Copyright © 1998 by Perceptual and Motor Skills. Reprinted with permission.

This report provides descriptive statistics (mean, mode, median, range, and standard deviation) and reliability estimates for the Chapman-Cook Speed of Reading Test obtained from college students. Also,
5   correlations between scores on the Chapman-Cook test and four other measures of reading and verbal ability are reported.

The Chapman-Cook test is a timed test of 25 short paragraphs, each containing one word that is
10   disconcordant with the paragraph's meaning. Test takers are instructed to find as many disconcordant words as possible in 2.5 min. Chapman and Cook (1923) suggested that the test may assess both comprehension and speed of reading. At the present,
15   psychometric and normative data are not available. A literature review indicated that only two studies, Muncer and Jandreau (1984), and Giroux, Salame, Bedard, and Bellavance (1992) have employed this test for research purposes, evaluating the effect of text
20   presentation on reading and cognitive abilities.

The Chapman-Cook test was administered to 116 college students (63 women, 53 men, M_{age} = 18 years) on three different occasions at 2-wk. intervals. The mean, mode, median, range, and standard deviations
25   obtained for the three test administrations are summarized in Table 1. Analysis of frequencies of correct responses indicates that 37 subjects at Time 1 accurately identified all disconcordant words in the 25 paragraphs, compared with 76 and 90 subjects at Times

30   2 and 3, respectively. These results suggest a strong practice effect. A ceiling effect was apparent at Time 1, which limits the test for discriminating reading ability in college students. Test-retest reliability between Times 1 and 2, Times 1 and 3, and Times 2 and 3
35   yielded correlations of .82, .63, and .69, respectively.

To assess the relation between scores on the Chapman-Cook test and other measures of reading ability and intellectual functioning, a different group of 22 college students (11 women, 11 men, M_{age} = 19 yr.)
40   were administered five tests. Scores of each subject on the two administrations over a 2-wk. interval of the Chapman-Cook test were averaged and then correlated with scores on the other four tests.

Table 1
Descriptive Statistics for the Chapman-Cook Speed of Reading Test ($N = 116$)

Statistics	Test 1	Test 2	Test 3
M	20	23	24
Mdn	22	25	25
Mode	25	25	25
Range	0–25	0–25	12–25
SD	5.6	4.3	2.0

The Shipley Institute of Living Scale has been used
45   to estimate general intellectual functioning in adults and adolescents and to assist in detecting cognitive impairments in individuals with normal premorbid intelligence (Zachary, 1992). The scale consists of two subtests, a 40-item vocabulary test and a 20-item test of
50   abstract thinking. For normative data including reliability and validity indices refer to Zachary (1992).

The Gray Oral Reading Test measures reading speed, accuracy, and comprehension. It consists of two alternate, equivalent forms, each containing 13
55   increasingly difficult passages that are followed by five comprehension testing questions. Normative data for those 7 to 18 years of age, including reliability and validity indices, are given by Wiederholt and Bryant (1992).

Table 2

Pearson Correlations for Number Correct Responses on the Chapman-Cook Test and Other Measures of Reading and Verbal Abilities

		r		Kaufman Brief Intelligence Test: Composite IQ		
Measure	2	3	4	Full Scale	Matrices	Verbal Scale
1. Chapman-Cook Test	.60	.55	.60	.60	.23	.53
2. Gray Oral Reading Test: Quotient		.37	.58	.62	.33	.63
3. National Adult Reading Test Revised: Estimated Full Scale IQ			.24	.50	.11	.70
4. Shipley Institute of Living Scale: Estimated Full Scale IQ				.51	.14	.61

60   The Kaufman Brief Intelligence Test is a brief, individually administered measure of intelligence used primarily for screening and related purposes (e.g., Donovick, Burright, Burg, Davino, Gronedyke, Klimczak, Mathews, and Sardo, 1996). The subtests,
65 Vocabulary and Matrices, respectively, measure crystallized and fluid intelligence. For normative data, including reliability and validity indices, refer to Kaufman and Kaufman (1990).

The National Adult Reading Test Revised has been
70 used to estimate verbal skills of premorbid cognitive functioning (Berry, Carpenter, Campbell, & Schmit, 1994). It consists of a list of 61 words which the test taker is required to read aloud. Points are given for correct pronunciation of words of increasing difficulty.

75   Pearson correlations between scores on the Chapman-Cook test with those on the four tests are listed in Table 2. The indices employed for the correlations in Table 2 are Number of Correct Responses for the Chapman-Cook test, Oral Reading
80 Quotient for the Gray Oral Reading Test, Estimated Full Scale IQ for The National Adult Reading Test Revised, Estimated IQ for the Shipley, and Verbal Standard score, Matrices Standard score, and the Composite IQ score for The Kaufman Brief
85 Intelligence Test. With the exception of the Matrices subtest in the Kaufman Brief Intelligence Test, correlations between the Chapman-Cook test and the other measures of reading ability and intellectual functioning ranged from .53 to .60. These results
90 suggest that about 25% to 30% of the variance in these scores can be predicted by scores on the Chapman-Cook test. Therefore, some information not available from tests currently used in assessment of reading and verbal intelligence may be provided by the Chapman-
95 Cook test. The results also suggest that the Chapman-Cook test may not be considered as a substitute for the currently used reading tests but as an additional source of information about reading ability. The short administration time of the Chapman-Cook test makes it
100 attractive for quick screening of reading. Research aimed at assessing psychometric properties and obtaining normative data for this test is warranted.

References

Berry, D. T-R., Carpenter, G. S., Campbell, D. A., Schmit, F. A., Helton, K., & Lipke-Molby, T. (1994). The New Adult Reading Test Revised: Accuracy in estimating WAIS-R IQ scores obtained 3.5 years earlier from normal older persons. *Archives of Clinical Neuropsychology, 9*, 239–250.

Chapman, J. C., & Cook, S. (1923). A principle of the single variable in a speed of reading cross-out test. *Journal of Educational Research, 8*, 389–396.

Donovick, P. J., Burright, R. G., Burg, J. S., Davino, S., Grone-Dyke, J., Klimczak, N., Mathews, A., & Sardo, J. (1996). The K-BIT: A screen for IQ in six diverse populations. *Journal of Clinical Psychology in Medical Settings, 3*, 131–139.

Giroux, L., Salame, R., Bedard, M., & Bellavance, A. (1992). Performances neuropsychologiques de personnes âgées normales en fonction de l'âge, de la scolarité et de la profession. *Reveu Quebecoise de Psychologie, 13*, 3–27.

Kaufman, A. S., & Kaufman, N. L. (1990). *Kaufman Brief Intelligence Test.* Minneapolis, MN: American Guidance Service.

Muncer, S. J., & Jandreau, S. (1984). Morphemes and syllables, words and reading. *Perceptual and Motor Skills, 59*, 14.

Wiederholt, J. L., & Bryant, B. R. (1992). *Gray Oral Reading Tests* (3rd ed.). Austin, TX: Pro-Ed.

Zachary, R. A. (1992). *Shipley Institute of Living Scale–Revised, Manual.* Los Angeles, CA: Western Psychological Services.

About the authors: Roee Holtzer, Environmental Neuropsychology Laboratory, State University of New York at Binghamton. Lynanne M. McGuire, Environmental Neuropsychology Laboratory, State University of New York at Binghamton. Richard G. Burright, Environmental Neuropsychology Laboratory, State University of New York at Binghamton. Peter J. Donovick, Environmental Neuropsychology Laboratory, State University of New York at Binghamton, and Department of Psychology & Neurosciences, United Health Services Hospitals, Johnson City, New York.

Address correspondence to: Peter J. Donovick, Ph.D., Environmental Neuropsychology Laboratory, Department of Psychology, State University of New York at Binghamton, Binghamton, NY 13902-6000.
E-mail: bg4473@bingvmb.cc.binghamton.edu

Exercise for Article 28

Factual Questions

1. What is the time limit for the Chapman-Cook Test?

2. How many college students participated in the part of the study in which Chapman-Cook Test scores were correlated with other measures of reading ability and intellectual functioning?

3. Based on the information in Table 1, the distribution of scores on which test administration (Test 1, Test 2, or Test 3) has the least variability? Explain the basis for your answer.

4. For Test 1 in Table 1, which measure of central tendency (i.e., average) has the highest value?

5. What is the value of the correlation coefficient for the relationship between the Chapman-Cook test and the Shipley Institute of Living Scale?

6. The weakest correlation coefficient in Table 2 has what value?

Questions for Discussion

7. Would you be interested in knowing more about why the Chapman-Cook test was selected for examination in this study? Explain.

8. Explain in your own words what the researchers probably mean by the term "practice effect." (See lines 30-31.)

9. Explain in your own words what the researchers probably mean by the term "ceiling effect." (See lines 31-33.)

10. Would you characterize the relationship between the Chapman-Cook Test and the Gray Oral Reading Test as "very weak"? If no, how would you characterize it?

11. Do you think that it would be desirable to conduct a replication of this study? Why? Why not?

Quality Ratings

Directions: Indicate your level of agreement with each of the following statements by circling a number from 5 for strongly agree (SA) to 1 for strongly disagree (SD). If you believe an item is not applicable to this research article, leave it blank. Be prepared to explain your ratings.

A. The introduction establishes the importance of the study.

SA   5   4   3   2   1   SD

B. The literature review establishes the context for the study.

SA   5   4   3   2   1   SD

C. The research purpose, question, or hypothesis is clearly stated.

SA   5   4   3   2   1   SD

D. The method of sampling is sound.

SA   5   4   3   2   1   SD

E. Relevant demographics (for example, age, gender, and ethnicity) are described.

SA   5   4   3   2   1   SD

F. Measurement procedures are adequate.

SA   5   4   3   2   1   SD

G. All procedures have been described in sufficient detail to permit a replication of the study.

SA   5   4   3   2   1   SD

H. The participants have been adequately protected from potential harm.

SA   5   4   3   2   1   SD

I. The results are clearly described.

SA   5   4   3   2   1   SD

J. The discussion/conclusion is appropriate.

SA   5   4   3   2   1   SD

K. Despite any flaws, the report is worthy of publication.

SA   5   4   3   2   1   SD

Article 29

Two-Year Comparison of Income, Education, and Depression Among Parents Participating in Regular Head Start or Supplementary Family Service Center Services

Robert H. Poresky
Kansas State University

Ann Michelle Daniels
South Dakota State University

ABSTRACT. Changes after 2 years in a Head Start Family Service Center Demonstration Project were assessed through pre-implementation and postimplementation interviews with 80 parents of Head Start children to evaluate changes during the project noted for the children's parents. Compared with parents in regular Head Start, parents in the supplementary Family Service Center project reported more contact with staff, increased functional literacy scores, and increased family incomes. The percentage of these parents with high depression scores decreased. These changes encourage implementation of more intensive social services within Head Start programs as a means of effectively assisting Head Start parents.

From *Psychological Reports*, *88*, 787–796. Copyright © 2001 by Psychological Reports. Reprinted with permission.

In March 1993, a two-year longitudinal study of the effectiveness of a Head Start Family Service Center Demonstration project was initiated to examine whether supplementary case management services
5 would be associated with improved outcomes for Head Start parents. The Family Service Center project was similar to the Child and Family Resource Program of the late 1970s in that it provided services to the parents of Head Start children and assessed the needs and
10 strengths of the parents through individualized plans (Affholter, Connell, & Nauta, 1983). It differed from the Child and Family Resource Program in that it focused on three specific areas with the parents: increasing literacy, employability, and decreasing substance
15 abuse. The Family Service Center project potentially provides new data and information on some rural Head Start parents and effective ways of assisting their development, an area that has not been well researched (Anziano, 1995). The Family Service Center was de-
20 signed to meet the specific needs and concerns of Head Start parents by having the case managers individually assess the strengths, concerns, and needs of each parent with emphasis on employability, assess the type and

amount of resources the parent had, and help link the
25 parents with available community resources.

One important employability factor is functional literacy. Functional literacy is more complex than merely having the ability to read. It encompasses the abilities to read, comprehend, and perform arithmetic
30 skills specific to living in one's society (Tewksbury & Vito, 1994). Low literacy has been linked to high dropout rates, poverty, crime, and unemployment (Cronan, Walen, & Cruz, 1994; Tewksbury & Vito, 1994). To increase employability, functional literacy must be
35 increased for many parents. The Family Service Center focused on literacy by linking parents with programs in the community that provided literacy services such as GED classes. It also focused on literacy by providing parents reading materials such as newspapers and
40 magazines. In addition, the case managers also provided gas or taxi vouchers for parents who participated in a literacy program and needed help with transportation.

Depression is another employment-related factor.
45 Shea (1998) reported that people who suffer from depression generally have a difficult time with their perception of the world, cognitive processes, thought content, and psychodynamic defenses. Depressive symptoms often carry into the employment, educational, and
50 familial realms. Although depression was not a primary focus area of the Family Service Center program, people who show depressive symptoms are less likely to be able to cope with the stress of finding and keeping a job and are less likely to have the energy for self-
55 improvement activities such as attending literacy classes. They may also have more difficulty in connecting with community resources (Roggman, Moe, Hart, & Forthun, 1994). Depression could have a significant effect upon the employment focus by impacting par-
60 ents' interaction and connection with their case manager, community resources, and potential employers. The Family Service Center program was designed to address depression directly by the contacts between the

Table 1

Frequency of Parent Contact with Family Service Center or Head Start Staff During the First and Second Years as Reported at Follow-Up Times 1 and 2

| Frequency of Contact | Follow-up Time 1 | | | | Follow-up Time 2 | | | |
| | Family Service | | Head Start | | Family Service | | Head Start | |
	n	%	n	%	n	%	n	%
2–3 times a week	7	19	7	20	4	13	0	0
Once a week	8	23	0	0	11	38	3	11
2–3 times a month	12	32	3	10	2	6	7	22
Once a month	6	17	9	25	11	38	7	22
Less than once a month	3	7	16	45	2	6	13	44

case managers and the parents and indirectly by referral to community service agencies.

The services for parents were provided during the 9-mo Head Start program. Support services were also available in the summer for parents who desired to continue. The evaluation was coordinated on a national level by ABT Associates, Inc., and three participating Head Start centers within one rural Head Start grantee were selected as a site for the national evaluation. These centers provided a rural aspect to the national evaluation since most of the other Head Start centers chosen for the national evaluation were located in urban areas. The centers were in three rural Kansas counties with populations ranging from 11,000 to 64,000 persons. None of the counties had public transportation (i.e., buses, subways, trains, etc.). The study spanned all three years from pre-implementation (baseline) through the first- and second-year follow-ups for both the Family Service Center group (treatment group), which included parents who received services from both the Family Service Center and the regular Head Start program, and the regular Head Start (nontreatment group), which included parents who only received services from the regular Head Start centers.

The Family Service Center's case managers had the role of facilitators and also served as support persons for the Head Start parents in the Family Service Center program. Specifically, case managers were to link the parents to community resources that would help them find employment, attain higher literacy, and help the parents avoid substance abuse. The Family Service Center focused on literacy by linking parents with programs in the community that provided literacy services such as GED classes. It has also focused on literacy by providing parents reading material, such as newspapers and magazines. In addition, the case managers also provided gas or taxi vouchers for parents who participated in a literacy program and needed help with transportation. These objectives were to be achieved through regularly scheduled appointments with the parents. This report focuses on the employment-related areas of depression and literacy since no current substance abuse, other than tobacco use, was reported during the parents' interviews.

This report's primary focus is on the experimental effects associated with the implementation of the Family Service Center project for parents of children in Head Start. Longitudinal comparisons were made of the children's parents who were provided services by the Family Service Center or by the regular Head Start portion at the end of Year 1 and Year 2 follow-up interviews. The changes in parents' outcomes served by Family Service Center and Head Start staff, regardless of which portion of the study they participated in, were also examined.

Research Design

Intervention

Between the baseline and first annual follow-up interviews, the Family Service Center case managers developed and implemented formalized case plans for their parents. These plans included an assessment of parental strengths in which the case manager assessed the resources that could help parents become employed or reach their literacy goals. Such resources included previous experience, education, community resources, familial resources, and personal strengths such as the willingness to learn and the courage to try.

The case managers then worked with the parents on a goal plan. These goal plans included small, intermediate goals such as keeping appointments and larger goals such as getting a General Education Degree or Associate's degree. The case managers then tried to meet weekly with the parents to assist them and to assess progress toward their goals. The case managers also helped link the parents with relevant community resources as Head Start social service coordinators have done in the past. The community resources included religious, governmental, and civic entities, which provide supportive services to families.

Sample

The Head Start parents were recruited during the spring and summer of 1993. Eighty respondents volunteered and were then randomly assigned to the two groups for the study. The parents were randomly assigned by ABT Associates, Inc. to the Family Service Center (treatment) and regular Head Start (nontreatment) groups after the initial baseline interviews were

Table 2
Annual Household Income: Percentage of Family Service Center and Regular Head Start Parents as Reported at Interviews

Income Bracket	Baseline		Follow-up Time 1		Follow-up Time 2	
	Family Service	Head Start	Family Service	Head Start	Family Service	Head Start
n Reporting	40	40	36	35	30	30
< $15,000	83	90	72	86	57	77
$15,000 +	10	8	22	12	40	20
Don't Know/Refusal	8	3	6	3	3	3

Note. Some percentages do not add to 100% due to rounding.

completed.

The Family Service Center and regular Head Start
150 groups were similar in their ethnic diversity. The majority of the parents were Euro-American, and their
ethnic profile is similar to the ethnic profile of people
in northeastern Kansas. The sample included 2 Asian
Americans, 16 African Americans, 3 Native Ameri-
155 cans, 4 Hispanic Americans, 53 Euro-Americans, and 2
from other ethnic groups.

The parents in the study were predominantly female. Mothers and grandmothers comprised 94% of the
combined sample, and fathers accounted for only 6%.
160 Fifty percent of the Family Service Center group said
they were legally married in contrast to only 23% of
the regular Head Start group at the Baseline. A majority of the families said they lived in a house rather than
an apartment or a trailer. Approximately 80% of the
165 families said they rented their residences.

Data Collection

The 2-yr longitudinal evaluation was based on interviews conducted at the time the families were recruited for the program (Baseline), after their first year
in the program (Time 1), and a year later (Time 2).
170 Whenever possible, the interviews were face-to-face
personal interviews, which were conducted using standard preprinted interview forms. When face-to-face
interviews could not be arranged, the interviews were
conducted by telephone. The number of families inter-
175 viewed at baseline was 80; this declined to 71 at Time
1 follow-up and then to 60 at Time 2.

Measures

Basic demographic data on income and other employment-related aspects were collected in each interview. Literacy was assessed by using the Comprehen-
180 sive Adult Student Assessment System, a functional
reading test that consists of an appraisal section and
detailed assessments at four different testing levels
with two alternative forms for each level. The Comprehensive Adult Student Assessment System has been
185 validated and approved by the U.S. Department of
Education (Tewksbury & Vito, 1994). A score above
225 is considered to be high school proficiency. During
the baseline interviews, parents were given an appraisal
test and then assessed with the appropriate detailed test

190 version. The scaled score from the detailed test was
used as the literacy measure. Detailed test levels in
subsequent years were based on the parents' prior level
of functioning. If the parent had exceeded the highest
level on the Comprehensive Adult Student Assessment
195 System, the parent was not administered an examination at the following interviews but was assigned a
scaled score of 500, which is above the test's ceiling.

Depression was assessed by using the Center for
Epidemiological Studies–Depression Scale (Radloff,
200 1977, 1991), a 20-item inventory on which the respondent rates how often she experienced a feeling in the
past week. The questions are designed to measure
symptoms of depression, such as hopelessness, leth-
argy, appetite loss, sleep problems, and sadness. Possi-
205 ble ratings ranged from "little or none of the time" to
"most or all of the time." Each of the 20 items is scored
on a 4-point scale from 0 to 3 with some items reverse
scored. The total score on the CES–Depression was
calculated by reversing selected items' scores and add-
210 ing them together with the other items to generate total
scores from 0 to 60. A score of 16 or above on the
CES–Depression indicates that the respondent is depressed (Radloff, 1977). The reliability of the CES–
Depression has been well documented in the literature.
215 Radloff (1977) found a Cronbach alpha of .85 when
used with the general population. Roberts (1980) found
the inventory worked well with different ethnic populations. He reported Cronbach alphas of .85 for Euro-
American respondents, .85 for African American re-
220 spondents, and .87 for Hispanic respondents. Siantz
and Smith (1994) reported Cronbach alpha of .84 for
mothers and .77 for fathers. In this study, Cronbach
alphas of .86 for the Baseline sample (*n* = 80), .92 for
the Time 1 sample (*n* = 71), and .89 for the Time 2
225 sample (*n* = 60) were found (Poresky, Clark, &
Daniels, 2000). Poresky, et al. (2000) also found the
total score to be a much stronger measure of depression
than the CES–Depression factor scores.

Results

Process Findings

Three-quarters of the Family Service Center clients
230 met with their case managers at least two times a
month in contrast to regular Head Start parents of

193

Table 3
Educational and Job Preparation of Family Service Center and Regular Head Start: Percent of Respondents

Parents' Education	Baseline		Follow-up Time 1		Follow-up Time 2	
	Family Service	Head Start	Family Service	Head Start	Family Service	Head Start
n Reporting	40	40	36	35	30	30
High School Diploma	53	48	53	54	53	60
GED	18	30	19	23	30	17
Business School	5	10	3	11	7	10
Trade School	33	20	39	37	33	27
Associate's Degree	3	3	3	3	7	3
Bachelor's Degree	9	3	0	0	3	0

Note. Due to multiple degrees, percentages may exceed 100%.

whom only 30% had contact with Head Start staff twice a month or more as reported at the first follow-up. The contact data indicate that the Family Service Center clients had a higher frequency of contact with their case managers and Head Start staff than the matched Head Start control group did with Head Start staff ($\chi_{40}^2 = 9.68$, $p < .01$). Table 1 shows the contact data for both groups.

Treatment and Control Outcome Findings

The overall purpose of Head Start is to help children and their families improve their well-being. One aspect of family well-being is family income. At the beginning of the project, the families' annual income ranged from below $3,000 to over $15,000, with 10% of the Family Service Center families and 8% of the Head Start families having incomes of $15,000 or more. At Time 2, 40% of the Family Service Center families and 20% of the Head Start families had incomes over $15,000. The gain in the proportion of families with incomes over $15,000 for the Family Service Center parents was statistically significant ($\chi_{30}^2 = 8.27$, $p < .01$), but the change in income for the Head Start parents was not significant. Table 2 presents the family income reported by the parents for all three measurement times.

Another pathway to improved family well-being is increased educational preparation. Education was obtained by asking respondents at the Baseline interview to report their formal educational attainment. The majority of respondents reported having obtained a high school diploma or high school equivalence diploma (GED) prior to the baseline interview. At Time 2, the Family Service Center group showed an increase in the percent of persons who had obtained a GED or high school diploma. Seventy-one percent of the Family Service Center group had a high school diploma or GED at baseline, and 83% had one at Time 2, while 78% of the Head Start group had one at Baseline, and 77% had a diploma or GED at Time 2. The Family Service Center educational gain was not statistically significant based on a chi-square analysis. The Family Service Center group went from 41% having advanced

education or training certificates at the time of the Baseline interview to 50% at Time 2, and the Head Start group increased from 36% having advanced education or training certificates at Baseline to 40% at Time 2. Table 3 presents the educational status or job preparation of the two groups of parents for all three interviews.

In counties with no general public transportation, a concern for these families is access to transportation. The case managers worked with the parents to help them arrange transportation with neighbors and family members and even provided gasoline funds. The Family Service Center families were able to increase their access to a car from 73% at Baseline to 90% at Time 2.

Table 4
Longitudinal Comprehensive Adult Student Assessment Scale Scores for Head Start and Family Service Center Groups

Group	*n*	Baseline	Follow-up Time 1	Time 2
Head Start	23	250.52	251.13	250.83
Family Service Center	29	259.52	283.34	301.34

In the longitudinal analysis, the Family Service Center group showed a 24-point increase in their Comprehensive Adult Student Assessment Scale scores between Baseline and Time 1 and an additional 18-point increase between Times 1 and 2, whereas the Head Start group showed no change for those who were assessed at each time (see Table 4). This greater gain by the Family Service Center group was statistically significant ($F_{2,100} = 3.14$, $p < .05$).

Depression can impede family well-being both through its direct effect on other family members and its adverse effect on employment performance. High depression was indicated by scores of 16 and above on the CES–Depression. The percent of Family Service Center clients with CES–Depression scores above 16 decreased from 48% at the time of the Baseline interview to 39% at Time 1 and 23 % at Time 2. For the Head Start group, the corresponding rates were 35%, 23%, and 33%, respectively. The greater decline in the

194

Table 5
Center for Epidemiological Studies–Depression Scale High and Low Scores of Family Service Center and Regular Head Start Parents

Depression Score	Baseline				Follow-up Time 1				Follow-up Time 2			
	Family Service		Head Start		Family Service		Head Start		Family Service		Head Start	
	n	%	n	%	n	%	n	%	n	%	n	%
16 or above (Depressed)	19	48	14	35	22	39	8	23	7	23	10	33
Below 16 (Not depressed)	21	53	26	65	14	61	27	77	23	77	20	66

Note. Due to rounding, some percentages exceed 100%.

proportion of parents with high depression scores was significant for the Family Service Center group ($\chi_{20}^2 = 4.29$, $p < .05$), but no change on distributions was found in the Head Start group. Table 5 presents the distribution of the high CES–Depression scores.

Employment remained a problem. The Family Service Center group had a 53% employment rate at Baseline and 53% at Time 2. The Head Start group had an initial employment rate of 40% at Baseline and a 43% employment rate at Time 2.

None of the respondents said they had used drugs within the past 30 days, and only a few said that they had ever used drugs in the past. There was also an absence of alcohol or drug abuse in the topics the clients reported discussing with their case managers. Approximately half of the Family Service Center and regular Head Start parents smoked cigarettes, but at Time 2 the number of days the Family Service Center smokers reported smoking was significantly lower at 24 days in the past month compared to 30 days in the past month for Head Start parents ($F_{1,33} = 4.82$, $p < .05$). A similar pattern was found for the parents' partners, with 53% of the Head Start partners smoking and 22% of the Family Service Center partners smoking at Time 2 ($F_{1,36} = 4.27$, $p < .05$).

Staff Contact

The number of months and amount of Aid to Families of Dependent Children received in the last year was associated with the amount of contact the parents had with Family Service Center or Head Start staff. The parents who reported more contact with staff in the second year received AFDC payments for an average of 7.77 mo. in contrast to the parents with less contact who reported receiving payments for 11.71 mo. ($F_{1,25} = 7.14$, p < .01). Those who had more staff contact received greater monthly amounts (M = $455.15) than those with less contact (M = $361.64; $F_{1,25} = 4.38$, p < .05). The projected annual AFDC payments were $3,549 for those with more contact and $4,223 for those with less contact with a Family Service Center or regular Head Start staff member. In addition, those who met with staff showed a decline in the proportion with high depression scores ($t_{24} = 2.75$, p < .01) while those who did not meet with a case manager showed no change.

Attrition

Twenty participants dropped out between the Baseline and second-year follow-up (Time 2) interviews. They were evenly distributed between the Family Service Center program and regular Head Start experimental groups. No significant differences on the key measures were found between the small numbers of dropouts and those who continued for the full project.

Discussion

The three focus areas of the Family Service Center Demonstration Project were literacy, employability, and substance abuse. In the area of literacy, those who received services from both the Family Service Center and Head Start showed a 42-point increase in their Comprehensive Adult Student Assessment System scores in contrast to the lack of change for the group who received services only from regular Head Start. There were significantly greater gains in literacy for the Family Service Center clients.

Employment remained a problem, with both the Family Service Center and Head Start groups showing a fairly steady employment rate of about 50%. However, since the focus area of the Family Service Center was employability, other areas such as gaining access to a car and lowering depression factor into employability. The Family Service Center group showed a large increase in the percent of parents who had access to a car. A statistically significant increase in their income and some nonsignificant gains in educational achievements were also reported for the Family Service Center group. The Family Service Center group also showed a statistically significant reduction in the percent of those who scored high on the depression scale.

During the three consecutive annual interviews, no recent use of illegal substances or abuse of alcohol was reported. However, decreases in cigarette smoking by the parents and the parent's partners were observed during contacts.

Further findings include changes associated with the increased contact with Family Service Center case managers and regular Head Start staff. These included reduced welfare costs and reduced depression rates for those clients who had more contact with their primary case manager or Head Start worker.

In conclusion, the results indicate that the Family
Service Center case manager component of the Head
395 Start program both enhanced some of the services accessed by the parents and that some gains in the focal
areas were measurable. The more substantial improvements were seen in literacy with improvements in
Comprehensive Adult Student Assessment System
400 scores, depression with reductions in the percent of
parents with high depression scores, and gains in family income. These results show both the potential for
change and suggest the difficulty of attaining changes
in the employment of Head Start parents. Further re-
405 search is needed to identify those program components
that contributed the most to these changes and to specify techniques for overcoming the continuing obstacles
for employment that these parents of limited income
face.

References

Affholter, D. P., Connell, D., & Nauta, M. J. (1983) Evaluation of the child and
family resource program: early evidence of parent-child interaction effects.
Evaluation Review, 7(1), 65–79.

Anziano, M. C. (1995) The role of the Family Service Center Demonstration in
the future of Head Start. Paper presented at the Annual Training Conference
of the National Head Start Association, Washington, DC, April.

Cronan, T. A., Walen, H. R., & Cruz, S. G. (1994) The effects of community-
based literacy training on Head Start parents. *Journal of Community Psychology*, 22, 248–258.

Poresky, R. H., Clark, K., & Daniels, A. M. (2000) Longitudinal characteristics
of the Center for Epidemiologic Studies in Depression scale. *Psychological
Reports*, 86, 819–826.

Radloff, L. (1977) The CES in D scale: self-report depression scale for research in the general population. *Journal of Applied Psychological Measurement*, 1, 385–401.

Radloff, L. (1991) The use of the Center for Epidemiologic Studies–
Depression Scale in adolescents and young adults. *Journal of Youth and
Adolescence*, 20, 149–166.

Roberts, R. E. (1980) Reliability of the CES–D scale in different ethnic contexts. *Psychiatry Research*, 2, 125–134.

Roggman, L. A., Moe, S. T., Hart, A. D., & Forthun, L. F. (1994) Family
leisure and social support: relations with parenting stress and psychological
well being in Head Start parents. *Early Childhood Research Quarterly*, 9,
463–480.

Shea, S. C. (1998) *Psychiatric interviewing: the art of understanding.* (2nd ed.)
Philadelphia, PA: Saunders.

Siantz, M. L. D., & Smith, M. S. (1994) Parental factors correlated with developmental outcome in the migrant Head Start child. *Early Childhood Research Quarterly*, 9, 481–503.

Tewksbury, R. A., & Vito, G. F. (1994) Improving the educational skills of jail
inmates: preliminary program findings. *Federal Probation*, 58, 55–59.

Address correspondence to: Robert H. Poresky, Ph.D., School of
Family Studies and Human Services, College of Human Ecology,
Kansas State University, Manhattan, KS 66506-1403.

Exercise for Article 29

Factual Questions

1. The researchers say that "functional literacy" is
more complex than merely having the ability to
read. Rather, they state that it "encompasses"
what?

2. The researchers used what method to assign parents to the treatment and nontreatment groups

(i.e., how did they decide which parents would be
assigned to each group)?

3. "Time 1" refers to how much time after the Baseline?

4. What score on the CES–Depression Scale indicates depression (i.e., at what score level and
above is depression indicated)?

5. Was gain in the proportion of families with incomes over $15,000 for the Family Service Center
parents statistically significant? If yes, at what
probability level was it significant?

6. What was the average score for the Family Service Center parents on the Adult Student Assessment Scale at Baseline? What was the average
score at Time 2?

7. The researchers report that during the evaluation,
the employment rate for both groups was "fairly
steady" at what percentage (i.e., about what percentage were employed)?

Questions for Discussion

8. In your opinion, is the "Intervention" described in
lines 119–140 described in sufficient detail? If no,
what additional information would you like to
have about the intervention?

9. When face-to-face interviews could not be arranged, the researchers conducted interviews by
telephone. In your opinion, are there advantages
and disadvantages to both methods of collecting
data? Explain. (See lines 172–174.)

10. Data on income and substance use (i.e., tobacco,
alcohol, and drugs) were collected via self-reports.
In your opinion, how likely is it that such self-
reports are accurate?

11. Twenty of the 80 original parents dropped out
between the Baseline and Time 2. Do you think
that this attrition might have affected the results?
Explain. (See lines 351–357.)

12. The evaluation does not report on changes in children's behavior. Despite this lack of information,
do you think that this research article makes a
valuable contribution to our understanding of
Head Start and Family Service Center Services?
Explain.

Quality Ratings

Directions: Indicate your level of agreement with each of the following statements by circling a number from 5 for strongly agree (SA) to 1 for strongly disagree (SD). If you believe an item is not applicable to this research article, leave it blank. Be prepared to explain your ratings.

A. The introduction establishes the importance of the study.

SA   5   4   3   2   1   SD

B. The literature review establishes the context for the study.

SA   5   4   3   2   1   SD

C. The research purpose, question, or hypothesis is clearly stated.

SA   5   4   3   2   1   SD

D. The method of sampling is sound.

SA   5   4   3   2   1   SD

E. Relevant demographics (for example, age, gender, and ethnicity) are described.

SA   5   4   3   2   1   SD

F. Measurement procedures are adequate.

SA   5   4   3   2   1   SD

G. All procedures have been described in sufficient detail to permit a replication of the study.

SA   5   4   3   2   1   SD

H. The participants have been adequately protected from potential harm.

SA   5   4   3   2   1   SD

I. The results are clearly described.

SA   5   4   3   2   1   SD

J. The discussion/conclusion is appropriate.

SA   5   4   3   2   1   SD

K. Despite any flaws, the report is worthy of publication.

SA   5   4   3   2   1   SD

Article 30

Telehealth in the Federal Bureau
of Prisons: Inmates' Perceptions

Philip R. Magaletta
Federal Bureau of Prisons

Thomas J. Fagan
CorEx Group

Mark F. Peyrot
Loyola College

ABSTRACT. Nationally, correctional psychologists are being asked to use behavioral telehealth interventions with mentally ill inmates. Beyond anecdotal stories, no information is available on which inmates might be best suited for such interventions. This article examines inmates' ($N = 75$) satisfaction with telehealth consultations, reporting initial satisfaction with the consultation process, more comfort with the process over time, and a willingness to return for follow-up. Inmates with thought disorders and inmates with mood disorders were satisfied with telehealth, but difficulties were noted when inmates became frustrated and angry. These difficulties may be accommodated by technological upgrades and spending more time preparing inmates for consultation.

From *Professional Psychology: Research and Practice, 31*, 497–502. Copyright © by the American Psychological Association. Reprinted with permission.

Although most psychologists in corrections have heard about behavioral telehealth—the use of telecommunications and information technology to provide behavioral health services (Nickelson, 1998)—few
5 have practiced it. Those who have, however, are beginning to ask for a delineation and refinement of the potential benefits. More specifically, they wish to understand which patients respond best to this mode of service delivery and under what conditions (Rabasca,
10 1998; Sleek, 1997; Stamm, 1998). Furthermore, although it has been clearly established that telehealth holds significant promise for cost containment in correctional facilities (Brecht, 1998; Brunicardi, 1998; Grigsby et al., 1998; McCue et al., 1997; National In-
15 stitute of Justice, 1999; Zincone, Doty, & Balch, 1997), the issue of how inmates will respond to telehealth consultations remains less clear.

Behavioral telehealth offers substantial benefits for inmates, correctional administrators and institutions,
20 and the communities in which the institutions are located. Inmates are afforded greater access to community specialists, thus offering them a quality of care that may not otherwise be available. Telehealth provides the correctional institution with greater predictability
25 and control in scheduling appointments and frequently allows emergency cases to be addressed more quickly. These aspects of telehealth translate into substantial cost savings that benefit the correctional administrators who are charged with operating the correctional institu-
30 tion. Finally, community safety factors are enhanced because inmates are not required to be moved to, through, and from the community for treatment (Magaletta, Fagan, & Ax, 1998). The breadth of such outcomes, in which all levels of the correctional system
35 benefit (i.e., the community, administration, service providers, and inmates), is a rarity. These positive outcomes can be reinvested to yield a more efficient and higher quality correctional product. With almost one-quarter of the 1.8 million incarcerated individuals in
40 the United States today (Office of Justice Programs, 1999) being seriously mentally ill, telehealth offers the opportunity to radically alter and enhance the services that can be offered to this underserved population.

The Federal Bureau of Prisons'
Telehealth Pilot Program

Seeking the aforementioned benefits, the Federal
45 Bureau of Prisons' Telehealth Pilot Program emerged from a collaboration between the U.S. Department of Justice and the U.S. Department of Defense. The project was operational from September 1996 through Spring 1999. A recently published report on outcomes
50 of the project (National Institute of Justice, 1999) revealed numerous benefits, including substantial cost savings. On the basis of benefits identified in that report, the Federal Bureau of Prisons' administrative staff decided to expand the use of telehealth within the
55 agency and are now in the process of installing telehealth technology in other correctional facilities around the country (P. Wise, personal communication, August 31, 1999).

During the pilot project, a hub site (Federal Medical
60 Center, Lexington, KY) was connected with two remote sites (U.S. Penitentiary, Lewisburg, PA, and U.S. Penitentiary, Allenwood, PA). Mental health consultations were focused solely on medical management of the inmates. Inmates' attendance at the consultation
65 was voluntary, and there was no consequence for refusing a consultation. Each consultation lasted between 10 and 30 minutes and occurred with the inmate, the referring psychologist, and a telehealth coordinator (i.e., person who operates the telehealth equipment) meeting

70 in a room at the remote site. This site had previously been connected to the hub site where the psychiatrist and their telehealth coordinator were located. All consultations during the assessment period at the remote site were conducted in the same exact room for all in-
75 mates. This room was approximately 10 feet by 19 feet, carpeted but not soundproof, and painted powder blue to decrease reflection. Also, the psychiatrists at the hub site conducted all of their consultations from the same exact room during the assessment period.

80 The telehealth system that connected the two sites operated on 336-kilobits/second bandwidth and produced an audiovisual product with a 1-second delay. Bandwidth is a term that indicates both the speed and the amount of data that can be transferred across the
85 phone lines between the remote and hub sites. It is the interaction of telehealth hardware, phone lines, and bandwidth that determines the amount of delay that is produced during a telehealth consultation.

Before the initial telehealth consultation, inmates
90 were given a brief face-to-face explanation by the psychologist that the consultant was a psychiatrist from the Federal Medical Center in Lexington, KY; that he would appear to them on a TV screen; that the psychologist, the psychiatrist, and two telehealth coordina-
95 tors would be sitting in during the consultations; and that the consultation was confidential and was not being broadcast or taped. During the consultation, the psychiatrist appeared to the inmate on a TV screen, and the inmate appeared to the psychiatrist on a computer
100 screen. The main camera used for viewing was a single-chip, remote-controlled camera mounted on top of the viewing TV at the remote site and on top of the computer at the hub site. This camera had the ability to move up and down, zoom in and out, and focus near
105 and far from either the remote or the hub site, without making any audible noise. During the consultation, the inmates did not have access to equipment; the image of the consultant was remotely controlled by either the hub or the remote site telehealth coordinators.

Inmates' Assessment

110 Psychologists have played a critical consultation–liaison role during each inmate's telehealth consultation with psychiatrists. To date, several psychologists have participated in well over 1,000 mental health consultations. These psychologists have been responsible
115 for interviewing the inmate, determining the inmate's need for service, triaging the case, preparing the inmate for the consultation, forwarding relevant case information to the psychiatrist before the consultation, sitting in on the consultation, and disseminating relevant in-
120 formation to appropriate treatment and custody staff after the consultation.

In addition to the consultation–liaison role, psychologists assigned to the U.S. Penitentiary in Allenwood, PA, developed a simple six-item questionnaire
125 (see Table 1). Inmates were asked to voluntarily com-

plete a questionnaire after each telehealth consultation. Questionnaires were distributed for an 18-month period beginning in January 1997. This questionnaire assessed each inmate's general satisfaction with the telehealth
130 medium and process. It also served as a quality assurance and feedback monitoring tool for psychology staff assigned to the telehealth project. Each questionnaire item was scored on a 7-point Likert scale with responses ranging from most positive (3) to most nega-
135 tive (–3). The value of 0 was "neutral" for Items 1 through 4 and Item 6; for Item 5, 0 indicated that telehealth treatment was the same as face-to-face treatment that was received outside the prison. A composite variable for overall satisfaction with the consultation was
140 created by averaging the individual items. The internal consistency reliability for this composite measure was .86.

Table 1

Descriptive Statistics for the Consultation Questionnaire Completed by the Inmates

Item	M	SD	p^a
1. Could you see the person on the TV very well? ($N = 75$)	2.44	1.42	< .001
2. What did you think about the TV sound? ($N = 75$)	2.04	1.51	< .001
3. Did you feel the doctor could give you good treatment over the TV? ($N = 73$)	2.04	1.56	< .001
4. How do you feel about coming back to be seen by a doctor on TV? ($N = 75$)	2.29	1.58	< .001
5. How does this treatment compare with psychiatric treatment received outside the jail? ($N = 57$)	0.47	1.85	ns
6. Would you recommend TV treatment to other inmates? ($N = 69$)	1.58	2.09	< .001

Note. Responses to the items ranged from most positive (3) to most negative (–3), with 0 as the scale midpoint.
[a] Indicates the probability that the mean was greater than 0.

At the conclusion of the data collection period, the inmates ($N = 75$; all male) rated at least one session.
145 Inmates could rate multiple sessions, with six sessions being the highest number rated. Many inmates ($n = 33$) rated more than one session. The average number of sessions rated was 1.88. Unless otherwise noted, data

199

are reported only for the initial session rated. For 52 of these inmates, their initial session was also the first time that they had been exposed to telehealth.

Throughout the 18-month period, inmates using the telehealth system received diagnoses from both the institution psychologist and the telehealth psychiatrist. On the basis of these diagnoses and for the purposes of statistical comparison, inmates were grouped into one of three diagnostic categories: thought disorder, affective disorder, or "other." Inmates were grouped into the thought disorder category ($n = 17$) when either the psychologist or the psychiatrist provided a diagnosis included in the "Schizophrenia and Other Psychotic Disorders" classification from the *Diagnostic and Statistical Manual of Mental Disorders* (4th ed.; *DSM-IV*; American Psychiatric Association, 1994). If both the psychologist and the psychiatrist agreed on a diagnosis included in either the "Mood Disorders or Anxiety Disorders" section of *DSM-1V* (or an adjustment disorder with anxiety or depressed mood), then the inmate was placed in the affect disorder group ($n = 26$). Finally, if an inmate was not included in either category, he was then placed in the other category (personality disorders, substance abuse disorders, etc.; $n = 32$).

Using the aforementioned data, this study sought to answer the following four questions: (a) Are inmates generally satisfied with the telehealth medium and process? (b) Do the perceptions of inmates who have seen a psychiatrist in person at any time before or during their incarceration differ from those of inmates who have had no previous experience with a psychiatrist prior to their telehealth consultation? (c) Do inmates' perceptions regarding the telehealth process change over time? and (d) Does satisfaction with the telehealth process vary among inmates with differing diagnoses?

This study also attempted to answer a fifth question (i.e., Why do some inmates refuse to be seen through the telehealth medium?) by informally interviewing inmates who were referred but refused to participate in a psychiatric telehealth session. We believe that these inmates might hold important clues as to how telehealth technology might be better used or how resistance to telehealth might be more effectively countered.

Inmates' Perceptions

Descriptive data on each of the questionnaire items are presented in Table 1. All of the items had means greater than zero, indicating that inmates endorsed a positive rating of the telehealth program. For five of the six items, the ratings were significantly greater than zero. In terms of the overall quality of treatment that was delivered over telehealth (see Item 3), most inmates (81%) rated treatment positively, and 83% reported that they would come back to be seen by a doctor over telehealth. Also, more than two-thirds (71%) stated that they would recommend telehealth to other inmates (Item 6).

A major factor with any telecommunications technology is the "hard variables"—audio and visual quality. Although most inmates in the sample reported positive perceptions along both dimensions, a difference in the distribution of scores for positive response between the audio and the visual questions was noted (see Table 1); a statistically significant difference was found between these two items, $t(73) = 2.43$, $p = .017$. The difference in the distribution of scores for the audio and visual transmission suggests that audio quality was the more sensitive and salient variable in the inmates' overall perceptions of telehealth. The implications of this finding are discussed later in the Implications for Practice section.

Of the inmates who had received face-to-face psychiatric treatment outside of prison and who answered Item 5 ($n = 57$), almost half (46%) felt that being evaluated over telehealth was comparable to the outside treatment they had received. The remaining inmates were divided in their responses, between telehealth treatment being better than face-to-face treatment received outside the prison (35%) and telehealth treatment being worse (19%), a difference that was not statistically significant. It is interesting to note that in most cases in which telehealth treatment was perceived as being worse than outside treatment, it was not bad enough to generate a future refusal. In terms of group comparisons on the composite satisfaction variable, there was no significant difference in satisfaction between those inmates who had and those who had not previously seen a psychiatrist face-to-face at the U.S. Penitentiary in Allenwood, PA, prior to telehealth.

To determine whether inmates' perceptions of telehealth changed over time, we calculated the correlation between each of the session ratings and the place of the session in the series of ratings (first visit rated through sixth visit rated, coded as 1 through 6). For the composite variable, there was a significant correlation ($r = .20$, $p = .018$). Among the individual questionnaire items, only Item 5, which compared perceptions of telehealth with face-to-face treatment received outside of prison, was separately significant ($r = .36, p < .001$). Both of these findings suggest that inmates' perceptions regarding the telehealth program became more positive over time.

It is possible that a practice effect, which increased the inmates' ability to accommodate the speech delay, contributed to the aforementioned finding. It is also probable that the group of professionals who facilitated and participated in the telehealth consultations became more cohesive as a team and more competent in their use of the equipment and their troubleshooting skills over time. Ghosh, McLaren, and Watson (1997) noted in their case study of ongoing psychotherapy via a videolink, that both the patient and the provider displayed an ability to accommodate and adjust to the medium over time.

When inmates were grouped into diagnostic categories (thought disorder, affective disorder, and other), no differences emerged on the composite variable. However, when these diagnostic groups were compared on how telehealth compared with face-to-face treatment received outside the prison, the group with thought disorders reported a higher level of satisfaction with telehealth treatment inside of prison than did the group with affective disorders (1.35 ± 1.73 vs. -0.02 ± 1.46), $t(41) = 2.79, p = .008$.

Of the 394 consultations scheduled between August 1996 and June 1998, only 20 inmates (5% of the total scheduled consultations) refused to attend their session. Eleven of these inmates reported that they did not want any consultation with a psychiatrist, either face-to-face or over telehealth. Two inmates indicated that they were angry with the telehealth psychiatrist and therefore refused their follow-up sessions, and 1 inmate did not provide an explanation. The remaining 6 inmates (1.5% of the total scheduled consultations) reported that they did not attend the session because of the medium that was being used. More specifically, 2 of these 6 (and 1 other inmate who was never scheduled and therefore did not have the opportunity to refuse) were suspicious that "the government" would make an audio or video recording of their session and use it against them at some later date. Another inmate did not want to return after he had a nightmare about the psychiatrist chasing him with a video camera. Three other inmates reported that they felt nervous about being evaluated over telehealth and requested to be seen face-to-face. At the time of their refusal, such an option was possible. We should note that the psychologists' primary diagnostic impressions for all 6 inmates who refused because of the telehealth medium were made on Axis II. These men were not believed to have a formal thought disorder. The chronic nature of Axis II disorders, and particularly those found with regularity among samples of high-security inmates (i.e., antisocial, paranoid, and narcissistic), made these inmates difficult to treat regardless of the mode of service delivery (Joseph, 1997).

Finally, several cautions concerning our instrumentation are in order. There were no controls for response bias, and the items included in the questionnaire were somewhat simplistic. Future endeavors will need to delineate questions that lend conceptual clarity to the "overall satisfaction with telehealth" outcome (see Mekhjian, Turner, Gailiun, & McCain, 1998). Perhaps any "special" or unique experience that occurs to one in prison is magnified in light of the typically self-eroding and downtrodden experience of incarceration. It is also possible that telehealth helps inmates feel as if they are more a part of society by partaking in the "technological revolution" that is occurring outside of prison. As an older inmate said, "Doc, last time I was out, Pac-Man was the latest video game."

Implications for Practice

Our personal experience with conducting telehealth consultations suggests that audio quality is the most important variable in perceiving telehealth services as beneficial, particularly for inmates who present in a state of high affective arousal and who have a history of acting out. For example, as these patients begin to express anger, rage, and other chaotic emotions, it becomes necessary for the consultant to provide accurate and immediate (i.e., real-time) visual and verbal feedback. It may even become necessary to verbally interrupt the patient to initiate a de-escalation process. With the 1-second delay in transmission, it becomes difficult to implement these objectives.

In terms of the visual delay and the less-than-perfect resolution, the typical nonverbal cues that emerge when anger is experienced may be difficult for the provider to detect. Because the emotion of anger usually involves physiological changes in the person experiencing it, being able to see nonverbal cues is critical for making a quick and accurate assessment (Matsakis, 1998). Covert cues such as a shift in eye gaze or initial flushing of the face may be difficult to detect, and overt behaviors such as clenched fists may simply be out of range on the provider's TV or computer screen (Heath & Luff, 1992).

In terms of the audio delay, Fussell and Benimoff (1995) noted that when there is a delay in transmission, the area of communication most likely to be affected is the "turn-taking" between sender and receiver. Although we did not empirically capture this interaction, we did observe that during heated exchanges the patient and the provider often attempted to talk in real time but actually "walked" on the transmitted speech of one another. In these scenarios, neither patient nor provider hears one another. This further frustrates the patient, escalating emotional turmoil and increasing affective expression. Fueling this escalation is the fact that, as emotion begins to be expressed, the patient loses the ability to concentrate or focus on accommodating the delay in speech. Our hypothesis is that feeling inwardly overwhelmed, the patient becomes less able to outwardly accommodate the medium being used.

There are several ways of working with this problem. First, the health care provider at the hub site should have a greater degree of awareness when working with volatile or angry patients during consultation. Being vigilant in ensuring that these types of patients are done speaking before responding to them, and perhaps limiting affectively charged topics, are likely to pay dividends. Second, increasing bandwidth can decrease the delay in speech and video and may be worth pursuing for those patients who present with a high degree of affective arousal. Third, extra time and effort can be spent preparing these types of patients for consultation. Coaching them about the delay in speech and

375 separating this out from how the psychiatrist feels about them are worth the effort. Finally, if a last measure is needed, the consulting psychologist can "step in"—live and in person—and begin immediate work to de-escalate the patient.

380 We should note that in the scant literature and case vignettes that exist regarding behavioral telehealth, there is no mention of the aforementioned phenomena. It is possible that our experiences reflect the reality that high-security inmates have a lower frustration toler-

385 ance and more overt anger than a lower security or a nonincarcerated population might have. For high-security correctional institutions, it may be advisable to purchase telehealth equipment and phone lines that favor precision in audio quality.

390 It is of particular interest that those who can receive the most benefit from psychiatric intervention, those with thought disorders, had such positive perceptions of telehealth. Clinicians often express appropriate hesitation about the possible negative interaction of

395 real technology with delusions or other psychotic processes. Some anecdotal evidence exists to suggest that clinicians should be cautious about using telehealth with those who have a history of delusions of reference from communications technology (McLaren, Ball,

400 Summerfield, Watson, & Lipsedge, 1995). Other literature suggests that no caution is needed—individuals with thought disorders do not experience an exacerbation of delusions when seen over telehealth (Dongier, Tempier, Lalinec-Michaud, & Meunier,

405 1986). Finally, Zarate et al. (1997) reported that at least half of their sample of patients with schizophrenia actually preferred telehealth interviews to live ones, and similar to our finding, their respondents with schizophrenia reported equal or more positive

410 perceptions of telehealth than did a sample of respondents with obsessive-compulsive disorder.

Two examples of inmates with thought disorders from our sample are worthy of note. One was an inmate who had consistently expressed his delusions of

415 reference from the TV in his housing unit. For this reason, we were particularly hesitant to have him evaluated over telehealth. When the consultation occurred despite this hesitation, the inmate's only comment was "See, I told you the television talks to me!" This was

420 used as an opportunity to discuss the difference between real-time television and television that is broadcast after taping. However, the inmate's delusional system still was not altered. Although telehealth did not exacerbate his delusion, it may have served to reinforce

425 it. In another case, a schizophrenic inmate saw his picture on the screen and believed that it was his imposter (the one he had been telling us about). After this incident, we decided not to use the "picture in picture" option (where the inmate simultaneously sees a full

430 image of the consultant as well as a smaller image of himself in the corner of the screen) as part of our consultation with patients with thought disorders. In both cases, it was clear that although there was an

cases, it was clear that although there was an interaction between technology and the delusional system of

435 the patient, sound treatment could still be provided.

Several ideas about the reason for thought-disordered patients' positive perceptions have been presented. One is that individuals with thought disorders are overstimulated in social and interpersonal rela-

440 tionships, and telehealth gives them enough interpersonal distance to decrease their anxiety. When Zaylor (1998) saw his patients over telehealth, they had control over how close or how far away they wanted him to appear on their TV. He reported that letting the

445 thought-disordered individual have this control of the "interpersonal space" is calming. Stamm (1999) also discussed the idea of telehealth providing restraint in the interpersonal environment and suggested that thought-disordered individuals are less anxious when

450 the environment is structured or constrained. This also lends some credence to our observation that those who present in a high state of affective arousal, for example, those who are angry, do less well over telehealth—they rebel when they perceive constraint; it only serves to

455 fuel their already hot affect.

Although much has been said about the interaction of diagnosis, inmates, and technology, we have yet to discuss the attitudes of the health care providers themselves toward telehealth. As professionals at the core of

460 any telehealth operation, their attitudes can either facilitate or negate the successful implementation of a telehealth system. It is not uncommon to find initial resistance to "distance" treatment approaches among psychologists. Most psychologists were trained in

465 models that inherently assumed that the consumer would receive services face-to-face, in the same room. Many professionals have had repeated exposures to the pairing of interpersonal and physical "space." For most psychologists, the "therapeutic relationship" describes

470 an attachment with a very concrete manifestation—the client physically comes to an office, and the relationship is born there. In some instances, therapists have felt that their clients would not agree to "distance" approaches to treatment. At this time, it seems that for the

475 majority of clients who have been evaluated over telehealth, this belief may simply be more salient for the provider (Dankins, 1997; Magaletta, 1997; McLaren & Ball, 1997; Ruskin et al., 1998; Wheeler, 1998; Zarate et al., 1997).

480 Another aspect of professional resistance that is rare but that should be noted comes from telehealth's ability to increase access to care. This feature expands the market for other professionals to provide services. In terms of correctional psychology, this is much less

485 of a concern for traditional correctional psychologists who, by the very nature of their duties, must be in the correctional institution. However, psychologists who have correctional "specialties" (e.g., forensic assessments, counseling of HIV-positive inmates, sex of-

490 fender treatment and assessment, early parole assess-

ments) are likely to experience increased competition in the delivery of services.

In addressing professional resistance, we have several recommendations. First, clinicians should receive standardized training prior to using telehealth. Such training should emphasize the critical element of developing a collaborative team approach if more than one person will be involved in the telehealth consultation process (Magaletta et al., 1998). This can be facilitated by giving the providers ample time to get to know one another. They should also be coached to pay particular attention to the types of information they might need from one another prior to conducting a consultation with a given client. Training should also present information on the limits of telehealth. For example, in correctional work, training might include cautioning clinicians about the use of telehealth with affectively aroused inmates.

Regarding the emergence of a successful therapeutic relationship over telehealth, we have one core recommendation. Consistency is likely to be the key factor lending itself to a successful therapeutic relationship, not the distance between the provider and the consumer. We hypothesize that stability and consistency in the rooms where both the provider and the client are viewed are essential. It may be the case that the stability of rooms, being seen in the same room across sessions, does much to ameliorate the perception of distance and thus helps form the membrane of the therapeutic relationship.

Finally, instead of fearing increased market competition, we encourage clinicians to look toward those they serve and determine in what other ways telehealth might benefit them. Although most studies that currently exist on telehealth in corrections have concerned the medical management of mentally ill inmates, other areas of psychological services are expanding. B. Sutton (personal communication, February 12, 2000), with the California Department of Corrections, has been successful in conducting a psychoeducational anger management group over telehealth. Magaletta et al. (1998) mentioned the potential for more inmates to be seen in specialty services such as neuropsychological, geriatric, and sex offender assessments and treatment. Family visits may also be managed with telehealth technology and may ameliorate the problem of geographically remote prisons. As in any visiting scenario, the issue of who organizes and supervises such visits would have to be explored. A final area that is well matched for telehealth is prerelease planning and preparation for inmates being released back into the community. To be able to build a technological bridge from behind the wall to the community that will receive the inmate would do much to ensure a smoother transition back to society. Inmates would clearly benefit from having a chance to meet, review, and discuss their release conditions and plans with those who will be helping with this process.

It is clear that telehealth is positioned to be the premier vehicle for health care delivery in corrections. Correctional psychologists are among the first to have access to and to explore the limits and opportunities that such a system can offer those whom they serve. Heeding Stamm's (2000) warning that telehealth is a service delivery mechanism and not a treatment protocol, we urge psychologists to maintain a pioneering spirit and navigate this vehicle toward those we serve.

References

American Psychiatric Association. (1994). *Diagnostic and statistical manual of mental disorders* ((4th ed.). Washington, DC: Author)

Brecht, R. M. (1998). Correctional telemedicine. (In *Telemedicine sourcebook* (pp. 146–151). New York: Faulkner & Gray.)

Brunicardi, B. O. (1998). Financial analysis of savings from telehealth in Ohio's prison system. *Telehealth Journal, 4,* 49–54.

Dankins, D. R. (1997, June). Market targets 1997. *Telemedicine and Telehealth Networks,* 25–29.

Dongier, M., Tempier, R., Lalinec-Michaud, M., & Meunier, D. (1986). Telepsychiatry: Psychiatric consultation through two-way television. A controlled study. *Canadian Journal of Psychiatry, 31,* 32–34.

Fussell, S. R., & Benimoff, I. (1995). Social and cognitive processes in interpersonal communication: Implications for advanced telecommunications technologies. *Human Factors, 37,* 228–250.

Ghosh, G. J., McLaren, P. M., & Watson, J. P. (1997). Evaluating the alliance in videolink teletherapy. *Journal of Telemedicine and Telecare, 3,* Suppl. 1 33–35.

Grigsby, J., Sandberg, E. J., Kaehny, M. M., Kramer, A. M., Schlenker, R. E., & Shaughnessy, P. W. (1998). Analysis of expansion of access to care through use of telemedicine and mobile health services. (In *Telemedicine sourcebook* (pp. 173–189). New York: Faulkner & Gray.)

Heath, C., & Luff, P. (1992). Media space and communicative asymmetries: Preliminary observations of video-mediated interaction. *Human–Computer Interaction, 7,* 315–346.

Joseph, S. (1997). *Personality disorders: New symptom-focused drug therapy.* (New York: Haworth Medical Press)

Magaletta, P. R. (1997, November). Endorsing telehealth [Letter to the editor]. *APA Monitor, 6*

Magaletta, P. R., Fagan, T. J., & Ax, R. K. (1998). Advancing psychology services through telehealth in the Federal Bureau of Prisons. *Professional Psychology: Research and Practice, 29,* 543–548.

Matsakis, A. (1998). *Managing client anger.* (Oakland, CA: New Harbinger)

McCue, M. J., Mazmanian, P. E., Hampton, C., Marks, T. K., Fisher, E., Parpart, F., & Krick, R. S. (1997). The case of Powhatan Correctional Center/Virginia Department of Corrections and Virginia Commonwealth University/Medical College of Virginia. *Telehealth Journal, 3,* 11–17.

McLaren, P., & Ball, C. J. (1997). Interpersonal communications and telemedicine: Hypotheses and methods. *Journal of Telemedicine and Telecare, 3,* Suppl. 1 5–7.

McLaren, P., Ball, C., Summerfield, A. B., Watson, J. P., & Lipsedge, M. (1995). An evaluation of the use of interactive television in an acute psychiatric service. *Journal of Telemedicine and Telecare, 1,* 79–85.

Mekhjian, H., Turner, J. W., Gailiun, M., & McCain, T. (1998). Patient satisfaction with telemedicine in a prison environment: A matter of context. *Journal of Telemedicine and Telecare, 5,* 55–61.

National Institute of Justice. (1999). *Telemedicine can reduce correctional health care costs: An evaluation of a prison telemedicine network* ((Report No. NCJ 175040). Washington, DC: U.S. Department of Justice)

Nickelson, D. W. (1998). Telehealth and the evolving health care system: Strategic opportunities for professional psychology. *Professional Psychology: Research and Practice, 29,* 527–535.

Office of Justice Programs. (1999). *Mental health and treatment of inmates and probationers* ((Report No. NCJ 174463). Washington, DC: U.S. Department of Justice)

Rabasca, L. (1998, August). Study probes how patients are affected by telehealth. *APA Monitor, 31*

Ruskin, P. E., Reed, S., Kumar, R., Kling, M. A., Siegel, E., Rosen, M., & Hauser, P. (1998). Reliability and acceptability of psychiatric diagnosis via telecommunication and audiovisual technology. *Psychiatric Services, 49,* 1086–1088.

Sleek, S. (1997, August). Providing therapy from a distance. *APA Monitor,* 1–38.

Stamm, B. H. (1998). Clinical applications of telehealth in mental health care. *Professional Psychology: Research and Practice, 29,* 536–542.

Stamm, B. H. (1999, August). Discussant. (In M. Mahue & R. Ax (Cochairs), *Telehealth and the legal system–Corrections.* Symposium conducted at the 107th Annual Convention of the American Psychological Association, Boston.)

Stamm, B. H. (2000, Winter). Telehealth puts public service caregiving in focus. *Public Service Psychology, 25,* 19 1

Wheeler, T. (1998, April). Thoughts from tele-mental health practitioners. *Telemedicine Today,* 38–40.

Zarate, C. A., Weinstock, L., Cukor, P., Morabito, C., Leahy, L., Burns, C., & Baer, L. (1997). Applicability of telemedicine for assessing patients with schizophrenia: Acceptance and reliability. *Journal of Clinical Psychiatry, 58,* 22–25.

Zaylor, C. (1998, August). Planning and implementation of an interactive televideo clinic. (In M. Maheu & A. Anker (Cochairs), *Telehealth II–A beginner's blueprint for effective program design.* Symposium conducted at the 106th Annual Convention of the American Psychological Association, San Francisco.)

Zincone, L. H., Doty, E., & Balch, D. C. (1997). Financial analysis of telehealth in a prison system. *Telehealth Journal, 3,* 247–255.

Note: The views expressed in this article are those of the authors and do not necessarily represent the official policy or opinions of the Federal Bureau of Prisons or the Department of Justice.

Address correspondence to: Philip R. Magaletta, Federal Bureau of Prisons, 320 First Street, NW, Washington, DC, 20534. E-mail: pmagaletta@bop.gov

Exercise for Article 30

Factual Questions

1. Of the 1.8 million incarcerated in a recent year, what percentage was estimated to be seriously mentally ill?

2. On the 7-point scale for each questionnaire item, what was the score for the most positive response?

3. What was the mean score for the questionnaire item about how they feel about coming back to be seen by a doctor on TV?

4. Were all of the inmates males?

5. For how many of the six items in Table 1 were the ratings significantly greater than zero?

6. For Item 5, the researchers correlated the session numbers with the responses to the question. They found a positive value of *r*, which indicates that in later sessions, the responses to Item 5 were more favorable. What was the value of *r* that the researchers reported?

7. In the section of their report on implications, the researchers point out that most psychologists were trained in models that inherently assumed what?

Questions for Discussion

8. In the evaluation of this pilot program, there was no control group. In your opinion, how important would it be to include a control group (receiving in-person treatment) in a future, more definitive study? Explain.

9. In lines 272–303, the researchers describe the reasons why some inmates refused to attend their sessions. Do you think that this is important information? Why? Why not?

10. The researchers describe their questionnaire as "somewhat simplistic." Assuming this is correct, do the statistics generated by using the questionnaire provide interesting information? Useful information? Explain. (See lines 305–307.)

11. To what extent has this research convinced you of the value of the telehealth method for delivering psychiatric care for inmates? Explain.

12. If you were to conduct a study on the same topic, what changes in the methodology, if any, would you make?

Quality Ratings

Directions: Indicate your level of agreement with each of the following statements by circling a number from 5 for strongly agree (SA) to 1 for strongly disagree (SD). If you believe an item is not applicable to this research article, leave it blank. Be prepared to explain your ratings.

A. The introduction establishes the importance of the study.

SA   5   4   3   2   1   SD

B. The literature review establishes the context for the study.

SA   5   4   3   2   1   SD

C. The research purpose, question, or hypothesis is clearly stated.

SA   5   4   3   2   1   SD

D. The method of sampling is sound.

SA   5   4   3   2   1   SD

E. Relevant demographics (for example, age, gender, and ethnicity) are described.

SA   5   4   3   2   1   SD

F. Measurement procedures are adequate.

SA   5   4   3   2   1   SD

G. All procedures have been described in sufficient detail to permit a replication of the study.

SA   5   4   3   2   1   SD

H. The participants have been adequately protected from potential harm.

SA   5   4   3   2   1   SD

I. The results are clearly described.

SA   5   4   3   2   1   SD

J. The discussion/conclusion is appropriate.

SA   5   4   3   2   1   SD

K. Despite any flaws, the report is worthy of publication.

SA   5   4   3   2   1   SD

Article 31

Project ARM: Alcohol Risk Management to Prevent Sales to Underage and Intoxicated Patrons

Traci L. Toomey
University of Minnesota

Alexander C. Wagenaar
University of Minnesota

John P. Gehan
Policy and Communications

Gudrun Kilian
University of Minnesota

David M. Murray
University of Memphis

Cheryl L. Perry
University of Minnesota

ABSTRACT. Clear policies and expectations are key to increasing responsible service of alcohol in licensed establishments. Few training programs focus exclusively on owners and managers of alcohol establishments to reduce the risk of alcohol service. Project ARM: Alcohol Risk Management is a one-on-one consultation program for owners and managers. Participants received information on risk level, policies to prevent illegal sales, legal issues, and staff communication. This nonrandomized demonstration project was implemented in five diverse bars. Two waves of underage and pseudo-intoxicated purchase attempts were conducted pre- and postintervention in the five intervention bars and nine matched control bars. Underage sales decreased by 11.5%, and sales to pseudo-intoxicated buyers decreased by 46%. Results were in the hypothesized direction but not statistically significant. A one-on-one, outlet-specific training program for owners and managers is a promising way to reduce illegal alcohol sales, particularly to obviously intoxicated individuals.

From *Health Education & Behavior, 28,* 186–199. Copyright ©
2001 by SOPHE. Reprinted with permission.

Alcohol is associated with many public health problems, including traffic crashes, homicides, suicides, drownings, and sexual assaults.[1-6] Extant research suggests that changing environments that promote risky
5　patterns and rates of alcohol use can create long-term reductions in alcohol-related problems.[7] One component of the social environment that influences alcohol use is the serving practices of licensed alcohol establishments.

10　Many alcohol establishments have serving practices that promote risky drinking. For example, sales to underage or intoxicated individuals are known *to* occur in one-half to three-fourths of all retail alcohol outlets.[8-10] One-third to two-thirds of intoxicated drivers report
15　purchasing their alcohol at a licensed alcohol outlet immediately prior to their intoxicated driving.[11-12]

To reduce the number of illegal alcohol sales to youth and intoxicated patrons, training programs for alcohol outlet staff, such as servers, are frequently used
20　throughout the United States. The best server training programs provide outlet staff with the skills necessary to refuse illegal alcohol sales, slow down service of alcohol, and promote the sale of food and nonalcoholic beverages.[13-14]

25　Although server training programs may reduce the risk of patron intoxication and decrease alcohol-related traffic crashes,[13,15-21] server training programs by themselves do not appear to be effective in stopping alcohol sales to underage or intoxicated customers.[16,18] To
30　make server training programs more effective, outlet staff may need to be encouraged and supported by their management to serve alcohol responsibly.[16,17,22,23]

One way management can support responsible server and seller behavior may be to establish and en-
35　force clearly written policies that create an environment promoting responsible service of alcohol. Effects of server training programs may be improved if an alcohol establishment's policies and the behaviors of owners and managers are consistent with messages
40　provided in server training to employees. Written policies may be a useful tool for management to clearly communicate expectations about alcohol sales, given that high staff turnover in these alcohol establishments tends to make server training programs difficult to im-
45　plement. Wolfson and associates[24,25] found that establishment policies and practices were significantly associated with fewer alcohol sales to purchasers who appeared to be under age 21.

Outlet-specific and management-specific training
50　programs may be necessary to help owners and managers reduce risky practices by identifying, implementing, and enforcing effective alcohol policies for their establishments. However, few training programs exist for outlet managers. Among 22 recently reviewed local
55　and national server training programs, only 9 had at

206

least one component that appeared to target owners or managers of alcohol establishments.[14] Only 1 of these programs (consisting solely of a videotape) exclusively targeted owners and managers.

Although increasing responsible alcohol sales may require changes in the behavior of both outlet staff and management, few server and manager training programs include theoretically based behavior change techniques.[14] Two theoretical models that may be applied to these training programs are the health belief model and social learning theory.[14,26,27] According to the health belief model, behavior change is predictable based on certain belief patterns, including (1) believing there is risk if behavior is not changed, (2) perceiving this risk or consequence as serious, and (3) believing that the benefits of the behavior change outweigh the costs. In addition, there must be a "cue to action" or a motivating force to encourage the individual to alter his or her behavior.[28] Similarly, social learning theory posits that behavior results from an expectation about outcomes and a response to environmental cues.[27] However, social learning theory also suggests that self-efficacy, or the belief that one has the skills to change behavior, is necessary for behavior change. Self-efficacy may be increased through practice of the behavior, vicarious experience, and verbal persuasion.[29]

If these behavior change theories are applied to management training programs for alcohol establishments, the resulting training program would need to persuade owners and managers that (1) there could be serious consequences for making an illegal alcohol sale, (2) the benefits of adopting and implementing written alcohol policies far outweigh the potential costs of implementing such policies, and (3) such a program will provide skills to develop effective policies. Many managers and owners currently do not believe they will face any consequences, serious or otherwise, for selling alcohol to underage or intoxicated individuals.[9,24] Also, owners and managers may not have the skills necessary to identify problem areas and policy solutions and to implement establishment policies.

As a result of the lack of theoretically based training programs targeting owners and managers of alcohol outlets, we developed Project ARM: Alcohol Risk Management. This article reports on the Project ARM intervention and an initial evaluation of its effects on service to underage and intoxicated patrons.

Method

Intervention Design

The ARM intervention was composed of five one-on-one consultation sessions for owners and managers of bars. The goal of this project was to work with owners or managers to (1) develop and implement written establishment policies that encourage responsible alcohol sales and (2) inform and discuss new alcohol policies with staff. Consultation sessions and written materials were tailored specifically to each establishment,

allowing each establishment to obtain information most relevant to its structure, location, operations, and clientele. Each consultation session lasted 1 to 2 hours. Sessions were implemented once a week during a 5-week period.

The public health goal of Project ARM was to change those actions of alcohol establishments—sales to minors and sales to patrons already significantly impaired by alcohol—that can lead to death, injury, and damage. However, we recognized that the program might not be attractive to the managers on that basis alone. The program needed to be promoted to alcohol establishments in a different manner to gain the buy-in of bar owners and managers. Focus group discussions with owners and managers of alcohol establishments suggest that owners and managers believe that individual drinkers, not alcohol establishments, should be held responsible for alcohol-related problems.[30] So we designed a program that could answer questions that owners and managers may ask, such as the following: Why should the establishments participate in the program? Why should new establishment policies be developed and enforced? Will these new policies decrease their profits?

Following the behavior change principles outlined above, we identified and emphasized the management's self-interest of decreasing risk and economic loss and minimizing potential liability that results from illegal alcohol sales to underage and intoxicated customers. Our focus group discussions indicated that owners and managers fear lawsuits and decreased alcohol sales.[30] We also provided supportive materials and verbal persuasion to increase their confidence and skills in implementing new alcohol policies in their establishments.

Risk assessment. To facilitate discussions on the need for new establishment policies, ARM consultants showed owners and managers how their establishment compared with similar establishments in terms of (1) potential risk of illegally selling alcohol, (2) methods to slow service of alcohol to prevent patron intoxication, and (3) methods of communication with staff. ARM consultants asked the participating owner or manager at each establishment to complete a 68-item self-administered risk assessment survey. ARM consultants calculated risk scores based on responses to these items and presented the scores to owners and managers. The risk assessment survey included items that assessed both policies and practices.

Policy items on the risk assessment survey measured types of existing establishment policies that affect alcohol sales to underage and obviously intoxicated patrons, customer intoxication, and management communication with staff. For example, we asked whether establishments had policies regarding carding customers, denying service to obviously intoxicated customers, not announcing last call, and attending regular staff meetings. In addition, the survey asked how these policies were communicated to employees. Some establishments develop written policies that are distributed to employees. Other establishments post policies on an employee bulletin board. Still others place policies in files but do not communicate their existence to staff. Some establishments communicate policies orally but do not put the policies in written form. Other establishments may not have any policies at all.

Based on independent ratings by a panel of 10 server training and alcohol policy experts, a priori weights were assigned to each type of policy distribution. Weights were assigned because different forms of distribution of policies may have a differential effect on serving practices in an establishment. Weights for policy distribution were 1 for no policies, 3 for unwritten policies or written policies on file, 4 for written policies that were posted in the establishment, and 5 for written policies that were individually distributed to each employee. These weights assume that having a written policy that has been distributed to all staff may be more effective than an unwritten "policy" that is only shared orally.

The practice items measured frequency of occurrence of an establishment practice, such as how often staff card customers who appear to be younger than age 30, serve an obviously intoxicated customer, or notify incoming staff about the intoxication level of a customer. Establishments may have policies, but the policies may not be well understood or enforced. This could result in establishment practices or behaviors that are very different from those specified by establishment policies. Frequency of each type of practice was measured on a scale from 1 (never) to 5 (always).

Both the policy items and practice items addressed a wide range of issues that could affect responsible service of alcohol in a given establishment—from posting warning signs to not making last call for alcohol to checking age identification. The current research literature indicates that not all policies and practices are equally effective in reducing illegal alcohol sales or alcohol-related problems.[24,25] Therefore, both policy items and practice items were weighted based on a panel of judges' ratings of the likely effectiveness of the policy or practice in reducing the risk of making an illegal alcohol sale or experiencing alcohol-related problems. For example, a policy to post warning signs was judged less effective in reducing sales to underage people than a policy to check all age identification of customers who appear younger than age 30. A priori weightings for judged effectiveness ranged from 0.5 to 2, as determined by the panel of 10 experts.

Weighted responses to the risk assessment survey were summed to create a total risk score (possible range: 126.0 to 551.5), with lower scores indicating higher risk. In addition, risk scores were calculated for each of four subareas: (1) preventing sales to underage people (possible range: 29.5 to 99.0), (2) preventing sales to intoxicated patrons (possible range: 37.5 to 157.5), (3) dealing with intoxicated customers (possible range: 30.5 to 152.5), and (4) communicating with outlet staff (possible range: 28.5 to 142.5). Each of these four indices was developed a priori based on the existing research literature and recommendations of the expert panel. Using baseline data from the five intervention sites and four pilot establishments, we calculated Cronbach's alpha coefficients for each of the indices, and results were encouraging—all coefficients were above 0.90. Caution should be used when interpreting these coefficients, however, since the sample size was small.

ARM consultation sessions. During the first session, the risk assessment survey was administered to the participating owner or manager. In addition, the ARM consultant showed the owner or manager a videotape that included peer testimonials about the benefits of having written establishment policies. The consultant then gave an overview of state alcohol laws and the potential liability that establishments face for an illegal alcohol sale.

The risk assessment scores generated from data gathered in session 1 were used to guide discussions during sessions 2 and 3. The consultant presented the risk scores for the manager's outlet compared with the average risk of other, similar establishments. Using outlet risk scores as a guide, Project ARM consultants recommended up to 19 model alcohol policies. If an establishment's score was elevated in one of the four risk areas, emphasis was placed on adoption of policies that target that area. For example, if an establishment had a higher risk score for sales to underage people than other establishments, the consultant stressed the importance of policies such as checking age identification of everyone younger than age 30. As each policy was discussed, the consultant provided the owner or manager with resource materials that would help with implementation. For instance, a calendar that indicated the date of birth that is the cutoff for a legal alcohol sale was provided to help a server determine if someone is underage.

During session 4, the consultant cofacilitated an establishment staff meeting with the owner or manager. During the staff meeting, the consultant showed the ARM videotape that addressed the importance of policies and reviewed state alcohol laws and liability issues. The owner or manager presented the new establishment policies and asked for input from staff on implementation of these policies. By discussing new policies with the staff before they were finalized, the consultant, along with the owner or manager, attempted to increase the staff's support for and compliance with the new policies.

During session 5, the consultant and the owner or manager discussed changes in any of the selected policies. The *consultant* provided information on how to make the new policies effective, particularly through active monitoring and enforcement. Owners and man-

285 agers were encouraged to arrange server training for their employees and were given a list of local server training programs. The consultant also recommended that regular staff meetings be held to discuss the effec-
290 tiveness of policies and impediments that servers face when trying to responsibly serve alcohol. At the end of session 5, the owner or manager completed the risk assessment survey again. Change in the risk score was an intermediate outcome for the assessment of the ARM program.

Evaluation Design

295   As part of this demonstration project, Project ARM was implemented and evaluated in five bars located in a major metropolitan area. Pre- and postintervention underage and pseudo-intoxicated purchase attempt rates from the five intervention bars were compared
300 with rates in nine matched control bars. All research protocols were approved by the University of Minnesota's Internal Review Board.

    Establishments. We recruited a diverse group of five bars, based on location, customer type, outlet size,
305 and their perceived risk of illegal sales of alcoholic beverages (membership vs. nonmembership in a high-risk insurance pool). Project ARM consultants initiated recruitment through telephone contact followed by face-to-face meetings. Recruitment was targeted to one
310 individual in each outlet whom we identified as having the most influence regarding decision making and policy implementation in that outlet. Participating owners and managers received $300 as an incentive to complete the program. In the five intervention bars, one
315 owner and four managers who had decision-making authority agreed to participate.

    Fifty percent of all establishments contacted agreed to participate. Most owners and managers who declined to participate did so because of perceived lack of
320 need, lack of time, or because of their belief that the risks involved with alcohol sales are unavoidable. The intervention sample included a college bar, a suburban bar, an urban bar, a high-risk bar, and a nightclub located in a suburban entertainment complex. Of the five
325 bars that refused to participate, two were neighborhood bars, two were urban bars, and one was a high-risk bar. All participating bars completed all components of the training program. ARM consultants all had experience in the hospitality industry and were able to build a rela-
330 tionship with each owner or manager. Trainers held all sessions with owners and managers at their establishments and accommodated their schedules to ensure full participation.

    We matched control sites to increase baseline comp-
335 arability in the absence of randomization. Each of the five intervention bars was matched with two control establishments based on similar type and location. One control site was visited only once for data collection because of potential danger to researchers attempting to
340 purchase alcohol, resulting in nine control sites in the

analyses. The resulting study sample consisted of (1) three college bars, serving a primarily young clientele, located adjacent to a university; (2) three suburban bars serving a mixed clientele, including older patrons and
345 families; (3) three urban bars serving a working-class clientele; (4) two high-risk bars; and (5) three nightclubs located in suburban entertainment complexes. All control bars were within 5 miles of the intervention bars; we chose bars in close proximity to decrease the
350 likelihood of differential community-based enforcement across intervention and matched control bars.

    To evaluate the effects of Project ARM on the propensity of participating establishments to sell alcohol illegally, two waves of both pseudo-intoxicated and
355 underage purchase attempts were made in both the pre- and postintervention periods. All purchase attempts were made within 4 to 6 weeks before and after the intervention in each of the five intervention bars and their matched control establishments. All purchase
360 attempts were completed on a Friday or Saturday between 3:00 p.m. and 10:00 p.m. The purchase attempts were balanced in terms of time and day of purchase. Neither intervention nor control bars were aware that these unobtrusive observations were being made; noti-
365 fying the bars about these observations might have artificially reduced the sales rates in all establishments, biasing the results of the study.

    Underage purchase attempts. Six women, ages 18 to 20 years old, were hired to make alcohol purchase
370 attempts (in the state where this project was implemented, it is legal for a bona-fide university-based research team to use underage buyers). To ensure that all buyers looked underage, potential buyers were screened by a panel of 10 individuals; those buyers
375 who appeared 18 or 19 years old were selected for the study. Only female buyers were used to achieve more homogeneity across purchase attempts. All buyers were accompanied by another woman who also appeared to be younger than age 21. Both dressed casually (i.e., did
380 not attempt to appear older) and did not carry age identification. Both team members were trained on research protocol and safety measures and were blinded as to treatment condition.

    During each purchase attempt, the buyer and the
385 companion entered the establishment together and sat at a table. The buyer attempted to purchase an alcoholic drink while the companion ordered a nonalcoholic beverage. If the server asked for age identification, the buyer explained that her identification was in
390 the car. If asked her age, the buyer was instructed to state her real date of birth and, if pushed further, to state her real age. Buyers were instructed not to attempt to persuade the server to serve them alcohol. If service was refused, both team members left the establishment.
395 If served alcohol, the buyer was instructed to leave the establishment without consuming any of the drink. The underage purchase attempt protocol used in this study is well developed, based on a protocol we have used on

hundreds of occasions in other studies.[8,31] Previous studies[8,31] indicate that purchase rates vary by buyer; therefore, we controlled for this "buyer effect" in our analyses.

Pseudo-intoxicated purchase attempts. Pseudo-intoxicated buyers were three male actors ages 30, 34, and 44, specifically hired and trained for this role. Pseudo-intoxicated buyers performed the intoxicated protocol before a panel of judges, which rated the actors' skill at feigning intoxication. The panel consisted of 10 individuals, most of whom had experience in the hospitality industry. The remaining panel members represented the "reasonable person" recognized by law as the standard by which conduct is judged. In addition to the buyer, a staff person served as an observer during each purchase attempt. The observer entered the establishment separately prior to the purchaser, observed the interaction between the server and the pseudo-intoxicated buyer, and recorded a variety of data regarding the purchase attempt and the environment of the establishment.

Pseudo-intoxicated buyers exhibited clear intoxication behaviors (e.g., loss of coordination, fumbling with items in the pocket, acting disoriented) while entering the establishment and then staggered to the bar to find a seat. Before ordering, the buyer asked the server several confused questions while demonstrating slow, slurred speech, inappropriate laughter, and forgetfulness. After asking what kind of beer they serve, the buyer ordered a double vodka. If the buyer's request was refused, he asked for a beer instead. If still refused, the buyer asked for the time and made an excuse to leave. If the buyer was served, he asked twice how much he owed, paid for the drink, and then asked for directions to the restroom where he would leave his drink, untouched. After 5 minutes, the buyer returned to the bar and ordered a second double vodka from the same server while continuing to exhibit drunken behavior. This second purchase attempt provided greater assurance that the server had an opportunity to recognize the intoxication and also facilitated evaluation of whether there would be repeated service to someone who was clearly intoxicated. If the second request was refused, the buyer made an excuse and left. If served the second time, the buyer waited a few minutes, left the drink on the bar, and exited the establishment. If at any time the buyer was asked for identification, he presented his real identification. If asked if he was driving, he said he was meeting someone who would give him a ride. No car keys were displayed. Indications that bar staff or other customers were aware of the buyers' apparent intoxication level were noted by observers at nearly every visit.[32]

The observer left the establishment immediately after the buyer to ensure that the buyer was not at risk for assault. The observer never acknowledged knowing the buyer unless the service or security staff detained the buyer in any way. In such cases, the observer stepped in, pretending to be a friend or relative, and volunteered to take the buyer home. Pseudo-intoxicated buyers were trained to closely follow this protocol. Buyers were blinded to the treatment condition. The pseudo-intoxicated purchase attempt protocol was adapted from a protocol used by McKnight.[33] To decrease potential confounding of an individual actor's ability to feign intoxication, each establishment had the same buyer at baseline and follow-up. Since follow-up purchase attempts occurred 4 to 6 weeks after the baseline purchase attempts, the risk that a buyer would be recognized at an establishment was small. In addition, we controlled for potential buyer effects in all analyses to ensure that any systematic differences by the buyer were not inadvertently attributed to the intervention.

Dependent variables. Two visits were made by an underage buyer to each establishment during each of two survey periods (pretest, posttest), with a single purchase attempt at each visit. One dependent variable was defined from each visit, reflecting whether the underage confederate was able to purchase an alcoholic beverage during that visit (1 = sold, 0 = not sold). In addition, two visits were made by a pseudo-intoxicated buyer to each establishment during each survey period, with up to two separate purchase attempts at each visit. Two dependent variables were defined from the combination of two purchase attempts at each visit. The first focused on whether the pseudo-intoxicated buyer was able to purchase alcohol at least once (1 = ever sold, 0 = never sold). The second focused on whether the pseudo-intoxicated buyer was refused on either attempt (1 = ever refused, 0 = never refused). With 14 establishments (5 intervention, 9 control), 56 observations were available for each dependent variable.

Analyses. The evaluation design of Project ARM was a traditional repeated-measures design with two within-subjects factors and one between-subjects factor.[34] The case or respondent was the alcohol establishment. Period and visit were within-subjects factors because each establishment was observed at each visit and each period. Condition was a between-subjects factor because each establishment was assigned to one condition (intervention treatment vs. control). Condition, period, visit, and their interactions were fixed effects, while establishment was a random effect. The traditional ANOVA model specifies two error terms for this design[34]—here, establishment within conditions and period by visit by establishment within condition. This model is readily extended to an ANCOVA model to allow regression adjustment for covariates.

We fit that model using SAS PROC MIXED, version 6.12,[35] a general mixed-model regression program that is well suited to design and data structures of this kind.[36,37] We included as additional fixed effects the buyer ID, approximate number of patrons in the establishment at the time of the purchase attempt, job category and perceived age of seller, and whether the purchase attempt was made from a table or at the bar. We

Table 1

Recommended Model Policies and Status of Policy by Establishment After the Project Arm Intervention

Recommended Model Policies	Establishment				
	1	2	3	4	5
1. Check identification of customers appearing to be under the age of 30.	Y	M	Y	Y	Y
2. Confiscate false age identification.	Y	Y	M	Y	Y
3. Consider age as a criterion when hiring alcohol servers.	R	R	R	Y	R
4. Monitor all areas of the establishment.	R	R	M	Y	R
5. Limit the number of people coming into your establishment.	Y	R	Y	R	Y
6. Do not offer drink promotions that encourage excessive drinking.	Y	Y	Y	Y	Y
7. Serve only measured drinks.	Y	R	R	Y	R
8. Notify other servers about the status of customers at the end of shift.	Y	Y	Y	Y	Y
9. Do not announce last call; stop service half hour before closing.	Y	M	Y	Y	Y
10. Promote food and nonalcoholic beverages.	Y	R	Y	Y	Y
11. Do not serve obviously intoxicated customers.	Y	Y	Y	Y	R
12. Guarantee 15% gratuity if service is refused and guest doesn't leave a tip.	R	Y	R	M	NA
13. Arrange alternative transportation.	Y	M	Y	Y	Y
14. Record all questionable incidents in an incident log.	Y	Y	M	Y	Y
15. Require annual server training.	Y	Y	Y	Y	M
16. Prohibit drinking on the job.	Y	Y	M	Y	Y
17. Have manager/lead worker on duty at all times.	Y	Y	Y	Y	M
18. Hold regular staff meetings.	Y	Y	Y	Y	Y
19. Distribute written copies of policies to all staff; post policies in visible area.	Y	Y	Y	Y	Y
Total policies adopted	16	14	16	18	14

Note. Y = adopted, R = refused, M = adopted but modified, NA = not applicable to that business.

515 included these variables because we knew from previous research[8,31] that the purchase attempt buy rates vary among buyers and across levels of the other covariates. To the extent that those variables were unevenly distributed across establishments, they would induce con-
520 founding if ignored; to the extent that they were balanced across the establishments, they would reduce power if ignored. Each analysis employed a two-tailed Type I error rate of 5%, and no correction was made for multiple testing because there were only three de-
525 pendent variables and because we had a priori expectations for each.

Because the MIXED procedure assumed that the residual errors are distributed normally, we repeated the final model using the SAS GLIMMIX macro. This
530 analysis provided a logistic regression equivalent to the ANCOVA model fit by MIXED and so avoided any question about the normality of errors assumption that is attached to the ANCOVA model. For each dependent variable, the results from the mixed-model logistic
535 regression analysis were equivalent to those from the ANCOVA model; because most readers will be more familiar with the ANCOVA model and its results, we present only the results from the ANCOVA.

We present the adjusted means for each dependent
540 variable later in Table 3. Intervention effects were estimated as the adjusted net difference among the four condition means for each dependent variable: net change = $(I_{\text{follow-up}} - I_{\text{baseline}}) - (C_{\text{follow-up}} - C_{\text{baseline}})$. Results are also presented in terms of relative change:
545 relative change = (net change/I_{baseline}) • 100.

Results

Intermediate outcomes. Prior to Project ARM, only two of the five bars had established any written alcohol policies. One outlet had two and the other seven written policies at baseline. Following management train-
550 ing, all five bars had written policies, adopting 14 to 18 of the 19 model policies (or modified versions of a model policy; see Table 1). Before adopting a policy, some bars worked with the ARM consultants to modify a recommended policy to fit the individual establish-
555 ment. For example, one bar adopted a policy to check age identification of people appearing younger than 25 rather than 30. While we preferred policies to be adopted as we had written them, we determined it was preferable that managers adopt a modified version of a
560 policy, moving toward more control over alcohol service, than to not take any action at all. Some bars chose not to adopt certain policies, such as the policy to serve only measured drinks, because they believed they would lose business. Two bars adopted 18 of the 19
565 model policies, the exception being the policy related to the minimum age of server. Most bars did not want to consider age when hiring alcohol servers because they depend on 18- to 20-year-olds to staff their estab-

211

Table 2

Average Prerisk/Postrisk Scores for Intervention Outlets

	Prerisk		Postrisk	
	Mean	Standard Deviation	Mean	Standard Deviation
Overall risk	332.6	74.9	431.1	30.2
Sales to underage customers	72.9	10.5	84.5	8.1
Preventing intoxication	79.0	13.3	109.6	15.0
Handling intoxication	99.2	25.7	125.3	4.0
Staffing and communication	81.5	32.2	111.7	19.4

Note. Higher score equals lower risk.

lishments and felt that this policy may be viewed as age discrimination.

Mean risk scores across intervention bars improved after the Project ARM training, suggesting a decrease in risk of illegal alcohol sales (see Table 2). Aggregate mean scores for each of the four subcategories—sales to the underage customers, preventing intoxication, handling intoxication, and staffing and communication—also changed in the expected direction after the intervention.

Purchase attempt results. Underage purchase rates within the two conditions were similar at baseline (intervention [I] = 46.0%, control [C] = 48.0%). Following the intervention, the purchase rate went up slightly in the control condition (to 49.4%) and down in the intervention condition (to 42.0%). The 11.5% relative decrease was in the hypothesized direction but not statistically significant (see Table 3).

A similar pattern was observed for sales to pseudo-intoxicated buyers. At baseline, the pseudo-intoxicated purchase rates for the first purchase attempt were comparable, although the controls were slightly higher (I = 68.4%, C = 70.1%). Following the intervention, the pseudo-intoxicated purchase rate was slightly higher in the control condition (72.9%) and substantially lower in the intervention condition (40.0%). The 45.8% relative decline was in the hypothesized direction; however, given the small sample size, the result was not statistically significant.

The baseline rate for refusals to pseudo-intoxicated buyers on either the first or second purchase attempt was much higher in the intervention than the control bars (I = 83.1%, C = 63.0%). The refusal rate in the intervention bars decreased slightly to 80.3% but decreased much more in the control establishments at follow-up (54.8%). As a result, the 6.5% relative change was in the expected direction.

Discussion

Since this was a demonstration project, the goal was to develop the intervention program and conduct preliminary testing to see whether the program was feasible, was well received by participants, and held promise of being able to change serving practices. Process evaluation data indicate that owners and managers enjoyed and valued participation in Project ARM. Outlet employees also expressed appreciation for Project ARM, indicating they liked having clear rules about what is acceptable or not in terms of serving alcohol to underage or intoxicated customers.

Project ARM was effective in changing establishment policies. Fourteen to 18 of the model policies were adopted in each of the five intervention bars. Each of the participating owners and managers orally introduced and discussed the selected policies with their staff and provided each staff person with a written copy of these policies.

The main results of this demonstration project are encouraging. Although not statistically significant, we observed a net change in the hypothesized direction for all three outcome variables. Compared with control establishments, bars that participated in the ARM consultation program sold alcohol to project buyers less often. Significant differences were not expected because the sample size was small, limiting the statistical power of this demonstration effort.

To achieve statistical significance for the observed relative decrease of 45.8% for pseudo-intoxicated buys, we would need participation of 20 bars per condition (i.e., 20 intervention and 20 control). To reach statistical significance for a decrease in sales to underage buyers, we would have needed 830 bars per condition. The magnitude of observed effects suggests that Project ARM may be effective in preventing sales to obviously intoxicated patrons but is less likely to affect sales to underage people.

Project ARM may be more successful in reducing sales to obviously intoxicated patrons than underage individuals for several reasons. First, intoxicated customers may be more common in bars than underage purchasers, making discussions of sales to intoxicated individuals more salient. Second, intoxication may be more easily identifiable than age. Our pseudo-intoxicated buyers were instructed to act out clear and obvious signs of substantial intoxication, such as slurred speech and staggered walking. Skills needed to identify these signs may be much easier to develop than judging whether an individual is potentially underage. A standard recommendation is to check age identification of anyone who appears younger than age

Table 3
Results of Repeated ANCOVA Analyses of Effect of Intervention on Alcohol Service Behavior

Outcome Measure	Intervention Pre (%)	Intervention Post (%)	Control Pre (%)	Control Post (%)	Net Difference	Relative Change	Standard Error	t-Ratio	p Value
Ever sold to underage	46.0	42.0	48.0	49.4	-5.3	-11.5	0.30	-0.18	0.86
Ever sold to pseudo-intoxicated	68.4	40.0	70.1	72.9	-31.3	-45.8	0.27	-1.17	0.27
Ever refused pseudo-intoxicated	83.1	80.3	63.0	54.8	5.4	6.5	0.22	0.24	0.81

30. Servers may need more skills to identify signs of age or more external pressure from their management or the community to ask for age identification.

While the ARM intervention may be promising for decreasing sales to intoxicated customers, the intervention did not substantially alter the rate of refusals to pseudo-intoxicated purchasers on the first or second purchase attempt. One explanation for this may be that the baseline rate of ever being refused was quite high in the intervention bars (83%), so there may have been a ceiling effect. The fact that intervention bars were more likely to refuse alcohol sales to the pseudo-intoxicated buyers on the first or second purchase attempt than control bars, even at baseline, may reflect a selection bias artifact. However, control bars were very similar to intervention bars at baseline in terms of implemented alcohol policies and illegal sales rates.

The interpretation and generalizability of these results are limited by threats of selection bias introduced from two design limitations. First, only half of the establishments we contacted agreed to participate in the program. Although the establishments that refused to participate were similar in terms of type to those that agreed to participate, we do not know if nonparticipants differed in other important ways that could influence the effectiveness of the program.

Second, establishments were not randomly assigned to condition. Intervention bars may have been more concerned about responsible serving practices than control establishments, even at baseline. However, the intervention outlets had few written alcohol service policies prior to the intervention and were similar to the controls in terms of two of the three outcomes—sales to underage and sales to pseudo-intoxicated patrons. In addition, control bars were matched to intervention bars on size and location of outlet to increase baseline similarity.

Implications for Practice

An important issue for both researchers and practitioners is how to increase participation rates. Assuming that a program such as Project ARM can reduce illegal alcohol sales, practitioners need to have as many estab-lishments as possible participate in the program to substantially prevent illegal sales in a community. Establishments may resist participation in this type of program for several reasons, including lack of time and belief that they do not have a problem. Many establishments may also distrust organizations that are not part of the hospitality industry or feel that alcohol establishments are being unfairly targeted.

One way to increase participation may be to develop an effective program that takes less time to complete. Another is to increase credibility and trust by hiring consultants or trainers who have experience in the hospitality industry, such as former bartenders and servers. Offering incentives may also increase participation rates; however, despite being offered $300, only half of the outlets we contacted agreed to participate. When developing and marketing a program, it is also important to consider the self-interest of the manager and owner. They want a program that will help them run a better business—decreasing risk of problems while maintaining profits. On completion of the program, all of the participants indicated that given the value of information provided in the program, they would have completed the program even without incentive money.

It should be noted that in the "real world," the ARM intervention would most likely be implemented within a context of increased community concern about alcohol problems, stepped-up enforcement levels, and other conditions that would motivate outlets to participate in a training program. Some outlets may be motivated to participate in a training program and to comply with laws out of concern about preventing alcohol-related problems. Others, however, may only be motivated to participate because of active enforcement efforts and community pressure to comply.

Community enforcement efforts and interventions such as ARM may complement each other. Implementing the ARM intervention in the context of increased enforcement levels and community pressures may increase the effectiveness of the program by increasing participation rates and motivating owners and managers to encourage responsible service of alcohol among their staff. Interventions such as ARM may help with enforcement efforts by increasing the political feasibility of making enforcement actions against alcohol retailers.

745   Despite limitations, results of this demonstration project are encouraging for practitioners and researchers. Studies of other training programs have shown limited effects on illegal alcohol sales. A program de-
750 veloped from key behavior change principles that specifically targets owners and managers of alcohol establishments (rather than service staff) may prevent illegal alcohol sales to obviously intoxicated patrons. However, a larger randomized trial is needed to fully determine the effectiveness of this type of program. In addi-
755 tion, further research is needed to assess the long-term effects of Project ARM. In the current study, follow-up purchase attempts were completed within 4 to 6 weeks of the completion of the intervention. Effects of the program may increase or diminish over time, depend-
760 ing on the level of commitment to and enforcement of the policies by outlet management.

References

1 Baker SP, O'Neill B, Ginsburg MJ, Li G: *The Injury Fact Book* (2nd ed.). New York, Oxford University Press, 1992.

2 Hayward L, Zubrick SR, Silburn S: Blood alcohol levels in suicide cases. *J Epidemiol Community Health* 46:256–260, 1992.

3 Roizen J: Estimating alcohol involvement in serious events, in: *Alcohol and Health Monograph 1: Alcohol Consumption and Related Problems*. Washington, DC, Government Printing Office, 1982, pp. 179–219.

4 Roizen J: Issues in the epidemiology of alcohol and violence, in: Martin SE (ed.): *Alcohol and Interpersonal Violence, Monograph 24: Fostering Multidisciplinary Perspectives*. Washington, DC, Government Printing Office, 1993, pp. 3–36.

5 Leigh BC: The relationship of substance use during sex to high-risk sexual behavior. *J Sex Res* 27(2):199–213, 1990.

6 Stall R, Wiley JA, McKusick L, Coates TJ, Ostrow D: Alcohol and drug use during sexual activity and compliance with safe sex guidelines for AIDS. *Hlth Educ Q* 13:359–371, 1986.

7 Edwards G, Anderson P, Babor TF, Cassell S, Ferrence R, Giesbrecht N, et al: *Alcohol Policy and the Public Good*. New York, Oxford University Press, 1994.

8 Forster JL, Murray DM, Wolfson M, Wagenaar AC: Commercial availability of alcohol to young people: Results of alcohol purchase attempts. *Prev Med* 24:342–347, 1995.

9 McKnight AJ, Streff FM: The effect of enforcement upon service of alcohol to intoxicated patrons of bars and restaurants. *Accid Anal Prev* 26(1):79–88, 1994.

10 Preusser DF, Williams AF: Sales of alcohol to underage purchasers in three New York counties and Washington, D.C. *J Pub Hlth Policy* 13(3):306–317, 1992.

11 Foss RD, Perrine MW, Myers AM, Musty RE, Voas RB: A roadside survey in the computer age, in Perrine MW (ed.): *International Committee on Alcohol, Drugs, and Traffic Safety—T-89*. Chicago, National Safety Council, 1990.

12 O'Donnel M: Research on drinking locations of alcohol impaired drivers: Implementations for prevention policies. *J Pub Hlth Policy* 6(4):510–525, 1985.

13 Saltz RF: The roles of bars and restaurants in preventing alcohol-impaired driving: An evaluation of server intervention. *Eval Hlth Professions* 10:5–28, 1987.

14 Toomey TL, Kilian GR, Gehan JP, Wagenaar AC, Perry CL, Jones-Webb R: Qualitative assessment of responsible alcohol service training programs. *Pub Hlth Rep* 113(2):62–169, 1998.

15 Gliksman L, Single E: *A Field Evaluation of a Server Intervention Program: Accommodating Reality*. Paper presented at the Canadian Evaluation Society Meetings, Montreal, Canada, May 1988.

16 Howard-Pitney B, Johnson MD, Altman DG, Hopkins R, Hammond N: Responsible alcohol service: A study of server, manager, and environmental impact. *Am J Pub Health* 81(2):197–199, 1991.

17 McKnight AJ: *An Evaluation of a Host Responsibility Program*. Washington, DC, U.S. Department of Transportation, National Highway Traffic Safety Administration, 1987.

18 McKnight AJ: Factors influencing the effectiveness of server-intervention education. *J Stud Alcohol* 52(5):389–397, 1991.

19 Molof MJ, Kimball C: *A Study of the Implementation and Effects of Oregon's Mandatory Alcohol Server Training Program*. Eugene, OR, Integrated Research Services, 1994.

20 Russ NW, Geller ES: Training bar personnel to prevent drunken driving: A field evaluation. *Am J Public Health* 77:952–954, 1987.

21 Holder HD, Wagenaar AC: Mandated server training and reduced alcohol-involved traffic crashes: A time series analysis of the Oregon experience. *Accid Anal Prev* 26(l):89–97, 1994.

22 National Highway Traffic Safety Administration: *TEAM: Techniques of Effective Alcohol Management: Findings from the First Year*. Washington, DC, Department of Transportation, 1986.

23 Saltz RF: Where we are in the evaluation of responsible beverage service program evaluations. *Alcohol Drugs Driving* 10(3-4):277–285, 1994.

24 Wolfson M, Toomey TL, Forster JL, Murray DM, Wagenaar AC: Alcohol outlet policies and practices concerning sales to underage people. *Addiction* 91(4):589–602, 1996.

25 Wolfson M, Toomey TL, Forster JL, Wagenaar AC, McGovern PG, Perry CL: Characteristics, policies and practices of alcohol outlets and sales to underage persons. *J Stud Alcohol* 57:670–674, 1996.

26 Glanz K, Lewis FM, Rimer BK (eds.): *Health Behavior and Health Education*. San Francisco, Jossey-Bass, 1997.

27 Bandura A (ed.): *Social Learning Theory*. Englewood Cliffs, NJ, Prentice Hall, 1977.

28 Green LW, Kreuter MW: *Health Promotion Planning: An Educational and Environmental Approach*. Mountain View, CA, Mayfield, 1991.

29 Rosenstock IM, Strecher VJ, Becker MH: Social learning theory and the health belief model. *Hlth Edu Q* 15(2):175–183, 1988.

30 Gehan JP, Toomey TL, Jones-Webb R, Rothstein C, Wagenaar AC: Alcohol outlet workers and managers: Focus groups on responsible service practices. *J Alcohol & Drug Ed*, 44(2): 60–71, 1999.

31 Forster JL, McGovern P, Wagenaar AC, Wolfson M, Perry CL, Anstine P: The ability of young people to purchase alcohol without age identification. *Addiction* 89:699–705, 1994.

32 Toomey TL, Wagenaar AC, Kilian GR, Fitch OB, Rothstein C, Fletcher L: Alcohol sales to pseudo-intoxicated bar patrons. *Pub Hlth Rep* 114(4):337–342, 1999.

33 McKnight AJ: *Development and Field Test of a Responsible Alcohol Service Program: Vol. III. Final Results*. Washington, DC, U.S. Department of Transportation, National Highway Traffic Safety Administration, 1989.

34 Winer BJ, Brown DR, Michels K: *Statistical Principles in Experimental Design*. New York, McGraw-Hill, 1991.

35 SAS Institute: *SAS/STAT Software: Changes and Enhancements Through Release 6.1.2*. Cary, NC, SAS Institute, 1997.

36 Little RC, Milliken GA, Stroup WW, Wolfinger RD: *SAS System for MIXED Models*. Cary, NC, SAS Institute, 1996.

37 Murray DM: *Design and Analysis of Group-Randomized Trials*. New York, Oxford University Press, 1998.

About the authors: Traci L. Toomey, Alexander C. Wagenaar, Gudrun Kilian, and Cheryl L. Perry are with the Division of Epidemiology, University of Minnesota, Minneapolis. John P. Gehan is with Policy and Communications, St. Paul, Minnesota. David M. Murray is with the Department of Psychology, University of Memphis, Tennessee.

Address correspondence to: Traci L. Toomey, Ph.D., Division of Epidemiology, University of Minnesota, 1300 South 2nd Street, Ste. 300, Minneapolis, MN 55454-1015. Phone: (612) 626-9070; fax: (612) 624-0315. E-mail: toomey@epi.umn.edu

Acknowledgments: Preparation of this article was assisted by a grant from the Robert Wood Johnson Foundation, Princeton, NJ (grant 028812; Alexander C. Wagenaar, principal investigator). A project of this nature could not be accomplished without the hard work and cooperation of many people. We thank Gudrun R. Kilian and Orville (Bud) Fitch II for helping with the development and implementation of the intervention; Linda Fletcher for coordinating field data collection; Rebecca Mitchell for editing; and finally, the owners and managers who participated in the program. We also thank our colleagues James Mosher, James Peters, and Miles Canning for their valuable comments.

Exercise for Article 31

Factual Questions

1. The review of 22 local and national server training programs revealed how many that exclusively targeted owners and managers?

2. The researchers' focus group discussions indicated that owners and managers feared what two things?

3. During which one of the ARM consultation sessions did staff meet with the owner/manager?

4. Most of the owners and managers who declined to participate in this project did so because of what?

5. Were the underage buyers instructed to attempt to persuade the server to serve them alcohol?

6. The pre-intervention percentage for "Ever sold to pseudo-intoxicated" was 68.4%. What was the post-intervention percentage?

7. The researchers found changes in the hypothesized direction for all three outcome measures. Were these changes statistically significant?

Questions for Discussion

8. The underage purchase attempts were all made by females. Note that this simplified the study since gender of purchaser did not need to be considered in the analysis (i.e., results for females did not need to be compared to results for males). In your opinion, did this simplification impact the validity of the study? Explain.

9. The underage buyers were "blinded" to the treatment condition, that is, they were not told which bars had the intervention and which were the control bars. Is this an important feature of this study? Explain. (See lines 459–460.)

10. The researchers point out that the generalizability of the results is limited because only half the establishments they contacted agreed to participate in the program. In your opinion, is this an important limitation? Explain.

11. The researchers note that the failure to randomly assign bars to conditions is a limitation of this study. Do you agree? Explain. (See lines 683–693.)

12. The researchers call for larger studies that cover a longer time span. Do you think this would be worthwhile? Why? Why not? (See lines 752–761.)

Quality Ratings

Directions: Indicate your level of agreement with each of the following statements by circling a number from 5 for strongly agree (SA) to 1 for strongly disagree (SD). If you believe an item is not applicable to this research article, leave it blank. Be prepared to explain your ratings.

A. The introduction establishes the importance of the study.

SA   5   4   3   2   1   SD

B. The literature review establishes the context for the study.

SA   5   4   3   2   1   SD

C. The research purpose, question, or hypothesis is clearly stated.

SA   5   4   3   2   1   SD

D. The method of sampling is sound.

SA   5   4   3   2   1   SD

E. Relevant demographics (for example, age, gender, and ethnicity) are described.

SA   5   4   3   2   1   SD

F. Measurement procedures are adequate.

SA   5   4   3   2   1   SD

G. All procedures have been described in sufficient detail to permit a replication of the study.

SA   5   4   3   2   1   SD

H. The participants have been adequately protected from potential harm.

SA   5   4   3   2   1   SD

I. The results are clearly described.

SA   5   4   3   2   1   SD

J. The discussion/conclusion is appropriate.

SA   5   4   3   2   1   SD

K. Despite any flaws, the report is worthy of publication.

SA   5   4   3   2   1   SD

Article 32

Effects of Distraction on Children's Pain and Distress During Medical Procedures: A Meta-Analysis

Charmaine Kleiber
University of Iowa

Dennis C. Harper
University of Iowa

ABSTRACT.

Background: It is difficult to determine the usefulness of distraction to decrease children's distress behavior and pain during medical procedures because many studies use very small samples and report inconsistent findings.

Objectives: To investigate the mean effect sizes across studies for the effects of distraction on young children's distress behavior and self-reported pain during medical procedures.

Method: Hunter and Schmidt's (1990) procedures were used to analyze 16 studies (total *n* = 491) on children's distress behavior and 10 studies (total *n* = 535) on children's pain.

Results: For distress behavior, the mean effect size was 0.33 (±0.17), with 74% of the variance accounted for by sampling and measurement error. For pain, the mean effect size was 0.62 (±0.42) with 35% of the variance accounted for. Analysis of studies on pain that limited the sample to children 7 years of age or younger (total *n* = 286) increased the amount of explained variance to 60%.

Conclusions: Distraction had a positive effect on children's distress behavior across the populations represented in this study. The effect of distraction on children's self-reported pain is influenced by moderator variables. Controlling for age and type of painful procedure significantly increased the amount of explained variance, but there are other unidentified moderators at work.

From *Nursing Research*, 48(1), 44–49. Copyright © 1999 by Lippincott Williams & Wilkins, Inc. Reprinted with permission.

Children consistently name invasive medical procedures as the cause of the most painful experiences (Hester, 1993). Younger children are particularly in need of intervention because they report more pain
5   (Lander & Fowler-Kerry, 1991; Vessey, Carlson, & McGill, 1994) and display more behavioral distress during medical procedures (Dahlquist, Power, Cox, & Fernbach, 1994; Humphrey, Boon, van Linden van den Heuvell, & van de Wiel, 1992; Jay, Ozolins, Elliott, &
10   Caldwell, 1983; Katz, Kellerman, & Siegel, 1980). One of the most frequently used nonpharmacological interventions for acute pain management is distracting the child's attention away from the medical procedure (McCarthy, Cool, Petersen, & Bruene, 1996). How-
15   ever, the results of research on the effects of distraction are mixed. In a review of the literature completed by these authors, 33% of the studies on distraction and distress behavior reported statistically insignificant results, and 75% of the studies on distraction and pain
20   reported insignificant results. It is unknown whether the statistical insignificance was due to small sample sizes, small effect sizes, or the variability in the effectiveness of distraction. This study investigates the effect of distraction on children's distress behavior and
25   self-reported pain across study populations, using meta-analysis methodology to control for sample size.

Relevant Literature

Distraction is a class of cognitive coping strategies that divert attention from a noxious stimulus through passively redirecting the subject's attention or by ac-
30   tively involving the subject in the performance of a distractor task (Fernandez, 1986). Thus, distraction involves the *cognition*, expectancies, or appraisals of an individual, and results in a modification of the individual's behavior. According to McCaul and Malott
35   (1984), distraction affects pain perception because: (a) pain perception is partially a cognitively controlled process; and (b) distraction consumes part of an individual's finite attentional capabilities, leaving less attention or focus available to perceive pain.
40   McGrath (1991) suggests that distraction affects the perception of pain because it directly interferes with neuronal activity associated with pain. The *gate control* theory of pain (Melzack & Wall, 1965; Wall, 1978) suggests that pain is modulated by a gating mechanism
45   that opens and closes nerve impulses to the brain. The gating mechanism is influenced by cognitive processes, such as attention to the noxious stimuli. The relationship between cognitive processes and the perception of pain has been questioned by others, however. Willis &
50   Coggeshall (1991) suggest that there may be dual neu-

ronal pathways for the sensation of pain and the reaction to pain, and cite studies reporting that patients who have had frontal lobotomy feel pain but are not "concerned" by it, and that patients who have had spinal
55 transection do not feel pain but continue to have a vigorous flexor response to painful stimuli. In a descriptive study of pain after major surgery, Beyer, McGrath, and Berde (1990) found discordance between the intensity of children's perceived pain and behavioral reac-
60 tions to pain. The relationships between pain stimulation, pain-related behavior, and perceived pain are probably more complex than previously thought.

Some researchers use distress behaviors (e.g., crying, moaning, fighting, and verbal resistance) as a
65 proxy for pain. However, behavior can be influenced by many things other than pain (e.g., fear, anxiety, and temperament). Therefore, the research on the use of distraction with children during medical procedures should be explored and judged for its separate effects
70 on pain and on behavioral distress, as put forth in this analysis.

The purpose of this analysis is to quantitatively estimate the effect of distraction interventions on young children's perceived pain and observed distress behav-
75 ior during medical procedures. The research questions are: (a) What are the average effect sizes for pain and distress behavior among the studies included in the analysis?; (b) What is the variability among the effect sizes?; and (c) How much of the observed variance is
80 due to sampling and measurement error?

Method

Sample

Standard search procedures were used to locate published and unpublished studies. Electronic databases searched were Cancerlit (1992–August 1996), Healthstar (1994–September 1996), Medline (1966–
85 October 1996), and CINAHL (1982–August 1996), using the key terms *pain, distraction, imagery,* and *attention,* and was limited to the age group *infant to 12 years* and to the *English* language. A hand search of the CINAHL database from 1970 to 1982 was conducted
90 using the key terms *pain* and *children.* Additional sources included the Psychology Database at the University of Iowa libraries (containing journal articles from 1967 to October 1996 and book chapters from 1967 to 1980 and 1987 to 1996); the Periodical Ab-
95 stracts Database (indexing articles from 1,600 common journals from 1986 to 1996); ERIC (an index of education-related literature); and Wilson Database (WLS). The search strategy for those databases included the keywords *imagery* or *imagination, attention, distrac-*
100 *tion, pain,* and *child age* group. Unpublished studies were discovered by searching the Dissertation Abstracts database for 1961 to 1996 using an intentionally broad search strategy with the keywords *child* and *pain* or *distraction* or *distress.* Although this strategy cap-
105 tured a large number of studies, very few of them dealt with medical procedures. Reference lists accompanying research and review articles on children and pain were scanned for any studies missed through the database searches. The searches resulted in a large number
110 of citations for initial screening: 192 from Medline; 784 from Dissertation Abstracts; and 136 from the psychological databases.

Study Selection

The inclusion criteria were: (a) mean age of subjects was under 12 years; (b) study designs were ran-
115 domized clinical trials (RCT) or repeated measures (RM) designs; (c) means and standard deviations (*SD*s) for both control and experimental conditions were available for the outcome variables *self-reported pain* or *observed behavioral distress*; and (d) distraction was
120 the intervention. For the purposes of this analysis, distraction was defined as *any intervention intended to focus the subject's attention away from pain or discomfort.*

Nineteen studies (see Table 1) met all of the inclu-
125 sion criteria. Seventeen studies included published means and *SD*s and two authors (S. Arts, personal communication, May 12, 1997; R. Blount, personal communication, June 2, 1997) provided the unpublished statistics. An additional eight authors, whose
130 published works were missing group means and *SD*s, either did not have the information available or did not respond to inquiries.

Hunter and Schmidt's (1990) method for meta-analysis differs from some other methods in that the
135 individual results of studies are not weighted according to the methodological strength of the research. This method argues that all relevant studies should be retained to provide the largest possible database. Methodological inadequacies should be considered if theo-
140 retically plausible moderator variables fail to account for unexplained variance.

Study Descriptions

The studies used in the meta-analyses are summarized in Table 1. The mean age for subjects was 6.6
145 years, with a range of 3 to 15 years. The medical procedures varied in complexity and painfulness. The rationale for accepting studies with varying procedures was that this was an effort to sample the universe of painful experiences that children encounter. Therefore,
150 the intensity of the medical procedure experience was not restricted through the choice of studies included in the analysis.

The distraction interventions (independent variable) varied in complexity, from simple things that could be
155 manipulated, such as a kaleidoscope, to a package of distraction techniques that included concentrating on breathing, imagery, and nonprocedural talk. The consistent intent of the distraction interventions was to divert the child's attention away from the medical procedure.

217

Table 1
Effects of Distraction on Children's Self-reported Pain and Observed Distress Behavior

Author	Year	Design	Total N	Mean Age (years)	Age Range	Procedure	Control Condition	Experimental Treatment Condition	Pain Scale	Pain Effect Size	Distress Scale	Distress Effect Size
Arts	1994	RCT	80	9.7	4–12	Intravenous (IV) before surgery	Placebo cream at IV site	Music via earphones	FACES	+.04347	Global Distress Scale	+.06666
Blount	1992	RCT	60	5	3–7	Injection (well child)	Usual treatment	Distraction with party blower	FACES	+.12121	OSBD	-.20905
Broome	1992	RM	14	6.6	3–15	Bone marrow aspiration or lumbar puncture (BMA/LP)	Usual treatment	Imagery, breathing, rehearsal	FACES	-.90275	OSBD	-.214285
Gonzalez	1993	RCT	28	4.7	3–7	Injection (well child)	Usual treatment	Nonprocedural talk by parent	OUCHER	-.86890	OSBD	-.87363
Manne	1990	RCT	23	4.7	3–9	Venipuncture (oncology)	Usual treatment	Distraction with party blower	FACES	-1.50710	PBRS	-.72607
Smith	1996	RM	27	4.5	3–8	Venipuncture (hematology or oncology)	Usual treatment	Distraction using a toy	Child's Global Rating Scale	-.31679	OSBD	+.07117
Vessey	1994	RCT	100	7.4	3–12	Venipuncture (well child)	Usual treatment	Distraction with kaleidoscope	FACES	-.65404	CHEOPS	-.44490
Fowler-Kerry	1987	RCT	160	5.5	4–7	Injection (well child)	Usual treatment	Music via earphones	VAS	-.51333	NA	NA
McGrath	1986	RM	15	7.6	3–11	BMA/LP	Usual treatment	Imagery, breathing, nonprocedural talk, and concentrating	VAS	-1.35980	NA	NA
Smith	1989	RCT	28	10.75	6–18	BMA/LP	Sensory information	Nonprocedural talk by a professional	VAS	+.07710	NA	NA
Elliot	1983	RM	4	8.2	5–12	Burn treatment	Usual treatment	Distraction, relaxing images, reinforcement	NA	NA	Burn Treatment Distress Scale	-.81554
Foertsch[a]	1992	RM	13	5.8	3–12	Burn treatment	Usual treatment	Imagery	NA	NA	OSBD	-.21318
Jay	1985	RM	5	4.5	3–7	BMA/LP	Usual treatment	Imagery, reinforcement	NA	NA	OSBD	-1.07331
Olsen[a]	1991	Sequential	60	6.9	4–9	Venipuncture (general pediatrics)	Usual treatment	Story via headphones	NA	NA	Child Behavior Observation Code	-.72607
Powers	1993	RM	4	4	3–5	Venipuncture (hematology, oncology)	Usual treatment	Distraction and breathing	NA	NA	OSBD	-.660
Schur[a]	1986	RM	17	4.9	4–9	BMA/LP	Usual treatment	Music with headphones	NA	NA	OSBD	-.67270
Stark	1989	RM	4	5.4	4–7	Dentistry procedure	Usual treatment	Distraction with story and poster	NA	NA	Anxiety and Disruptive Behavior Code	-.3123
Winborn[a]	1987	RCT	20	6.9	4–9	Dental procedure	Usual treatment	Distraction with music	NA	NA	BRPS	-.25721
Zabin[a]	1982	RCT	32	7.8	6–11	Venipuncture or finger stick (general pediatrics)	Cartoon before procedure	Cartoon during procedure	NA	NA	Total Disruptive Behavior	+.18202

[a] Unpublished dissertation.

NA = not applicable; RCT = randomized clinical trial, independent control and experimental groups; RM = repeated measures, one group measured at baseline and in experimental condition; OSBD = Observation Scale of Behavioral Distress; CHEOPS = Children's Hospital of Eastern Ontario Pain Scale; PBRS = Procedural Behavior Rating Scale; BRPS = Behavioral Rating Profile Scale.

160   The self-reported pain measures used in these studies are generally visual one-item scales. Most of the behavioral distress scales used in these studies are adaptations of the Behavior Rating Profile Scale created by Melamed (Melamed, Hawes, Heiby, & Glick,
165   1975). Behaviors such as crying, whining, grimacing, and thrashing were coded as either present or absent at varying intervals throughout the procedure and a final total score was given for behavioral distress.

Meta-Analysis Procedure

    An effect size statistic (*d*) for each study was com-
170   puted directly from means and *SD*s. Cohen's (1977) formula for *d* ([mean of experimental condition – mean of control condition)/pooled group *SD*] was used for RCT design studies. For RM studies, the denominator of the equation was the control condition *SD* (Hunter &
175   Schmidt, 1990, p. 352). Reported means and *SD*s were always used for calculating *d* when available, which was the case for 14 studies. One study reported results in logged form; the numbers were anti-logged for use in this analysis. Four studies reported results in graphic
180   form. The authors of this review independently transformed graphed data into numeric data. One hundred percent agreement was reached on the transformed numbers. Means and *SD*s were then calculated for each study.
185   Hunter and Schmidt's (1990) meta-analytic technique was used to calculate the mean effect size weighted by sample size

$$(\overline{d} = \frac{\Sigma[nidi]}{\Sigma\,ni});$$

the observed variance of the *d* values

190
$$(S^2{}_d = \frac{\Sigma[ni(di - \overline{d})^2]}{\Sigma\,ni});$$

and sampling error.

$$(S^2{}_{ed} = \left\{\frac{n-1}{n-3}\right\} \frac{4[1+\frac{\overline{d}^2}{8}]}{n}$$

For studies with RM dependent group designs, a different formula

195
$$(S^2{}_{ed} = \frac{2(1-r)}{n} + \frac{\overline{d}^2}{2n})$$

was used to calculate sampling error because it is affected by the correlation between pretest and post-test scores (Becker, 1988). When the size of the correlation between the scores is unknown, the relationship can be
200   estimated from data given in the studies (Dunlap, Cortina, Vaslow, & Burke, 1996). Seventeen sets of baseline and control condition scores for 17 children reported in the studies by Elliott and Olson (1983); Jay, Elliott, Ozolins, Olson, and Pruitt (1985); Powers,
205   Blount, Bachanas, Cotter, and Swan (1993); and Stark

et al. (1989) were used to calculate a correlation coefficient (*r* = .55).

    Correction for measurement error was accomplished through procedures described by Hunter and
210   Schmidt (1990, pp. 313–316). Because none of the studies in this analysis reported reliability for self-reported pain, previous studies of parallel forms reliability for self-report of pain in children 3–7 years old were used to estimate measurement error. Beyer,
215   McGrath, and Berde (1990) reported correlations ranging from .87 to .98 between the Oucher Scale and a chromatic visual analogue scale. Keck, Gerkensmeyer, Joyce, and Schade (1996) reported a correlation of .63 for children's ratings on the FACES and a word
220   graphic visual analogue scale. Reliabilities for behavioral scales are usually determined with interrater agreement percentages, using number of agreements divided by total number of observations, or Cohen's kappa statistic. Jay, Elliott, Katz, and Siegel (1987)
225   reported an interrater reliability of .98 for the Observed Scale of Behavioral Distress (OSBD). Manne et al. (1990) reported a mean kappa coefficient of .86 for the items in the Procedure Behavior Rating Scale (PBRS).

Results

    The results are reported in Table 2. The effect sizes
230   for both pain and behavioral distress had negative signs, meaning that distraction decreased self-reported pain and observed distress behavior. Because readers are used to thinking of beneficial effects as positive, the absolute values of the effect sizes are used in this
235   report.

Pain

    The average effect size (absolute value) for the 535 children who reported on perceived pain was 0.62 (±0.42), indicating that the mean pain score for chil-
240   dren who received distraction was more than half of one standard deviation below the mean pain score for the control group. The large *SD* of $\overline{d}$ and the wide credibility interval indicate that there is some variability in children's responses to the distraction intervention. The percent of variance accounted for by sam-
245   pling error alone is calculated as 30.58%. Measurement error accounted for another 4.3% of the variance.

    As stated previously, younger children tend to report more pain with medical procedures. Therefore, a subanalysis was conducted on the three studies with
250   subjects exclusively between the ages of 3 and 7 years (Blount et al., 1992; Fowler-Kerry and Lander, 1987; Gonzales, Routh, & Armstrong, 1993). Because all of the subjects had injections as part of well-child care, this subanalysis also controlled for the type of medical
255   procedure. For the 268 children in these three randomized clinical trials, the average effect size was .47 (±0.26). Sampling and measurement error accounted for 60% of the variance in the effect size. Thus, it ap-

219

Table 2

Meta-Analysis Results of the Effects of Distraction on Pain and Observed Distress

	Self-report of Pain, All Subjects	Self-report of Pain, Subjects ≤7 Years Old	Observed Behavioral Distress, All Subjects
Total no. of studies (subjects)	10 (535)	3 (268)	16 (491)
No. of subjects in RCT designs; RM designs	479; 56	268; 0	403; 88
Absolute value of mean effect size $\pm SD$	.62 ± .42	.47 ± .26	.33 ± .17
Observed variance of the effect size	.18818	.09212	.09613
Sampling error variance	.05751	.05026	.07060
Measurement error variance	.00813	.0046	.00038
Variance accounted for by sampling error and measurement error	35%	60%	74%
90% credibility intervals	−.07−+1.31	−.01−+.91	+.05−+.61

pears that moderator variables other than age and procedure type influence the effectiveness of distraction.

Distress

The analysis for behavioral distress shows an average effect size (absolute value) of 0.33 (±0.17) for the 491 children in the sample studies. The credibility interval for $\bar{d}$ does not include zero, indicating that distraction has a positive effect on children's distress behavior. Sampling error and measurement error accounted for 73.44% and .4% of the observed variance, respectively. Hunter and Schmidt (1990) suggest that when approximately 75% of the observed variance is accounted for, the remaining variance is likely to be caused by a combination of other statistical artifacts, namely reliability of the independent variables, study differences in range restriction, and instrument validity.

Discussion

This meta-analysis found a moderate effect size for the influence of distraction on observed distress behavior in children. Sampling and measurement error accounted for almost 74% of the observed variance among the studies, indicating that the positive effect of distraction on distress behavior is seen across the populations sampled by the studies.

For the effect of distraction on self-reported pain, the 90% credibility interval was wide and encompassed zero. Credibility intervals are calculated with the corrected standard deviation of the mean effect size and are used in meta-analyses to determine whether or not moderator variables are operating (Whitener, 1990). When the interval includes zero, variability in the effect size might be due to remaining statistical artifacts or to moderator variables. Because only about 35% of the observed variance was accounted for by sampling error and measurement error, a subanalysis that controlled for age and type of medical procedure was completed. Although substantially more of the ob-

served variance was accounted for in this subanalysis, there is still some variability left to explain. Possible moderator variables that come to mind are inconsistencies in the distraction interventions and variations in the characteristics of the children.

Research has shown that the child's innate temperament influences distress behavior during painful procedures (Corbo-Richert, 1994; Lee & White-Traut, 1996; Schechter, Bernstein, Beck, Hart, & Scherzer, 1991; Young & Fu, 1988). However, the relationships between child temperament and perceived pain have not been explored. The child's history of bad experiences with procedures is another possible moderator. In a study of preparation methods for medical procedures, Dahlquist et al. (1986) found a significant main effect for quality of previous medical experience on the behavioral distress of children during throat culture. The amount of past exposure to medical procedures was not related to behavioral distress. Thus, it appears that it is the *quality* of the child's experiences and not the quantity that matters. Systematic inquiry is needed to explore the influences of temperament and prior experience on children's responses during medical procedures, and to search for additional moderator variables.

Using distraction with children during medical procedures will reduce the amount of observed distress behavior for most children. The magnitude of the benefit will vary from child to child. Distraction is a low-cost intervention that has no risk to the patient and has a measurable benefit.

References

References marked with an asterisk (*) indicate studies included in the meta-analysis.

*Arts, S. E., Abu-Saad, H. H., Champion, G. D., Crawford, M. R., Fisher, R. J., Juniper, K. H., & Ziegler, J. B. (1994). Age-related response to lidocaine-prilocaine (EMLA) emulsion and effect of music distraction on the pain of intravenous cannulation. *Pediatrics, 93*(5), 797–801.

Becker, B. J. (1988). Synthesizing standardized mean-change measures. *British Journal of Mathematical and Statistical Psychology, 41*, 257–278.

Beyer, J. E., McGrath, P. J., & Berde, C. B. (1990). Discordance between self-report and behavioral pain measures in children aged 3–7 years after surgery. *Journal of Pain and Symptom Management, 5*, 350–356.

*Blount, R. L., Bachanas, P. J., Powers, S. W., Cotter, M. C., Franklin, A., Chaplin, W., Mayfield, J., Henderson, M., & Blount, S. D. (1992). Training children to cope and parents to coach them during routine immunizations: Effects on child, parent, and staff behaviors. *Behavior Therapy, 23*, 689–705.

*Broome, M. E., Lillis, P. P., McGahee, T. W., & Bates, T. (1992). The use of distraction and imagery with children during painful procedures. *Oncology Nursing Forum, 19*, 499–502.

Cohen, J. (1977). *Statistical power analysis for the behavioral sciences* (revised ed.). New York: Academic Press.

Corbo-Richert, B. H. (1994). Coping behaviors of young children during a chest tube procedure in the pediatric intensive care unit. *Maternal-Child Nursing Journal, 22*, 134–146.

Dahlquist, L. M., Gil, K. M., Armstrong, F. D., DeLawyer, D. D., Greene, P., & Wuori, D. (1986). Preparing children for medical examinations: The importance of previous medical experience. *Health Psychology, 5*, 249–259.

Dahlquist, L. M., Power, T., Cox, C., & Fernbach, D. (1994). Parenting and child distress during cancer procedures: A multi-dimensional assessment. *Children's Health Care, 23*, 149–166.

Dunlap, W. P., Cortina, J. M., Vaslow, J. B., & Burke, M. J. (1996). Meta-analysis of experiments with matched groups or repeated measures designs. *Psychological Methods, 1*, 170–177.

*Elliott, C. H., & Olson, R. A. (1983). The management of children's distress in response to painful medical treatment for burn injuries. *Behaviour Research and Therapy, 21*(6), 675–683.

Fernandez, E. (1986). A classification system of cognitive coping strategies for pain. *Pain, 26*, 141–151.

*Foertsch, C. E. (1993). *Investigation of an imagery-based treatment for the control of children's behavioral distress during burn dressing changes.* Unpublished doctoral dissertation, University of Iowa.

*Fowler-Kerry, S., & Lander, J. R. (1987). Management of injection pain on children. *Pain, 30*, 169–175.

*Gonzalez, J. C., Routh, D. K., & Armstrong, F. D. (1993). Effects of maternal distraction versus reassurance on children's reactions to injections. *Journal of Pediatric Psychology, 18*(5), 593–604.

Hester, N. O. (1993). Pain in children. In J. Fitzpatrick & J. Stevenson (Eds.) *Annual review of nursing research: Vol. 11* (pp. 105–142). New York: Springer.

Humphrey, G. B., Boon, C. M., van Linden van den Heuvell, G. E், & van de Wiel, H. B. (1992). The occurrence of high levels of acute behavioral distress in children and adolescents undergoing routine venipunctures. *Pediatrics, 90*, 8–91.

Hunter, J. E., & Schmidt, F. L. (1990). *Methods of meta-analysis: Correcting error and bias in research findings.* Newbury Park, CA: Sage.

Jay, S. M., Elliott, C. H., Katz, E., & Siegel, S. E. (1987). Cognitive-behavioral and pharmacologic interventions for children's distress during painful medical procedures. *Journal of Consulting and Clinical Psychology, 55*(6), 860–865.

*Jay, S. M., Elliott, C. H., Ozolins, M., Olson, R. A., & Pruitt, S. D. (1985). Behavioral management of children's distress during painful medical procedures. *Behaviour Research and Therapy, 23*, 513–520.

Jay, S. M., Ozolins, M., Elliott, C. H., & Caldwell, S. (1983). Assessment of children's distress during painful medical procedures. *Health Psychology, 2*, 133–147.

Katz, E. R., Kellerman, J., & Siegel, S. (1980). Behavioral distress in children with cancer undergoing medical procedures: Developmental considerations. *Journal of Consulting and Clinical Psychology, 48*, 356–365.

Keck, J. F., Gerkensmeyer, J. E., Joyce, B. A., & Schade, J. G. (1996). Reliability and validity of the Faces and Word Descriptor Scales to measure procedural pain. *Journal of Pediatric Nursing, 11*, 368–374.

Lander, J., & Fowler-Kerry, S. (1991). Age differences in children's pain. *Perceptual and Motor Skills, 73*, 415–418.

Lee, L. W., & White-Traut, R. C. (1996). The role of temperament in pediatric pain response. *Issues in Comprehensive Pediatric Nursing, 19*, 49–63.

*Manne, S. L., Redd, W. H., Jacobsen, P. B., Gorfinkle, K., Schorr, O., & Rapkin, B. (1990). Behavioral intervention to reduce child and parent distress during venipuncture. *Journal of Consulting and Clinical Psychology, 58*, 565–572.

McCarthy, A. M., Cool, V. A., Petersen, M., & Bruene, D. A. (1996). Cognitive behavioral pain and anxiety interventions in pediatric oncology centers and bone marrow transplant units. *Journal of Pediatric Oncology Nursing, 13*, 3–12.

McCaul, K. D., & Malott, J. M. (1984). Distraction and coping with pain. *Psychological Bulletin, 95*, 516–533.

McGrath, P. A. (1991). Intervention and management. In J. P. Bush & S. W. Harkins (Eds.), *Children in pain.* New York: Springer-Verlag.

*McGrath, P. A., & deVeber, L. L. (1986). The management of acute pain evoked by medical procedures in children with cancer. *Journal of Pain and Symptom Management, 1*(3), 145–150.

Melamed, B., Hawes, R., Heiby, E., & Glick, J. (1975). The use of film modeling to reduce uncooperative behavior of children during dental treatment. *Journal of Dental Research, 54*, 797–801.

Melzack, R., & Wall, P. D. (1965). Pain mechanisms: A new theory. *Science, 150*, 971–979.

*Olsen, B. R. (1991). *Brief interventions for routine use with children in a phlebotomy laboratory.* Unpublished doctoral dissertation, West Virginia University.

*Powers, S. W., Blount, R. L., Bachanas, P. J., Cotter, M. W., & Swan, S. C. (1993). Helping preschool leukemia patients and their parents cope during injections. *Journal of Pediatric Psychology, 18*(6), 681–695.

Schechter, N. L., Bernstein, B. A., Beck A., Hart, L., & Scherzer, L. (1991). Individual differences in children's response to pain: Role of temperament and parental characteristics. *Pediatrics, 87*, 171–177.

*Schur, J. M. (1986). *Alleviating behavioral distress with music or Lamaze pant-blow breathing in children undergoing bone marrow aspirations and lumbar punctures.* Unpublished doctoral dissertation, University of Texas Southwestern Medical Center at Dallas.

*Smith, J. T., Barabasz, A., & Barabasz, M. (1996). Comparison of hypnosis and distraction in severely ill children undergoing painful medical procedures. *Journal of Counseling Psychology, 43*(2), 187–195.

*Smith, K. E., Ackerson, J. D., & Blotcky, A. D. (1989). Reducing distress during invasive medical procedures: Relating behavioral interventions to preferred coping style in pediatric cancer patients. *Journal of Pediatric Psychology, 14*(3), 405–419.

*Stark, L. J., Allen, K. D., Hurst, M., Nash, D. A., Rigney, B., & Stokes, T. F. (1989). Distraction: Its utilization and efficacy with children undergoing dental treatment. *Journal of Applied Behavior Analysis, 22*(3), 297–307.

*Vessey, J. A., Carlson, K. L., & McGill, J. (1994). Use of distraction with children during an acute pain experience. *Nursing Research, 43*, 369–372.

Wall, P. D. (1978). The gate control theory of pain mechanisms. A re-examination and re-statement. *Brain, 101*, 1–18.

Whitener, E. (1990). Confusion of confidence intervals and credibility intervals in meta-analysis. *Journal of Applied Psychology, 75*, 315–321.

Willis, W. E., & Coggeshall, R. E. (Eds.) (1991). *Sensory mechanisms of the spinal cord* (2nd ed.). New York: Plenum Press.

*Winborn, M. D. (1987). *Associative and dissociative preparatory strategies for children undergoing dental treatment.* Unpublished doctoral dissertation, Memphis State University.

Young, M. R., & Fu, V. R. (1988). Influence of play and temperament on the young child's response to pain. *Children's Health Care, 18*, 209–217.

*Zabin, M. A. (1982). *The modification of children's behavior during blood work procedures.* Unpublished doctoral dissertation, West Virginia University.

About the authors: Charmaine Kleiber is a doctoral student, College of Nursing, University of Iowa, and an advanced practice nurse, University of Iowa Hospitals and Clinics, Iowa City, Iowa. Dennis C. Harper is a professor at the Department of Pediatrics, College of Medicine, University of Iowa, Iowa City, Iowa.

Acknowledgments: The authors thank Sue Gardner, RN, Ph.D.(c), and Barbara Rakel, RN, Ph.D., for their assistance with this analysis. This research was supported by National Institute of Nursing Research, National Institutes of Health, Individual Predoctoral Fellowship # NR07170-02.

Address reprint requests to: Charmaine Kleiber, RN, MS, 1819 Flanigan Street, Iowa City, IA 52246; e-mail: charmaine-kleiber@uiowa.edu

Exercise for Article 32

Factual Questions

1. According to the researchers, are behaviors such as crying and moaning always good proxies for pain?

2. How did the researchers "discover" unpublished studies?

3. All studies selected for this meta-analysis had what as the "intervention"?

4. For the purposes of this study, how was "distrac-

tion" defined?

5. When distraction with a party blower was used in Manne's (1990) study, what was the Pain Effect Size?

6. When Zabin (1982) used the cartoon during the procedure, what was the Distress Effect Size?

7. What was the average effect size (absolute value) for the 535 children who reported on perceived pain?

Questions for Discussion

8. Do you believe that the search procedure described in lines 81–112 is described in sufficient detail?

9. In lines 113–132, the researchers describe their inclusion criteria (i.e., the criteria used to determine whether a study would be included in this meta-analysis). The criteria specifically did not include "methodological strength of the research." (See lines 133–141.) Do you believe that methodological strength should have been included? Explain.

10. Examination of Table 1 reveals a large number of different experimental treatment conditions. Do you believe that this is a strength or weakness of this meta-analysis? If you had been conducting this meta-analysis, would you have restricted it to studies that involved similar experimental treatment conditions? Explain.

11. Given the overall average effect size for perceived pain, do you think that this study makes a strong case for using distraction with children? (See lines 236–241.)

12. Overall, how well did this meta-analysis help you understand the effects of distraction on children's pain and distress during medical procedures?

Quality Ratings

Directions: Indicate your level of agreement with each of the following statements by circling a number from 5 for strongly agree (SA) to 1 for strongly disagree (SD). If you believe an item is not applicable to this research article, leave it blank. Be prepared to explain your ratings.

A. The introduction establishes the importance of the study.

SA 5 4 3 2 1 SD

B. The literature review establishes the context for the study.

SA 5 4 3 2 1 SD

C. The research purpose, question, or hypothesis is clearly stated.

SA 5 4 3 2 1 SD

D. The method of sampling is sound.

SA 5 4 3 2 1 SD

E. Relevant demographics (for example, age, gender, and ethnicity) are described.

SA 5 4 3 2 1 SD

F. Measurement procedures are adequate.

SA 5 4 3 2 1 SD

G. All procedures have been described in sufficient detail to permit a replication of the study.

SA 5 4 3 2 1 SD

H. The participants have been adequately protected from potential harm.

SA 5 4 3 2 1 SD

I. The results are clearly described.

SA 5 4 3 2 1 SD

J. The discussion/conclusion is appropriate.

SA 5 4 3 2 1 SD

K. Despite any flaws, the report is worthy of publication.

SA 5 4 3 2 1 SD

Article 33

A Review of Teen-Tot Programs: Comprehensive Clinical Care for Young Parents and Their Children

Lara J. Akinbami
Children's National Medical Center

Tina L. Cheng
Children's National Medical Center

Dana Kornfeld
Children's National Medical Center

ABSTRACT. Comprehensive clinical programs for teenage mothers and their children, also known as teen-tot programs, have been a promising intervention to improve outcomes of teenage childbearing and parenting. However, much remains unknown regarding the efficacy of such programs. We reviewed four published evaluations of programs that provided medical care, counseling, contraception, guidance for parenting, and assistance with staying in school. The evaluations reported moderate success in preventing repeat pregnancies, helping teen mothers continue their education, and improving teen and infant health over 6 to 18 months. However, the evaluations had limitations that may have reduced or accentuated observed effectiveness. Teen-tot programs will continue to face the challenges of sustaining adequate long-term interventions and evaluations, and reducing the high attrition rate among program participants. It is concluded that increased support and funding for teen-tot programs and more complete evaluations are warranted.

From *Adolescence*, 36, 381–393. Copyright © 2001 by Libra Publishers, Inc. Reprinted with permission.

Teenage childbearing poses risks for teenage mothers, such as higher risk of inadequate education and living in poverty, and their infants, including poor birth outcomes and long-term learning and behavior prob-
5 lems (Card & Wise, 1978; Furstenberg, Brooks-Gunn, & Morgan, 1987; Baldwin & Cain, 1990; Fraser, Brockert, & Ward, 1995; Jekel, Harrison, Bancroft, Tyler, & Klerman, 1975). Furthermore, repeat pregnancy rates among teenage mothers of low socioeco-
10 nomic status may be as high as 39% within one year of delivery (Linares, Leadbeater, Jaffe, Kato, & Diaz, 1992) and 50% within two years of delivery (Polit & Kahn, 1986). Each additional childbirth increases the chance that a teenage parent and her children will live
15 in poverty for a longer period of time by postponing the teenager's return to school or reducing her ability to find employment (Furstenberg et al., 1987). Despite the declining rate of repeat births to teenagers, in 1998, nearly 110,000 births (22% of all births to teenagers)
20 occurred among teenagers who were already mothers

(Ventura, Martin, Curtin, Mathews, & Park, 2000).

Teen-tot programs were established to prevent poor outcomes for teenage parents and their children. These comprehensive clinic-based programs serve teenage
25 mothers and their infants in a single setting and typically offer health care, family planning, counseling, encouragement for teenage mothers to continue their education, assistance with obtaining services, and social support. By providing "one-stop shopping" for this
30 high-risk population, the teen-tot model is designed to remove barriers to receiving care that exist in traditional care models, such as transportation difficulties, lack of continuity of care, and lack of case management. A central goal is to prevent rapid repeat preg-
35 nancy by simplifying access to contraception, discouraging school dropout, and encouraging the pursuit of careers that provide economic security. In addition, components of these programs are designed to improve infant and teen health and parenting practices.

40 Concern has been raised about the inadequate evaluation of programs for teenage mothers (Stahler & DuCette, 1991; Stahler, DuCette, & McBride, 1989). Previously published reviews of teenage parent program evaluations have not specifically focused on
45 postnatal clinic-based interventions targeted at both mother and child (Scholl, Hediger, & Belsky, 1994; O'Sullivan, 1991). We sought to review the experience of teen-tot programs in meeting the goals of improving outcomes and preventing repeat pregnancies.

Method
50 Published medical literature was systematically searched via computerized databases. Medline, Popline, and Health Star were searched from January 1980 to August 2000 using the terms "pregnancy in adolescence," "parents," and "program evaluation." The Psy-
55 chInfo database was searched using the terms "adolescent mothers," "adolescent pregnancy," and "program evaluation." Two investigators independently reviewed the results of each search to identify articles that were potentially eligible for inclusion. In addition, bibliog-
60 raphies of articles identified through the search were examined for additional eligible articles. Initial criteria

included a title and abstract, if available, that described a comprehensive program for pregnant and/or parenting teenagers and their children.

65   Potentially eligible articles were reviewed in entirety by three investigators to determine which described a comprehensive clinical teen-tot program, that is, a program including clinical health supervision, family planning, and support for teen parents, such as

70   assistance with staying in school or obtaining community services. Each article describing a comprehensive teen-tot program was rated in four areas: (1) statement of goals used to develop the program, (2) statement of the intervention content (i.e., the parameters, intensity,

75   and target of the intervention, as well as the staff involved in conducting the intervention), (3) description of study design: size and characteristics of the target group and the comparison group (randomized, matched, or convenience), program duration, and data

80   collection procedures and intervals, and (4) program impact evaluation: use of reliable outcome measures and appropriate impact analyses, including statistical significance (Bauman, Drotar, Leventhal, Perrin, & Pless, 1997; personal communication, L. J. Bauman).

Results

85   The literature search identified 46 articles describing interventions that met initial criteria for closer review. Most of these articles were excluded because they did not clearly describe a clinical component or described outcomes in descriptive terms only. Four

90   studies met eligibility criteria: the Teen-Tot Clinic (TTC) (Nelson, Key, Fletcher, Kirkpatrick, & Feinstein, 1982), the Queens Hospital Center (QHC) (Rabin, Seltzer, & Pollack, 1991), the Teen Mother and Child Program (TMCP) (Elster, Lamb, Tavare, & Ralston, 1987), and the Special Care Program (SCP)

95   (O'Sullivan & Jacobsen, 1992) (see Table 1). The SCP evaluation did not describe on-site clinical services for the adolescent participants, but is included in this review because it is the only example we found of a randomized study.

100

All four programs were conducted in hospital clinics or academic centers in urban areas. Participants were recruited from hospital clinics (TTC, SCP), prenatal adolescent programs (QHC), or were self-referred

105   (TMCP). TTC, SCP, and QHC drew participants from socioeconomically disadvantaged minority groups, while the participants in TMCP were predominantly white and 35% came from higher socioeconomic groups. Control groups were created through randomi-

110   zation (SCP), by matching characteristics of a group of mothers who delivered one year earlier with those of the participants (TTC), or by drawing a convenience sample of teenagers concurrently receiving care in traditional programs (TMCP, QHC).

115   Each program limited duration of participation either by infant or maternal age. Evaluators of the TTC and QHC did not provide data for average duration of

program participation or attrition rate. TMCP reported a high attrition rate, with complete data available for

120   42% of participants and 49% of controls at the 26-month postpartum evaluation. SCP also reported a high attrition rate: at 18 months, 40% of participants and 18% of controls were still attending the well-baby clinic. However, 91% of the original participants and

125   controls were interviewed at 18 months. None of the four evaluations provided data on attendance for individual program components.

Outcome data were gathered at varying intervals (TTC, TMCP, and QHC) or at the conclusion of the

130   intervention (SCP). Sources of outcome data included chart reviews (TTC, QHC, TMCP, and SCP), interviews of participants and controls (TTC, TMCP, SCP), developmental and maternal knowledge test scores (TMCP), assessment of home environment (TMCP),

135   and school attendance records (SCP).

We analyzed the efficacy of these programs in meeting three goals they had in common: (1) preventing repeat pregnancies and school dropout, (2) improving infant and teen health outcomes, and (3) improving

140   the adequacy of teenagers in the parental/caretaking role. All four programs reported decreased repeat pregnancy rates among participants compared to controls between 12 and 26 months postpartum (for TMCP, the difference between participants and controls did not

145   reach a level of statistical significance). Outcomes for maternal school attendance varied. TTC and QHC reported that participants were significantly more likely to be attending school, and QHC reported significantly greater rates of employment among participants com-

150   pared to controls. However, TTC reported outcomes at 6 months postpartum, a relatively short interval for evaluation, and QHC failed to specify a time period at all. There was no difference in school attendance between participants and controls in the TMCP or SCP.

155   In general, reported infant health outcomes were favorable. Higher rates of clinic attendance (QHC, SCP), immunization completion (TTC, TMCP, SCP), adequate weight- and height-for-age (TTC), and lower rates of injury and illness (QHC) were reported for

160   participants compared to controls. However, TMCP reported minimal impact on infant growth, development, and medical outcomes among participants. Only QHC reported maternal health outcomes; maternal morbidity was significantly lower among program par-

165   ticipants. None of the evaluators of the four programs specified whether record-keeping for clinic attendance, immunizations, or hospitalizations was uniform between participant and control sites. Some programs did not report data necessary to adequately evaluate out-

170   comes. For example, TTC and TMCP did not report rates of clinic attendance for participants and controls.

Only TMCP reported outcomes for interventions designed to improve caretaking skills. The evaluators measured the use of preventive health behaviors such

175   as using car seats. There were no significant differ-

Table 1
Teen-Tot Program Characteristics, Interventions, and Outcomes

Program	Intervention	Evaluated Outcomes	Strengths and Weaknesses
TEEN-TOT CLINIC. Nelson, Key, Fletcher, Kirkpatrick, & Feinstein (1982) • Duration: 18 mos postpartum. • Participants (n = 35): age < 17 yrs, race 91% black. Referred from urban hospitals. • Control group (n = 70): matched for maternal and child characteristics. Received care at public clinics.	1. Well-child health visits, developmental assessment, nutrition counseling, WIC, referral to community services. 2. Group sessions on child developmental and parenting skills. 3. Contraceptive counseling and services. 4. Assistance with education, employment, living arrangements, goals, and relationships.	1. 91% vs. 46% controls fully immunized (6 mos). * 97% vs. 83% controls between 5th–95th growth percentiles (6 mos).* [2. None reported] 3. Contraceptive use (6 mos): 91% vs. 63% controls.* Repeat pregnancy (18 mos): 16% vs. 38% controls.* 4. School enrollment (6 mos): 86% vs. 66% controls.*	↑ Matched control group. No difference between participant and control group characteristics. ↓ No analysis of attrition. ↓ Many outcomes reported only at 6 mos. ↓ Small number of participants.
QUEENS HOSPITAL CENTER. Rabin, Seltzer, & Pollack (1991) • Duration: until mother 20 yrs old. • Participants (n = 498): age < 20 yrs, race not specified. Recruited from clinical adolescent program. • Control group (n = 91): from adult obstetric clinic. Received care in pediatric and adult family planning clinic.	1. 24-hour "on-call" system, each teen-infant pair assigned to one interdisciplinary team. 2. Family life education program with bi-weekly classes for participants, their partners and families. 3. Comprehensive services available on-site (mental health center, WIC, housing office, high school equivalency program, day care center).	1. Clinic attendance: 75% vs. 18% of controls.* Maternal morbidity† and infant morbidity‡ lower among participants.* 2. Contraceptive use: 85% participants vs. 22% of controls.* Repeat pregnancy: 9% participants vs. 70% controls.* 3. School attendance: 77% participants vs. 38% controls.* School completion: 95% participants graduated from high school. Employment: 48% participants vs. 22% controls.*	↑ No difference between participant and control group characteristics. ↓ Length of participation not specified. ↓ No discussion of attrition or dropout characteristics. ↓ Intervals of outcome evaluation not specified.
TEEN MOTHER AND CHILD PROGRAM. Elster, Lamb, Tavare, & Ralston (1987) • Duration: 2 yrs postpartum. • Participants (n = 125): age < 18 yrs, race > 80% white. 35% from high socioeconomic group. Self-referral, community referral. • Control group (n = 135): Recruited from WIC site. Received care from community providers.	1. Prenatal care, education, psychosocial and nutritional assessments. 2. Health care for infants and teen mothers. Staff on call. WIC referral. 3. Individual counseling about financial management, school, and work. Referrals for vocational training, education. 4. Contraceptive education. 5. Infant health and development education. 6. Counseling on parenting, interpersonal relationships, and stress. Outreach to fathers.	1. Participants had more prenatal visits.* No difference in preterm or low birthweight. 2–6. Participants had better composite score at 12 and 26 mos postpartum* (repeat pregnancy, school/job attendance, receipt of entitlements, ER visits, hospitalizations, immunizations, maternal preventive health efforts, child developmental knowledge, and General Well-Being Schedule scores). Greater immunization completion among participants.* No significant difference in infant growth and development or repeat pregnancy rates.	↔ Participants more likely to have higher income, attend school, graduate, or be working at time of enrollment. Multiple regression used to control for differences. ↓ High attrition rate.
SPECIAL CARE PROGRAM. O'Sullivan & Jacobsen (1992) • Duration: 18 mos. • Participants (n = 120): age < 18 yrs, race 100% black. Recruited from urban teaching hospital. • Random assignment to control group (n = 123). Received routine care.	1. Well-baby visits. Participants received reminders if appointment missed. 2. Social worker reviewed family planning methods, made referrals to birth control clinic. 3. Health care provider asked about mother's plan to return to school. 4. Health teaching in the waiting room. Infant care and appropriate ER use education.	1. Clinic attendance (18 mos): 40% vs. 22% of controls. Immunizations (18 mos): 33% vs. 18% of controls.* 2. Repeat pregnancy (18 mos): 12% vs. 28% of controls.* 3. Return to school: > 50% of both participants and controls (no significant statistical difference). 4. ER use: 75% vs. 80% for controls (no significant statistical difference).	↑ Randomized study. ↑ Outcomes analyzed among dropouts. ↔ High attrition rate, but 91% of original participants and controls interviewed at 18 mos.

* Statistically significant difference using chi-square test (95% confidence level).
† Disease state of pelvic organs, upper respiratory, hematologic or gastrointestinal systems requiring multiple doctor visits or hospitalizations.
‡ Includes maternal morbidity definition plus any accident in a child under 2 years of age.
ER: emergency room
WIC: Women Infant Children program

ences between participants and controls at either 12 or 26 months into the intervention. Unfortunately, no program reported outcomes for interventions designed to improve parenting practices.

180   While there was no statistically significant difference between many outcomes for participants and controls in the TMCP, a composite score was calculated for 10 outcomes. The score was significantly better for participants compared to controls at both the 12- and 26-month evaluations. The score was also robust: mothers with a low (better) score at 12 months also had a low score at 26 months. The authors concluded that a broad range of events should be studied when evaluating programs for teenage parents.

Discussion

190   It is disappointing but not surprising that only four studies met inclusion criteria for this review. Although many programs for teenage parents and their children exist, few are truly comprehensive, and fewer still are evaluated. In 1976, the National Alliance Concerned with School-Age Parents listed 1,132 programs for sexually active and parenting teenagers, of which only 54 offered comprehensive medical and social services (Weatherley, Perlman, Levine, & Klerman, 1986). Comprehensive programs may be rare because they face major constraints, including inadequate financial support, insufficient health and social welfare infrastructure, and negative public attitudes toward the target population (Weatherley et al., 1986). The inadequate assessment of comprehensive programs for pregnant and parenting adolescents has been widely acknowledged, and attributed in part to the precedent set by the legislative limit on resources for evaluation of federally funded programs (Stahler & DuCette 1991; Stahler et al., 1989; O'Sullivan, 1991). Although the federal legislation of the early 1980s called for program evaluation, a maximum of 5% of the total program budget can be used for evaluation under Title XX (Stahler et al. 1989). Another barrier to rigorous evaluation might be the perception of program managers that allocating resources for evaluation siphons them away from participants.

The four studies we identified were able to conduct fairly rigorous evaluations given the constraints. And on the surface, the evaluations suggest that comprehensive programs are more successful than traditional health care in addressing some of the risks teenage mothers and their children face. One of the most important successes is postponing repeat pregnancies, because studies have shown an association between short interpregnancy intervals and poor birth outcomes (Khoshnood, Lee, Wall, Hseih, & Mittendorf, 1998; Rawlings, Rawlings, & Read, 1995) and higher risk of poor birth outcomes for second births to teenage mothers compared to older mothers (Santelli & Jacobsen, 1990; Akinbami, Schoendorf, & Kiely, 2000). Of the four programs that reported various outcomes for infant health, three found a positive impact. In contrast, the results for other important outcomes, such as parenting skills, mastering knowledge of child development, and outcomes for child development, were disappointing. The achievements of these programs are theoretically the result of providing "one-stop shopping" and fostering greater communication and trust between teen parents and health care workers. By removing barriers both to access to services and to bonding with providers, greater compliance with contraception and clinic visits can be realized, and greater efficacy from health education, anticipatory guidance, and counseling can be achieved.

Unfortunately, in addition to having only four evaluations on which to base conclusions about the efficacy of teen-tot programs, there are also shortcomings in these evaluations that make it difficult to judge how well program goals were met. For example, reported immunization rates are dependent on numerous factors in addition to clinic attendance and patient compliance, such as provider behavior and record keeping (Morrow, Crews, Caretta, Altaye, Finch, & Sinn, 2000; Taylor, Darden, Slora, Hasemeier, Asmussen, & Wasserman, 1997). Furthermore, the knowledge that immunization completion rates would be evaluated might have changed the behavior of the health providers in the evaluated teen-tot programs. Thus, it is unclear if higher immunization rates in teen-tot programs can be attributed to specific interventions or are due to biases introduced by the study design. Another example is inadequate longitudinal assessment of teenage mothers' education. Evaluating long-term outcomes such as school completion and employment, rather than rates of school enrollment, is necessary to fully analyze the success of education interventions. School enrollment in the short term is important since teenagers who obtain additional schooling after a first birth may be less likely to have a closely spaced second birth (Kalmuss & Brickner Namerow, 1994). However, a review of community programs found that immediate gains in education among teenage participants were short-lived (Corson Jones, 1991). Since teenage mothers are more likely than their childless peers to have poor academic records even before becoming pregnant (Card & Wise, 1978; Brooks-Gunn & Chase Landsdale, 1991), it is important to determine which interventions are most effective in helping teenage mothers obtain an adequate education.

In addition to these issues, these studies also have more general limitations that might have introduced bias into the findings. The randomized study design, which is optimal because it minimizes systematic differences in baseline characteristics between participant and control groups, is rare among published evaluations. Just as devoting funds to evaluation might be seen as depriving participants of services they might otherwise receive, randomly enrolling eligible teenage mothers in a control arm of a study might be seen as

290 denying benefits to those in need. Given the difficulties in creating sustainable programs for teenage mothers and their children, it might be too optimistic to expect randomized studies to be undertaken. As seen with one of the included studies (TTC), it is possible to mini-
295 mize differences between participants and controls by matching characteristics of controls otherwise ineligible for participation with those of participants.

Probably more vital to minimizing bias in a study is minimizing attrition rates. The teenagers who drop out
300 of a study are likely to have different characteristics than those who remain, and these characteristics may affect the risk of repeat pregnancy or compliance with prenatal care and well-child visits. High attrition also hampers program sustainability and statistical power of
305 evaluation. Not only should programs strive to minimize attrition, but in order to assess bias, it is also necessary to evaluate outcomes and background characteristics among controls and participants who drop out of the program. However, dropouts are notoriously hard
310 to follow (Stahler et al., 1989). Funds devoted to such efforts should be included in both intervention and evaluation budgets (e.g., staff and resources to track participants and controls, home visits, reminder postcards and phone calls, and financial incentives).
315 O'Sullivan and Jacobsen (1992) have provided an analysis of SCP outcomes among dropouts from both the participant and control groups. This analysis revealed important information; for example, there were significantly increased immunization rates and de-
320 creased inappropriate emergency room visits among participants remaining in the program but not among dropouts, and differences in repeat pregnancy timing and frequency between dropouts and participants.

Misclassifying participants might have led to biases
325 through measurement error. As acknowledged by Elster et al. (1987), most programs are unable to quantify the individual services a participant receives. Classifying a teen as a participant assumes she has attended all program components and thus is in a position to bene-
330 fit. Including teens with poor attendance as participants will underestimate program impact. A related problem arises from failing to measure participation in each separate program component—it is unclear which elements of the program are related to the observed ef-
335 fects. For example, it is not possible to determine if an impact on pregnancy rates is primarily related to attendance at family planning sessions, clinic attendance in which contraceptive measures are prescribed, encouragement to continue with school, or to a combination
340 of these interventions. And while the use of a composite score in the evaluation by Elster et al. (1987) may be useful in detecting small impact in many areas, this approach compounds the problem of linking observed impacts to specific interventions.
345 A source of bias common among programs located in resource-rich areas is the difficulty of isolating a true "no treatment" control group. When the provision of a wide array of community and public services to control groups occurs, the observed difference in impact be-
350 tween control and intervention groups is diminished (Stahler & DuCette, 1991). In general, authors were careful to specify that they were comparing comprehensive delivery of services to traditional delivery of services rather than to absence of services. O'Sullivan
355 and Jacobsen (SCP) (1992) delineated what services the control group received *within* their program, but, like the other studies, did not specify if controls had received additional outside services. To conduct a comparative study of impact or cost-effectiveness, it is
360 necessary to know the alternative services provided, their impact, and the costs involved.

Many of the above limitations are likely to lead to an underestimation of the true benefit of teen-tot programs. Publication bias may lead to an overestimation
365 of the positive impact of teen-tot programs. Studies that demonstrate positive impact are more likely to be published than those showing little or no impact. As a result of this bias and other numerous obstacles to conducting adequate evaluations, we have limited evidence
370 upon which to judge the performance of teen-tot programs. A more representative picture of the experience of teen-tot programs could be obtained by adopting multisite evaluations, as proposed by Stahler and DuCette (1991). Several programs could devote time
375 and effort to collecting outcome data from participants and to documenting services actually received. Recruitment of matched controls and analysis of program outcomes could be undertaken by a third party with a full-time qualified staff and a separate budget (see
380 Stahler & DuCette, 1991, for a discussion of third-party evaluation).

Conclusions

Although rates of teenage childbearing have been decreasing in recent years, the risks faced by teenage mothers and their children in a new era of welfare re-
385 form increases the urgency of implementing effective interventions among this still large and vulnerable group. Given the positive outcomes for teenage mothers and their children that have been observed, and also the substantial limitations that hamper efforts to con-
390 duct rigorous program evaluations, continued support and funding for teen-tot interventions and evaluation are warranted. Specifically, questions remain about the efficacy of separate program components, sustainability of benefits in the long run, the success of programs
395 in resource-poor areas, and how to best address the high attrition rates that teen-tot programs face. The challenge to adequately evaluate programs for pregnant and parenting teens that was raised over a decade ago still remains.

References

Akinbami, L. J., Schoendorf, K. C., & Kiely, J. L. (2000). Risk of preterm birth in multiparous teenagers. *Archives of Pediatrics and Adolescent Medicine, 154,* 1101–1107.

Baldwin, W., & Cain, V. S. (1990). The children of teenage parents. *Family Planning Perspectives, 12*(1), 34–43.

Bauman, L. J., Drotar, D., Leventhal, J. M., Perrin, E. C., & Pless, I. B. (1997). A review of psychosocial interventions for children with chronic health conditions. *Pediatrics, 100(2),* 244–251.

Brooks-Gunn, J., & Chase Lansdale, P. L. (1991). Children having children: Effects on the family system. *Pediatric Annals, 20(9),* 467–481.

Card, J. J., & Wise, L. L. (1978). Teenage mothers and teenage fathers: The impact of early childbearing on the parents' personal and professional lives. *Family Planning Perspectives, 10(4),* 199–205.

Corson Jones, L. (1991). Community-based tertiary prevention with the adolescent parent and child. *Birth Defects, 27*(1), 57–71.

Elster, A. B., Lamb, M. E., Tavare, J., & Ralston, C. W. (1987). The medical and psychosocial impact of comprehensive care on adolescent pregnancy and parenthood. *Journal of the American Medical Association, 258*(9), 1187–1192.

Fraser, A. M., Brockert, J. E., & Ward, R. H. (1995). Association of young maternal age with adverse reproductive outcomes. *New England Journal of Medicine, 332*(17), 1113–1117.

Furstenberg, F. F., Brooks-Gunn, J., & Morgan, S. P. (1987). Adolescent mothers and their children in later life. *Family Planning Perspectives, 19*(4), 142–151.

Jekel, J. F., Harrison, J. T., Bancroft, D. R. E., Tyler, N. C., & Klerman, L. V. (1975). A comparison of the health of index and subsequent babies born to school age mothers. *American Journal of Public Health, 65*(4), 370–374.

Kalmuss, D. S., & Brickner Namerow, P. (1994). Subsequent childbearing among teenage mothers: The determinants of a closely spaced second birth. *Family Planning Perspectives, 26*(4), 149–153, 159.

Khoshnood, B., Lee, K., Wall, S., Hseih, H., & Mittendorf, R. (1998). Short interpregnancy intervals and the risk of adverse birth outcomes among five racial/ethnic groups in the United States. *American Journal of Epidemiology, 148,* 798–805.

Linares, L. O., Leadbeater, B. L., Jaffe, L., Kato, P. M., & Diaz, A. (1992). Predictors of repeat pregnancy outcome among Black and Puerto Rican adolescent mothers. *Journal of Developmental and Behavioral Pediatrics, 13*(2), 89–94.

Morrow, A. L., Crews, R. C., Caretta, H. J., Altaye, M., Finch, A. B., & Sinn, J. S. (2000). Effect of method of defining active patient population on measured immunization rates in predominantly Medicaid and non-Medicaid practices. *Pediatrics, 106*(1), 171–176.

Nelson, K. G., Key, D., Fletcher, J. K, Kirkpatrick, E., & Feinstein, R. (1982). The teen-tot clinic: An alternative to traditional care for infants of teenage mothers. *Journal of Adolescent Health, 3,* 19–23.

O'Sullivan, A. L. (1991). Tertiary prevention with adolescent mothers: Rehabilitation after the first pregnancy. *Birth Defects, 27*(1), 57–71.

O'Sullivan, A. L., & Jacobsen, B. S. (1992). A randomized trial of a health care program for first-time adolescent mothers and their infants. *Nursing Research, 41*(4), 210–215.

Polit, D. F., & Kahn, J. R. (1986). Early subsequent pregnancy among economically disadvantaged teenage mothers. *American Journal of Public Health, 76,* 167–171.

Rabin, J. M., Seltzer, V., & Pollack, S. (1991). The long-term benefits of a comprehensive teenage pregnancy program. *Clinical Pediatrics, 30*(5), 305–309.

Rawlings, J. S., Rawlings, V. B., & Read, J. A. (1995). Prevalence of low birth weight and preterm delivery in relation to the interval between pregnancies among white and black women. *New England Journal of Medicine, 332,* 69–74.

Santelli, J. S., & Jacobsen, M. S. (1990). Birth weight outcomes for repeat teenage pregnancy. *Journal of Adolescent Health Care, 160,* 240–247.

Scholl, T. O., Hediger, M. L., & Belsky, D. H. (1994). Prenatal care and maternal health during adolescent pregnancy: A review and metanalysis. *Journal of Adolescent Health, 15,* 444–456.

Stahler, G. J., & DuCette, J. P. (1991). Evaluating adolescent pregnancy programs: Rethinking our priorities. *Family Planning Perspectives, 23*(3), 129–133.

Stahler, G. J., DuCette, J. P., & McBride, D. (1989). The evaluation component in adolescent pregnancy care projects: Is it adequate? *Family Planning Perspectives, 21*(3), 123–126.

Taylor, J. A., Darden, P. M., Slora, E., Hasemeier, C. M., Asmussen, L., & Wasserman, R. (1997). The influence of provider behavior, parental characteristics, and a public policy initiative on the immunization status of children followed by private pediatricians: A study from Pediatric Research in Office Setting. *Pediatrics, 99*(2), 209–215.

Ventura, S. J., Martin, J. A., Curtin, S. C., Mathews, T. J., & Park, M. M. (2000). *Births: Final data for 1998* (National Vital Statistics Reports, Vol. 48, No.3). Hyattsville, MD: National Center for Health Statistics.

Weatherley, R. A., Perlman, S. B., LeVine, M. H., & Klerman, L. V. (1986). Comprehensive programs for pregnant teenagers and teenage parents: How successful have they been? *Family Planning Perspectives, 18*(2), 73–78.

About the authors: This work was started while Lara J. Akinbami was a pediatric resident at Children's National Medical Center, Washington, D.C; Tina L. Cheng, Department of General Pediatrics and Adolescent Medicine, Children's National Medical Center, Washington, D.C., and George Washington University School of Medicine and Public Health, Washington, D.C.; Dana Kornfeld, Department of General Pediatrics and Adolescent Medicine, Children's National Medical Center, Washington, D.C.

Address correspondence to: Lara J. Akinbami, National Center for Health Statistics, 6525 Belcrest Road, Room 790, Hyattsville, MD 20782.

Exercise for Article 33

Factual Questions

1. The authors state the "central goal" of teen-tot programs. What is this goal?

2. The authors searched the PsychInfo database for relevant articles using what terms?

3. The literature search identified how many articles describing interventions that met initial criteria for closer review?

4. The letters SPC stand for what words?

5. According to Table 1, which programs evaluated immunizations?

6. According to Table 1, which program reported a statistically significant difference in school attendance between participants and controls?

7. Were the authors surprised that only four studies met inclusion criteria for their review?

Questions for Discussion

8. The authors state that two investigators independently reviewed the results of the computerized literature search. What is your understanding of the term "independently reviewed"? In your opinion, was it a good idea to have more than one person review the results? Explain.

9. Does it surprise you that only one of the studies used random assignment? In your opinion, how important is randomization in studies of programs? Explain. (See lines 96–100.)

10. Evaluators of two of the programs did not provide data for average duration of program participation or attrition. Do you think these are important omissions? Explain.

11. Two of the evaluations did not report rates of

clinic attendance for participants and controls. In your opinion, is it important to report such rates? Why? Why not? (See lines 170–171.)

12. In your opinion, would it be desirable to conduct more rigorous evaluations of teen-tot programs even if some of the resources for evaluation might reduce resources for direct assistance to participants? Explain. (See lines 213–216.)

13. Do you agree with the statement that "Including teens with poor attendance as participants will underestimate program impact."? Explain. (See lines 330–331.)

14. Given that only four evaluations met the authors' criteria and that the authors are critical of the methodology used in these evaluations, is this review likely to be of help to those who are responsible for designing and implementing teen-tot programs? Explain.

Quality Ratings

Editor's note: Because this article is a review of previously published research (and all the others in this book are reports of original research), the following items for quality ratings differ from those for the other articles in this book.

Directions: Indicate your level of agreement with each of the following statements by circling a number from 5 for strongly agree (SA) to 1 for strongly disagree (SD). If you believe an item is not applicable to this research article, leave it blank. Be prepared to explain your ratings.

A. The authors have provided convincing reasons for reviewing literature on teen-tot programs.

SA   5   4   3   2   1   SD

B. The term "teen-tot program" is adequately defined.

SA   5   4   3   2   1   SD

C. The method for locating articles for potential review is clearly described.

SA   5   4   3   2   1   SD

D. The criteria for selecting the final four articles (out of the original 46) are clearly described.

SA   5   4   3   2   1   SD

E. The authors have made it easy to compare the interventions and outcomes, as well as strengths and weaknesses of the four programs.

SA   5   4   3   2   1   SD

F. The authors described important limitations of the evaluations that they reviewed.

SA   5   4   3   2   1   SD

G. Despite any flaws, this review of literature is worthy of publication.

SA   5   4   3   2   1   SD

Appendix A

Reading Research Reports:
A Brief Introduction

David A. Schroeder   David E. Johnson   Thomas D. Jensen

To many students, the prospect of reading a research report in a professional journal elicits so much fear that no information is, in fact, transmitted. Such apprehension on the part of the reader is not necessary,
5 and we hope that this article will help students understand more clearly what such reports are all about and will teach them how to use these resources more effectively. Let us assure you that there is nothing mystical or magical about research reports, although they
10 may be somewhat more technical and precise in style, more intimidating in vocabulary, and more likely to refer to specific sources of information than are everyday mass media sources. However, once you get beyond these intimidating features, you will find that the
15 vast majority of research reports do a good job of guiding you through a project and informing you of important points of which you should be aware.

A scientific research report has but one purpose: to communicate to others the results of one's scientific
20 investigations. To ensure that readers will be able to appreciate fully the import and implications of the research, the author of the report will make every effort to describe the project so comprehensively that even a naive reader will be able to follow the logic as he or
25 she traces the author's thinking through the project.

A standardized format has been developed by editors and authors to facilitate effective communication. The format is subject to some modification, according to the specific needs and goals of a particular author for
30 a particular article, but, in general, most articles possess a number of features in common. We will briefly discuss the six major sections of research articles and the purpose of each. We hope that this selection will help you take full advantage of the subsequent articles
35 and to appreciate their content as informed "consumers" of social psychological research.

Heading

The heading of an article consists of the title, the name of the author or authors, and their institutional

affiliations. Typically, the title provides a brief descrip-
40 tion of the primary independent and dependent variables that have been investigated in the study. This information should help you begin to categorize the study into some implicit organizational framework that will help you keep track of the social psychological
45 material. For example, if the title includes the word *persuasion*, you should immediately recognize that the article will be related to the attitude-change literature, and you should prepare yourself to identify the similarities and differences between the present study and
50 the previous literature.

The names of the authors may also be important to you for at least two reasons. First, it is quite common for social psychologists to use the names of authors as a shorthand notation in referring among themselves to
55 critical articles. Rather than asking, "Have you read 'Videotape and the attribution process: Reversing actors' and observers' points of view'?", it is much easier to say, "Have you read the Storms (1973) article?" In addition, this strategy gives the author(s) credit for the
60 material contained in the article. Second, you will find that most researchers actively pursue programs of research that are specific to a particular area of interest. For example, you will eventually be able to recognize that an article written by Albert Bandura is likely to be
65 about social learning processes, while an article by Leonard Berkowitz is probably going to discuss aggression and violence. Once you begin to identify the major researchers in each area, you will find that you will be able to go beyond the information presented
70 within an article and understand not only how a piece of research fits into a well-defined body of literature but also how it may be related to other less obvious topics.

Abstract

The Abstract is a short (often less than 150 words)
75 preview of the contents of the article. The Abstract should be totally self-contained and intelligible without any reference to the article proper. It should briefly convey a statement of the problem explored, the methods used, the major results of the study, and the con-
80 clusions reached. The Abstract helps to set the stage and to prepare you for the article itself. Just as the title helps you place the article in a particular area of inves-

tigation, the Abstract helps pinpoint the exact question or questions to be addressed in the study.

Introduction

85   The Introduction provides the foundation for the study itself and therefore for the remainder of the article. Thus, it serves several critical functions for the reader. First, it provides a context for the article and the study by discussing past literature that is relevant to 90 and has implications for the present research. Second, it permits a thorough discussion of the rationale for the research that was conducted and a full description of the independent and dependent variables that were employed. Third, it allows the hypotheses that were tested 95 to be stated explicitly, and the arguments on which these predictions were based to be elucidated. Each of these functions will be considered in detail.

The literature review that is typically the initial portion of the Introduction is not intended to provide a 100 comprehensive restatement of all the published articles that are tangentially relevant to the present research. Normally, a selective review is presented—one that carefully sets up the rationale of the study and identifies deficiencies in our understanding of the phe-105 nomena being investigated. In taking this approach, the author is attempting to provide insights into the thought processes that preceded the actual conducting of the study. Usually, the literature review will begin by discussing rather broad conceptual issues (e.g., major 110 theories, recognized areas of investigation) and will then gradually narrow its focus to more specific concerns (e.g., specific findings from previous research, methods that have been employed). It may be helpful to think of the Introduction as a funnel, gradually draw-115 ing one's attention to a central point that represents the critical feature of the article.

Following the review of the past literature, the author typically presents the rationale for his or her own research. A research study may have one of several 120 goals as its primary aim: (1) It may be designed to answer a question specifically raised by the previous literature but left unanswered. (2) It may attempt to correct methodological flaws that have plagued previous research and threaten the validity of the conclu-125 sions reached. (3) It may seek to reconcile conflicting findings that have been reported in the literature, typically by identifying and/or eliminating confounding variables by exerting greater experimental control. (4) It may be designed to assess the validity of a scientific 130 theory by testing one or more hypotheses that have been deduced or derived from that theory. (5) It may begin a novel line of research that has not been previously pursued or discussed in the literature. Research pursuing any of these five goals may yield significant 135 contributions to a particular field of inquiry.

After providing the rationale for the study, the author properly continues to narrow the focus of the article from broad conceptual issues to the particular variables that are to be employed in the study. Ideally, 140 in experimental studies, the author clearly identifies the independent and dependent variables to be used; in correlational studies, the predictor and criterion variables are specified. For those readers who do not have an extensive background in research methodology, a 145 brief explanation of experimental and correlational studies may be in order.

Experimental studies. An experimental study is designed to identify cause-effect relationships between independent variables that the experimenter systemati-150 cally manipulates and the dependent variable that is used to measure the behavior of interest. In such a study, the researcher controls the situation to eliminate or neutralize the effects of all extraneous factors that may affect the behavior of interest in order to assess 155 more precisely the impact of the independent variables alone. In most instances, only the tightly controlled experimental method permits valid inferences of cause-effect relationships to be made.

Correlational studies. In some circumstances, the 160 researcher cannot exert the degree of control over the situation that is necessary for a true experimental study. Rather than giving up the project, the researcher may explore alternative methods that may still permit an assessment of his or her hypotheses and predictions. 165 One such alternative is the correlational approach. In a correlational study, the researcher specifies a set of measures that should be related conceptually to the display of a target behavior. The measure that is used to assess the target behavior is called the criterion vari-170 able; the measure from which the researcher expects to be able to make predictions about the criterion variable is called the predictor variable. Correlational studies permit the researcher to assess the degree of relationship between the predictor variable(s) and the criterion 175 variable(s), but inferences of cause and effect cannot be validly made because the effects of extraneous variables have not been adequately controlled. Correlational studies are most frequently used in naturalistic or applied situations in which researchers must either tol-180 erate the lack of control and do the best they can under the circumstances or give up any hope of testing their hypotheses.

After the discussion of these critical components of the study, the author explicitly states the exact predic-185 tions that the study is designed to test. The previous material should have set the stage sufficiently well for you as a reader to anticipate what these hypotheses will be, but it is incumbent on the author to present them nonetheless. The wording of the hypotheses may vary, 190 some authors preferring to state the predictions in conceptual terms (e.g., "The arousal of cognitive dissonance due to counterattitudinal advocacy is expected to lead to greater attitude change than the presentation of an attitude-consistent argument.") and others preferring 195 to state their predictions in terms of the actual operationalizations that they employed (e.g., "Subjects who received a $1 incentive to say that an objectively boring task was fun are expected to subsequently evaluate the task as being more enjoyable than subjects who were offered a $20 incentive to say that the task was interesting.").

In reading a research report, it is imperative that you pay attention to the relationship between the initial literature review, the rationale for the study, and the statement of the hypotheses. In a well-conceived and well-designed investigation, each section will flow logically from the preceding one; the internal consistency of the author's arguments will make for smooth transitions as the presentation advances. If there appear to be discontinuities or inconsistencies throughout the author's presentation, it would be wise to take a more critical view of the study—particularly if the predictions do not seem to follow logically from the earlier material. In such cases, the author may be trying to present as a prediction a description of the findings that were unexpectedly uncovered when the study was being conducted. Although there is nothing wrong with reporting unexpected findings in a journal article, the author should be honest enough to identify them as what they really are. As a reader, you should have much more confidence in the reliability of predictions that obtain than you do in data that can be described by postdictions only.

Method

To this point, the author has dealt with the study in relatively abstract terms, and has given little attention to the actual procedures used in conducting it. In the Method section, the author at last describes the operationalizations and procedures that were employed in the investigation. There are at least two reasons for the detailed presentation of this information. First, such a presentation allows interested readers to reconstruct the methodology used, so that a replication of the study can be undertaken. By conducting a replication using different subject populations and slightly different operationalizations of the same conceptual variables, more information can be gained about the validity of the conclusions that the original investigator reached. Second, even if a replication is not conducted, the careful description of the method used will permit you to evaluate the adequacy of the procedures employed.

The Method section typically comprises two or more subsections, each of which has a specific function to fulfill. Almost without exception, the Method section begins with a subject subsection, consisting of a complete description of the subjects who participated in the study.[1] The number of subjects should be indicated, and there should be a summary of important demographic information (e.g., numbers of male and female subjects, age) so that you can know to what populations the findings can be reasonably generalized. Sampling techniques that were used to recruit subjects and incentives used to induce volunteering should also be clearly specified. To the extent that subject characteristics are of primary importance to the goals of the research, greater detail is presented in this subsection, and more attention should be directed to it.

A procedures subsection is also almost always included in the Method section. This subsection presents a detailed account of the subjects' experiences in the experiment. Although other formats may also be effective, the most common presentation style is to describe the subjects' activities in chronological order. A thorough description of all questionnaires administered or tasks completed is given, as well as any other features that might be reasonably expected to affect the behavior of the subjects in the study.

After the procedures have been discussed, a full description of the independent variables in an experimental study, or predictor variables in a correlational study, is typically provided. Verbatim description of each of the different levels of each independent variable is presented, and similar detail is used to describe each predictor variable. This information may be included either in the procedures subsection or, if the description of these variables is quite lengthy, in a separate subsection.

After thoroughly describing these variables, the author usually describes the dependent variables in an experimental study, and the criterion variables in a correlational study. The description of the dependent and/or criterion variables also requires a verbatim specification of the exact operationalizations that were employed. When appropriate and available, information about the reliability and validity of these measures is also presented. In addition, if the investigator has included any questions that were intended to allow the effectiveness of the independent variable manipulation to be assessed, these manipulation checks are described at this point. All of this information may be incorporated in the procedures subsection or in a separate subsection.

After you have read the Method section, there should be no question about what has been done to the subjects who participated in the study. You should try to evaluate how representative the methods that were used were of the conceptual variables discussed in the Introduction. Manipulation checks may help to allay one's concerns, but poorly conceived manipulation checks are of little or no value. Therefore, it is important for you as a reader to remember that you are ultimately responsible for the critical evaluation of any research report.

Results

Once the full methodology of the study has been described for the reader, the author proceeds to report the results of the statistical analyses that were con-

---

[1] *Editor's note:* Many researchers prefer the terms *participants* or *respondents* to the term *subjects*.

ducted on the data. The Results section is probably the most intimidating section for students to read, and often the most difficult section for researchers to write. You are typically confronted with terminology and
310 analytical techniques with which you are at best unfamiliar, or at worst totally ignorant. There is no reason for you to feel bad about this state of affairs; as a neophyte in the world of research, you cannot expect mastery of all phases of research from the start. Even
315 experienced researchers are often exposed to statistical techniques with which they are unfamiliar, requiring them either to learn the techniques or to rely on others to assess the appropriateness of the procedure. For the student researcher, a little experience and a conscien-
320 tious effort to learn the basics will lead to mastery of the statistical skills necessary.

The author's task is similarly difficult. He or she is attempting to present the findings of the study in a straightforward and easily understood manner, but the
325 presentation of statistical findings does not always lend itself readily to this task. The author must decide whether to present the results strictly within the text of the article or to use tables, graphs, and figures to help to convey the information effectively. Although the
330 implications of the data may be clear to the researcher, trying to present the data clearly and concisely so that the reader will also be able to discern the implications is not necessarily assured. In addition, the author is obligated to present all the significant results obtained
335 in the statistical analyses, not just the results that support the hypotheses being tested. Although this may clutter the presentation and detract from the simplicity of the interpretation, it must be remembered that the researcher's primary goal is to seek the truth, not to
340 espouse a particular point of view that may not be supported by the data.

Discussion

The Discussion section is the part of the manuscript in which the author offers an evaluation and interpretation of the findings of the study, particularly as they
345 relate to the hypotheses that were proposed in the Introduction. Typically, the author will begin this section with a brief review of the major findings of the study and a clear statement of whether the data were consistent or inconsistent with the hypotheses. The Discus-
350 sion will then address any discrepancies between the predictions and the data, trying to resolve these inconsistencies and offering plausible reasons for their occurrence. In general, the first portion of the Discussion is devoted to an evaluation of the hypotheses that were
355 originally set forward in the Introduction, given the data that were obtained in the research.

The Discussion may be seen as the inverse of the Introduction, paralleling the issues raised in that section in the opposite order of presentation. Therefore,
360 after discussing the relationship of the data with the hypotheses, the author often attempts to integrate the

new findings into the body of research that provided the background for the study. Just as this literature ini-
365 tially provided the context within which you can understand the rationale for the study, it subsequently provides the context within which the data can be understood and interpreted. The author's responsibility at this point is to help you recognize the potential import of the research, without relying on hype or gimmicks to
370 make the point.

The Discussion continues to expand in terms of the breadth of ideas discussed until it reaches the broad, conceptual issues that are addressed by the superordinate theoretical work that originally stimulated the past
375 research literature. If a particular piece of research is to make a significant contribution to the field, its findings must either clarify some past discrepancy in the literature, identify boundary conditions for the applicability of the critical theoretical work, reconcile differences of
380 opinion among the researchers in the field, or otherwise contribute to a more complete understanding of the mechanisms and mediators of important social phenomena.

Once the author has reached the goals that are
385 common to most journal articles, attention may be turned to less rigorous ideas. Depending on a particular journal's editorial policy and the availability of additional space, the author may finish the article with a brief section about possible applications of the present
390 work, implications for future work in the area, and with some restraint, speculations about what lies ahead for the line of research. Scientists tend to have relatively little tolerance for conclusions without foundation and off-the-cuff comments made without full consideration.
395 Therefore, authors must be careful not to overstep the bounds of propriety in making speculations about the future. But such exercises can be useful and can serve a heuristic function for other researchers if the notions stated are well conceived.

Conclusion

400 Finally, particularly if the article has been relatively long or complex, the author may decide to end it with a short Conclusion. The Conclusion usually simply restates the major arguments that have been made throughout the article, reminding the reader one last
405 time of the value of the work.

As we suggested earlier, not all articles will follow the format exactly. Some latitude is allowed to accommodate the particular needs of the author and the quirks of the research being described. Given that the goal is
410 effective communication of information, it would not be reasonable for the format to dictate what could and could not be included in a manuscript. We hope that this introduction will help to demystify research articles and provide you with some insights into what an
415 author is trying to accomplish at various points in the report.

Let us end with a word of encouragement: Your en-

420   joyment of social psychology will be enhanced by your fuller appreciation of the sources of the information to which you are being exposed, and, to the extent that you are able to read and understand these original sources for yourself, your appreciation of this work will be maximized.

Reference

Storms, M. D. (1973). Videotape and the attribution process: Reversing actors' and observers' points of view. *Journal of Personality and Social Psychology, 27*, 165-175.

Appendix B

Fundamental Principles for Preparing Psychology Journal Articles

Harry F. Harlow
University of Wisconsin

Reprinted from Harlow, H. F. (1962). *Journal of Comparative and Physiological Psychology, 55,* 893-896.

As retiring editor of the *Journal of Comparative and Physiological Psychology,* I feel that I have one remaining responsibility to my psychological colleagues. Having passed judgment on about 2,500 original manuscripts and almost as many revisions in my 12 years as editor, I believe I should bequeath to posterity some principles of scientific reporting that I have formulated only through countless hours of moonlighting.

Covering Letter

In plotting the publication of a manuscript, the prospective author should think first about the covering letter. It is an unforgivable error to write, "I am submitting a manuscript for your consideration...." This evasive method gets you nowhere with editors. Even if the nondirective technique works with many patients, there are some sick people who are best approached using positive pressures.

There are a number of general principles underlying a good covering letter, and they can be illustrated by example. I offer the following:

Dear Harry:

I am submitting the manuscript, "Creative Thinking by Paramecia," for publication in *JCPP.* My chairman has assured me that upon acceptance of this manuscript he will recommend me for promotion to associate professor. Two recipients of the Distinguished Psychologist Award have reviewed this paper and recommend it highly.

I am pleased to see that you are one of the five candidates for president of the American Psychological Association. As you know, I have nominated you for many years and will probably give you my support in the future.

Because of the unusual significance of these researches, I would like early publication, which I will finance from my National Institute of Mental Health grant.

Warm regards,

John Hopeful
Assistant Professor

The battle is now half won. You will get a fair shake.

Introduction

Almost all scientific papers include an introduction even though large parts of it are frequently buried in the sections labeled Method and Results. However, the total omission of an introduction constitutes a glaring error, and, anyway, it is fun to write introductions—one is not constrained by facts.

One way to write an introduction is simply to state what the experiment is all about and make predictions about the outcome. Since the data will already have been collected and processed, you will have no difficulty in making insightful predictions. As all famous historians know, one can predict the past with great precision. However, prediction is one of the great booby traps into which young and inexperienced psychologists often fall. All their predictions are confirmed; older men know that this never happens. The proper technique is to select the prediction of minimum import, or throw in a completely extraneous one, and have this prediction fail. Honesty is the best policy.

Although some psychologists write simple, straightforward introductions, this is commonly considered to be *déclassé.* In the sophisticated or "strip-tease" technique, you keep the problem a secret from the reader until the very last paragraph. Indeed, some very sophisticated authors keep the problem a secret forever. Since I am interested in readers as well as authors, I advise that readers always approach introduction sections using the Chinese technique—begin at the end and read backward.

The function of the introduction is to impress your colleagues with your scholarship and erudition—academic appointments are seldom made on the basis of a Results section. Scholarly one-upmanship is attained with an unending number of nonspecific references, such as:

"The up-and-down effect was first discovered by _____ (1762), and this study led to many fruitful investigations (_____, 1804; _____, 1827; _____, 1844; _____, 1861; _____, 1874; _____, 1888; _____, 1894; _____, 1911; _____, 1917; _____, 1928; _____, 1937; _____, 1944; and _____, 1952). Beyond these researches, the broad implications of this discovery led to related studies on the in-and-out phenomenon (____, 1829; ____, 1855; ____, 1888; ____, 1914; ____, 1927; and ____, 1950) and the around-and-about law (____, 1884; ____, 1914; ____, 1933; ____, 1947; ____, 1952; and ____, 1960)."

Often, but not often enough, young and lazy authors are frightened away from this technique simply because they are appalled by the amount of work involved in reading the literature, especially if part is written in some foreign language. However, there is no excuse for this attitude; the author should remember that he is not reading the literature—just citing it. Anyway, he can always rely on some scholarly article in *Psychological Bulletin* as a secondary source to provide an impressive reference list with almost no effort.

Occasionally, editors object to overly extended, striptease introductions and to long lists of nonspecific references. At this point, the author should take the bull by the horns and write the editor a nasty letter accusing him of rigidity, illiteracy, and lack of scholarly interests. Editors are busy and editors are human. They can be broken—don't pamper them.

Method

To write a good Method section, one must be an idealist. If this section is to be understood, it must be clear, orderly, and systematic. The best way to achieve this is not to tell what really happened, or if you must tell, wait as long as is physically possible. Your four groups of *Ss* should always add to 20 or 30 each. If 7 *Ss* in Group 2 died of pneumonia and 19 *Ss* in Group 3 were suffocated, don't put it in the Method section. The death of these *Ss* was not planned but resulted, and the information obviously belongs in the Results. There is also good reason for putting this information in the Discussion because you can then meditate on how different the results might have been had the *Ss* lived.

A mechanical problem that often creeps up in Method relates to the spelling and meaning of words such as "maize," "liman," and "maccaccuss resus." Fortunately there is a fundamental rule. Writing manuscripts is a tedious process and time means money. You must protect your time in every possible manner. If you cannot spell or do not know the meaning of a word, don't look it up in *Webster's Third International Dictionary*. If the word isn't in Thorndike and Barnhart, 95% of your psychological audience won't know the meaning of the word or how to spell it anyway. Moreover, that's the editor's responsibility. Let well enough alone.

Results

The Results section comes in a very convenient place, and one way to start it is to put the procedures that you inadvertently omitted from the Method section —which you are too lazy to rewrite—at the very beginning of the Results.

If the editor objects, point out that you are doing this for the sake of continuity. The next problem can only be resolved by reference to the Procedure. Reread the Procedure section and find out the order that you said you were going to follow; then, carefully rearrange that order in the Results. If you write succinctly and clearly, there is a real danger that the reader will only read your manuscript once, and every psychologist worth his salt recognizes the importance of overlearning. Then, too, if he has to struggle to understand it, he will naturally attribute the difficulties to the abstruseness of the problem.

The most important items in the Results will probably be the figures. Authors seldom realize the importance of figures and consequently fail to give them sufficient attention. It is absolutely imperative that the figures be of professional quality. This may cost a little money, but even with academic salaries what they are, the cost is cheap compared with the value of the man-hours spent in gathering and processing the data. The ordinate and abscissa should be boldly drawn, and the curves should stand out like sore thumbs, which they frequently really are.

Now we are at a critical point. It is important to make sure that all legends, all numbers on the ordinate and abscissa, and all titles are completely unreadable. If you fail to do this, there is a real danger that editors and readers will compare the information given in the graph with what is written in the Results and Discussion and call the discrepancies to your attention. Fortunately, your figures can be made unreadable at a high academic level by following a few simple rules. Draw the figure on paper 2 ft sq and never purchase templates with letters more than 1/4 in high. Then when the figures are reduced in size for journal publication, the data will remain a personal secret. You can subsequently let out the data you are not trying to hide by personal correspondence.

Even authors who follow this rule—and the general principle is widely understood—frequently make a completely unforgivable error by sending glossy prints of their figures to the editor. If the editor has already recognized the fact that he has presbyopia and has purchased glasses, he may insist that the graphs be redrawn, and then the jig is up. However, if you send the original drawings and simply scratch out in pencil the copy for the carbon that some editors require, you have a high chance of success. A better technique is to send the carbon without figures. Most editors will relay this carbon to a consulting editor without checking for figures, and a single favorable review frequently ensures publication.

Another good technique is to supplement the figures by presenting the data for individual animals in lengthy tables without means, medians, or standard deviations. No reader, and certainly no editor, will ever take the trouble to make the necessary computations to check your curves or statements of significance. The additional advantage is that long, detailed tables carry the implication that you engaged in an overwhelmingly complicated piece of research.

Discussion

Whereas there are firm rules and morals concerning the collection and reporting of data that should be placed in the Results, these rules no longer are in force when one comes to the Discussion. Anything goes— shoot the moon—the sky's the limit!

Even though one is going far afield, the endeavor should not be random, but the deception should be achieved with skill and grace. The most important fundamental guiding principle is to repeat the predictions made in the introduction—elaborating them if possible—and then to describe the importance of your work in broad generic terms and never get down to mundane fact. In Discussion sections, one does not discover things about maze performance, minutes to run down a straight alley, 48 hrs of food deprivation, or the number of mechanical puzzle devices opened—one makes breath-taking discoveries about learning, drive reduction, motivation, and curiosity. After all, this is the way psychologists are going to talk when they present and discuss their work at scientific meetings, and no man attains fluency in the jargon without practice.

Very occasionally, some psychologist makes the mistake of saying what is worth saying in the Discussion and then stopping. This is interpreted by other psychologists as indicating that the person lacks verbal skill and creativity. Anyone can talk effectively about data that actually exist.

If your experiment has any merit whatsoever, and little is required, there is the likelihood that someone else will do it later and do it better. To save face, it is important to engage in the alibi-in-advance technique. Endless Discussion pages can be consumed by describing how you would do the experiment if you were to do it over, and the joy of this device is that no data need be collected. You have the fellow who is going to be so cold and calculating as to check your results, on the run, and if you are smart enough, no matter what he obtains, it will be a dry run.

Even if you have only completed a single experiment, you can greatly augment your data by several pages of descriptions of the results you would have obtained had you done a long series of related experiments. Furthermore, a clarity is achieved by describing the experiments that were not done instead of those that were because the results in the imaginary experiments come out in an integrated, orderly manner that is seldom achieved in the laboratory. Remember that data collection is a routine process, and the brilliant scientist will rise above it when he comes to the Discussion.

Nothing is now left except to find a way to end the Discussion section, which has become so long and so confused that most readers will have forgotten what the original problem was about anyway. Discussion should be concluded in a friendly, charitable, and slightly condescending manner. First, say a few little things about the difficulties of doing research, particularly research in your chosen area. Then point out that there are a few little technical problems and research odds and ends that need to be picked up before your area of choice is completely neat and tidy. Finally, explain that once the research trail has been broken, less strong bodies can follow along.

Footnotes

Finally, one comes to the footnotes. Footnotes are always on a separate page (or pages) and there is a chance that the editor will miss them, particularly if the typewritten material is single-spaced and turned upside down. Thus, here is an opportunity to introduce a couple of additional pages of complete trivia. If the editor should discover them, nothing will be lost, for paper is cheap. Remember that this is your last chance to get in some padding, and never forget the fact that promotion is the prerogative of deans and final decisions are frequently weighed on scales other than those of justice.

Special attention should be given to one footnote — the acknowledgment. It is this one that separates the men from the boys. Since most experiments are not worth doing and the data obtained are not worth publishing, great care should be taken to protect one's reputation when one's name is associated with the conventional potboiler. This can be achieved by a simple and honest footnote:

"The author (or authors) had very little to do with this research. The idea was stolen from Dr. _____, the experimental design was proposed by my (our) statistical consultant, Dr. _____, the Ss were run by Mr. _____ and Miss _____, the data were processed by the mathematical computing center, and the paper was completely rewritten by Editor _____, on the basis of extensive notes and suggestions made by Consulting Editor _____, whose name was inadvertently left off the masthead of the *Journal of _____*."

Editorial Policy

Faced with a mounting flood of uninspired researches and watching publication lag continuously mount despite multiple allotments of additional journal pages, I came to realize that my editorial policies, even though rigid and unreasonable, were incomplete or else in error. For a long time, I thought there was no solution, and then I realized that I was wrong. I established a new *JCPP* policy and formalized it with a rubber stamp, only to realize that my term as editor had already expired. But at least I have the rubber stamp that I planned to use on a large number of manuscripts: "Not read but rejected."

Appendix C

Criteria for the Evaluation of Educational Research

Suggested Scale

5–Excellent (A model of good practice.)
4–Good (A few minor defects.)
3–Mediocre (Not good, not bad.)
2–Poor (Some serious defects.)
1–Completely incompetent (A horrible example.)

Title

1. Title is well related to content of article.

Problem

2. Problem is clearly stated.
3. Hypotheses are clearly stated.
4. Problem is significant.
5. Assumptions are clearly stated.
6. Limitations of the study are stated.
7. Important terms are defined.

Review of Literature

8. Coverage of the literature is adequate.
9. Review of literature is well organized.
10. Studies are examined critically.
11. Source of important findings is noted.
12. Relationship of the problem to previous research is made clear.

Procedures

13. Research design is described fully.

14. Research design is appropriate to solution of the problem.
15. Research design is free of specific weaknesses.
16. Population and sample are described.
17. Method of sampling is appropriate.
18. Data-gathering methods of procedures are described.
19. Data-gathering methods of procedures are appropriate to the solution of the problem.
20. Data-gathering methods or procedures are used correctly.
21. Validity and reliability of data gathering procedures are established.

Data Analysis

22. Appropriate methods are selected to analyze data.
23. Methods used in analyzing the data are applied correctly.
24. Results of the analysis are presented clearly.
25. Tables and figures are effectively used.

Summary and Conclusions

26. Conclusions are clearly stated.
27. Conclusions are substantiated by the evidence presented.
28. Conclusions are relevant to the problem.
29. Conclusions are significant.
30. Generalizations are confined to the population from which the sample was drawn.

Form and Style

31. Report is clearly written.
32. Report is logically organized.
33. Tone of the report displays an unbiased, impartial, scientific attitude.

Appendix D

A Reader's, Writer's, and Reviewer's Guide to Assessing Research Reports in Clinical Psychology

Brendan A. Maher
Harvard University

Maher, B. A. (1978). A Reader's, Writer's, and Reviewer's Guide to Assessing Research Reports in Clinical Psychology. *Journal of Consulting and Clinical Psychology, 46,* 835–838. Published by the American Psychological Association. This material may be reproduced in whole or in part without permission, provided that acknowledgment is made to Brendan A. Maher and the American Psychological Association.

Many detailed responses to a first draft were reviewed. Particular acknowledgment is due Thomas Achenbach, George Chartier, Andrew Comrey, Jesse Harris, Mary B. Harris, Alan Kazdin, Richard Lanyon, Eric Mash, Martha Mednick, Peter Nathan, K. Daniel O'Leary, N. D. Reppucci, Robert Rosenthal, Richard Suinn, and Norman Watt.

Requests for reprints should be sent to Brendan A. Maher, Department of Psychology and Social Relations, Harvard University, Cambridge, MA 02138.

The editors of the *Journal of Consulting and Clinical Psychology* who served between 1974 and 1978 have seen some 3,500 manuscripts in the area of consulting and clinical psychology. Working with this number of manuscripts has made it possible to formulate a set of general guidelines that may be helpful in the assessment of research reports. Originally developed by and for journal reviewers, the guidelines are necessarily skeletal and summary and omit many methodological concerns. They do, however, address the methodological concerns that have proved to be significant in a number of cases. In response to a number of requests, the guidelines are being made available here.

Topic Content

1. Is the article appropriate to this journal? Does it fall within the boundaries mandated in the masthead description?

Style

1. Does the manuscript conform to APA style in its major aspects?

Introduction

1. Is the introduction as brief as possible given the topic of the article?
2. Are all of the citations correct and necessary, or is there padding? Are important citations missing? Has the author been careful to cite prior reports contrary to the current hypothesis?
3. Is there an explicit hypothesis?
4. Has the *origin* of the hypothesis been made explicit?
5. Was the hypothesis *correctly* derived from the theory that has been cited? Are other, contrary hypotheses compatible with the same theory?
6. Is there an explicit rationale for the selection of measures, and was it derived logically from the hypothesis?

Method

1. Is the method so described that replication is possible without further information?
2. *Subjects*: Were they sampled randomly from the population to which the results will be generalized?
3. Under what circumstances was informed consent obtained?
4. Are there probable biases in sampling (e.g. volunteers, high refusal rates, institution population atypical for the country at large, etc.)?
5. What was the "set" given to subjects? Was there deception? Was there control for experimenter influence and expectancy effects?
6. How were subjects debriefed?
7. Were subjects (patients) led to believe that they were receiving "treatment"?
8. Were there special variables affecting the subjects, such as medication, fatigue, and threats that were not part of the experimental manipulation? In clinical samples, was "organicity" measured and/or eliminated?
9. *Controls*: Were there appropriate control groups? What was being controlled for?
10. When more than one measure was used, was the order counterbalanced? If so, were order effects

actually analyzed statistically?

11. Was there a control task(s) to confirm specificity of results?

12. *Measures*: For both dependent and independent variable measures—was validity and reliability established and reported? When a measure is tailor-made for a study, this is very important. When validities and reliabilities are already available in the literature, it is less important.

13. Is there adequate description of tasks, materials, apparatus, and so forth?

14. Is there discriminant validity of the measures?

15. Are distributions of scores on measures typical of scores that have been reported for similar samples in previous literature?

16. Are measures free from biases such as
    a. Social desirability?
    b. Yeasaying and naysaying?
    c. Correlations with general responsivity?
    d. Verbal ability, intelligence?

17. If measures are scored by observers using categories or codes, what is the interrater reliability?

18. Was administration and scoring of the measures done blind?

19. If short versions, foreign-language translations, and so forth, of common measures are used, has the validity and reliability of these been established?

20. In correlational designs, do the two measures have theoretical and/or methodologies independence?

Representative Design

1. When the stimulus is human (e.g., in clinical judgments of clients of differing race, sex, etc.), is there a *sample* of stimuli (e.g., more than one client of each race or each sex)?

2. When only one stimulus or a few human stimuli were used, was an adequate explanation of the failure to sample given?

Statistics

1. Were the statistics used with appropriate assumptions fulfilled by the data (e.g., normalcy of distributions for parametric techniques)? Where necessary, have scores been transformed appropriately?

2. Were tests of significance properly used and reported? For example, did the author use the *p* value of a correlation to justify conclusions when the actual size of the correlation suggests little common variance between two measures?

3. Have statistical significance levels been accompanied by an analysis of practical significance levels?

4. Has the author considered the effects of a limited range of scores, and so forth, in using correlations?

5. Is the basic statistical strategy that of a "fishing expedition"; that is, if many comparisons are made, were the obtained significance levels predicted in advance? Consider the number of significance levels as a function of the total number of

comparisons made.

Factor Analytic Statistics

1. Have the correlation and factor matrices been made available to the reviewers and to the readers through the National Auxiliary Publications Service or other methods?

2. Is it stated what was used for communalities, and is the choice appropriate? Ones in the diagonals are especially undesirable when items are correlated as the variables.

3. Is the method of termination of factor extraction stated, and is it appropriate in this case?

4. Is the method of factor rotation stated, and is it appropriate in this case?

5. If items are used as variables, what are the proportions of yes and no responses for each variable?

6. Is the sample size given, and is it adequate?

7. Are there evidences of distortion in the final solution, such as single factors, excessively high communalities, obliqueness when an orthogonal solution is used, linearly dependent variables, or too many complex variables?

8. Are artificial factors evident because of inclusion of variables in the analysis that are alternate forms of each other?

Figures and Tables

1. Are the figures and tables (a) necessary and (b) self-explanatory? Large tables of nonsignificant differences, for example, should be eliminated if the few obtained significances can be reported in a sentence or two in the text. Could several tables be combined into a smaller number?

2. Are the axes of figures identified clearly?

3. Do graphs correspond logically to the textual argument of the article? (E.g., if the text states that a certain technique leads to an *increment* of mental health and the accompanying graph shows a *decline* in symptoms, the point is not as clear to the reader as it would be if the text or the graph were amended to achieve visual and verbal congruence.)

Discussion and Conclusion

1. Is the discussion properly confined to the findings, or is it digressive, including new post hoc speculations?

2. Has the author explicitly considered and discussed viable alternative explanations of the findings?

3. Have nonsignificant trends in the data been promoted to "findings"?

4. Are the limits of the generalizations possible from the data made clear? Has the author identified his/her own methodological difficulties in the study?

5. Has the author "accepted" the null hypothesis?

6. Has the author considered the possible methodological bases for discrepancies between the results reported and other findings in the literature?